The Greater German Reich and the Jews

War and Genocide

General Editors: Omer Bartov, Brown University
A. Dirk Moses, University of Sydney

There has been a growing interest in the study of war and genocide, not from a traditional military history perspective, but within the framework of social and cultural history. This series offers a forum for scholarly works that reflect these new approaches.

"The Berghahn series Studies on War and Genocide *has immeasurably enriched the English-language scholarship available to scholars and students of genocide and, in particular, the Holocaust."* — **Totalitarian Movements and Political Religions**

For a complete series listing, please see page 424.

THE GREATER GERMAN REICH AND THE JEWS

Nazi Persecution Policies in the Annexed Territories 1935–1945

Edited by

Wolf Gruner and Jörg Osterloh

Translated by Bernard Heise

berghahn
NEW YORK • OXFORD
www.berghahnbooks.com

First published in 2015 by
Berghahn Books
www.berghahnbooks.com

©2015, 2017 Wolf Gruner and Jörg Osterloh
First paperback edition published in 2017

German-language edition
©2010 Campus Verlag
*Das "Großdeutsche Reich" und die Juden:
Nationalsozialistische Verfolgung in den "angegliederten" Gebieten*

All rights reserved.
Except for the quotation of short passages for the purposes
of criticism and review, no part of this book may be reproduced in any form
or by any means, electronic or mechanical, including photocopying, recording,
or any information storage and retrieval system now known or to be invented,
without written permission of the publisher.

The translation of this work was funded by Geisteswissenschaften
International—Translation Funding for Humanities and Social Sciences
from Germany, a joint initiative of the Fritz Thyssen Foundation, the German
Federal Foreign Office, the collecting society VG WORT and the Börsenverein
des Deutschen Buchhandels (German Publishers & Booksellers Association)

Library of Congress Cataloging-in-Publication Data
Grossdeutsche Reich und die Juden. English
 The greater German Reich and the Jews : Nazi persecution policies in the annexed territories 1935–1945 / edited by Wolf Gruner and Jörg Osterloh.
  pages cm — (Studies on war and genocide ; volume 20)
 Includes bibliographical references and index.
 ISBN 978-1-78238-443-4 (hardback : alk. paper) — ISBN 978-1-78533-503-7 (paperback) — ISBN 978-1-78238-444-1 (ebook)
 1. Jews—Persecutions—Europe, Central—History—20th century. 2. Jews—Persecutions—Europe, Eastern—History—20th century. 3. Jews—Europe, Central—History—20th century. 4. Jews—Europe, Eastern—History—20th century. 5. Holocaust, Jewish (1939–1945)—Europe, Central. 6. Holocaust, Jewish (1939–1945)—Europe, Eastern. 7. Germany—Politics and government—1933–1945. 8. Antisemitism—Europe—History—20th century. 9. Europe, Central—Ethnic relations. 10. Europe, Eastern—Ethnic relations. I. Gruner, Wolf, 1960– editor. II. Osterloh, Jörg, 1967– editor. III. Title.
 DS135.E83G677 2015
 940.53'18—dc23

2014019672

British Library Cataloguing in Publication Data
A catalogue record for this book is available from the British Library.

ISBN: 978-1-78238-443-4 hardback
ISBN: 978-1-78533-503-7 paperback
ISBN: 978-1-78238-444-1 ebook

Contents

List of Illustrations	vii
Acknowledgments	ix
Introduction Wolf Gruner and Jörg Osterloh	1
Chapter 1. Saar Region Gerhard J. Teschner	13
Chapter 2. Austria Albert Lichtblau	39
Chapter 3. Sudetenland Jörg Osterloh	68
Chapter 4. Protectorate of Bohemia and Moravia Wolf Gruner	99
Chapter 5. Memel Territory Ruth Leiserowitz	136
Chapter 6. Danzig-West Prussia Wolfgang Gippert	157
Chapter 7. Wartheland Ingo Loose	189

Chapter 8. Zichenau   219
Andreas Schulz

Chapter 9. East Upper Silesia   239
Sybille Steinbacher

Chapter 10. Eupen-Malmedy   267
Christoph Brüll

Chapter 11. Luxembourg   289
Marc Schoentgen

Chapter 12. Alsace-Lorraine   316
Jean-Marc Dreyfus

Conclusion   340
Wolf Gruner and Jörg Osterloh

Review of the Literature and Research on the Individual Regions   371
Wolf Gruner and Jörg Osterloh

Glossary   387

Notes on Contributors   393

Selected Bibliography   397

Index of Places   411

Index of Names   419

ILLUSTRATIONS

Maps

Map 0.1. "Borderland Germandom" in a 1934 school atlas	5
Map 2.1. Austria, 1938	40
Map 3.1. Sudetenland and the Protectorate of Bohemia and Moravia, 1938/39	69
Map 5.1. Memel Territory, 1939	137
Map 6.1. Danzig-West Prussia and Wartheland, 1939	172
Map 8.1. Government District of Zichenau, 1939	220
Map 9.1. East Upper Silesia, 1939	240
Map 10.1. Eupen-Malmedy, Luxembourg, and Alsace-Lorraine, 1940	277

Figures

Figure 1.1. *Our Saar*—A propagandistic text regarding the Saarland plebiscite (so-called *Grenzkampf-Schrift*) by Heinrich Schneider, 1934	17
Figure 2.1. Anti-Semitic propaganda exhibition *The Eternal Jew*, 1938	50
Figure 3.1. Renaming the "Judengasse" in Eger, November 1938	77
Figure 4.1. "Not accessible to Jews"—a municipal playground in Prague, 1939	110
Figure 5.1. Expulsion of Jews from Memel, spring 1939	149

Figure 6.1. Anti-Semitic posters at the burned-out
    Danzig synagogue, 1939   158
Figure 7.1. Jews in the Warthegau prior to their
    deportation, 1942   195
Figure 8.1. Rounding up the Jews from the Zichenau
    ghetto, 1941/42   225
Figure 9.1. Jewish forced laborers in Bendzin
    marked by armbands, 1939/40   246
Figure 10.1. Parade by the Segelfliegerverein
    (glider pilot association) in Eupen, 1938/39   268
Figure 11.1. Postcard with portraits of Josef Bürckel
    (Head of the Civil Administration in Lorraine) and
    Gustav Simon (Head of the Civil Administration in
    Luxembourg), 1940   295
Figure 12.1. "Jews not wanted"—notice at
    a Strasbourg tavern, 1940   324

Tables

Table 2.1. The Jewish and Non-Jewish Residential
    Population in the Austrian Federal States and
    their Capitals, According to the 1934 Census   41
Table 2.2. Countries of Asylum for Austrian Jews
    Expelled up to the Start of the War, by Continent   53
Table 2.3. Deportations from Austria   58

Acknowledgments

In 2012 the German edition of this volume, which appeared in 2010 in the Fritz Bauer Institute's *Wissenschaftliche Reihe* (academic series), received a prize awarded by the Börsenverein des Deutschen Buchhandels (German Publishers & Booksellers Association) to support the "translation of outstanding publications in the humanities and social sciences," making this English edition possible.

In preparation for the translation, the articles and editorial contributions have all been updated, in some cases with additional content as well. The editors would like to thank the authors not only for their contributions, but also for their patience and understanding in light of our numerous queries, and for revising, updating, and sometimes even expanding their texts for the English translation; Sabine Lachmann for producing the maps; Gerd Fischer and Sabine Grimm for carefully copy editing the German version; Volker Zimmermann for his knowledgeable comments on a number of selected chapters; the members of the German Historical Studies Group in Los Angeles for their stimulating discussion of an early version of the introduction; and also Christoph Dieckmann and Michael Wildt for their helpful criticism of a later version of the introduction to the German edition.

The editors would like to thank Omer Bartov, Marion Berghahn, and Dirk Moses for including the volume in the War and Genocide series published by Berghahn Books in New York, the anonymous reviewers for their suggestions, which have influenced the English edition, Bernard Heise for his very circumspect translation, and also Ann Przyzycki DeVita and Adam Capitanio for masterfully supervising the project on behalf of the publisher.

INTRODUCTION
Wolf Gruner and Jörg Osterloh

In early 2005 the President of the EU Commission, José Manuel Barroso, referred in an essay to "Auschwitz-Birkenau in Poland" but failed to mention Nazi Germany's responsibility for the camp, sparking fierce protests in Poland.[1] Polish reactions looked very much the same when the President of the United States, Barack Obama, in a speech honoring Jan Karski in May 2012, described Auschwitz as a "Polish death camp."[2] Of course, Barroso and Obama can hardly be suspected of harboring revisionist tendencies; even so, these examples reveal how references to the extermination camp have been beset by increasingly common and gravely misleading linguistic imprecisions, reflecting the steadily fading public awareness of the dimensions attained by the "Greater German Reich" during the Second World War. At its height, the "Greater German Reich" included the border regions of France and Belgium, all of Luxembourg and Austria, the Bohemian and Moravian parts of Czechoslovakia, western Poland, and the northern Slovenian territories. To be sure, from today's perspective, the town of Oświęcim—named Auschwitz[3] during the Nazi period—correctly lies in Poland; but from fall 1939 to early 1945, the National Socialist state had appropriated and annexed the region of East Upper Silesia, including the town. Thus the SS established the Auschwitz concentration—and later extermination—camp on the territory of the Third Reich.

The influence of the German Reich's territorial expansion on the persecution of the Jews—that is, on the policies of the perpetrators, the situation of the respective Jewish populations, and the behavior of the other inhabitants—has thus far hardly been systematically explored. Yet more or less each time the German Reich annexed another territory, the various architects of the Nazi regime's policies of racial persecution confronted new questions.[4] While between 1933 and 1938, the Nazis had managed to reduce the number of Jewish Germans[5] in the "Old Reich" from 520,000 to 240,000 by expelling them or inducing them to flee, in 1938/39 the annexations of Austria and the Sudetenland respectively brought an additional 190,000 and 29,000 religious Jews into the Reich, and the founding of the Protectorate of Bohemia and Moravia further increased their number by 118,000. The conquest of large parts of Poland created an entirely new situation; now more than 2 million Polish Jews found themselves under German dominion, 600,000 of them living in regions directly incorporated by the Reich. By comparison, only a few Jews lived in the territories annexed in the West in 1940.[6]

Updated and expanded for the English version, this volume for the first time systematically assembles the most important facts regarding the persecution of Jewish populations in the context of Nazi occupation policy with respect to the territories "annexed" or "incorporated"[7] by Germany. Each chapter is organized into three sections. The first section focuses on the situation prior to the territory's annexation, assessing the situation of both the Jews and non-Jews and elucidating the social, demographic, economic, political, and governmental circumstances after the First World War. The second section addresses the immediate German military occupation, the persecutions during the first weeks, and the initial constitutional measures implemented under Nazi rule. The authors investigate—among others—the following questions: Did violent actions occur during the first phase? What German and/or indigenous institutions initiated persecutory measures? What role did local ethnic Germans play in the respective region? How did the non-German/non-Jewish parts of the population behave? The third section deals with the territory's integration into the German Reich, the establishment of its most important administrative institutions, and the anti-Jewish policies implemented in the region until the end of the Nazi regime. The key questions for this section include: Which individuals and institutions advanced anti-Jewish policies in the annexed territory? When did jurisdictional competencies emerge, and what kind of breaks and shifts can be identified? What impact did Nazi ethnic policies—toward ethnic Germans, but also toward Czechs, Poles, and the French, for example—have on the persecution of the

Jews? In light of the demographic realities—for example in Poland—
to what extent did the Nazis successfully create a National Socialist
Volksgemeinschaft in the annexed territories?

The authors have all approached these questions on the basis of
the most recent scholarship and—in most cases—their own primary
research.[8] In a few instances, the lack of adequate sources or an insufficient level of preexisting research has led authors to adjust their
focus. Whereas Andreas Schulz and Ruth Leiserowitz primarily elucidate the prehistory of the annexations in the Regierungsbezirk (government district) of Zichenau (Ciechanów) and the Memel Territories
(Klaipėda Region), respectively, Ingo Loose and Sybille Steinbacher, in
their respective chapters about the Warthegau and East Upper Silesia, concentrate on the history of the occupation. Most of the chapters,
however, foreground the period until 1941, since afterward—except for
the Warthegau, East Upper Silesia, Austria, and the Protectorate—
few Jewish inhabitants remained in the annexed regions, due to the
expulsions and deportations.

For a long time historians in Germany and in the countries affected
by the Nazi annexations almost unanimously assumed that, as a rule,
German occupying authorities simply transferred existing anti-Jewish policies as developed at the time of each respective annexation
from Germany to the annexed territory. Exemplifying this view, Eva
Schmidt-Hartmann's thesis regarding the Protectorate of Bohemia
and Moravia maintains that the Protectorate featured "similar and basically the same arrangements" that obtained "in all of the other countries occupied by Germany."[9] The chapters presented here, however,
show that certain measures were introduced in various territories at
very different times (in some cases they were not even implemented at
all) and adjusted in accordance with regional circumstances, the international situation, and Germany's changing interests.

Previous scholarship has almost completely ignored questions regarding the possibility that the persecution of the Jews underwent
independent developments in the annexed territories, whether at the
hands of occupying Germans or indigenous neighbors. At the same
time it is obvious that the population's complex constellation—Jewish
and non-Jewish inhabitants, resident ethnic Germans, newly arriving Reich Germans—in most of the annexed territories must have
had consequences. An analysis of the occupation, the competent authorities, and the individuals they employed reveals as untenable any
assumption that Berlin or even the NSDAP solely determined the lines
of action in the annexed regions.[10] In March 1939, for example, Hitler

decided to leave the development of anti-Jewish policy in the Protectorate of Bohemia and Moravia to the Czech government. Indeed, local and regional conditions, constellations, institutions, and players shaped anti-Jewish policies—and thus at the same also their impact on the respective Jewish populations—far more pervasively than previously assumed.[11]

As the book will show, the persecution of the Jews did not continuously become more radical from one annexation to the next—from Austria through the Protectorate and Poland, to the territories in the West.[12] Anti-Jewish policy did not, in fact, result solely from ideological directives centrally issued from Berlin; rather, local players—Germans and non-Germans—reacted to specific economic, social, demographic, and political constellations. Thus in Vienna the "Aryanization" of Jewish property degenerated into a race among Nazi party members for personal enrichment; in response, Austrian Minister Hans Fischböck developed government expropriation plans for Austria, which were subsequently adapted by Göring for the entire Reich.[13] In our opinion, the key to understanding the intensification of anti-Jewish policy in the course of the Nazi regime's annexations, on the one hand, and the inconsistency of regional measures, on the other, lies precisely in these mutual actions between local, regional, and central persecutory measures.

Twentieth-century Europe was marked by shifting boundaries, transitions of power, changing political systems, and the creation of new states. For countless numbers of people this meant forced emigrations, the loss of homelands, and changing national citizenships. After the First World War, the peace negotiations in Paris and the resulting "Paris Peace Treaties" of 1919/20 fundamentally reconfigured the political map of Central and Eastern Europe, and as such they are considered one of the twentieth century's key events. As a result of the Versailles Treaty of 28 June 1919, the German Reich had to cede extensive territories in the North, West, and especially in the East, as well as acquiesce to restrictions of its sovereignty and pay reparations. Concluded on 10 September 1919, the Treaty of Saint-Germain-en-Laye prohibited the Austrian Republic, which emerged from the remains of the Habsburg Danubian Monarchy, from unifying with Germany; Austria also had to acknowledge the now independent states of Czechoslovakia, Poland, Hungary, and Yugoslavia and concede the associated territorial losses.[14]

The National Socialists made the revision of these treaties—which they referred to as the "shameful peace"—one of their major objectives.

Map 0.1. "Borderland Germandom" in a 1934 school atlas

Already in its "Twenty-Five Point Program" of 1920, the NSDAP prominently called for "the consolidation of all Germans into a Greater Germany on the basis of the peoples' [*Völker*] right to self-determination," demanding "equal rights of the German Reich vis-à-vis the other nations and the repeal of the Treaties of Versailles and St. Germain."[15] In making such demands, the NSDAP in Germany—and Austria—did not stand alone; rather, these demands reflected widespread sentiments within the population.

Two years after the National Socialists assumed power in the Reich in 1933, the opportunity arose for the first time to revise borders and repatriate Germans (see map 0.1). A plebiscite was supposed to help resolve the future of the Saar region, which, in accordance with the Versailles Treaty, stood under the League of Nations' supervision for fifteen years. In 1935, Germany—and thus the Nazi regime—emerged from the plebiscite as the triumphant victor and took over the territory. Two years later in November 1937, Hitler instructed the Wehrmacht to prepare for an invasion of Austria and Czechoslovakia. In the process, he was pursuing long-term goals: along with strategic gains of space and resources, millions of people were supposed to be expelled and the territories slated for annexation were to be extensively Germanized.[16]

The "Greater German Reich"—de facto and in terms of self-perception, but by no means de jure—emerged in 1938 as a result of the annexations of Austria in the spring and the Sudetenland in the fall, both carried out "peacefully" in the end. For Hitler, however, the Munich Agreement signed on 30 September 1938, through which Great Britain, France, Italy, and Germany forced Czechoslovakia to cede the Sudetenland, also involved bitter disappointment, for he had been counting on a military destruction of the ČSR. On 15 March 1939, the Wehrmacht finally marched into the *Resttschechei* (Nazi jargon for the rump Czech state) and Hitler proclaimed the newly created Protectorate of Bohemia and Moravia to be a part of the Reich. In so doing, the Third Reich for the first time raised a claim to a territory where most of the population did not consist of Germans.[17] Just one week later, Lithuania had to surrender the Memel Territory, an event largely overlooked due to the developments in Prague. These constituted the last "peaceful" conquests of the German Reich, although in all of these cases—with the exception of the Saar—Berlin had exerted immense political pressure and threatened the deployment of military means.

The Nazi regime created the preconditions for territorial expansion by force of arms with the surprising German-Soviet Nonaggression Pact of 23 August 1939 and the associated additional secret protocol.[18] Only a few days later, on 1 September, with its invasion of Poland, the German Reich began pursuing its further territorial objectives through violence. After the Polish military's quick defeat, Hitler dismembered the conquered country. The Reich annexed West Prussia, the "Free City" of Danzig (which had been under the protection and supervision of the League of Nations), the Wartheland, and East Upper Silesia, and also parts of Northern Mazovia as the Regierungsbezirk of Zichenau. Starting on 17 September, the Soviet Union occupied eastern Poland within days, and on 28 September the two conquering states agreed on the course of their new common border in Poland.[19] The Nazi regime consolidated the rest of the former Polish state under its control into the General Government for the Occupied Polish Territories (Generalgouvernement für die besetzten polnischen Gebiete), which neither de facto nor in terms of constitutional or international law belonged to the German Reich.[20] This is why this book does not deal with the districts in the General Government, even though many of the authors refer in their chapters to the numerous connections between the annexed regions and the other Polish territories.

The next annexations would expand the German Reich westward. After the Wehrmacht conquered the Netherlands, Belgium, Luxembourg, and large parts of France within a span of only a few weeks in May/June 1940, the Nazi state annexed—de jure or de facto—Eupen-Malmedy, Luxembourg, and Alsace and Lorraine. The last annexations occurred in 1941. Within just a few days after the German attack on Yugoslavia and Greece on 6 April 1941, northeastern Slovenia came under German administration. On 26 April, Hitler directed Maribor (Marburg an der Drau) to "make [the country] German again."[21] However, by the end of the war the planned constitutional integration into the German Reich had still not taken place. After the invasion of the Soviet Union in June 1941, the Nazis formed the Bezirk (district) of Białystok from parts of the former Polish territory.[22]

After the tide turned against the Germans in the Second World War, the Allies began reconquering the annexed regions from the German Reich. First, American and British troops liberated the Grand Duchy of Luxembourg in fall 1944, as well as Alsace-Lorraine and Eupen-Malmedy, which were reintegrated into the French and Belgian states, respectively. In the East, the Red Army captured the town of Memel (Klaipėda) in early 1945 and in the following weeks quickly overran the annexed regions of western Poland and the eastern parts of Germany. In the beginning of May 1945, only Prague (Prag, Praha), along with parts of the Protectorate and the Sudetengau, still remained in the hands of the German occupiers, who soon officially capitulated.[23]

Scholarship in both parts of Germany as well as in the countries affected by the Nazi annexations has neglected most of the regions assimilated by the Reich, along with the history of their annexations. Smaller annexations in particular, such as those of the Memel Territory or Eupen-Malmedy, have receded from view as a result of the focus on the Wehrmacht's military campaigns in the East. In a striking contrast to these scholarly omissions, in 1944 Raphael Lemkin developed his still influential definition of genocide as a punishable international crime on the basis of an analysis of the history of Nazi occupation and persecution in both the eastern and western parts of the German Reich.[24] Referring to the Nazi state's long-term interest in systematically Germanizing these territories, Lemkin soberly maintained that it had destroyed the local and/or national institutions and traditions in the annexed regions, introducing German administrative structures in their stead. He noted that in western Poland the population had to abandon its homes to make room for Germans from the Baltic, other parts of Poland, Bessarabia, and last but not least from the Reich itself; in Alsace-Lorraine and Luxembourg, on the other hand, persecution policies developed along different lines, since the Nazis viewed Luxembourgers as people with "related" blood.[25]

Even more than a modern comparative history of Nazi occupations,[26] we still today lack comparative studies of persecution and extermination in the "annexed" territories. In fact, studies on this topic are not even available for all the individual territories. While more or less comprehensive studies exist for Austria, the Sudetenland, the Protectorate of Bohemia and Moravia, East Upper Silesia, and the Warthegau, gaps still remain above all for the annexed regions in the West and Southeast.[27] During the Second World War and its immediate aftermath, these developments still garnered attention, particularly from the respective governments in exile and Jewish organizations in the United States. Along with Lemkin's study, other books also appeared that first documented Nazi persecution in individual annexed countries and throughout Europe, concentrating either on anti-Jewish policies or on "racial policy" as an element in "greater German" expansion and Germanization.[28]

After the Second World War, in the individual countries that had been occupied by the German Reich, interest focused more on the fate of the majority population and its resistance, in order to stabilize societies shaken by the war and occupation. Remarkably, in this respect it is difficult to distinguish between the policies of (non)commemoration in Western states—for example, Austria, France, and Belgium—and in Socialist countries such as Poland and Czechoslovakia. The same applies to the cultivation of national victimhood myths.[29] While scholarship in each respective nation joined to unanimously condemn Germany as an occupying power, it ignored the participation of indigenous persons in the persecution of the Jewish minority—this against its better judgment, for in the first postwar phase, most countries had implemented proceedings against collaborators, which often ended with drastic sentences. Thus the first to tread the minefield-riddled terrain of persecution and collaboration were often the survivors of the mass murder themselves.[30] In the 1990s, however, this situation finally changed in almost all of these countries.[31] Within a decade the research landscapes in the formerly occupied countries had dramatically altered, transformed by a new generation of frequently multilingual historians (insufficient language skills had also previously hindered the international reception of national scholarship), the opening of archives in the states of the former "Eastern Bloc," international discussions about restitution and compensation for the victims of Nazi rule in Europe, and changing political and academic interests. The transformation occurred against a background largely formed by the redefinition of many former Socialist countries after the end of the Cold War, the rising importance of the European Union in the West and the fundamental efforts by scholarly communities to find a place for their own nations within an integrating Europe. In this connection, the Holocaust acquired a major role in European commemoration policies, which strongly influenced most national historiographies.[32]

The systematic and comparative survey offered in this volume—in numerous cases, given the absence of preliminary work, made possible only as a result of the authors' own primary research—for the first time provides insights into the similarities and differences between anti-Jewish policies in the various regions of the "Greater German Reich" that were annexed or incorporated by the Nazi regime. In the conclusion that follows the chapters, the editors discuss and weigh these new findings. In addition, they analyze the continuities and discontinuities, as well as the social, political, and economic conditions of the surprisingly frequent autonomous local, regional, and national developments. They assess the interactions between the annexed territories and the previously often overlooked influence of these regional initiatives on the overall policies of the regime in Berlin, the transfer and development of persecutory knowledge by individual persons and institutions from one annexation to the next, as well as the establishment of regional authorities. Finally, the editors identify unresolved questions and outline key issues and areas for future research into anti-Jewish policy and its impact on the persecuted groups and overall societies in the annexed regions of the "Greater German Reich."

Los Angeles/Frankfurt, August 2014

Notes

1. José M. Barroso, "A United Europe Can Heal the Holocaust Wounds," *European Voice* (27 January 2005); Maciej Gertych, "Barroso Prompts Auschwitz Row," *European Voice* (3 February 2005).
2. See, for example, "Obama Angers Poles with 'Death Camp' Remark," *BBC News Europe* (30 May 2012), http://www.bbc.co.uk/news/world-europe-18264036.
3. The chapters in this anthology will initially refer to places commonly referenced in English—Prague, for example—by their English names, followed by their German and indigenous names enclosed in parentheses. When first mentioned, all other

places will generally be referred to by their names prior to the occupation and then their German name in parentheses. In other respects, depending on the context, the text usually uses the English or German name.

4. Mark Mazower, *Hitler's Empire: How the Nazis Ruled Europe* (New York, 2008), 83.
5. The introduction and the individual chapters frequently use generalized terms such as Germans, Jews, Poles, Czechs, the French, and Austrians. The editors and authors are very much aware of the problems associated with such usage but see no practical alternatives, even though these collectives were usually very heterogeneous and moreover often resorted to using religion, nationality, native language, and state citizenship merely as ethnic features. For the National Socialists the term "Pole," for example, usually referred to state citizenship during the initial occupation phase; only later did it refer increasingly to the racial categories of the Deutsche Volksliste (German People's List); in contrast, within the borders of the Reich, the designation "Jew" was based on the Nuremberg Race Laws. Thus when the following texts refer to Jews, the authors consequently always mean those people who fell under these laws, regardless of whether they viewed themselves as Jews or not.
6. On these figures, see Wolfgang Benz, ed., *Dimension des Völkermords: Die Zahl der jüdischen Opfer des Nationalsozialismus* (Munich, 1991).
7. The terms "annexation," "incorporation," and "integration" are used synonymously throughout this volume. They refer to the constitutional integration of the respective occupied territories into the German Reich through the introduction and application of Reich laws and the establishment of an administrative structure identical to the Reich's. This occurred as a process and was implemented in the individual regions in various forms and periods, but was basically distinguished from the "mere" occupation of territories like France, which remained under military administration, and the creation of the Generalgouvernement, which had its own specific administration and where the laws of the German Reich did not apply. When the following texts refer to "annexed" regions, they therefore mean both territories that de jure became Reich territory as well those that the Reich de facto annexed.
8. A survey of the current state of research with respect to individual countries and territories can be found at the end of the volume.
9. Eva Schmidt-Hartmann, "Tschechoslowakei," in *Dimension des Völkermords*, ed. Benz, 353–379, here 359.
10. As, for example, with Diemut Majer, *"Non-Germans" under the Third Reich: The Nazi Judicial and Administrative System in Germany and Occupied Eastern Europe with Special Regard to Occupied Poland, 1939–1945* (Baltimore, 2003) (German original: Boppard am Rhein, 1981).
11. The existence of significant local and regional differences in the development of Jewish policy within the Old Reich has since been sufficiently proven. Frank Bajohr has impressively demonstrated how foreign-trade concerns in Hamburg for a long time mitigated local "Aryanizations." Frank Bajohr, *"Aryanisation" in Hamburg: The Economic Exclusion of Jews and the Confiscation of their Property in Nazi Germany* (New York, 2002) (German original: Hamburg, 1997). And Wolf Gruner has demonstrated that the degree of pressure on Jewish populations depended on the initiative of the municipalities. Idem, *Öffentliche Wohlfahrt und Judenverfolgung: Wechselwirkung lokaler und zentraler Politik im NS-Staat (1933–1942)* (Munich, 2002).
12. On this, see the chapters in this volume.
13. Hans Safrian, "Expediting Expropriation and Expulsion: The Impact of the 'Vienna Model' on Anti-Jewish Policies in Nazi Germany 1938," *Holocaust and Genocide Studies* 14, no. 3 (2000): 390–414.

14. The Treaty of Trianon of 4 June 1920 also stipulated the separation of Slovakia and Croatia-Slavonia from Hungary. A concise overview is provided by Eberhard Kolb, *Der Frieden von Versailles* (Munich, 2005); see also Gerd Krumeich, ed., *Versailles 1919: Ziele—Wirkung—Wahrnehmung* (Essen, 2001); Magda Adám, *The Versailles System and Central Europe* (Aldershot, 2004); Alan Sharp, *The Versailles Settlement: Peacemaking in Paris, 1919* (New York, 1991).
15. Gottfried Feder, *Das Programm der NSDAP und seine weltanschaulichen Grundlagen*, 22nd printing (Munich, 1930), 8.
16. Oberst Hoßbach, "Niederschrift über die Besprechung in der Reichskanzlei am 5.11.1937 vom 10.11.1937," in *Der Prozeß gegen die Hauptkriegsverbrecher vor dem Internationalen Militärgerichtshof Nürnberg 14.11.1945–1.10.1946*, 42 vols. (Nuremburg, 1947–1949), here vol. 25, doc. 386-PS, pp. 402–413, here p. 410.
17. Thus rendering obsolete the legitimation of the annexations by the right of the Germans to self-determination as invoked by Hitler; Mazower, *Hitler's Empire*, 53.
18. Jan Lipinsky, *Das Geheime Zusatzprotokoll zum deutsch-sowjetischen Nichtangriffsvertrag vom 23. August 1939 und seine Entstehungs- und Rezeptionsgeschichte von 1939 bis 1999* (Frankfurt, 2004); Manfred Sapper and Volker Weichsel, eds., *Der Hitler-Stalin-Pakt: Der Krieg und die europäische Erinnerung: Osteuropa* 59, no. 7–8 (2009).
19. Through an exchange of territories, Germany subsequently acquired the district of Suwałki (as of 1939, Suwalken; as of 1941, Sudauen), integrating it into the East Prussian Regierungsbezirk of Gumbinnen. Unfortunately, a chapter on this region could not be acquired for this volume.
20. According to Martin Broszat, the Generalgouvernement was an "ad hoc constructed German 'Nebenland' [Nazi term for a directly dependent land], lacking the quality of a state, [and] with stateless inhabitants of Polish ethnicity." On the status of the Generalgouvernement, see Martin Broszat, *Nationalsozialistische Polenpolitik 1939–1945* (Stuttgart, 1961), 68–70, quote on 70.
21. Joachim Hösler, "Sloweniens historische Bürde," *Aus Politik und Zeitgeschichte*, no. 46 (2006), 31–38, here 32f. On Slovenia see also Holm Sundhaussen, *Geschichte Jugoslawiens 1918–1990* (Stuttgart, 1982); Rolf Wörsdörfer, *Krisenherd Adria 1915–1955* (Paderborn, 2004); Tamara Griesser-Pecar, *Das zerrissene Volk: Slowenien 1941–1946* (Vienna, 2003).
22. Unfortunately, chapters on the regions of Lower Styria (Untersteiermark), Upper Carniola (German: Oberkrain; Slovene: Gorenjska), and Białystok could not be recruited for this volume.
23. After the war, the occupied Polish regions were allocated to the Polish state, which at Stalin's behest was shifted substantially westward and now integrated former German regions. The Sudeten regions as well as Bohemia and Moravia were returned to Czechoslovakia. In 1948, the Memel Territory was constitutionally integrated into the Lithuanian Soviet Republic.
24. Raphael Lemkin, *Axis Rule in Occupied Europe: Laws of Occupation, Analysis of Government, Proposals for Redress*, reprint of the original 1944 edition, 2nd edition (Clark, NJ, 2008), especially 79–95. On Lemkin and his importance to scholarship, "Raphael Lemkin: The 'Founder of the United Nation's Genocide Convention' as a Historian of Mass Violence," special issue, *Journal of Genocide Research* 7, no. 4 (2005).
25. Lemkin, *Axis Rule*, 82 f., 86.
26. The most recent general overview on this topic, Mark Mazower's *Hitler's Empire*, likewise fails to offer any systematic comparison of the occupation regimes.
27. On the research situation with respect to the individual regions, see the literature review at the end of the volume.

28. See, for example, Institute of Jewish Affairs of the American Jewish Congress, World Jewish Congress, *Hitler's Ten-Year War on the Jews* (New York, 1943); Gerhard Jacoby, *Racial State: The German Nationalities Policy in the Protectorate of Bohemia-Moravia* (New York, 1944); The Jewish Black Book Committee, *The Black Book: The Nazi Crime against the Jewish People* (New York, 1946).
29. On this, see Gerhard Paul, "Von Psychopathen, Technokraten des Terrors und 'ganz gewöhnlichen Deutschen': Die Täter der Shoah im Spiegel der Forschung," in *Die Täter der Shoah. Fanatische Nationalsozialisten oder ganz normale Deutsche*, ed. Gerhard Paul (Göttingen, 2002), 13–90, here 14; Mazower, *Hitler's Empire*, 6f. See also the individual chapters in Jan Eckel and Claudia Moisel, eds., *Universalisierung des Holocaust? Erinnerungskultur und Geschichtspolitik in internationaler Perspektive*, Beiträge zur Geschichte des Nationalsozialismus, vol. 24 (Göttingen, 2008).
30. On the historiography, see Dieter Pohl, "Die Holocaust-Forschung und Goldhagens Thesen," *Vierteljahrshefte für Zeitgeschichte* 45 (1997): 1–48, here 3f.; Christoph Dieckmann and Babette Quinkert, "Einleitung," in *Kooperation und Verbrechen: Formen der 'Kollaboration' im östlichen Europa 1939–1945*, ed. Babette Quinkert et al., Beiträge zur Geschichte des Nationalsozialismus, vol. 19 (Göttingen, 2003), 9–21.
31. On the historiographical developments in the respective countries, see the literature review at the end of this volume.
32. On this, see Eckel and Moisel, *Universalisierung des Holocaust?*

CHAPTER 1

SAAR REGION
Gerhard J. Teschner

Prior to Reintegration into the German Reich

The territory designated as the Saar Region or Saarland after the end of the First World War did not previously exist as a political administrative unit. Most of the so-called Saar Basin had belonged to Rhenish Prussia and a smaller portion to the Bavarian Palatinate. Based on the supra-regional economic importance of the local coal mining and steel industries, the 1919 Peace Treaty of Versailles, which imposed a number of territorial losses on the German Reich, created the Saar Region as a territory with a special status. It consisted, on the one hand, of parts of the Prussian Regierungsbezirk (government district) of Trier—namely, the city of Saarbrücken, the Landkreise (rural districts) of Saarbrücken, Saarlouis, and Ottweiler, and sections of the Kreise (districts) of Merzig and Wendel—and, on the other hand, parts of the Bavarian Palatinate, namely, the Bezirksamt (district) of St. Ingbert and sections of the Bezirksämter of Homburg and Zweibrücken.[1]

A Government Commission controlled by the newly created League of Nations henceforth administrated the Saar Region.[2] The League of Nations had appointed the Frenchman Victor Rault as the commission's president, and he received support from the commissioners

Adam Gottlob Carl Moltke-Hvitfeldt from Denmark, Jacques Lambert from Belgium, Richard Deans Waugh from Canada, and Alfred von Boch from the Saarland.[3] France tried to use the formation of the Saar Region to secure an unlimited influence on the aforementioned industrial sectors, in large part because of the extensive destruction of the industrial region in northern France, where most of the fighting between the Germans and the French had occurred.[4] In accordance with the new Saar Statute, France took over the sixty-six coal mines and their operations.[5] The Saar Statute in the Versailles Treaty stipulated that, after fifteen years (thus, in 1935), the region's population was supposed to participate in a plebiscite to decide its political future, namely, whether to retain the status quo, join France, or reintegrate with the German Reich.[6]

During the League of Nations' fiduciary administration, German jurisprudence and legislation[7]—respectively, their Prussian or Bavarian embodiments—remained in effect in the former Prussian and Bavarian-Palatine regions. Notwithstanding its economic incorporation with France, which for all citizens manifested itself in the introduction of French currency as of May 1921,[8] the Saar Region's purely German population remained bound to the German Reich in many respects: through the bureaucracy, for instance, which remained in the region and was taken over by the Government Commission; through the continued existence of ecclesiastical connections with the Catholic bishoprics of Speyer and Trier; and through the school system, because the Saar Region did not have its own university, which meant that high school graduates had to study at universities in Germany. The Saar Region's citizens also retained their German nationality.[9]

The Reich's Foreign Office was officially responsible for Germany's relations with the Government Commission, but the Reich as well as the states of Prussia and Bavaria had a number of additional individual bodies that maintained connections with the Saar Region.[10] In turn, a Landesrat (parliament) represented the population vis-à-vis the Government Commission, but only in an advisory capacity, not a legislative one. Initially, the parliament's members consisted chiefly of representatives from the liberal German-Saarland People's Party (Deutsch-Saarländische Volkspartei; DSVP), the Catholic Center Party, the Social Democratic Party, and the Communist Party. These parties unequivocally defined themselves by virtue of their close relationship with the German Reich and their parent parties operating in Germany. In contrast, until the end of the 1920s, radical right-wing parties, as well as Francophile groups, were irrelevant.[11]

In 1919, 705,445 people lived in the Saar Region, including 3,933 members of the Jewish faith. By 1927, the population had increased to 770,030, including 4,038 religious Jews. The Jewish portion of the population thus decreased slightly from 0.56 percent to 0.52 percent; compared to the rural districts, the city of Saarbrücken stood out, with 1,721 Jewish residents in 1927, which corresponded to 42 percent of the Saar Region's entire Jewish population.[12]

Jews had lived in the Saar Region as early as the Middle Ages. In 1935, the region featured seventy-two Jewish communities, organized into eighteen synagogue communities, namely, eleven corporations under public law and seven associations. Predominantly middle-class, the Jewish population contributed strongly to the liberal professions and commerce. Jews played an important role in the wholesale and retail textile and footwear trade and the livestock and grain trade. Jewish entrepreneurs operated in paper and metal processing, engineering, and the textile and chemical industries. Within the liberal professions, many Jews practiced medicine and law, whereas fewer worked for the civil service. Jewish businesspeople and entrepreneurs employed approximately 7,000 people.[13] The 1920s did not feature any noticeable tensions between Jews and Christians. Jews actively participated in public life as delegates from various political parties and as mandated representatives of associations and federations.[14]

After its appointment by the League of Nations, the Government Commission set up an administration independent of Germany. Its sometimes discordant relations with the Saar Region's population precipitated a large strike in 1923, resulting in an investigation by the League of Nations. Consequently, the Government Commission adopted a less pro-France course; in 1926, the French Chairman Victor Rault was replaced by the Canadian George Washington Stephens, who by 1935 had been followed by two Britons, Ernest C. Wilton and Sir Geoffrey George Knox.[15]

Despite the fifteen-year waiting period—stipulated in the Treaty of Versailles—until the plebiscite regarding the Saar Region's future, discussions about an earlier return of the Saar to the German Reich without a plebiscite had already begun in 1926 after a meeting in Thoiry between German Foreign Minister Gustav Stresemann and his French counterpart Aristide Briand, but these deliberations ended without any results due to France's opposition.[16] A renewed round of French-German negotiations regarding an early reintegration occurred between November 1929 and July 1930, but remained unsuccessful. Discussions focused primarily on the repurchase price for the coal mines as well as customs matters. The 1930 world economic crisis also discouraged further negotiations.[17] Notwithstanding a few other contacts with the French that failed, however, to produce any progress (through Reich Chancellor Franz von Papen, for example, in 1932), the German government and diplomatic corps henceforth prepared for the plebiscite anticipated in 1935.[18]

Adolf Hitler's appointment as Reich Chancellor on 30 January 1933 profoundly affected Germany's Saarland policies—not surprisingly, since the National Socialists had made revising the Versailles Treaty a primary political objective (see figure 1.1). In addition, after the Nazi seizure of power in the Reich, efforts also predominated to invigorate the NSDAP in the Saar Region, since prior to 1933 it had played only an extremely minor role in the region, despite having already been mentioned for the first time in 1923.[19] On 1 January 1927, with the Government Commission's approval, the NSDAP founded the Saarland Gau under the first Gauleiter Jakob Jung. The party had acquired 261 members by 1930,[20] but its membership then increased to more than 2,550 by the end of 1932. During the 1932 parliamentary elections, the NSDAP obtained 6.7 percent of the votes, thus winning two parliamentary seats.[21] On 8 November 1932, however, the Government Commission, which felt obligated to maintain law and order, banned all Nazi organizations in the Saar Region.[22] Consisting at the time of the British Knox (as President), the Finn Leo Ehrnrooth, the Frenchman Jean Morize, the Saarlander Bartholomäus Koßmann, and the Yugoslav Milovan Zoricic, the commission also rejected the application by the Saar Region's NSDAP on 20 February 1933 to have the ban revoked.[23]

Along with Knox, Koßmann played an important role in the Government Commission's relations with the German Reich. From the opposite direction, connections with the Saar Region were maintained by Heinrich Schneider as the Prussian and Reich Interior Ministry's Saar advisor and, on the part of the Bavarian Palatinate, initially by Heinrich Jolas (retired in 1932) as the Bavarian Staatskommissar (State Commissioner) for the Palatinate and subsequently by Richard Binder, who would also act as an advisor to the Palatinate's NSDAP Gauleiter Josef Bürckel. Karl Barth, a former member of the High Consistory of the established regional Church of the Palatinate, also worked for Bürckel, becoming his personal advisor as well in August 1934. In order to bring the Saar policies of Reich-German agencies together under one roof, on 14 November 1933 the Reich Chancellor created the Office of the Saarbevollmächtigte (Saar Commissioner), appointing Vice

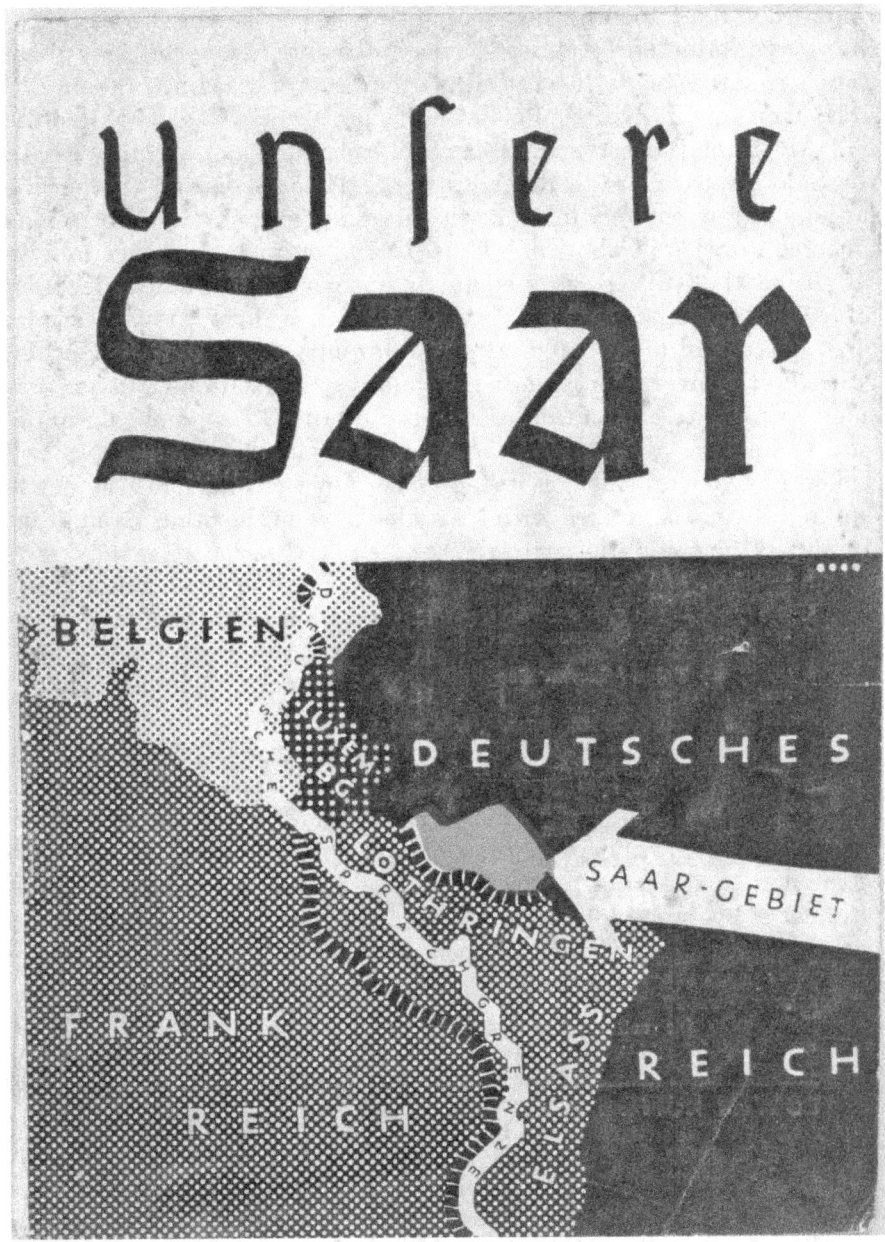

Figure 1.1. *Our Saar*—A propagandistic text regarding the Saarland plebiscite (so-called *Grenzkampf-Schrift*) by Heinrich Schneider, 1934. *Source:* Archive Wolf Gruner.

Chancellor von Papen to the position. Bürckel took over the office less than a year later, on 7 August 1934: a half a year before the Saar plebiscite, the stage was set for the Gauleiter's ever increasing influence.[24]

Hitler's appointment as Reich Chancellor tremendously boosted the NSDAP in the Saar Region itself. Since people generally anticipated the Saar's return to the Reich after the 1935 plebiscite, the party's influence grew not only in professional organizations and associations but also directly in politics.[25] Thus during municipal by-elections in July 1933, the NSDAP attained an increase in votes in Ludweiler from 50 to 786 (now 31 percent of all votes) and in Nalbach from 83 to 601 (46.4 percent of all votes).[26] After 30 January 1933, the influence of NSDAP supporters and members in many organizations and associations soon led to a situation referred to by the Government Commission as an *administration clandestine*.[27] In the process, the NSDAP exploited two methods for its advance. On the one hand, it deftly equated the national idea with Nazi ideology; on the other hand, it intimidated the population with references to the period after the Saar's return to the Reich.[28] The Government Commission responded to such intimidation by issuing various ordinances that subjected those engaging in threats, boycotts, and terror to severe punishment—to the disapproval, however, of a large part of the population and almost all of the political parties.[29]

On 14 July 1933, the NSDAP, DSVP, German National People's Party (Deutschnationale Volkspartei; DNVP), and the Catholic Center Party came together to form the "German Front" to jointly prepare for the 1935 plebiscite and at the same time enable the continued existence of the non-Nazi parties.[30] However, this objective was rendered obsolete just a few months later, since the DNVP dissolved on 20 September 1933, the DSVP on 6 October, and the Center Party—after harsh internal conflict—on 13 October 1933. The Center Party's demise was especially important for the National Socialists, for it bereft the Catholic portion of the population of political representation.[31] At the instigation of the Palatinate's Gauleiter Bürckel, the Saar NSDAP disbanded in spring 1934 so that, at least outwardly, the former parties and their representatives appeared as equal participants in the German Front. Jakob Pirro from Homburg, one of Bürckel's confidants, was elected as the German Front's regional leader.[32] By dissolving, the Saarland's nationalist parties followed the example set a few months earlier by their parent/affiliated parties in the Reich, which had admittedly approved the Enabling Act on 27 March 1933 but without managing to win any gratitude from the new Nazi rulers.[33]

As the sole remaining democratic party, the Social Democratic Party sought a five- or ten-year postponement of the Saar Region's impending plebiscite, since the guarantees for a free vote and for the personal freedom of opponents after the return to the German Reich seemed insufficient. Neither wanting nor able to amend the provisions of the Treaty of Versailles, the German Front as well as the Council of the League of Nations, the Government Commission, and France opposed the Social Democratic Party's recommendation. On 4 June 1934, the Council of the League of Nations scheduled the plebiscite regarding the Saar Region's future for 13 January 1935.[34]

So on 6 June 1934, the Social Democratic Party exhorted the population to retain the status quo "until the day on which a Germany, having become free again, in an honest and sustained willingness to communicate with a similar such France, makes possible a final political and economic allocation of the Saar between the two peoples [*Völker*]."[35] The Communist Party had issued the same appeal regarding the plebiscite on 2 June 1934 in the *Arbeiterzeitung*. On 4 July 1934, both parties, as a "Freedom Front," published an exhortation signed by their two respective chairmen.[36]

Since spring 1933, the Jews in the Saar Region had also found themselves exposed to increasing anti-Semitic pressure, even though the German Front, largely to avoid giving the Government Commission any reason to intervene, exercised restraint. The Nazi newspaper *Saardeutsche Volksstimme* stood at the forefront of the anti-Semitic agitation, writing in an extremely insulting manner about Jewish influence at the Saarbrücken theater, for example.[37]

The anti-Jewish laws in the Reich also directly affected a number of Jews in the Saar Region. For example, they now applied to the region's Jewish legal professionals who were completing part of their training at the Oberlandesgericht (Higher Regional Court) of Cologne; they could only finish their training by means of a special arrangement through the Reich Ministry of Justice.[38] The persecution of Jews in the Reich as of February 1933 also led to an increase in the number of Jewish emigrants in the Saar Region, who had to be cared for by the Jewish religious communities. Reports by these people, notably by a number of journalists and authors, provided Jewish Saarlanders with authentic knowledge regarding conditions in the German Reich.[39]

The Committee of Jewish Delegations in Paris also performed critically important work during the period both immediately before and after the plebiscite. In a memorandum to the League of Nations on 6 February 1934, the Committee requested guarantees for the implementation of a free plebiscite without any impediments for those who sympathized with retaining the status quo or joining France. And, more importantly, it demanded that the Reich's anti-Jewish laws not be introduced in the event that Germany annexed the Saar, insisting instead that the rules established by the League of Nations on 21 September 1922 for the protection of minorities be applied to the Saar Region's Jews. Citing numerous examples, the memorandum documented the preexisting anti-Semitic attitudes and practices that prevailed both in part of the population and in the Saar Region's administration.[40] This memorandum was joined in support by a petition in the same tone signed by the chairpersons of the Joint Foreign Committee of the Board of Deputies of British Jews and the Anglo-Jewish Association and submitted to the British government.[41]

In two expert reports written for the Council of the League of Nations, the American Manley O. Hudson and the Swiss citizen Maurice Bourquin emphasized the League of Nations' obligation under § 34 of the Appendix to Article 50 of the Treaty of Versailles to ensure a "free, secret, and independent plebiscite."[42] Both experts also pointed out that, according to § 35 of the Appendix, the "League of Nations shall decide under which state sovereignty the territory would be placed, taking into consideration the desire expressed through the plebiscite."[43] Thus, the course of action after the plebiscite did not automatically proceed from the plebiscite's results; rather, the League of Nations made the final decision, which could also be subject to conditions, such as protections for minorities. This had been standard practice since the end of the war for other regions, such as in the territories ceded by Germany to Poland.[44]

On 1 September 1934, in a new memorandum, the Committee of Jewish Delegations recommended areas to the League of Nations where the latter could impose conditions on the respective state that would take over the Saar Region after the plebiscite, suggesting among other things a guarantee for one's free choice of nationality, the freedom to leave the country with one's possessions, the right to freely pursue one's profession and continue an already initiated school or university education, and the prohibition of legislation banning Jewish kosher slaughter (*shechita*).[45]

The League of Nations had already deployed a three-person committee chaired by the Italian diplomat Baron Pompeo Aloisi for the Saar plebiscite on 20 January 1934. During the course of 1934, this committee dealt with the demands for a guarantee declaration, negotiating repeatedly with the German and French governments with such guarantees in mind. Following two declarations—the first by the Reich Foreign Minister Konstantin Freiherr von Neurath on 2 June and the second by him on 3 December after Hitler's personal decision on 27 November—the German Reich approved a special regulation for the Saar Region's Jews that for the period of one year after reintegration—that is, until 29 February 1936—exempted the Saar Region from German "Aryan" legislation and allowed Saarland Jews to emigrate freely with their assets. In the Rome Agreement of 3 December 1934, Germany also concluded arrangements with France regarding the future of the Saar Region's mines.[46] Even though the Agreement failed to meet the full approval of the Committee of Jewish Delegates,[47] it substantially helped create the conditions that allowed many of the Saar Region's Jews to escape the Nazi regime.

The First Year of the Reintegration

On 13 January 1935, with a voter participation rate of 97.88 percent, the people of the Saar Region voted 90.53 percent for reunifying the Saar Region with Germany, 8.83 percent for retaining the status quo, and 0.40 percent for unifying with France.[48] Many observers viewed these results as an unexpectedly broad approval for reunification with the German Reich. People had generally anticipated a higher percentage of votes in favor of retaining the status quo, largely because even though many voters wanted the region to return to Germany, they did not want it to return to Hitler's German Reich. Assessed against the allocation of seats resulting from the last parliamentary election, in which the parties advocating the retention of the status quo (Social Democrats and Communists) had managed to win 37 percent of the seats, the approximately 9 percent of the votes for retaining the existing status proved bitterly disappointing.[49] We can assume that most Jews voted to retain the status quo, but this cannot be documented.[50] In light of the plebiscite's results, on 17 January 1935 the Council of the League of Nations approved the reunification of the Saar Region with the German Reich, stipulating 1 March as the designated date.[51]

Notwithstanding Bavarian and Prussian efforts to reinstate the status that existed prior to the Saar Region's creation, the Law on the Preliminary Administration of the Saarland retained the Saarland's integrity.[52] Bürckel had already received a commitment from Hitler in December 1934 that he would be given control of the Saar Region after the plebiscite victory. When the law went into force on 1 March 1935,

Bürckel was appointed as the Reich Commissioner for the Reintegration of the Saarland (Reichskommissar für die Rückgliederung des Saarlandes) and the Saarland—even though not expressly designated as such—became a state of the Reich. A number of Bürckel's confidants from the Palatinate obtained good posts—the aforementioned Binder and Barth, for example, as Regierungsdirektoren (government directors)—in the leading sections of his commissarial office (in a certain sense, the Saarland's government), which was not always well received in the Saarland itself.[53]

On 23 March 1935, Reich Interior Minister Frick informed the highest Reich and state authorities about the guarantees provided by the Reich in the Rome Agreement to protect minorities, but in particular about the right of persons residing in the Saarland on 3 December 1934 to leave the Saarland with their assets without incurring any levies if they registered their emigration in writing with the Reich Commissioner by 31 August 1935 and emigrated by 29 February 1936.[54] The Würzburg state revenue office, responsible for the former Bavarian part of the Saarland, had already informed the Saarland revenue offices on 5 March 1935 that the Reich Flight Tax could not be imposed on this specific group of people until February 1936.[55] The Supreme Plebiscite Court in Saarbrücken, a League of Nations institution, monitored compliance with the guarantees until the transitional period expired in spring 1936.[56]

How, then, did the Saarland's Jews react to the reintegration? Rabbi Dr. Lothar Rothschild, a Saarlander originally from Basel, presented his views on the situation of the Jews along the Saar in a Viennese newspaper on 21 January 1935, anticipating difficult times above all for poor Jews, because the wealthy could emigrate more easily, as could young people, who would go to Palestine. The community had to get ready for a large-scale welfare operation in order to help those "who today . . . as employees and workers live from their salaries, from hand to mouth, and who one day, bereft of all employment opportunities, will stand baffled and helpless in the street."[57]

Officials complied in various ways with the guarantees provided by the German Reich, as shown by the appeals submitted to the Supreme Plebiscite Court against the German authorities, especially at lower administrative levels.[58] Already on 2 April 1935, Reich Commissioner Bürckel issued an order requiring Saarland officials to substantiate their "Aryan" lineage. This order had to be rescinded on 20 May, however, after the Foreign Office and the Reich Ministry of Justice intervened, seeing here a violation of Rome Agreement. Consequently,

Bürckel no longer demanded any formal "Aryan certification" through birth or baptism certificates, but he still had all officials fill out a general questionnaire that also solicited information regarding their "Aryan" lineage.[59]

The number of appeals to the Supreme Plebiscite Court sheds light on the treatment of protected groups of people during the period after reintegration. By 29 February 1936, 371 appeals were submitted to the court, including 366 directed against German authorities or private individuals. In an additional ninety-four cases, the German state representative Heinrich Welsch, director of the Trier Gestapo, managed to thwart an official appeal. Only forty-one people who raised an appeal still lived in the country. The number of Jewish claimants amounted to seventy-seven, approximately 20 percent of the plaintiffs. The many complaints brought before the court demonstrate that the admonishments issued by various Reich German authorities to local agencies did not always ensure compliance with the Rome Agreement at the local level.[60]

The facts listed in a 21 September 1935 petition submitted to the Council of the League Nations in Geneva by Reich-German emigrants illustrate the conduct of the Saarland authorities and NSDAP organizations. The petition was formulated by the Saarland Social Democrat Max Braun, the authors Heinrich Mann, Lion Feuchtwanger, and Ernst Toller, the former floor leader of the SPD in the Reichstag Rudolf Breitscheid, as well as various emigrant organizations in Paris. Regarding the treatment of the Jewish population, explicitly protected by the Rome Agreement, they reported on the incarceration of a Jewish businessman, Erich Oppenheimer, for "racial defilement," and the ejection of thirty Jews from the Deutschmühlen municipal swimming pool, specifically mentioning a businessman named Kahn; in Saarbrücken, the windows of a Jewish hairdresser on Ludwigstraße were broken, patrons at the Café Assmann were hassled because they were suspected to be Jews, and customers of Jewish stores that had been posted with signs had been insulted and photographed.[61] Even though the Foreign Office and the Ministries of Justice and the Interior urged scrupulous compliance with the guarantees provided in the Rome Agreement, everyday life for the Jewish population in the Saarland now hardly differed from that of the Jews in the Reich. Even Reich Commissioner Bürckel did not strongly oppose such activities.

Quite the contrary: the Reich Commissioner's administration very quickly took action in another area, namely, the school system. Adopting a decree by the Reich and Prussian Minister for Science, Education, and National Culture on 10 September 1935, the Reich Commissioner pointed out to Saarland authorities on 23 September 1935 that "children of Jewish descent form a strong impediment to the unity of the classroom community and the undisrupted implementation of a National Socialist youth education," therefore making it necessary to think about establishing Jewish schools.[62] Responses from the individual school boards drew attention to the statutory basis—existing in part since the nineteenth century—for founding and maintaining Jewish elementary schools. The statement by the Saarbrücken II School District concluded: "They [the Jews] are obligated to set up Jewish elementary schools in centrally situated localities in accordance with actual needs," but that in the event of insufficient finances these schools could be supported by the respective municipalities or by the state.[63] In another circular to the Saarland's school directors and school district administrators from 11 November 1935, the Reich Commissioner demanded that "in all schools particular attention [was] to be given to racial-political enlightenment." The "fateful significance of race," he insisted, must be handled in the entire curriculum and not only in special classes.[64]

According to the census on 1 January 1933, 4,638 Jews lived in the Saar Region, corresponding to 0.56 percent of the entire population.[65] On 25 June 1935 in the first census after reintegration with the German Reich, the number of Jews had already declined to 3,117 persons,[66] leading to the conclusion that a significant portion of the Jewish population living in the Saar Region had emigrated not only during the first four months after reintegration but also earlier. Josef Bürckel took stock of the emigration declarations in a report written to the Reich Interior Ministry dated 25 May 1936—thus after the Rome Agreement's one-year guarantee period had expired. His office had received 2,350 such declarations, accepting 2,225 of them. By the expiration of the deadline on 29 February 1936, 317 were withdrawn, including 265 from Saarland Jews. The remaining 1,908 valid declarations, however, pertained to a far larger number of emigrants, since only one declaration had to be made per family.[67] Another survey of police authorities arranged by Bürckel tallied a total of 4,644 emigrating persons, including 2,014 Jews.[68]

However much the emigration of Jews conformed with the Reich government's desire to render the Reich "Jew free" as quickly as possible,[69] the fiscal authorities faced the problem of procuring foreign currency for Jews emigrating from the Saarland, because, on the one hand, these Jews were exempt from the Reich Flight Tax and, on the other hand, they could transfer their personal assets abroad without incurring any deductions. The authorities carefully ensured that the assets registered by emigrants actually belonged to their personal property and were not being moved abroad by third parties using this method. Since the Nazi seizure of power, the scarcity of foreign currency constituted a constant problem for the Nazi economy, which was dependent on imports.[70]

Overall, the Saarland's population benefited from the guarantees issued for the first year, especially if we compare the reintegration of the Saar Region into the German Reich with later annexations. Above all, the activities of the Supreme Plebiscite Court during this period must have had a positive impact, particularly since, as a result of the existing legal situation, its decisions were rarely appealed.[71]

The Saar Region as a Fully Integrated Part of the German Reich

As of 1 March 1936, the Jews in the Saar Region received the same treatment as Jews in the rest of the Reich, that is, they faced the same degree of discrimination and persecution. The so-called Nuremberg Laws—namely, the Law for the Protection of German Blood and German Honor (Gesetz zum Schutze des deutschen Blutes und der deutschen Ehre), enacted on 15 September 1935 at the Nuremberg Rally, and the Reich Citizen Law (Reichsbürgergesetz) from that same date——now also applied to the Saarland's Jews.[72] A confidential circular order from the Reich Commissioner on 20 January 1936 drew attention to the application of the provisions. In the same order, however, Bürckel reminded officials that, even after 29 February, persecuting or retaliating against persons who had adopted a different political stance during the League of Nations' administration of the Saar Region would not be permitted.[73]

Naturally, Saarland authorities now applied all of the other laws and ordinances enacted in the Reich since 1933 to exclude the Jews from public service and certain professions. These laws and ordinances included the Law for the Restoration of the Professional Civil Service (Gesetz zur Wiederherstellung des Berufsbeamtentums) and the Law on the Admission to the Legal Profession (Gesetz über die Zulassung zur Rechtsanwaltschaft) of 7 April 1933, and the Ordinance on the Admission of Doctors for Work at Healthcare Funds (Verordnung über die Zulassung von Ärzten zur Tätigkeit bei den Krankenkassen) of

22 April 1933, as well as regulations governing school and university attendance and religious practices like the slaughtering of animals. For example, on 15 June 1936 the Reich Ministry of Justice issued an ordinance for the Saarland that—applying the corresponding law of 1933—revoked the admission of "non-privileged non-Aryan legal attorneys to the legal profession by 30 September 1936."[74] Because the Rome Agreement's guarantees had expired during preparations for the August 1936 Olympics in Berlin, Reich authorities made an effort to prevent extreme attacks against German Jews in order to avoid creating the impression that Jews suffered discrimination in Germany.[75]

The facts verify the predictions made in 1935 by Rabbi Rothschild from Saarbrücken.[76] A substantial number of Jews emigrated from the Saarland, even after 29 February 1936. This weakened the Jewish communities, which in many cases could no longer economically sustain their synagogues or appoint enough board members to comply with legal standards, which in the Prussian part of the Saarland were still based on a law from 23 July 1847. Thus the synagogue community in Saarwellingen requested permission to sell a schoolhouse,[77] and the Jewish communities in the Kreis of Saarbrücken and the community in Merzig applied to the Office of the Reich Commissioner to request the appointment of a commissioner because they could no longer fill their board positions.[78] By 30 October 1936, state commissioners had to be appointed for a large number of communities—Saarbrücken, Neunkirchen, Illingen, Saarwellingen, Saarlautern (Saarlouis), Dillingen, Merzig, Schönbruch, Rehlingen, and Wallerfangen—which affected virtually all of the former Prussian parts of the Saarland with largest Jewish populations.[79] Just a few months later, on 4 April 1937, the Jewish communities in Illingen, Neunkirchen, and Merzig merged,[80] while in March 1937 St. Wendel's synagogue community still existed but with only nineteen members.[81] The Law on the Legal Status of Jewish Religious Associations was issued on 28 March 1938, which revoked the status of Jewish communities as corporations under public law, halting the activities of state commissioners on their behalf.[82] Henceforth these communities had to be registered as associations under civil law.[83]

Meanwhile, the German Reich's Anschluss of Austria had changed Germany's political landscape. On 12 March 1938, German troops advanced into Austria, and the Law on the Reunification of Austria with the German Reich entered into force on 13 March.[84] A plebiscite on 10 August 1938 sanctioned the Anschluss with 99.7 percent of the votes. The Anschluss of Austria advanced Josef Bürckel's career, leading to his appointment on 13 March 1938 as the Reich Commissioner for Austria's Reunification with the Reich (Reichskommissar für die Wiedervereinigung Österreichs mit dem Reich). As a result of his activities as the Reich Commissioner in the Saarland and the region's successful reintegration, he seemed predestined for this new assignment. A number of his staff from the Saarland accompanied him to Vienna, including the aforementioned Regierungsdirektor Karl Barth.[85]

Apart from his other activities, Bürckel founded the Central Office of Jewish Emigration (Zentralstelle für jüdische Auswanderung) in Vienna on 20 August 1938, led by SS-Standartenführer Dr. Walter Stahlecker and also employing Adolf Eichmann. The so-called Nisko operation in October 1939, involving the deportation of approximately 5,000 Czech and Austrian Jews to the eastern part of the General Government, created after the occupation of Poland, occurred during the tenures of Bürckel in Vienna and Eichmann in Prague.[86]

On the basis of his experiences in Vienna, Bürckel later realized his idea of a political unification of the Bavarian Palatinate and the Saarland. The order to merge the two regions was issued on 8 April 1940—and Bürckel became Reich Commissioner for the Saar-Palatinate (Reichskommissar für die Saarpfalz).[87] Bürckel had ceased his work as the Reich Commissioner in Vienna on 15 March, but he remained in the city until the appointment of a Reich Governor (Reichsstatthalter) in the summer, returning to the Saarland on 4 August 1940. During his absence, Deputy Gauleiter Ernst Ludwig Leyser had been responsible for the Palatinate and Saarland.[88]

Bürckel's absence did nothing to change the fate of the Saarland's Jews, who were harassed to the same degree as Jews throughout the entire Reich and robbed of their livelihoods. During the Night of Broken Glass on 9 November 1938, synagogues also burned in the Saarland, and stores and residences were plundered. Thus SA Brigade 151 reported the next day that the synagogue in Saarbrücken had been set ablaze and the synagogues in Dillingen, Merzig, Saarlouis, Saarwellingen, and Brotdorf had been destroyed; all of the synagogues in the districts of Ottweiler and St. Wendel were damaged as well. Many Jews were taken into so-called protective custody.[89] As in the rest of the Reich, the surviving synagogue communities had to arrange and pay for the final demolition of the damaged synagogues; in Saarbrücken, municipal authorities confiscated 10,000 RM for this purpose from one of the community's bank accounts, transferring the funds to the city treasury.[90]

In particular, Nazi officials repeatedly surveyed and discussed the landed property of Jews during the period from 1938 to 1940/41. On

13 December 1938, the Reich Commissioner for the Saarland sent the Reich Minister for Nutrition and Agriculture an "Overview of the Settlement Capacity of Saarland Landed Property in Jewish Hands," which listed the corresponding communities, albeit without specifying the sizes of the properties.[91] On 6 February 1940 (thus after the start of the war) the Reich Commissioner formulated a similar report to the same ministry in far more concrete terms, specifying an agricultural area of 231 hectares for the Saarland. The report itemized the properties individually according whether their owners were from hostile countries, neutral countries, or German state subjects, as well as combinations of these three categories, noting however that "considering the predominance of non-German property, obstacles will probably continue to impede the practical exploitation of the Jewish property. . . ." According to the report, the diverse range of property relations resulted from the Agreement on the Saarland's reintegration, which had facilitated Jewish efforts to emigrate and obtain foreign citizenship.[92] On 18 October 1940, at a "Conference on the Dejudaization of Agricultural Landed Property," representatives and high officials from the Reich Ministry of Nutrition extensively discussed the issue of exploiting Jewish landed property, but without reaching any general solutions. They noted that Jewish owners were entitled to treatment in accordance with the applicable laws and, in the event of a sale, to proper proceeds, "which could be about 10 percent lower than the general market value. . . . If the Jew is not paid the market value, then, for his part, he cannot pay the Reich Flight Tax and the Jew levy. Furthermore, the opportunity to emigrate will be taken from him if he cannot retain the means to do so."[93] A document from 31 December 1941 finally recorded the 216.44 hectares of originally Jewish agricultural property in the Saarland in tabulated form, broken down according to Kreise, and an area of 10.36 hectares—thus 4.8 percent—that had since been transferred into "Aryan" ownership. For three years, and despite substantial efforts, practically no progress had been achieved—at least from the perspective of the authorities dealing with the matter.[94]

The Jews continued to emigrate. Thus the census of the "Greater German Reich" on 17 May 1939 registered only 494 persons of the Jewish faith in the Saarland.[95] Accordingly, since the census on 25 June 1935—that is, within four years—the Saarland's Jewish population had drastically decreased by more than 2,500 persons. Of these, 1,062 had emigrated between 1 January and 25 May 1936; for the second half of 1935 and after May 1936, Hans-Walter Herrmann has calculated an additional 1,200 to 1,300 emigrations and approximately eighty deportations to Poland.[96] Just over a third of the remaining Jews—namely, 177—lived in Saarbrücken; 39 still lived in Merzig/Brotdorf, 36 in Illingen, and 34 in Saarlouis.[97]

The German invasion of Poland on 1 September 1939 and France's declaration of war against Germany two days later affected the Jewish (as well as the "Aryan") population insofar as the inhabitants of the "red zone" near the border (including the cities of Saarbrücken, Saarlouis, and Merzig) were evacuated to the German Reich's interior, primarily to Thuringia and Upper Franconia. After the success of the German military campaign in France, non-Jewish residents were able to return to their towns and villages in August 1940, but the Jews were not. At the beginning of the war the latter were housed primarily in collective quarters in Halle an der Saale and Dessau. Later they were transferred to camps in Mark Brandenburg, where they had to perform forced labor.[98] The non-evacuated remainder of the Jewish population in Saarland communities located farther from the border lived primarily in Homburg and Ottweiler, as well as in a few communities in the Kreis of Saarlouis.[99]

On 22 October 1940, the Nazis deported all of the Jews from the Gaue of Baden and the Saar-Palatinate—a total of 6,507—to unoccupied France. Even though these measures involved far more Jews from Baden than from the Palatinate and the Saarland, they were referred to as the "Bürckel Operation." According to a contemporary list, the Nazis deported 134 persons from the Saarland; Hans-Walter Herrmann has revised this figure to 145 persons.[100]

This deportation operation had been well prepared in secret. On the morning of 22 October, various police forces (Schutzpolizei, Kriminalpolizei, and the Gendarmerie) located the Jewish families (registered in lists) and notified them of the deportation order. According to the order, the deportees officially had two hours (in many cases, substantially less time) to assemble fifty kilograms of baggage per person, a complete set of clothing, one wool blanket per person, food for a number of days, eating and drinking utensils, all personal identification papers, and cash in the amount of 100 RM in preparation for the transport. They had to leave behind any cash, various valuables, and other property exceeding this amount.[101] The police forces designated for the seizures had received a sheet of printed instructions stipulating how they were to handle property that was left behind.[102] Only Jews who were married to an "Aryan" spouse or, by chance, were not found in their homes on the respective date, escaped the deportation.[103]

The Saarland Jews, who chiefly came from locations far from the border, were brought to the Gestapo office in Saarbrücken, where they signed over their real estate to the Reich Association of Jews in Germany (Reichsvereinigung der Juden in Deutschland). They were then taken to Forbach and subsequently deported by rail to southern France, probably together with Palatinate Jews in the same train.[104]

The border crossing from the occupied zone in France to the non-occupied zone occurred at the train stations of Chalon-sur-Saône and Mâcon. Eichmann, who probably organized the deportation's entire logistics, waited here in person; he was visibly relieved to have gotten rid of Germany's undesired Jews by deceiving the French authorities—for he had declared the trains Wehrmacht transports.[105]

After the trains arrived in Lyon, the French government in Vichy, the Ceasefire Commission in Wiesbaden, and the German government engaged in fierce communications—on the one hand, the unnotified French had to find accommodations for the deportees; on the other hand, they protested to the German Foreign Office against having to accept the deportees, whom they viewed as German citizens.[106] For its part, the Foreign Office first needed to make inquiries at the Reich Security Main Office (Reichssicherheitshauptamt) and received a letter from Heydrich dated 29 October 1940 that listed the number of Jews and the circumstances surrounding the deportation: "The Führer ordered the deportation of the Jews from Baden via the Alsace and Jews from the Palatinate via Lorraine. After the implementation of the operation, I can inform you that from Baden on 22 and 23/10/1940, with seven transport trains, and from the Palatinate on 22/10/1940, with two transport trains, 6,507 Jews, in agreement with local duty stations of the Wehrmacht, without previously informing the French authorities, were moved to the unoccupied part of France via Chalon-sur-Saône."[107] The French government now had to rapidly decide where to send the trains from Germany. It chose a camp at the foot of the Pyrenees—Gurs, in the Département Basses-Pyrénées (Prefecture Pau), which had been quickly built from scratch at the end of the Spanish Civil War in spring 1939 for fighters on the side of the Spanish Republic who had been interned in France. Consisting of a number of sectors separated by barbed wire, the internment camp was setup under the French army's administration. The basic component was a lightly constructed simple cabin—unheated, poorly lit, and with extremely limited space (approximately 0.75 x 2.0 meters per person)—accommodating sixty inmates.[108]

Together with deportees from Baden and the Palatinate, the 145 Saarlanders—ninety women and fifty-five men—arrived at the

Oloron-Sainte-Marie train station on 25 and 26 October. Army trucks brought them to Gurs, where the men were consigned to one block and the women and children to another. Built to provide temporary housing for young soldiers, the camp was by no means suitable for accommodating these refugees, over a third of whom were over sixty.[109] Apart from the poor accommodations (the camp did not even have enough straw mattresses for everyone), the camp lacked adequate medical services, medicine, doctors, and a sufficiently varied food supply. In the cold and damp weather during the onset of winter at the foot of Pyrenees and especially in the poor sanitary conditions, with unenclosed wash stations at each cabin and an unenclosed toilet facility for each block that often could only be reached through ankle-deep mud, the deportees found life difficult to bear. The separation of families according to gender further aggravated their situation—with very few passes that allowed people to move from block to block, married couples managed to see each other only after weeks or months.[110] Many of the deportees from Baden and the Saar-Palatinate died, starting from day one. By 18 January 1941 alone—that is, in just under three months—564 people had perished, predominantly due to old-age infirmity, intestinal infections, and heart failure, according to death certificates issued by the camp's few doctors.[111]

The arrival of the German Jews completely overwhelmed the French authorities, especially since the camp's administration was simultaneously being transferred from the army to the civil government, that is, the prefecture in Pau and the interior ministry in Vichy. During the course of the following months, the food supply improved and some of the inmates were transferred to other camps, some of them new: the elderly to Noé and Le Récébédou near Toulouse, and families to Rivesaltes in the vicinity of Perpignan.[112] At the same time, French Jews and French and international aid organizations—such as the Red Cross, the Quakers, Swiss Children's Aid, and Protestant Church relief organizations—undertook measures that brought small improvements in nutrition and medical support for the camp inmates.[113] During the course of spring 1941, these measures began having a positive effect on the lives of the deportees: during the entire month of July, "only" nine people died in Gurs. Thus for the Jews from Baden and the Saar-Palatinate, camp life assumed a certain "normality." Incidentally, the French authorities never discriminated against these Jews because of their "race"—setting aside the latter's internment in camps, which was covered by the French law on "foreign nationals of the Jewish race" of 4 October 1940 and provided for the internment of foreign Jews in camps according the discretion of the respective department prefects.[114] Some of the deportees continued to pursue emigration efforts, in part with the support of authorities in Germany, who later, however, impeded such efforts because they wanted to reserve the few emigration opportunities during the war for Jews in the Reich.[115]

This "normality," however, came to end when the Nazis began deporting the Jews from France "to the East." At the so-called Wannsee Conference on 20 January 1942,[116] the architects of the operation made plans to comb through Europe from west to east and "evacuate" the Jews from all of the countries within the German sphere of influence. With respect to France, they assumed that there were 165,000 Jews in the occupied zone and 700,000 Jews in the unoccupied zone.[117] After the first arrests in the occupied zone, the deportations to the extermination camps began with the transport from Compiègne on 27 March 1942.[118] In summer 1942, the Gestapo headquarters in Paris expanded the arrests to the unoccupied territory with the assistance of the French police. The camps housing the Jews from Baden, the Palatinate, and the Saarland constituted a convenient reservoir from which to fill the trains destined for Auschwitz. On 6 and 8 August, two transports each with 1,000 Jews left Gurs for the Drancy collection camp near Paris, whence, just a few days later, transport numbers 17 through 21[119] left for Auschwitz with a large number of Jews from Baden and the Saar-Palatinate. In the meantime, Jews from the rest of the camps had been brought to Drancy. The transports from Gurs and the other camps continued into October. In keeping with the age distribution of the camp inmates, very few of the deportees survived their arrival at the extermination camps by being selected for forced labor—the large majority died in the gas chambers.[120]

Hans-Walter Herrmann has endeavored to discover the fate of the 145 Jews deported from the Saarland on 22 October 1940. Thirty of them died in French camps and elsewhere in France; sixty-four died or disappeared in the eastern European camps; eleven emigrated or fled; seventeen survived in France and one in Auschwitz. The fate of twenty-two people remains unknown.[121]

Without a doubt, many of the Jews from the Saarland who were evacuated from the "red zone" to central Germany at the beginning of the war shared the fate of their coreligionists who were deported to France. With the liquidation of the forced labor camps in 1942 and 1943, the Gestapo deported the younger people to Auschwitz and those over sixty-five years old to Theresienstadt (Terezin).[122] Even so, we can assume that approximately 90 percent of the Jews living in the Saar Region in 1933 survived the Holocaust, thanks largely to the guarantees negotiated prior to the region's reintegration into the German Reich.

Conclusion

The Saar Region was formed as a distinct territory after the Treaty of Versailles in 1919 from sections of the Prussian Rhine Province and the Bavarian Palatinate and, for a period of fifteen years until 1935, was placed under the administration of the League of Nations, which appointed a Government Commission for this purpose. The main reason for the creation of the Saar Region lay in the French demand to obtain compensation for damages suffered as a result of the war by taking over the Saar mines.

The region's German population and its political representatives expected that the region would be reintegrated into the German Reich after the plebiscite planned for 1935, which also, however, included the options of joining France or maintaining the status quo. After the National Socialists seized power in Germany on 30 January 1933, the Saar Region's hitherto weak NSDAP grew vigorously and, together with other nationalist parties, conducted an intensified propaganda campaign in support of reintegration. At the same time, the Saarland exhibited continually increasing anti-Semitic tendencies. This prompted Jewish organizations to argue to the League of Nations that, in the event of the Saar's reintegration with Germany, the region's approximately 4,600 Jews needed special protection. In the Rome Agreement negotiated with the League of Nations, the German Reich declared its willingness for a period of a year—that is, until 29 February 1936—not to implement the German anti-Jewish laws in the Saar Region and to allow people the freedom to emigrate without any loss of their assets. After the plebiscite, which decided in favor of Germany with 90 percent of the vote, on 1 March 1935 the Palatinate Gauleiter Josef Bürckel assumed control the Saarland as Reich Commissioner. Despite a few violations of the Rome Agreement's guarantees, prior to and during the period from 1 March 1935 to 29 February 1936, thousands of Jews managed to leave the Saarland.

As of 1 March 1936, all of the Reich's laws that discriminated against the Jews and progressively expelled them from public life applied in the Saarland as well; and in November 1938, synagogues also burned along the Saar. After the war broke out, the Jews from areas near the border were brought to central Germany. Following the victory over France, on 22 October 1940 the Gestapo deported the 145 Jews still remaining in the Saarland to the Gurs internment camp in southern France. Thirty of them died at the camp; sixty-five were transported to Auschwitz in summer 1942, of whom only one survived. Nothing is known about the fate of twenty-two of the deported Saarland Jews, while the rest managed to flee or belatedly emigrate.

Notes

1. *Treaty of Peace with Germany* (New York, 1919), Article 48.
2. Ibid., Article 50, Annex §§ 16 to 21, 40–41.
3. *Journal Officiel de la Société des Nations* (1920), 47ff.
4. *Treaty of Peace with Germany*, Article 45, 32–33.
5. *Treaty of Peace with Germany*, Art. 45 and Art. 50.
6. Ibid., Art. 49 and Art. 50, Annex § 34.
7. The Reich Court also remained the competent court of appeal for civil matters in the Saar Region; Fritz Jacoby, *Die nationalsozialistische Herrschaftsübernahme an der Saar: Die innenpolitischen Probleme der Rückgliederung des Saargebietes bis 1935* (Saarbrücken, 1973), 26.
8. As of 1 May 1921, miners received their wages in francs; they were followed somewhat later by steelworkers and railway and postal employees. As of 30 April 1921, the Saar Region's postage stamps were issued in French currency; Maria Zenner, *Parteien und Politik im Saargebiet unter dem Völkerbundsregime 1920–1935* (Saarbrücken, 1966), 44.
9. *Treaty of Peace with Germany*, Art. 50, Annex §§ 27 and 28.
10. Jacoby, *Herrschaftsübernahme*, 31.
11. Ibid., 38f.
12. Dieter Muskalla, *NS-Politik an der Saar unter Josef Bürckel: Gleichschaltung, Neuordnung, Verwaltung* (Saarbrücken, 1995), 614. On the demographic developments of the Saarland's Jewish population, see (with slighty different figures) Albert Marx, *Die Geschichte der Juden an der Saar: Vom Ancien Régime bis zum Zweiten Weltkrieg* (Saarbrücken, 1992), 160–162.
13. Jacoby, *Herrschaftsübernahme*, document 25, 355.
14. Hans-Walter Herrmann, "Das Schicksal der Juden im Saarland 1920 bis 1945," in *Dokumentation zur Geschichte der jüdischen Bevölkerung in Rheinland-Pfalz und im Saarland von 1800 bis 1945*, vol. 6, published by the Landesarchivverwaltung Rheinland-Pfalz in conjunction with the Landesarchiv Saarbrücken (Koblenz, 1974), 264.
15. Jacoby, *Herrschaftsübernahme*, 27.
16. Ibid., 56ff.
17. Ibid., 67–79.
18. Ibid., 80ff.
19. Zenner, *Parteien*, 251.
20. Ibid., 253, note 24.
21. Ibid., 254.

22. Jacoby, *Herrschaftsübernahme*, 86f.
23. Ibid., 87.
24. Ibid., 92–98.
25. On the consequences of the Saarland's "plebiscite battle" in 1933–1935 for anti-Jewish terror, see Marx, *Geschichte*, 176–178.
26. Zenner, *Parteien*, 259f.
27. *Journal Officiel de la Société des Nations* 14, no. 3 (1934): 303, quoted in Zenner, *Parteien*, 260.
28. Zenner, *Parteien*, 261.
29. Ibid., 262.
30. Ibid., 269.
31. Ibid., 288–291.
32. Ibid., 298f.
33. The DNVP—as of May 1933 the Deutschnationale Front—dissolved on 27 June, the Center Party in July, and the DSVP (associated with Deutsche Volkspartei) on 4 July 1933.
34. Zenner, *Parteien*, 296f., 300ff.
35. Quoted in ibid., 303.
36. Ibid., 303f.
37. Herrmann, "Schicksal," 265f. and doc. no. 9, 268ff. (attacks by the Nazi newspaper *Saardeutsche Volksstimme* against the directors and the general music director of the Saarbrücken theater).
38. Memorandum by the Saarland Israelite Junior Lawyers to the Government Commission, 28 June 1933, ibid., 267 and doc. no. 17, 312ff.
39. Ibid., 269.
40. Ibid., doc. no. 25, 329–344.
41. Supplication by the Chairs of the Foreign Committee of the Board of Deputies of British Jews and the Anglo-Jewish Association, 1 March 1934, ibid., doc. no. 26, 344–349.
42. *Treaty of Peace with Germany*, Appendix § 34 and Article 50.
43. Ibid., Appendix § 35.
44. Legal opinion by Manley O. Hudson, 30 June 1934, ibid., doc. no. 31, 353–362; Legal opinion by Maurice Bourquin, September 1934, ibid., doc. no. 33, 363–370.
45. Ibid., doc. no. 34, 370–373.
46. Jacoby, *Herrschaftsübernahme*, 152–156; *Documents on German Foreign Policy 1919–1939*, series C, vol. 3, no. 373, 706.
47. Resolution of the Committee of Jewish Delegates to the League of Nations, 28 December 1934, Herrmann, "Schicksal," doc. no. 43, 383.
48. Muskalla, *NS-Politik*, 46.
49. Ibid., 47ff.
50. Dieter Muskalla's correlation of plebiscite results and religious affiliation admittedly indicates a status-quo result of 12.27 percent for the city of Saarbrücken with a 1.28 percent Jewish population; but this is not supported by the status-quo result of 9.11 percent for the rural district of Saarbrücken with a Jewish population of only 0.12 percent. On the other hand, the status-quo result for the District of Merzig was only 4.77 percent (the smallest of all), even though, at 0.70 percent, the Jewish portion of the population was the second highest of all the districts. The reason for these disproportions probably resulted from the different proportions of left-wing voters in the districts. Muskalla, *NS-Politik*, 65, table. 4: correlation of plebiscite results and religious affiliation in the districts.
51. Ibid., 141.

52. Gesetz über die vorläufige Verwaltung des Saarlandes from 30 January 1935; RGBl. 1935 I, 66ff.
53. Jacoby, *Herrschaftsübernahme,* 160–164.
54. Herrmann, "Schicksal," doc. no. 50, 390f.
55. Ibid., doc. no. 48, 388. The Reich Flight Tax was introduced on 8 December 1931 to tax the assets of people who left the Reich. As a rule, it amounted to 25 percent of the exported capital. RGBl. 1931 I, 699–745.
56. Jacoby, *Herrschaftsübernahme,* 172ff.
57. Herrmann, "Schicksal," doc. no. 47, 386f., from *Wiener Sonn- und Montagszeitung,* no. 3 (21 January 1935), 3.
58. Jacoby, *Herrschaftsübernahme,* 172ff.
59. Ibid., 171.
60. Ibid., 173f.
61. Ibid., 241–246, appendix of selected sources, document no. 18.
62. Herrmann, "Schicksal," doc. no. 54, 395f.
63. Ibid., doc. no. 60, 399ff.
64. Ibid., doc. no. 64, 403f., Circular order by the Reich Commissioner for the reintegration of the Saarland, 11 November 1935.
65. Ibid., doc. no. 25, 334.
66. Muskalla, *NS-Politik,* table on p. 614, and Jacoby, *Herrschaftsübernahme,* 182, based on the Reich Commissioner's report from 4 March 1936.
67. Jacoby, *Herrschaftsübernahme,* 181.
68. Muskalla, *NS-Politik,* 425.
69. "The emigration of Jewish Saarlanders was evidently encouraged on the part of officials, since Jewish emigration declarations were processed very quickly. . . ." Jacoby, *Herrschaftsübernahme,* 182.
70. Adam Tooze, *The Wages of Destruction: The Making and Breaking of the Nazi Economy* (UK edition, London, 2006), passim.
71. Jacoby, *Herrschaftsübernahme,* 185.
72. Joseph Walk, ed., *Das Sonderrecht für die Juden im NS-Staat: Eine Sammlung der gesetzlichen Maßnahmen und Richtlinien; Inhalt und Bedeutung,* 2nd ed. (Heidelberg, 1996), 127. On the introduction of the Reich's anti-Jewish laws, see also Marx, *Geschichte,* 198–200.
73. Herrmann, "Schicksal," doc. no. 71, 409f.
74. Walk, *Sonderrecht,* 165.
75. Decree by the Reich Minister of the Interior of 3 December 1935: "In order not to endanger the 1936 Olympic Games in Berlin, all anti-Jewish signs and posters in the area of Garmisch-Partenkirchen . . . are to be removed." Also from the Order of the Deputy of the Führer from 29 January 1936: "To prevent bad impressions for visitors from abroad, signs with extreme content are to be taken down; signs such as 'Jews are undesired here' are sufficient." Ibid., 143, 153.
76. Herrmann, "Schicksal," doc. no. 47, 386f., from *Wiener Sonn- und Montagszeitung,* no. 3, 21 January 1935, 3.
77. Ibid., doc. no. 72, 410ff.
78. Application by the Board of the Synagogue Community of the District of Saarbrücken from 10 March 1936, ibid., doc. no. 74, 412f.; Request by the Former Chair of the Council of Representatives of the Merzig Synagogue Community from 16 June 1936, ibid., doc. no. 81, 420.
79. Ibid., doc. no. 88, 431.
80. Articles of Association of the United Synagogue Communities of Illingen, Neunkirchen, and Merzig from 5 April 1937, ibid., doc. no. 91, 433.

81. Report of the district administrator on St. Wendel, ibid., doc. no. 96, 438.
82. Gesetz über die Rechtsverhältnisse der jüdischen Kultusvereinigungen from 28 March 1938; RGBl., 1938 I, 338.
83. Walk, *Sonderrecht*, 219; Revocation of the Appointment of the District Administrator of Saarbrücken as the State Commissioner of the Synagogue Community of the District of Saarbrücken from 13 July 1938, Herrmann, "Schicksal," doc. no. 106, 450.
84. Gesetz über die Wiedervereinigung Österreichs mit dem Deutschen Reich from 13 March 1938, RGBl., I 1938, 237f.
85. Jacoby, *Herrschaftsübernahme*, 202.
86. Wolf Gruner, "Von der Kollektivausweisung zur Deportation der Juden aus Deutschland (1938–1945): Neue Perspektiven und Dokumente," in *Die Deportation der Juden aus Deutschland: Pläne, Praxis, Reaktionen 1938–1945*, Beiträge zur Geschichte des Nationalsozialismus, vol. 20 (Göttingen, 2004), 21–62, here 31–35; Hans Safrian, *Die Eichmann-Männer* (Vienna, 1993), 73–80; Gerhard J. Teschner, *Die Deportation der badischen und saarpfälzischen Juden am 22. Oktober 1940* (Frankfurt, 2002), 95.
87. Muskalla, *NS-Politik*, 307f.
88. Ibid., 302.
89. Note on the telephonic announcement of SA Brigade 151 Saarbrücken regarding the destruction of the synagogues, Herrmann, "Schicksal," doc. no. 108, 452. On the excesses in Homburg, see Dieter Blinn, *Juden in Homburg: Geschichte einer jüdischen Lebenswelt 1330—1945* (Homburg-Saarpfalz, 1993), 153–157.
90. Ibid., doc. no. 113, 457f.
91. Ibid., doc. no. 111, 454f.
92. Ibid., doc. no. 120, 463–466.
93. Ibid., doc. no. 123, 468–471.
94. Ibid., doc. no. 135, 486f.
95. Hans-Walter Herrmann, "Die Deportation nach Gurs," in *Oktoberdeportation 1940*, ed. Erhard R. Wiehn (Konstanz, 1990), 493–510, here 506.
96. The eighty deportations presumably refer to Jews with Polish passports, who were deported to the Polish border at the end of October 1938; Hans-Walter Herrmann, "Beiträge zur Geschichte der saarländischen Emigration 1935–1939," *Jahrbuch für westdeutsche Landesgeschichte* 4 (1978): 357–412, here 382.
97. Herrmann, "Deportation nach Gurs," 506.
98. Ibid., 499f. In order to return, people needed a "return certificate" [Heimkehrerschein] issued by the Saar-Palatinate's Gauleiting at the place of evacuation. On the camp in Halle and the labor camps in Mark Brandenburg, see chapter two in Wolf Gruner, *Jewish Forced Labor under the Nazis: Economic Needs and Racial Aims 1938–1944* (New York, 2006).
99. Herrmann, "Deportation nach Gurs," 506. On Homburg, see Blinn, *Geschichte*, 158–172.
100. Ibid., 498.
101. Teschner, *Deportation*, 72f.
102. Information sheet for officials for use during the deportation of the Palatinate Jews, Herrmann, "Schicksal," doc. no. 124, 472f.
103. The precise number of these people and their subsequent fate remains unknown. Herrmann, "Deportation nach Gurs," 503.
104. The seven trains from Baden traveled over Mülhausen (Mulhouse), Dijon, Mâcon, Lyon, and Toulouse. We can assume that, after Dijon, the trains from the Saar-Palatinate followed the same route. Herrmann, "Deportation nach Gurs," 495.

105. Teschner, *Deportation*, 102.
106. Ibid., 103.
107. Politisches Archiv des Auswärtigen Amtes Berlin, Inland II g 189, K 204459/60. There are numerous works—with various points of view—dealing with the prehistory and background of the entire action; see Teschner, *Deportation*, 90–100, and Gruner, "Kollektivausweisung," 41f.
108. Teschner, *Deportation*, 122–127.
109. Herrmann, "Deportation nach Gurs," 505 (table 1: age structure of the deportees).
110. Teschner, *Deportation*, passim.
111. Ibid., appendix 8, 357f. (Etat numérique des Décès survenus au Camp depuis le 25 Octobre 1940, Archives départementales Pau, 72 W 30.)
112. These resettlements occurred in February and March 1941.
113. Teschner, *Deportation*, 190–214.
114. *Journal Officiel de l'Etat Français*, 18 October 1940, 5324.
115. Teschner, *Deportation*, 214–218.
116. Copy of the Wannsee protocol as certified by the notary Dr. Wilhelm Dieckmann, Burgwedel, Bundesarchiv, R 58/1086. Protocol printed as doc. 24 in Kurt Pätzold, Erika Schwarz, *Tagesordnung: Judenmord. Die Wannsee-Konferenz am 20. Januar 1942* (Berlin, 1992), 102–120.
117. This number was massively exaggerated. In reality, approximately 140,000 Jews lived in the occupied zone; see Serge Klarsfeld, *Vichy—Auschwitz: Die Zusammenarbeit der deutschen und französischen Behörden bei der "Endlösung der Judenfrage" in Frankreich* (Nördlingen, 1989), 27f.
118. Ibid., 330ff.
119. According to Klarsfeld's calculations.
120. Teschner, *Deportation*, 275–295 and appendix 12, 364.
121. Herrmann, "Deportation nach Gurs," 505, table 3.
122. On the liquidation of the labor camps, see Gruner, *Forced Labor*, 75–80.

CHAPTER 2

AUSTRIA
Albert Lichtblau

Prior to the Annexation

Austria played an important role in the persecution of the Jewish population in the Third Reich. On the one hand, it was the country that socialized Adolf Hitler and produced many of the extermination machinery's protagonists; on the other hand, after the Anschluss in 1938, the region was the source of many important impulses for the radicalization of anti-Jewish policy.[1]

The collapse of the Habsburg monarchy as a result of the First World War had serious consequences for the Jewish population's situation during the two decades prior to National Socialist rule in Austria. The organization of the Austro-Hungarian Empire's successor states ostensibly occurred according to national criteria; in Austria, a democratic republican form of government replaced the monarchy. The formation of these new states left the so-called First Republic of Austria with a predominantly urban Jewish population. In 1934, the final census conducted prior to the Anschluss indicated that almost 92 percent of the country's 191,481 registered persons of Jewish faith lived in Vienna.[2] If we also take into account the 6 percent of country's Jews living in Lower Austria and Burgenland (which bordered on Hungary and became a part of Austria in 1921), the proportion of Austria's total Jewish population living in the Republic's eastern part amounted to almost 98 percent. The scarcity of Jews living in the country's other regions resulted from settlement bans, which had lasted for centuries and were not repealed until the emancipations of 1848 and 1867.[3]

Since the implementation of the Law Regarding the Regulation of the External Legal Circumstances of the Israelite Religious Community on 21 March 1890,[4] Jewish communities in Austria were organized territorially; they included all religious Jews living within a region, regardless of the particular orientation of their faith. Orthodox groups tried in vain to dissociate themselves from these compulsory communities. An exception was Burgenland, which after joining Austria retained traditions established by Hungarian legislation; despite its small population, Burgenland featured eleven Israelite religious communities. Most of Austria's Israelite religious communities—namely, fifteen—existed in Lower Austria; there were two in Upper Austria; the other federal states each had one. The fact that none existed in Vorarlberg resulted from the decline of rural Jewry and the end of the tradition-steeped Hohenemser community (see map 2.1).[5]

The Jewish population's awareness of Austria was still informed by the traditions of the Habsburg monarchy. On the other hand, the truncated state's German-speaking majority viewed its national

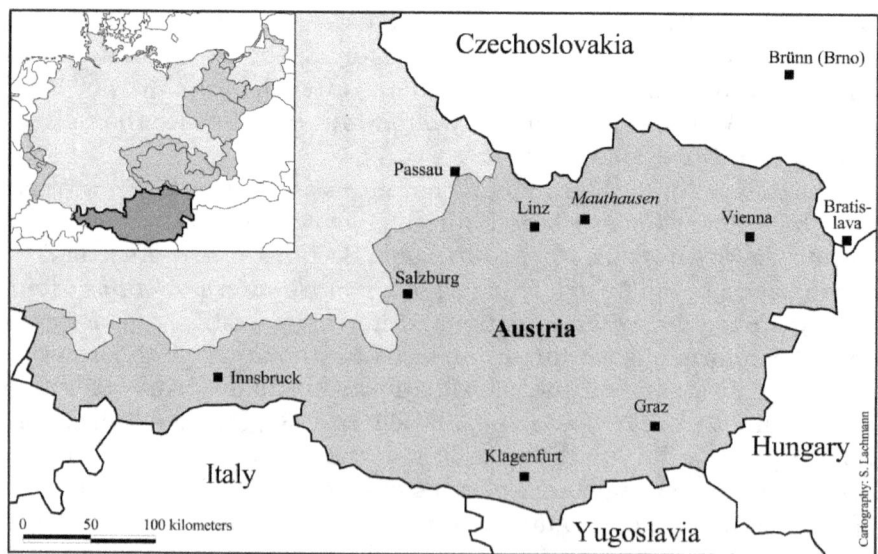

Map 2.1. Austria, 1938

Table 2.1. The Jewish and Non-Jewish Residential Population in the Austrian Federal States and their Capitals, According to the 1934 Census

	Non-Jewish Population	Jewish Population	Percentage of Jews as Part of the Population of the Federal States and their Capitals
Vienna	1,698,096	176,034	9.39
Lower Austria	1,501,360	7,716	0.51
Upper Austria	901,352	966	0.11
Linz	108,299	671	0.6
Salzburg	245,562	239	0.10
City of Salzburg	40,034	198	0.5
Styria	1,012,911	2,195	0.22
Graz	151,121	1,720	1.1
Carinthia	404,860	269	0.07
Klagenfurt	29,491	180	0.6
Tyrol	348,733	365	0.10
Innsbruck	60,688	317	0.5
Vorarlberg	155,360	42	0.03
Bregenz	56,303	1	0.0
Burgenland	295,815	3,632	1.21
Eisenstadt	4,782	204	4.3
Austria total	6,568,752*	191,481**	2.83

* including 4,703 without a fixed address
** including 23 without a fixed address

affiliation in a tradition based on the marginalization of other peoples and the fiercely waged *Nationalitätenstreit*—that is, ethnic struggle—for hegemony. The majority of the population would in all likelihood have voted in favor of unification with Germany. But in 1919 in St.-Germain-en-Laye, the victorious powers of the First World War prohibited unification and compelled the government of the state originally designated as the "Republic of German-Austria" to eliminate "German" from the country's name. During unofficial plebiscites in Tyrol and Salzburg, almost 100 percent supported an Anschluss. When the National Socialists came to power in 1933, it became obvious that the Austrian "national identity" could do little to oppose the "*Anschluss* idea" propagated by Germany and supported by many Austrians. Parts of the Jewish population also very much reflected a predominantly German self-awareness. For example, the liberal organization that until 1933 dominated elections in the Vienna Israelite Community referred to itself in its newspaper *Die Wahrheit* as the Union of German-Austrian Jews (Union deutschösterreichischer Juden) until 12 June 1931; only after this date did the term "German" disappear from its name.[6]

Even prior to the end of the Habsburg monarchy, the city of Vienna had witnessed repeated conflicts regarding the Jewish population. Elected in a Galician voting district, Rabbi Joseph Samuel Bloch was considered the most pugnacious Jewish delegate in the Austrian parliament from 1883 to 1895, refusing to shy away from conflicts with the anti-Semitic theologian and priest August Rohling, who promulgated legends of Jewish ritual murder.[7] The success of the anti-Semitic Christlichsoziale Partei (Christian Social Party) under Karl Lueger, who began serving as Vienna's mayor in 1897, also compelled Vienna's Jewish community to adopt a more self-assertive course.[8] After 1918, the First Republic lacked a prominent Jewish political proponent like Rabbi Bloch, for the Jewish electorate proved to be too weak to push through candidates on autonomous Jewish lists in parliamentary elections. The only exception was the Zionist Robert Stricker, who as a representative of a Jewish list briefly held a seat in the constitutive national assembly at the beginning of the Republic.[9]

By means of election law reform, the Republic of Austria implemented fundamental changes to the power constellation in the representative bodies. In Vienna, the hitherto unchallenged governing anti-Semites now fell behind, whereas the Social Democratic Workers' Party (Sozialdemokratische Arbeiterpartei) managed to achieve absolute majorities in every election in the city.[10] The transformation from an "anti-Semitic" to a "red" Vienna stood for modernity and a new beginning, despite the depression after the First World War, and offered politicians of Jewish descent a field of activity. Since the decline of the Liberals resulted in a lack of electable non-anti-Semitic alternatives, most of the Jewish electorate voted for the Social Democrats. Even so, the Social Democratic Party remained passive—if not hostile—with regard to the Jewish population's interests. For one, this distanced stance was linked to the efforts of individual leading politicians like Viktor Adler to dissociate themselves from their Jewish origins; for another, the party greatly feared being denounced as a "Jewish protection party."[11]

During the First World War, the number of Jews living in Vienna had increased substantially due to the influx of refugees from the former Habsburg territories Galicia and Bukovina. These Jewish war refugees saw themselves exposed to intense hostility from the anti-Semitic parties, who found their preconceptions of the Jews as "foreigners"—as "others" from the East or even the Orient—confirmed by the arrival of these poor and religiously devout (and accordingly dressed) people.[12] Anti-Semitism combined with a xenophobic reflex that gripped even the Social Democratic Workers' Party. With an Announcement Regarding the Forced Emigration of Persons Not Entitled to Reside in German-Austria (Kundmachung betreffend die Abreisendmachung der in Deutschösterreich nicht heimatberechtigten Personen) on 9 September 1919, the Social Democratic Governor of Lower Austria, Albert Sever, endeavored to counter the food and housing shortage by deporting Jewish refugees from Austria.[13] The same year witnessed the founding of the German-Austrian Protection Club Anti-Semite League (Deutschösterreichische Schutzverein Antisemiten-Bund), which in 1921 issued invitations to participate in an international "Anti-Semite Conference" in Vienna. At the time, the association included sixty-two organizations with a total of 400,000 members.[14]

The First Republic's anti-Semitism differed from that of the imperial period because it was more firmly rooted in society and more radical; the imperial period's predominantly verbal anti-Semitism gave way during the First Republic to one that was action-based and even criminal. Anti-Semitism's broader social roots drew their support from its resonance among the educated classes. An anti-Semitically socialized elite had come to hold the levers of power in the political, economic, and education systems. In the 1920s, the anti-Semitic radical wing managed to dominate voting in important associations. Its racist strategy—namely, adding so-called Aryan paragraphs to organizations' articles of association—chiefly targeted recreational and sports clubs; the strategy was exemplified above all by its successes in the Alps Association (Alpenverein), the Austrian Tourist Club (Österreichische Touristenklub), the Austrian Ski Federation (Österreichische Skiverband), and the German Gymnast Federation (Deutsche Turner-Bund), which in 1942 included 70,000 adult and 45,000 child members.[15] Many municipalities that relied on tourism also believed that they could promote themselves by announcing that Jewish guests were unwelcome.[16]

The situation was tense, because after the elimination of the Social Democrats in October 1920, the various Austrian governments consisted almost exclusively of representatives from anti-Semitic parties, such as the Christian Social Party (Christlichsoziale Partei), the Greater German People's Party (Großdeutsche Volkspartei), the Rural League (Landbund), and the Home Guard (Heimwehr).[17] Increasing acts of violence, including murder, lent anti-Semitism a new alarming quality. One prominent victim was the journalist and author of the visionary novel *The City without Jews,* Hugo Bettauer, who on 10 March 1925 was shot by the National Socialist Otto Rothstock, dying soon thereafter as a result of the attack.[18] Unbridled anti-Semitic excesses repeatedly erupted in the universities, but also following anti-Semitic demonstrations, such as the protest against the Zionist Congress held in Vienna in 1925.[19] The murder of the Jewish jeweler Norbert Futterweit on 12 June 1933 occurred during a phase when Austrian National Socialists increasingly resorted to terroristic methods.[20]

It is impossible to generalize about how the Jewish population handled these developments, because the findings vary. Anti-Semitism affected them especially in public places, thus above all in schools and universities. Memoirs mention that many Jews withdrew into their private spheres to avoid unpleasant experiences with anti-Semites. Austrian anti-Semitism did not appear exceptional when compared to the rest of Europe. Jewish media reported extensively on the enmity toward Jews in other countries. Presumably, many Austrian Jews thought that the situation was even worse elsewhere, such as in neighboring Hungary.[21]

After 1918, Jewish life—particularly Jewish associations—experienced a heyday. The sports club SC Hakoah Vienna (*Hakoah* means "the power" in Hebrew) managed to impart Jewish self-awareness to young people who were now only loosely associated through their religion and at the same time counter somewhat the anti-Semitic cliché of the "weak Jew." When the Hakoah soccer team won the Austrian championships during the 1924/25 season, the club scored points even among Jewish community members largely uninterested in sports. The impressive contribution to cultural life by many Jewish artists played an important role in the relationships between Austria's Jewish and non-Jewish populations. But even this apparently tolerant segment of society was already interspersed with individuals who would later offer their services to the National Socialist rulers.[22]

The National Socialists' seizure of power in Germany intensified the situation in Austria. During multiple elections in 1932, the Austrian National Socialists had not only shredded the German-National camp but also gained support from members of the Christian Social Party. During the 23 April 1933 Innsbruck municipal council by-elections, the NSDAP managed to increase its portion of votes tenfold compared to the 1931 election, triumphing with 36.1 percent as the strongest party.[23] In June 1933, the Austrian Republic banned the National Socialist Party—as it had earlier already prohibited the Communist Party—and the National Socialists went underground. In February 1934, a civil war erupted between the militant wing of the Social Democrats, on the one hand, and the Christian Social Party—governing as part of a coalition—and the Home Guard, on the other hand, that finally destroyed the country's democratic structures. After the Socialists were defeated in battle, the stalwartly democratic Social Democratic Workers' Party was also banned; leading party politicians either fled or were arrested. Under Federal Chancellor Engelbert Dollfuß, the Christian Social Party attempted to establish a fascist state—whether it should be designated as an authoritarian corporative state or Austrofascism continues to be fiercely debated.[24]

The Jewish population remained largely undisturbed by these political interventions, since social democracy hardly played any role in Israelite Community elections or Jewish association activity. Nonetheless, the situation was peculiar, for the ruling Christian Social Party now had to guarantee the equal treatment of the country's Jewish population and at the same time cater to the deeply rooted anti-Semitism of its supporters. Politicians sporadically resorted to anti-Semitic measures—such as calls for boycotts, obstructions in the field of academic employment, and efforts to introduce segregated schooling (motivated by protests and then abandoned).[25] On the other hand, wholly in keeping with the corporatist concept of the state, Jewish representatives—preferably Zionists—were appointed to the highest state government and Viennese municipal committees, which is how the President of the Vienna Israelite Community, Desider Friedmann, became a member of the State Council (Staatsrat).[26]

National Socialist Germany exerted enormous political and economic pressure on Austria. The "thousand mark ban" from 27 May 1933 sought to stop German tourism.[27] The influence of Austria's economically dominant neighbor also affected the Austrian film industry, which unofficially introduced an "Aryan" paragraph in order to remain in the German market. The National Socialists' escalation policy culminated in the failed coup and the murder of Federal Chancellor Engelbert Dollfuß on 25 July 1934. Afterward, German policy shifted to a grueling "evolutionary path," which led to the Austro-German Agreement of 11 July 1936, as a result of which National Socialists were amnestied and moderate Nazi exponents entrusted with political offices.²⁸ In comparison with other fascist states, Austrofascism appeared weak, with its veneration of the only marginally popular "martyr" Dollfuß, its uncharismatic "Führer" Kurt Schuschnigg, its feebly developed national identity and therefore unconvincing invocation of the Fatherland, as well as its inability to reintegrate the former left-wing electorate.

Even though Jewish refugees from Germany brought alarming news, most Jews living in Austria apparently did not take the dangers emanating from National Socialism very seriously, since very few took precautionary measures. Viewed in retrospect, the declarations of patriotic loyalty made by Jewish organizations during the time of Austrofascism—above all, by the League of Jewish Frontline Soldiers (Bund jüdischer Frontkämpfer)—were like strings plucked without a soundboard within Austrian society. Very few non-Jews worked publicly to oppose the country's anti-Semitism and the threats of National Socialism; exceptions were the political outsider Irene Harand and the World Movement Against Racial Hatred and Human Suffering (Weltbewegung gegen Rassenhass und Menschennot), founded by Harand and the Jewish lawyer Moriz Zalman in 1933.²⁹

The First Weeks of the Annexation

Germany's political pressure on Austria increased. After a meeting with Hitler on 12 February 1938, Federal Chancellor Kurt Schuschnigg found himself forced to fill government positions with ministers friendly toward National Socialism, most significantly Arthur Seyß-Inquart as Minister of the Interior. On 9 March 1938, Schuschnigg made the surprise announcement that a plebiscite on Austrian independence would be held on 13 March. In the name of the Jewish community, Desider Friedmann handed over a check for 800,000 Schillings in support Schuschnigg's campaign for independence, and the Jewish press published the appeal: "With Schuschnigg for Austria."³⁰

But *Anschluss* had become inevitable; Europe's major powers signaled their reluctance to get involved and Germany's pressure became overwhelming.³¹ Schuschnigg resigned and in a radio speech on 11 March 1930—often described in the autobiographies of Austrian Jews—took his leave "from the Austrian Volk with a German word and heartfelt desire: God protect Austria!" The Austrian Armed Forces were ordered not to mount any resistance "because we are not willing, not for any price, even in this grave hour, to spill German blood. . . ."³²

Interior Minister Seyß-Inquart thereupon took over government affairs on 12 March 1938 until Austria's formal annexation: the Anschluss was regulated by the Federal Constitutional Law on the Reunification of Austria with the German Reich and an analogous German Reich law,[33] both from 13 March 1938. On 10 April 1938, a plebiscite—resulting in a triumph for Hitler—ratified these developments, which were accompanied by the "integration of Austria into the German Reich" at the administrative level.[34]

With a single blow, the Jewish population found itself in a precarious position. In contrast to when the Nazis came to power in Germany, the National Socialist foot soldiers and their numerous supporters directed their unleashed political energy against the Jewish population, especially in Vienna. The unrestrained terror also impacted non-Jews who, to the National Socialists, looked typically Jewish or had supposedly Jewish names. The Anschluss pogrom's acts of violence ranged from personal enrichment through intimidation and robbery to the confiscation of commercial enterprises by self-appointed commissars, and the publicly celebrated *Hetz* (Austrian: amusement), during which Jews—preferably orthodox-looking men and well-dressed women—were forced to wash off the slogans related to the plebiscite for Austrian independence from building walls and pavements for the amusement of a surrounding public audience.[35] The Austrian National Socialists, who had previously generated anxiety and terror through their acts of violence, now presented themselves as guarantors for overcoming the chaos. In a reversal of blame, they accused not only political opponents but also the Jewish population of being responsible for the preceding unrest.

The Jewish population's biggest shock was the experience of helplessness that began with the Anschluss, for Jews could no longer expect state protection. The implementation of the Nazi regime proceeded abruptly. Already on 12 March 1938, Reichsführer-SS Heinrich Himmler and Chief of the Security Police (Sicherheitspolizei; SiPo) Reinhard Heydrich flew to Vienna to carry out the "cleansing" of the Austrian police and the first arrests of the new regime's critics.[36] The Nazi leadership's initial retinue, the administrative officials, security forces, and the Wehrmacht were also accompanied by the Security Service (Sicherheitsdienst; SD) of the SS, in part to centralize "Jewish policy." On 15 March, a Gestapo headquarters was set up in Vienna; the next day at the Heldenplatz, Himmler had the Vienna police swear an oath to Hitler.[37]

Born and raised in Austria, Adolf Eichmann summoned the functionaries of Zionist organizations to the devastated Palestine Office[38] as early as 15 March 1938. On 18 March, the Gestapo raided the Vienna

Israelite Community, arresting functionaries and shutting down the Israelite Community and its facilities.[39] Eichmann later appointed the community's office director, Josef Löwenherz, as the director of the Israelite Community, which did not reopen until 2 May 1938.[40] Subsequently, its activities concentrated on providing welfare services and facilitating the flight of persons in distress.

On 15 March 1938, Hitler spoke at the so-called liberation rally in Vienna before approximately 250,000 listeners, giving what he described as the "greatest implementation report of [his] life": "As Führer and Chancellor of the German nation and Reich, I now report before history the entry of my homeland into the German Reich." Since the National Socialists managed to wrest an endorsement from the Viennese Cardinal Theodor Innitzer and the well-known Social Democratic politician Karl Renner, it must have seemed as if the objective of creating a greater German *Volksgemeinschaft* had been reached for society as a whole.[41]

As early as 13 March 1938, Hitler appointed Josef Bürckel—the Gauleiter of Saar-Palatinate—as the "provisional director [kommissarischer Leiter] of the NSDAP in Austria." Because of his success with the Saar plebiscite, Bürckel seemed to be the ideal candidate for Hitler's planned plebiscite regarding the Anschluss of Austria, and he brought a number of trusted officials from the Saarland to Vienna for his staff.[42] The conduct of the elite arriving from Germany and the new Nazi bureaucracy provoked annoyance on the part of Austrians, who quickly perceived them as arrogant. The developments were incongruous with the idea of the *Volksgemeinschaft,* reviving instead the historically based animosities between Austria and Prussia.[43] On 23 April 1938, Hitler formally appointed Bürckel to the Office of the Reich Commissioner for the Reunion of Austria with the German Reich (Reichskommissar für die Wiedervereinigung Österreichs mit dem Deutschen Reich).[44]

Since the annexation, the violence against the Jewish population and known opponents of the Nazis proceeded simultaneously from "above" and "below," even if the two were not hand in hand. Through the violence perpetrated from "below," the participating Austrians demonstrated to their new rulers that anti-Jewish measures would not encounter any resistance worth mentioning in the population; rather, they would find broad support. The violence from "above" signaled that the state wanted to proceed with all of its power against any form of dissent. Gestapo agents began arresting political opponents and well-known Jews right from the outset. The first deportation of 151 inmates in "protective custody" to Dachau—carried out on 1 April 1938—included sixty Jews, among them the former Zionist Gemeinderat (municipal counselor) Jakob Ehrlich, the Zionist politician and author Robert Stricker, and the President of the Vienna Israelite Community, Desider Friedmann. Of the 120 people in the Dachau transport on 23 May 1938, fifty were of Jewish origins. Jakob Ehrlich became the first prominent Jewish victim of Nazi rule in Austria, dying that same month. After returning from the concentration camp, Stricker and Friedmann remained imprisoned as hostages in Vienna; in 1942, they were deported to Theresienstadt (Terezín) and in 1944 murdered with their wives in Auschwitz.[45]

An article in the *Völkischer Beobachter* on 28 April 1938 demanded that the "Jewish element in Vienna [had to be] eradicated and made to disappear" by 1942.[46] Such statements also appeared in provincial Austrian newspapers, which promised that the individual Gaue would soon be "Jew-free." For the time being, the worst National Socialist rampages occurred in Burgenland, where widespread expulsions had begun already by the end of March 1938. In Frauenkirchen, Nazis and their supporters locked the local Jewish residents in a barn overnight, plundered their businesses, and forced the Israelite Community's director to guarantee that the entire community would emigrate.[47] A decree stipulated that the Jewish population was still supposed to leave Burgenland in March 1938, but this could not be realized so quickly. Fear motivated many to flee to Vienna on their own accord; others were immediately forced by the Gestapo to cross the border into Hungary.[48]

In Austria, the policies that the Nazis began implementing with the Anschluss—classifying Jews as dangerous and alien "others"; bureaucratically registering them in order to subsequently impoverish and segregate them—encountered an anti-Semitism anchored in the center of society (see figure 2.1). These policies involved, on the one hand, introducing anti-Jewish measures already legislatively enacted in Germany, and on the other hand, compelling Jews to categorize themselves as such. These anti-Jewish measures included, for example, immediately having the civil service swear an oath to Hitler that explicitly excluded all Jews, and the introduction of the Nuremberg laws on 20 May 1938. In turn, not wearing a swastika on one's clothing or avoiding the Hitler salute effectively made Jews identifiable as such in public.[49]

Figure 2.1. Anti-Semitic propaganda exhibition *The Eternal Jew,* 1938. *Source:* sz-photo, image no. 317372

The Period of the Occupation

Developments in Austria were preceded by an intensification of anti-Jewish policies in Germany, which were further strengthened by the Anschluss.[50] Thus the "wild Aryanizations" in Austria, for example, forced the Nazi leadership in Berlin to take greater control of the expropriation process so that it would benefit the regime. The private "Aryanizations" and the widespread use of commissars for business takeovers went too far for the rulers. In May 1938, they established a Property Transaction Office (Vermögensverkehrsstelle) in the Austrian Ministry of Economics and Labor, which cooperated with Reich Commissioner Bürckel and henceforth centrally monitored all "Aryanizations" within the country, a model that was later adopted for Germany.[51] The official body with 200 employees was initially directed by Walter Rafelsberger, an Austrian SS member and at the time the State Commissioner for Private Industry (Staatskommissar für Privatwirtschaft).[52] The state profited from a series of levies and "Aryanizations." Approximately one-third of the "Aryanizers" in Vienna were NSDAP members; others had to submit reports certifying their political reliability.[53] One special feature was the Law for the Protection of the Austrian Economy,[54] intended to curb the existing "Aryanization hunger" of interested parties from Germany, who were better funded than the Austrians.[55] Most "Aryanizations" had been completed by the start of the war, whereupon in November 1939 the Property Transaction Office was changed into a Settlement Office (Abwicklungsstelle).[56]

The predatory enterprise did not restrict itself to the Jewish population's private assets. In order to restructure the entire system of Jewish organizations—and also to enable direct access to the assets of Jewish associations, foundations, and funds—Bürckel had already installed a Liquidation Commissar for Associations, Organizations and Societies (Stillhaltekommissar für Vereine, Organisationen und Verbände) on 18 March 1938. The Stillhaltekommissar operated until December 1939, after which his responsibilities were assumed by the Aufbaufonds-Vermögensverwaltung GmbH (literally, construction fund asset management) and subsequently—starting in 1942—by a Settlement Agent (Abwickler). The Stillhaltekommissar's functions applied to all associations that had been prohibited from undertaking any organizational activities from 16 March 1938 until the plebiscite on 10 April 1938. There were a number of procedural methods for dealing with Jewish associations. A few of these organizations—in particular, Zionist associations and the orthodox party Agudas Jisroel (Union of Israel)—were "exempted" to support the expulsion policy by assisting with emigration. The Stillhaltekommissar entrusted the assets of most of the dissolved welfare and charitable associations to the Vienna Israelite Community, but did not entrust real estate, which he often confiscated and resold. The money for the Israelite Community was first used to finance emigration and provide ever more extensive charitable support for the increasingly impoverished members, and later also to finance deportations. Above all, the Stillhaltekommissar confiscated the assets of well-funded associations such as B'nai B'rith. During the initial period, he also dealt with a number of "wild Aryanizations" of association assets that conflicted with the interests of Nazi policy.[57]

Much like the Stillhaltekommissar, the Central Office for Jewish Emigration (Zentralstelle für jüdische Auswanderung), too, would point the way for subsequent annexations; as a result, the institution would contribute to what we refer to today as the "Vienna model" of Jewish persecution. Although the exact course of this important authority's organizational development has yet to be adequately elucidated, a decree from 20 August 1938 by Josef Bürckel—the Reich Commissioner for the Reunion of Austria with the German Reich—played a decisive role in its formation.[58] The Central Office—at first formally directed by the Inspector of the SiPo and the SD in the SD Higher Administrative Section Danube (SD-Oberabschnitt Donau), Dr. Walter Stahlecker—was located in the requisitioned Palais Rothschild and constituted a kind of assembly line for completing elaborate emigration formalities. Section II/112 of the Security Service in Berlin—responsible for "Jewish questions"—had sent Adolf Eichmann, later the Central Office's managing director, to Vienna just a few days after the Anschluss. In Austria, the Security Service took advantage of the ambiguous division of competencies between the Security Service and the Gestapo in dealing with the Jewish population. Eichmann saw an opportunity to coordinate anti-Jewish policy in the SS Higher Administrative Section Austria (SS-Oberabschnitt Österreich). In Vienna, he and his team established a division of labor policy between the SS, other participating Nazi authorities, and the Jewish community, which was rendered compliant through relentless pressure and also forced to finance the expulsion policy. The extorted collaboration between the religious community and the Central Office was supposed to make the process as efficient as possible—and it was thoroughly successful. Since the start of the war in fall 1939, the Central Office came under the newly formed Reich Security Main Office (Reichssicherheitshauptamt) in Berlin. Additional Central Offices were opened in Prague and Amsterdam, while a Reich Center for Jewish Emigration (Reichszentrale für jüdische Auswanderung) was located in Berlin.[59]

Due to local power constellations, the procedures undertaken against Jewish rural communities deviated from those in Vienna. The communities were dissolved at different times—the Salzburg Israelite Community, for example, in May, with the Linz community being appointed as its legal successor. An order issued on 30 March 1940 finally appointed Josef Löwenherz from the Vienna Israelite Community as the legal successor to all Israelite Communities that at that point had not yet been dissolved.[60] Even though, for example, the Kärntner Israelite Community continued to exist, the Gestapo confiscated its assets. In many places, Jewish associations were dissolved and their functionaries arrested or intimidated. In Linz, the Gestapo took Israelite Community President Karl Schwager into custody by March 1938, assigning the organization's provisional leadership to Max Hirschfeld, the director of the Jewish burial society Chevra Kadisha (holy society).

Like his colleagues elsewhere, Hirschfeld found himself forced to co-operate with SS emigration offices and the Gestapo, including Franz Stangl, who later became the commandant of the Treblinka extermination camp.[61]

The race for spoils began outside of Vienna as well. The formerly "illegal" National Socialists felt entitled to take Jewish property as compensation for their sacrifices for the party. The limited availability of Jewish property in the countryside intensified the battle for the distribution of resources. Plunder, violence, and segregation increased the pressure—which had been enormous from the outset—on Austria's unprotected Jewish population. Until the November pogrom, relatives in Germany were often unwilling to believe the severity of the Austrian

Table 2.2. Countries of Asylum for Austrian Jews Expelled up to the Start of the War, by Continent

Continent/Country of Asylum	Number of Jews	Percentage of Jews
Europe	55,505	43.9
Great Britain	*30,850*	*24.4*
Italy	*4,460*	*3.5*
Belgium	*4,270*	*3.4*
Switzerland	*2,265*	*1.8*
Poland	*2,260*	*1.8*
Yugoslavia	*1,644*	*1.3*
France	*1,615*	*1.3*
The Netherlands	*1,151*	*0.9*
Hungary	*915*	*0.7*
North America	28,700	22.7
United States	*28,615*	*22.6*
Central & South America	11,580	9.2
Asia, Middle East	28,172	22.3
Palestine	*9,195*	*7.3*
China/Shanghai	*18,124*	*14.3*
Australia/ New Zealand	1,880	1.5
Africa	644	0.5
Total	126,481	100

circumstances. Because of their small number, Jews outside of Vienna were especially exposed. A number of families even sent their children to Germany, since it seemed safer.[62] Even though the new rulers had initially stopped the first wave of refugees after the Anschluss in order to enable greater control over emigration, starting in May 1938—after the bureaucratic plunder and its implementation had been legalized— the policy of expulsion was fully implemented, allowing two-thirds of the Austrian Jews to escape in time.[63]

Although many steps in the radicalization of Jewish persecution in Austria and Germany occurred simultaneously, such as preparing for the organized plunder by issuing the Ordinance on the Registration of the Assets of Jews on 26 April 1938,[64] policy developments were not synchronized.

The Austrian policy of exclusion, initially directed toward expulsion, had already affected the youngest Jews. After the Anschluss, according to many survivor reports, Jewish children were harassed in a number of different ways. By mid May, they had begun to be removed from state and municipal schools and institutionalized in facilities with a high proportion of Jewish students, resulting in overfilled classrooms and long school routes. Jewish students and teachers were excluded just as rapidly from the universities; in the 1938 summer semester, Jewish students were permitted to enroll only to complete their study programs.[65] In addition, in June 1938 the City of Vienna terminated the tenancies of approximately 2,000 Jewish renters in Vienna's community housing.[66]

The organized violence in November 1938, as well the individual acts of plunder, evoked hardly any sympathy or dissent from many Austrians.[67] In Vienna, the SS primarily destroyed synagogues and prayer houses; the SA attacked apartments and business operations.[68] Austria's capital witnessed the destruction of forty-two prayer houses and numerous other Jewish community facilities through hand grenades and arson, the closing of 4,083 stores, the eviction of tenants from 1,950 apartments, and the arrest of 7,800 individuals, including—albeit in smaller numbers—women as well as people already in possession of emigration documents.[69] The pogrom in Tyrol's capital Innsbruck was especially brutal, resulting in the murders of four people. In Graz, tormentors brought Rabbi David Herzog to the Jewish cemetery to dig his own grave, beating him unconscious in front of the closed cemetery.[70] Of the approximately 6,547 men arrested in Vienna on 10 November, approximately 3,700 were deported to Dachau,[71] initiating a race against time for stricken families to secure the release of internees from the concentration camp by proving they had emigration documents.

With a single blow, the November pogrom again dramatically increased the pressure of expulsion. The arrests of the men, the plundering, the evictions, the terror against the few Jews still residing in rural communities, the tightening of restrictions by expanding the authority of governors and mayors to spatially and temporally limit the residency of the Jewish population, the revoking of the freedom to pursue gainful employment, the liquidation of stores, the special levies, and so on clearly indicated to most Jewish Austrians that life in Austria no longer held any prospects.[72] Many young men left the country because they were deemed to be especially at risk; which also explains why the eventual victims of National Socialist extermination policy included disproportionately large numbers of women and elderly people.[73]

The crowding of Jews into progressively smaller residential areas formed an important part of the centralized and radicalized policy after the pogrom. In spring 1939, the city of Vienna autonomously carried out a large "Jewish resettlement operation." Exploiting the Law concerning Jewish Tenancies of 30 April 1939,[74] the Municipal Housing Authority's newly established Office for Jews (Dienststelle für Juden) gave thousands of Jewish renters the ultimatum to either move "voluntarily" or face "compulsory relocation." The city's goal was to herd them into "Jewish" houses. In parallel with these developments, the Reich Commissioner was already planning to establish a large camp to accommodate Jewish families from Vienna and employ them as forced laborers.[75]

With the beginning of the Second World War, the Nazis again fundamentally radicalized their anti-Jewish policies, and Austria once more became the testing ground for new measures. While policy thus far had been directed toward expulsion and the use of forced labor in individual camps, the war's rapid success in Poland created new prospects for the deportation of Greater Germany's entire Jewish population to Poland, plans for which began immediately after the outbreak of war, with Hitler calling for the deportation of 300,000 German and Austrian Jews.[76] In early October, Eichmann—now the director of the Central Office for Jewish Emigration in Prague—received the assignment from the Chief of the Gestapo Heinrich Müller to first deport 70,000 to 80,000 people from the regions of Kattowitz (East Upper Silesia) and Moravian Ostrava. Eichmann traveled to Austria, where he discussed the intention to "resettle" Vienna's Jews in Poland within eighteen months with the special commissioner for Jewish questions on Bürckel's staff[77] and ordered the Jewish community to prepare for this initial deportation. Its representatives were led to believe that the "resettlement" to Nisko near Lublin was in the best interests of those affected and that Nisko offered employment opportunities. Two transports with 1,584 persons left Vienna on 20 and 26 October 1939, but then Himmler personally interrupted the operation due to technical difficulties.[78]

Afterward, the National Socialists continued pursuing their policy of segregation and control—that is, the ongoing eviction of Jews from residences and their displacement from provincial locations (where very few Jews lived anyway) to Vienna. Now the Vienna Municipal Housing Authority's motto stated that the Jewish population was to be herded into "Jewish houses," without regard to family circumstances or gender. The concentration of Vienna's Jews in a sort of half-ghetto along specific house-lined streets was a precondition that facilitated the subsequent deportations. Moreover, since the beginning of the war, Jews had only been permitted to shop at certain times and in certain stores, a regulation that was further tightened in 1940 by a curfew, among other things. During the course of 1940, the NSDAP increasingly interfered with the concentration of Jewish renters in "Jewish houses." At the request of Reich Governor (Reichsstatthalter) and Gauleiter Baldur von Schirach—who had replaced Bürckel—Vienna's Deputy Gauleiter Karl Scharitzer ordered the resumption of a "systematic [*planvoll*] and drastic resettlement of the Jews."[79]

The second deportation wave from Vienna began in February 1941. In October 1940 during a briefing at the Führer Headquarters, Baldur von Schirach had advocated to Hitler the final removal of the Jews still living in Vienna. Hitler issued his approval in December 1940, whereupon in February and March 1941 the Gestapo deported more than 5,000 people from Vienna to Poland. As with the Nisko transports, the Nazis made no preparations for food or accommodations. The Israelite Community endeavored to mitigate the deportees' desperate plight. This operation against Vienna's Jews was also interrupted, this time because of the logistical situation during the lead-up to the invasion of the Soviet Union. But the National Socialists adhered to their plans to make Vienna and also Berlin *judenrein* (cleansed of Jews).[80] After the second deportation wave in February and March 1941, the Central Office informed the Israelite Community in May that the Jewish population was henceforth permitted to live only in Vienna's second, ninth, and twentieth districts, which bordered each other, and that every move to a different residence now had to be approved.[81]

The invasion of the Soviet Union marked the beginning of the policy of extermination, which, with the third deportation wave starting in October 1941, also seized those Jews still living in Austria. The destinations for the deportations were initially ghettos such as Łódź (Litzmannstadt), Izbica, Riga, and Minsk, and soon thereafter extermination camps such as Sobibór and Auschwitz. As in other regions, no considerations were made regarding gender, illness, or disability, although the Gestapo brought the elderly to Theresienstadt in the Protectorate of Bohemia and Moravia. After the end of the final large deportation wave at the end of 1942 until the end of Nazi rule, deportations from Vienna were destined exclusively for Theresienstadt and Auschwitz.[82]

Like everywhere else, the extermination machinery exploited the victims themselves as assisting agents; as previously mentioned, in Austria the Nazis developed this strategy at a very early stage. The basis for enabling German authorities to carry out subsequent measures—such as expropriations, forced labor conscriptions, resettlements, and deportations—was created primarily by the compilation of card indexes and the repeatedly ordered censuses of the Jewish population, both of which were conducted with the help of the Vienna Israelite Community. The Central Office itself selected the individuals slated for the third deportation wave, which started in fall 1941, but its director at the time, Alois Brunner, forced the Vienna Israelite Community to provide a Jewish steward service (Ordnerdienst) for the "roundups." The director of the community, Josef Löwenherz, initially refused. But when the Gestapo then rounded up the Jews with extreme brutality that included theft, extortion, and rape, the Israelite Community complied, providing 400 to 500 "stewards." From the perspective of the Nazi authorities, this procedure worked so well that three employees from the Vienna Israelite Community were brought to Berlin in order to pass along their experiences. But in contrast to Vienna, according to their report, such "roundups" in Berlin encountered resistance from the non-Jewish population.[83] In Vienna, on the other hand, onlookers still subjected the Jews to malicious insults when the Gestapo brought its victims from the collection points in the city center to the train station during daylight hours.[84]

During the deportations, the Central Office and the municipal administration intensified their repressive policies. Bypassing the labor office, the Gestapo forced men and women to perform additional work on Sundays for the NSDAP or the Wehrmacht. Beginning in summer 1942, the Gestapo increasingly also deported inmates of labor camps in Austria and Germany to the East. The last Austrian forced laborers were removed from the camps and brought to Vienna in October.[85] At the end of the large deportation wave, in October 1942 the Gestapo finally also deported approximately 1,500 employees of the Israelite Community and their families, after which the Vienna Israelite Community was dissolved.[86] A Council of Elders of the Jews in Vienna (Ältestenrat der Juden in Wien) took its place as of 1 November 1942. On 31 March 1943, the Central Office was closed as well, with the Gestapo assuming its responsibilities and organizing the subsequent, smaller deportations until the end of the war.[87]

In numerous instances, Austria played a pioneering role in the Nazi government's anti-Jewish policy, including the "segregated labor deployment" (geschlossene Arbeitseinsatz)—that is, the deployment of segregated labor groups. Here the innovation resulted from an interaction between regional labor management, state governments and the specifically affected Reich ministries, the Central Office, the Gestapo, and the Jewish communities. Labor offices already began procuring officially unemployed Jews to perform forced labor for private firms—even in Germany—in fall 1938.[88] The "segregated labor deployment" became the model for the Reich Labor Administration, which adopted it in December 1938 for application throughout the Reich. Vienna's Jews toiled as forced laborers in private brick works and municipal waste removal, in the construction of the Reich Autobahn and dams in various regions of Austria, and in road and dam construction in northern Germany. Plans to intern Austrian Jews as forced laborers in labor camps scattered

Table 2.3. Deportations from Austria

Year	Number of Deportees
1939	1,584
1940	0
1941	13,015
1942	32,445
1943	1,303
1944	478
1945	22
No year indicated	206
Total	49,053

throughout the German Reich were rendered obsolete by the war and the immediate initiation of deportation planning. Yet during the course of the Second World War, the groups of people affected by the forced labor policy progressively expanded. From the outset, the process included numerous forms of discrimination, reflected by poor food supplies, meager pay, the segregation of Jewish and non-Jewish workers, numerous prohibitions—restricting the freedom of movement, for example—and appalling work hours. Even before the Nazis introduced the "yellow star" for all Jews in September 1941, Jewish forced laborers were given special identifying marks. When the Vienna labor office assigned a few hundred Jews to a labor camp in Eisenerz at the end of 1940, the town's mayor ordered their marking by a yellow armband with a black star on their right arm. In other camps, Jewish forced laborers had to wear a rectangular red fabric patch on their backs.[89]

After most of the Austrian Jews had been deported, in 1943 the forced labor deployments finally conscripted Jews living in "mixed marriages." Even though the Gestapo supervised the Council of Elders, the labor administration retained important functions. At the end of 1944, approximately 90 percent of all Jews remaining in Austria performed forced labor, including children, youth, and persons over sixty-five years of age (of the latter, approximately one in five worked).[90] Plans to deport all of the Jews living in "mixed marriages" throughout the Reich—as ordered by the Reich Security Main Office—fell through in Vienna in February 1945 due to transportation problems.[91]

Although the extermination machinery raged until the Third Reich's final hours, in the end the Nazi regime pursued its initially broadcast promise to render the Gaue "cleansed of Jews" with an absurd logic. With Hitler's approval, Hungarian Jews were being deployed as forced laborers in Austria since 1944; moreover, the "evacuation marches" brought Jewish concentration camp survivors into the country as well. The former consisted, first, of approximately 7,500 Hungarian Jews from Auschwitz, who were brought to the Mauthausen concentration camp and its satellite camps starting in May 1944. In June 1944, they were followed by an estimated more than 15,000 *Austauschjuden* (exchange Jews)[92] from the Hungarian ghettos of Szeged, Szolnok, Debrecen, and Baja, who were deported to the Strasshof concentration camp, whence they were allocated to perform forced labor in Vienna and the Reichsgau Lower Danube.[93] A third group consisted of the so-called *Leihjuden* (borrowed Jews),[94] employed primarily to dig trenches for military fortifications. Estimates vary between 30,000 and 50,000 persons, whereby the Austrian Historical Commission assumes 40,000 persons, including 3,500 to 4,000 women.[95] In light of the chaos of war and the arbitrary murders during the "evacuation marches," the number of fatalities can only be estimated; the Historical Commission estimates at least 8,000 persons.[96] Massacres occurred in numerous Austrian municipalities. Notwithstanding a few local historical studies, we still lack a comprehensive body of local research.[97]

Many protagonists of National Socialist extermination policy came from Austria, like Adolf Eichmann and many of his employees, and like various commandants of concentration and extermination camps, as well as Odilo Globocnik, the director of "Operation Reinhardt" for the systematic murder of the Jews in the General Government.[98] The proportion of Austrians involved in the extermination policy continues to be discussed.[99] The fact that there was hardly any resistance in Austria to the persecution of the Jewish population and that many profited from the Nazi regime—whether through private plunder or by taking over abandoned rental apartments—made the deflection of guilt after the war especially grotesque. After an initial anti-fascist consensus, the parties soon began vying for the voices of former Nazis. During the Cold War, communism replaced the short-lived enemy construct of National Socialism. Austrian society successfully created a myth of Austria as the first victim of Hitler's Germany, which completely undermined initial efforts to legally prosecute the crimes of the Nazi period and persisted until the mid 1980s.[100] Not until the international debate surrounding the candidacy of former United Nations Secretary-General Kurt Waldheim for the Office of Austria's State President did the victim myth collapse, setting in motion a change of paradigms. The topic has by no means been fully dealt with in Austria; opinion surveys reveal the society's internal tensions when dealing with the Nazi past, as well as the survival of anti-Jewish resentment. In fact, in the meantime taboos against anti-Jewish attitudes in public (and thus also private) communication have noticeably broken down. In Austria, the politics of remembrance regarding the Nazi past and solid, respectable representations of the history of expulsion and mass murder still collide with feelings of guilt, political demagoguery, and unresolved generational conflicts within families.[101]

Conclusion

At the time of the Anschluss, the National Socialists had already discriminated against and excluded Germany's Jewish population for five years. One and a half years still remained before the outbreak of the Second World War, a phase during which anti-Jewish policies enormously accelerated. The Anschluss pogroms signaled to the Nazi rulers a willingness within the Austrian population to proceed openly against the Jews and that solidarity with the threatened group was extremely minimal. To keep the situation under control, the German authorities quickly introduced measures that at the very least were supposed to centralize and manage the "Aryanization" campaign of plunder.

In a state of shock, the Jewish population in Austria recognized the hopelessness of its plight more quickly than the Jews in Germany, which is why the wave of flight began here long before the November pogrom of 1938. By the beginning of the Second World War, 126,481 Austrian Jews had managed to emigrate. Between the outbreak of the war and the emigration ban at the end of 1941, only approximately 11,000 persons managed to flee. However, countries that were later occupied by German troops became new traps that cost the lives of many who had fled—the historian Jonny Moser refers to a figure of 16,692 persons.[102]

Because of the anti-Jewish policies developed on its soil, Austria played a pioneering role in the persecution of the Jews. The establishment of new organizational structures, such as the Central Office for Jewish Emigration and the Property Transaction Office, as well as the introduction of forced labor and the coerced cooperation of "religious communities" that were rendered compliant by the Nazis, constituted important radicalizing measures that served as models for other regions later "annexed" by the Reich. Austria offered a field of action for numerous National Socialist careerists, including Adolf Eichmann, who as one of the most ambitious advanced to become a central figure in organizing the mass murder.[103]

The first deportation trains already left Vienna shortly after the outbreak of the Second World War. Even though the operation was soon aborted, it taught the National Socialists fundamental lessons for later deportations, such as those in February and March 1941. Various Vienna authorities now crowded the Jewish population into ever-shrinking residential areas and restricted their range of movement. Of the Jews living in Austria prior to National Socialism, approximately 65,000 persons—that is, almost one-third—were murdered.[104] Yet at the end of the Second World War, the National Socialists pursued their promise to deliver an "*Ostmark* cleansed of Jews" with an absurd logic, bringing into the country Hungarian Jews for forced labor and Jewish survivors from evacuated camps, many of whom died from the strain of the forced labor or marches, or in massacres shortly before the end of the war.

Notes

1. Brigitte Hamann, *Hitler's Vienna: A Portrait of the Tyrant as a Young Man* (London, 2010) (German original: Munich, 1996).
2. *Die Ergebnisse der österreichischen Volkszählung vom 22. März 1934*, Statistik des Bundesstaates Österreich, no. 1 (Vienna, 1935), 45.
3. Eveline Brugger et al., *Geschichte der Juden in Österreich*, supplementary volume to Österreichische Geschichte, ed. Herwig Wolfram (Vienna, 2006).
4. Gesetz vom 21. März 1890, betreffend die Regelung der äußeren Rechtsverhältnisse der israelitischen Religionsgesellschaft; RGBl, (Austria) 15 April 1890, 103.
5. Overview of the Jewish organizations in the land of Austria, the Central Archives for the History of the Jewish People Jerusalem (CAHJP), A/W 299.
6. See *Die Wahrheit: Jüdische Wochenschrift*, nos. 24 and 25 (12 and 19 June 1931).
7. Joshua Shanes, *Diaspora Nationalism and Jewish Identity in Habsburg Galicia* (New York, 2012).
8. John W. Boyer, *Karl Lueger (1844–1910): Christlichsoziale Politik als Beruf: Eine Biografie* (Vienna, 2010).
9. Dieter J. Mühl, "'Immer war Wahlkampf': Robert Stricker (1879–1944); Ein Beitrag zur jüdischen Politik in Österreich," *Aschkenas* 11, no. 1 (2001): 121–160; Harriet Pass Freidenreich, *Jewish Politics in Vienna 1918–1938* (Bloomington and Indianapolis, 1984), 61–65.
10. Maren Seliger, Karl Ucakar, *Wahlrecht und Wählerverhalten in Wien 1848–1932: Privilegien, Partizipationsdruck und Sozialstruktur* (Vienna, 1984), 145–157.
11. Robert Wistrich, *Socialism and the Jews: The Dilemmas of Assimilation in Germany and Austria-Hungary* (London 1982), 249.
12. See Beatrix Hoffmann-Holter, *"Abreisendmachung": Jüdische Kriegsflüchtlinge in Wien 1914 bis 1923* (Vienna, 1995).
13. Christoph Hinteregger, *Der Judenschwindel* (Vienna, 1923), 70–72.
14. Bruce F. Pauley, *From Prejudice to Persecution: A History of Austrian Anti-Semitism* (Chapel Hill, NC, 1992), 82; Günter Fellner, *Antisemitismus in Salzburg 1918–1938* (Vienna, 1979), 128ff.
15. See Andrea Wachter, "Antisemitismus im österreichischen Vereinswesen für Leibesübungen 1918–1938 am Beispiel der Geschichte ausgewählter Vereine" (diss., University of Vienna, 1983); Rainer Amstädter, *Der Alpinismus: Kultur, Organisation, Politik* (Vienna, 1996); Pauley, *From Prejudice to Persecution*, 119; Hanno Loewy and Gerhard Milchram, eds. *"Hast du meine Alpen gesehen?": Eine jüdische Beziehungsgeschichte* (Hohenems, 2009).
16. Robert Kriechbaumer, ed., *Der Geschmack der Vergänglichkeit: Jüdische Sommerfrische in Salzburg* (Vienna, 2002), 127–173; see also Frank Bajohr,*"Unser Hotel ist judenfrei": Bäder-Antisemitismus im 19. und 20. Jahrhundert* (Frankfurt, 2003).
17. See Klaus Berchtold, ed., *Österreichische Parteiprogramme 1868–1966* (Vienna, 1967); Emmerich Tálos et al., eds., *Handbuch des politischen Systems: Erste Republik 1918–1933* (Vienna, 1995), 143–316; Pauley, *From Prejudice to Persecution*, 174–183.
18. Murray G. Hall, *Der Fall Bettauer* (Vienna, 1978), 80–133.
19. Pauley, *From Prejudice to Persecution*, 108–116.

20. Gerhard Botz, *Gewalt in der Politik: Attentate, Zusammenstöße, Putschversuche, Unruhen in Österreich 1918 bis 1938*, 2nd ed. (Vienna, 1983).
21. There were repeated reports about the *numerus clausus* and anti-Semitism in Hungary; see, for example, *Die Wahrheit: Unabhängige Zeitschrift für jüdische Interessen* 36 no. 15 (10 September 1920): 13; ibid., no. 17 (20 October 1920): 12f.; ibid., no. 21 (15 December 1920): 9.
22. Oliver Rathkolb, *Führertreu und gottbegnadet: Künstlereliten im Dritten Reich* (Vienna, 1991), 44ff., 235ff.
23. Dirk Hänisch, *Die österreichischen NSDAP-Wähler: Eine empirische Analyse ihrer politischen Herkunft und ihres Sozialprofils* (Vienna, 1998), 110ff.
24. Emmerich Tálos and Wolfgang Neugebauer, eds., *Austrofaschismus: Politik—Ökonomie—Kultur 1933–1938*, 5th ed. (Vienna, 2005); Ernst Hanisch, "'Christlicher Ständestaat' und autoritäre/faschistische Systeme," in *Mensch, Staat und Kirchen zwischen Alpen und Adria 1848–1938*, ed. Werner Drobesch et al. (Klagenfurt, 2007), 177–181.
25. Pauley, *From Prejudice to Persecution*, 268–273.
26. Sylvia Maderegger, *Die Juden im österreichischen Ständestaat 1934–1938* (Vienna, 1973); Angelika Königseder, "Antisemitismus 1933–1938," in *Austrofaschismus*, ed. Tálos and Neugebauer, 54–65.
27. Until this economic sanction was lifted in July 1936, German citizens had to pay a fee of 1,000 RM before undertaking a trip to Austria.
28. Winfried R. Garscha, "Nationalsozialisten in Österreich 1933–1938," in *Austrofaschismus*, ed. Tálos and Neugebauer, 100–120.
29. Christian Klösch et al., *"Gegen Rassenhass und Menschennot": Irene Harand—Leben und Werk einer ungewöhnlichen Widerstandskämpferin* (Innsbruck, 2004).
30. Pauley, *From Prejudice to Persecution*, 279; *Die Wahrheit: Jüdische Wochenschrift* 54, no. 11 (11 March 1938): 1.
31. See Gerald Stourzh and Birgitta Zaar, eds., *Österreich, Deutschland und die Mächte: Internationale und österreichische Aspekte des "Anschlusses" vom März 1938* (Vienna, 1990); Werner Welzig, ed., *"Anschluss"—März/April 1938 in Österreich* (Vienna, 2010).
32. http://www.mediathek.at/akustische-chronik//Popups_4/Schuschnigg_Ruecktritt_1 (accessed 26 December 2009).
33. Bundesverfassungsgesetz über die Wiedervereinigung Österreichs mit dem Deutschen Reich from 13 March 1938; BGBl, (Austria), 13 March 1938, 259.
34. Hanns Haas, "Der 'Anschluss,'" in *NS-Herrschaft in Österreich: Ein Handbuch*, ed. Emmerich Tálos et al. (Vienna, 2001), 26–54.
35. Gerhard Botz, *Nationalsozialismus in Wien: Machtübernahme, Herrschaftssicherung, Radikalisierung 1938/39* (Vienna, 2008), 126ff.; Gerhard Botz, "The Jews of Vienna from the Anschluss to the Holocaust," in *Jews, Antisemitism and Culture in Vienna*, ed. Ivar Oxaal, Michael Pollak, and Gerhard Botz (London, 1987), 185–204; George Eric Rowe Gedye, *Als die Bastionen fielen: Die Errichtung der Dollfuß-Diktatur und Hitlers Einmarsch in Wien und den Sudeten; Eine Reportage über die Jahre 1927 bis 1938* (Vienna, 1981) (Original: *Betrayal in Central Europe: Austria and Czechoslovakia: The Fallen Bastions* [New York, 1939]); Hans Safrian and Hans Witek, *Und keiner war dabei: Dokumente des alltäglichen Antisemitismus in Wien 1938* (Vienna, 1988).
36. Peter Longerich, *Heinrich Himmler: A Life* (Oxford, 2011), 403f. (German original: Munich, 2008).
37. Thomas Mang, *"Gestapo-Leitstelle-Wien: Mein Name ist Huber" Wer trug die lokale Verantwortung für den Mord an der Juden Wiens?* (Münster, 2003).

38. Gabriele Anderl and Angelika Jensen, "Zionistische Auswanderung nach Palästina vor 1938," in *Auswanderungen aus Österreich: Von der Mitte des 19. Jahrhunderts bis zur Gegenwart*, ed. Traude Horvath and Gerda Neyer (Vienna, 1996), 187–209.
39. Herbert Rosenkranz, *Verfolgung und Selbstbehauptung: Die Juden in Österreich 1938–1945* (Vienna, 1978), 48ff.
40. Doron Rabinovici, *Eichmann's Jews: The Jewish Administration of Holocaust Vienna, 1938–1945* (Cambridge, 2011), 40f. (German original: Frankfurt, 2000).
41. Quoted in Botz, *Nationalsozialismus in Wien*, 102.
42. Gerhard Botz, *Die Eingliederung Österreichs in das Deutsche Reich: Planung und Verwirklichung des politisch-administrativen Anschlusses (1938–1940)*, 2nd ed. (Linz, 1976), 49ff.; idem, *Nationalsozialismus in Wien*.
43. Evan Burr Bukey, *Hitler's Austria: Popular Sentiment in the Nazi Era, 1938–1945* (London, 2000).
44. RGBl. 1938 I, 407.
45. Rosenkranz, *Verfolgung und Selbstbehauptung*, 37; Evelyn Adunka, "Jakob und Irma Ehrlich," *Chilufim: Zeitschrift für jüdische Kulturgeschichte*, no. 2 (2009).
46. *Völkischer Beobachter*, 28 April 1938, 2. On the interpretation of the quote, see Botz, *Nationalsozialismus in Wien*, 321f.
47. Rosenkranz, *Verfolgung und Selbstbehauptung*, 45ff.
48. Jonny Moser, *Wallenbergs Laufbursche: Jugenderinnerungen 1938–1945* (Vienna, 2006), 20ff.; Gerhard Baumgartner et al., *"Arisierungen," beschlagnahmte Vermögen, Rückstellungen und Entschädigungen im Burgenland* (Vienna, 2004).
49. On 20 May 1938, the Nuremberg Laws were adopted by Austria. See Dieter Kolonovits et al., *Staatsbürgerschaft und Vertreibung*, Veröffentlichungen der Österreichischen Historikerkommission: Vermögensentzug während der NS-Zeit sowie Rückstellungen und Entschädigungen seit 1945 in Österreich, vol. 7 (Vienna, 2004), 287–306.
50. Peter Longerich, *Holocaust: The Nazi Persecution and Murder of the Jews* (Oxford, 2010), 98ff.
51. Botz, *Nationalsozialismus in Wien*, 324ff.
52. Gertraud Fuchs, "Die Vermögensverkehrsstelle als Arisierungsbehörde jüdischer Betriebe" (master's thesis, University of Vienna, 1989), 29–53.
53. Botz, *Nationalsozialismus in Wien*, 329.
54. Gesetz zum Schutz der österreichischen Wirtschaft from 14 April 1938; Gesetzblatt für das Land Österreich, 1938, 145.
55. The research on the "Aryanizations" and restitutions is summarized in Clemens Jabloner et al., *Schlussbericht der Historikerkommission der Republik Österreich: Vermögensentzug während der NS-Zeit sowie Rückstellungen und Entschädigungen seit 1945 in Österreich* (Vienna, 2003).
56. Botz, *Nationalsozialismus in Wien*, 324ff.
57. Shoshana Duizend-Jensen, *Jüdische Gemeinden, Vereine, Stiftungen und Fonds: "Arisierung" und Restitution* (Vienna, 2004). On the activity of the Stillhaltekommissar in the Sudetenland, see Jörg Osterloh's contribution to this volume.
58. Gabriele Anderl and Dirk Rupnow, *Die Zentralstelle für jüdische Auswanderung als Beraubungsinstitution* (Vienna, 2004), 113–122.
59. Raul Hilberg, *The Destruction of the European Jews*, 3rd ed. (New Haven, 2003); Ervin Staub, *The Roots of Evil: The Origins of Genocide and Other Group Violence* (Cambridge, 1989), 84. On the Central Office in Prague, see Wolf Gruner's contribution to this volume.
60. Rosenkranz, *Verfolgung und Selbstbehauptung*, 221.

61. August Walzl, *Die Juden in Kärnten und das Dritte Reich* (Klagenfurt, 1987); Daniela Ellmauer et al., *"Arisierungen," beschlagnahmte Vermögen, Rückstellungen und Entschädigungen in Oberösterreich* (Vienna, 2004), 323–336.
62. Daniela Ellmauer et al., eds., *Geduldet, geschmäht und vertrieben: Salzburger Juden erzählen* (Salzburg, 1998), 137f., 154.
63. Peter Eppel, "Österreicher in der Emigration und im Exil 1938 bis 1945," in *Vertriebene Vernunft: Emigration und Exil österreichischer Wissenschaft 1930–1940*, ed. Friedrich Stadler (Vienna, 1988), vol. 2, 69f.
64. Verordnung über die Anmeldung des Vermögens von Juden from 26 April 1938; RGBl., I 1938, 414.
65. Rosenkranz, *Verfolgung und Selbstbehauptung*, 38, 140f.
66. Herbert Exenberger et al., *Kündigungsgrund Nichtarier: Die Vertreibung jüdischer Mieter aus den Wiener Gemeindebauten in den Jahren 1938–1939* (Vienna, 1996), 28ff.
67. Kurt Schmid and Robert Streibel, eds., *Der Pogrom 1938: Judenverfolgung in Österreich und Deutschland* (Vienna, 1990), 18f.
68. Rosenkranz, *Verfolgung und Selbstbehauptung*, 162.
69. Ibid., 159.
70. David Herzog, *Erinnerungen eines Rabbiners 1932–1940*, ed. by Walter Höflechner on the basis of a master's thesis by Andreas Schweiger (Graz, 1995), 45ff.
71. Schmid and Streibel, eds., *Der Pogrom 1938*, 31.
72. Rosenkranz, *Verfolgung und Selbstbehauptung*, 164ff.
73. Ibid., 189.
74. Gesetz über Mietverhältnisse mit Juden from 30 April 1939; RGBl., 1939 I, 864.
75. Wolf Gruner, *Zwangsarbeit und Verfolgung: Österreichische Juden im NS-Staat 1938–45* (Innsbruck, 2000), 97–123.
76. Wolf Gruner, "Von der Kollektivausweisung zur Deportation der Juden aus Deutschland (1938–1945): Neue Perspektiven und Dokumente," in *Die Deportation der Juden aus Deutschland: Pläne, Praxis, Reaktionen 1938–1945*, Beiträge zur Geschichte des Nationalsozialismus, vol. 20, ed. Birthe Kundrus and Beate Meyer (Göttingen, 2004), 21–62. On Austria in detail, see Gruner, *Zwangsarbeit und Verfolgung*, 128–141.
77. Longerich, *Holocaust*, 151ff.
78. Gruner, "Kollektivausweisung," 34.
79. Gruner, *Zwangsarbeit und Verfolgung*, 189–192. Gerhard Botz has calculated that the expulsions, deportations, and expropriations freed up the same number of apartments that the Social Democrats had constructed through their impressive municipal housing construction program between 1919 and 1934; Gerhard Botz, *Wohnungspolitik und Judendeportation in Wien 1938 bis 1945: Zur Funktion des Antisemitismus als Ersatz nationalsozialistischer Sozialpolitik* (Vienna, 1975), 60, 120–124; see also Rabinovici, *Eichmann's Jews*, 96ff.
80. Rosenkranz, *Verfolgung und Selbstbehauptung*, 255–262.
81. Gruner, *Zwangsarbeit und Verfolgung*, 222.
82. Martin Niklas, "... *die schönste Stadt der Welt": Österreichische Jüdinnen und Juden in Theresienstadt*, Schriftenreihe des Dokumentationsarchivs des österreichischen Widerstandes zur Geschichte der NS-Gewaltverbrechen, vol. 7 (Vienna, 2009), 30–45.
83. Rabinovici, *Eichmann's Jews*, 129ff.
84. Ibid., 135ff.
85. Gruner, *Zwangsarbeit und Verfolgung*, 255–269. See idem, *Jewish Forced Labor under the Nazis: Economic Needs and Racial Aims (1938–1944)*, (New York, 2006), 132–134.

86. Jonny Moser, *Demographie der jüdischen Bevölkerung Österreichs 1938–1945* (Vienna, 1999), 80ff.
87. Ibid.
88. Gruner, *Zwangsarbeit und Verfolgung*, 107; idem, *Jewish Forced Labor under the Nazis*, 109–112.
89. Gruner, *Zwangsarbeit und Verfolgung*, 73–92, 164–186; idem, *Jewish Forced Labor under the Nazis*, 112–128.
90. Gruner, *Zwangsarbeit und Verfolgung* 283f.; idem, *Jewish Forced Labor under the Nazis*, 134–136.
91. Evan Burr Bukey, *Jews and Intermarriage in Nazi Austria* (Cambridge, 2011), 189.
92. Under certain conditions, *Austauschjuden* should have been released in return for services rendered; see Eleonore Lappin-Eppel, *Ungarisch-Jüdische Zwangsarbeiter und Zwangsarbeiterinnen in Österreich 1944/45- Arbeitseinsatz—Todesmärsche—Folgen* (Vienna, 2010).
93. Eleonore Lappin, "Strukturen der Verantwortung: Volksgerichtsverfahren wegen Verbrechen gegen ungarische Juden in österreichischen Zwangsarbeitslagern des Sondereinsatzkommandos der Sicherheitspolizei und des SD in Ungarn, Außenkommando Wien," *Zeitgeschichte* 35, no. 6 (2007): 351–371.
94. *Leihjuden* were Jews delivered to Germany by the Arrow Cross, that is, the Hungarian fascists; they were supposed to be deployed for work that was "important for the war" until the end of the war—an obvious camouflage; see Eleonore Lappin-Eppel, *Ungarisch-Jüdische Zwangsarbeiter.*
95. Florian Freund et al., *Zwangsarbeiter und Zwangsarbeiterinnen auf dem Gebiet der Republik Österreich 1939–1945* (Vienna, 2004), 183; Szabolcs Szita, *Verschleppt, verhungert, vernichtet: Die Deportation von ungarischen Juden auf das Gebiet des annektierten Österreich 1944–1945* (Vienna, 1999); Eleonore Lappin et al., *Ungarisch-jüdische Zwangsarbeiterinnen und Zwangsarbeiter in Niederösterreich 1944/45* (St. Pölten, 2006).
96. See Götz Aly and Christian Gerlach, *Das letzte Kapitel: Der Mord an den ungarischen Juden 1944/45* (Stuttgart, 2002), 355–367; Eleonore Lappin, "The Death Marches of Hungarian Jews Through Austria in the Spring of 1945," *Yad Vashem Studies*, 38 (2000): 203–242; Eleonore Lappin, "Die Rolle der Waffen-SS beim Zwangsarbeitseinsatz ungarischer Juden im Gau Steiermark und bei den Todesmärschen ins KZ Mauthausen (1944/45)," in *Jahrbuch 2004,* ed. Dokumentationsarchiv des österreichischen Widerstandes (Vienna, 2004), 77–112; Eleonore Lappin, "Das Schicksal der ungarisch-jüdischen Zwangsarbeiter in Österreich 1944/45," in *Studien zur Geschichte der Juden in Österreich*, vol. 2, ed. Eleonore Lappin and Martha Keil (Bodenheim, 1996), 141–168; Claudia Kuretsidis-Haider, *Verbrechen an ungarisch-jüdischen Zwangsarbeitern vor Gericht: Die Engerau-Prozesse vor dem Hintergrund der justiziellen "Vergangenheitsbewältigung" in Österreich (1945–1955)* (diss., University of Vienna, 2003).
97. Walter Manoschek, ed., *Der Fall Rechnitz: Das Massaker an Juden im März 1945* (Vienna, 2009); Jacob M. Perschy, ed., *Das Drama Südostwall am Beispiel Rechnitz: Daten, Taten, Fakten, Folgen* (Eisenstadt, 2009).
98. Hans Safrian, *Eichmann's Men* (Cambridge, 2009); Bogdan Musiał, ed., *"Aktion Reinhardt": Der Völkermord an den Juden im Generalgouvernement 1941–1944* (Osnabrück, 2004).
99. See the lead story "Hitlers Heimat: Waren die Österreicher die radikaleren Nazis? Die Fakten und die Mythen," *Profil: Das unabhängige Nachrichtenmagazin Österreichs*, 11 May 2009.

100. Siegfried Göllner, *Die politischen Diskurse zu "Entnazifizierung," "Causa Waldheim" und "EU-Sanktionen": Opfernarrative und Geschichtsbilder in Nationalratsdebatten* (Hamburg, 2009); Thomas Albrich et al., *Holocaust und Kriegsverbrechen vor Gericht: Der Fall Österreich* (Innsbruck, 2006).
101. See, for example, the table in Heinz P. Wassermann, "Zwischen Stagnation und Modernisierung: Antisemitismus in Österreich," in *Feindbild Judentum: Antisemitismus in Europa*, ed. Lars Rensmann and Julius H. Schoeps (Berlin, 2008), 251.
102. Moser, *Demographie*, 27f., 57–79.
103. David Cesarani, *Becoming Eichmann: Rethinking the Life, Crimes, and Trial of a "Desk Murderer"* (Cambridge, 2007).
104. Jonny Moser, "Österreich," in *Dimension des Völkermords: Die Zahl der jüdischen Opfer des Nationalsozialismus*, ed. Wolfgang Benz (Munich, 1991), 67–93; Florian Freund and Hans Safrian, "Die Verfolgung der österreichischen Juden 1938–1945: Vertreibung und Deportation," in *NS-Herrschaft in Österreich*, ed. Tálos et al., 767–788.

CHAPTER 3

SUDETENLAND

Jörg Osterloh

Prior to the Annexation

After the First World War, the world familiar to the approximately 3.2 million German residents of Bohemia and Moravia collapsed within weeks.¹ The Austro-Hungarian Empire's disintegration was followed by their homeland's incorporation into the Republic of Czechoslovakia. The provinces of German Bohemia and Sudetenland, proclaimed in October 1918, went unrecognized, and the desire to unite the territories with the Republic of German-Austria went unheeded. Instead, the Czech military marched into the German settlement areas. All German efforts in Bohemia and Moravia to claim the right of national self-determination as announced by President Woodrow Wilson failed. A request for a referendum made to the Entente powers in mid December 1918 was rejected. The conclusion of the peace treaty between the victorious powers and German-Austria in Saint-Germain-en-Laye on 10 September 1919 finally sealed the incorporation of the disputed territories with the newly founded Czechoslovak Republic.²

Now living in a country dominated by Czechs, the Germans in particular were caught unprepared by the profound shift in the

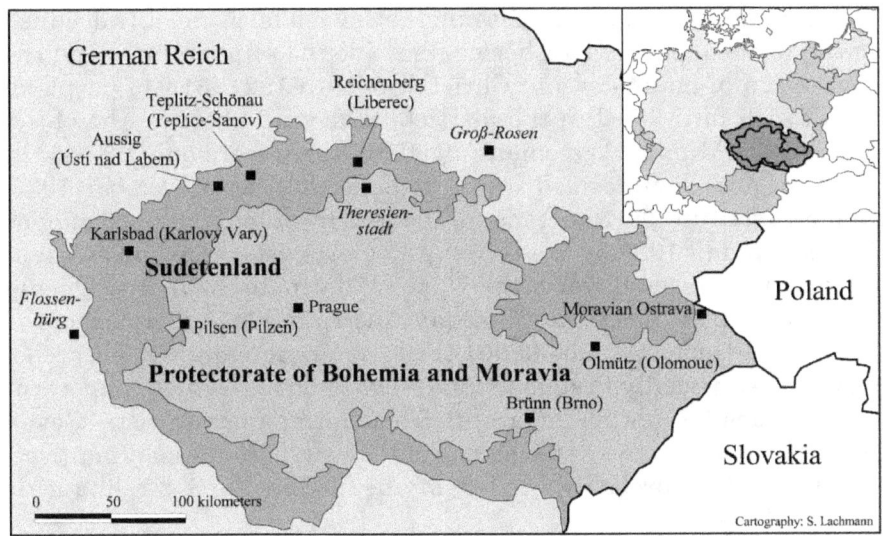

Map 3.1. Sudetenland and the Protectorate of Bohemia and Moravia, 1938/39

ethnic-national balance of power. Their fragmented settlement patterns near the new state's boundaries with Germany, Austria, and Poland now became obvious, as did the lack of their own independent party system, for the German parties of Austria-Hungary had operated entirely in the empire's western half. Nor was there a shared self-awareness, for the collective term *Sudetendeutsche* (Sudeten Germans) referring to all Germans in Bohemia and Moravia only gradually became part of the vernacular.[3]

The Sudeten Germans never accepted their minority status—they fought either for recognition as a *Staatsvolk* (constitutive people) or for their "right of self-determination." In so doing, they aligned themselves increasingly with the German Reich, the only remaining potential advocate for their interests. In the "revenge-seeking, radical-nationalistic German world," the topos of the *Volksgemeinschaft*—an ideologically laden term referring to an ethnic-national "people's community"—soon gained central significance. The now incipient radical process of self-discovery also generated a similarly strict dissociation from everything "foreign,"[4] which, moreover, the *völkisch* (ethnically minded) nationalists combined with a rejection of the Jews. Already during the Habsburg monarchy, political anti-Semitism had suggested that "the Jews" threatened the existence of the German *Volk*.[5]

The number of people professing the Jewish faith steadily declined in the western part of Czechoslovakia, due to low birth rates and the conversion of many Jews to Christianity.[6] In 1921, 31,945 people of the Jewish faith lived in the districts that would become the object of the 1938 Munich Agreement; by 1930, there were only 29,045. In 1930, 24,505 Jews resided in the regions that, as of October 1938, would constitute the Sudetengau; the rest lived in the border regions annexed in fall 1938 by the German Regierungsbezirke (government districts) of Lower Bavaria the Upper Palatinate (539), and Oppeln (410), as well as the *Ostmark* (former Austrian) Länder (states) of the Lower and Upper Danube (3,961).[7] In any event, since 1933, Czechoslovakia—especially Prague (Praha)—was one of the most important destinations for Jewish emigrants from Germany and Austria, even if usually only as a way station en route to supposedly safe countries. Many refugees probably settled in the Sudetenland for linguistic reasons.[8]

A Czech government ordinance pertaining to the implementation of a census had granted members of the Jewish minority the right to profess their own nationality since 1920.[9] Jews in the Sudetenland, however, predominantly spoke German as their native language, understood themselves culturally as belonging to *Deutschtum* (Germandom) and—unless they professed "Jewish nationality"—mostly described themselves as Germans.[10] The largest Jewish communities in the Sudeten region lived in Teplitz-Schönau (Teplice-Šanov) with 3,213 members (approximately 10 percent of the residents), Karlsbad (Karlovy Vary) with 2,115 persons (approximately 9 percent), and Reichenberg (Liberec) with 1,392 persons (approximately 3.6 percent). Therefore, until the 1930s the Jewish portion of the population, especially in Teplitz-Schönau and Karlsbad, bore a significance that it did not even have in the large cities of the German Reich and Austria, with the exception of Vienna.[11] The professional and social position of the Jewish population differed little from that of the *Westjuden* (western Jews), according to a contemporary assessment in the Zionist Prague periodical *Selbstwehr* (self-defense).[12] In the Sudetenland, too, the Jews represented, according to Avraham Barkai, the "old middle class," which essentially consisted of owners of small and mid-sized stores and small companies, their employees, and liberal professionals.[13] In the cities, Jewish economic success and influence was represented above all by well-known Jewish industrial magnates; this was especially the case with respect to the families of the "coal barons" Petschek and Weinmann in Aussig (Ústí nad Labem).[14]

Enmity against the Jews was also widespread in Bohemia and Moravia, in the first instance for religious reasons. A radical minority in the Sudetenland, however, had already advocated a racially motivated anti-Semitism since the late nineteenth century. It played an important role in the conflict between German and Czech nationalities during the Habsburg monarchy and also during the first Czechoslovak Republic, albeit with fluctuating intensity. Especially significant was the German National Socialist Workers' Party (Deutsche Nationalsozialistische Arbeiterpartei; DNSAP), founded in Czechoslovakia at the end of 1919. Its ideological leader, Rudolf Jung, would also be very important for the National Socialists in the German Reich.[15] The party's base existed among Germans living in the Bohemian border regions, who for a long time had also provided the basis for the anti-Semitic Schönerer movement during the Habsburg monarchy.[16] The DNSAP adopted a blatantly anti-Semitic posture, cultivating close links with the NSDAP in Germany, which it openly espoused at the beginning of the 1930s. When threatened with a ban by the Czechoslovak government in 1933, the party voluntarily dissolved.[17] The Sudeten German Home Front (Sudetendeutsche Heimatfront), founded soon thereafter, absorbed most of the DNSAP members; in 1935, at the behest of Prague, it changed its name to the Sudeten German Party (Sudetendeutsche Partei; SdP). Led by Konrad Henlein, a gymnastics instructor from Asch (Aš), it soon became the most important political factor in the Sudetenland. For a long time, the Sudeten German Party avoided taking official positions on the "Jewish Question," strongly repudiating any accusations of having an anti-Semitic disposition. Under the watchful eyes of the government in Prague, the Sudeten German Party was compelled to develop an external democratic mimicry. In actual fact, however, it was anti-liberal, anti-democratic, anti-Semitic, anti-Slavic, and pro-National Socialist. Starting in fall 1937, the party once and for all followed in wake of Germany's National Socialist regime.[18]

The radical Sudeten-German parties stood in close ideological proximity to the *völkisch* and nationalistically minded middle classes. Thus a number of the bourgeois Sudeten-German parties refused to accept Jews, making no secret of their enmity toward them. However, their actions were for most part dependent on their political fortunes at the moment. The German Christian Social People's Party (Deutsche Christlichsoziale Volkspartei), for instance, curbed its anti-Jewish rhetoric during phases when it formed part of the government in Prague.[19] Only the German Social Democratic Workers' Party (Deutsche sozialdemokratische Arbeiterpartei), the liberal German Democratic Freedom

Party (Deutschdemokratische Freiheitspartei), and the Communist Party of the ČSR campaigned for Jewish votes, had Jewish members, and registered Jewish candidates on their electoral lists.[20]

Society reflected these developments. Large and influential clubs and associations more or less openly advocated an anti-Semitic mindset. Thus the German Gymnastics League (Deutsche Turnverband), whose membership included approximately one of every twenty Sudeten Germans, introduced an "Aryan paragraph" in its articles of association, refusing to accept Jews as members.[21] Anti-Slavism and anti-Semitism were also widespread among Sudeten-German students, who often behaved even more radically than their fellow students in the German Reich. At the German university in Prague, where most of them studied, racial anti-Semitic attitudes had prevailed quite early in the student societies. Thus the future elite of the Sudetenland's German community grew up in a climate shaped by hate and intolerance of the Jews. But racial anti-Semitism was not yet capable of gaining broad support. While tens of thousands of Sudeten Germans tacitly accepted the exclusion of their Jewish neighbors, most of them prioritized the "nationality struggle" with the Czechs.[22]

The German Reich's *Anschluss* of Austria in March 1938 also marked a turning point for the Sudetenland. At the end of April, the Sudetendeutsche Partei openly proclaimed its commitment to National Socialism, henceforth blatantly aligning its policies according to the Third Reich and also taking a clear position regarding the "Jewish Question" by including an "Aryan paragraph" in its articles of association. The party, which modeled its structures on the organization of the NSDAP, grew rapidly and by July 1938 had more than 1.3 million members.[23]

Starting in March 1938, violence against Jews, Czechs, and Sudetenland democrats erupted repeatedly in the Sudeten region, often led by SdP members.[24] In a few places, they demanded—referring to the excesses in Austria—that the Jews sell their property and flee. The agenda of Henlein and his party no longer included a peaceful solution. With the "Sudeten crisis" in September 1938, the pressure on the Jews finally reached a high point. Hitler's speech at the NSDAP's national party convention in Nuremberg contributed decisively to the further radicalization of the Sudeten Germans. After considering the *Kampfzeit* (period of struggle), Hitler explained that the "creation of a cohesive and united *Volksgemeinschaft*" had been made possible only through the "neutralization" of the Jews in Germany. At the end of his speech, which at its core revolved around the ČSR, he declared: "The

Germans in Czechoslovakia are neither defenseless, nor are they forsaken. This should be taken into consideration."[25]

On 14 September 1938, Hitler received Konrad Henlein in Berlin. A day later, Henlein would pronounce the rallying cry: *Heim ins Reich* (back home to the Reich), whereupon the government in Prague immediately banned the Freiwillige Schutzdienst (literally, voluntary protection service)—namely, a Sudeten-German group of meeting-hall brawlers modeled on the SA—followed by the Sudeten German Party itself on 16 September. Reacting to these measures, the next day Hitler ordered the formation of the Sudeten-German Free Corps (Sudetendeutsches Freikorps; SFK).[26] Consisting of Sudeten Germans who had fled into the Reich, the armed unit under Henlein's leadership was supposed to protect Sudeten Germans and incite further unrest in the border region.[27] Apart from the desired conflicts with the Czechs, these events simultaneously unleashed the most severe assaults to date on Jews in the Sudetenland. Thus, among other things, Jewish businesses were demolished in Eger (Cheb), Karlsbad, and Asch.[28] Whether the Freikorps controlled these operations remains unknown. The radical actions quickly made an impact. Already by September, the localities of Warnsdorf (Varnsdorf) and Komotau (Chomutov) boasted that they were "Jew-free"; in 1930 Warnsdorf still had 226 Jewish residents and Komotau, with 444, had even more.[29]

However, expulsion and flight were no longer limited to isolated locations. The large-scale migration toward the Czechoslovakian interior already began during the weeks prior to the conference in Munich. While many Jews in the Old Reich had been unable to precisely assess the dangers in 1933,[30] Hitler's five-year regime of terror and the pogrom-like excesses in Austria in spring 1938 forewarned the Sudeten-German Jews about the consequences of annexation.

The First Weeks of the Annexation

In the early morning hours of 30 September 1938, representatives of Germany, Italy, France, and Great Britain signed the Munich Agreement, stipulating the transfer of the Sudetenland from Czechoslovakia to the German Reich[31] (see map 3.1). As per the Agreement, the Czechoslovakian army vacated the region between 1 and 10 October, whereupon the Germans moved in. For the time being, the Wehrmacht took over executive power in the occupied region.[32]

Responsibility for the "reorganization of affairs" fell in the first instance to the Heads of the Civil Administration (Chefs der Zivilverwaltung; CdZ), experienced administration officials from the Old Reich and Austria who marched in with the Army Groups: Regierungspräsident (government district president) Rüdiger from Oppeln accompanied Army Group Command 1; Regierungspräsident Friedrich Bachmann from Schneidemühl accompanied Army Group Command 3; Ministerialdirektor (ministerial director) Harald Turner from the Prussian Finance Ministry accompanied Army Group Command 4; Regierungspräsident Hetzel from Ansbach accompanied Army Group Command z.b.V. (*zur besonderen Verwendung*; for special employment); and Oberregierungsrat (senior government councilor) Kummer from the state government of Lower Austria accompanied Army Group Command 5.[33]

The massive persecution of actual and supposed opponents of the Nazi regime got under way even as the majority of Sudeten Germans frenetically welcomed the Wehrmacht's soldiers as "liberators."[34] During the brief and largely lawless period between the departure of the Czechs and the Wehrmacht's entry, arbitrary actions, excesses, and acts of revenge by SdP supporters were the order of the day. Along with Sudeten-German opponents of the annexation, the border region's Jewish and Czech residents particularly suffered as a result of the violence. In a number of cities, such as Aussig, for example, attackers once again targeted Jewish businesses. In other places such businesses were identified with abusive placards, while, at the same time, the first signs indicating "German-Aryan"—sometimes also "Czech-Aryan"—stores also appeared.[35]

An "unbridled terror"[36] gripped the Sudetenland, spread at first primarily by the Sudetendeutsche Freikorps. The wave of violence quickly proved to be a problem even for the new rulers. Upon the request of the Sudeten-German politician Karl Hermann Frank, Hitler supposedly promised three days of "hunting freedom" after the entry of German troops. Admittedly, this was largely curtailed; nonetheless, due to numerous complaints (even from abroad), on 4 October the Freikorps once again had to be explicitly forbidden from undertaking actions on its own authority.[37]

Yet, as had already occurred in Austria, the central role in fighting all of the potential enemies of the Nazi regime fell to the Einsatzgruppen, special police units that marched into the Sudetenland immediately behind the Wehrmacht. During the first phase of the occupation, they took over security-police and intelligence responsibilities, such as the "security of the new order against all attacks and disruptions, [and] the arrest of all persons known to be enemies of the Reich."[38]

Their activity marked the transition to the systematic persecution of the regime's opponents. The Security Service (Sicherheitsdienst; SD) of the SS had already developed plans in June 1938, preparing lists—the so-called *Mobilisationskartei* (mobilization file)—of known opponents of the Nazis. These were supplemented by an index of alleged enemies of the state that the Security Service had received on 23 September from the SdP. Even though orders did not yet expressly call for taking action against the Jewish population, the terror unleashed by the Einsatzgruppen affected many Jews. The thorough preparation of the terror agencies resulted in a large wave of arrests. The Gestapo field office in Eger on 14 October reported the internment of 971 persons. On 7 November, the Karlsbad Gestapo reported 1,157 detainees.[39] But Sudeten-German fanatics so severely influenced the number of arrests that even the Chief of the Security Police (Sicherheitspolizei; SiPo) and the SD Reinhard Heydrich intervened in December 1938 to moderate their influence.[40] Social Democrats, Communists, Czechs, and Jews filled not only concentration camps in the Old Reich (by December 1939, 2,500 Sudeten Germans had been sent to the Dachau concentration camp alone)[41]—but also detainment camps in the Sudetenland. By spring 1939, approximately 10,000 people had lost their freedom,[42] including an unknown number of Jews.

The new rulers immediately intensified the anti-Semitic propaganda. Whereas earlier the German-Czech *Volkstumskampf* (ethnic-national struggle) had dominated the Sudetenland press, now the "Jewish Question" (along with settling accounts with the "Czech rulership") advanced to the fore. The propaganda was accompanied by the terrorization of the Jewish populace. Businesses were pasted over with defamatory posters, windows smashed, and people abused. Those responsible also included members and supporters of SdP.[43]

Starting at the end of October 1938, Gestapo officials in a number of localities searched out local Jewish residents, compelling them to sign declarations obligating them to leave the Reich's territory within six days. To increase the pressure, the Gestapo was ordered to search the homes of all Jews for "subversive material" and "stolen goods," wording left deliberately vague to avoid obstructing the officials' initiative. If any incriminating material was actually found, the persons to whom it supposedly belonged had to be turned over to the Gestapo control center. Without a doubt, the goal of anti-Jewish policy in the Sudetenland at this point in time was to make the region largely "Jew-free." By the beginning of November 1938, at least 12,000 of the region's 28,000 resident Jews had fled to the interior of Bohemia.[44]

The terror of the "annexation period" merged more or less seamlessly with the November pogroms.[45] Here, too, synagogues burned on the night of 9–10 November 1938, stores were plundered, homes devastated, and people abused.[46] An unknown number (which will probably never be precisely clarified) of Jews were murdered. In Dux (Duchcov), the pogrom also seized upon the Czech population; to justify assaults on Czechs, the latter were accused of having made common cause with the Jews against the Reich—thus an allegation that abruptly inverted the anti-Semitic logic of the first weeks following the annexation, which maintained that the Jews had made a pact with the Czechs. The order to carry out the "Jewish action" was issued to the same addressees as elsewhere in the Reich: to the Gestapo and to the party with its formations, particularly the SA. Himmler's directive prohibiting the involvement of the SS also applied here (although it was disregarded in many cases, of course).[47] As in the Reich, the Gestapo, police, and SA arrested a large number of Jews in the Sudetenland as well. Some remained detained in improvised camps in the Sudetenland itself. One such camp located in Espenthor (Olšová Vrata), approximately eight kilometers from Karlsbad, imprisoned around 300 people.[48] No such "wild" camps had been created in the Old Reich after the pogroms.

By mid November, the *Marienbader Zeitung* could already announce in large font on its front page: "Marienbad is Jew-free."[49] In many places, the traces still remaining of Jewish life were erased from public space—for example, by renaming streets (see figure 3.1). After all, by December 1938 more than half of the Jews residing in the Sudetenland had left their hometowns; officials in Prague registered 15,186 "Israelites" who had fled from the border region.[50] They had been expelled using methods resembling those employed in the Old Reich and Austria. The decisive difference was that the Sudetenland's Jewish population could be forced to flee into the *Resttschechei* (the Nazi designation for the rump Czech state), whereas similar "refuge areas" did not exist for Jews elsewhere in the Reich.

While local powers merely saw the chance to "cleanse" their precincts of all Jews and also a large number of Czechs, ambitious spatial planners in Berlin pursued more extensive goals. According to their ideas, an ethnically homogenous population was to be created in the Sudetenland, since the supposed *Volkstumsgrenze* (ethnic-national boundary) between the Germans and Czechs ran through the region. For the "racial experts" in the Race and Settlement Main Office (Rasse- und

Figure 3.1. Renaming the "Judengasse" in Eger, November 1938. *Source:* Jitka Chmelikova, *Osudy chebskych Židů: Chebšti Žide od 2. Poloviny 19. stoleti do současnosti* (Cheb, 2000), 81.

Siedlungshauptamt) of the SS, it was clear that "the Sudeten lands . . . [are among] the most racially weakened regions of Germany, because for a century they have not received an influx of healthy blood from the German motherland, in contrast they have lost much valuable blood due to emigration."[51]

The burdens created for the *Resttschechei* by the influx of refugees served to destabilize the country. The Nazi regime especially hoped that the large numbers of Jewish refugees would invoke a widespread anti-Semitic movement in the ČSR;[52] yet notwithstanding all of the National Socialist propaganda reports, this failed to materialize to the desired extent. Nonetheless, anti-Semitic activities in the second Czechoslovak Republic noticeably increased.[53]

The Period of the Occupation

Parallel to the military occupation and administration of the Sudetenland, the German Reich pressed ahead at full speed with the reorganization of the state administration. Hitler had already appointed Konrad Henlein as the Reich Commissioner (Reichskommissar) for the Sudeten-German territories, directly under his command, assigning him the task of "ensuring the political organization—[in accordance with Hitler's] general directives—as well as the state, economic, and cultural organization—according to the specific directives from the Reich ministers—of the Sudeten-German regions."[54]

Reich Interior Minister Wilhelm Frick was in charge of the reorganization. On 8 October 1938, he declared the Reich Commissariat (Reichskommissariat) to be the supreme administrative and state-police authority in the Sudeten-German regions.[55] For the most part, Henlein successfully asserted his demand that Sudeten Germans occupy all representative positions;[56] thus, among others, he appointed Karl Hermann Frank as his deputy, Wilhelm Sebekovsky as the Head of the Reich Commissioner's Office, and Fritz Köllner as the Party organization's representative (Beauftragter).[57] Upon Henlein's recommendation, in November Reich Interior Minister Frick ultimately also appointed Sudeten-German politicians to lead the rest of the Reich Commissariat's departments: Anton Kreißl, for example, took over the Interior Department; Wolfgang Richter the Economics Department; and Franz Höller the Propaganda Department.[58]

However, in each instance officials from the Old Reich functioned in advisory capacities. Thus on 17 October 1938, Reich Economics Minister Walther Funk sent Regierungsrat (Government Councilor) Gustav Fremerey to Reichenberg, where, as a "specialized technical consultant," he was supposed to help set up the economics department.[59] In addition, the director of the especially important Subsection for Domestic Affairs (Unterabteilung Inneres) was a Reich German named

Koch. Likewise, Reich Germans were also appointed to key positions in the police department: General Karl von Pfeffer-Wildenbruch took over Subdivision A (Order Police); SS-Oberführer Heinz Jost assumed command of Subdivision B (Security Police).[60] Thus Reich Germans held all of the institutions in the Sudetenland relevant to security matters. At the same time, their areas of responsibility included important aspects of Jewish policy; among other things, Koch was responsible for "population matters, state membership, Reich citizenship, racial legislation, and blood-protection legislation."[61] Heinrich Himmler had made the appointments in his capacity as the head of the German police.[62]

At the behest of Reich Interior Minister Frick, during the last stage of the statutory integration of the Reich's new Sudeten territories in March 1939, the southern Bohemian and southern Moravian regions bordering on Bavaria or Lower and Upper Austria would be joined with the districts of Lower Bavaria and the Upper Palatinate, or, respectively, the districts of the *Ostmark*. For the time being, however, they continued to be under the authority of the Reich Commissioner for the Sudeten-German regions, who availed himself of the Regierungspräsident (government district president) in Regensburg and the Landeshauptmänner (governors) in Linz and Vienna as his "representatives" when carrying out his tasks.[63]

Because of the Sudetenland's specific geographical circumstances, the Reich Interior Ministry felt it necessary to set up an intermediate authority in the region between the Reich Commissioner and the Landräte (district administrators). On 18 October, Frick ordered the appointment of "representatives of the Reich Commissioner"[64]—these posts were assigned to the Heads of the Civil Administration: Turner in Karlsbad, Bachmann in Aussig, and Rüdiger in Troppau (Opava).[65] The preconditions for administrating the Reich's new territories having been established within only a few days, on 21 October 1938 in Reichenberg, Henlein officially took over administrative affairs as the Reich Commissioner for the Sudeten-German territories.[66] On 7 November, the Interior Ministry appointed the "representatives" as Regierungspräsidenten;[67] shortly thereafter, the three Sudeten-German and former SdP/ DNSAP politicians—Hans Krebs in Aussig, Wilhelm Sebekovsky in Karlsbad, and Friedrich Zippelius in Troppau—replaced the provisional officer holders. Appointed as their deputies were the Reich Germans Harry von Craushaar (Aussig), Karl Müller (Karlsbad), and Jost von Schönfeldt (Troppau).[68]

Berlin expedited the Sudetenland's *Angliederung* (incorporation) with the Reich. Even before the military occupation ended, on 8 October 1938

Reich Interior Minister Frick ordered that all future Reich laws also applied for the Sudetenland, unless the region was explicitly exempted from their entry into force.[69] The applicable laws of the German Reich finally went into effect for the Sudeten region on 1 July 1939. Various exemption provisions still obtained until 30 June, particularly in the regions of southern Bohemia and southern Moravia.[70] In Berchtesgaden on 14 April 1939, Hitler signed the so-called Sudetengau Act (Sudetengaugesetz), which officially gave the region the status of a Reichsgau.[71] The Reichsgau Sudetenland was thus simultaneously an administrative district of the Reich and a self-regulatory body. It was led by a Reich Governor (Reichsstatthalter), who directed the government apparatus as a Reich administration under the official supervision of the Reich Interior Ministry according to the technical instructions from the competent departments. Hitler appointed Henlein as the Reich Governor in the Reichsgau Sudetenland. The Reichsgau was supposed to symbolize the unity between the party and the state[72]—the Sudetenland was henceforth regarded as the "model Gau" for the Reich.[73]

When reorganizing the Sudetenland's administration, however, Berlin also referred to lessons learned in Austria just a few months earlier. On 14 October 1938, while the military administration was still in control, the army's supreme commander Generaloberst Walther von Brauchitsch ordered the deployment of a Liquidation Commissioner for Associations, Organizations and Societies in the Sudeten-German Region (Stillhaltekommissar für Organisationen im sudetendeutschen Gebiet) who was supposed to review all clubs and associations and either transfer them into the Reich's corresponding organizations or dissolve them.[74] With the agreement with the Reich's Ministers of the Interior and Finance, he appointed Albert Hoffmann—the Reich Office Leader at the staff of deputy to the Führer—to this post. of the Deputy to the Fuhrer Albert Hoffmann to this post.[75]

As early as the next day, Hoffmann announced that all Sudetenland organizations were obligated to register by 25 October 1938.[76] The Stillhaltekommissar's apparatus in Reichenberg worked fast, since Hoffmann could rely on a team that, in part, had already worked together during the "processing" of all of the Austrian organizations.[77] Gauamtsleiter Hermann Neuburg functioned as Hoffmann's deputy. Unit II C, led first by a department head named Linnemann and later by Günther Scholz, processed faith-based associations, included all Jewish associations.[78] Since the agency's employees completely lacked local knowledge, in rapid succession Hoffmann appointed honorary "general representatives" (Generalbeauftragte) for certain organizations, usually SdP functionaries who were familiar with local conditions, allocating them to the agency's corresponding unit.[79]

The Stillhaltekommissar's responsibility for the south Bohemian Landkreise (rural districts) of Markt Eisenstein (Železná Ruda Městys), Bergreichenstein (Kašperské Hory) and Prachatitz (Prachatice) in the Gau Bavarian Ostmark constituted an anomaly, because these were the only areas of the Old Reich where he could operate. Apart from Austria and the Sudetenland, his agency would later also control all of the associations and foundations in the Protectorate of Bohemia and Moravia, Alsace, Lorraine, and the Netherlands.[80] By 20 February 1940, the Stillhaltekommissar had "processed" 66,408 organizations in the Sudeten regions, dissolving 10,960 of them, including all of the Jewish ones. In total, he processed assets worth almost 142 million RM, confiscating approximately 18 million RM, including the assets of the Jewish associations.[81] The Stillhaltekommissar's responsibilities were subsequently taken over by the Aufbaufonds-Vermögensverwaltung GmbH (construction fund-asset management), founded by Hoffmann; starting already in January 1939, it assumed the responsibility as a trust company for liquidating non-liquid assets.[82]

As of October 1938, anti-Semitism became institutionalized as state doctrine in the Sudetenland as well.[83] The Old Reich's anti-Jewish laws were introduced within a few short weeks. To start with, Interior Minister Frick prohibited the Jews in the "annexed territory" from "raising the Reich and national flag and displaying the Reich's colors."[84] On 19 October, Goebbels expanded the scope of the Editor Act (Schriftleitergesetz) to include the Sudeten region, thereby limiting journalistic employment exclusively to those with "German or a related type of blood, and, if [they are] married, [have] a spouse with German or a related type of blood."[85]

The measures ordered in the wake of the November pogroms for the rest of the Reich's territories also applied for the Sudetengau, such as the Ordinance on an Atonement Tax on the Jews of German Nationality, which obligated the Jews to surrender 20 percent of their assets.[86] The next step involved implementing the "race laws" in the Sudeten-German regions. On 27 December 1938, Frick issued the Ordinance on the Introduction of the Nuremberg Race Laws in the Sudeten-German Territories.[87] The now relentless terror, the November pogroms, and the statutory discrimination triggered a second large wave of refugees, heading mostly toward inner Bohemia. According to the Reich Office for Statistics (Statistisches Reichsamt), on 17 May 1939 only 2,363 *Volljuden* (Full Jews) and 2,183 *Mischlinge*

1. Grades (1st degree Hybrids) and 1,396 *Mischlinge 2. Grades* (2nd degree Hybrids) still lived in the Reichsgau Sudetenland.[88]

Even as the Sudetenland was being organizationally "annexed" by the Reich, Göring had determined on 14 October 1938 that the "Jewish Question" needed to be tackled "with all means," for the Jews had to "get out of the economy."[89] With that he announced the decisive round of the "Aryanization" of Jewish property. The Ordinance regarding the Elimination of the Jews from German Economic Life issued on 12 November 1938 prohibited Jews—including those in the Sudetenland—from the "operation of retail sales locations" and the "independent operation of a trade."[90] According to the Ordinance regarding the Registration of the Assets of Jews in the Sudeten-German Regions issued by Göring on 2 December 1938, Jews had to register their assets by 31 January 1939.[91] The Ordinance regarding the Utilization of Jewish Assets followed only one day later on 3 December for the entire Reich.[92]

Thus in the Sudeten-German regions, the comprehensive "Aryanization" of Jewish property ranked first among the anti-Jewish measures. In 1930 Jews had owned four to five thousand industrial or mercantile companies.[93] Because of the large-scale flight, hundreds of abandoned stores, skilled trade firms, and industrial companies were left behind, which the new rulers began to register, manage, and exploit immediately after the Wehrmacht marched into the region. Many jobs—in some places, even the provisioning of the population—depended on resuming their operation.[94] A substantial portion of the Jewish population was expelled between September and November 1938, facilitating the predatory takeover of their property.[95] In Teplitz-Schönau alone, 200 stores, as well as 511 houses and apartments, stood empty; work in most of the 89 business operations must have come to a standstill.[96]

Following the Ordinance regarding the Elimination of the Jews from German Economic Life, on 12 November 1938 Konrad Henlein ordered the appointment of provisional managers for all "Jewish" firms in the Sudetenland. Commissioners appointed since the annexation had to seek approval from the respective Regierungspräsidium (government district presidium) in Troppau, Aussig, or Karlsbad.[97] The system of "wild" commissars deployed in Austria in spring 1938, where party members personally enriched themselves on a large scale from Jewish property, had served as a warning to authorities in Berlin and Reichenberg to avoid a similar situation in the Sudetenland.[98] An order from 19 January 1939 provided for the use of commissars to head commercial operations "if proper business management is not guaranteed due to the absence of persons hereto entitled."[99] This, however, opened the door widely to arbitrary action. At the end of January 1939, commissars managed approximately 100 operations in the Regierungsbezirk of Troppau, around 800 in Aussig, and approximately 1,000 in Karlsbad.[100]

On the basis of the ordinance from 2 December 1938, Regierungspräsident Wilhelm Sebekowsky in Karlsbad announced that all Jews still living in his Regierungsbezirk had to register their assets; the Landräte were responsible for compiling the names and statistics.[101] Parallel to this, the NSDAP Gauwirtschaftsberater (Gau economic advisor) in the Sudetengau instructed Wolfgang Richter and the NSDAP Kreisleiter (district leaders) to inform him about all Jewish commercial operations.[102] After the registration of Jewish assets, the Reich Governor and the three Regierungspräsidenten began the expropriations. An exemption provision applied for objects that had been confiscated by the Gestapo, which were later allocated to the competent Oberfinanzpräsidien (regional finance presidiums) in Karlsbad and Troppau. Almost all land property was transferred to the Oberfinanzpräsidentens' (regional finance presidents') real estate divisions. The Karlsbad-Fischern (Karlovy Vary-Rybaře) branch of the German Settlement Society (Deutsche Ansiedlungsgesellschaft) managed most of the agricultural properties confiscated for the benefit of the Reich. They were supposed to be used for the "new formation of the German peasantry." By the end of February 1941, the Reich Governor had registered 781 agricultural properties in the Sudetengau confiscated from Jewish assets.[103]

In order to maintain a semblance of legality, the responsible parties adhered to legal formalities during the "Aryanization" process. Basically, as evident from instructions in the January 1939 *Anzeiger der Industrie- und Handelskammern im Sudetengau* (the gazette for the Sudetengau's chamber of commerce and industry) the seller or authorized representative and the acquirer were supposed to conclude sales contracts.[104] Subject to certain conditions, prospective buyers who could not come up with the necessary funds to acquire a Jewish business operation had the opportunity to apply for an "Aryanization loan" as part of the Reich Economic Assistance Program (Reichswirtschaftshilfe) for the Sudetenland.[105] The Reich Economics Ministry controlled the "dejudaization" and "reorganization" of the Sudeten-German economy and, with respect to a number of important industries—such as mining, energy, steel, and the financial system—reserved the right to decide on the sale of companies, whereas in the Old Reich the ministry functioned solely as an appellate body, even during the highpoint of "Aryanization" in 1938/39.[106]

Yet the authorities and the party soon discovered that not enough local residents were interested in "Aryanizing" Jewish—or "Germanizing" Czech—businesses. Therefore, the ministry no longer generally excluded prospective buyers from the Old Reich from acquiring companies in the Sudetenland.[107] "Aryanization" advanced swiftly, allowing Regierungspräsident Krebs to announce in Aussig in June 1940, during a visit by Reich Governor Henlein, that the Reparations and Aryanization Department (Wiedergutmachungs- und Arisierungsabteilung) in his agency had completed its work.[108] To be sure, the Sudeten-German Jews had meanwhile been expropriated, almost without exception; but many operations, stores, and real estate properties remained under fiduciary management. Sales or liquidations often dragged on for months, even years; a number of cases remained undecided even at the end of the war.

The diverging interests of Berlin and the Sudeten-German authorities proved to be a fundamental problem. The Reich primarily wanted to harness the Sudeten-German industrial potential for the arms industry. For the Reich Economics Ministry, "Aryanization" also served as an instrument for economic structural policy. In contrast, the Sudeten-German authorities primarily wanted to create work for unemployed *Volksgenossen* (ethnic-national comrades) and preserve jobs in the factories of Jewish entrepreneurs.[109] The course of "Aryanization" created deep resentment among the Sudeten-Germans. The authorities and population in the Sudetenland both complained that the domestic economy was being "taken over by the Old Reich." This was partially true. Sudeten-Germans only managed to acquire appreciable Jewish factories in the largely outdated textile and food industries. But in sectors critical for the war effort, opportunities usually went to prospective buyers from the Old Reich. Meanwhile, most of the retail companies owned by Jews or Czechs were shut down. Thus the Sudeten-German economy profited primarily from the easing of competitive pressure.[110] By the end of 1940, the value of "Aryanized" assets in the Sudetenland was assessed at approximately 8.7 billion Kč—namely, around 1 billion RM.[111]

The state's coercive measures against the Jews who still remained in the Reichsgau Sudetenland were no different from the Jewish policies in the Old Reich. In June 1940, only 1,886 Jews still lived in the Sudetengau;[112] their number remaining relatively constant until April 1942 (1,614).[113] In the Reichsgau Sudetenland, the "concentration" of Jews in "Jew houses" had already begun in mid 1939,[114] after the government of the Reich created the legal basis for owners to terminate Jewish tenants with the Law concerning Rental Relationships with Jews on 30 April 1939. At the same time, Jews who still had their own premises were obligated to take in homeless Jewish families.[115] Berlin promptly introduced the law on 10 May 1939 in the Reichsgau Sudetenland as well.[116] The apartments and houses of Jews who had fled in 1938/39 had already been placed with new tenants, and the Sudeten-German authorities had only been waiting for a starting signal that allowed them to requisition additional Jewish residential space.[117] In August 1940, the municipal administration of Teplitz-Schönau finally concentrated the city's remaining resident Jews "almost without exception in very small apartments (one to two rooms)."[118] Finally, so-called Jew houses (their exact number remains unknown) were created in most cities that still had several dozen Jewish residents.

Following the model provided by corresponding measures in the Reich, starting in summer 1941 the Gestapo also forged plans for collectively accommodating all Jews from Aussig and its environs in a camp, choosing an empty, dilapidated castle in the village of Schönwald (Krásný Les) in the Erzgebirge, distanced some thirty kilometers from Aussig. The new residents had to repair the building at their own expense.[119] At the end of 1941, the Landrat from Leitmeritz (Litoměřice) began implementing his plans to concentrate some of the Jews residing in the Kreis, making use of the nearby Dlaschkowitz (Dlažkovice) castle.[120] In total, these forced resettlements impacted around 100 people in the case of Schönwald, and presumably several dozen in the case of Dlaschkowitz (exact figures are unknown). By expelling Jews from their residences, the authorities pursued a number of goals: freeing up residential space; along with that, the further pauperization of the Jews; the concentration of as many Jews as possible in only a few locations, making them more easily available for further "measures"; and their extensive isolation from the population.[121]

Parallel to resettlements within the Gau, the marking of all the Jews took place throughout the Reich. The police ordinance "on the marking of the Jews" issued by Reinhard Heydrich on 1 September 1941, obligating the Jews to wear a "Jewish star," also affected the Reichsgau Sudetenland.[122]

Like elsewhere in the Reich, the authorities in the Reichsgau Sudetenland needed the remaining locally resident Jews for forced labor.[123] Even children were fastidiously registered and, upon reaching the age of fourteen, forced to work.[124] But their deployment did little to alleviate the labor shortage, for the expulsions had depleted their numbers too severely. In contrast to the Old Reich and the *Ostmark,* where dozens of Jewish work camps were erected during the first half of 1939, not a single such camp was set up in Sudetenland.

The use of forced labor—notwithstanding the goal of finally making the Gau "Jew-free"—brought large numbers of Jews from elsewhere into the Sudetenland: Himmler's instigation led to the founding of "Organization Schmelt"—named after its director SS-Oberführer Albrecht Schmelt, the former Breslau Polizeipräsident (police president)—in the industrial region of East Upper Silesia in fall 1940. Schmelt operated a lucrative business for the SS, renting Jewish forced laborers to the Reich Autobahn Directorate (Reichsautobahnbaudirektion) and various industrial companies. Organization Schmelt extended all the way across Wehrkreis (military district) VIII, respectively the SS Higher Administrative Section Southeast (SS-Oberabschnitt Südost)—thus across Upper Silesia, Lower Silesia, and parts of the Reichsgau Sudetenland. In the beginning of 1943, Schmelt presided over 177 camps with more than 50,000 Jewish forced laborers. Nineteen camps were established in the Sudetenland for non-German Jews. The living and working conditions in the Schmelt camps differed little from most concentration camps.[125] Schmelt had Jewish females trained in factories in the East Upper Silesian cities of Sosnowitz (Sosnowiec) and Bendsburg (Będzin) that produced clothing for the Wehrmacht, preparing them for mass deployment in Silesian and Sudeten-German flax mills.[126] Organization Schmelt was particularly active in the textile industry in Kreis Trautenau (Trutnov),[127] where 1,215 female forced laborers were employed in fall 1942.[128]

The deportations of Jews began somewhat later in the Sudetenland than elsewhere. We can only speculate as to the reasons, although presumably this was related to the small number of remaining Jews. Between July 1942 and February 1943, around 400 people were initially "evacuated" directly from the Reichsgau Sudetenland to the extermination camps in the East. The first transport left Aussig on 13 July 1942 as part of the fourth "deportation wave" from the German Reich,[129] which differed from previous waves because the deportees were no longer brought to ghettos but rather murdered immediately in most cases. In June 1942 alone, the Gestapo deported 361 people from the Sudetenland to the extermination camps in the East, reducing the number of Jews in the Reichsgau to 1,197.[130] The subsequent transports from the Sudetenland went to Theresienstadt in the Protectorate of Bohemia and Moravia, designated as an *Altersghetto* (old-age ghetto) or, euphemistically, as a *Vorzugslager* (privileged ghetto), and used to accommodate protectorate members as well as privileged and older Jews from the Reich.[131] By the end of 1944, 460 had been brought to Theresienstadt from the Reichsgau Sudetenland.[132]

While, on the one hand, the deportations of resident Jews continued until the Gau was deemed to be virtually "Jew-free," on the other hand, the SS brought thousands of Jewish prisoners from its empire of camps to the Sudetenland. Admittedly, none of the large concentration camps were located either here or in the Protectorate of Bohemia and Moravia, yet the camp system metastasized in these regions as well. The first satellite camps of Flossenbürg, Ravensbrück, and Groß-Rosen were erected in the Sudetenland in 1942, in part emerging from the camps of Organization Schmelt. Starting in mid 1943, the undertow of a new deportation wave also took Jewish forced laborers from the Schmelt camps, whereupon a number of camps in the Sudeten region were shut down and others placed under the control of the concentration camp system.[133]

In fall 1944, a network of concentration camp satellites and outposts stretched across the Sudetengau, considered to be the last region in the Reich that was safe from bombing. Not all camps housed Jewish prisoners; sometimes Jews only arrived there in the last months of the war with the evacuation transports from Auschwitz and other camps. One of the Sudeten region's largest concentration camp satellites was Leitmeritz, where underground production facilities for Auto-Union AG and Osram AG were supposed to be built in the tunnel system of a former lime and brick works. A camp complex was created—a "gigantic subsystem of KZ Flossenbürg"—with presumably 18,000 prisoners (16,541 are documented); roughly 4,500 of them died there. Approximately 3,000 of the slave laborers were Jews whom the SS had shifted to Leitmeritz from Dachau, Flossenbürg, and Groß-Rosen, among other places.[134]

In 1944, the number of resident Jews still registered in the Reichsgau Sudetenland was only 587.[135] The last chapter of the deportations from the German Reich, and thus also from the Sudetenland, began in January 1945. In a final large-scale operation, the Reich Security Main Office (Reichssicherheitshauptamt) in Berlin planned to deport all of the Jews who had thus far been spared, namely, those who lived in so-called mixed marriages.[136] Between 6 February and 7 March, the Gestapo again deported another 157 people from the Reichsgau Sudetenland to Theresienstadt.[137] Thus when the Third Reich surrendered in May 1945, no more than 400 Jews still lived in the Sudeten region.

Conclusion

When developing and pursuing their anti-Jewish policies in the Sudetengau, the National Socialists built on their experiences in Austria. This became clear in October and November 1938, when the Gestapo forced the Jewish population in a number of places to make written commitments to leave the country, a strategy first used during the expulsions from Burgenland in spring 1938.[138] They also paid heed to lessons learned from their experiences in Austria when carrying out the "Aryanizations." Whereas Austria during March and April witnessed the emergence of an untamed Aryanization process exploited by "wild" commissars for personal enrichment, in the Sudetengau the authorities implemented measures right from the start to ensure that the management of expropriated businesses and companies benefited the state. The rapid exodus of the Jewish population greatly facilitated the "Aryanizations" in the Gau.

The Nazi regime felt very little need to make tactical compromises when annexing the Sudetenland; consequently, by the end of 1939, the region's resident Jews had been almost completely stripped of their rights. This radicalization occurred in the immediate context of the foreign policy victories in 1938, namely, the annexations of Austria and, of course, the Sudetenland itself by the German Reich. Yet in contrast to Austria, the Reichsgau Sudetenland did not become another "testing ground" for Jewish policy, nor did the preconditions for such testing exist, for most of the Jews either fled or were expelled in 1938. Within a very short time, Berlin introduced to the "incorporated" region of Sudetenland a body of anti-Jewish laws and ordinances that had taken five years to prepare and implement in the Old Reich. Without governing bodies in the Sudetenland that—in contrast to postwar myths—employed large numbers of indigenous officials in leading positions, the rapid implementation of anti-Semitic laws and policies would not have been possible. Many Sudeten Germans profited from the Nazi regime's Jewish policies—particularly as a result of "Aryanization"—and therefore willingly accepted the persecution of their Jewish neighbors for "reasons of group selfishness."[139]

Flight and expulsion led a large proportion of the Sudeten-German Jews to seek refuge in the interior of Bohemia. In December 1938, the number of those who had fled to this region already totaled more than 15,000. Most of them fell into the hands of the Nazi regime when the Wehrmacht marched into the *Resttschechei* on 15 March 1939. The situation for the Jews remaining in the Sudetenland was comparable to that of their suffering counterparts in the Reich. They were stripped of their rights, crowded into "Jew houses," and plundered to the point of total poverty; all persons capable of work had to perform forced labor. The deportations of the Jews from the Reichsgau Sudetenland began in July 1942—at first, directly to the death camps in the East; then, starting in spring 1943, to Theresienstadt, which as a rule, however, was just a way station on the route to extermination. Only 400 of what were formerly 24,500 Jews survived the Holocaust in the Reichsgau Sudetenland itself.

Notes

1. The article is based on the author's study *Nationalsozialistische Judenverfolgung im Reichsgau Sudetenland 1938–1945* (Munich, 2006).
2. Jörg K. Hoensch, *Geschichte der Tschechoslowakei*, 3rd ed. (Stuttgart, 1992), 32f. However, there were also voices surmising that a referendum would not necessarily have produced a majority in favor of incorporation with Germany. See, for example, Prague Consul General von Gebsattel to the foreign office, 27 November 1918, in *Akten zur deutschen auswärtigen Politik 1918–1945* (ADAP), Series A: *1918–1925*, vol. 1: *9. November 1918 bis 4. Mai 1919* (Göttingen, 1982), 67–70 (doc. 44), here 69. Evidently, at least some of the Sudeten Germans were not averse to an interim arrangement with the new situation. See Volker Zimmermann, *Die Sudetendeutschen im NS-Staat: Politik und Stimmung im Reichsgau Sudetenland (1938–1945)* (Essen, 1999), 35.
3. Rudolf Jaworski, *Vorposten oder Minderheit? Der sudetendeutsche Volkstumskampf in den Beziehungen zwischen der Weimarer Republik und der ČSR* (Stuttgart, 1977), 33; Ronald Smelser, *The Sudeten Problem, 1933–1938: Volkstumspolitik and the Formulation of Nazi Foreign Policy* (Middletown, CT, 1975) 42; Christoph Boyer and Jaroslav Kučera, "Die Deutschen in Böhmen, die Sudetendeutsche Partei und der Nationalsozialismus," in *Nationalsozialismus in der Region*, ed. Horst Möller et al. (Munich, 1996), 273–285, here 274; Jörg Osterloh, *Nationalsozialistische Judenverfolgung im Reichsgau Sudetenland 1938–1945* (Munich, 2006), 11 including note 1, 49f.
4. Hoensch, *Geschichte*, 33; Boyer and Kučera, "Die Deutschen in Böhmen," 274. From the period, see Josef Pfitzner, *Sudetendeutsche Einheitsbewegung: Werden und Erfüllung*, 2nd ed. (Karlsbad; Leipzig, 1937), 34. For a critical social democratic perspective, see Josef Fischer et al., *Ihr Kampf: Die wahren Ziele der Sudetendeutschen Partei* (Prague, 1937), quote on page 35.
5. See here, for instance, Peter Pulzer, *The Rise of Political Anti-Semitism in Germany and Austria* (New York, 1964).
6. For more detail on this and the Jewish population in the ČSR, see the chapter by Wolf Gruner in this volume.
7. *Čechoslovakische Statistik*, vol. 9, series VI (census 1), part I: *Volkszählung in der Čechoslovakischen Republik vom 15. Februar 1921* (Prague, 1924), 86–97; *Čechoslovakische Statistik*, vol. 98, series VI (census 7), part I: *Volkszählung in der Čechoslovakischen Republik vom 1. Dezember 1930* (Prague, 1934), 82–99. On the decline of the Jewish population, see Franz Friedmann, "Židé v Čechach [Jews in Bohemia]," in *Die Juden und Judengemeinden Böhmens in Vergangenheit und Gegenwart: Ein Sammelwerk*, ed. Hugo Gold (Brünn and Prague, 1934), 720–735, here 729; Theodor Haas, "Statistische Betrachtungen über die jüdische Bevölkerung Mährens," in *Juden und Judengemeinden Mährens*, ed. Hugo Gold (Brünn, 1929), 591–597, here 594.
8. On Jewish emigration from Germany and Austria, see Peter Heumos, *Die Emigration aus der Tschechoslowakei nach Westeuropa und dem Nahen Osten 1938–1945: Politisch-soziale Struktur, Organisation und Asylbedingungen der tschechischen,*

jüdischen, deutschen und slowakischen Flüchtlinge während des Nationalsozialismus; Darstellung und Dokumentation (Munich, 1989), 15–55; Kurt R. Grossmann, "Refugees to and from Czechoslovakia," in *The Jews of Czechoslovakia: Historical Studies and Surveys,* vol. 2 (Philadelphia and New York, 1971), 565–581; Eva Schmidt-Hartmann, "Tschechoslowakei," in *Dimension des Völkermords: Die Zahl der jüdischen Opfer des Nationalsozialismus,* ed. Wolfgang Benz (Munich, 1991), 353–379, here 355.

9. Ordinance issued by the government of the Czechoslovak Republic, dated 30 October 1920. Excerpts printed in Emil Sobota. *Das Tschechoslovakische Nationalitätenrecht* (Prague, 1931), 279–282. On the deliberations of the census committee, see *Čechoslovakische Statistik,* vol. 9, 9*, 64*. See also Wolf Gruner's chapter in this volume.

10. *Čechoslovakische Statistik,* vol. 98, XLIII. This is also substantiated by research into the position of the Jews with respect to the Germans and the Czechs. German was the predominant vernacular among Bohemian Jews. Only after the founding of the ČSR did they gradually draw closer to the Czechs, but without any fundamental shift of priorities in the border region. See Wilma A. Iggers, "Juden zwischen Tschechen und Deutschen," *Zeitschrift für Ostforschung* 37 (1988): 428–442.

11. In 1933, 160,564 Jews lived in Berlin (3.78 percent of population). Similar proportions also obtained in Frankfurt and Breslau, as well as in a series of small and mid-sized towns. See Ino Arndt and Heinz Boberach, "Deutsches Reich," in *Dimension,* ed. Benz, 23–65, here 23ff. In Vienna, on the other hand, the Jewish portion of the population amounted to approximately 9 percent. See Gerhard Botz, "Arisierungen in Österreich (1938–1940)," in *Die politische Ökonomie des Holocaust: Zur wirtschaftlichen Logik von Verfolgung und "Wiedergutmachung,"* ed. Dieter Stiefel (Vienna and Munich, 2001), 29–56, here 31.

12. "Juden in den Grenzgebieten der Tschechoslowakei," *Selbstwehr,* 30 September 1938.

13. Avraham Barkai, *From Boycott to Annihilation: The Economic Struggle of the German Jews, 1933–1943* (Hanover, NH, 1989), 2 (German original: Frankfurt, 1987). Czechoslovakian occupational statistics do not make it possible to determine whether these were employees in small, mid-sized, or large companies. See here also Gustav Otruba, "Der Anteil der Juden am Wirtschaftsleben der böhmischen Länder seit dem Beginn der Industrialisierung," in *Die Juden in den böhmischen Ländern: Vorträge der Tagung des Collegium Carolinum in Bad Wiessee vom 27. bis 29. November 1981,* ed. Ferdinand Seibt (Munich, 1983), 209–268, here 220.

14. On the Petschek and Weinmann companies, see *Compaß: Finanzielles Jahrbuch; Čechoslovakei,* 71st year, (Prague, 1938). Lists of well-known and/or significant Jewish industrialists in the most important industries in Bohemia and Moravia-Silesia can be found in Otruba, "Anteil," 222–268, and Joseph Pick, "Economy," in *Jews of Czechoslovakia,* vol. 1 (Philadelphia, 1968), 359–438.

15. On the DNSAP in general, see Andreas Luh, "Die Deutsche Nationalsozialistische Arbeiterpartei im Sudetenland: Völkische Arbeiterpartei und faschistische Bewegung," *Bohemia* 32 (1991): 23–38.

16. On Georg Ritter von Schönerer and his role in the Habsburg monarchy, see Andrew G. Whiteside, *The Socialism of Fools: Georg von Schönerer and Austrian Pan-Germanism* (Berkeley, 1975).

17. Smelser, *The Sudeten Problem,* 52–54.

18. Zimmermann, *Die Sudetendeutschen im NS-Staat,* 39–57; Ralf Gebel, *"Heim ins Reich!" Konrad Henlein und der Reichsgau Sudetenland 1938–1945* (Munich, 1999), 25–60.

19. On the DCVP, see Jaroslav Šebek, "Der Antisemitismus im sudetendeutschen katholischen Milieu 1918–1938," in Židé v Sudetech / Juden im Sudetenland, published by the Česká křesťanská akademie and the Ackermann-Gemeinde (Prague, 2000), 93–99.
20. Osterloh, Judenverfolgung, 104ff.
21. On the Deutsche Turnverband, see Andreas Luh, Der Deutsche Turnverband in der Ersten Tschechoslowakischen Republik: Vom völkischen Vereinsbetrieb zur volkspolitischen Bewegung (Munich, 1988).
22. On the situation of the Jews at the German university in Prague, see Osterloh, Judenverfolgung, 108–128.
23. On the development of the SdP in 1938, see Detlef Brandes, Die Sudetendeutschen im Krisenjahr 1938 (Munich, 2008); Boyer and Kučera, "Die Deutschen in Böhmen," 275, 281ff.
24. "Henlein Nazi rehearse," in The Jewish Chronicle, 5 June 1938.
25. Adolf Hitler, Hitler: Reden und Proklamationen 1932–1945: Kommentiert von einem deutschen Zeitgenossen, part 1: Triumph, vol. 2: 1935–1938, ed. Max Domarus (Wiesbaden, 1973), 896. On the speech, ibid., 897–906, quote on 905; "Deutschlands Forderung für die Sudetendeutschen," Völkischer Beobachter, North German edition, 14 September 1938, 3–5. See also Saul Friedländer, Nazi Germany and the Jews, vol. 1, The Years of Persecution, 1933–1939 (New York, 1997), 249.
26. Martin Broszat, "Das Sudetendeutsche Freikorps," Vierteljahrshefte für Zeitgeschichte 9 (1961): 30–49, here 34f.; on the Freiwilliger Schutzdienst, see Gebel, "Heim ins Reich!", 57.
27. Zimmermann, Die Sudetendeutschen im NS-Staat, 63.
28. Rudolf M. Wlaschek, Juden in Böhmen: Beiträge zur Geschichte des europäischen Judentums im 19. und 20. Jahrhundert, 2nd ed. (Munich, 1997), 68.
29. Gebel, "Heim ins Reich!", 78; Čechoslovakische Statistik, vol. 98, 84f., 92f.
30. Situation report Turner, 24 November 1938, Bundesarchiv (BArch), R 15.01/6080; Zimmermann, Die Sudetendeutschen im NS-Staat, 387.
31. Agreement between Germany, the United Kingdom, France, and Italy, concluded in Munich on 29 September 1938, in ADAP, series D, vol. 2: Deutschland und die Tschechoslowakei (1937–1938) (Baden-Baden, 1950), 812–814 (doc. 675).
32. Decree of the Führer and Reich Chancellor on the administration of the Sudeten region. from 1 October 1938, RGBl. 1938 I, 1331f. Also published in Verordnungsblatt für die sudetendeutschen Gebiete 1938, 1f., on 4 October 1938. See also Hans Umbreit, Deutsche Militärverwaltungen 1938/39: Die militärische Besetzung der Tschechoslowakei und Polens (Stuttgart, 1977), 32–48.
33. Special instructions regarding the order for the occupation of territorial portions separated from Czechoslovakia, Appendix 1, October 1938, Bundesarchiv-Militärarchiv (BA-MA), RH 64/37, fol. 7–12; ibid., fol. 14, Beilage 1, 1 October 1938.
34. Gebel, "Heim ins Reich!", 69–80; Zimmermann, Die Sudetendeutschen im NS-Staat, 71–82.
35. Vladimír Kaiser, "Die jüdische Gemeinde in Aussig/Ústí nad Labem im 19. und 20. Jahrhundert," in Židé v Sudetech, 235–254, here 239; Gebel, "Heim ins Reich!", 75; Deutschland-Berichte der Sozialdemokratischen Partei Deutschlands (Sopade) 1934–1940, Fünfter Jahrgang 1938 (Salzhausen and Frankfurt, 1980), 1041, 1064, 1068.
36. Boyer and Kučera, "Die Deutschen in Böhmen," 285.
37. On the SFK see Broszat, "Das Sudetendeutsche Freikorps"; Werner Röhr, "Das Sudetendeutsche Freikorps—Diversionsinstrument der Hitler-Regierung bei der Zerschlagung der Tschechoslowakei," Militärgeschichtliche Mitteilungen 52 (1993):

35–66. On the excesses of the SFK, see Helmut Krausnick, *Hitlers Einsatzgruppen: Die Truppe des Weltanschauungskrieges 1938–1942* (Frankfurt, 1985), 21; Zimmermann, *Die Sudetendeutschen im NS-Staat*, 96f.
38. Quoted in Krausnick, *Einsatzgruppen*, 17. See also Hans Buchheim, "Die SS—Das Herrschaftsinstrument," in *Anatomie des SS-Staates*, vol. 2, ed. Hans Buchheim et al. (Olten and Freiburg im Breisgau, 1965), 13–253.
39. Zimmermann, *Die Sudetendeutschen im NS-Staat*, 90ff.; *Deutschland-Berichte 1938*, 1042.
40. Miroslav Kárný, "Der Holocaust und die Juden in Böhmen und Mähren," in *Tschechen, Deutsche und der Zweite Weltkrieg: Von der Schwere geschichtlicher Erfahrung und der Schwierigkeit ihrer Aufarbeitung*, ed. Robert Maier (Hannover, 1997), 39–56, here 47; Martin Broszat, "Nationalsozialistische Konzentrationslager 1933–1945," in *Anatomie*, vol 1., ed. Buchheim et al., here 94.
41. Gebel, *"Heim ins Reich!"*, 72. This number presumably also includes the Jews arrested after the November pogroms.
42. Groscurth to Vizeadmiral Canaris, 12 October 1938, in Helmuth Groscurth, *Tagebücher eines Abwehroffiziers 1938–1940: Mit weiteren Dokumenten zur Militäropposition gegen Hitler*, ed. Helmut Krausnick and Harold C. Deutsch, with collaboration by Hildegard von Kotze (Stuttgart, 1970), 327–329 (Appendix 1), here 327; Zimmermann, *Die Sudetendeutschen im NS-Staat*, 94f.
43. Osterloh, *Judenverfolgung*, 187ff.
44. Ludomír Kocourek, "Das Schicksal der Juden im Sudetengau im Licht der erhaltenen Quellen," *Theresienstädter Studien und Dokumente* (1997): 86–104, here 86f.; Heumos, "Emigration," 16f. According to other information—which, however, is not confirmed by Czechoslovakian statistics—17,000 Jews had already fled from the Sudetenland to the interior of Bohemia by October 1938. Wilma A. Iggers, "Die Emigration der deutschen und österreichischen Juden in die Tschechoslowakei," in *Judenemanzipation—Antisemitismus—Verfolgung in Deutschland, Österreich-Ungarn, den Böhmischen Ländern und in der Slowakei*, ed. Jörg K. Hoensch et al. (Essen, 1999), 143–154, here 153. See also Wolf Gruner's chapter in this volume.
45. On the November pogroms, see Hermann Graml, *Reichskristallnacht: Antisemitismus und Judenverfolgung im Dritten Reich*, 3rd ed. (Munich, 1998); Wolfgang Benz, "Der Novemberpogrom 1938," in *Die Juden in Deutschland 1933–1945: Leben unter nationalsozialistischer Herrschaft*, ed. Wolfgang Benz, 3rd ed. (Munich, 1993), 499–544; Peter Longerich, *Holocaust: The Nazi Persecution and Murder of the Jews* (Oxford, 2010), 109–113 (German original: Munich, 1998); Alan Steinweis, *Kristallnacht 1938* (Cambridge 2009).
46. See, for example, the short report by Arnold Budlowsky on the abuses and the destruction of the synagogue in Gablonz (Jablonec nad Nisou) in Ben Barkow, Raphael Gross, and Michael Lenarz, eds., *Novemberpogrom 1938: Die Augenzeugenberichte der Wiener Library, London* (Frankfurt, 2008), 483f.
47. *Deutschland-Berichte 1938*, 1196; Zimmermann, *Die Sudetendeutschen im NS-Staat*, 103f.; Peter Longerich, *Die braunen Bataillone: Geschichte der SA* (Munich, 1988), 237.
48. Kocourek, "Schicksal," 88, refers to the "Espetov" camp. This is evidently a former Czech name of the community. The official directory does not include a community called Espetov, but it does include the community of Espenthor (924 residents) in Kreis Karlsbad, *Das Ortsbuch für das Deutsche Reich: Ergänzungsband: Ostmark, Sudetengau, Memelland*, published in association with the Deutsche Reichsbahn and the Deutsche Reichspost (Berlin, 1940), 81.

49. "Marienbad judenfrei," *Marienbader Zeitung*, 16 November 1938, printed in *Die Verfolgung und Ermordung der europäischen Juden durch das nationalsozialistische Deutschland 1933–1945* [*VEJ*], vol. 2: *Deutsches Reich, 1938-August 1939*, ed. Susanne Heim (Munich, 2009), 462f.
50. Heumos, "Emigration," 246f.
51. Quoted in Isabel Heinemann, *"Rasse, Siedlung, deutsches Blut": Das Rasse- und Siedlungshauptamt der SS und die rassenpolitische Neuordnung Europas* (Göttingen, 2003), 177. Now see also Detlef Brandes, *"Umvolkung, Umsiedlung, rassische Bestandsaufnahme": NS-"Volkstumspolitik" in den böhmischen Ländern* (Munich, 2012).
52. "Oase des Judentums verschwindet," *Völkischer Beobachter*, North German edition, 22 October 1938.
53. See here Helena Krejčová, "Spezifische Voraussetzungen des Antisemitismus und antijüdische Aktivitäten im Protektorat Böhmen und Mähren," in *Judenemanzipation*, ed. Hoensch, 175–194, here, 181ff. A critical view of Czechoslovakia's position with regard to Jewish refugees can be found in Michal Frankl and Kateřina Čapková, *Nejisté útočiště: Československo a uprchlíci před nacismem, 1933–1938* (Prague, 2008). See also Wolf Gruner's chapter in this volume.
54. Decree of the Führer and the Reich Chancellor on the administration of the Sudeten-German territories, 1 October 1938, RGBl. 1938 I, 1331f.; for an introduction, see Umbreit, *Militärverwaltungen*, 32–45.
55. Ordinance on the decree of the Führer and the Reich Chancellor on the administration of the Sudeten-German territories, 8 October 1938, RGBl. 1938 I, 1348, 2; Draft of allocation of duties of the authority of the Reichskommissar for the Sudeten-German territories, undated, BArch, R 43 II/1370, fol. 41f.
56. Stuckart to RMdI, Fs., 12 October 1938, BArch, R 1501/5414, fol. 143.
57. At the same time, Herbert David (legal office), Franz Höller (propaganda director) and Richard Lammel (personnel office), among others, were appointed to the Party's Hauptleitung (main directorate); Deutsches Nachrichtenbüro, morning edition, 12 October 1938, BArch, R 43 II/1370, fol. 8.
58. "Berufungen in das Reichskommissariat," *Sudetendeutsche Tageszeitung*, 16 November 1938.
59. RWM to RMdI, 17 October 1938, Rossijskij Gosudarstvennij Voennyj Archiv v Moskve (RGVA—Russian Government Military Archive, Moscow), 1458–10–243, fol. 57.
60. Memorandum, 17 October 1938, BArch, R 43 II/1370, fol. 10ff., here fol. 11. Prior to the annexation of the Sudetenland, as head of the SD's Auslandsnachrichtendienstes (foreign intelligence service) Jost had been responsible for monitoring Henlein; see Gebel, *"Heim ins Reich!"*, 114.
61. SS-Sturmbannführer Regierungsrat Kernert became the director of StaPo Reichenberg; Entwurf der Geschäftsverteilung der Behörde des Reichskommissars für die sudetendeutschen Gebiete, undated, BArch, R 43 II/1370, fol. 41. Reich Germans also sometimes presided over local police presidiums. The new Karlsbad police chief, Polizeidirektor Mählich, for example, came from Hamm in Westphalia. "Neuer Polizeichef in Karlsbad," *Die Zeit*, 16 December 1938.
62. "Sicherheitsdienst durch die Polizei," *Der Freiheitskampf*, 24 October 1938; BArch, R 43 II/1367 b, fol. 76; Deutsches Nachrichtenbüro, evening edition, 22 October 1938, BArch, R 43 II/1367b, fol. 76.
63. Bavarian prime minister to RMdI, 21 December 1938, Bayerisches Hauptstaatsarchiv (BayHStA), Reichsstatthalter Epp, 28.
64. Reich Interior Minister to the Reichskommissar for Sudeten-German regions, 18 October 1938, BArch, R 43 II/1370, fol. 66f. See also Gebel, *"Heim ins Reich!"*, 97f., 101.

65. "Regierungspräsidenten für Karlsbad, Aussig und Troppau," *Der Freiheitskampf*, 7 November 1938.
66. On 20 October 1938 von Brauchitsch allocated the administrative responsibilities to the Reichskommissar. Decree of the Supreme Commander of the Army to the Sudeten Germans, 20 October 1938, in *Verordnungsblatt für die sudetendeutschen Gebiete 1938*, 33. At the same time, Henlein announced that upon the "expiration of the 20th of October 1938" the "entire administration in the Sudeten-German regions" would transfer to him. Decree of the Reichskommissars for the Sudeten-German Territories to the Sudeten Germans, 20 October 1938, in ibid., 34.
67. Reich Interior Minister to the Reichskommissar for Sudeten-German regions, 4 November 1938, with appendix: business allocation plan for Regierungspräsidenten in the Sudeten-German regions, RGVA, 1458–10–218, fol. 70ff.
68. Zimmermann, *Die Sudetendeutschen im NS-Staat*, 150f.
69. Ordinance on the decree of the Führer and the Reich Chancellor on the administration of the Sudeten-German territories, 8 October 1938, RGBl. 1938 I,1345, 1.
70. RGBl. 1939 I, 745f. Until 14 April 1939, Reich laws that went into force in the Reichsgau Lower Danube and the Reichsgau Upper Danube did not go into effect in the Sudeten regions until 1 July 1939. In contrast, Reich laws introduced in the Lower and Upper Danube as of 15 April 1939 also went into immediate effect in the Sudetenland.
71. Law on the Establishment of the Administration in the Reichsgau Sudetenland (Sudetengaugesetz), 14 April 1939, RGBl. 1939 I, 780ff. The *Ostmarkgesetz* (*Ostmark* Law), published in parallel, likewise designated the former Austrian lands as *Reichsgauen*; Gesetz über den Aufbau der Verwaltung in der Ostmark, 14 April 1939, RGBl. 1939 I, 777ff.
72. "Gesetz über Ostmark und Sudetengau," *Deutsche Allgemeine Zeitung*, 21 April 1939. On the right to issue instructions to the Reichssonderverwaltungen (Reich Special Administrations), see RMdI to the obersten Reichsbehörden, 1 November 1938, RGVA, 1458–10–213, fol. 2.
73. Gebel, *"Heim ins Reich!"*, 100.
74. *Verordnungsblatt für die sudetendeutschen Gebiete 1938*, 18. On the following, see ibid. See also Deutsches Nachrichtenbüro, Meldung no. 1694, 18 October 1938 (BArch, R 2501/3341, fol. 56).
75. On Albert Hoffmann, see SS-Offizierspersonal-Akten, Film 107-A, BArch, BDC.
76. Stiko Reichenberg, Anordnung 1/38, Durchführungsbestimmungen, 15 October 1938, Österreichisches Staatsarchiv/Archiv der Republik (ÖStA/AdR), Stiko Wien, Kt. 922.
77. Referat II D (Gottfried Dorer) was responsible for foundations and funds. The leading functionaries in Abteilung IV B (Finanzwesen der Vereine, Organisationen und Verbände) under Egon Meiler were all Reich Germans. Hermann Neuburg (Abt. IV Aa) and Max Warsow (Abt. IV Ad) had already worked as Abteilungsleiter (department heads) in Vienna. Gertrude Rothkappl, "Die Zerschlagung österreichischer Vereine, Organisationen, Verbände, Stiftungen und Fonds: Die Tätigkeit des Stillhaltekommissars in den Jahren 1938–1939" (diss., Universität Wien, 1996), 32ff. On the creation and the activities of the authority in Austria, see Verena Pawlowsky et al., *Vereine im Nationalsozialismus: Vermögensentzug durch den Stillhaltekommissar für Vereine, Organisationen und Verbände und Aspekte der Restitution in Österreich nach 1945* (Vienna, 2004).
78. Statement Neuburg, undated, Archiv ministerstva vnitra (AMV—interior ministry archive, Prague), 301–139–1, fol. 229; Übersicht über die Dienststelle des Stiko,

undated, Státní Oblastní Archiv v Litoměřicich (SOAL—State Territorial Archive Leitmeritz) pobočka Most (Brüx regional office), Stiko, Kt. 1.
79. A detailed list of the Generalbeauftragte in: Übersicht über die Dienststelle des Stiko, undated, SOAL pobočka Most, Stiko, Kt. 1.
80. Pawlowsky et al., *Vereine*, 18f., 43.
81. Reorganization of the association system, undated, SOAL pobočka Most, Stiko, Kt. 1; Zimmermann, *Die Sudetendeutschen im NS-Staat*, 169f.; Gebel, *"Heim ins Reich!"*, 123f. On 15 September 1940 the Stilhaltekommissar ceased his activities in the Sudetenland; a settlement agency remained responsible for unresolved issues; "Die Tätigkeit des Stillhaltekommissars beendet," *Die Zeit*, 9 March 1941; "Stiko, Abwicklungsstelle," *Amtliches Nachrichtenblatt*, no. 49, 14 September 1940.
82. Osterloh, *Judenverfolgung*, 273f.
83. Ludolf Herbst, *Das nationalsozialistische Deutschland, 1933–1945: Die Entfesselung der Gewalt: Rassismus und Krieg* (Frankfurt, 1996), 37; in general on the following, see Osterloh, *Judenverfolgung*, 187ff.
84. Ordinance on the decree of the Führer and the Reich Chancellor on the administration of the Sudeten-German territories, 8 October 1938, RGBl. 1938 I, 1345, 1.
85. Ordinance on the Introduction of the Editor Act in the Sudeten-German Territories, 19 October 1938, RGBl. 1938 I, 1447.
86. Ordinance on an Atonement Tax on Jews of German State Membership, 12 November 1938, RGBl. 1938 I,1579. Ordinance of the Elimination of the Jews from German Economic Life, 12 November 1938, *Verordnungsblatt für die sudetendeutschen Gebiete, 1938*, 168.
87. Ordinance on the Introduction of the Nuremberg Race Laws in the Sudeten-German Territories, RGBl. 1938 I, 1997; *Verordnungsblatt für die sudetendeutschen Gebiete, 1938*, 145. This ordinance brought the "Reich Citizenship Law" and the "Law for the Protection of German Blood and German Honor" (both enacted on 15 September 1935) into force in January 1939. See also "Blutschutzgesetz im Sudetengau," *Duxer Zeitung*, 6 December 1938.
88. *Statistik des Deutschen Reiches*, vol. 552, no. 4: *Die Bevölkerung des Deutschen Reiches nach den Ergebnissen der Volkszählung 1939: Die Juden und jüdischen Mischlinge im Deutschen Reich* (Berlin, 1944), 4, 38f.
89. Meeting with Göring on 14 October 1938 in the RLM, in *Der Prozeß gegen die Hauptkriegsverbrecher vor dem Internationalen Militärgerichtshof Nürnberg, Nürnberg 14. November 1945—1. Oktober 1946*, vol. 27 (Nuremberg, 1948), 160–164 (doc. 1301-PS), quote on 163.
90. RGBl. 1938 I, 1580.
91. RGBl. 1938 I, 1703.
92. RGBl. 1938 I, 1709.
93. This figure is an approximate calculation based on the data from ten cities; a comprehensive overview of the economic and social situation of the Jewish population in the Sudetenland does not exist. *Čechoslovakische Statistik*, vol. 116, series VI (Berufsstatistik, no. 4), part 2: Volkszählung in der Čechoslovakischen Republik vom 1. Dezember 1930 (Prague, 1935), 174–195 (table 5). As such, the figures essentially corresponded with those in the Old Reich, which in 1933 had approximately 520,000 resident Jews and around 100,000 independent Jewish firms, including 50,000 retail stores. See Avraham Barkai, "Die deutschen Unternehmer und die Judenpolitik im 'Dritten Reich,'" in *Die Deutschen und die Judenverfolgung im Dritten Reich*, ed. Ursula Büttner (Hamburg, 1992), 207–229, here 209 including note 10. For a criticism of Barkai's figures, see Frank Bajohr, *"Aryanization" in Hamburg: The Economic Exclusion of Jews and the Confiscation of their Property*

in *Nazi Germany* (New York and Oxford, 2001) (German original: Hamburg, 1997), 108.
94. Zimmermann, *Die Sudetendeutschen im NS-Staat*, 388.
95. Franz Svatosch, "Das Grenzgebiet unter dem Hakenkreuz: Die sozialökonomischen Veränderungen Nord- und Nordwestböhmens während der ersten Phasen der hitlerfaschistischen Okkupation (Oktober 1938 bis Mitte 1942)," (diss., Potsdam, 1969), 305.
96. Dr. Paul Wanie, city archivist, "Die Chronik der Stadtgemeinde Teplitz-Schönau nach der Heimkehr des Sudetenlandes ins Grossdeutsche Vaterland," (1938–1940), manuscript in Státní okresní Archiv Teplice (SOkA Teplice—Staatliches Kreisarchiv Teplitz-Schönau), inv. č. 462, kniha 473, 419.
97. Zimmermann, *Die Sudetendeutschen im NS-Staat*, 205.
98. Longerich, *Holocaust*, 109; Jonny Moser, "Das Unwesen der kommissarischen Verwalter," in *Arbeiterbewegung, Faschismus, Nationalbewußtsein*, ed. Helmut Konrad and Wolfgang Neugebauer (Vienna, 1983), 89–97.
99. RWM to the Reichskommissar for the Sudeten-German regions, 2 March 1939, appendix: guidelines for the appointment, confirmation, and dismissal of commissarial directors, 19 January 1939, RGVA, 1458-10-240.
100. Wolfgang Braumandl, *Die Wirtschafts- und Sozialpolitik des Deutschen Reiches im Sudetenland 1938–1945* (Nuremberg, 1985), 295.
101. Ibid., 302; Zimmermann, *Die Sudetendeutschen im NS-Staat*, 205.
102. Directive from the Gauwirtschaftsberater K-2, Reichenberg, 12 December 1938, SOAL, Župní vedení NSDAP, inv. č. 24, kt. 29.
103. Reichsstatthalter to RMEuL, 22 January 1941 with appendix 1: general overview of the status of the Aryanization of agricultural properties as at 1 January 1941, BArch, R 3601/3267, fol. 402ff.
104. Svatosch, "Das Grenzgebiet unterm Hakenkreuz," 307; Braumandl, *Die Wirtschafts- und Sozialpolitik*, 303.
105. On this see Osterloh, *Judenverfolgung*, 363–391.
106. Draft of an order regarding the approval procedure according to the "ordinance regarding the protection of the Sudeten-German economy" for the portfolio of the Reich Economics Ministry, January 1939, RGVA, 1458–10–218, fol. 99; RWM to the Reichskommissar for the Sudeten-German regions, 14 January 1939, RGVA, 1458–10–218, fol. 105f. In the Old Reich, the Reich Economics Ministry only claimed decision-making rights with respect to companies with more than 1,000 employees. See also Frank Bajohr, "'Arisierung' und Restitution: Eine Einschätzung," in *"Arisierung" und Restitution: Die Rückerstattung jüdischen Eigentums in Deutschland und Österreich nach 1945 und 1989*, ed. Constantin Goschler and Jürgen Lillteicher (Göttingen, 2002), 39–59, here 40.
107. The ministry worked on an "order regarding the approval procedure according to the ordinance regarding the protection of the Sudeten-German regions." RWM, express letter, 4 January 1939, RGVA, 1458–10–218, fol. 98.
108. Zimmermann, *Die Sudetendeutschen im NS-Staat*, 205.
109. On the diverging interests, see Osterloh, *Judenverfolgung*, 307ff. On the importance of preserving jobs, see, for example, the argumentation in: Kreditausschusssitzung für die Reichswirtschaftshilfe, 9 January 1939, Vorbericht Firma RA Dr. Erich Hermann, Deutsch-Gabel, BArch, R 2/16174, fol. 116, 3.
110. Osterloh, *Judenverfolgung*, 399–426, 439–482.
111. Czechoslovakia, in Jewish Record, XII/1940, Národní archiv (NA—State Archive, Prague), Zahraniční tiskový archiv, Karton 586, inventarní čislo 492, E-14; Zimmermann, *Die Sudetendeutschen im NS-Staat*, 205. This assessment was based on

the assumption of 25,000 affected Jews in the Sudetenland and estimated assets worth the equivalent of 40,000 RM per person. But the assessment appears to have been too high, since historians have assessed the total value of Jewish property in the Old Reich for 1933 at approximately 12 billion RM; Avraham Barkai, "The Fateful Year 1938: The Continuation and Acceleration of Plunder," in *November 1938: From 'Reichskristallnacht' to Genocide*, ed. Walter H. Pehle (New York, 1991), 95–122, here 99 with footnote 15 (German original: Frankfurt, 1988); Graml, *Reichskristallnacht*, 172. This assessment is made on the basis of 525,000 Jews in the German Reich in January 1933 and assumes assets worth approximately 23,000 RM per person. The fact that the figures in the "Jewish Record" are probably too high is also substantiated by the figures presented in Helen B. Junz, *Where Did All the Money Go? The Pre-Nazi Era Wealth of European Jewry* (Amsterdam, 2001), 86, according to which 550,000 "racial Jews" (as per the classification of the Nuremberg Laws) in the German Reich in 1933 owned assets worth 160 billion RM (around 29,000 RM per person). Regarding Junz's figures, see also Constantin Goschler and Jürgen Lillteicher, "Einleitung," in *"Arisierung,"* ed. Goschler and Lillteicher, 12.
112. RVJD to RMdI, 2 July 1940, RGVA, 500–1-431, fol. 200.
113. Übersicht zur Bevölkerungsentwicklung in den Kultusvereinigungen und Bezirksstellen der Reichsvereinigung ("Altreich" einschließlich Sudetenland und Danzig), May 1941 (BArch, R 8150/26, fol. 1) and April 1942 (BArch, R 8150/27, fol. 46).
114. The essential work on the "Jew houses" is still Marlis Buchholz, *Die hannoverschen Judenhäuser: Zur Situation der Juden in der Zeit der Ghettoisierung und Verfolgung 1941 bis 1945* (Hildesheim, 1987). On developments in various large cities, see Wolf Gruner, "Local Initiatives, Central Coordination: German Municipal Administration and the Holocaust," in *Networks of Nazi Persecution: Bureaucracy, Business, and the Organization of the Holocaust*, ed. Gerald D. Feldman and Wolfgang Seibel (New York and Oxford, 2005), 269–294, here 276 and 283.
115. RGBl. 1939 I, 864f.
116. Ordinance on the Introduction of the Law on Rental Relationships with Jews in the Sudeten-German Territories, 10 May 1939, RGBl. 1939 I, 907.
117. Aussig Regierungspräsident to the region's Landräte, 11 May 1940, SOkA Teplice, AMT, inv.č. 451, Hefter: 123/11.
118. Bürgermeister to Landrat of Teplitz-Schönau, situation report for August 1940, undated, SOkA Teplice, LRT, Kt. 8, Hefter: Pol. X.
119. LKA Baden-Württemberg, Sonderkommission—Zentrale Stelle–, Vernehmungsniederschrift L.O., 24 September 1964, BArch Ludwigsburg, 505 AR-Z 17/61, vol. I, fol. 147; see also Tomáš Fedorovič, "Die Gemeinde Schönwald und ihre unfreiwilligen Einwohner," in *Theresienstädter Studien und Dokumente* (2001): 269–286, here 270. Regarding the general background for the construction of such work and residential camps for Jewish families starting in summer 1941, as well for more details on Schönwald, see Wolf Gruner, *Jewish Forced Labor under the Nazis: Economic Needs and Racial Aims 1938–1944* (New York, 2006), 61–74.
120. Aussig Regierungspräsident, situation report for April 1942, dated 1 May 1942, SOAL, ÚVP, PS, Kt. 30.
121. Osterloh, *Judenverfolgung*, 486–493.
122. RGBl. 1941 I, 547.
123. See the general overview by Wolf Gruner, *Der Geschlossene Arbeitseinsatz deutscher Juden: Zur Zwangsarbeit als Element der Verfolgung 1938–1943* (Berlin, 1997).
124. Witness testimony of G.K., 29 October 1963, office for the investigation of Nazi violent crime at state headquarters in Israel, BArch Ludwigsburg, 505 AR-Z 17/61, vol. I, fol. 45.

125. Wolf Gruner, "Juden bauen die 'Straßen des Führers': Zwangsarbeit und Zwangsarbeitslager für nichtdeutsche Juden im Altreich 1940 bis 1943/44," *Zeitschrift für Geschichtswissenschaft* 44 (1996): 789–808, here 806ff.; cf. Gruner, *Jewish Forced Labor*, 196–229; see also Osterloh, *Judenverfolgung*, 546ff. On the "Organisation Schmelt," see also Sybille Steinbacher's chapter in this volume.
126. Situation report of Rüstungsinspektion VIII, 14 November 1941, BA-MA, RW 20-8/21, fol. 163f.; Gruner, "Juden bauen," 805; Gruner, *Jewish Forced Labor*, 222; Sybille Steinbacher, *"Musterstadt" Auschwitz: Germanisierungspolitik und Judenmord in Ostoberschlesien* (Munich, 2000), 149f.
127. NSDAP, Kreisleitung Trautenau, political situation report for November 1941, dated 2 December 1941, SOAL, ŽV, inv.č. 13 Kt. 3. On the camps in Kreis Trautenau, see Miroslav Kryl and Ludmila Chládková, eds., *Pobočky koncentračního tábora Gross-Rosen ve lnářských závodech Trutnovska za nacistické okupace* (Trutnov, 1981).
128. NSDAP, Kreisleitung Trautenau, political situation report for September 1942, dated 15 October 1942, SOAL, ŽV, inv.č. 13 Kt. 3, Kocourek, "Schicksal," 96f., mentions 1,300 women.
129. File note dated 8 July 1942, SOkA Teplice, AMT, inv.č. 5569, Kt. 496.
130. RVJD, inventory report dated 4 August 1942, BArch, R 8150/27, fol. 88; LKA Baden-Württemberg, Vernehmungsniederschrift E. W., 18.4.1966, BArch Ludwigsburg, 505 AR-Z 17/61, vol. II, fol. 285; Longerich, *Politik*, 488.
131. H. G. Adler, *Theresienstadt 1941–1945: Das Antlitz einer Zwangsgemeinschaft; Geschichte, Soziologie, Psychologie* (Tübingen, 1955), 58.
132. Institut Theresienstädter Initiative, ed., *Theresienstädter Gedenkbuch: Die Opfer der Judentransporte aus Deutschland nach Theresienstadt 1942–1945* (Prague, 2000), 84ff.
133. Gruner, "Juden bauen," 806; Gruner, *Jewish Forced Labor*, 228; Steinbacher, *Auschwitz*, 328.
134. Jörg Skriebeleit, "Die Außenlager des KZ Flossenbürg in Böhmen," in *KZ-Außenlager—Geschichte und Erinnerung*, special issue, *Dachauer Hefte* 15: (1999): 196–217, here 199–208, quote on 208; Miroslava Benešová, "Das Konzentrationslager in Leitmeritz und seine Häftlinge," *Theresienstädter Studien und Dokumente* (1995): 217–240. On KZ Groß-Rosen and its satellite camps, see Bella Gutterman, *A Narrow Bridge to Life: Jewish Forced Labor and Survival in the Gross-Rosen Camp System, 1940–1945* (New York and Oxford, 2008), 130–230.
135. RVJD, overview of the number of Jews on 1 November 1944, BArch, R 8150/32, fol. 39; RVJD, Sudetenland regional office, status of the Jewish population in the Aussig Regierungsbezirk on 1 January 1945, BArch, R 8150/33, fol. 2.
136. Longerich, *Holocaust*, 387.
137. *Theresienstädter Gedenkbuch*, 88f.
138. Longerich, *Holocaust*, 99.
139. Anton Otte, "Einführung," in *Židé v Sudetech*, 11.

CHAPTER 4

PROTECTORATE OF BOHEMIA AND MORAVIA
Wolf Gruner

Prior to the Annexation

As was the case with Germany, the end of the First World War, whose consequences dramatically changed the maps and power relationships of Central and Eastern Europe, also contained the seeds for later developments in Bohemia (Čechy) and Moravia (Morava). The new Czechoslovak Republic, founded as one of the successor states of the Austro-Hungarian Empire, included most of the Czech and Slovak peoples, as well German, Jewish, Hungarian, Polish, and Ruthenian minorities.[1] The independence declaration on 28 October 1918 guaranteed equal rights and political representation for all population groups, including minorities. At the same time, by recognizing Jewish nationality, the new government pursued the political goal of weakening the country's German and Hungarian contingents; the former included many of the new republic's 354,000 Jews, the large majority of whom spoke German.[2]

In 1921, more than 13 million people lived in the Czechoslovak Republic; along with 6,840,000 Czechs, almost 2 million Slovaks, and just over 3 million Germans.[3] By the end of 1930, the number of inhabitants had risen to almost 15 million, most of whom were living in the west—that is, Bohemia, Moravia, and Silesia—and 4 million in the east, namely, in Slovakia and Carpathian Ruthenia. The capital Prague (Praha) had 900,000 residents at the time.[4]

In Bohemia, Czechs made up two-thirds of the population, while Germans comprised one-third; in Moravia, Czechs accounted for 74 percent, while Germans comprised almost 23 percent. But the German share of the population was declining due to lower birth rates.[5] Whereas Czechs and Slovaks gained cultural and political freedoms under the new state, the Germans lost the privileged status they had enjoyed during the Habsburg period. Many therefore rejected the young republic, even demanding the unification of German-speaking Bohemian regions with the recently founded Republic of German-Austria.[6] Along with the new official languages, Czech and Slovak, minorities could officially use their own languages to communicate with local authorities in areas where these minorities comprised at least one-fifth of the inhabitants. Germans received additional minority rights, including representation in parliament and municipal councils, as well as access to culture and education; in 1935, 97 percent of their children attended German schools.[7]

The national euphoria of the immediate postwar period also fueled an already existing anti-Semitism in Bohemia and Moravia, but it remained marginal compared to that in neighboring countries.[8] In any event, isolated demonstrations occurred, and stores and apartments were plundered in Prague. In the small town of Holešov (Holleschau), members of a nearby army unit, together with local residents, devastated apartments and administrative offices. Three Jews died as a result of a three-day pogrom. Later, in 1927, a fascist party based on the Italian model formed in the ČSR and anti-Semitic agitation began gradually gaining ground in the press.[9] But the country's founder, President Tomáš G. Masaryk, fought against such trends with all available means.[10]

Of the 354,000 Jews living in Czechoslovakia in 1921, half described their nationality as Jewish (11,251 of 79,777 in Bohemia; 19,016 of 45,306 in Moravia); the rest viewed themselves as Czechs, Germans, or Hungarians.[11] Many spoke multiple languages. The concept of cultural hybridity applied above all for the Jews in Prague,[12] who lived in close proximity to the other groups in Czech society.[13] The republic's founding was accompanied by the formation of a Czech-Jewish movement that advocated universal assimilation. The diverse Jewish population included Zionists as well, who encouraged Jewish immigration to Palestine and advocated the creation of a Jewish state, and large numbers of Orthodox Jews who strongly opposed both assimilation and the Zionist agenda.[14] Indeed, most of the Jews lived in the republic's eastern part—in Slovakia and Carpathian Ruthenia—where they constituted 14 percent of the inhabitants; with 90 percent of Jews in this region describing their nationality as Jewish, they tended to advocate orthodox religious positions.[15]

After 1918, three Jewish umbrella organizations existed in Czechoslovakia, representing—respectively—the communities of Greater Prague as well as the Czech-speaking and German-speaking communities. In 1926, these organizations joined with the Moravian communities to form the Supreme Council, which promoted the study of Jewish history, religion, and culture, for the Jewish population had been steadily declining since the end of the nineteenth century, due to conversions, the secularization of Czech society, and the increasing number of interfaith marriages (already 30 percent in 1933)—all signs of the strong acculturation of Jews and their acceptance by Czech society. In 1930, a total of 356,830 Jews lived in Czechoslovakia; of these, 7,301 (21.5 percent) resided in Bohemia and 41,250 (11.5 percent) in Moravia and Silesia, in 150 Jewish communities.[16]

Of the approximately 10 million inhabitants of Bohemia and Moravia, the 117,551 Jews comprised only 1 percent.[17] Most of the Jews inhabited the large cities; in Bohemia, almost 50 percent (35,403) lived in Prague alone; in Moravia, 25 percent (11,103) lived in Brno (Brünn) and 15 percent (6,865) in Moravian Ostrava (Mährisch-Ostrau; Moravská Ostrava). More than half of all the Jews in both provinces existed in five cities with more than 50,000 inhabitants. The proportion of Jews amounted to 4.2 percent of the population in Prague and Brünn, 5.5 percent in Mährisch-Ostrau, 2.4 percent in Pilsen, and 3.3 percent in Olmütz (Olomouc). As in most of Western Europe, the majority—that is, 60 percent—of Czech Jews worked in trade and commerce, 14 percent in the public sector, and only a few in agriculture. Many Jews had established good reputations in culture and politics.[18]

The new republic had formed a political landscape with a diverse range of parties. The Czechoslovak Social Democratic Worker's Party, Czechoslovak Socialist Party (as of 1926, the National Socialist Party), Czechoslovak People's Party, Czechoslovak National Democratic Party, and the Republican Party of Agricultural and Smallholder People (the so-called Agrarian Party) regularly contributed the lion's share of parliament representatives.[19] The German minority was also represented in parliament—indeed, quite conspicuously, with three of the "German parties" taking part in government starting in 1926. But when a National Socialist movement developed in the Sudeten territory in the 1930s, the Prague government reacted with political pressure that led to the dissolution of radical parties. After 1933, most of their members joined the newly founded Sudeten German Home Front (Sudetendeutsche Heimatfront) under Konrad Henlein; later renamed the Sudeten German Party (Sudetendeutsche Partei), in light of Hitlers's "success" it won more than a million votes in the 1935 parliamentary election and emerged as the Sudeten Germans' strongest political force. After the annexation of Austria, when Henlein called for all Germans in the ČSR to join his party, a number of German parties, such as the Farmers' League (Bund der Landwirte) and the German Christian Social People's Party (Deutsche Christlichsoziale Volkspartei), disbanded. Henlein now openly propagated policies inspired by the Nazi state and its anti-Semitism.[20]

Anti-Semitic agitation in the ČSR had generally gained momentum since the mid 1930s, directed against "Jewish Bolshevism" and especially against the large number of refugees, for since 1933 thousands of politically and racially persecuted persons—first from the Reich and then from Austria—sought refuge in Czechoslovakia. Initially, both the government and the population welcomed the first refugees. But as of the mid 1930s, growing pressure from right-wing political forces led to more restrictive ČSR immigration policies.[21]

The Nazi state viewed itself as the representative of the "Greater German *Volksgemeinschaft*" and therefore felt entitled to intervene in the life and politics of other states.[22] The Czechoslovak government, in contrast, understood such intervention as an expression of a traditional pan-German imperialism.[23] Both externally and internally, the pressure increased on the ČSR, whose founding president, Masaryk, had resigned in 1935 and died in 1937. The situation intensified in summer 1938 after the expiration of the German-Polish Accord for Upper Silesia in 1937[24] and the annexation of Austria in March 1938. Nazi agitation, organized violence, as well as boycotts against Jewish and Czech businesses dominated in the Sudeten region.[25] Even though the ČSR had granted Germans many important liberties at the end of September 1938 (although never any autonomy), Great Britain and France, rightly fearing war, conceded to Hitler's demand—explicitly declared in Nuremberg—for the self-determination of the Sudeten Germans and the cession of territory. The Munich Dictate de facto divided the young republic into three parts. Slovakia obtained extensive autonomy. Czechoslovakia lost not only three-tenths of its territory, a quarter of its population, and countless natural resources to Germany, but also its thousand-year-old (and well-fortified) border. In the newly annexed Sudeten region, during the next days and weeks the Gestapo arrested tens of thousands of "enemies of the Reich," triggering a large wave of refugees.[26]

In November 1938, Czechoslovakia registered 12,392 Jewish refugees in terms of religious affiliation; by December that number had increased to 15,186, many of whom, however, viewed their nationality as Czech.[27] According to the Prague statistical office, more than 259,000 persons of Jewish faith lived in the truncated Czech state; apart from the refugees, 99,000 lived in Bohemia, Moravia, and Silesia, 87,000 in Slovakia, and 66,000 in Carpathian Ruthenia. Installed by Edvard Beneš before going into exile at the end of September, the government under Jan Syrový now led the Second Republic in an authoritarian style, banning the Communist Party and creating a single trade union organization. The end of November 1938 witnessed Emil Hácha's election as state president and the formation of Rudolf Beran's government. Nevertheless, pressure from within by so-called *Volksdeutsche* (ethnic Germans) and from without by the Nazi regime increased.[28]

The need to shelter and provision hundreds of thousands of Czech and German refugees generated severe social and political tensions within Czech society. Hitler, for his part, had no interest in accepting the ethnic Germans from the territories of the Czech state; as far as he was concerned, they were supposed to contribute to the further destabilization of the ČSR. The expulsion of many Jews from the Sudeten region and their flight to the ČSR contributed to the growing anti-Semitism. On 27 January 1939, the Prague government ordered the deportation of Jews who had immigrated since 1914, including state citizens. The army placed Jewish officers on leave; Jewish doctors were supposed to surrender their positions in public hospitals. German universities, schools, and daily newspapers dismissed their Jewish lecturers, teachers, and journalists. Czech newspapers began publishing anti-Semitic articles. As a result of the expulsion, 14,000 Jews left the republic. This decision, in fact, saved many of their lives,[29] for by October 1938, Hitler had already instructed the German Wehrmacht to prepare for the violent "finishing-off the *Resttschechei* [rump Czech state]."[30]

The First Weeks of the Annexation

On the morning of 15 March 1939—after President Hácha and Foreign Minister František Chvalkovský had been summoned to Berlin and complied with Hitler's ultimatum to allow an unopposed occupation[31]—the Wehrmacht marched into the remaining territory of the ČSR. The day before, the Slovakian part of the republic had announced its independence under German protection.[32] Hitler traveled to Prague, where the next day he declared that "the Bohemian-Moravian lands" had belonged to the "*Lebensraum* of the German *Volk*" for a thousand years, and that they would henceforth form part of the Greater German Reich as the Protectorate of Bohemia and Moravia. He also announced that he would promptly grant Reich citizenship to Germans living in the region, and that from now on they were subject exclusively to German jurisdiction. Thus, as so-called *Protektoratsangehörige* (protectorate subjects), Czechs and Jews, even those of German origin, held the status of second-class citizens.[33]

In contrast, the Germans in the Protectorate were granted representation in the now so-called Greater German Reichstag, as had also occurred with the reintegration of the Saarland and the annexation of the Sudetenland.[34] In the long term, Hitler sought to fully Germanize the Bohemian-Moravian region by settling German peasants.[35] But in the short term he did not view this as an option; therefore, he annexed the Czech regions to the German Reich, but granted them political autonomy.[36]

Initially, the German army exercised executive authority in the Protectorate. Notably, the Sudeten German Konrad Henlein functioned as the Head of the Civil Administration (Chef der Zivilverwaltung; CdZ) in Bohemia. Josef Bürckel held this position in Moravia—he had experience with annexations, having served as the Reich Commissioner for the Reintegration of the Saarland (Reichskommissar für die Rückgliederung des Saarlandes) and subsequently as the Reich Commissioner in Vienna. The Heads of the Civil Administration were supposed to establish a German administration, supervise the still-existing Czech authorities, and assume responsibility for the police. Thus the Gestapo and SS fell initially under the army's command.[37] The so-called Einsatzgruppen of the Security Police (Sicherheitspolizei; SiPo) and Security Service (Sicherheitsdienst; SD) of the SS had advanced directly behind the Wehrmacht—in Bohemia under Dr. Otto Rasch (Inspector of the Security Police in Kassel), and in Moravia under Dr. Franz Walter Stahlecker (Inspector of the Security Police in Vienna), who had previously already led an Einsatzgruppe in the Sudetenland.[38] Later during the occupation of the Soviet Union, both would lead Einsatzgruppen that perpetrated systematic mass murder of Jews.

On 18 March 1939, Hitler appointed Freiherr Konstantin von Neurath, the former German foreign minister, as Reich Protector

(Reichsprotektor) for Bohemia and Moravia.[39] But the Wehrmacht did not transfer executive authority to him until the middle of April.[40] As State Secretary, Karl Hermann Frank—since 1937 the deputy chairman of the Sudeten German Party and since 28 March 1939 a Higher SS and Police Leader (Höherer SS- und Polizeiführer)—received de facto the post of deputy protector. Born in 1898 in Karlsbad (Karlovy Vary), after abandoning his law studies and completing a business apprenticeship in Prague, Frank worked for the municipal administration of Witkowitz (Vítkovice) until 1920, and later as an independent accountant. A member of the German National Party (Deutschnationale Partei) prior to 1933, as of 1934 he worked full-time for the Sudeten German Home Front in Eger (Cheb).[41]

The Office of the Reich Protector in Prague was structured as a central administration and four main divisions: I Administration, Justice, and Education; II Economics and Finances; III Transportation; and IV Cultural Policy. It also included the posts of the commander of the Security Police and Security Service, as well as the commander of the Order Police (Ordnungspolizei). The thirty-five Oberlandräte (regional administrators), who had already been appointed by the army's supreme commander and controlled the lower-level Czech authorities, became the Reich Protector's regional agents.[42] The NSDAP did not create any independent organizations in the occupied territories. The Protectorate's local NSDAP regional offices were subordinate to the bordering Gaue in the Sudetenland, the Bavarian *Ostmark*, and the Upper and Lower Danube.[43]

In contrast to Austria and the Sudetenland, the Protectorate was granted an independent legal status, which did not extend, however, to foreign policy, military matters, or transportation and communication issues.[44] The Czech government remained in place, although it was controlled by the Reich Protector, and Czechs continued to head the Ministries of the Interior, Finance, Education and Culture, Justice, Public Works, Agriculture, Commerce and Skilled Trades, and Health and Social Affairs.[45]

President Emil Hácha, who likewise stayed in office, dissolved the Czech parliament on 21 March 1939. Thus, Hácha, a conservative Catholic, symbolized the end of democracy. He approved anti-Jewish measures, but at the same time remained connected with the Czech underground, as well as with exiled confidants of Beneš.[46] Still in March, Hácha founded the National Partnership (Národní souručenství), a unifying movement that replaced the Czech parties and was supposed to function as a national assembly and political organization. Jews and women were excluded from membership. The National Partnership soon had more than 2 million members, amounting to 98.5 percent of all Czech men in the Protectorate.[47] On 27 April, Hácha restructured a number of positions in the Czech government; General Alois Eliáš took over the government's leadership and was confirmed by the Reich Protector. While the political persuasions of Eliáš—formerly a delegate at the League of Nations and most recently the Minister of Transportation under Beran—resembled those of Hácha (for whom he also cultivated ties with exiled Czechs), Justice Minister Jaroslav Krejčí enthusiastically paid homage to Nazi rule.[48]

At this time, 118,310 Jews (perhaps even more), organized in 136 communities, lived in the remaining territories of the former Czech state annexed by Germany.[49] During the beginning of Germany's occupation in March 1939, anti-Jewish violence erupted in a number of different locations. In Olomouc (Olmütz), Germans—and evidently also Czechs—burned down the local synagogue. In Vsetín (Wesetin), the synagogue succumbed to flames on the day the Germans arrived. The city of Iglau (Jihlava) prohibited Jews from using the streetcars and forced them to clear snow; there the synagogue burned down at the end of March. Synagogues were also simultaneously destroyed in Moravian Ostrava (Mährisch-Ostrau) and Kynšperk nad Ohří (Königsberg an der Eger), presumably by Czech fascists. During the first weeks of the occupation, the Gestapo arrested more than 1,000—and a short time later more than 4,600—Communists, Social Democrats, and German refugees. A quarter of them, mostly Jewish emigrants, wound up in concentration camps in the Reich.[50]

In Prague, the Protectorate's future capital, Jewish facilities were shut down or brought under Gestapo control, as had also occurred in Vienna during the first few days following the *Anschluss*.[51] Otakar Klapka continued to govern as Prague's Primator (lord mayor); but as of 16 March 1939, the Sudeten German historian and politician Josef Pfitzner, appointed as the Regierungskommissar (government commissioner) for the municipal administration, acted at his side. Born in Petersdorf (Silesia) in 1901, Pfitzner taught eastern European history in Prague. A member of the Sudeten German Party in mid 1930s, he had represented the party in the Prague municipal parliament since May 1938.[52]

Henceforth, a number of different agencies engaged in the persecution of Jews: the Office of the Reich Protector and the Gestapo, the Oberlandräte, the Czech government, the municipalities, and later the Central Office for Jewish Emigration (Zentralstelle für jüdische

Auswanderung).⁵³ The Czech government initiated the first formal anti-Jewish measures while still under Prime Minister Rudolf Beran. On 17 March 1939, it issued an ordinance that stripped Jewish physicians and lawyers of their practices, removed Jews from leadership positions in industry and social organizations, and arranged for the marking of "Aryan" businesses.⁵⁴ Three days later the regime ordered that authorities could deploy trustees in companies if necessary for the "public interest." The regional district authorities were supposed to prepare lists of Jewish companies that were eligible for "Aryanization."⁵⁵

Approximately thirty thousand businesses and companies, according to German estimates, existed in the Protectorate.⁵⁶ To prevent the kind of "wild Aryanization" that had occurred the previous year in Vienna, on 16 March 1939 the Commissioner for the Four-Year Plan, Hermann Göring, ordered that significant property ownership changes in the Protectorate (for example, regarding real estate or commercial businesses) were henceforth to be monitored by the Reich Ministry of the Economy.⁵⁷ In the Protectorate itself, the Heads of the Civil Administration—Henlein and Bürckel—promptly issued corresponding orders. By the end of March, they had prohibited Jews from selling companies and real estate in Moravia and Bohemia.⁵⁸ On 20 March 1939, they had already forbidden the appointment of commissars and custodians in sole proprietorships.⁵⁹

Thus, at first, who would control anti-Jewish policy remained a matter of dispute. But then a conference at the Reich Interior Ministry on 25 March 1939 resolved that it would "basically be left to the government of the Protectorate" to determine "whether and what measures it undertakes against the Jews." To be sure, Hitler had decided that "the Jews were to be excluded from the Protectorate's public life," but the "implementation of this task should be the responsibility of the government of the Protectorate and not the direct task of the Reich."⁶⁰

On 17 April 1939, seven Jewish religious associations in Prague agreed to join forces, for the Czech government's measures were maneuvering the Jewish population into a difficult economic and social situation. In addition, opportunism and approval of the anti-Jewish policies were spreading rapidly among the economic elite, as well as within the Czech public service sector, the police, and the remnants of the Czech army, which had been reduced to 7,000 men. The associations representing merchants, lawyers, and physicians began shutting out their Jewish colleagues.⁶¹ On 1 June 1939, a report by the Jewish community in Prague stated: "The number of those requiring support is growing day by day. Jewish employees are being dismissed, the Jewish middle class, which supports all the social work and the Jewish communities, is becoming steadily impoverished. . . ."[62] In a parallel process, Jews and their establishments increasingly became the victims of attacks by Czech fascists, who hereby sought to challenge President Hácha. In May and June, synagogues burned in Brno, Olmütz, Uherský Brod (Ungarisch Brod), Chlumec (Kulm), Náchod (Nachod), Pardubice (Pardubitz), and Moravian Ostrava. In its bulletin *Arisjký boj* (Aryan Struggle), Flag (Vlajka)—the most radical organization of Czech fascists—was already demanding the ghettoization of the Jews.[63]

More and more Jews now wanted to emigrate, yet they were prevented not only because of their growing poverty but—for the time being and in contrast to practices in the Reich and Austria—also by the Security Police itself. In May 1939, Heydrich had instructed the Security Police to prevent any "Jewish emigration" from the Protectorate at the expense of the Old Reich's emigration quota. For this reason, Heydrich insisted, no Central Office for Jewish Emigration would be established in Prague.[64]

But the guidelines issued by Hitler in March 1939 (which he reemphasized in May when the Reich Protector spoke with him about potentially introducing the Nuremburg Laws) still applied, namely, "that the Czechs should regulate the Jewish question themselves, and that we should not meddle." Reich Protector von Neurath was subsequently of "the opinion that, as a result of the given dynamic, the Jewish question will ultimately proceed in terms of the Nuremburg laws."[65] Admittedly, this dynamic was not "given," but rather produced by various parties. Already by the end of March 1939, the Czech Aryan Union had demanded that President Hácha exclude Jews from Protectorate citizenship. According to the Aryan Union, a Jew was anyone who adhered to the Jewish faith, maintained social contact with Jews, or had sinned against the nation or the "Aryan race." The organization maintained that Jews should be stigmatized with a marking.[66] The Security Service had internally recommended such a symbol for Germany in the context of the 1938 November pogroms, but Hitler rejected the idea for foreign policy reasons.[67] A few weeks later, the National Partnership also recommended that the government strip the Jews of various rights and introduce an official definition of Jew based on religious affiliation.[68] On 11 May, Prime Minister Eliáš informed the Reich Protector that the Czech regime was intensely preoccupied "with a draft of a government ordinance on the Jewish question." He suggested personal contacts in order to coordinate the measure's contents.[69] According to the draft, Jews were not fully entitled state citizens of the Protectorate. A Jew was anyone who stemmed from four Jewish grandparents, but only if he had belonged to a Jewish religious community since 1918. The draft provided for the removal of Jews from public agencies, corporations, and schools, as well as from administrations, courts, stock exchanges, the arts, and medicine.[70]

The proposed government ordinance became the first test of Czech autonomy. On 22 May 1939, representatives from every division in the Office of the Reich Protector discussed the Czech proposal, criticizing its definition of Jew as being far too mild.[71] Instead of the Czechs, the Reich Protector himself issued a more radical definition on 21 June. Like the Nuremberg race laws, his ordinance on the "Regulation of the Jewish Question" determined that, in the Protectorate, a Jew was any person who had three grandparents of the Jewish faith, regardless of that person's religious denomination. The definition served above all to limit the Jews' power of disposition over their assets. As in Germany and Austria, they had to register their property. The Reich Protector also reserved the right to install trustees in Jewish businesses. The ordinance from 21 June explicitly superseded the Head of the Civil Administration ordinances from 20 and 22 March on the prohibition of the sale of Jewish property.[72]

With this early show of force, the Reich Protector ended the conflict of interest regarding the "Aryanization" of Jewish companies brought to light by this case, a conflict that had smoldered since the parallel Czech and German measures of March 1939. Local groups of the National Partnership had been preparing lists of Jewish businesses since May. Problems arose in places like Olmütz, because while the local National Partnership group, the Chamber of Trade and Commerce, and the city were jointly supposed to install Czech trustees in Jewish firms, the German occupation administration had deployed receivers in these firms at the same time.[73] In the summer, the Germans increased pressure in numerous ways. In the Office of the Reich Protector, the "Commercial Economy" group established a "Dejudaization" department, directed initially by Oberregierungsrat (senior government councilor) Siegfried Ludwig from the Reich Interior Ministry, who was responsible for "Aryanization questions."[74] Moreover, with the Neurath ordinance from 21 June 1939, the Reich had secured a further position of strength, for German authorities were now allowed to install trustees not only in Jewish but also non-Jewish businesses, provoking Hácha to lodge a protest with the Reich Protector against this obvious "instrument of Germanization under the cloak of Aryanization."[75]

Figure 4.1. "Not accessible to Jews"—a municipal playground in Prague, 1939. *Source:* Bildarchiv Preußischer Kulturbesitz, image no.: 30025479

The Period of the Occupation

Between October 1938 and the end of July 1939, 20,000 Jews—including German and Austrian refugees—had left the country.[76] On 21 June 1939, the day of the path-breaking Neurath ordinance, Heydrich decided at last to establish a Central Office for the Promotion of Jewish Emigration (Zentralstelle zur Förderung der jüdischen Auswanderung) in Prague, albeit under the condition of using Czech money to facilitate the emigration of Jews living in the Old Reich.[77] Founded by a Reich Protector's decree on 15 July 1939 and structured according to the Austrian model, the Central Office was subordinate to the Security Main Office (Sicherheitshauptamt)[78] in Berlin and initially responsible only for Prague and the surrounding region. Directed by Stahlecker, the Commander of the Security Police in Prague, it was supposed to combine all "Jewish emigration questions" and supervise the Jewish organizations.[79] This was also the reason for ordering Adolf Eichmann—who had developed this model in Vienna—to Prague.[80]

Together with the Protectorate's Czech government, they agreed on an institution directed by the Security Service as well as the competent Czech ministries in Prague, which were to delegate independent employees. The Czechs then ratified the establishment of the new authority on 20 July.[81]

The Central Office soon stipulated to the Prague Jewish community that 30,000 Jews had to leave the Protectorate by the end of 1939 and 70,000 Jews by the end of 1940.[82] By no means, however, did Eichmann and the Central Office hereby emerge as the sole authority for anti-Jewish policy,[83] nor did Reich Protector von Neurath.[84] On 4 July 1939, the Czech government issued an ordinance on the exclusion of Jews from all juridical and administrative capacities, public authorities, and occupations such as the liberal professions.[85] The division of powers also became clear on 3 August 1939 when, in response to many local initiatives, an ordinance issued not by the new Central Office but rather by the Czech Interior Ministry instituted the segregation of Jews in restaurants, swimming pools, hospitals, and sanatoriums and stipulated the marking of Jewish enterprises and stores.[86]

This again clearly demonstrated that municipalities and Oberlandräte actively advocated their own interests in anti-Jewish policy (see figure 4.1). On 3 July 1939, the Reich Protector had installed German commissioners as chief municipal authorities in Brünn, Iglau, Mährisch-Ostrau, Olmütz, and Budweis (České Budějovice), all large cities with a strong German contingent.[87] Henceforth, the Protectorate was organized into nineteen Oberlandratsbezirke (regional administrative districts): twelve in Bohemia and seven in Moravia.[88]

The Nazi state's occupation of Poland fundamentally changed the basic political conditions for anti-Jewish policy. The Nazi leadership decided as early as September 1939 to resettle all of the Jews from the Greater German Reich to the new domains in the East, registering the Jewish population for this purpose.[89] On 1 October 1939, 90,147 Jews, including 80,139 religious Jews, still lived in the Protectorate.[90] Using this information, Eichmann—now working in the recently founded Reich Security Main Office (Reichssicherheitshauptamt; RSHA)[91] prepared for the "deportation" of the Jews from the German Reich. The first transport with 901 men left Czech territory on 18 October. Departing from Mährisch-Ostrau, it was accompanied by border police and SS personnel from the Vienna and Prague Central Offices all the way to Nisko in the eastern part of occupied Poland.[92] Prior to the second transport, Czech women protested against the deportations of the Jews.[93] The third and, for the time being, final train from the

Protectorate with over 300 Jewish "prisoners" from Prague made it only as far as Sosnowitz (Sosnowiec) in East Upper Silesia on 1 November.[94] Himmler interrupted the "emigration action," which had resulted in the deportation of several thousand Czech, Polish, and Austrian Jews, until February 1940, since "for technical reasons" the target zone could no longer be reached.[95]

The now growing Czech solidarity with the Protectorate's Jewish residents—protests against the deportations had also occurred in Prague[96]—was based in an increasingly radical atmosphere. Mass anti-German demonstrations had taken place in October and November 1939, which were crushed by the occupying power.[97] Many Protectorate Germans welcomed the harsh response, some even believing that it had not gone far enough.[98] However, tensions between Reich Germans and Germans from Czech regions increased as well; there were common allegations that the former were buying up everything in the Protectorate due to the strong Reichsmark while the latter were providing most of the trustees.[99]

Anticipating that the interrupted deportations would resume in early 1940, the commander of the Security Police expanded the competency of the Central Office for Jewish Emigration from Prague to the Protectorate's entire territory.[100] However, when on 19 February Heydrich postponed the Czech transports to allow the deportation of Polish Jews from the annexed Polish territories instead,[101] the initiative shifted back to the Protectorate. Yet, even though the Prague Central Office had now extended its controlling authority to all Jewish communities, this did not mean that it had exclusively taken control of the "Jewish question" in the Protectorate of Bohemia and Moravia.[102] On 20 February, for example, the Landesbehörde (regional authority) in Prague, which reported to the Czech Ministry of Interior, banned Jews from visiting cinemas and theaters.[103] And on 5 March 1940, the Reich Protector stipulated that Jewish communities must now also provide support for all so-called racial Jews as per the definition from 21 June 1939, while assets from dissolved communities or organizations were to be transferred into an emigration fund that would be established by the Central Office.[104]

As a result of occupational and business bans, and dismissals from "Aryanized" and other companies, an increasing number of Protectorate Jews found themselves bereft of employment and income opportunities.[105] On 23 October 1939, the Reich Protector had ordered the dismissal of all Jewish salaried employees, and on 26 January 1940, he ordered that Jews could be banned from corporate management. On the same day, he prohibited Jews from managing firms trading in textiles, shoes, and leather goods.[106] As of 7 February, business assets of Jewish companies had to be registered; as of 16 March the private assets of Jewish entrepreneurs had to be registered as well.[107] This increased the momentum of the "Aryanization" process, which was advanced chiefly by Germans. Whereas Czechs usually applied in vain to become trustees, German entrepreneurs and banks—even non-specialists—found themselves competing for worthwhile "Aryanization objects."[108]

On 24 April 1940, the Czech government expelled the Jews from jurisprudence, administrations, schools, pharmacies, the press, and medicine.[109] Earlier on 19 March 1940, a Czech government ordinance had established new rules for unemployment benefits, shifting responsibility from the Czech trade unions to labor offices that had been established the previous year under the Czech Ministry for the Administration of Social Affairs and Health.[110] As Jews registered en masse as unemployed, the labor offices began recruiting them for forced labor. The first sizable group of Jews receiving unemployment benefits was evidently put to work incinerating waste in Prague. In contrast to the centralized forced labor program for unemployed Jews in the Reich established at the end of 1938, the compulsory labor in the Protectorate remained locally organized for the time being.[111]

The Protectorate did not receive any clear signals from Berlin regarding the intended direction of future Germanization policies. On 1 March 1940, 189,000 Germans lived in the Protectorate; on 1 September that number had already reached 245,000, including 40,000 Sudeten-German migrants and 20,000 former Czechs of German origin who had taken advantage of their opportunity to acquire German citizenship. In total, however, Germans constituted only around 3.3 percent of the Protectorate's 7,380,000 inhabitants.[112] At first, the National Socialists sought to create closed settlement enclaves in Moravia in order to form a so-called *Volkstumsbrücke*—an ethnic German "bridge"—between Silesia and Austria; later, they favored scattered settlements, including around Iglau. When allocating Jewish companies and houses, they gave preferential treatment to the Protectorate's Germans to increase their economic vitality.[113] Because settling Germans from outside the Protectorate did not seem feasible during the war, the competent agencies in Berlin and Prague now discussed—instead of German resettlement—the "racial" assimilation of the Czechs as an alternative approach for Germanization.[114]

Of course, this did not apply for Jewish Czechs. In the course of 1940, the Reich Protector received Czech and German petitions requesting the marking of the Jews. But despite having approved such measures for the Polish regions within the Reich, the Nazi government in Berlin did not yet want see them instituted in the Protectorate.[115] Meanwhile, the National Partnership had forbidden its members from cultivating social contacts with Jews. Yet many Czechs did not comply, although probably not so much because they lacked anti-Semitic resentments but because of their enmity toward the Germans.[116]

In June 1940, the NSDAP Kreisleitung (district office) in Olmütz recommended restricting the times during which Jews were allowed to shop; the Oberlandrat passed this information along to Reich Protector. On 9 July, however, the Czech Interior Minister directed the local authorities to prohibit Jews from shopping at certain times of day.[117] Thereupon in Prague, the Polizeipräsident (police president) restricted Jewish shopping in "Aryan" stores to the period from 11 A.M. to 1 P.M. and 3 P.M. to 4:30 P.M.[118] On 7 August 1940, the Czech government ordered the exclusion of Jewish children from public schools.[119]

In early July 1940, Eichmann had informed the Jewish communities in Berlin, Prague, and Vienna "that after the end of the war an overall solution to the European Jewish question would prospectively have to be striven for."[120] Anticipating new deportations, German authorities increased their efforts to control anti-Jewish policy in the Protectorate. Because many local initiatives were "not coordinated with the concerns of the rest of the Reich's territories," on 17 August 1940 the commander of the Security Police requested all Oberlandräte to implement anti-Jewish measures only after consultation with the Central Office, which was under his authority. He informed them that he had prompted the Czech government to prohibit the Jews from visiting parks and attending sporting events, restrict their use of trains and streetcars, and limit their shopping times, but that the repeated requests to establish ghettos "currently cannot be taken into consideration."[121]

The example of the shopping times clearly shows that the commander of the Security Police in Prague had not been informed about the measures undertaken by Czech authorities in the meantime.[122] At the same time, the Central Office—in anticipation of the deportations—successfully pushed for control in additional areas previously managed by the Czechs. In fall 1940, it began supervising the "Jewish housing market." Thus in September in Prague and in October in Brünn, all "Jewish" residences were visited and registered. Henceforth in Prague, the city government, Central Office, and NSDAP jointly implemented the concentration of Jewish tenants in so-called Jewish houses,[123] a process they began in the spring of 1941. In a parallel process, the authorities organized resettlements from smaller localities in the Oberlandratsbezirke to the larger cities.[124]

Meanwhile, the German administrative bodies had been selectively expanded. Starting in 12 December 1939, Bohemian cities were subject to the same principles as those stipulated by the 1935 German Municipal Code (Gemeindeordnung), thus abolishing the democratic form of city government.[125] The Reich Protector installed German mayors and Kreishauptmänner (district chiefs) and also ensured the employment of more Germans by the police, railway, and post.[126] At the end of December 1939, 95 municipalities had a German directorate; one year later that number had increased to 125. Germans consequently governed all localities with more than 25,000 inhabitants, apart from Prague and Pilsen, where Germans acted as deputy mayors. In summer 1941, after the dissolution of the Czech regional committees and commissions and the installation of the Oberlandräte, the Reich Protector declared that there should no longer be any mention of Czech authorities. Nonetheless, besides the 15,000 Germans in the occupation administration and Czech government bodies, approximately 400,000 Czechs worked in the public service sector.[127]

On 28 February 1941, German radio in Prague issued a warning to the Protectorate's population: anyone who continued to cultivate good relations with Jews would be punished as an enemy of the country.[128] Due to the German Reich's continuously accelerating demand for manpower[129] and the repeated postponement of the deportations slated for the Protectorate, the Protectorate's authorities—both German and Czech—introduced forced labor for the Jews. First, on 10 January 1941, the Reich Protector had forbidden the Jews in his domain from engaging in virtually any kind of independent economic activity.[130] Then on 23 January the Czech government issued its first ordinance on the work requirement for Jews between the ages of eighteen and fifty. In April, the Reich Protector instructed the Czech officials to align their forced labor assignments in accordance with the Reich's standard practices. On 9 May 1941, the Czech Ministry for Social Affairs and Health Administration declared that the labor offices would organize the segregated labor deployments according to the ministry's instructions.[131]

After Germany's invasion of the Soviet Union, the Protectorate's labor administration intensified the forced labor deployment. On 29 August 1941, the ministry expanded the deployment to include Jews between the ages of sixteen and sixty. At this time, 11,700 Jewish men had work assignments, including 6,892 working in the agricultural sector or for construction companies.[132] In parallel with this development, the Protector shifted the public obligation to provide poor relief to the Jewish religious communities, thereby excluding Jews from the government welfare system, as already practiced in Germany and Austria since the end of 1938.[133] In the meantime, the Reich Interior Ministry had introduced the Law for the Protection of German Blood in the Protectorate in July 1941, effective retroactively as of March 1939. It now also applied for Protectorate subjects—both German and Czech.[134]

The alignment of forced labor and social welfare practices epitomized the endeavor to centralize anti-Jewish policy in the Reich's greater German territory in light of the revived deportation plans. In late July and early August, Hitler had decided to resume the deportation of Jews from the German Reich, beginning with operations in the large cities.[135] The ordinance from early September introducing the "Jewish Star," which stigmatized the Jews and prohibited them from leaving their residential communities, signaled the transition to concrete deportation preparations.[136] From Prague, State Secretary Frank had already suggested the marking of Jews in July because "from a viewpoint of policy and policing, transactions with Jews [must] be made as difficult as possible for the Czechs."[137] During the deportation preparations, the Commander of the Security Police and Security Service Horst Böhme dispatched a circular on 17 September 1941 in which he reserved any anti-Jewish measures in the Protectorate exclusively for his office.[138]

On 25 September 1941, Reinhard Heydrich took over the affairs of Reich Protector Neurath.[139] The main reason for the shuffle probably had less to do with the planned deportations than with growing Czech resistance since the invasion of the Soviet Union. After arriving in Prague, Heydrich resorted to draconian measures to quell this dangerous development within the territory of the Greater German Reich. By November, his new policies had cost the lives of 404 people.[140] Deposed by Heydrich, on 1 October 1941 Prime Minister Eliáš was sentenced to death by a German *Volksgerichtshof* (people's court) in Prague for resistance and joint machinations with Otakar Klapka, the Primator of Prague. But whereas the Germans quickly executed Klapka, they spared Eliáš because they wanted to keep him as a hostage. Subsequently in January 1942, State President Hácha appointed a new government under Justice Minister Krejči, in which Colonel František Moravec, a Czech advocate for the union with the German Reich, directed the Ministry of Education and new Ministry for Popular

Enlightenment.[141] A Reich German, Walter Bertsch—formerly responsible for labor deployment in the Office of Reich Protector—took over the Ministry for the Economy and Employment.[142]

Undertaken against the background of deportation planning, the personnel change in the Office the Reich Protector entailed an intensified and more centralized anti-Jewish policy. In one of his first official acts, on 29 September 1941 Heydrich placed Jewish partners in "privileged mixed marriages" with Czechs in the Protectorate on an equal footing with other Jews, closed all synagogues because of an alleged whispering campaign, and threatened "Jew sympathizers" with severe punishments.[143] Although Heydrich seemed to have taken anti-Jewish measures in his own hand, his presence failed to prevent further radical local initiatives, as the National Partnership demanded that the Czech government ghettoize the Jews.[144] When on 6 October 1941 President Hácha recommended their isolation to his interior minister, the latter refused because the Commander of the Security Police and Security Service had reserved all measures for his own office and the transports were already underway.[145]

In preparation for the transports, the Jewish population in the territories of the Greater German Reich had been registered anew. According to racial criteria, approximately 88,000 Jews still lived in the Protectorate, including 46,800 in Prague.[146] On 10 October, Heydrich met with Frank, Böhme, and Eichmann in the Prague castle to elaborate the following plans: starting on 15 October, 5,000 Jews would be deported from Prague; those who initially remained would be consigned to ghettos, where, for the time being, they would have to perform forced labor; later they would be transported to the East.[147] Only two days later, Heydrich ordered that the assets of Jews were to be "transfer[red]" (meaning expropriated) upon their "evacuation."[148]

In Prague, the Gestapo, in cooperation with the Central Office for Jewish Emigration, was responsible for implementing the deportations. On 16 October 1941, the first of five planned transports left the Czech capital bound for the Litzmannstadt ghetto in the Warthe district.[149] But because the Litzmannstadt ghetto lacked sufficient intake capacity for the subsequent transports, Hitler himself chose Riga and Minsk as the next destinations.[150] The second suboperation was supposed to deport the Jews from the Czech provinces, with the first transport leaving Brünn on 16 November for Minsk.[151]

On 3 November 1941, against the background of these new deportations, Commander of the SiPo and SD Böhme once again clearly informed Czech Interior Minister Josef Ježek that in the future all anti-Jewish measures were a matter for the Security Police.[152] But that was only partially correct, for while the Gestapo had deported thousands of Jews to Poland since October, the labor offices had also intensified their forced labor deployments.[153]

By mid November 1941, Nazi expulsion and deportation policies had reduced the number of Jews in Germany, Austria, and the Protectorate from an original 890,000 to 281,000.[154] In the meantime, the Nazi leadership planned on shifting from suboperations within Greater Germany to the deportation and murder of all the Jews in Europe as a whole. At the Wannsee Conference, which took place on 20 January 1942, Heydrich explained the plans for Europe: "The Reich territory, including the Protectorate of Bohemia and Moravia, will have to be handled in advance, if only for . . . social-political necessities."[155]

The conference attendees also learned that Theresienstadt (Terezin) was being designated as an old-age ghetto for German Jews.[156] In the interim, the Security Police had established a ghetto in the Protectorate. Situated at the confluence of the Ohře and Elbe rivers near the border with the Sudetengau, the eighteenth-century fortress town of Theresienstadt served first as a place for concentrating Jews from throughout Bohemia and Moravia.[157] At the end of November 1941, the Gestapo deported the first 350 men to the fortress to begin erecting the ghetto.[158] On 15 December 1941, Heydrich himself signed a circular decree "re: evacuation Jews," stipulating the following: the commander of the Security Police would determine which regions to clear, while the Central Office would arrange the transports; the latter would also take over the assets.[159] With the start of the deportations, a so-called Trustee Office (Treuhandstelle) was established at the Jewish community of Prague, directed by Salo Krämer, the former head of the Jewish community of Moravian Ostrava. Later, on behalf of this office, hundreds of Jews had to gather the property of the deportees from their abandoned homes and prepare them for sale—hundreds of thousands of books, tens of thousands of pictures, hundreds of pianos, as well as massive quantities of furniture, tableware, carpets, and clothing.[160]

In December 1941, the Gestapo deported more than 7,000 people from Prague, Pilsen, Brünn, and other places to Theresienstadt, which from the outset had been conceived as a transit camp. The first train already left Theresienstadt for Riga in January 1942.[161] But because the fortress was too small to accept all of the Protectorate Jews, the Reich Protector transformed the entire city into a ghetto. The German residents had to leave and were compensated by the Central Office from the so-called emigration fund with Jewish property.[162]

Notwithstanding the ongoing deportations, in February 1942 the Protectorate's labor offices registered more than 14,000 Jewish forced laborers. The Prague labor office alone had placed more than 5,000 workers, who were used among other things for snow removal. More than 2,000 Jews cleared snow from the roads in Brünn as well. But because of new transports, these deployments had to be stopped. The Brünn labor office at least managed to gain the release "until further notice" of Jewish forced laborers working in the mines. The Ministry of Labor had provided 250 men from the "Theresienstadt collection camp" to the Kladno labor office. Ghetto inmates were now dispatched to locations within the Protectorate—1,000 women were sent to Rakovnik (Rakonitz) to plant trees, for example. Some of these labor detachments existed until fall 1943.[163]

Earlier on 6 March 1942 at a conference at the Reich Security Main Office, Eichmann had announced that an additional 20,000 people would be "evacuated" from Prague.[164] Even though the number of available Jews quickly declined as a result of new transports, in May the labor offices managed to increase the number of forced laborers to over 15,000 men and almost 1,000 women. This marked the zenith of the forced labor deployments in the Protectorate.[165]

A report by the Prague underground to the Czechoslovak government-in-exile in London stated that parts of the population believed that the Jews deserved their fate.[166] Meanwhile, working from London, Beneš had prepared an attack on Heydrich. Symbolically chosen, a Czech, a Slovak, and a Ruthenian carried out the assault on 27 May 1942 in Prague. The National Socialists subsequently imposed martial law on the Protectorate, and ethnic Germans attacked Czech stores for revenge.[167] On 29 May, the Reich Security Main Office informed the Jewish community of Prague that the decision had been made for the "complete evacuation of the Jews from the Old Reich, the *Ostmark*, and the Protectorate"; Jews under the age of sixty-five would be brought to the East, while older Jews would be brought to Theresienstadt for "permanent residence."[168]

On 4 June 1942, Heydrich died from his severe injuries. Hitler appointed Kurt Daluege, Chief of the Order Police in the Reich, as the Deputy Reich Protector. Himmler traveled with him to Prague, where they implemented draconian measures. Many of the individuals involved in the assassination—but also many who were not, such as Prime Minister Eliáš, who had been imprisoned since fall 1941—were shot to death. Two thousand non-Jewish and 1,000 Jewish Czechs presumably succumbed to the wave of terror.[169] Ethnic Germans had demanded harsh retaliations and the dissolution of the Protectorate, reported the Security Service. Very few expressed regrets about the victims or worried about the consequences for the future coexistence of Germans and Czechs in Bohemia and Moravia.[170]

Whereas the mass deployment of Jewish forced laborers in Germany had already peaked in 1941, the high point in the Protectorate did not occur until 1942, precipitating deliberations on whether to officially legalize forced labor in the Protectorate by instituting special labor legislation, as had occurred in the Old Reich. The Government Ordinance on the Treatment of the Jews under Labor Law in the Protectorate of Bohemia and Moravia of 17 July excluded Jews from receiving social security, overtime pay, and vacation. In contrast to the Reich, the provisions made no exceptions for "privileged" Jews in mixed marriages.[171] Due to the ongoing transports, however, fewer and fewer Jews remained in the Protectorate for the forced labor assignments. In fall 1942, the Gestapo deported 18,000 people in ten transports from Theresienstadt to Treblinka.[172] In Prague itself, however, approximately 1,000 Jews still worked in armaments factories, among other places.[173]

By the end of 1942, the Gestapo had "evacuated" 69,677 Jewish men and women from the Protectorate. Only 15,530 still remained, 13 percent of the figure from 1939.[174] Toward the end of the deportations—and thus quite late—the Reich Interior Ministry issued an Ordinance on the Loss of Protectorate Citizenship. Modeled on the eleventh ordinance of the Reich Citizenship Law,[175] it stipulated that Jews residing abroad would lose their Protectorate citizenship and that their assets would be transferred to the German Reich,[176] thereby enabling the expropriation of all Jews who had thus far been deported from the Protectorate, except for those who had been brought to Auschwitz. Since the Auschwitz death camp was located within the Reich, the property of persons brought to this camp was confiscated on the basis of laws from 1933 regarding enemies of the *Volk* or the state.[177]

The end of the deportations simultaneously meant the end of the Jewish community council of Prague. On 28 January 1943, a Jewish Council of Elders under Salo Krämer took its place. The last representatives of the old community had to relocate to Theresienstadt.[178] In May, Himmler ordered that the transports from the Reich's Greater German territories needed to be completed by the end of the following month.[179] And in June 1943, the last large deportation train with 4,000 community employees and their families left Prague.[180] Thereupon the Council of Elders received new leadership once again: František Friedmann and Erich Kraus. Themselves living in "mixed marriages," they were supposed to look after the fate of the few remaining Jews in mixed marriages and the so-called half-Jews.[181]

At this time, Hitler relieved Daluege from his office as the Deputy Reich Protector and finally removed Reich Protector von Neurath, who had been on leave, from his post. He appointed Reich Interior Minister Frick as Reich Protector and Karl Hermann Frank as the German Minister of State for Bohemia and Moravia, a new capacity equivalent to the rank of a Reich Minister. From 1939 until the end of the war, Frank, whose long-term efforts targeted the Germanization of the Czech regions, formed the backbone of the German Protectorate policy. After the liberation, he was executed in Prague on 6 September 1945 because of his role.[182]

In the meantime, the few remaining Jews who had not been imprisoned in the Theresienstadt ghetto—most of whom lived in "mixed marriages"—had also been conscripted for forced labor. In Prague, Jewish women had to split mica in the athletic grounds of the former Jewish association Hagibor.[183] In 1944, hundreds of Jewish men from "mixed marriages" were brought to labor camps outside of Prague.[184] At the end of 1944, only 6,795 Jews still officially lived in the Protectorate.[185] As in the Reich, at the beginning of 1945 the Gestapo also revoked the "mixed marriage" protections that had thus far obtained in the Protectorate. In January and February, the Gestapo once again deported 3,570 people, including the members of the Council of Elders.[186] Meanwhile, however, the Allies bombed Prague. The Czech uprising under the looming shadows of the approaching Allied armies expelled the German occupiers in the beginning of May 1945.

Conclusion

In Prague, only 424 Jews survived the occupation in hiding.[187] The scholarship estimates approximately 80,000 Jewish victims in the Protectorate of Bohemia and Moravia. Because Jewish emigration was first prevented by the Security Police after the occupation began in March 1939 and shortly thereafter by the outbreak of war, by October 1941 only approximately 25,000 people managed to escape the Protectorate. In total, 265,000 Jews from all of the former Czechoslovak regions lost their lives, accounting for more than three-quarters of all Czech victims of the German occupation.[188]

As a result of long-term intentions to Germanize the region, the Nazi leadership's plans to deport the Jews from the German Reich in 1939 included the Protectorate as well. Thus Jews from the Protectorate fell victim both to the first transports in October 1939 as well as those in October 1941. While a few transports traveled directly to the eastern regions, from 24 November 1941 to 16 March 1945 the Gestapo initially transported 73,608 Jews to the Theresienstadt ghetto.[189] When in early 1942 Theresienstadt was chosen to be an "old-age ghetto" for German Jews, the deportation of Jews from Theresienstadt to the extermination camps accelerated.

A variety of institutions at all government levels played an active role in the persecution of Jews in the Protectorate. In March 1939, Hitler himself had formulated the goal of segregating the Protectorate's Jews, but had assigned this task to the Czech government. Consequently, the Protectorate's Czech government, the Office of the Reich Protector, the Oberlandräte, the municipal administrations, as well the Central Office for Jewish Emigration founded in July 1939 all actively participated in the exclusion of the Jews, first from the economy and culture, later from all public life.

While the Reich Security Main Office centrally controlled the deportations since the start of the war, other areas of so-called Jewish policy remained the Protectorate's responsibility. The Reich Protector and the Security Police pushed ahead with the "Aryanization" of Jewish firms; the Czech Protectorate government, Oberlandräte, and municipalities orchestrated the segregation of the Jewish population in public life. The use of forced labor deployments initially occurred at the local level, until it was organized by the Czech Ministry for the Administration of Social Affairs and Health and the labor offices starting in 1941. A number of Protectorate initiatives—the marking of the Jews, for example— even expedited key decisions for the Greater German Reich. Only after the resumption of mass deportations and the ensuing centralization of anti-Jewish measures in fall 1941 did the Security Police take over Jewish persecution in the Protectorate, but this did not rule out local initiatives or independent developments in areas like the use of forced labor. The creative freedom within Jewish policy flourished well into the war, opening up wide-ranging opportunities for German and Czech officials to become personally involved—but therefore also personally responsible. Through their measures, they decisively shaped the victims' experiences of persecution.[190]

Notes

1. On the debates of both Czech and also German nationalists, see Peter Haslinger, *Nation und Territorium im tschechischen politischen Diskurs 1880–1938* (Munich, 2010).

2. Livia Rothkirchen, *The Jews of Bohemia and Moravia: Facing the Holocaust* (Lincoln, NE, and Jerusalem, 2005), 26–28; Jeremy King, *Budweisers into Czechs and Germans: A Local History of Bohemian Politics, 1848–1948* (Princeton, 2005), 159–163.
3. Konrad Henlein, "The German Minority in Czechoslovakia," *International Affairs* 15, no. 4 (1936): 561–572, here 563; Rothkirchen, *The Jews of Bohemia and Moravia*, 29.
4. Emanuel Čapek, "Racial and Social Aspects of the Czechoslovak Census," *Slavonic and East European Review* 12, no. 35 (1934): 596–610, here 596 and 605.
5. Ibid., 598.
6. German-Austria initially designated the German-speaking regions of Austria-Hungary, then in 1918 the new republic. After the 1919 Treaty of Saint-Germain-en-Laye, the name and the intention to unify with Germany had to be abandoned.
7. Robert William Seton-Watson, "The German Minority in Czechoslovakia," *Foreign Affairs* 16 no. 4 (1938): 651–666, here 654–657; Elizabeth Wiskemann, "Czechs and Germans after Munich," *Foreign Affairs* 17, no. 2 (1939): 291–304, here 297; Emil Sobota, "Czechs and Germans: A Czech View," *Slavonic Review* 14, no. 41 (1936): 301–320, here 304. On this and the following, Chad Bryant, *Prague in Black: Nazi Rule and Czech Nationalism* (Cambridge, MA, 2007), 18–20; King, *Budweisers into Czechs and Germans*, 154–157; Rothkirchen, *The Jews of Bohemia and Moravia*, 31; as well as, in detail, Jaroslav Kučera, *Minderheit im Nationalstaat: Die Sprachenfrage in den tschechisch-deutschen Beziehungen 1918–1938* (Munich, 1999); and also Michaela Marek et al., eds., *Kultur als Vehikel und als Opponent politischer Absichten: Kulturkontakte zwischen Deutschen, Tschechen und Slowaken von der Mitte des 19. Jahrhunderts bis in die 1980er Jahre* (Essen, 2010).
8. See Helena Krejčová, Alena Mišková, "Anmerkungen zur Frage des Antisemitismus in den Böhmischen Ländern Ende des 19. Jahrhunderts," in *Judenemanzipation—Antisemitismus—Verfolgung in Deutschland, Österreich-Ungarn, den Böhmischen Ländern und in der Slowakei*, ed. Jörg K. Hoensch et al. (Essen, 1999), 55–62; also by the same authors, "Die antijüdischen bzw. antideutschen Kundgebungen und Demonstrationen in Böhmen und Mähren (1899)," in *Judenemanzipation—Antisemitismus—Verfolgung*, 63–84. See also the special edition of *Judaica Bohemiae* 46, no. 2 (2011) which is dedicated to the anti-Semitic essays by the prominent author Jan Neruda (1834–1891) published in a large daily newspaper and their historical context.
9. Rothkirchen, *The Jews of Bohemia and Moravia*, 27, 45–46; Heidrich Bodensieck, "Das Dritte Reich und die Lage der Juden in der Tschecho-Slowakei nach München," *Vierteljahrshefte für Zeitgeschichte* 9, no. 3 (1961): 249–261, here 249. See the detailed discussion in Ines Koeltzsch, "Antijüdische Straßengewalt und die semantische Konstruktion des 'Anderen' im Prag der Ersten Republik," *Judaica Bohemiae* 46, no. 1 (2011): 73–99.
10. Martin Schulze Wessel, "Czech Anti-Semitism in the Context of Tensions Between National and Confessional Programs, and the Foundation of the Czechoslovak National Church," *Bohemia, Zeitschrift für Geschichte und Kultur der böhmischen Länder* 46, no. 1 (2005): 102–107. On Masaryk's ideas and political concepts, see Eva Schmidt-Hartmann, *Thomas G. Masaryk's Realism: Origins of a Czech Political Concept 1882-1914* (Munich, 1984); Valentina von Tulechov, *Tomas Garrigue Masaryk: Sein kritischer Realismus in Auswirkung auf sein Demokratie- und Europaverständnis* (Göttingen, 2011).

11. *Čechoslovakische Statistik*, vol. 9, series VI (Volkszählung 1), part I: *Volkszählung in der Čechoslovakischen Republik vom 15. Februar 1921* (Prague, 1924), 86–97. See Rothkirchen, *The Jews of Bohemia and Moravia*, 29. On the problem of self-conceptions, see the detailed discussion in Kateřina Čapková, *Czechs, Germans, Jews? National Identity and the Jews of Bohemia* (New York, 2012).
12. Scott Spector, "Mittel-Europa? Some afterthoughts on Prague Jews, 'Hybridity,' and Translation," *Bohemia* 46, no. 1 (2005): 28–37, here 30.
13. Kateřina Čapková, "Czechs, Germans, Jews—Where is the Difference? The Complexity of National Identities of Bohemian Jews, 1918–1938," *Bohemia* 46, no. 1 (2005): 7–14, here 10f. On the Jews in Bohemia, see generally Hillel J. Kieval, *The Making of Czech Jewry: National Conflict and Jewish Society in Bohemia, 1870–1918* (New York, 1988). On Prague, see Ines Koeltzsch, *Geteilte Kulturen: Eine Geschichte der tschechisch-jüdisch-deutschen Beziehungen in Prag (1918–1938)* (Munich, 2012).
14. On the Zionists since 1918, see Tatjana Lichtenstein, "Racializing Jewishness: Zionist Responses to National Indifference in Interwar Czechoslovakia," *Austrian History Yearbook* 43 (April 2012): 75–97, and by the same author "'Making' Jews at Home: Zionism and the Construction of Jewish Nationality in Inter-war Czechoslovakia" *East European Jewish Affairs* 36, no. 1 (June 2006): 49–71. Cf. Čapková, *Czechs, Germans, Jews?*, 169–241.
15. Čapek, "Racial and Social Aspects," 603; Rothkirchen, *The Jews of Bohemia and Moravia*, 29.
16. *Čechoslovakische Statistik*, vol. 98, series VI (Volkszählung 7), part I: *Volkszählung in der Čechoslovakischen Republik vom 1. Dezember 1930* (Prag, 1934), 82–99. See Rothkirchen, *The Jews of Bohemia and Moravia*, 34–36.
17. Moses Moskowitz, "The Jewish Situation in the Protectorate of Bohemia and Moravia," *Jewish Social Studies* 4, no. 1 (Jan. 1942): 17–44, here 31, 33.
18. Rothkirchen, *The Jews of Bohemia and Moravia*, 32–39.
19. Ibid., 30.
20. For more detail, see the chapter by Jörg Osterloh in this volume. See also Bryant, *Prague in Black*, 22–25. Cf. Caitlin E. Murdock, *Changing Places: Society, Culture, and Territory in the Saxon-Bohemian Borderlands, 1870–1946*, Ann Arbor: University of Michigan Press, 2010.
21. Bryant, *Prague in Black*, 23–25; Rothkirchen, *The Jews of Bohemia and Moravia*, 46f., 53f., 73–77. For a general discussion of the Czechoslovak republic and the refugees between 1933 and 1938, see Kateřina Čapková and Michal Frankl, *Nejisté útočiště. Československo a uprchlíci před nacismem, 1933–1938* (Prague, 2008).
22. Max Hildebert Boehm, *Volkstheorie und Volkstumspolitik der Gegenwart* (1935), quoted in Sobota, "Czechs and Germans," 312.
23. Sobota, "Czechs and Germans," 312; Wiskemann, "Czechs and Germans after Munich," 303f.
24. See the chapter by Sybille Steinbacher in this volume.
25. Jörg Osterloh, *Nationalsozialistische Judenverfolgung im Reichsgau Sudetenland 1938–1945* (Munich, 2006), 136–165; Rothkirchen, *The Jews of Bohemia and Moravia*, 60f.
26. See the detailed discussion in Osterloh, *Nationalsozialistische Judenverfolgung im Reichsgau Sudetenland*, 185–203, as well as his contribution to this volume.
27. Peter Heumos, "Flüchtlingslager, Hilfsorganisationen, Juden im Niemandsland: Zur Flüchtlings- und Emigrationsproblematik in der Tschechoslowakei im Herbst 1938," *Bohemia* 25, no. 2 (1984): 243–275, here 247–252; Rothkirchen, *The Jews of Bohemia and Moravia*, 80f. In general on the flight and expulsions from the

annexed territories, see Jan Benda, "Okupace pohraničí a nucená imigrace v letech 1938–1939 (The Occupation of the Border Regions and Forced Emigration between 1938–1939)," *Český Časopis Historický* (*The Czech Historical Review*) 110, no. 2 (2012): 329–347.

28. Vojta Beneš and Roderick Aldrich Ginsburg, *10 Million Prisoners (Protectorate Bohemia and Moravia)* (Chicago, 1940), 14; Bodensieck, "Das Dritte Reich," 249–257; Rothkirchen, *The Jews of Bohemia and Moravia*, 75–90; Bryant, *Prague in Black*, 25.
29. Beneš and Ginsburg, *10 Million Prisoners*, 15; Bodensieck, "Das Dritte Reich," 257–261; Rothkirchen, *The Jews of Bohemia and Moravia*, 91–93; Bryant, *Prague in Black*, 25. On the discrimination of the Jews and Roma during this phase and the growing chauvinism, see also Mary Heimann, *Czechoslovakia: The State That Failed* (New Haven, 2011), 100f.
30. Adolf Hiter, *Hitler: Reden und Proklamationen 1932–1945*, part I, vol. 2, *1935–1938*, ed. Max Domarus (Munich, 1965), 960.
31. See the description by the Minister for the Administration of Social Affairs and Health Vladislav Klumpar in Wilhelm Dennler, *Die Böhmische Passion* (Freiburg i. Br., 1953), 95–98. Dennler's diary was probably written after the war in an attempt at self-exoneration. A high official in the Office of the Reich Protector and later Deputy Minister in the Czech government, Dennler represents himself as having been critical of the Nazi leadership, yet does not once mention the persecution of the Jews and describes the German treatment of the Czechs as friendly, apart from a few "excesses." According to Dennler, there was no forced labor; rather, the Czechs had pushed their way into the "Reich."
32. Beneš and Ginsburg, *10 Million Prisoners*, 22f.; Bryant, *Prague in Black*, 28.
33. Decree by the Führer and Reich Chancellor regarding the Protectorate of Bohemia and Moravia, of 16 March 1939, RGBl. 1939 I, 485.
34. Law of 13 April 1939, RGBl. 1939 I, 762. See Joachim Lilla, "Die Vertretung des 'Reichsgaus Sudetenland' und des 'Protektorats Böhmen und Mähren' im Großdeutschen Reichstag," *Bohemia* 40, no. 2 (1999): 436–471, here 444.
35. According to Helmut Rauschning, *Gespräche mit Hitler* (New York, 1940), 42; Petr Němec, "Das tschechische Volk und die nationalsozialistische Germanisierung des Raumes," *Bohemia* 32, no. 2 (1991): 424–455, here 426.
36. Decree by the Führer and Reich Chancellor regarding the Protectorate of Bohemia and Moravia, of 16 March 1939, RGBl. 1939 I, 485.
37. Hans Umbreit, *Deutsche Militärverwaltungen 1938/39: Die militärische Besetzung der Tschechoslowakei und Polens* (Stuttgart, 1977), 34–56.
38. Klaus Michael Mallmann, "Menschenjagd und Massenmord: Das neue Instrument der Einsatzgruppen und -kommandos 1938–1945," in *Die Gestapo im Zweiten Weltkrieg: "Heimatfront" und besetztes Europa*, ed. Gerhard Paul and Klaus-Michael Mallmann (Darmstadt, 2000), 291–316, here 292–294; Oldřich Sládek, "Standrecht und Standgericht. Die Gestapo in Böhmen und Mähren," in ibid., 317–339, here 322–326.
39. Beneš and Ginsburg, *10 Million Prisoners*, 30; Rothkirchen, *The Jews of Bohemia and Moravia*, 99. See also Ernst Frank, *Karl Hermann Frank: Staatsminister im Protektorat*, 2nd expanded edition (Heusenstamm, 1971), 76.
40. He was appointed to the office by the Wehrmacht on 5 April 1939; he did not receive executive powers until ten days later. See Umbreit, *Militärverwaltungen*, 59.
41. For a detailed treatment, see René Küpper, *Karl Hermann Frank (1898–1946): Politische Biographie eines sudetendeutschen Nationalsozialisten* (Munich, 2010). In contrast, very apologetic with regard to his own biography, Frank, *Karl Hermann Frank*.

42. Initially, Rasch functioned as Befehlshaber der Sipo und des SD (BdS) in Prague, but Stahlecker replaced him after five weeks; see Sládek, *Standrecht und Standgericht*, 322–326. See Livia Rothkirchen, "The Protectorate Government and the 'Jewish Question', 1939–1941," *Yad Vashem Studies* 17 (1999): 331–362, here 336.
43. Detlef Brandes, "Nationalsozialistische Tschechenpolitik im Protektorat Böhmen und Mähren," in *Der Weg in die Katastrophe: Deutsch-tschechoslowakische Beziehungen 1938–1947*, ed. Detlef Brandes and Václav Kural (Essen, 1994), 39–56, here 43.
44. Decree by the Führer and Reich Chancellor regarding the Protectorate of Bohemia and Moravia, of 16 March 1939, RGBl. 1939 I, 486f.
45. Rothkirchen, "The Protectorate Government," 336; Jan Björn Potthast, *Das jüdische Zentralmuseum der SS in Prag: Gegnerforschung und Völkermord im Nationalsozialismus* (Frankfurt, 2002), 56–60.
46. Bryant, *Prague in Black*, 42.
47. Beneš and Ginsburg, *10 Million Prisoners*, 67f.; Moses Moskowitz, "Three Years of the Protectorate of Bohemia and Moravia," *Political Science Quarterly* 57, no. 3 (September 1942): 353–375, here 372; King, *Budweisers into Czechs and Germans*, 180; Bryant, *Prague in Black*, 45.
48. Brandes, "Nationalsozialistische Tschechenpolitik," 42; Bryant, *Prague in Black*, 44; Rothkirchen, *The Jews of Bohemia and Moravia*, 100, 141.
49. Central Office report from 2 October 1941, appendix, table 1, in *Deutsche Politik im "Protektorat Böhmen und Mähren" unter Reinhard Heydrich 1941–1942: Eine Dokumentation*, ed. Miroslav Kárný et al. (Berlin, 1997), doc. no. 23, 125. For a critique of the figure, see Miroslav Kárný, "Zur Statistik der jüdischen Bevölkerung im sogenannten Protektorat," *Judaica Bohemiae* 12, no. 1 (1986): 9–19; also Eva Schmidt-Hartmann, "Tschechoslowakei," *Dimension des Völkermords: Die Zahl der jüdischen Opfer des Nationalsozialismus*, ed. Wolfgang Benz (Munich, 1991), 353–379, here 358; Rothkirchen, *The Jews of Bohemia and Moravia*, 116.
50. Josef Bartož, "Die Arisierung jüdischen Vermögens in Olmütz im Jahre 1939," *Theresienstädter Studien und Dokumente* (2000): 282–296, here 283; Jens Hampel, "Das Schicksal der jüdischen Bevölkerung der Stadt Iglau 1938–1942," *Theresienstädter Studien und Dokumente* (1998): 70–99, here 74; Rothkirchen, *The Jews of Bohemia and Moravia*, 100f.; Bryant, *Prague in Black*, 34.
51. Dr. Franz Friedmann's report: "Rechtsstellung der Juden, Protektorat, Stand 31.7.1942," in *Židé v Protektorátu. Hlášení Židovské náboženské obce v roce 1942: Dokumenty*, ed. Helena Krejčová et al. (Prague, 1997), doc. no. 15, 234. See also Rothkirchen, *The Jews of Bohemia and Moravia*, 99f. On Vienna, see Wolf Gruner, *Zwangsarbeit und Verfolgung: Österreichische Juden im NS-Staat 1938–1945* (Innsbruck, 2000), 23–25.
52. See Vojtěch Šustek, "Die nationalsozialistische Karriere eines sudetendeutschen Historikers," in *Josef Pfitzner a protektorátní Praha v letech 1939–45*, vol. 1, ed. Alena Míšková and Vojtěch Šustek (Prague, 2000), 71–109; Detlef Brandes and Alena Míšková, eds., *Vom Osteuropa-Lehrstuhl ins Prager Rathaus: Josef Pfitzner 1901–1945* (Essen, 2013).
53. On this and the following, see Wolf Gruner, "Das Protektorat Böhmen und Mähren und die antijüdische Politik 1939–1941: Lokale Initiativen, regionale Maßnahmen, zentrale Entscheidungen im 'Großdeutschen Reich,'" *Theresienstädter Studien und Dokumente* (2005): 27–62.
54. Cabinet committee to the Office of the Reich Protector on 24 July 1940, mentioned in United States Holocaust Memorial Museum/Archives (USHMM) Washington, RG 48.005M, Reel 5 (Prague State Archive, I 3b-5800 carton 387, no. 18, no fol.). See Rothkirchen, "The Protectorate Government," 340.

55. Bartož, "Die Arisierung jüdischen Vermögens in Olmütz," 285; Christoph Kreutzmüller and Jaroslav Kučera, "Die Commerzbank und die Vernichtung der jüdischen Gewerbetätigkeit in den böhmischen Ländern und den Niederlanden," in *Die Commerzbank und die Juden 1933–1934*, ed. Ludolf Herbst and Thomas Weihe (Munich, 2004), 173–222, here 199. On this and the following see Jörg Osterloh and Harald Wixforth, "Die 'Arisierung' im Protektorat Böhmen und Mähren: Rahmenbedingungen und gesetzliche Vorgaben," in *Die Expansion der Dresdner Bank in Europa*, by Harald Wixforth with the collaboration of Johannes Bär et al. (Munich, 2006), 306–348; Miroslav Kárný, "Die Protektoratsregierung und die Verordnungen des Reichsprotektors über das jüdische Vermögen," *Judaica Bohemiae* 29 (1993): 54–66.
56. In actual fact, the number was probably closer to 20,000, see Osterloh and Wixforth, "'Arisierung' im Protektorat," 306.
57. Printed in full in *Die Verfolgung und Ermordung der europäischen Juden durch das nationalsozialistische Deutschland 1933–1945* (*VEJ*), vol. 3: *Deutsches Reich und Protektorat September 1939—September 1941*, ed. Andrea Löw (Munich, 2012), doc. no. 237, 569–570; and in *Europa unterm Hakenkreuz: Die faschistische Okkupationspolitik in Österreich und der Tschechoslowakei (1938–1945)*, document selection and introduction by Helma Kaden (East Berlin, 1988), doc. no 32, 106. See also Drahomir Jančík, "Die 'Arisierungsaktivitäten' der Böhmischen Escompte Bank im Protektorat Böhmen und Mähren 1939–1945," in *Banken und "Arisierungen" in Mitteleuropa während des Nationalsozialismus*, ed. Dieter Ziegler (Stuttgart, 2002), 143–173, here 145.
58. Ordinance of the CdZ for Moravia of 20 March 1939, USHMM, RG 48.005M, Reel 1 (Prague State Archive, Bodenamt: Judenvorschriften), no. 3, no fol.; Ordinance of the CdZ for Bohemia of 29 March 1939, USHMM, RG 48.005M, Reel 1 (Prague State Archive, Bodenamt: Judenvorschriften), no. 2, no fol. See Jaroslava Milotová, "Die Zentralstelle für jüdische Auswanderung in Prag: Genesis und Tätigkeit bis zum Anfang des Jahres 1940," *Theresienstädter Studien und Dokumente* (1997): 7–30, here 20; Potthast, *Zentralmuseum*, 60.
59. Osterloh and Wixforth, "'Arisierung' im Protektorat," 307.
60. Minutes of the state secretary conference on 25 March 1939 and appendix in: *VEJ/3*, doc. no. 240, 574–580, here 579; appendix only printed in *Europa unterm Hakenkreuz Österreich und Tschechoslowakei*, doc. no. 36, 110–112: see Milotová, "Zentralstelle," 7; Potthast, *Zentralmuseum*, 62; Umbreit, *Militärverwaltungen*, 54.
61. Beneš and Ginsburg, *10 Million Prisoners*, 135; Rothkirchen, *The Jews of Bohemia and Moravia*, 102, 117.
62. Letter by Böhme (SD headquaters Prague) to head of Securitry Main Office from 8 June 1939 with report by the Jewish Religious Community of Prague from 1 June 1939, BArch, R 58/6401, fol. 231–234.
63. Beneš and Ginsburg, *10 Million Prisoners*, 136f.; Rothkirchen, *The Jews of Bohemia and Moravia*, 101f.; Bryant, *Prague in Black*, 44.
64. Note SD II 112 Dannecker 10 July 1939 following note by Hagen from 2 May 1939, BArch, R 58/6401, fol. 260; note by Hagen 16 June 1939 regarding submissions to Leiter II (Six), BArch, R 58/6401, fol. 243–24. On this and the following, see Gruner "Das Protektorat Böhmen und Mähren," 34–37. See also Hans Safrian, *Eichmann's Men* (New York, 2009), 50 (German original: Vienna, 1993). For Heydrich's biography, see Robert Gerwarth, *Hitler's Hangman: The Life of Heydrich* (New Haven, 2011).
65. Note Reich Protector (Burgsdorff) from 2 May 1939, USHMM, RG 48.005M, Reel 5 (Prague State Archive), I 3b-5803 carton 388, no. 3, no fol.; printed in: *VEJ/3*, doc. no. 245, 592. Also quoted in Milotová, "Zentralstelle," 8.

66. Draft law quoted in Beneš and Ginsburg, *10 Million Prisoners*, 136.
67. Michael Wildt, ed., *Die Judenpolitik des SD 1935–1938: Eine Dokumentation* (Munich, 1995), 60.
68. King, *Budweisers into Czechs and Germans*, 181.
69. Head of the government to protector with draft on 11 May 1939, USHMM, RG 48.005M, Reel 5 (Prague State Archive), I 3b-5803 carton 388, no. 5, no fol.; printed in *VEJ/3*, doc. no. 246, 593.
70. Draft of government ordinance on 11 May 1939, 1–22, USHMM, RG 48.005M, Reel 5 (Prague State Archive), I 3b-5803 carton 388, no. 4, no fol. See also Rothkirchen, *The Jews of Bohemia and Moravia*, 144.
71. Draft of the minutes of the meeting at the Reich Protector on 22 May 1939, 1, USHMM, RG 48.005M, Reel 5 (Prague State Archive), I 3b-5803 carton 388, no. 2, no fol.
72. *Verordnungsblatt des Reichsprotektors in Böhmen und Mähren* (1939), 45–48; printed in *VEJ/3*, doc. no. 247 593–596. See SD headquarters Prague B 1 (Böhme) to CdS on 23 June 1939, BArch, R 58/6401, fol. 255. Regarding the ordinance, see Jaroslava Milotová, "Zur Geschichte der Verordnung Konstantin von Neuraths über das jüdische Vermögen," *Theresienstädter Studien und Dokumente* (2002): 75–115. On legislation in general, see John G. Lexa, "Anti-Jewish Laws and Regulations in the Protectorate of Bohemia and Moravia," in *The Jews of Czechoslovakia: Historical Studies and Surveys*, vol. 3, ed. Avigdor Dagan (Philadelphia, 1984), 75–103. On the economic aspects, see Eduard Kubů, "Die Verwaltung von konfisziertem und sequestriertem Vermögen—eine spezifische Kategorie des 'Arisierungs-Profits': Die Kreditanstalt der Deutschen und ihre Abteilung 'F'," in *Banken und "Arisierungen"*, ed. Ziegler, 175–210, here 179; Kreutzmüller and Kučera, "Die Commerzbank und die Vernichtung der jüdischen Gewerbetätigkeit," 200f.
73. Kubů, "Die Verwaltung von konfisziertem und sequestriertem Vermögen," 177f.; Bartož, "Die Arisierung jüdischen Vermögens in Olmütz," 286–288.
74. In fall 1939, Ludwig was replaced by Dr. Rudolf Stier from the corresponding department at the Reichskommissar in the Sudetenland; Osterloh and Wixforth, "'Arisierung' im Protektorat," 307f.
75. Quoted in ibid., 309.
76. Arieh Tartakower and Kurt R. Grossmann, *The Jewish Refugee* (New York, 1944), 37.
77. SD II note from 22 June 1939, BArch, R 58/6401, fol. 261; see also note II 112 Dannecker from 10 July 1939, BArch, R 58/6401, fol. 260+RS. See Safrian, *Eichmann's Men*, 50.
78. The Sicherheitshauptamt was the precursor to the Reichssicherheitshauptamt, which was established in September 1939.
79. Circular Leiter SD-Amt II (Six) from 16 June 1939, BArch, R 58/6401, fol. 249f.; note Hagen from 16 June 1939 regarding submission to Leiter II (Six), BArch, R 58/6401, fol. 243–245; note SD II from 22 June 1939, BArch, R 58/6401, fol. 261; see also note II 112 Dannecker from 10 July 1939, BArch, R 58/6401, fol. 260+RS; also circular decree Reichsprotektor Freiherr von Neurath with letter to the prime minister in Prague from 15 July 1939, 1–5, USHMM, RG 48.005M, Reel 4 (Prague State Archive) I 3b-5811 Zentralstelle, no. 1, no fol.; letter printed in: *VEJ/3*, doc. no. 252, 609–610. On the founding of the Prague Central Office in July 1939, see Milotová, "Zentralstelle," 7–30; also Gabriele Anderl, "Die 'Zentralstellen für jüdische Auswanderung' in Wien, Berlin und Prag—ein Vergleich," *Tel Aviver Jahrbuch für deutsche Geschichte* 23 (1994): 276–299.

80. On Eichmann see David Cesarani, *Becoming Eichmann: Rethinking the Life, Crimes, and Trial of a "Desk Murderer"* (Cambridge, MA, 2004). On the Central Office in Vienna, see the contribution by Albert Lichtblau in this volume.
81. USHMM, RG 48.005M, Reel 4 (Prague State Archive) I 3b-5811 Zentralstelle, no. 11, no fol.: Notes Reich Protector I 3 regarding meeting on 19 July 1939, from 9 August 1939. For more details see Gruner, "Das Protektorat Böhmen und Mähren und die antijüdische Politik," 36; also Milotová, "Zentralstelle," 10–15.
82. Tartakower and Grossmann, *The Jewish Refugee*, 37.
83. See for this wrong assumption: Schmidt-Hartmann, "Tschechoslowakei," 359; Anderl, "Die 'Zentralstellen für jüdische Auswanderung,'" 279. Rothkirchen, too, maintains that even though many anti-Jewish ordinances continued to be issued by the Czech government, they hardly played a role any more in decision making; Rothkirchen, *The Jews of Bohemia and Moravia*, 145. See also Miroslav Kárný, "Die 'Judenfrage' in der nazistischen Okkupationspolitik," *Historica* 21 (1982): 137–192.
84. See for this opinion Bryant, *Prague in Black*, 50.
85. Institute of Jewish Affairs of the American Jewish Congress, ed., *Hitler's Ten-Year War on the Jews* (New York, 1943), 57.
86. Prague Ministry of the Interior ordinance of 3 August 1939, USHMM, RG 48.005M, Reel 1 (Prague State Archive, Innenministerium: Judenvorschriften), no. 11, no fol.; printed in *VEJ/3*, doc. no. 256, 616–618. See "Bericht eines Reisenden," in *Sopade—Deutschland-Berichte der Sozialdemokratischen Partei Deutschlands 1934–1940*, vol. 7 (1940), ed. Klaus Behnken (Salzhausen, 1989), 262–264.
87. Moskowitz, "Three Years of the Protectorate," 360; Detlef Brandes, *Die Tschechen unter deutschem Protektorat*, part I: *Besatzungspolitik, Kollaboration und Widerstand im Protektorat Böhmen und Mähren bis Heydrichs Tod (1939–1942)* (Munich, 1969), 165f.
88. Ordinance on the Establishment of the Administration and the German Sicherheitspolizei in the Protectorate of Bohemia and Moravia of 1 September 1939, RGBl. 1939 I, 1681; excerpt in *Europa unterm Hakenkreuz: Österreich und Tschechoslowakei*, doc. no. 51, 128f.
89. For a detailed discussion of the following, see Wolf Gruner, "Von der Kollektivausweisung zur Deportation der Juden aus Deutschland (1938–1945): Neue Perspektiven und Dokumente," in *Die Deportation der Juden aus Deutschland: Pläne, Praxis, Reaktionen 1938–1945*, ed. Birthe Kundrus and Beate Meyer (Göttingen, 2004), 21–62, here 30–35; also Peter Longerich, *Holocaust: The Nazi Persecution and Murder of the Jews* (New York, 2010), 151–154 (German original: Munich, 1998).
90. *Hitler's Ten-Year War*, 55. See, with slightly different figures (80,391 persons of Jewish faith and 9,828 non-religious Jews), Alena Hájková, "Erfassung der jüdischen Bevölkerung des Protektorats," *Theresienstädter Studien und Dokumente* (1997): 50–62, here 53.
91. The RSHA was formed as a result of a RFSS decree from 27 September 1939. On the personnel and history of this institution, see the detailed account by Michael Wildt, *An Uncompromising Generation: The Nazi Leadership of the Reich Security Main Office* (Madison, 2009) (German original: Hamburg, 2002).
92. Note for Eichmann from 18 October 1939, Yad Vashem (YV) Jerusalem, 051/no. 91 (Prague State Archive), fol. 22. See also the daily report Mährisch-Ostrau SD office (Dr. Heinrich) from 18 October 1939, YV Jerusalem, 051/no. 91 (Prague State Archive), fol. 22. Regarding the selection and transport, see Lukáš Přibyl, "Das Schicksal des dritten Transports aus dem Protektorat nach Nisko," *Theresienstädter Studien und Dokumente* (2000): 297–342, here 298.

93. Note from 23 October 1939, BArch, R 70 Böhmen und Mähren, no. 9, no fol.
94. YV Jerusalem, 051/no. 91 (Prague State Archive), fol. 38: Telex on 3 November 1939 with daily report (Dannecker) to Vienna headquarters from 1 and 2 November 1939. Most of these Jews were brought to a camp in Vyhne (Eisenbach) in Slovakia in 1940 as a "Jewish emigrant group" until they would emigrate, but in 1941 the camp was changed into a work camp; for more detail, see Přibyl, "Das Schicksal des dritten Transports"; Eduard Nižnansky, "Die Aktion Nisko, das Lager Sosnowiec (Oberschlesien) und die Anfänge des Judenlagers in Vyhne (Slowakei)," *Jahrbuch für Antisemitismusforschung* 11 (2002): 325–335.
95. Gruner, "Von der Kollektivausweisung zur Deportation der Juden," 34.
96. Gruner, "Das Protektorat Böhmen und Mähren und die antijüdische Politik," 38.
97. Beneš and Ginsburg, *10 Million Prisoners*, 155–157. For detail on the demonstrations, see Brandes, *Tschechen*, part I, 83–95.
98. Brandes, "Nationalsozialistische Tschechenpolitik," 55.
99. Bryant, *Prague in Black*, 46–48, 83.
100. Circular decree of the Reich Protector/Commander of the SiPo and SD II 308/40 from 29 January 1940, USHMM, RG 48.005M, Reel 4 (Prague State Archive), I 3b-5811 Zentralstelle, no. 2, no fol.
101. Götz Aly, *"Final Solution": Nazi Population Policy and the Murder of the European Jews* (London, 1999), 49 (German original: Frankfurt, 1995). See also the chapters by Ingo Loose and Sybille Steinbacher in this volume.
102. Vgl. Milotová, "Zentralstelle," 23.
103. Report "Rechtsstellung der Juden," *Židé*, doc. no. 15, 243–248.
104. English translation of the ordinance printed in Moskowitz, "The Jewish Situation in the Protectorate," 43f. See also the report from the Central Office from 2 October 1941, printed in *Deutsche Politik im "Protektorat Böhmen und Mähren"*, doc. no. 23, 123f.
105. Ibid., 127, appendix: table 2.
106. Osterloh and Wixforth, "'Arisierung' im Protektorat," 310. Ordinance of 26 January 1940 in *Verordnungsblatt des Reichsprotektors Böhmen und Mähren* (1940/7), 41f., excerpt in *Europa unterm Hakenkreuz: Österreich und Tschechoslowakei*, doc. no. 62, 139.
107. Moskowitz, "The Jewish Situation in the Protectorate," 26f.
108. At the end of June 1940 in the jurisdiction of the regional administrator of Prague, the trustees included 1,109 German but only 96 Czechs. For more detail see Osterloh and Wixforth, "'Arisierung' im Protektorat," 307, 310–331. See also Kárný, "Die 'Judenfrage' in der nazistischen Okkupationspolitik," 142, 150, 167; Rothkirchen, *The Jews of Bohemia and Moravia*, 107f. Recently, see Drahomír Jančík, Eduard Kubů, and Jiří Šouša, *Arisierungsgewinnler: Die Rolle der deutschen Banken bei der "Arisierung" und Konfiskation jüdischer Vermögen im Protektorat Böhmen und Mähren (1939–1945)*, with collaboration by Jiří Novotný (Wiesbaden, 2011).
109. Němec, "Das tschechische Volk," 446. See also Moskowitz, "The Jewish Situation in the Protectorate," 26.
110. Wilhelm Dennler, *Sozialpolitik im Protektorat Böhmen und Mähren* (Berlin, 1940), 4, 9.
111. On the use of forced labor, see Wolf Gruner, *Jewish Forced Labor under the Nazis: Economic Needs and Nazi Racial Aims 1938–1944* (New York, 2006) 141–173.
112. Brandes, "Nationalsozialistische Tschechenpolitik," 52; Petr Němec, "Die Lage der deutschen Nationalität im Protektorat Böhmen und Mähren unter dem Aspekt der 'Eindeutschung' dieses Gebiets," *Bohemia*, 32 no. 1 (1991): 39–59, here 39f.
113. Němec, "Die Lage der deutschen Nationalität," 40–55.

114. Němec, "Das tschechische Volk," 443f.; Bryant, *Prague in Black,* 116–125.
115. Handwritten submission (Rudolf Pitzak) to the Office of the Reich Protector (February 1940), USHMM, RG 48.005M, Reel 4 (Prague State Archive, carton I-3b-5851), no. 1, no fol.; Narodni Arijeká Kulturni Jednotav [National Aryan Cultural Association] Prague to Reich Protector von Neurath on 12 June 1940, ibid., no. 6, no fol.; Olmütz regional administrator to Reich Protector on 13 June 1940, ibid., no. 4, no fol.; and Reich Protector/BdS to Gruppe I/3 at the Reich Protector on 5 March 1940, ibid., no. 3, no fol.; this last documented printed in *VEJ/3,* doc. no. 272, 664.
116. King, *Budweisers into Czechs and Germans,* 181.
117. Olmütz regional administrator to Reich Protector on 13 June 1940, USHMM, RG 48.005M, Reel 4 (Prague State Archive carton, I-3b-5851), no. 4, no fol.; printed in *VEJ/3,* doc. no. 280, 677; also circular decree of the Prague Ministry of the Interior on 9 July 1940, USHMM, RG 48.005M, Reel 1 (Prague State Archive, Innenministerium: Judenvorschriften), no. 44, no fol.
118. *Jüdisches Nachrichtenblatt,* Prague edition from 13 August 1940; Ruth Bondy, "Chronik der sich schließenden Tore: Jüdisches Nachrichtenblatt—Židovské Listy (1939–1945)," *Theresienstädter Studien und Dokumente* (2000): 86–103, here 95.
119. Report "Rechtsstellung der Juden," *Židé,* doc. no. 15, 246f., 261f. See *Hitler's Ten-Year War,* 58.
120. Report of the Israeli Religious Community Vienna 1938–1944/45 (Löwenherz report), 25, Central Zionist Archives, Jerusalem (CZA), S 26, no. 1191g, no fol.; see Safrian, *Eichmann's Men,* 66.
121. Circular decree Reich Protector/Commander of the SiPo and SD II 1305–6/40 (signed by Frank) from 17 August 1940, USHMM, RG 48.005M, Reel 3 (Prague State Archive), no. 60, no fol.; printed in *VEJ/3,* doc. no. 286, 689–690.
122. More examples proving this are provided in Gruner, "Das Protektorat Böhmen und Mähren und die antijüdische Politik," 42.
123. Report "Sonderaktionen" by Jewish Religious Community in Prague (1942), *Židé,* doc. no. 14, 227; report "Rechtsstellung der Juden," in *Židé,* ed. Krejčová et al., doc. no. 15, 246f., 256; *Hitler's Ten-Year War,* 59; Bondy, "Chronik," 94f.
124. Copy of monthly report by SD-Leitabschnitt Prague March 1941, 57, USHMM, RG 11.001 M.23, Reel 91 (OSOBI, 1488–1-15), fol. 7; monthly report SD-Leitabschnitt Prague (May 1941) from 1 June 1941, 46, USHMM, RG 11.001 M.15, Reel 83 (OSOBI, 1322–2-391), fol. 49.
125. Moskowitz, "Three Years of the Protectorate," 357.
126. According to the report on the successful *Volkstum* work of the regional administrators on 5 October 1940, reference in Němec, "Das tschechische Volk," 452.
127. Brandes, *Tschechen,* part I, 165f.; idem, "Nationalsozialistische Tschechenpolitik," 52.
128. Moskowitz, "The Jewish Situation in the Protectorate," 18.
129. Central Office report from 2 October 1941, *Deutsche Politik im "Protektorat Böhmen und Mähren",* doc. no. 23, 123.
130. *Jüdisches Nachrichtenblatt,* Prague edition from 21 February 1941; English translation printed in Moskowitz, "The Jewish Situation in the Protectorate," 41.
131. For more detail, see Gruner, *Jewish Forced Labor,* 152–158.
132. For more detail, see ibid., 158–164.
133. After being published on 22 August 1941, the Reich Protector's ordinance from 5 August 1941 went into effect on 1 September 1941; handwritten notice on the draft of the Reich Protector ordinance from June 1941, USHMM, RG 48.005M, Reel 4 (Prague State Archive), I 3b-5812 Armenfürsorge für Juden, no. 2–3, no fol.
134. Third ordinance on the implementation of the Law for the protection of German Blood and German Honor, of 5 July 1941, RGBl. 1941 I, 384; printed in *VEJ/3,* doc.

no. 309, 732–733. See also *Verordnungsblatt des Reichsprotektors* from 5 July 1941, 403; Němec, "Das tschechische Volk," 446.
135. See Gruner, "Von der Kollektivausweisung zur Deportation der Juden," 46–51.
136. Police order on the marking of the Jews, of 1 September 1941, RGBl. 1941 I, 547.
137. State Secretary Frank to Lammers on 16 July 1941 (excerpt), *Verfolgung, Vertreibung, Vernichtung. Dokumente des faschistischen Antisemitismus 1933–1942*, ed. Kurt Pätzold (Leipzig, 1983), doc. no. 269, 294.
138. Jaroslava Milotová, "Der Okkupationsapparat und die Vorbereitung der Transporte nach Lodz," *Theresienstädter Studien und Dokumente* (1998): 40–69, here 41; Potthast, *Zentralmuseum*, 133.
139. Gerwarth, *Hitler's Hangman*, 218–277.
140. Rothkirchen, "The Protectorate Government," 353; Detlef Brandes, *Die Tschechen unter deutschem Protektorat*, part II: *Besatzungspolitik, Kollaboration und Widerstand im Protektorat Böhmen und Mähren von Heydrichs Tod bis zum Prager Aufstand (1942–1945)* (Munich, 1975), 10; Miroslav Kárný, "Reinhard Heydrich als Stellvertretender Reichsprotektor in Prag," in *Deutsche Politik im "Protektorat Böhmen und Mähren"*, 9–75, here 9–12; Bryant, *Prague in Black*, 129–143.
141. Brandes, "Nationalsozialistische Tschechenpolitik," 45; Moskowitz, "Three Years of the Protectorate," 373; Bryant, *Prague in Black*, 145.
142. It had probably been anticipated since December 1941 that a German would enter the Czech government. This formed part of the planned administrative reform that was also supposed to include the creation of a German state ministry, which in fact was not established until 1943; Dennler, *Die Böhmische Passion*, 65–68.
143. Circular decree of the Reich Protector/Commander of the SiPo and SD on 29 September 1941, USHMM, RG 48.005M, Reel 4 (Prague State Archive), carton, I-3b-5851, no. 21, no fol. See *Deutsche Politik im "Protektorat Böhmen und Mähren"*, 97, doc. no. 14. See Milotová, "Okkupationsapparat," 57.
144. Quoted in Milotová, "Okkupationsapparat," 56.
145. Dr. Kliment to Josef Ježek (Minister of the Interior) on 6 October 1941, *Deutsche Politik im "Protektorat Böhmen und Mähren"*, 128; see Milotová, "Okkupationsapparat," 41; Ministry of the Interior statement, undated, *Deutsche Politik im "Protektorat Böhmen und Mähren"*, 128f.
146. Central Office report from 2 October 1941, appendix: table 1, *Deutsche Politik im "Protektorat Böhmen und Mähren"*, 125, doc. no. 23.
147. Record of the security police conference in Prague on the "solution of the Jewish question" in the protectorate, 10 October 1941, *Deutsche Politik im "Protektorat Böhmen und Mähren"*, 137–141, doc. no. 29. Also printed in Peter Longerich, ed., *Die Ermordung der europäischen Juden: Eine umfassende Dokumentation des Holocaust 1941–1945* (Munich, 1989), doc. no. 64, 172–176.
148. Circular decree of the Reich Protector/Commander of the SiPo and SD I 2776/41 of 12 October 1941, USHMM, RG 48.005M, Reel 3 (Prague State Archive), no. 9, no fol.
149. Milotová, "Okkupationsapparat," 60f.
150. Gruner, "Kollektivausweisung," 51.
151. Hájková, "Erfassung der jüdischen Bevölkerung," 54; Milotová, "Okkupationsapparat," 46; Schmidt-Hartmann, "Tschechoslowakei," 361; Rothkirchen, *The Jews of Bohemia and Moravia*, 125.
152. Meeting Ježek with Böhme on 3 November 1941, *Deutsche Politik im "Protektorat Böhmen und Mähren"*, 174, doc. no. 44: 11. See Milotová, "Okkupationsapparat," 42; Potthast, *Zentralmuseum*, 133.
153. For more detail, see Gruner, *Jewish Forced Labor*, 162–166.

154. Table: Age distribution of Jews from 14 November 1941, Leo Baeck Institute Archive New York, Max Kreutzberger, Research Papers, AR 7183, box 2, folder 2, fol. 32.
155. Conference protocol, in Kurt Pätzold and Erika Schwarz, *Tagesordnung: Judenmord: Eine Dokumentation zur Organisation der "Endlösung"* (Berlin, 1992), doc. no. 24, 102–112, citation: 107. On the conference's goals, with various interpretations, see Pätzold and Schwarz, *Tagesordnung: Judenmord*, 44–46; Longerich, *Politik*, 466–472; Christian Gerlach, "Die Wannsee-Konferenz, das Schicksal der deutschen Juden und Hitlers politische Grundsatzentscheidung, alle Juden Europas zu ermorden," *WerkstattGeschichte* 18 (1997): 7–44; Mark Roseman, *The Wannsee Conference and the Final Solution: A Reconsideration* (New York, 2002).
156. Pätzold and Schwarz, *Tagesordnung: Judenmord*, 107.
157. For detail on the following see H. G. Adler, *Theresienstadt 1941–1945: Das Antlitz einer Zwangsgemeinschaft: Geschichte, Soziologie, Psychologie* (Tübingen, 1955); idem, ed., *Die verheimlichte Wahrheit: Theresienstädter Dokumente* (Tübingen, 1958).
158. Report by the Jewish Religion Community in Prague, "Arbeit" (undated; mid 1942), Krejčová et al., *Židé*, doc. no. 5, 108. On the construction unit and the status of these men in the subsequent ghetto hierarchy, see Anna Hájková, "Die fabelhaften Jungs aus Theresienstadt: Junge tschechische Männer als dominante soziale Elite im Theresienstädter Ghetto," in *Im Ghetto 1939–1945: Neue Forschungen zu Alltag und Umfeld*, ed. Christoph Dieckmann and Babette Quinkert (Beiträge zur Geschichte des Nationalsozialismus, vol. 25) (Göttingen, 2009), 116–135.
159. Circular decree of the Reich Protector/Commander of the SiPo and SD I 3098/41 on 15 December 1941, USHMM Washington, RG 48.005M, Reel 3 (Prague State Archive), no. 10, no fol.
160. Rothkirchen, *The Jews of Bohemia and Moravia*, 129.
161. Vojtěch Blodig, *Theresienstadt in der "Endlösung der Judenfrage" 1941–1945: Führer durch die Dauerausstellung des Ghetto-Museums in Theresienstadt* (Terezin, 2003), 32f.; Schmidt-Hartmann, "Tschechoslowakei," 362; Rothkirchen, *The Jews of Bohemia and Moravia*, 127f. On the fate of the transport, see Andrej Angrick and Peter Klein, *The "Final Solution" in Riga: Exploitation and Annihilation, 1941–1944* (New York, 2009), 215, 219–225 (German original: Darmstadt 2006).
162. *Verordnungsblatt des Reichsprotektors*, no. 7, 1942 on 28 February 1942, facsimile in *Europa unterm Hakenkreuz: Österreich und Tschechoslowakei*, illustration 22. See Heydrich to Frick on the ordinance of 16 February 1942, *Deutsche Politik im "Protektorat Böhmen und Mähren"*, doc. no. 82, 237. On the Bohemian and Moravian emigration fund, see Gabriele Anderl and Dirk Rupnow, *Die Zentralstelle für jüdische Auswanderung als Beraubungsinstitution. Nationalsozialistische Institutionen des Vermögensentzuges*, editorial collaboration by Alexandra-Eileen Wenck (Munich, 2004).
163. Gruner, *Jewish Forced Labor*, 166–169; also report by Prague Deputy Primator Josef Pfitzner Prag to State Secretary Frank for 1 November to 31 December 1942, from 12 January 1943, in Míšková and Šustek, *Pfitzner*, doc. no. 17, 327.
164. Düsseldorf Gestapo report from 9 March 1942 regarding meeting on 6 March 1942 in Amt IV B 4, ed. Helmut Eschwege, *Kennzeichen J. Bilder, Dokumente, Berichte zur Geschichte der Verbrechen des Hitlerfaschismus an den deutschen Juden 1933–1945* (Berlin, 1981), 193; *Deutsche Politik im "Protektorat Böhmen und Mähren"*, doc. no. 85, 241.
165. Gruner, *Jewish Forced Labor*, 170–172.

166. Eva Hahn, "Verdrängung und Verharmlosung: Das Ende der jüdischen Bevölkerungsgruppe in den böhmischen Ländern nach ausgewählten tschechischen und sudetendeutschen Publikationen," in *Der Weg in die Katastrophe*, ed. Brandes and Kural, 135–150, here 147.
167. King, *Budweisers into Czechs and Germans*, 187; Bryant, *Prague in Black*, 167–172.
168. Report Israelite Religious Community Vienna 1938–1944/45 (Löwenherz report), 41, CZA Jerusalem, S 26, no. 1191g, no fol. See notice regarding visit in the RSHA on 29–30 May 1942; quoted in Safrian, *Eichmann's Men*, 118; also Reich Association comment from 29 May 1942, BArch, R 8150, no. 8, fol. 109.
169. King, *Budweisers into Czechs and Germans*, 187; Bryant, *Prague in Black*, 167–172.
170. Brandes, "Nationalsozialistische Tschechenpolitik," 55f.
171. Regierungsverordnung über die arbeitsrechtliche Behandlung der Juden im Protektorat Böhmen und Mähren, mentioned in Gruner, *Jewish Forced Labor*, 170f.
172. Bryant, *Prague in Black*, 151.
173. Report by Prague Deputy Primator Josef Pfitzner Prag to State Secretary Frank for 1 September to 31 October 1942, from 2 November 1942, in Míšková and Šustek, *Pfitzner*, doc. no. 16, 308.
174. Report by the Inspector for Statistics at the Reichsführer SS, status 1 January 1943 (Korherr report), 5, Leo Baeck Institute Archive New York, Microfilms: Wiener Library London, 500 series, no. 526. See Jewish Black Book Committee, *The Black Book: The Nazi Crime against the Jewish People* (New York, 1946), 178.
175. Ordinance of 25 November 1941, RGBl. 1941 I, 722.
176. "Verordnung über den Verlust der Protektoratsangehörigkeit"; RGBl. 1942 I, 637.
177. "Gesetz über die Einziehung kommunistischen Vermögens" from 26 May 1933 and "Gesetz über die Einziehung volks- und staatsfeindlichen Vermögens" from 14 July 1933, RGBl. 1933 I, 293 und 479.
178. Rothkirchen, *The Jews of Bohemia and Moravia*, 130.
179. Yaacov Lozowick, *Hitler's Bureaucrats: The Nazi Security Police and the Banality of Evil* (London, 2000), 107f., 113.
180. Bryant, *Prague in Black*, 151.
181. Rothkirchen, *The Jews of Bohemia and Moravia*, 130–135.
182. René Küpper, "Karl Hermann Frank als Deutscher Staatsminister für Böhmen und Mähren," in *Geteilt, besetzt, beherrscht: Die Tschechoslowakei 1938–1945; Reichsgau Sudetenland, Protektorat Böhmen und Mähren, Slowakei*, ed. Monika Glettler, Lubomir Lipták, and Alena Míšková (Essen, 2004), 31–52.
183. Berta Landré, "Jüdische Zwangsarbeit in Prag," *Zeitgeschichte* 9 no. 11/12 (1982): 365–377.
184. Ludomír Kocourek, "Das Schicksal der Juden im Sudetengau im Licht der erhaltenen Quellen," *Theresienstädter Studien und Dokumente* (1997): 86–104, here 96; Rothkirchen, *The Jews of Bohemia and Moravia*, 157.
185. However, at this time many Polish and Hungarian Jews were among the tens of thousands of KZ inmates who had been brought to the protectorate for the construction of armament factories. At least thirty-seven KZ satellite camps existed in Bohemia between 1942 and 1945. Jörg Skriebeleit, "Die Außenlager des KZ Flossenbürg in Böhmen,"in *KZ-Außenlager—Geschichte und Erinnerung*, special issue *Dachauer Hefte* 15 (1999): 196–217, here 199–208; Miroslava Benešová, "Das Konzentrationslager in Leitmeritz und seine Häftlinge," *Theresienstädter Studien und Dokumente* (1995): 217–240; as well as, recently, Alfons Adam, *"Die Arbeiterfrage soll mit Hilfe von KZ-Häftlingen gelöst werden": Zwangsarbeit in KZ-Außenlagern auf dem Gebiet*

der heutigen Tschechischen Republik (Berlin, 2013)—I would like to thank Jörg Osterloh for the reference.
186. Rothkirchen, *The Jews of Bohemia and Moravia*, 133.
187. Bryant, *Prague in Black*, 151.
188. Miroslav Kárný, "Die tschechischen Opfer der deutschen Okkupation," in *Der Weg in die Katastrophe*, ed. Brandes and Kural, 151–164, here 152f.
189. Rothkirchen, *The Jews of Bohemia and Moravia*, 134.
190. On the prosecution of Czechs who participated in the protectorate policy, see Benjamin Frommer, *National Cleansing: Retribution against Nazi Collaborators in Postwar Czechoslovakia* (New York, 2004).

CHAPTER 5

MEMEL TERRITORY
Ruth Leiserowitz

Prior to the Annexation

The designation "Memel Territory" was coined in 1919 at the peace conference in Versailles, referring to the northern strip of East Prussia, bordered on the south by the Memel River and extending to the village of Nimmersatt (Nemirsatė) on the Baltic coast. The territory had an area of 2,416 square kilometers and 141,000 inhabitants in 1919.[1] Article 99 of the Treaty of Versailles finally stipulated the cession of the Memel Territory from the German Reich[2] (see map 5.1). When the Reich government protested, the Allies responded with a letter signed by French Prime Minister George Clémenceau stating: "the region has always been Lithuanian. The majority of the population is Lithuanian in terms of origin and language. The fact that large parts of the city of Memel itself are German does not justify keeping the entire region under German sovereignty, particularly because the harbor of Memel is Lithuania's only access to the sea."[3]

According to the Lithuanian government, the peace conference had called for the territory's cession for national and economic reasons; according to the German interpretation, the decisive considerations were chiefly economic.[4] There was no occupation statute for the territory; France administered the territory from the moment that the

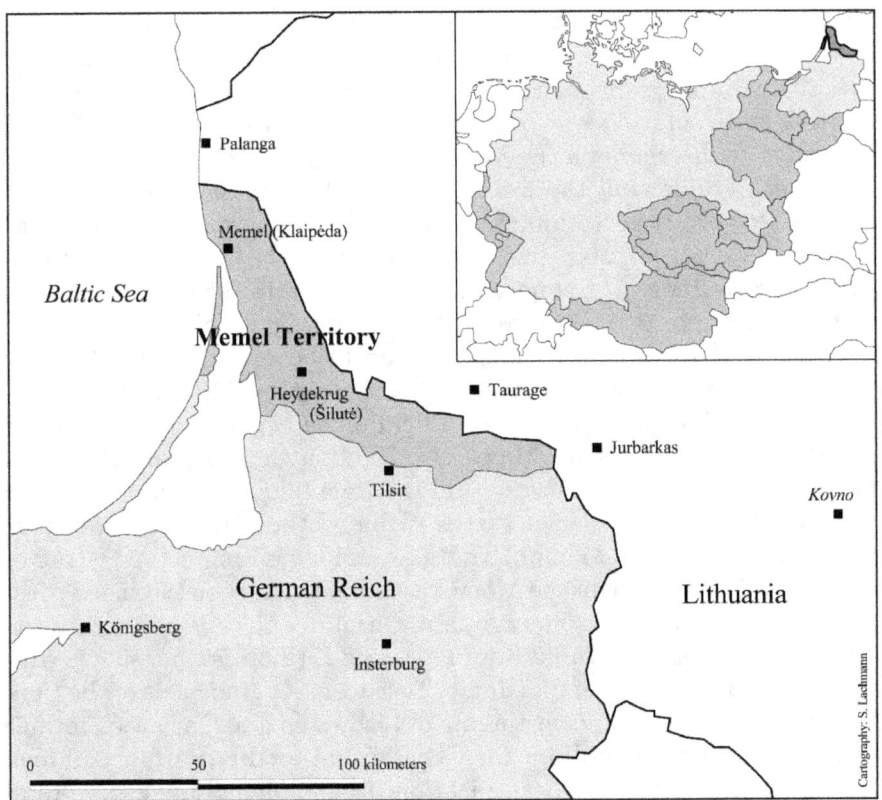

Map 5.1. Memel Territory, 1939

peace treaty took effect until 15 January 1923. During that period, the territory constituted an independent customs district, but it retained the Reichsmark as its currency.[5] As understood by Germany, Memel's inhabitants continued to be German citizens; the Allies, on the other hand, referred to them in 1920 as "citoyens de Memel"; the Lithuanians called the town "Klaipėda."[6] That same year in February, a French occupation contingent was stationed in Memel under Brigade General Dominique Joseph Odry, who assumed the post of the Governor of Memel.[7]

The region's future seemed undecided at first. Discussions included a proposal to create a free state in Memel modeled on the example of Danzig, an idea that appealed above all to the city's business circles.[8] The German government, however, feared that a realization of this proposal would lead to a plebiscite that would sanction the cession of the territory, thereby clearly undermining Berlin's position that the people of Memel did not accept the arrangement stipulated in Versailles.[9] Yet the Lithuanian government in Kovno (Kaunas) also clearly felt that the free state solution was contrary to its interests;[10] thus in fall 1922 it decided to intervene in the Memel Territory.[11]

Evidently following the example of the Polish undertaking in the Vilnius Region,[12] the Lithuanians decided on an occupation that was supposed to be disguised as an uprising by the Memel Territory's Lithuanian minority. Kovno (Kaunas) and Berlin secretly consulted on the matter, for both Lithuanian and German politicians agreed that French influence in the Memelland had to be contained.[13] After the Lithuanian militia had achieved a fait accompli on 15 January 1923, the Entente Powers and Lithuania held tense negotiations that led to the Memel Convention of 8 May 1924. The Convention guaranteed Memelland extensive autonomy within the Republic of Lithuania. Visible signs of the region's special status included the establishment of its own parliament—the Memel Landtag—and a supreme administrative body—the Directorate of the Memel Region. A governor exercised Lithuanian sovereignty.[14] Lithuanian and German enjoyed equal status as official languages. The inhabitants received Lithuanian passports with the addendum "citizen of the Memel Territory." On the basis of the Convention, signed by the governments of Lithuania and Germany, former German nationals could opt for German nationality within eighteen months of the Convention's ratification; 13,238 Memellanders—a total of 10 percent of the population—decided to do so, most of whom (9,792) retained their residency in the Memel Territory as foreigners.[15] In the census, which took place at the same time, 59,315 of the inhabitants described themselves as German, 37,626 as Lithuanian, and an additional 34,337 as Memellanders.[16]

Germany and Lithuania considered the situation temporary. The German Reich endeavored to secure the territory's permanent repatriation; Lithuania, on the other hand, wanted to fully integrate the region into its state. In the early 1930s, positions became entrenched. After Hitler's seizure of power in Germany at the end of January 1933, two parties affiliated with National Socialism formed in the Memel Territory at the same time, both of which were popular: the Christian-Socialist Working Group (Christlich-Sozialistische Arbeitsgemeinschaft) led by the pastor Theodor Freiherr von Saß; and the Socialist People's Community (Sozialistische Volksgemeinschaft), headed by the veterinarian Dr. Ernst Neumann.[17]

Even though the Lithuanian government declared a state of emergency in the Memel Territory, which lasted from 1926 to 1938 and restricted the freedom of assembly, National Socialism nonetheless gained large support among the Memel Germans. Many of them could barely wait to adopt the new world view from the Reich and create the corresponding organizations.[18] The NSDAP Kreisleiter in Tilsit, Hans Moser, who functioned as a liaison between the Memelland National Socialists and Germany, repeatedly received orders from the Nazi leadership in Germany to curb such plans, since according to Berlin the foreign policy situation did not allow them to rush ahead. In this regard, Vygantas Vareikis even refers to a "National Socialist cultural space" in the region.[19]

In actual fact, between 1920 and 1937, Memel constituted a region with a German cultural and economic life; the autonomous authorities undertook no anti-Semitic measures whatsoever until 1937. At first, the region's unresolved future entailed more advantages than disadvantages for the Jewish population.[20] After the separation of the Memel Territory from Germany, in 1920 the French governor abolished all restrictions pertaining to the acquisition of citizenship by Jews.[21] Article 99 of the Treaty of Versailles also obligated Germany "to accept the settlement made by the Principal Allied and Associated Powers in regard to these territories, particularly in so far as concerns the nationality of the inhabitants."[22] Jews living in Memel and who until this point in time did not possess German citizenship now received it.[23] The governor had appointed a four-person commission, in which two Jews—Moritz Altschul and Leon Rostovsky—and a German discussed the applications under the leadership of a French officer. Consequently, the number of Jews with German citizenship rapidly increased. Presumably, the governor granted them German citizenship because—despite French references to "Memel citizens"—no other alternative existed. Precise figures, however, remain unknown.

Despite—or precisely because—of the unresolved situation, the city attracted new residents: the number of inhabitants rapidly grew from 32,000 in 1920 to 35,000 by the end of 1922.[24] On the census date—20 September 1920—Memelland enumerated 1,350 Jews, a number, however, that Rudolfas Valsonokas, a lawyer living in Memel, described as implausible in 1932.[25] Numerous factors, such as the harbor, trade, favorable conditions for industrial development, opportunities to learn a trade, and good emigration opportunities led to the settlement of many Jews in Memel. New arrivals included Jewish traders from the surrounding region who opened stores in the town; Jewish doctors and lawyers from Kovno, who had obtained their diplomas in Germany; and Jews from Russia. In the early 1920s, many Jews who settled in Memel believed in the harbor town's economic future. Lithuania's annexation of Memelland did not change matters; most of them had no desire to leave Memelland and live in other less attractive parts of Lithuania. Last but not least, the steady influx of Lithuanian Jews underscored the economic and cultural gap between the Memel Territory and Lithuania. The 1930s witnessed above all the settlement of workers from the provinces, who, despite the general economic crisis, were able to find employment in Memel's industrial operations.[26] The new arrivals primarily included Jewish families that were originally from western Lithuania but had been forcibly evacuated to the Russian interior by czarist officials during the First World War prior to the arrival of the German army. When they obtained approval from the Russian authorities to return to Lithuania in the early 1920s, they discovered new owners living in their former homes. So they reoriented themselves—toward Memel.[27] The Lithuanian government, meanwhile, welcomed the influx of Jews to Memel, for, together with the Lithuanians, they noticeably decreased the German majority. By 1928 the number of Jews in the Memel Territory already totaled 4,500—most of them, therefore, were new arrivals.[28] This influx occurred against the background of the city's rapid development, which grew from 20,884 inhabitants in 1918 to 47,412 as of 1 January 1936.[29]

How did the relationships between the various population groups develop in the 1920s and 1930s? Important areas in this respect were professional and neighborly environments, as well as schools and associations. But as was already the case prior to the First World War, Jewish-German-Lithuanian contacts took place primarily in business. Jewish merchants and entrepreneurs played a particularly large role in important sectors like the lumber trade, flax exports, fertilizer imports, the local foodstuffs and indulgence foods industry, but also in tobacco processing and the textile industry.[30] According to a government overview, in 1931 the city of Memel had 471 stores, of which 119 (25 percent) were owned by Jews. Of the city's 151 industrial operations, 31 (20 percent) belonged to Jews; there were also additional operations with mixed ownership.[31] In total, in Memel during the period between 1925 and 1935, Lithuanian Jews founded nine cotton and wool weaving companies, including what would later be the city's largest employer, Israelit & Co., Litauische Garn-Manufaktur "Liverma."

Jewish merchants and entrepreneurs also held important positions in professional associations, such as the Memel Chamber of Commerce, whose vice president was Nathan Nafthal. The Chamber of Commerce appointed the long-time head of the Jewish community, Kommerzienrat (counselor of commerce) Leopold Alexander, as an honorary member.[32] The banks owned by Efim Konikoff and Feiwel Jawschitz played an important role in the city, as did the Jüdische Volksbank (Jewish Volksbank) founded in 1925, which by 1929 already had more than 300 members. The extent of the Jewish merchants' and industrialists' influence on the city's economy became clear when in 1938 they began relocating their businesses to Lithuania or abroad.[33]

Another area where Jews and Christians encountered each other was school. Traditionally, the city's Jewish children—regardless of their origins—attended German schools; the boys, for example attended the Luisen Gymnasium, the girls the Auguste-Viktoria Lyceum. In contrast, the Lithuanian high school had very few Jewish students. Jews' memories of school varied. Maurice Hillmann, whose family had previously lived in Penza in the Soviet Union during the evacuation, recalled good times: "In Memel I had a happy youth: good teachers, good friends, lots of sports in Jewish sports clubs, good music teachers of Polish descent. . . ."[34] Cherie Goren (Sara Fleischmann) noted: "My sister Fanny and I went to a German school. . . . We memorized Goethe and Schiller. We sang song [sic] by Heinrich Heine. . . . A great portion of Jews identified with the Germans and their culture."[35] Hilde Sturmann (nee Nafthal), who also attended the Auguste-Viktoria Lyceum, recalls her friends including many "German girls."[36] Trudi Birger, who arrived in Memel from Frankfurt already in 1933, reports: "I cannot recall having experienced any anti-Semitic incidents in school, even though we Jewish students were few. The teachers treated us fairly."[37] Other Jews, especially from families who had arrived during the interwar periods, remembered having experienced anti-Semitism even as children. They did not make any non-Jewish friends and were not invited to birthday parties.[38] Thus fine distinctions obtained between long-established and immigrant Jews in Memel society.

In the 1930s, the climate in the schools changed dramatically. German children became involved in German nationalist groups. To be sure, a Hitler Youth per se was not yet officially permitted, yet bandwagon effects were undeniable.[39] In response, the Jewish children, too, drew closer together. In 1936—against the explicit opposition of both the Directorate and the German-oriented Jews—the Jewish primary school Tarbut was founded, based on the model of a widespread network of schools in Lithuania; its language of instruction was Hebrew.[40]

Non-Jews and Jews also encountered each other in veterans' organizations, such as the Memel Warriors' Association (Kriegerverein Memel), as well as at sporting events. Yet the extent to which Jews belonged to non-Jewish sports clubs is unknown. The Jewish associations, on the other hand, were well known and respected. Their members not only ranked among the leaders at large sports events such as the Memelland championships, but also participated in the Maccabiah Games, the Olympics for Jewish athletes.[41] In 1935, the fifteenth anniversary of the Bar Kochba sports club, where German and Lithuanian Jews practiced sports, was celebrated with a large party. The successful club must have been an annoyance for many non-Jews.[42] Other locally conspicuous features of Jewish social life in Memel included the Hanukkah festivities in the *Schützenhaus* (shooting club clubhouse) and the large formal dances held at the *Schützenhaus* and the Hotel Victoria—at the time, the city's most preeminent establishment—on Purim and other Jewish holidays.[43] In the mid 1930s, the Bar Kochba began quite deliberately to stage-manage its presence in the city through sports festivals and parades, thereby temporarily reclaiming the public space for Jews.

Memel's synagogue congregation, naturally, played a central role Jewish life. Its rights continued to be based in the Prussian law "on the circumstances of the Jews" of 23 July 1847, combined with additional clauses from the autonomy legislation of 1924. Thus congregation employees were subordinate to the Directorate, which also paid their salaries. In actual fact, two Jewish factions existed in the Memel community: a German-oriented faction and an orthodox faction whose members supported Agudat Israel.[44] This traditional party fought against the Zionists as well as generally all modernization efforts. After Lithuania annexed the Memel Territory, the Zionists soon comprised the majority in Memel's Jewish community, which until that point had predominantly been German-Jewish.[45]

Even though the influence of the Lithuanian Jews grew and they constituted a numerical majority by the end of the 1920s, Memel's Jewish society retained its German character. Many felt themselves drawn to German culture, notwithstanding the growing pervasiveness of National Socialism. Numerous recollections indicate that a diverse Jewish life developed in Memel during the interwar period. Economically, many of Memel's inhabitants were doing well and the city flourished in a liberal climate. It was a heyday in Memel's cultural life that benefited every segment of the population.

The Memel Jews received the first reports of growing anti-Semitism in the German Reich from neighboring East Prussia even before Hitler took over power, when East Prussian students, expelled in 1933 from Königsberg University because they were Jews, arrived in Memel as refugees.[46] But by 1934, the first daubings of swastikas and words like "Memel awake!" appeared on Jewish businesses, windows, and fences.[47] The German Consulate General began to harass the Jews. Thus, for example, instead of receiving his requested multiple-entry visa, Consul Nafthal was now only issued single-entry visas for the German Reich and was monitored by the Gestapo.[48] In 1935, National Socialists in Memel were charged with hooliganism, evoking reactions very similar to those in the Reich not only from Memelland's National Socialist newspapers but from Lithuanian newspapers as well. They declared that the accused were "victims of a Jewish conspiracy," since Jewish judges and Jewish state attorneys participated in this criminal case. News of the introduction of the Nuremberg Laws in Germany also aggrieved the Jews in Memel.[49] In the same year, Reich German authorities prohibited German traders from traveling to Memel's annual market.[50] The Memel Jews began rethinking their relationship to Germandom. Against the background of National Socialist policies and their impact on the Memel Territories, most of them neither could nor wanted to maintain the commitment to German nationality.[51] A more and more vigorous Zionist identity developed predominantly among members of the younger generation, who increasingly lent their intellectual and financial support to local Jewish organizations. On the occasion of the Jewish holidays in fall 1936, all of Memel's Jewish stores made a show of closing their doors, which had never happened in Memel before.[52]

Many began preparing to leave. The Memel Jews cultivated far-reaching contacts with relatives, friends, and professional associates in Germany, Latvia, Lithuania, and much further afield. Cherie Goren reported on one of her father's trips in 1936: "He returned from England, after meeting Aunt Rachel from America, and announced papers were being prepared for us."[53] Her family finally left Memel in November 1938 after they heard about the pogrom in Germany.[54] Quite a few Jews, however, especially those who had fought for Germany during the First World War, still placed confidence in their democratic rights. Cherie Goren remembered things this way as well: "The whole town was German, even the Jews. My Uncle Nahnny, who fought for the Kaiser and earned the Iron Cross, said that they wouldn't bother us and were only after the *Ostjuden*. Everybody seemed to agree, except my Papa."[55]

Jewish families that had arrived after 1923 rarely made any escape plans. As a rule, they assumed that, if necessary, they could return to Lithuania.[56] On 26 February 1937, the Memel city council passed a law restricting the professional practice of Jewish judges. Synagogue windows were now being repeatedly smashed. In the summer, German youths attacked young Jewish vacationers in the village of Schwarzort (Juodkrantė) on the Curonian Spit, a long-time favorite vacation destination among Jews. That same year, ten Jewish students at the business school and Memel's pedagogical institute became victims of assaults by Lithuanian students. The German propaganda also influenced the Lithuanians; they fully admired the "modern" Germans, who dared to formulate their anti-Semitic attitude so clearly. Of course, this admiration also tied into premodern Lithuanian anti-Semitism, which was strongly shaped by Catholicism. A letter written by the Jewish Memel resident Erna Segalowitz, the wife of a flax dealer, to her sister in New York in May 1938 also reflected the city's menacing mood: "If only one could live a little more peacefully here. Particularly these days, one is in dreadful uncertainty. What will happen?"[57]

In fall 1938, the situation worsened for the Memel Jews, as Germans daubed swastikas on Jewish businesses and prevented shoppers from entering Jewish stores. After the Munich Agreement, whose signatories were identical with those that signed the Memel Convention, fears that there might be a National Socialist putsch in Memel intensified—Jews began to emigrate, some to Lithuania, others to other countries.[58] On 1 November 1938, under pressure by German politicians, the Lithuanian government had to end the state of emergency—which had been in effect for twelve years—and press censorship. To celebrate this occasion, supporters of the Socialist People's Community's leader Neumann assembled for a torchlight procession and a rally. The Memel German Security Service (Memeldeutsche Ordnungsdienst), modeled on the SA, was founded a few days later, whereupon it soon marched through Memel. Also in November, 30,000 Memel residents participated in an event commemorating the "savior of East Prussia" Paul von Hindenburg. Viewing these developments with trepidation, many Jews now resolved to emigrate. In November alone, they withdrew 2.5 million litas from the city's banks.[59] The feverish search for emigration opportunities began, but for most applicants it was already too late, since many countries had already imposed a visa ban or instituted long waiting lists.

Lithuanians encouraged Jews to vote Lithuanian in the 11 December 1938 Landtag elections with the following text:

> Jewish Citizens! One-hundred-and-ten Jewish cemeteries have been devastated by Hitler gangs in Germany! This does not happen in Lithuania. Fifty synagogues have been defiled by Hitler gangs in Germany, and not in Lithuania. Lithuanians were not the ones who drew off the blood of Jewish merchants in Übermemel [a community in Kreis Pogegen (Pagėgiai)]. Hitler-minded persons want to displace the Jews, not Lithuanians. Jews work for Lithuanian authorities and for the commandant in Memel. Rathenau, a Jewish minister in Germany, was blindly murdered in cowardly fashion by Hitler gangs. Therefore, Jews, eyes open! Elect list 3![60]

Nonetheless, the Memel German list, with Neumann as its lead candidate and invoking the German *Volksgemeinschaft* in its campaign, won almost 87 percent of the ballots cast, with a voter participation rate of 96.8 percent,[61] which thus delivered Memel into German hands, so to speak. Official incorporation with the German Reich now seemed to be only a matter of time.

By 1 December 1938, the Directorate had already prohibited all closeout sales, yet the dissolution of Jewish businesses increased.[62] The headline of a newspaper in Kovno soon read: "Jewish firms are being liquidated in Klaipėda."[63] In her memoirs, a merchant's wife recalled:

> In Memel, the National Socialistic character revealed itself more and more. Increasingly, in the streets one heard the demands to throw off the Lithuanian yoke, to join with the Führer; Nazi songs were sung very loudly. For us Jews, these were certainly not pleasant sounds. Having many female friends among Christian Memel women, I had to notice that some of them turned their heads away so as not to greet me. But I have by no means forgotten that a few them—because I myself now turned my head away—called out "good day" to me and stopped me, in order to show that in their eyes I was still the same person. My sixteen-year-old daughter, who is blonde and blue-eyed, was often called out to by young people: "Heil Hitler, come to the Ferdinandplatz today, there will be an assembly." That very much frightened me. At the time, my husband had already travelled on business to England and he no longer returned. I had to make all of the decisions.[64]

For this Memel resident as well, in the end her only option was escaping to Lithuania.[65]

The First Weeks of the Annexation

In 1938, 6,000 Jews lived among Memel's 51,000 inhabitants—that is, 12.5 percent; by 1939 their numbers had even increased to 7,000 (14 percent).[66] Of course, the actual total figure can no longer be determined because of immense fluctuations. Approximately 9,000 Jews are said to have left the Memel Territories in 1939 alone.[67] Since Jewish emigration from the region had already demonstrably started in 1938, the reasons why the number of Jewish inhabitants for early 1939 nonetheless initially increased must be reexamined. Presumably, many Jews only stayed in the city temporarily to complete their requisite Hachscharah training for emigration to Palestine. In addition, probably hundreds of refugees from Germany and Austria lived in Memel prior to the annexation.[68]

In early 1939, more than half of Memel's Jews left the city and moved chiefly to western Lithuanian villages and towns such as Palanga (Polangen), Krėtinga (Crottingen), Darbėnai, Jurbarkas (Georgenburg), Tauragė (Tauroggen), Šiauliai (Schaulen), and Kovno. They brought with them from Memel assets valued at an estimated 100 million litas.[69] In 1939, Memel's Jewish residents still operated 330 factories and enterprises—grain and lumber mills; textile, soup, cigarette, and chocolate manufacturing facilities; breweries; amber processing workshops, and more—employing 70 percent of the Memel workforce. The estimated value of Jewish assets prior to reincorporation with the German Reich totaled 300 million pounds sterling.[70] Many Jews sold their property cheaply to Germans. As evidence increased that the city and region would soon be annexed by Germany, almost all of Memel's remaining Jews fled to Lithuania. The first refugees probably included the city's wealthiest Jews; they were able to move their entire movable assets into safety without any problems. Later, as capital flight increased, the Memel authorities placed obstacles in their way and demanded special export permits. Finally, in early December 1938 they generally prohibited the export of property.[71]

Germany incorporated the Memel Territory on 22 March 1939. The move had been preceded by an ultimatum presented two days earlier by the German government to the Lithuanian Foreign Minister Juozas Urbšys during his passage through Berlin. After deliberations by the Lithuanian Cabinet, on 22 March Lithuania concluded a treaty with Germany on the return of Memelland.[72] SS and police units advanced into Memel on 23 March, even before the Wehrmacht.[73] On the same day, Adolf Hitler—on board the pocket battleship *Deutschland* en route to

Memel—issued the Law on the Reunification of Memelland with the German Reich, effective retroactively as of 22 March 1939.[74] After arriving in Memel, the Reich Chancellor gave an address from the theater balcony facing the Theaterplatz. Cheering Germans, including SA men and Hitler Youth members brought in from nearby East Prussia, above all from Tilsit, crowded into the city, with swastika flags visible everywhere.[75]

Erich Koch, Oberpräsident (Upper President) of East Prussia, functioned as the Überleitungskommissar (transition commissar) for the time being, with Neumann as his deputy.[76] Memelland became a part of the German Reich, effective immediately, and was henceforth subordinate to the Gumbinnen Regierungspräsident (Government District President) Dr. Herbert Rohde, whose East Prussian administrative district absorbed Memelland on 1 April 1939.[77] Use of the term "Memelland" was henceforth prohibited. On 1 May 1939, Reich law in its entirety took effect in the Memel Territory. The Lithuanian authorities and their representatives hastily left the city. East Prussian institutions dispatched delegates in order to reinstate German institutions, often merely integrating the Memel Territory into existing East Prussian structures.[78]

The new power relations had a prompt and serious impact on the Jewish population. By order of the new National Socialist rulers, the last remaining Jews had to leave the city within fourteen days, with local authorities threatening to arrest those who wanted to remain.[79] On 23 March 1939, under the headline "Swastika Flags over Memelland," the *Völkischer Beobachter* reported:

> In the early morning already, two trains overfilled with Jews departed Memel once more; yesterday evening a train likewise left Memel that was so overfilled with Jews that some of the passengers stood on the running boards. The population of Memel gave these Jewish freeloaders, under whose influence it has suffered for decades, their farewell. Upon news of the large flight of the Jews, thousands of people appeared at the train station, and the numerous taxis that arrived, packed with household goods, bedding, etc. were greeted with all kinds of hilarious acclamations. Groups of chanters formed on the railway platform, calling to the Jews: "We wish you a good trip and never-see-you-again!" or "Travel to Abraham!" etc.[80]

In 1958, on the other hand, Dr. Wilhelm Brindlinger, a Memel-German jurist who held the post of Memel's Oberbürgermeister from 1931 to 1934 and from 1936 to 1944, testified the following as a witness in the Ulm Einsatzgruppen trial in response to questions regarding the relationship of the city's population with the Jews: "This outflow [that is, the flight of the Jews from Memel; R.L.] lasted around ten days. I was proud of the fact that during this departure, the Memel residents comported themselves with dignity and without hatefulness. In my opinion, not a single person was molested"[81] (see figure 5.1).

For Memel Jews who had fled to Lithuania, in spring 1939 the only other escape opportunities still available involved faraway destinations like the United States, Canada, or South Africa. None of the countries neighboring Lithuania would have provided safe emigration opportunities. Matters were made worse by the fact that, after the Third Reich had annexed the Memel Territory, Lithuania no longer had any harbors that would have enabled Jewish emigrants to choose sea routes to other countries. The outbreak of war in September intensified the problem of obtaining visas. Most of the Memel refugees crowded into the Lithuanian capital of Kovno, which was already accommodating Jewish emigrants from the German Reich, Austria, and the Czechoslovak Republic. Beset by immense helplessness, the refugees searched hectically for alternatives; above all, they needed new passports, for their Memelland papers became invalid at the end of 1939.[82]

On 23 March 1939—the day after the annexation—the Reich government issued a law stipulating that Memellanders who on 30 July 1924 had been Lithuanian citizens and on 22 March 1939 resided in the Memel Territories or in Germany were once again members of the German state.[83] In late March 1939, the Lithuanian foreign ministry instructed its embassy in Berlin, as well as the consulate in Memel and consular general in Königsberg, that no papers for entry into Lithuania were to be issued to Memellanders who were now deemed to be Germans "and are not Aryans."[84]

While emigration opportunities for Memelland Jews steadily deteriorated, the Memel authorities endeavored to transfer the German Reich's anti-Jewish legislation to the Memel Territory as quickly as possible, focusing initially on the "Aryanization" of Jewish property. On 27 March 1939, Willy Betke, a former Landtag and Directorate member, began acting as the "Trustee for Jewish Property in the City of Memel."[85] On 30 March 1939, the *Memeler Dampfboot* newspaper already announced the introduction of the Reich German ordinance on the registration of Jewish property, and all Jews still living in the city were ordered to surrender any precious metals and jewelry by 31 May. These radical measures prompted the last fifty or so remaining Jews to leave the city and the territory.[86]

Figure 5.1. Expulsion of Jews from Memel, spring 1939. *Source:* Ullstein-Image, image no: 53578

The Period of the Occupation

With the German annexation of the Memel Territory, the Lithuanian government's attitude changed, because State President Antanas Smetona became personally involved on behalf of the Jews. The Lithuanians now introduced measures to protect the Jews as much as possible from the Germans' grasp. As part of the negotiations for a German-Lithuanian treaty on the state membership of the Memellanders—signed on 9 July 1939 in Kovno—both parties finally agreed that all persons seeking Lithuanian citizenship could apply for such citizenship until 31 December 1939; this regulation also applied for Memelland Jews. Many took advantage of this opportunity, since they wanted to avoid German state membership at all costs. However, the regulation did not apply for Jews who had already been German citizens prior to August 1914.[87] This affected approximately 180 people, who jointly applied to the Lithuanian government for an exceptional regulation,[88] whereupon fifty of them, at any rate, obtained Lithuanian citizenship.[89]

In 1939/40, the Lithuanian passport still afforded Jews a certain degree of protection against the German Reich. Reich German revenue offices demanded that various Memel residents, including the Jewish businessmen Siegfried Rudeitzki and Nathan Nafthal, pay the Reich Flight Tax, issuing tax warrants. In Nafthal's case, the revenue office withdrew its claims after he was granted Lithuanian citizenship. In summer 1939, a number of Jews returned once more to Memel to collect their moveable belongings,[90] while various merchants dissolved their stores from Lithuania. However, entrepreneurs and store owners who fled from Memelland communities such as Heydekrug and Pogegen—and who did not apply for Lithuanian passports—were expropriated on the basis of the Reich's applicable laws, and their assets were managed by the Deutsche Allgemeine Treuhand GmbH in Königsberg or its subsidiaries in Memel.[91]

During the negotiations regarding the regulation of the Memellanders' state citizenship in summer 1939, the Germans complied with the Lithuanian desire to provide relief for persons affected by property issues. This regulation impacted primarily the property of Jews in the city of Memel. In this connection, in July 1939 the Reich Economics Minister instructed the Gumbinnen Regierungspräsident that "during the liquidation taking place of Lithuanian Jewish assets in Memelland . . . sufficient time for liquidation must be allowed" for the owners, since the "fulfillment of this commitment by the German government is indispensable for the undisrupted implementation of the German-Lithuanian economic agreements. . . ."[92] Therefore, the minister continued, Jews were to be treated as Lithuanian state citizens if any doubt prevailed regarding their state citizenship.

The German government showed unusual restraint in this matter, a fact that was met with incomprehension in Memel. In early January 1942, the authorities in Memel criticized:

> Upon the repatriation [*Heimkehr*] of the Memel Territory, the owners of the Jewish land parcels fled almost without exception, and their whereabouts cannot be determined; their assets are considered enemy assets . . . [;] this legal situation now results in that the developed property is deteriorating, since the appointed trustees (Treuhand GmbH and Finanzamt [revenue office] Memel) do not have sufficient maintenance funds at their disposal. In many cases, the rents are insufficient for this purpose. Beyond that, the renters are complaining that nothing is being done on their apartments and buildings.[93]

Thus far we have no knowledge about the continued operation of enterprises under trustee management. In any event, by this time, many of the Jewish owners who had fled to Kovno had already been murdered.

After Lithuania had granted the Red Army the right to station troops on its territory in fall 1939, the Soviet occupation in July 1940 came as no surprise. Stalin quickly arranged for the appointment of a new government and had the country declared a Soviet republic. All diplomatic missions in Kovno were promptly closed. Memelland Jews who had just recently received Lithuanian passports were deprived of all emigration opportunities. From August 1940 to May 1941, only foreigners or stateless persons were permitted to leave the Lithuanian Socialist Soviet Republic.[94] In the fall, Soviet documents replaced the Lithuanian passports. Their new passports, under the category of nationality (a feature common to the passports of all Soviet citizens), registered the Memel Jews as "Jew." Thus they were clearly "marked" in their new environment as well.

As early as 23 June 1941—thus even before the arrival of the first Wehrmacht combat units—pogroms lasting several days erupted in Kovno, during which Lithuanian partisans murdered an unknown number of Jews, including many men who had come from Memel.[95] The role played by Memel Jews in Kovno's society remains unclear. Was the population aware of them as a collective or not?[96] By mid August 1941, the German occupiers had constructed a ghetto in Kauen (as Kovno/Kaunas was renamed by the Germans during the occupation) for all the Jews. The inmates had to perform forced labor. Beginning in late November 1941, murder operations were conducted at various intervals.[97] As the front approached in summer 1944, the Kaunas ghetto was finally liquidated, with the women being sent to Stutthof and the men to Dachau. Most did not survive the end of the war in the unbearable prison conditions of these concentration camps.[98]

Back in Heydekrug, at the end of 1941 the local SS, on its own initiative, had established a work camp for Jews recruited by means of "procurement operations" in nearby small Lithuanian towns. The Jewish forced laborers were used predominantly in peat production and road construction. In spring 1943, the SS dissolved the illegal camp, deporting its inmates to Auschwitz.[99]

Conclusion

As a result of the Treaty of Versailles, Memel admittedly lost its geographical position as a border town; but simultaneously, for the first time in the city's history, Jews were able to migrate to the town without restrictions. During the interwar period, Jews settled primarily for economic reasons, whereby Jewish migration to Memel—referred to as

Klaipėda by the Lithuanians—was also supported by the Lithuanian state. It should be noted that during the interwar period, Jews in the Memel Territory lived largely undisturbed for almost two decades in the wind shadow of the German-Lithuanian disputes. Germans and Lithuanians were evidently so fixated on each other that for a long time they largely ignored the Jews, who formed the next largest group of inhabitants. In the process, the economic involvement of Jewish immigrants in the interwar period contributed to the city's economic boom. Only in 1930s, under the influences of the Nazi regime in the German Reich, did Memel residents appear to perceive their Jewish fellow citizens differently. The Lithuanian administration temporarily halted the effects of National Socialist ideas, which were now quickly migrating from the Reich over the largely open border to Memel. Nonetheless, in the 1930s the city gradually became less attractive for Jews, as the increase of National Socialist influences in the city and region became more obvious and the Jewish community no longer had any prospects there.

After the annexations of Austria and the Sudetenland by the Reich, a *Heim-ins-Reich* euphoria also began developing in fall 1938 among Memel Germans. The German Memel authorities endeavored on their own initiative to align their Jewish policies as quickly as possible with those of the Reich's Nazi government. With Lithuania's cancellation of the state of emergency in the Memel Territory and the subsequent pro-German electoral results, all prospects vanished for local Jewish society. Thus for thousands of Memel Jews, escape, usually to Lithuania, remained the only option. After the annexation was completed in March 1939, the German authorities plundered the few remaining Jews of their entire existence and extended the Reich's anti-Semitic legislation to the territory. In any event, hardly any alternatives remained. The nearby path across the border to Lithuania soon proved to be a dead end. Already by 1940, the Soviet occupation policy thwarted any further plans for the Memelland Jews to establish themselves or flee. After the German invasion of the USSR on 22 June 1941, the Nazis also quickly implemented their National Socialist policies of persecution and extermination in Lithuania, claiming most of the former Jewish inhabitants of the Memel Territory among their victims.

Notes

1. Ernst-Albert Plieg, *Das Memelland 1920–1939: Deutsche Autonomiebestrebungen im litauischen Gesamtstaat* (Würzburg, 1962); on the Memel Territory, see also

Petronėlė Žostaustaitė, *Klaipėdos kraštas 1923–1939* (Vilnius, 1992), which has a German summary.
2. *Treaty of Peace with Germany* (New York, 1919), Article 99.
3. Henry de Chambon, *La Lituanie moderne* (Paris, 1933), 83. For more detail see Joachim Tauber, *Die deutsch-litauischen Beziehungen im 20. Jahrhundert* (Lüneburg, 1993).
4. Gerhard Willoweit, *Die Wirtschaftsgeschichte des Memelgebietes*, 2 vols. (Marburg, 1969).
5. Walter Schätzel, *Das Reich und das Memelland: Das politische und völkerrechtliche Schicksal des deutschen Memellandes bis zu seiner Heimkehr* (Berlin, 1943), 107.
6. Christian-Alexander Schröder, "Die Entstehung des 'Territoire de Memel' und die Pläne der französischen Administration (1919–1923)," *Nordost-Archiv* 10 (2001): 45–74.
7. Friedrich Janz, *Die Entstehung des Memelgebietes: Zugleich ein Beitrag zur Entstehungsgeschichte des Versailler Vertrags* (Berlin, 1928), 74-78.
8. *Denkschrift der wirtschaftlichen Körperschaften und Verbände zur Selbständigkeit des Memelgebietes* (Memel, 1921); Schröder, "Entstehung," 51.
9. Karl Heinz Ruffmann, "Deutsche und litauische Memelpolitik in der Zwischenkriegszeit: Ein Vergleich," *Nordost-Archiv* 2 (1993): 217–234.
10. Vytautas Žalys, "Das Memelproblem in der litauischen Außenpolitik (1923–1939)," *Nordost-Archiv* 2 (1993): 235–278.
11. Ibid., 249–255; on the occupation of the Memel Territory, see Vygantas Vareikis, "Klaipėdos krašto užemimas," in *1923 metų sausio įvykiai Klaipėdoje*, ed. Klaipėdos Universiteto Vakarų Lietuvos ir Prūsijos istorijos centras (Klaipėda, 1995). The anthology deals with the events in Memel in 1923, but it does not provide any German or English summaries.
12. In 1920, Polish irregulars under General Lucjan Żeligowski had occupied the Vilnius region (which was also claimed by Lithuania). This allowed Poland to officially deny any responsibility.
13. Žalys, "Memelproblem," 258. See also Niels Joeres, *Der Architekt von Rapallo: Der deutsche Diplomat Ago von Maltzan im Kaiserreich und in der frühen Weimarer Republik* (diss., Ruprecht-Karls-Universität, Heidelberg, 2006) 240ff; http://www.ub.uni-heidelberg.de/archiv/6751 (accessed 12 November 2009).
14. Joachim Tauber, "Das Memelgebiet (1919–1944) in der deutschen und litauischen Historiographie nach 1945," *Nordost-Archiv* 10 (2001): 11–44, here 16.
15. Rudolfas Valsonokas, *Klaipėdos problema: Fotografuotinis leidinys* (Vilnius, 1989), 273.
16. British Empire, France, Italy, Japan, and Lithuania. Convention concerning the Territory of Memel, signed at Paris, 8 May 1924. http://www.worldlii.org/int/other/treaties/LNTSer/1924/194.pdf (accessed 13 April 2013); Valsonokas, *Klaipėdos problema*, 268.
17. Joachim Tauber, "Das Dritte Reich und Litauen 1933–1940," in *Zwischen Lübeck und Novgorod: Wirtschaft, Politik und Kultur im Ostseeraum vom frühen Mittelalter bis ins 20. Jahrhundert*, ed. Ortwin Pelc and Gertrud Pickhan (Lüneburg, 1996), 477ff.; Martin Broszat, "Die memeldeutschen Organisationen und der Nationalsozialismus," *Vierteljahrshefte für Zeitgeschichte* 5 (1957): 273–278.
18. See Ernst Rademacher, "Bericht über die Lage im Memelland vom 25.4.1933," *The Historical Journal* 39 (1996): 780–783.
19. Vareikis, "Klaipėdos krašto," 69.
20. Ruth Leiserowitz, *Sabbatleuchter und Kriegerverein: Juden in der ostpreußisch-litauischen Grenzregion 1812–1942* (Osnabrück, 2010), 287ff.

21. Josef Rosin, *Preserving Our Litvak Heritage: A History of 31 Jewish Communities in Lithuania* (League City, 2005), 98.
22. See *Treaty of Peace between the Allied and Associated Powers and Germany, and Protocol: signed at Versailles, June 28, 1919* (Ottawa, 1919).
23. For the years 1919 to 1923, the files of the Prussian Interior Ministry include only one application by a Jewish family from Memel. Records of other Memel citizens who demonstrably obtained German citizenship during this period cannot be found. This suggests that authorities in Memel made decisions separately and kept their own files.
24. Willoweit, *Wirtschaftsgeschichte*, vol. 2, 747ff.
25. Valsonokas, *Klaipėdos problema*, 270 (*nepatikimai mazas* means incredibly small).
26. Julius Žukas, "Soziale und wirtschaftliche Entwicklung Klaipėdas/Memels von 1900 bis 1945," *Nordost-Archiv* 10 (2001): 75–115; Claudia Sinnig, "Fluchtpunkt Klaipėda: Litauische Literaturen im Klaipėda der dreißiger Jahre," *Nordost-Archiv* 10 (2001): 279–306, here 287; Valsonokas, *Klaipėdos problema*, 275.
27. Interview with Itzchak Lipmann (Memel/Tel Aviv), 5 March 2004, Archive of the Verein Juden in Ostpreußen e.V. (JOP); interview with Mika Meller (Memel/Tel Aviv), 16 August 2003, JOP.
28. Joseph Shulman, "Memel," Mendel Sudarski and Uriah Katzenelenbogen, *Lite* (New York, 1951), 282; Valsonokas, *Klaipėdos problema*, 273.
29. Rosin, *Preserving Our Litvak Heritage*, 100.
30. Eginhard Walter, *Das Memelgebiet: Bevölkerung und Wirtschaft eines Grenzlandes* (Königsberg, 1939), 80.
31. Ibid., 82.
32. *Die Selbstverwaltung der Kaufmannschaft in Memel von ihren Anfängen bis zur Gegenwart aus Anlass ihres ersten Jahrzehnts der Industrie- und Handelskammer für das Memelgebiet 1919–1929* (Memel, 1929), 141.
33. Walter, *Memelgebiet*, 137.
34. Letter Maurice Hillmann to Ulla Lachauer, 17 July 1989, JOP.
35. Cherie Goren, *A Time To Keep: Grammy Cherie's Story* (Merion Station, 1999), 12.
36. Interview with Hilde Sturmann, née Nafthal (Memel/Jerusalem), 15 August 2003, JOP.
37. Trudi Birger, *Im Angesicht des Feuers: Wie ich der Hölle des Konzentrationslagers entkam* (Munich, 2002), 35.
38. Interview with Dora Love née Rabinowitz, Yad Vashem, 03/7504.
39. Ibid.
40. Lietuvos Centrinis Valstybės Archyvas (Lithuanian Central State Archive; LCVA), Vilnius, f. 378, Ap. 3, B. 3426, p. 140 (17 April 1934). "Tarbut," the Hebrew word for culture, was a synonym for secular Zionistic education.
41. Interview with Dora Love née Rabinowitz, Yad Vashem, 03/7504.
42. "Wo blieben die Memeler Juden?," *Memeler Dampfboot* 6 (June 1985): 91.
43. Zita Genienė, "Gastronomie, Tourismus und Feste in Klaipėda im 19. und der ersten Hälfte des 20. Jahrhunderts," *Nordost-Archiv* 10 (2001): 211–234.
44. Agudat Israel (Hebrew: לארשי תדו) (Union of Israel), an Ashkenazi ultra-Orthodox party, emerged from the eponymous movement founded in 1912.
45. Shulman, "Memel," 283.
46. Hans Adam Sturmann, "Der rettende Hafen: Erinnerungen an die Hachschara in Memel," *Israel-Nachrichten*, 11 March 1977.
47. LCVA,f. 378, Ap. 3, B. 3426, p. 382 (16 March 1934).
48. Ibid., 154 (15 March 1934).
49. Interview with Rahel Itzigsohn (Memel/Tel Aviv), 3 March 2004, JOP.

50. Newspaper of the Reichsverband Ambulanter Gewerbetreibender Deutschlands: *Wochenzeitschrift für Marktfahrer, Hausierer, Neuheiten-Verkäufer, Schausteller, Markthändler, Markthallen-Standinhaber und Straßenhändler, Berlin und Pößneck*, no. 14 (6 April 1935).
51. Interview with Itzchak Lipmann (Memel/Tel Aviv), 5 March 2004.
52. *Di Yiddishe Shtime* (Kaunas), 5 October 1936.
53. Goren, *A Time To Keep*, 31.
54. Ibid., 40.
55. Ibid., 35.
56. Interview with Itzchak Lipmann (Memel/Tel Aviv), 5 March 2004.
57. Letter Erna Segalowitz to Margot Lepehne, 25 May 1938, private possession of Ivar Segalowitz.
58. Shulman, "Memel," 283.
59. Valstybinė duomenų apie valiutą, 29 November 1938, 100.
60. Rosin, *Preserving Our Litvak Heritage*, 101.
61. Plieg, *Das Memelland*, 101. On the election and its preparations, see Christian Rohrer, *Nationalsozialistische Macht in Ostpreußen* (Munich, 2006), 503–507.
62. *Amtsblatt des Memelgebietes* 1938, no. 125 (1 December 1938), no. 1.
63. *Lietuvos žinios*, 31 December 1938.
64. Yad Vashem, 0–33/2182 (under the name Joseph Karmisch).
65. Interview with Mimi Itzigsohn (Memel/Rechovot), 17 August 2003, JOP.
66. Shulman, "Memel," 282. Other sources state 9,000 Jews for Memel: Kurt Benjamin, "Zur Geschichte der Juden in Memel," *Aufbau* (18 March 1984).
67. Dov Levin, *The Litvaks: A Short History of the Jews in Lithuania* (Jerusalem, 2000), 184.
68. Mika Rabinowitz referred, as an example, to this sports teacher, Fritz Marcuse, who went from Berlin first to Kaunas, then to Memel, and in 1939 to Šiauliai; Interview with Mika Rabinowitz (Memel/Ramat Gan), 14 November 1999, JOP.
69. In 1939, 6 litas equaled approximately 1 U.S. dollar.
70. Shulman, "Memel," S. 282.
71. *Amtsblatt des Memelgebietes*, 1938 no. 125 (1 December 1938), no. 1.
72. RGBl. 1939 II, 608. On the *Heimkehr des Memelgebiets* (repatriation of the Memel Territory), see the relevant chapter in Rohrer, *Nationalsozialistische Macht in Ostpreußen*, 513–532.
73. Rohrer, *Nationalsozialistische Macht in Ostpreußen*, 514.
74. Gesetz über die Wiedervereinigung des Memellandes mit dem Deutschen Reich, RGBl. 1939 I, 559.
75. Interview with George Birman (Memel/New York), 3 April 2003, JOP.
76. Rohrer, *Nationalsozialistische Macht in Ostpreußen*, 515.
77. *Amtsblatt des Regierungsbezirkes Gumbinnen*, Memel edition from 1 April 1939, no. 2.
78. More on this trial in Rohrer, *Nationalsozialistische Macht in Ostpreußen*, 516–521.
79. "Memel Now a Fortress. Why Jews Must Go," *Manchester Guardian*, 17 April 1939.
80. *Völkischer Beobachter*, 23 March 1939, 1 (emphasis in the original).
81. Testimony of Dr. Wilhelm Brindlinger, Oberbürgermeister (ret.) in Memel since June 1931, Bundesarchiv (BArch) Ludwigsburg, II 207 AR-Z 15/58, vol. 1, fol. 151.
82. RGBl. 1939 II, 999.
83. Ibid.
84. Letter from 31 March 1939, LCVA,f. 383, Ap. 7, B. 2180, L. 178.
85. Rohrer, *Nationalsozialistische Macht in Ostpreußen*, 526.

86. Interview with Marion Landau (Memel/Rechovot), 17 August 2003, JOP. The register "Juden in Memel 1939" only has one identification card, namely, for Rebekka Kaplan, Friedrichsmarkt 18/19, 61 years old, issued by the Ernährungs- und Wirtschaftsamt der Stadt Memel (Nutrition and Economics Office of the City of Memel); see LCVA,f. 645, Ap. 2, L 167. She was presumably the last Jew in Memel. Information regarding her future whereabouts is unavailable; neither is she registered in the Yad Vashem data bank.
87. Memorandum regarding Jews who have no right to Lithuanian citizenship, 13 August 1940, LCVA, R 1019, Ap. 1, B. 17, L. 38.
88. LCVA, R 1019, Ap.1, B. 17, L. 39. Anyone who relied on the opportunity of becoming stateless was viewed by the Lithuanians as lacking loyalty and encountered severe difficulties; see interview with Eva Glass née Maidenbaum (Memel/New York), 3 April 2004.
89. RGBl. 1939 II, 999.
90. Livio Isaak Sirovich, *Ihr Lieben, schreibt mir nicht alles: Eine jüdische Familie in Litauen 1935–1941* (Munich, 2001), 149. Originally, the Reichsfluchtsteuer introduced in 1931 was directed against the widespread capital flight from Germany; after 1933, however, the National Socialists used it specifically as an instrument of anti-Jewish policy. The tax became due when persons moved abroad, provided that the assets amounted to more than 200,000 Reichsmark and their annual earnings amounted to more than 20,000 Reichsmark.
91. "According to the resident registry, the Jewish merchant Mendel Kahn resided here in Pogegen since 9/7/1927. During the time of the reintegration of Memelland, he fled without deregistering, we do not know where. The business was transferred to German hands." LCVA,f. 1573, Ap. 6, B. 171, p. 10.
92. Reintegration of Memelland into the German Reich, letter of the Reich Economics Minister to the Government Region President Gumbinnen, 1 July 1939, Politisches Archiv des Auswärtigen Amtes (PA AA) Berlin, Deutsche Gesandtschaft Kaunas, p. 8.
93. Report no. 252 from 19 January 1942, in Heinz Boberach, ed., *Meldungen aus dem Reich: Die geheimen Lageberichte des Sicherheitsdienstes der SS 1938–1945*, vol. 9 (Herrsching, 1984), 3185f.
94. However, Germany meanwhile refused to issue transit visas for Jews who wanted to reach Palestine via Italy. See PA AA, DR 5, no. 36.
95. Yad Vashem Archives, Testimonies; Vincas Bartusevičius, Joachim Tauber, and Wolfram Wette, eds., *Holocaust in Litauen: Krieg, Judenmorde und Kollaboration im Jahre 1941* (Cologne, 2003).
96. Jürgen Matthäus, "Operation Barbarossa and the Onset of the Holocaust, June–December 1941," in *The Origins of the Final Solution: The Evolution of Nazi Jewish Policy, September 1939-March 1942*, ed. Christopher Browning (Lincoln, NE, 2007), 244–308. Documents in the Yad Vashem Archives prove that a large number of Jewish intellectuals from Memel were in the group that had already been murdered in June 1941. We will only be able determine whether the partisans selected them rather haphazardly or deliberately once the role of the Memel immigrants in Lithuania between the 1939 and 1941 has been more clearly described.
97. Wolfram Wette, "SS-Standartenführer Karl Jäger," in Bartusevičius et al, *Holocaust in Litauen*, 77–90, here 84.
98. Birger, *Im Angesicht des Feuers*; Solly Ganor (Sally Genkind), *Das andere Leben: Kindheit im Holocaust* (Frankfurt, 1997); Levin, *The Litvaks*, 217ff.
99. Leiserowitz, *Sabbatleuchter*, 369–387.

CHAPTER 6

DANZIG-WEST PRUSSIA
Wolfgang Gippert

As in other territories annexed by Germany during the Second World War, the "solution of the Jewish question" in Danzig-West Prussia developed in a continuous process. It began with the successive deprivation of the rights of Jews, combined with pogrom-like excesses and expulsions, and culminated in their collective expropriation, deportation, and murder. Because of the region's particular political-territorial situation in the interwar period—after 1918 in the course of reorganizing Central and Eastern Europe, Danzig (Gdańsk) was detached from Germany and proclaimed a "Free City" while most of West Prussia was allocated to the newly created Polish state—specific regional circumstances shaped the developments in this area, as they did in other annexed regions.

Thus, as a result of being forced to emigrate prior to the Free City's *Heimführung* (home bringing) into the "Greater German Reich," most of the German Jews in Danzig were able to save their own lives, whereas the Jews living in Polish territory—many of whom had emigrated from Eastern Europe—only managed to do so in what could only have been a few exceptional instances. On the other hand, the circle of people responsible for National Socialist Jewish policy resembled those in other annexed regions: along with members of the NSDAP leadership, the SA, and the SS, it also included Wehrmacht commanders and soldiers,

Figure 6.1. Anti-Semitic posters at the burned-out Danzig synagogue, 1939. *Source:* Getty Images no. 2628273

Einsatzgruppen and special units consisting of Gestapo, Security Police (Sicherheitspolizei; SiPo), and Order Police (Ordnungspolizei) that operated behind the front, paramilitary formations of the Volksdeutscher Selbstschutz (ethnic German self-defense force), as well as

German administration officials. Created in October 1939 as part of Nazi Germanization policies, the Reichsgau of Danzig-West Prussia came largely under the control of Albert Forster, the acting Gauleiter in Danzig since 1930. Forster set himself the ambitious goal of ethnically "cleansing" the Reichsgau so that he could declare Danzig-West Prussia to be the first of the newly created administrative units to be "Jew-free" and "Pole-free"[1] (see figure 6.1).

Prior to the Annexation

The development of the Jewish communities in Danzig-West Prussia since the eighteenth century was closely tied to changing political and constitutional circumstances; their histories were shaped by numerous migratory movements, especially in the nineteenth and twentieth centuries, which continuously altered both the size of these communities and their national and social composition.[2]

For a long time, the urban merchants and tradespeople living in the Hanseatic town of Danzig only granted Jews—their "bothersome competitors"—temporary residence rights. In contrast, Jews obtained settlement rights more easily in the surrounding villages under ecclesiastic, aristocratic, or royal rule, as well as in parts of the Polish aristocratic republic.[3] Danzig's magistrates did not abandon their restrictive policies until the eighteenth century when the economic situation of Danzig and the other Hanseatic towns steadily deteriorated, for they hoped that an increased influx of Jews, who were viewed as a key pillar of trade, would revive the economy. In 1792/93, following the first two partitions of Poland, the Prussian state incorporated Danzig along with other annexed Polish regions as the newly created province of West Prussia, resulting in multilayered changes for the Jewish communities, which, largely isolated from their non-Jewish surroundings, cultivated a religiously traditional way of life. When Prussian rule began, around 11,000 Jews lived in the formerly Polish Netze District, representing approximately 6 percent of the population. Around 3,600 Jews (1.1 percent) resided in the previously Prussian part of West Prussia, one-third of them in the suburbs of Danzig. In 1852, 24,447 Jews lived in West Prussia, accounting for 2.2 percent of the total population.[4]

In the nineteenth century, large parts of rural West Prussia lost almost all of their Jewish inhabitants, who either were expelled from their homeland or fled the oppressive poverty. Despite numerous immigrants from Eastern Europe, between 1871 and 1910 the Jewish population in West Prussia declined from 26,632 to 13,954.[5] Many of these Jews sought better living conditions in the larger, economically prosperous towns, leading to the progressive assimilation of these urban Jews into German society—for example, in Thorn (Toruń), Graudenz (Grudziądz), Elbing (Elbląg), and above all the harbor town of Danzig, which by the turn of the twentieth century had around 2,500 Jewish residents.[6]

At end of the First World War, the Jewish population in West Prussia underwent profound changes. Most of the West Prussian communities now belonged to the newly created Polish state, while the communities of Danzig, Zoppot (Sopot), Neuteich (Nowy Staw), and Tiegenhof (Nowy Dwór Gdański) henceforth lay in the Free City of Danzig. In the course of Europe's reorganization through the Treaty of Versailles, the Free City of Danzig was supposed to open a trade route to the Baltic for the newly created Polish state. The miniature state encompassed an area of approximately 1,950 square kilometers, bordering Poland in the south and west and Germany (East Prussia) in the east. Its population—the majority of the inhabitants were German and around 5 percent were Polish—increased from an original 360,000 to over 400,000 by 1929. The Free City received an independent constitution and government. However, under the protection of the League of Nations, the Free City of Danzig was linked politically and economically to the Polish state, a situation that proved a constant source of conflict during the interwar period.[7]

After the signing of the Versailles Treaty, hundreds of thousands of German inhabitants left the regions that had been ceded to Poland; the Jews, too, most of whom had opted for Germany, were drawn to the large German cities.[8] The influx of Jews from the regions of central and southern Poland fundamentally altered the internal structures of the Jewish communities, particularly in the Free City: above all, many Jews fled to Danzig from Russia and Poland during the revolutionary years to escape pogroms and poverty. During the interwar period, the harbor town, which lacked any immigration restrictions, developed into a gateway for large waves of Eastern European emigrants heading for the United States, Canada, and Palestine. In the period between 1920 and 1930, approximately 87,000 Jews emigrated via the port of Danzig. Some of the emigrants, however, remained in the Free City, which offered them economic prospects, leading to the steady growth of the local Jewish community.[9] Just a few years after the creation of the Free City, the number of eastern Jewish immigrants significantly exceeded that of the Jews native to Danzig.

The long-established Danzig Jews, many of whom worked in academia and commerce, were largely integrated into the German population. Religiously, they predominantly adopted reformist and liberal positions. Economically active Jews also figured among the immigrants: bankers and manufacturers, as well as shipping agents and wholesalers who played an important role above all in trading lumber, grain, and colonial goods. Most of the *Ostjuden* (eastern Jews), however, were destitute or low-income; they tried to support themselves as laborers, trade workers, or small-scale retailers.[10] Zionism played a dominant role in the immigrants' religious life, their poverty rendering them receptive to the idea of an independent Jewish state. They founded their own associations and organizations and published a Yiddish-language newspaper. However, the deep divide between the long-established German Jews and the newly arrived Russian and Polish Jews, between liberals and Zionists, persisted for a long time.[11]

As in other places, anti-Semitism had a long tradition in Danzig. The German Society for the Dissemination of Anti-Semitism in the Eastern Fatherland (Deutsche Gesellschaft zur Verbreitung des Antisemitismus im Osten des Vaterlandes) had established a local chapter in the harbor town early on, which held its first anti-Jewish rally in 1893.[12] Already by the turn of the century, anti-Jewish propaganda found a receptive audience within local military circles and lodges, as well as among conservative bourgeois officials and academics. In the 1920s, ethnic nationalist groups launched hate campaigns against the influx of Polish Jews into Danzig, which led to sustained conflict within the Jewish community between long-time residents and immigrants. Measured against the dismal situation in Poland, where the Jewish population suffered under excesses motivated by anti-Semitism,[13] the Free City, with its constitution guaranteed by the League of Nations, formed an island of freedom for the immigrants, despite Danzig's intensifying anti-Polish and anti-Jewish climate. But even the Jews native to the town, who viewed themselves as an inherent part of Danzig's German society, found themselves increasingly exposed to public hostility.

During the Versailles peace negotiations, Danzig's German population had protested against separating the town from Germany.[14] In the interwar period, the Free City's political culture was characterized by an underlying longing—but also very much by open demands—for reintegration into the "German"[15] that cut across all party lines and social strata. The NSDAP picked up on these sentiments. It managed to establish itself in Danzig as a mass party starting in the early 1930s, building on electoral votes from all social classes, occupational groups, and political camps, above all members of the so-called *alter Mittelstand*, namely, persons associated with small and mid-sized independently owned commercial, retail, and agricultural businesses.[16]

Right from the outset, Arthur Greiser played a role in the rise and consolidation of the NSDAP, the so-called *Gleichschaltung* (synchronization) and radicalization of public life in Danzig, and the expulsion of the Jews from the Free City.[17] In October 1930, Hermann Göring briefly commissioned him to provisionally administer the Danzig Gau, but the office was ultimately assigned to the 28-year-old Albert Forster.[18] With the arrival of the Gauleiter, who had been dispatched from the NSDAP Reichsleitung in Fürth, anti-Jewish propaganda in Danzig became more radical, with calls for boycotts against Jewish business, medical doctors, and lawyers being made publicly at assemblies, in the official party newspaper *Danziger Vorposten*, and on placards.[19]

After Hitler's seizure of power, the NSDAP won the Volkstag (the Free City's parliament) elections in May 1933. Under Head of State Hermann Rauschning,[20] Arthur Greiser became the Vice President of the Senate and at the same time the Senator for the Interior. The first National Socialist Senate pursued rather obscure policies against the Free City's Jews, who continued to play an important role in the Danzig's economic life. To avoid any Jewish counter-boycott, Rauschning, who as a farmer had himself been in business relationships with Jews, assured Jewish business leaders that all constitutional rights would be protected.[21]

In fact, Danzig had not yet undertaken an official legal approximation with the Reich, where on 7 April 1933 Jewish civil servants and employees had been expelled from a wide range of occupations, associations, and organizations. However, on 24 June 1933 the Danzig parliament passed an "enabling act"[22] that allowed the government to issue ordinances with the force of law in all administrative areas. In the following period, the government enacted a series of ordinances that admittedly did not explicitly target Jews but nonetheless paved the way for depriving the Jews in Danzig of their rights and gradually implemented an approximation with the legal situation in Germany.[23]

Just one week after the promulgation of the "enabling act," on 30 June 1933 authorities issued an ordinance to increase public security and order that included provisions regarding the laws governing associations, the banning of newspapers, and the newly introduced "protective custody," according to which individuals could be imprisoned up to three months without a court verdict.[24] An ordinance from

7 July 1933 stipulated that newly arriving medical doctors and dentists required official authorization in order to practice and that by the end of 1933 new arrivals would be completely banned from practicing.[25] In this way the Senate wanted to prevent the settlement of Jewish physicians who had lost their licenses in Germany. An ordinance from 14 July 1933 stipulated that notaries, who had previously been appointed by the judicial administration, would henceforth be appointed by a committee of NSDAP members. While not technically violating the constitution, this regulation nonetheless destroyed any prospects for Jews to be admitted to legal professions.[26] An ordinance from 4 August 1933 regarding professional associations under public law dissolved such existing chambers.[27] When the chamber committees were reorganized, Jews—some of whom had served for decades—were not reelected to their former positions. The Danzig Senate considered the dismissal of Jews from civil service positions to be a "state necessity." To avoid violating the constitution and applicable laws, the Nazis resorted to indirect methods, expelling the Jews from the public administration by restructuring agencies, ordering transfers, carrying out humiliations, and sometimes also by offering them settlements.[28]

The Danzig National Socialists tried in many ways to force the Jews out of their professions or at least make their lives difficult. Members of the NSDAP and its organizations were urged to no longer accept the assistance of Jewish doctors and lawyers and to sever their business relationships with Jews. They pressured companies and businesses to dismiss their Jewish workers and salaried employees. The Jews were also progressively shut out of Danzig's cultural life. After an ordinance from 11 August 1933 changed the city theater into a state theater, and the municipal administration dismissed all of the Jewish artists and employees working for the theater, the Zoppot Waldoper (forest opera), and radio station.[29] Editions of the *Danziger Echo*, a German-language Jewish newspaper, were repeatedly confiscated and the newspaper was finally banned in July 1936. Buildings that housed Jews and the facades of Jewish stores were smeared with insults such as "separatist sow" and "Juda die!" NSDAP Gauleiter Forster exploited every opportunity to publicly berate and degrade the Jewish citizenry. Jewish foreign trade companies formed an exception; because of their major economic importance for Danzig, they remained largely unmolested until 1936.[30]

These abuses, which affected German and Polish Jews alike, brought the various social classes and religious groups within Danzig's Jewish population together. In reaction to the anti-Jewish measures, the Jews established new organizations, primarily professional associations whose members united for the purpose of "self-defense."[31] Already created in summer 1933, the Association of Jewish Academics (Verein jüdischer Akademiker) filed numerous complaints with the Danzig government and later also appealed to the League of Nations. The Association of Jewish Employees (Vereinigung jüdischer Arbeitnehmer) developed into the organization with the largest membership. It sought to alleviate disputes between employers and employees; sometimes it also managed to negotiate severance settlements for terminated Jewish employees. Numerous Polish merchants, retailers, and tradespeople joined the newly founded Association of Jewish Business Operators and Trade Workers in the Free City of Danzig (Verband jüdischer Gewerbebetreibender und Handwerker in der Freien Stadt Danzig). The three abovementioned organizations elected a committee that also directed protest resolutions to the League of Nations in Geneva.[32]

The prohibition of the Catholic Center in October 1937 eliminated the last opposition party in Danzig and thus also any remnants of democracy in the Free City, after which National Socialist badgering of the Jews and the progressive deprivation of Jewish rights gave way to targeted violence against Jews. On 20 and 21 October 1937, by order of the Danzig Polizeipräsident (police president) Helmut Froböß, the police allocated the mostly Polish-Jewish traders at the weekly markets in Danzig, Langfuhr, and Zoppot to remote and isolated locations, where the traders were attacked and beaten and had their goods destroyed—presumably by out-of-uniform SA members—whereupon many of them returned to their home communities in Poland.[33] Two days later, violence erupted in the historical center of Danzig. Nazi gangs in plain clothes smeared the inscription "Jew" on stores, smashed windows, and destroyed or stole merchant displays. Around sixty Jewish stores and private residences were damaged, thirty of which were plundered. After these events, the Jewish community lodged strong protests with the Polizeipräsident, the Danzig Senate, and the acting local League of Nations commissioner, as well as with League of Nations via the Jewish World Congress. Nothing happened, however, because these agencies all contented themselves with pro forma repudiations by the competent authorities and assurances that the perpetrators, which included members of the SA and Hitler Youth, would be punished.[34]

Starting in fall 1937, other methods began being used as well in an effort to drive the Jews out of Danzig's economic life and thereby deprive them of their livelihoods.[35] In the course of the October excesses, the Gestapo arrested the director and senior executives of the Jewish

Public Bank on the charge of a currency offense. Many Jewish firms found themselves subject to tax audits lasting several weeks, which supposedly discovered "large irregularities." The often substantial tax arrears payments and penalties ruined some of the Jewish business owners. Other entrepreneurs were arrested on the suspicion of tax evasion and due to supposed flight risks; their assets and businesses were confiscated and "Aryanized." A report by the Senate Administration of the Free City of Danzig "on the matter of the exclusion of Jews from the economic life of the city" from 20 May 1939 lists the Jewish industrial companies and trading firms "Aryanized" since January 1938, including among others factories that produced paper, chocolate, vinegar, soap, paint, and amber products, as well as various textile retailers and wholesalers. In contrast, at the instigation of the Senate's Department of the Economy, a number of Jewish trading companies dealing in herring, lumber, grain, and furs that used Danzig not as a sales market but as a port of transit were initially placed on a "Jewish protection list," since by providing foreign currency they greatly benefited the city's economy.[36]

In sum, from the National Socialist perspective, the anti-Jewish excesses and repressive measures accomplished their intended goal. During the first large wave of emigration, which began in fall 1937, almost half of the more than 10,000 Jews living in Danzig left the Free City within a year. Most of the destitute Polish Jews fled back to their homeland, while wealthier Jews emigrated to Palestine, Canada, and the United States, as well as to Bolivia, Chile, Cuba, and Shanghai.[37]

Developments set in motion in 1933 entered their final phase in fall 1938, when the Danzig government passed blatantly anti-Jewish ordinances. By means of an ordinance from 23 September 1938, Danzig revoked the approbations of Jewish medical doctors and thus bereft them of their professional livelihoods.[38] Danzig's new Civil Servant Act from 2 November 1938 excluded Jews from the civil service.[39] When countless synagogues were burned, businesses destroyed, and people murdered on the Night of Broken Glass from 9 to 10 November in Germany, this also unleashed a new wave of abuse and violence against the Jewish population in Danzig. During the night from 12 to 13 November, the synagogue in the suburb of Langfuhr was broken into, its interior destroyed, and the building set on fire. The following night, the synagogue in nearby Zoppot burned as well. In Zoppot, Nazi thugs destroyed the display windows of Jewish stores and broke into Jewish residences, demolishing furnishings, looting, starting fires, and severely abusing numerous people. Panic stricken, many Jews left the city; during the following days, approximately 1,500 fled over the nearby Polish border. A short time later, authorities prohibited the Jews from settling in the seaside resort town of Zoppot.[40]

As it already had with regard to earlier excesses, the Danzig NSDAP party leadership officially distanced itself in November 1938 from the pogroms, referring to them as the result of "unleashed people's anger [*Volkszorn*]." At the same time, however, it made no secret of its goal to expel all of the Jews from the Free City as soon as possible.[41] As early as 21 November 1938, the Danzig Senate issued the Ordinance for the Protection of German Blood and German Honor as a pendant to the Nuremberg race laws, which among other things prohibited the conclusion of marriages between Jews and non-Jews under pain of punishment and revoked the right of Jews to vote on political matters or hold public office.[42]

In light of these developments, the board of the city's synagogue community demanded that the city stop the violent actions against the Jews to facilitate an orderly emigration. The Senate granted the Jewish community a "free departure," albeit with the condition that the Jews leave within a very short period and sell their landed property to the Danzig government to finance their emigration.[43] The issue sparked fierce conflicts within the synagogue community, yet the board nonetheless began preparing for the emigration. It sold the community's real estate to the Danzig government to enable Jews without assets to emigrate as well. In spring 1939, the Senate issued a series of ordinances that accelerated the forced emigration: assets belonging to Jews could be frozen and their land property in Danzig confiscated.[44] Approximately 1,000 interested parties registered for the first transport to Palestine.[45]

Jews living in the neighboring Polish port town of Gdingen also found themselves under increasing pressure at the end of the 1930s.[46] In 1937, Gdingen's Jewish community included approximately 5,000 individuals (4.4 percent of the town's total population), although many of these Jews were only temporary residents in Gdingen, since they wanted to emigrate via the port to Palestine. However, starting in September 1938, the Polish authorities began deporting the Jewish population from the town, since, as an "undesired element," they were not to be tolerated in areas near the border. In any event, many Jews who predicted the war moved to interior regions of Poland on their own accord. Just before the war broke out, numerous Jews likewise fled from their Jewish communities in Pomerelia to central Poland, so that, according to estimates, just under half of the Jewish inhabitants remained in Pomerelia.[47]

At the beginning of 1939, approximately 3,300 to 3,500 Jews[48] still lived in the port town of Danzig, most of them Danzig state citizens. As a rule, the Polish Jews, who suffered under the stigma of belonging to two undesirable minorities, had already returned to Poland.[49] The Jews who remained were either too poor to finance their emigration themselves, too old and frail to let themselves be uprooted, or belonged to that small group of individuals who, despite the emigration resolution, did not want to leave Danzig. In March 1939, the first transport organized by the synagogue community departed with 500 Jews for Palestine. Other groups shipped out in spring and summer to England, Shanghai, and South America, primarily Bolivia.[50] Thus in the first half of 1939, the Jewish community in Danzig largely dissolved. The Jewish school and the synagogue in center of town were closed. As a result of legal and illegal emigration—especially flight to Poland—the number of Jews in Danzig declined from 11,228 at the beginning of the 1930s to approximately 1,660 at the end of August 1939.[51]

The First Weeks of the Annexation

The German invasion of Poland and the concomitant "bringing home" of Danzig into the Reich marked the first step in a war with the declared goal of conquering *Lebensraum* in the East. The Free City of Danzig had already played an important role in German foreign policy during preparations for the destruction of the Polish state. The town's reintegration into the Reich was one of Germany's central demands regarding the revision of the Versailles Treaty; ultimately, the harbor town figured in the Nazi regime's plans as one of the means by which to provoke a war against Poland.[52]

The long-term preparations for an *Anschluss* with Germany should already have been evident in late 1937 and early 1938, according to the Polish historian Marek Andrzejewski. By this time, the National Socialist government in Danzig had long been following the lead of the German Reich with regard to legislation. It had harmonized its judicial, police, and administrative systems with German standards; it had largely eliminated freedoms of the press and association, destroyed the opposition parties, and suspended guarantees of personal freedom with the instrument of "protective custody." The construction of a National Socialist state system and the *Gleichschaltung* of political and public life took place under the eyes of the League of Nations and its local high commissioners, residing in Danzig, who were actually responsible for monitoring the constitutional-democratic conditions and disallowing any violation of the Danzig constitution.[53]

For the consolidating NSDAP, the tactic of repeatedly emphasizing the close bonds between Danzig and the German *Volksgemeinschaft* and for this purpose inviting prominent speakers and party bigwigs from the Reich to pompously staged rallies had already proven successful during the election campaigns.[54] Constantly stressing the "German character" of the people of Danzig, the NSDAP disseminated vast amounts of anti-Polish propaganda via the press and radio and affirmed the imminent "home bringing" of Danzig into the Reich. It was not entirely coincidental, for example, that in November 1938 the Reich Governor (Reichsstatthalter) of the *Ostmark* at the time, Arthur Seyß-Inquart, spoke at the Danzig exhibition hall, referring in his speech to the analogies between Austria prior to its *Anschluss* with the Reich and the Free City's situation.[55]

Parallel to this extensive construction of enemy stereotypes and the generation of a collective sense of "us" among the German-speaking residents, starting in spring 1939—and in violation of international law and the constitution—the Nazis in Germany pursued the city's military buildup while planning for "Case White," the code name for the planned attack on Poland.[56] On 11 June 1939, Generalmajor Friedrich Georg Eberhardt arrived in Danzig to set up a state police organization (Landespolizei). A second unit controlled by Eberhardt essentially consisted of SA members from Danzig.[57] In addition, the 300 men of the 3rd Battalion of SS-Totenkopfstandarte 4 from Berlin-Adlershof were secretly moved to Danzig,[58] followed by additional death-head (Totenkopf) units. With approximately 500 volunteers from Danzig, the formation assembled as the Danzig SS Home Guard (SS-Heimwehr Danzig) under the leadership of SS-Obersturmbannführer Hans-Friedemann Götze ultimately numbered approximately 1,500 men.[59] On 3 July, the Senate created the SS-Wachsturmbann (guard battalion) Eimann, a police auxiliary battalion with "special duties."[60] Under the direction of Max Pauly, later the commander of the Stutthof concentration camp, a section was created from this battalion that arranged the construction of prisons and camps for the arrests anticipated in Danzig for the beginning of the war: in July, the Victoria School in the vicinity of the Danzig police presidium was converted into a prison camp; the former barracks in harbor suburb of Neufahrwasser (Nowy Port) and the area of the gravel pit in Grenzdorf (Graniczna Wieś) were also intended as prison camps. In mid August 1939, inmates of the Danzig prison began initial preparations for building the Stutthof "civilian prisoner camp" in a marshy region near the Vistula Spit, around thirty-five kilometers east of Danzig.[61]

On 23 August 1939, NSDAP Gauleiter Albert Forster had himself appointed Head of State by means of a Senate resolution, in violation of Danzig's constitution.[62] Two days later, the German military training vessel *Schleswig-Holstein* arrived in the Danzig harbor, ostensibly for a goodwill visit. After SS detachments had staged incidents at the German-Polish border on the evening of 31 August, on the morning of 1 September 1939 the *Schleswig-Holstein* began bombarding the Westerplatte, a peninsula in the Danzig harbor and site of Polish military base.[63]

On this first day of the war, a series of constitutional and administrative actions integrated the Free City of Danzig into the German Reich. At 5:00 A.M., in a Danzig state radio broadcast, Albert Forster announced that he had issued and signed a Fundamental State Law (Staatsgrundgesetz) regarding Danzig's reunification with the Reich. With this law, Forster abolished the Free City's constitution. As the head of state, he transferred all legislative and executive power to himself and declared the Free City of Danzig to be a part of the German Reich. With the exception of the Danzig constitution, all statutes initially remained in effect.[64] In a telegram exchange, Hitler accepted the proclamation; the reunification act entered into force, effective immediately, and Forster was simultaneously appointed Head of the Civil Administration (Chef der Zivilverwaltung; CdZ) for the Danzig region. For the time being, however, the Gauleiter remained under the authority of the Third Army, commanded by General Georg von Küchler, who had been assigned executive power in the region of the former Free City. The Law on the Reunification of the Free City of Danzig with the German Reich, quickly passed by the German Reichstag on 1 September 1939 and taking effect immediately, finalized the constitutional changes, abolishing Danzig's Fundamental State Law and granting German citizenship to the citizens of Danzig "in accordance with more detailed provisions."[65] The High Commissioner of the League of Nations, Carl Jakob Burckhardt, was expelled on the very same day. In addition, on 1 September 1939 Forster issued multiple ordinances that abolished Polish rights in the former Free City, above all in the railway system and the harbor and customs administration. Additional ordinances regarding the confiscation of Polish and Jewish assets and real estate followed three days later.[66]

The military occupation of Poland was accompanied in Danzig by assaults on Polish establishments by the SS Home Guard, executions of Polish civilians, and mass arrests of Poles carried out by the Security Police and Wachsturmbann Eimann, using special search lists. The victims included above all employees of Polish institutions in Danzig—the Polish post office, the railway, the general commissariat of the Republic of Poland, the customs agency field office, the harbor and waterways council—as well as clergy, teachers, and functionaries of Polish organizations.[67] During the first days of the war, the Security Police and SS confined approximately 1,500 people in the Victoria School; they brought some of their prisoners to the nearby Stutthof internment camp, which was put into operation immediately after the war began.[68] A few of the Jews still living in Danzig, especially those considered Socialists, became victims of Gestapo and SS persecution immediately after the start of the war.[69] At the same time, many Jewish and non-Jewish Poles were arrested—and some of them shot to death—in nearby Gdingen (Gdynia) and in the Kreise (districts) of Dirschau (Tczew), Preußisch Stargard (Starogard Gdański), Karthaus (Kartuzy), Berent (Kościerzyna), and Putzig (Puck). Their precise numbers remain unknown; however, approximately 100 Danzig and Polish Jews were reportedly deported from neighboring Gdingen to Stutthof in mid September.[70]

In the days that followed, the Third Army under General Georg von Küchler and the Fourth Army under General Günther von Kluge marched into all of West Prussia,[71] marking the beginning of the widespread German terror against the Polish population. The Nazis built numerous containment camps (for displaced persons) and civilian prisoner camps, although in practice hardly any difference existed between the two types of camps.[72] During the military campaigns, regular Wehrmacht units committed countless crimes in all parts of the country against prisoners of war and Jewish and non-Jewish Polish civilians. The Germans carried out arbitrary executions and massacres as "retaliatory measures" and because they suspected their victims collectively as partisans. Wehrmacht soldiers ridiculed and humiliated Polish Jews, forcing them to perform cleanup work and dig ditches; likewise, they engaged in documented cases of plundering, rape, and mass executions.[73]

Apart from these acts of terror, the systematic murders committed by the Einsatzgruppen stood for the new character of this war. The special units, which recruited members of the Security Service (Sicherheitsdienst; SD) of the SS, the Security Police, and Order Police, and operated behind the German army formations in Poland, were tasked with "fighting all anti-Reich and anti-German elements in enemy territory to the rear of the fighting troops," a formulation that gave them carte blanche and a wide freedom to act.[74] The mass murders perpetrated by the Einsatzgruppen in the early phase of occupation primarily targeted the "Polish intelligentsia," namely, the stratum of people active in politics, the Church, and society that underpinned the Polish state. In the first instance, these measures were undertaken to prevent the formation of a Polish underground movement, but over the long term they were meant to degrade the Polish population into a nation of laborers devoid of leadership and culture. Provided with special search lists, the Einsatzgruppen initially came under army command and essentially conducted their murderous operations in the wake of the Wehrmacht. In Danzig-West Prussia alone, where Einsatzgruppe IV under SS-Brigadegeneral Lothar Beutel operated during the first weeks of September, the Germans murdered an estimated 30,000 Polish citizens by the end of 1939, primarily academics, clergy, senior civil servants, and federation and association functionaries, including many Jews.[75]

Operating independently, Einsatzkommando 16 (EK 16) committed most of the mass murders. Consisting of members of the Gestapo, the task force had been formed in Danzig on 12 September under the command of SS-Obersturmbannführer Rudolf Tröger, the head of the Danzig Gestapo.[76] EK 16 had a force of approximately 100 men and stationed units in larger towns such as Gotenhafen (formerly Gdynia/Gdingen), Thorn, and Bromberg (Bydgoszcz). This moment marked the beginning of the arrests and shootings in Danzig-West Prussia. In the district of Bromberg alone, a task force under the command of Kriminalrat (criminal investigator) Jakob Lölgen murdered around 5,000 Polish citizens as part of the "intelligentsia action."[77]

The command structures always included Gauleiter Albert Forster as well. During the first weeks after the annexation, as the Head of the Civil Administration, he was under the authority of the military commander in Danzig, yet he operated highly independently when establishing the region's new administrative structures. He filled important positions with Danzig party members who had earlier held key positions in the Gauleitung or Senate. In addition, starting on 7 September 1939, without consulting the military leadership, he issued a series of ordinances targeting Poles and Jews. Between 10 and 15 September, Forster convened an official meeting with all of Danzig-West Prussia's NSDAP district leaders, informing them that all "dangerous" Poles, Jews, and Polish clergy were to be "removed" by the special units.[78]

The Nazi leadership in Berlin, however, feared that Forster might lack the requisite severity when dealing with the "Polish intelligentsia."

At the behest of Heinrich Himmler, a decree from 21 September 1939 appointed Richard Hildebrandt as the Higher SS and Police Leader (Höherer SS- und Polizeiführer) in Danzig-West Prussia.[79] Appointed to serve at his side, SS-Oberführer Ludolf von Alvensleben, Himmler's personal adjutant, was supposed to take local control of establishing the Self-Defense Force (*Selbstschutz*), which consisted of militia-like units formed by small groups of ethnic Germans in many places immediately after German troops marched into western Poland. Officially, they were to ensure "peace and order" in local communities and

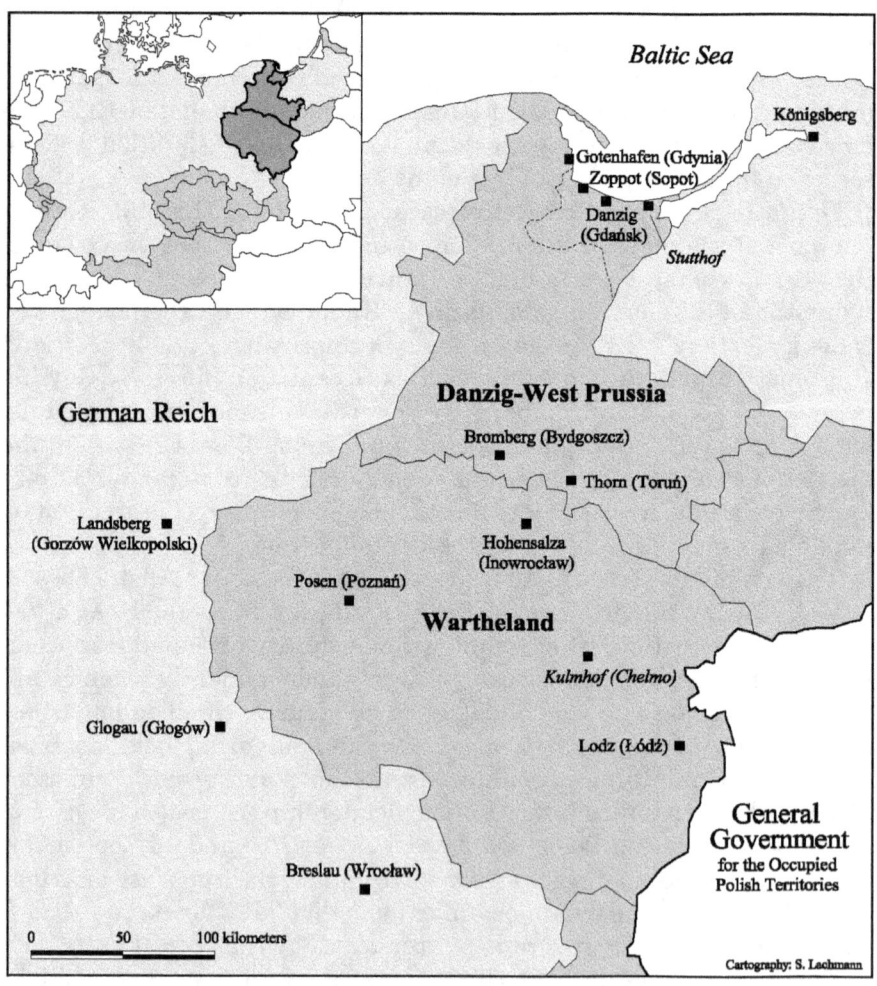

Map 6.1. Danzig-West Prussia and Wartheland, 1939

guard against aggressions by the Polish population and scattered Polish soldiers against the German-speaking minority. In actual fact, the Self-Defense Force became a pretext for acts of revenge perpetrated by embittered, fired-up, and criminal *Volksdeutsche* (ethnic Germans)—and, for the SS, an instrument in the destruction of the Polish upper class and the Jews.

In Danzig-West Prussia, the Self-Defense Force was organized into five inspectorates and twenty-three districts. In the beginning of October 1939, it had a force of 17,667 men. In Bromberg, von Alvensleben notified the inspectorate and Kreis (district) leaders that the Self-Defense Force was engaging in retaliation for crimes committed by Poles against *Volksdeutsche* and called for a "severe crackdown" against the Poles.[80] Like the Einsatzgruppen, during its killing operations the Self-Defense Force made no distinction between supposedly dangerous Poles and Jews, unleashing its combined anti-Polish and anti-Jewish resentments on an unprecedented scale. On 7 and 8 October 1939, for example, eighty-three Jewish and non-Jewish Poles—including twenty-eight women and ten children—were executed at the Jewish cemetery in Schwetz (Świecie).[81] Since Generalleutnant Max Bock, commander of Wehrkreis (military district) XX Danzig, felt that the more or less public executions endangered public security, and Albert Forster feared that the Self-Defense Force could develop into a state within the state, the units were ultimately disbanded in November 1939; nonetheless, violent independent actions took place well into spring 1940.[82]

The Period of the Occupation

After the fighting had ended, the occupiers dismembered Poland. The German Reich annexed the western and northeastern regions by means of the Decree of the Führer and Reich Chancellor on the Organization and Administration of the Eastern Regions of 8 October 1939.[83] The western parts were integrated into the Gaue of Danzig-West Prussia, Wartheland, and Upper Silesia; the central Polish heartland was proclaimed the General Government for the Occupied Polish Territories (Generalgouvernement für die besetzten polnischen Gebiete) and transformed into a German colony. As a new administrative unit, the Reichgau Danzig-West Prussia encompassed the territory of the former Free City of Danzig, part of the Pomeranian Voivodeship, a section of the Warsaw Voivodeship, and a number of Kreise from East

Prussia; it was organized into the Regierungsbezirke (government districts) of Danzig, Bromberg, and Marienwerder (see map 6.1). The military administration of the territory ended on 26 October 1939; on the same day, Hitler appointed Gauleiter Albert Forster as the Reich Governor of Danzig-West Prussia.[84] The integrated territories adopted the legal system and administrative structures of the German Reich. The law of Reich in its entirety and the law of the Prussian state entered into force on 1 January 1940. The new Reichsgau comprised an area of 26,055 square kilometers and numbered 2,179,000 inhabitants, 61 percent of whom were Poles. Yet there was a significant difference between the city of Danzig, occupied largely by Germans, and the other regions, whose inhabitants were up to 90 percent Polish.[85]

The western Polish regions incorporated into the German Reich were supposed to be ethnically "reorganized" by means of a *völkische Flurbereinigung*—an ethnic-national reallocation and consolidation of agricultural land. The goal was to shift Jews and Poles to the General Government as potential slave labor and replace them with ethnic German settlers from the East, thus "Germanizing" the region over the long term.[86] Whereas former Polish citizens were certainly able to continue living in the annexed region, provided they could prove their affiliation with the German *Volk* (*Volkszugehörigkeit*) or were classified as "racially valuable,"[87] first and foremost the new Reichgaue had to be rendered "Jew free." To do so, the German authorities in Danzig-West Prussia adopted methods similar to those used in the other annexed Polish regions: the Nazis expelled and plundered the Jewish population, exploited Jews as forced labor and repressed their cultural life, and ultimately expropriated and deported them.[88]

On 14 October 1939, a local West Prussian newspaper reported on a statement by Forster "that the Reichsgau Danzig-West Prussia can proudly claim that, of the four eastern Gaue, it is the only one that today already no longer has any Jews."[89] In fact, however, in fall 1939, the Danzig synagogue community still numbered approximately 1,200 members.[90] In August 1940, another transport organized by the Danzig community with more than 500 Jews left the town for Palestine; individually, however, Jews still managed to emigrate until spring 1941. The Jews remaining in Danzig were predominantly impoverished and elderly, with 200 of them still dying of natural causes after 1939.[91]

On 30 October 1939, Himmler ordered that all of the Jews and a large part of the Polish population had to be "de-settled" from the Reichsgau by the end of February 1940. The plans involved approximately 400,000 people.[92] As a countermove, ethnic Germans from the

Baltic states of Lithuania and Latvia were supposed to be brought to the region with the prospect of settling on a "German farm." As in Upper Silesia and the Warthegau, so-called Land Offices (Bodenämter) were created in cooperation with the Race and Settlement Main Office (Rasse- und Siedlungshauptamt) at the end of 1939, which were supposed to register and confiscate the commercial property of Poles and Jews—from industrial plants to small shops—along with farms and agricultural land, distributing these in part to ethnic German settlers.[93] In addition, in November 1940, Danzig received a branch office of the Central Emigrant Office (Umwandererzentralstelle), the Reich Security Main Office (Reichssicherheitshauptamt) agency that not only organized the expulsion of Poles from the west Polish territories but also extensively collaborated on the deportation of the Jews.[94]

Richard Hildebrandt's staff assumed responsibility for the mass deportations from Danzig-West Prussia; Himmler had appointed Hildebrandt as the region's Emissary of the Reich Commissioner for the Strengthening of Germandom (Beauftragter des Reichskommissars für die Festigung deutschen Volkstums). In October 1939, upon Hitler's instructions, the authorities had already started literally depopulating the harbor town of Gotenhafen, which was important for naval armaments. Within just a few weeks, a massive contingent of personnel from the military, Security Police, and SS-Wachsturmbann Eimann expelled over 40,000 of the Polish city's inhabitants—including the few remaining Jews—mostly to the General Government.[95] On 26 November 1939, Hildebrandt reported that 10,000 Jews and Poles need to be deported from West Prussia, since he expected the arrival an equal number of *Volksdeutsche* from Volhynia. To implement the evacuations, the Germans set up three collection camps in the Gau, namely, in Thorn, Potulitz (Potulice), and Dirschau. To begin with, they removed 1,400 people from Bromberg in May 1940. Other expulsions occurred in Gotenhafen, Danzig, Neustadt (Wejherowo), Dirschau, Graudenz, and Thorn. More than 7,000 people were destined for Lublin.[96] After a Central Emigrant Office had been established in Litzmannstadt, in December 1940 an additional 6,607 Poles and 3,259 Jews from Danzig-West Prussia were presumably transported to the Litzmannstadt ghetto.[97] Many of the people died from cold and hunger in the railway cars during the transports.

The General Government found itself hopelessly overburdened by the large number of deportees, who arrived to find supply shortages and housing scarcity in the ghettos. Conceived in January 1939 in the Reich Security Main Office, the Third Immediate Plan (*Nahplan*) for the General Government, which determined future population transfer objectives, envisaged the deportation of an additional 67,000 people from West Prussia. However, the plan would never be fully realized. Admittedly, deportations to the General Government continued at a reduced level, but they were increasingly superseded by internments in the Stutthof concentration camp.

When classified as a concentration camp in January 1942, the Stutthof camp had already existed for more than two years. Since the first days of the war, the camp had interned Jews and Poles who had not succumbed to pogroms or the "cleansing operations" of the Einsatzgruppen and German Self-Defense Force. In the subsequent period, the Germans used the camp above all to intern the Polish population of Danzig and West Prussia. Until the end of September 1941, Stutthof was classified as a "civilian prisoner camp." Together with camps in Grenzdorf, Neufahrwasser, and the Victoria School in Danzig, Stutthof stood under the control of the Commandant's Office of the Danzig prisoner camp. In turn, this office was directly subordinate to the Danzig police presidium, which answered to Head of the Civil Administration of the Reichsgau Danzig-West Prussia Albert Forster. In April 1940, by order of Higher SS and Police Leader Richard Hildebrandt, the SS Higher Administrative Section Weichsel (SS-Oberabschnitt Weichsel) took over the Stutthof camp's administration, with SS-Sturmbannführer Max Pauly as the camp's commander.[98] During its first two years, Stutthof was locally important and used to isolate Polish opponents of the regime and break them physically and psychologically. Very few of the political prisoners interned in the camp survived the constant abuse, countless punitive lineups, inhuman workloads, catastrophic sanitary conditions, diseases, and insufficient supplies. Along with "indirect" forms of destruction, the Germans also practiced horrendous forms of "direct" murder: shootings, hangings, phenol injections, drownings, beatings, and—as of 1944, in an unknown number of cases—gassings.[99] Starting in October 1941, Higher SS and Police Leader Richard Hildebrandt, jointly with the Inspector of the Security Police in Danzig Heinrich Willich, as per an order by Reichsführer-SS Heinrich Himmler, designated Stutthof an SS Special Camp (*SS-Sonderlager*) with the function of a work education camp. Max Pauly remained the camp's commander. Until the camp was dissolved starting in January 1945, approximately 10,000 "education prisoners" (*Erziehungshäftlinge*)— prisoners slated for reeducation—from various nations were forced to perform heavy slave labor at Stutthof, resulting in the death of 1,500 of these prisoners.[100]

An inspection by Heinrich Himmler on 23 November 1941 played a major role in the camp's further development. With a resolution on 7 January 1942, he assigned Stutthof the status of a "concentration camp," subordinating the camp to the Reich Security Main Office. Henceforth, the police authorities in Danzig-West Prussia were no longer the only authorities to arrange for the consignment of prisoners to the camp; from now on, the Nazi state's security and persecution apparatus deported prisoners to Stutthof from other occupied regions and other concentration camps as well. In addition, as of 1942, the Danzig Gestapo increasingly used the camp as a remand prison, especially since the "police prisoners" could be exploited at the camp for labor. War prisoners, deserters, conscientious objectors, and Polish resistance fighters were also brought to Stutthof.[101]

From the concentration camp, political prisoners, prisoners of war, and Jewish concentration camp prisoners were forced to perform slave labor in the territory of Danzig-West Prussia. During the occupation period, in more than two hundred satellite camps scattered throughout the entire Reichsgau, they had to perform extremely heavy physical labor under unspeakable conditions: in forestry and agricultural, in debris removal, in brickyards and cement factories, in road construction, in the Danzig shipyard, in industry, and for many private companies. Already in fall 1939, more than 3,000 prisoners from Stutthof had been literally leased out for agricultural labor in almost all of the villages in Danziger Werder. In 1941, more than 2,000 Polish Jews lived in forced labor camps in the region of the former Polish Corridor to build the Reich Autobahn Danzig–Stettin.[102]

In mid 1944, Stutthof joined in the destruction of Jewish prisoners. Consequently, Jewish men, women and children, above all from Eastern Europe, were brought to the camp. At first, the gas chamber was used to murder individuals who were not expected to provide any useful labor.[103] But when a typhus epidemic broke out in the beginning of November 1944, claiming an especially large number of victims in the "Jewish camp," Stutthof halted its gassing operations, for the epidemic had killed off more people than had been slated for destruction.[104]

From 2 September 1939 until the beginning of the camp's evacuation on 25 January 1945, approximately 110,000 prisoners were detained in Stutthof. The total number of fatalities amounted to between 63,000 and 65,000 persons, who died in the main camp, satellite camps, and on the death marches after the camp's liquidation. Approximately 43 percent of the fatalities were Jews. Between September 1939 and May

1945, 28,000 Jewish prisoners of the Stutthof concentration camp died, most of them (27,000) between July 1944 and 8 May 1945.[105]

In Danzig, well over 100 elderly and infirm persons of the Jewish faith had hoped to live out their days in a Jewish old-age home. But in August 1939, the NSDAP confiscated the building. The Jews—most of them over seventy—and others who had been expelled from their apartments were first housed in a community hall in the center of Danzig and then found temporary accommodations in an old warehouse that had previously been used as a penal camp. A few hundred Jews still lived there in 1940. In March 1941, some of them were brought to the Warsaw ghetto; the others were probably later transferred to the Majdanek-Lublin and Auschwitz extermination camps, or to Theresienstadt. Approximately twenty Jews reportedly still continued to live in Danzig until the end of the war.[106]

Conclusion

In Danzig-West Prussia, National Socialist "Jewish policy," "Polish policy," and "*Volkstums* policy" intertwined at many levels; the "solution of the Jewish question" in the region went hand in hand, so to speak, with the subjugation, murder, and expulsion of the Polish population. Ultimately, the Nazis sought to violently exclude the Jews and Poles from the racist construct of what they imagined to be an ethnically homogenous German *Volksgemeinschaft*.

During the time of the Free City, the emigration and influx of Eastern European Jews heavily swelled the size of the long-established German-Jewish community in Danzig, which numbered over 11,000 persons by the beginning of the 1930s. With the arrival of Gauleiter Albert Forster and the consolidation of the NSDAP in the Free City, as well as the progressive *Gleichschaltung* of public and political life under National Socialist Senate President Hermann Rauschning and Arthur Greiser, Jews were steadily deprived of their rights through the enactment of ordinances and expelled from the job market, the civil service, and cultural life. Public hate campaigns conducted in local organs of NSDAP propaganda, calls for boycotts, and ultimately the massive abuse and violence perpetrated by the Danzig SA under the protection of Polizeipräsident Helmut Froböß drove away Danzig's Jews. In light of the pogroms, which spared only economically important trading companies, many Polish Jews fled the harbor town for their homeland. Neither the League of Nations' high commissioners, who were locally deployed to protect the rule of law, nor the League of Nations itself undertook any measures to stem the violent activities, which also contravened international law and the constitution.

By 1 September 1939, when Second World War began and the German Reich incorporated the Free City, Danzig's Jewish community had already shrunk to less than 2,000. Most of the Danzig's wealthy, German-speaking Jews had already managed to save their lives by emigrating prior to the annexation, but emigrations still continued until spring 1941. In contrast, large numbers of the Jews living in the former Polish region of West Prussia—an estimated 2,000 individuals—fell victim to operations to imprison or murder the "Polish intelligentsia" during the first weeks of the war. Members of the Wehrmacht—special units from the SS, the Gestapo, the Security Police, and the Order Police—and above all SS-Wachsturmbann Eimann, Einsatzkommando 16 under SS-Oberführer Rudolf Tröger; and members of the *Volksdeutsche Selbstschutz* led by SS-Oberführer Ludolf von Alvensleben—all participated in the executions. At the regional leadership level, Reich Governor and Gauleiter Albert Forster and Higher SS and Police Leader Richard Hildebrandt bore responsibility for the mass murders, as well as for the subsequent deportation of Jews and Poles to the ghettos of the General Government and the labor and extermination camps. Both were among the few Nazi perpetrators convicted after 1945 for their crimes in the Reichsgau of Danzig-West Prussia.[107]

Notes

1. Dieter Schenk, *Hitlers Mann in Danzig: Albert Forster und die NS-Verbrechen in Danzig-Westpreußen* (Bonn, 2000), 206, 217.
2. On the history of the Jews in Danzig and West Prussia before the 1930s, see Max Aschkewitz, *Zur Geschichte der Juden in Westpreußen* (Marburg am Lahn, 1967); Grzegorz Berendt, *Migracje Żydów przez Gdańsk w XX w.* (Toruń, 1995) [Die Migration der Juden über Danzig im 20. Jahrhundert]; idem, *Żydzi na terenie Wolnego Miasta Gdańska w latach 1920–1945 (działalność kulturalna, polityczna i socjalna)* (Gdańsk, 1997) [Die Juden in der Freien Stadt Danzig 1920–1945 (die kulturelle, politische und soziale Arbeit)]; Michael Brocke, et al., eds., *Zur Geschichte und Kultur der Juden in Ost- und Westpreußen* (Hildesheim, 2000); Daniel Bogacz, *Fremde in einer freien Stadt: Deutsche, Polen und Juden in Danzig 1920–1939* (Bonn, 2004); Samuel Echt, *Die Geschichte der Juden in Danzig* (Leer, 1972); Sophia Kemlein, "Zur Geschichte der Juden in Westpreußen und Danzig (bis 1943)," in *Danzig—Gdańsk: Deutsch-polnische Geschichte, Politik und Literatur*, ed. Akademie für Lehrerfortbildung Dillingen (Dillingen, 1996), 94–109; Kamila Kozlowska, *Die Juden in der Freien Stadt Danzig: Integrations- und Ausgrenzungsprozesse zwischen 1919 und 1933* (Munich, 2011).

3. Under the protection of the Bishop of Kujawy, in the seventeenth century Jews formed the first Jewish community in the Kingdom of Prussia in Alt-Schottland (Stare Szkoty) outside the gates of Danzig; additional communities developed in the eighteenth century in the Danzig suburbs of Stolzenberg (Gdańsk-Choełm) and Langfuhr (Wrzesczcz). Kemlein, "Geschichte," 95.
4. Aschkewitz, *Geschichte*, 5f.
5. Between 1910 and 1920, approximately 15,000 Jews emigrated via Danzig to America. Kemlein, "Geschichte," 99ff.
6. In 1883, the Jewish communities in the suburbs and the Jews living in the Danzig itself joined together to form the synagogue community of Danzig. Shortly thereafter, they built the Great Synagogue in central Danzig. Separate synagogue communities formed in the towns of Zoppot, Tiegenhof, and Neuteich, as well in the suburb of Langfuhr. Berendt, "Danziger," 188.
7. On the history of the Free City, see Wolfgang Gippert, *Kindheit und Jugend in Danzig 1920–1945: Identitätsbildung im sozialistischen und im konservativen Milieu* (Essen, 2005).
8. In 1910, 7,680 Jews still lived in the region of the new Pomeranian Voivodeship, but by the time of the first Polish census in 1921 the number had declined to only 2,930 (merely 0.3 percent of the population). Kemlein, "Geschichte," 104.
9. Whereas Danzig's Jewish population consisted of approximately 2,200 people when the Free City was founded, by 1923 that number had already increased to more than 7,000 and by 1929 had reached approximately 10,500. Kemlein, "Geschichte," 106.
10. Echt, *Geschichte*, 96ff.; Berendt, *Migracje*, 181.
11. Kemlein, "Geschichte," 107.
12. Echt, *Geschichte*, 69.
13. Admittedly, the Polish constitutions of 1921 and 1935 ensured formal equal rights for all citizens and special rights for ethnic minorities, but the Jewish population found itself exposed to massive pressure from the camp of Polish National Democrats, who sought above all to restrict their economic activities. Yet in contrast to parts of Poland, few pogroms occurred in the Pomeranian Voivodeship, since in this region the national camp directed its opposition predominantly toward the well-organized German minority. Kemlein, "Geschichte," 105.
14. In spring 1919, up to 100,000 people gathered at multiple rallies held at the Danzig Heumarkt (hay market) to demonstrate against a possible integration of the town with the new republic of Poland and against its separation from Germany. Heinrich Sahm, *Erinnerungen aus meinen Danziger Jahren 1919–1930* (Marburg/Lahn, 1955), 1.
15. On the term *Volksgemeinschaft*, see the editors' introduction.
16. Even though, as a center of maritime trade, Danzig had always accommodated people of various nationalities, ethnicities, and religious beliefs—in 1929, 57 percent of population belonged to the Protestant and 37 percent to the Catholic Church—most of the inhabitants, cutting across party lines, had strong German-nationalistic inclinations. The multiple party system resembled that of the Weimar Republic and the 1927 Volkstag (the Free City's parliament) elections delivered the following results: SPD (and USPD) 33.8 percent, KPD 9.1 percent, Polish Party 3.1 percent, Catholic Center Party 14.3 percent, bourgeois centrist parties 8 percent, DNVP 20.6 percent, DSP 1.2 percent and NSDAP 0.8 percent. The NSDAP constantly gained more votes in the Volkstag (1930: 16.4 percent, 1933: 50.1 percent, and 1935: 59.3 percent); this was accompanied by the progressive consolidation and *Gleichschaltung* of political

and public life in the Free City. Marek Andrzejewski, *Opposition und Widerstand in Danzig 1933 bis 1939* (Bonn, 1994).
17. Arthur Greiser (1897–1946) was a member of the German nationalist "Stahlhelm" organization from 1924 to 1926. In 1929, he joined the NSDAP and the SA. In 1931, he transferred from the SA to the SS, where he later reached the rank of SS-Brigadeführer. After his provisional leadership of the Danzig Gau he worked full-time as a Gaugeschäftsführer (Gau business manager) for the NSDAP until 1933. From 1934 to 1939, Greiser was the Senate President of Free City and the Deputy Gauleiter of Danzig. In 1939 he was appointed to the office of Reich Governor of the neighboring Reichsgau Wartheland, where he was responsible for the mass murder of the Jewish population, for the mass deportations of Poles for forced labor, and for plundering the Polish people. Greiser was a key figure in the Germanization policies. Catherine Epstein, *Model Nazi: Arthur Greiser and the Occupation of Western Poland* (Oxford, 2010).
18. On Albert Forster (1902–1952) as a person, his "career" as the Gauleiter of Danzig-Westpreußen, and his responsibility for the crimes committed there, see the foundational study by Schenk, *Hitlers Mann*.
19. Erwin Lichtenstein, *Die Juden der Freien Stadt Danzig unter der Herrschaft des Nationalsozialismus* (Tübingen, 1973), 7.
20. Hermann Rauschning (1887–1982) was a moderate Nazi activist who during his term in office among other things pursued a policy of German-Polish rapprochement, which resulted in prolonged conflicts with the Danzig NSDAP leadership, notably with Albert Forster. Rauschning had already resigned from office as the Senate President by November 1934. His successor was the former Vice President of the Senate and Senator for the Interior Arthur Greiser. Andrzejewski, *Opposition*, 54ff.
21. Erwin Lichtenstein, "Die Juden in Danzig (1933–1939)," *Zeitschrift für die Geschichte der Juden* 4, no. 1 (1967): 201.
22. Senat der Freien Stadt Danzig, "Gesetz zur Behebung der Not von Volk und Staat," in *Gesetzblatt für die Freie Stadt 1933* (Danzig, 1933), 273ff.
23. On the contents of the ordinances, see Echt, *Geschichte*, 137ff. Individual cases documenting the regulatory expulsion of Jews from the areas of the general administration, judicial administration, the health-care system, the school system, cultural life, and the economy are also listed in Lichtenstein, *Juden der Freien Stadt*, 157–162.
24. Senat, "Rechtsverordnungen betr. Maßnahmen zur Erhöhung der öffentlichen Sicherheit und Ordnung," in *Gesetzblatt 1933*, 287ff.
25. Senat, "Rechtsverordnung betr. Genehmigungserfordernis für die Niederlassung zuziehender Ärzte, Zahnärzte und Heilkundiger," *Gesetzblatt 1933*, 321f.
26. "Verordnung zur Regelung der Rechtsverhältnisse der Notare," *Gesetzblatt 1933*, 333f.
27. Senat, "Verordnung über die Errichtung öffentlich-rechtlicher Berufsvertretungen der Industrie, des Handels, des Handwerks und des Gewerbes im Gebiet der Freien Stadt Danzig," *Gesetzblatt 1933*, 361ff.
28. Echt, *Geschichte*, 138.
29. Senat, "Verordnung zur Überleitung des Danziger Stadttheaters auf den Staat," in *Gesetzblatt 1933*, 381ff.; Echt, *Geschichte*, 139.
30. Echt, *Geschichte*, 139ff.; Ernst Sodeikat, "Die Verfolgung und der Widerstand der Juden in der Freien Stadt Danzig von 1933 bis 1945," *Bulletin des Leo Baeck Instituts* 8, no. 30 (1965): 107–149, here 113ff.

31. In 1934, a total of thirty-seven Jewish organizations existed in the Free City. Most of them had been founded in the 1920s or earlier. Kemlein, "Geschichte," 107.
32. Echt, *Geschichte*, 146ff.; Sodeikat, "Verfolgung," 116f. In May 1935, the Council of the League of Nations decided to commission a special report, assigning a committee to review the ordinances issued by the National Socialist Senate since 1933. In fact, the reviewers managed to prove constitutional violations. However, the League of Nations limited itself to making a few recommendations to the Free City on changing the situation of the Jews, but these were either rejected or ignored by the Danzig government. Echt, *Geschichte*, 156.
33. Sodeikat, "Verfolgung," 129.
34. Schenk, *Hitlers Mann*, 87.
35. Ingo Loose, *Kredite für NS-Verbrechen: Die deutschen Kreditinstitute in Polen und die Ausraubung der polnischen und jüdischen Bevölkerung 1939–1945* (Munich, 2007), 36–41.
36. Archiwum Państwowe w Gdańsku, 260/463, fol. 421–429; published by Marek Andrzejewski, "Antyżydowski terror w Wolnym Mieście Gdańsku (1937–1939): Materiały," Biuletyn Żydowskiego Instytutu Historycznego w Polsce 141 (1987): 123–126; see Echt, *Geschichte*, 172ff.
37. Echt, *Geschichte*, 174; Sodeikat, "Verfolgung," 131.
38. Senat der Freien Stadt Danzig, "Verordnung betreffend Abänderung der Rechtsverordnung betreffend den Erlaß einer Ärzteordnung vom 1. Dezember 1933," in *Gesetzblatt für die Freie Stadt 1938* (Danzig, 1938), 486.
39. Senat, "Danziger Beamtengesetz," in *Gesetzblatt 1938*, 549ff.
40. Lichtenstein, *Juden der Freien Stadt*, 77.
41. Ibid., 80ff.
42. Senat, "Verordnung zum Schutze des deutschen Blutes und der deutschen Ehre," in *Gesetzblatt 1938*, 616; Echt, *Geschichte*, 188f.
43. The financing of Jewish emigration was regulated by means of the Ordinance to Support and Ensure Jewish Emigration from the Territory of the Free City of Danzig of 3 March 1939. It placed all Jewish assets under a prohibition of disposition and sale, except for moveable items for personal use, household goods, and luxury items. By imposing appropriate requirements when Jewish real estate and assets were sold, the Senate commissioner for Jewish emigration could ensure that the Danzig government did not have to make any financial contributions for the emigrations it was forcing upon the Jews; Senat der Freien Stadt Danzig, "Verordnung zur Förderung und Sicherstellung der jüdischen Auswanderung aus dem Gebiet der Freien Stadt Danzig," in *Gesetzblatt für die Freie Stadt 1939* (Danzig, 1939), 89; Andrzejewski, *Antyżydowski terror*, 126.
44. Echt, *Geschichte*, 208. Through the Ordinance regarding the Dejudaization of the Danzig Economy and Danzig Land Ownership of 22, July 1939, the Senate authorized itself to confiscate Jewish firms and place them under the control of a trustee, which in practical terms amounted to the "Aryanization" of these commercial enterprises. Senat, "Verordnung betreffend die Entjudung der Danziger Wirtschaft und des Danziger Grundbesitzes," in *Gesetzblatt 1939*, 375.
45. Lichtenstein, "Juden in Danzig," 210ff.
46. On Gdynia, see Elżbieta Rojowska and Monika Tomkiewicz, *Gdynia 1939–1945 w świetle źródeł niemieckich i polskich: Aresztowania—egzekucje—wysiedlenia ludności cywilnej narodowości polskiej* (Gdynia, 2009).
47. Kemlein, "Geschichte," 105f.
48. This assessment comes from the report by the Danzig Senate on 20 March 1939. The Danzig synagogue community, on the other hand, estimated the number of

Jews still remaining in the town at this time to be around 2,800. Andrzejewski, *Antyżydowski terror*, 126.
49. From 1938 to September 1939, approximately 3,500 Jews returned to Poland in organized repatriation operations. "Geschichte," 108.
50. Lichtenstein, *Juden der Freien Stadt*, 99ff.
51. Schenk, *Hitlers Mann*, 217.
52. On Danzig's role in the Nazi government's foreign policy plans during the run-up to the Second World War, see Bernd-Jürgen Wendt, "Danzig—Ein Bauer auf dem Schachbrett nationalsozialistischer Außenpolitik," in *Hitler, Deutschland und die Mächte: Materialien zur Außenpolitik des Dritten Reiches*, ed. Manfred Funke (Düsseldorf, 1976), 774–794.
53. Andrzejewski, *Opposition*, 202; see also the detailed account of the last High Commissioner Carl Jakob Burckhardt, *Meine Danziger Mission 1937–193*, 3rd ed. (Munich, 1980).
54. Meanwhile, the Gau culture weeks, created by Albert Forster, featured appearances by Propaganda Minister Joseph Goebbels in spring 1937 and summer 1939. Schenk, *Hitlers Mann*, 81. His inflammatory speech from 17 June 1939 is printed in Helmut Heiber, ed., *Goebbels-Reden*, vol. 1: *1932–1939* (Düsseldorf, 1971), 333f.
55. Andrzejewski, *Opposition*, 203.
56. The League of Nations had allowed the Free City only a regular police force with just a few hundred personnel and a citizen's militia of approximately 3,000 men. However, the latter were considered badly trained and poorly equipped. After its victories in the May 1933 election, the NSDAP began systematically creating SA units in Danzig. However, after the conclusion of the German-Polish non-aggression pact in 1934, there was no further mention of setting up military formations in the Free City for the time being. See Horst Rohde, "Kriegsbeginn in Danzig—Planungen und Wirklichkeit," in *Der Zweite Weltkrieg: Analysen, Grundzüge, Forschungsbilanzen*, ed. Wolfgang Michalka (Munich, 1989), 463.
57. Rohde, "Kriegsbeginn," 465f.
58. Schenk, *Hitlers Mann*, 112.
59. The ceremonial banner presentation took place in Danzig on 18 August 1939, marking the formation's first public appearance. Rohde, "Kriegsbeginn," 469.
60. Kurt Eimann, the leader of the 530-man unit, had previously led SS-Standarte 36 in Danzig. After the beginning of the war, the "Wachsturm" developed into a mobile Einsatzkommando under Higher SS and Police Leader Richard Hildebrand, who had been ordered to Danzig and would perpetrate countless crimes against the Polish population in Danzig-West Prussia; Schenk, *Hitlers Mann*, 113, 179ff.
61. Janina Grabowska, "K.L. Stutthof: Ein historischer Abriß," in *Stutthof: Ein Konzentrationslager vor den Toren Danzigs*, ed. Hermann Kuhn (Bremen, 1995), 12f.; Karin Orth, *Das System der nationalsozialistischen Konzentrationslager: Eine politische Organisationsgeschichte* (Hamburg, 1999) 69.
62. Senat, "Verordnung betreffend das Staatsoberhaupt der Freien Stadt Danzig," in *Gesetzblatt 1939*, 413.
63. In 1924, the League of Nations had awarded Westerplatte to the Polish state for the transit of war material. This arrangement burdened relations between Danzig and Poland, especially since in March 1933 Poland stationed an armed military unit in Westerplatte, contravening international law. The bombardment of the Polish stronghold at 4:45 A.M. is generally viewed as the start of the Second World War. Rohde "Kriegsbeginn," 479, note 1.
64. Senat, "Veröffentlichung des Staatsgrundgesetzes," in *Gesetzblatt 1939*, 435. Hans Viktor Böttcher, *Die Freie Stadt Danzig: Wege und Umwege in die europäische*

Zukunft; Historischer Rückblick, staats- und völkerrechtliche Fragen (Bonn, 1995), 131, 368.
65. Reichsgesetzblatt (RGBl.) 1939 I, 1547. See also Böttcher, *Freie Stadt*, 131f., 370; Schenk, *Hitlers Mann*, 127ff. The "more detailed provisions" regarding the acquisition of German citizenship in the annexed Polish territories were regulated by the *Deutsche Volksliste* (German People's List), introduced on 4 March 1941, which excluded Jews. RGBl. 1941 I, 118.
66. Senat, "Verordnung betr. die Beschlagnahme polnischen Vermögens in Danzig" and "Zweite Verordnung betr. die Entjudung der Danziger Wirtschaft und des Danziger Grundbesitzes," *Gesetzblatt 1939*, 465f.
67. On the persecution and murder of the Polish and Jewish population in the occupied Polish territories, see Barbara Bojarska, *Eksterminacja inteligencji polskiej na Pomorzu Gdańskim: wrzesień-grudzień 1939* (Poznań, 1972); Bogdan Chrzanowski, *Eksterminacja ludności polskiej i żydowskiej na terenach okupowanych Polski w świetle wydawnictw podziemnych (1939–1945)* (Gdańsk, 1979); Jacek Andrzej Młynarczyk and Jochen Böhler, eds., *Der Judenmord in den eingegliederten polnischen Gebieten 1939—1945* (Osnabrück, 2010); Alexander B. Rossino, *Hitler Strikes Poland: Blitzkrieg, Ideology, and Atrocity* (Lawrence, KS, 2003).
68. The Neufahrwasser, Grenzdorf, and Stutthof camps held approximately 5,150 inmates at the beginning of February 1940. From 2 September 1939 until the end of March 1940, more than 9,000 people were held at these three camps, including Jews with Polish citizenship from Danzig and other towns and localities in West Prussia. Danuta Drywa, "Stutthof—Stammlager," in *Der Ort des Terrors: Geschichte der nationalsozialistischen Konzentrationslager*, vol. 6: *Natzweiler, Groß-Rosen, Stutthof*, ed. Wolfgang Benz and Barbara Distel (Munich, 2007), 490; idem, *The Extermination of Jews in Stutthof Concentration Camp 1939–1945* (Gdańsk, 2004).
69. Some of the detained Danzig Jews, including the cantor of the synagogue Leopold Schufftan and the Social Democrat Jakob Lange, were murdered in the Neufahrwasser, Grenzdorf, and Stutthof camps. Drywa, "Stutthof—Stammlager," 490.
70. Bogdan Chrzanowski, "Danzig-Westpreußen unter der NS-Besatzung (1939–1945)," in *Stutthof: Das Konzentrationslager* (Gdańsk, 1996), 33; Sodeikat, "Verfolgung," 143; Grabowska, "Stutthof," 15f.
71. Chrzanowski, "Danzig-Westpreußen," 26. On the various operating areas of the German Wehrmacht in Poland, see Jochen Böhler, *Auftakt zum Vernichtungskrieg: Die Wehrmacht in Polen 1939* (Frankfurt, 2006).
72. From 1 September 1939 to March 1940, units from the Wehrmacht, security police, and paramilitary *Selbstschutz* established a total of seventy-one internment camps in the occupied Pomeranian Voivodeship. Konrad Ciechanowski, "Entstehung des Lagers Stutthof—Internierungslager in Danzig-Westpreußen von September 1939 bis März 1940," in *Stutthof: Das Konzentrationslager*, 51f.
73. Młynarczyk and Böhler, *Judenmord*; Jochen Böhler, "'Tragische Verstrickung' oder Auftakt zum Vernichtungskrieg? Die Wehrmacht in Polen 1939," in *Genesis des Genozids: Polen 1939–1941*, ed. Klaus-Michael Mallmann and Bogdan Musiał (Darmstadt, 2004), 36–56. It is almost impossible to provide reliable statements regarding the number of Jews victimized by abuses committed by Wehrmacht soldiers in September 1939 in Danzig-West Prussia, especially since, compared to the other annexed regions of Poland, few Jews lived in the region. Frank Golczewski, for example, estimates that approximately 400,000 Jews lived in the neighboring Wartheland, but neglects the 1,800 Jews that reportedly lived in the new Reichsgau of Danzig-West Prussia. Frank Golczewski, "Polen," in *Dimension des Völkermords:*

Die Zahl der jüdischen Opfer des Nationalsozialismus, ed. Wolfgang Benz (Munich, 1991), 431.

74. At the end of August 1939, the Germans created five Einsatzgruppen (with twelve Einsatzkommandos) in the towns south, west, and north of the border, which marched into Poland when the war began. Klaus-Michael Mallmann et al., *Einsatzgruppen in Polen: Darstellung und Dokumentation* (Darmstadt, 2008), 16, quote on p. 18.

75. Bogdan Musiał, "Das Schlachtfeld zweier totalitärer Systeme: Polen unter deutscher und sowjetischer Herrschaft 1939–1941," in *Genesis*, ed. Mallmann and Musial, 15. Jews did not figure among the Polish state elite and thus in 1939 were not yet targeted as a group for systematic shooting. They were usually murdered in pogrom-like excesses or "retaliatory actions." Throughout Poland, approximated 7,000 Jews fell victim to German tyranny by the end of 1939. We know hardly any details about the fate of the West Prussian Jews. According to Berendt ("Danziger," 198), almost all of the Jews in the "Polish corridor" west of Danzig had been murdered by November 1939. Murawski states that the Jews living in West Prussia had already been take into "protective custody" in September 1939 and deported to newly erected ghettos in central Poland. Klaus-Eberhard Murawski, "Grundzüge der staatlichen Entwicklung in Ost- und Westpreußen," in *Zur Geschichte und Kultur der Juden in Ost- und Westpreußen*, ed. Michael Brocke et al. (Hildesheim, 2000), 35.

76. The jurist and Obersturmbannführer Dr. Rudolf Tröger, born in 1905, was summoned to Danzig in spring 1939 as the head of political police; in Danzig he was appointed as the inspector of the Security Police in November 1939. As a lieutenant in the reserves, he was killed in the campaign in France in June 1940. Mallmann et al., *Einsatzgruppen*, 41.

77. The destruction of the Polish intelligentsia claimed 60,000 to 80,000 victims, with the mass murders concentrated in Danzig-West Prussia. The NSDAP, the Gestapo, the security service, the SS, and the judiciary had already been able to set themselves up in this area prior to the invasion of Poland, whereas in the other occupied territories the corresponding organizations had not yet been established. EK 16 was disbanded on 7 November 1939 after a decree by Reinhard Heydrich and its personnel dispersed to the Gestapo offices in Danzig, Graudenz, and Bromberg; Schenk, *Hitlers Mann*, 170. At the end of November, when the Polish upper class had been almost completely liquidated, the other Einsatzkommandos were also dissolved and their members distributed among the police offices within the incorporated territories. They henceforth concentrated their activity on persecuting the Jewish population. Dorothee Weitbrecht, "Ermächtigung zur Vernichtung: Die Einsatzgruppen in Polen im Herbst 1939," in *Genesis*, ed. Mallmann and Musial, 67.

78. Quoted in Schenk, *Hitlers Mann*, 138ff., 147.

79. Along with Albert Forster, as the Higher Police Leader and Leader of SS Higher Administrative Section Weichsel, Richard Hildebrandt (1897–1952) was one of the most influential men in Danzig-West Prussia. He presided over the Inspectorate of the Security Police and the commanders of the Ordnungspolizei, thus: the Gestapo, the SD, the Criminal Police, and Gendarmerie. He bore responsibility for the crimes committed by the SS and SD as well as for the Stutthof concentration camp and its numerous satellite camps, and also for the massacres perpetrated by the Selbstschutz and the mass murder of the mentally handicapped. As an emissary of the Reichskommissar für die Festigung deutschen Volkstums, he shared responsibility with Forster for the forced deportations from the Reichsgau. Hildebrandt established his headquarters in a Danzig villa that had been confiscated from

a Jewish family. Formally, Hildebrandt remained subordinate to Reich Governor Forster, yet in actual fact he acted highly independently, which led to substantial tensions between the two men. As Himmler's protégé, Hildebrandt was almost untouchable. Schenk, *Hitlers Mann*, 222f.

80. On 5 October 1939, von Alvensleben sent an interim balance sheet of the murders to Berlin, according to which "sharpest measures" had been undertaken against 4,247 former Polish citizens. Schenk, *Hitlers Mann*, 157.
81. Schenk, *Hitlers Mann*, 217. Additional executions in West Prussian territory are known to have taken place in Bissau (Bysewo), Eggertshütte (Egiertowo), Sparau (Sporowo), and the forests of Piasnitz (Piaśnica) and Spengawsken (Szpęgawsk). Chrzanowski, "Danzig-Westpreußen," 33. National Socialist propaganda, which particularly in the summer months of 1939 had exposed supposed Polish atrocities against the German minority, also influenced spontaneous lynching operations. Reciprocal acts of retaliation, like the "Bloody Sunday of Bromberg," helped further escalate the prevailing mood of violence. Michael Alberti, "'Exerzierplatz des Nationalsozialismus': Der Reichsgau Wartheland 1939–1941," in *Genesis*, ed. Mallmann and Musial, 112.
82. Schenk, *Hitlers Mann*, 161.
83. RGBl. 1939 I, 2042.
84. Forster now held great power as an individual. As the Gauleiter, he bore political responsibility for his jurisdiction and held full disciplinary power over all of the party organizations in his territory; as the Reich Governor, he exercised general control over all branches of the administration. In addition, he presided over the judiciary. The Higher SS and Police Leader was also supposed to be personally and directly subordinate to the Reich Governor, but in the case of Richard Hildebrandt, who acted as the extended arm of Heinrich Himmler, this proved to be a fiction in practice. Schenk, *Hitlers Mann*, 142.
85. Czesław Madajczyk, *Die Okkupationspolitik Nazideutschlands in Polen 1939–1945* (Cologne, 1988), 35; Dieter Pohl, "Die Reichsgaue Danzig-Westpreußen und Wartheland: Koloniale Verwaltung oder Modell für die zukünftige Gauverwaltung?" in *Die NS-Gaue: Regionale Mittelinstanzen im zentralistischen "Führerstaat,"* ed. Jürgen John et al. (Munich, 2007), 397.
86. Hitler's secret decree on the "consolidation of Germandom" of 7 October 1939 formed the basis for the "Germanization policy." It stipulated the "home bringing" of so-called *Auslandsdeutsche* (German expatriates), the liquidation of national groups that ostensibly constituted a threat to the German Reich and its inhabitants, and the development of new German settlement regions as primary objectives. As the Reichskommissar zur Festigung des deutschen Volkstums, Heinrich Himmler was commissioned with coordinating these efforts. Chrzanowski, "Danzig-Westpreußen," 38. See the foundational studies by Isabel Heinemann, *"Rasse, Siedlung, deutsches Blut": Das Rasse- und Siedlungshauptamt der SS und die rassenpolitische Neuordnung Europas* (Göttingen, 2003); Andreas Strippel, *NS-Volkstumspolitik und die Neuordnung Europas: Rassenpolitische Selektion der Einwandererzentralstelle des Chefs der Sicherheitspolizei und des SD (1939—1945)* (Paderborn, 2011); and Gerhard Wolf, *Ideologie und Herrschaftsrationalität: Nationalsozialistische Germanisierungspolitik in Polen* (Hamburg, 2012).
87. The gateway for acceptance into the Volksgemeinschaft was the Deutsche Volksliste (German People's List): anyone included on the list obtained German citizenship. Jews, Sinti, and Roma were neither included in the Volksliste, nor could they become "protective members" of the Reich. In actual practice, the "recovery of German blood" in ethnically heterogeneous West Prussia proved to be difficult, since

distinguishing between *deutschstämmig* (of German origins) and *fremdvölkisch* (foreign-ethnic) Poles was almost impossible. Albert Forster had the ambition of declaring his Gau to be the first among the new administrative units to be "Jew free"; he therefore practiced a very generous policy of German assimilation, which led to conflicts with Himmler. Schenk, *Hitlers Mann*, 205.

88. Musial, "Schlachtfeld," 14. Michael Alberti, *Die Verfolgung und Vernichtung der Juden im Reichsgau Wartheland 1939–1945* (Wiesbaden, 2006); Sybille Steinbacher, *"Musterstadt" Auschwitz: Germanisierungspolitik und Judenmord in Ostoberschlesien* (Munich, 2000). See also the contributions by Ingo Loose and Sybille Steinbacher in this volume.
89. Quoted in Schenk, *Hitlers Mann*, 217.
90. Sodeikat, "Verfolgung," 144.
91. Kemlein, "Geschichte," 108.
92. Schenk, *Hitlers Mann*, 177. With a population of 1.3 million Poles (along with 817,000 Germans and fewer than 2,000 Jews), this was a utopian objective. In fact, by the end of 1942, the Germans had managed to expel 123,500 Poles, more than 53,000 of whom were resettled in the General Government. Heinemann, *"Rasse"*, 228.
93. If properties were proven to belong to Poles or Jews, upon the application of the Land Office they were confiscated by the Gestapo. In addition, SS Resettlement Offices and Task Groups (SS-Ansiedlungsstäbe and Arbeitsstäbe) were formed in March 1940 for deporting the undesired Poles and Jews and transferring businesses to ethnic German settlers. Heinemann, *"Rasse"*, 216f.
94. Heinemann, *"Rasse"*, 197f.
95. Chrzanowski, "Danzig-Westpreußen," 39; Schenk, *Hitlers Mann*, 177. We do not have precise figures for the Jewish population in Gdingen at this time. In 1937, 4,897 Jews lived in this harbor town neighboring Danzig; most of them had left the town for central Poland prior to the arrival of German troops. Berendt, "Danziger," 193, 198.
96. However, the numbers involved in the expulsions vary within the literature, particularly since researchers have based them on various different periods. According to Chrzanowski ("Danzig-Westpreußen," 39), a total of 30,758 people were expelled from Pomerania to the General Government by November 1940.
97. Götz Aly, *"Final Solution": Nazi Population Policy and the Murder of the European Jews* (London, 1999), 145 (German original: Frankfurt, 1995). Aly's study describes the chronology of the National Socialist deportation and extermination policies in detail.
98. Drywa, "Stutthof—Stammlager," 478.
99. Grabowska, "Stutthof," 61ff.; Danuta Drywa, "Direkte Extermination," in *Stutthof: Das Konzentrationslager*, 234ff.; see Maria Elżbieta Jezierska, "Straceni w obozie Stutthof [Die Hingerichteten im Lager Stutthof]," *Zeszyty Muzeum Stutthof* 7 (1987): 79–199.
100. Grabowska, "Stutthof," 19f.
101. Ibid., 20f.
102. Marek Orski, "Außenlager,"in *Der Ort des Terrors*, ed. Benz and Distel, 531–792; Grabowska, "Stutthof," 52ff.; Wolf Gruner, "Juden bauen die 'Straßen des Führers': Zwangsarbeit und Zwangsarbeitslager für nichtdeutsche Juden im Altreich 1940 bis 1943/44," *Zeitschrift für Geschichtswissenschaft* 44, no. 9 (1996): 789–808, here 794.
103. Aldo Coradello, *Co się działo w Stutthofie* (Warsaw, 2011), 34–41.
104. Drywa, "Stutthof—Stammlager," 501.

105. Ibid., 494 and 520.
106. The precise fate of the last Jews living in Danzig cannot be definitively reconstructed on the basis of the available sources, which are contradictory. Echt, *Geschichte,* 241ff.; Sodeikat, "Verfolgung," 147f.; Schenk, *Hitlers Mann,* 218.
107. The Polish Supreme National Tribunal sentenced Albert Forster to death on 29 April 1948; the execution presumably occurred on 28 February 1952. Richard Hildebrandt was likewise sentenced to death on 4 November 1949; the sentence was carried out on 10 March 1951. Schenk, *Hitlers Mann,* 287, 226.

CHAPTER 7

WARTHELAND
Ingo Loose

Prior to the Annexation

The National Socialists took over government in Germany in 1933 with the claim that they would reunite those Germans living outside the national borders with the Reich within the foreseeable future. This could be accomplished either by resettling these Germans within the Reich or through military expansion. Hitler had already prophesied in *Mein Kampf* that he wanted to "take up where we broke off six hundred years ago" and once more redirect the "endless German movement" toward the East.[1] Neither new nor genuinely National Socialistic, such plans merely marked a continuation, albeit radicalized, of the traditions of the nineteenth-century Prussian Settlement Commission. Considering the Reich's population density, resettlement was not an option at the time. Moreover, prior to 1939, the National Socialists primarily valued the German minority in Poland as a means of exerting political pressure and as a bargaining chip when conducting German foreign policy vis-à-vis Poland—a strategy that earlier had also formed the basis for the Weimar Republic's governments' policies regarding Poland.[2]

With respect to the borders of the later Reichsgau Wartheland, the number of Germans who remained in reconstituted Poland after 1919 instead of exercising their right to opt for Germany continuously decreased, as opposed to the population's Polish majority, which totaled just over 4 million people; by the beginning of the war in 1939 these Germans numbered around 325,000, most of them living in settlements concentrated in the part of central Poland which would later become the Regierungsbezirk (government district) of Litzmannstadt. The majority of the Jews viewed themselves as a national minority in Poland, with Yiddish or Hebrew as their mother tongue; however, a growing Jewish bourgeoisie existed above all in the towns, though characterized by substantially weaker efforts to assimilate than its counterparts in Western Europe.[3] Prior to 1 September 1939, the Warthegau's Jewish population numbered 435,000 people (8.8 percent), of whom 233,000 alone lived in Łódź. Most of them lived in the towns of later Reichsgau's eastern Regierungsbezirke of Litzmannstadt and Hohensalza. In contrast, most of the Jews from the former Province of Posen had emigrated to Germany after the First World War, and thus, during the interwar period, comparatively few Jews lived in what would become the Regierungsbezirk of Posen.[4]

Overall, Poland's German minority during the 1920s and 1930s cannot be described as a "fifth column" for the National Socialists. This minority undoubtedly included many who sympathized with the Nazi movement and also responded to its anti-Semitism, but most ethnic Germans—Polish citizens who spoke German as their native language or had a German identity—remained loyal to the Second Polish Republic. Although these ethnic Germans did not develop a uniform attitude toward the Polish Jews, their formative experience of anti-Semitism in Poland—which grew and escalated into violence and pogroms above all in the second half of the 1930s—would undoubtedly influence subsequent relationships between Germans, Poles, and Jews in the Reichsgau Wartheland.[5]

Thus, accepted by large parts of the country's population, anti-Semitism did not require the extensive Nazification of the Germans in Poland to gain strength. While Christian-motivated anti-Semitism constituted more of a rural phenomenon,[6] the political right in Poland—first and foremost the National Democratic Party (Endecja)—based its anti-Semitism on economically argued propaganda; Posen, which after 1939 became the *Gauhauptstadt*—that is, the Gau capital—of Wartheland, constituted a predominant National Democratic stronghold during the interwar period.[7] In contrast to the Nazi state, however, state-decreed anti-Semitism did not exist in the Second Polish Republic; moreover, making up 10 percent of the population—in Warsaw and Łódź even more than 30 percent—the Jews by no means formed a negligible quantity;[8] significantly, they were also represented by a range of political parties and notable politicians in political committees, the Sejm (the lower house of the Polish parliament), and regional parliaments.[9]

Accordingly, the few studies dealing with the tripartite relationship between the Poles, Jews, and Germans[10] indicate a mixture of distance and normality.[11] While the Polish public noticed the German minority's growing sympathy for National Socialism[12]—especially after the annexation of Austria in 1938—many Germans protested and repudiated the November pogrom in Germany;[13] hence the image of "the Germans" in Poland before 1 September 1939 is complicated. In recent years, Poland, too, has faced sensitive questions regarding the extent to which Poland's problematic minority policies during the 1930s cleared the way for collaboration or even just indifference to the fate of Polish Jews after 1939[14]—a connection already problematized by the Jewish historian Emanuel Ringelblum (1900–1944) in an essay written in 1943/44 in his Warsaw hideaway about Polish-Jewish relations during the Second World War, which also emphasized the efficacy of German methods—rewards and threats—intended to help induce the Polish population to give up hidden Jews.[15]

The First Weeks of the Annexation

Hitler clearly specified Germany's war aims in an address to the Wehrmacht's supreme commanders on 22 August 1939: " . . . I have placed my death-head formations at the ready with the order to mercilessly and pitilessly send men, women, and children of Polish descent and language to their deaths. . . . Poland shall be depopulated and settled with Germans."[16] Hitler's set phrase of depopulation and resettlement contained the heart of National Socialist occupation policy in Poland, especially in the Warthegau. The defamation, disfranchisement, and terrorization of the Jews in Old Reich prior to the war also clearly signaled right from the outset who would occupy the lowest level of the victim hierarchy in the annexed territories, even though the extensive "cleansing" operations during the first weeks of the German occupation chiefly victimized the Polish elite and not so much the Jews.

In fall 1939, under Wehrmacht control, the Einsatzgruppen of the Security Police (Sicherheitspolizei; SiPo) and Security Service (Sicherheitsdienst; SD) systematically exterminated the Polish leadership elite and intelligentsia, but they also had already massacred large numbers of

Jews and "elements hostile to the Reich and Germans." As Jochen Böhler and Alexander B. Rossino have convincingly demonstrated, these mass murders during the occupation's first months by no means constituted a radicalizing process but rather were motivated from the start by a manifest intent to kill.[17] Polish historiography, in particular, frequently refers to this process with the term "indirect destruction" (zagłada pośrednia), which clearly intimates that National Socialist operations in Poland *always* victimized Jews and Poles, sometimes in considerable numbers, and that this was also the Germans' intent.[18]

After the German invasion of Poland, the Nazis initially divided the occupied territory into four military districts (Militärbezirke)—Danzig-West Prussia, Posen, Łódź, and Kraków—and Hitler appointed a Head of the Civil Administration (Chef der Zivilverwaltung; CdZ) for each.[19] The previous Senate President of Danzig Arthur Greiser obtained the Head of the Civil Administration position for the military district of Posen in mid September 1939, advancing to become the Reich Governor (Reichsstatthalter) and Gauleiter for the entire region after the establishment of the Reichsgau Posen (renamed the Reichsgau Wartheland on 29 January), headquartered in the Gau capital Posen.[20]

Although far from completely Nazified prior to 1 September 1939, the German minority in Poland nonetheless committed a wide range of crimes against the Polish and Jewish population after the German attack on Poland. These included the numerous excesses of the *Volksdeutsche Selbstschutz*[21] (ethnic German self-defense units) as well as the "euthanasia operation," which recruited its personnel from the local Security Police and already began in the Warthegau at the end of October 1939, simultaneously with the establishment of the civil administration.[22] The Reichsgau Wartheland was also where a special unit under SS-Untersturmführer Herbert Lange first used gas vans to murder institutionalized persons, starting in January 1940. Thus Michael Alberti has rightly noted that nowhere else is the "connecting line between the 'euthanasia' murders and the genocide of the European Jews more clearly visible than in the Warthegau."[23]

From the very first days of the occupation, Jewish daily life—or, more appropriately, survival—proved catastrophic in every sense. As early as October 1939, the Polizeipräsident (Police President) in Łódź instituted a general work duty for Jews over the age of fourteen; and already by 13 October, thousands of Jews in the Warthegau were working on a daily basis without pay, predominantly for the Wehrmacht but also for numerous government bodies and other agencies.[24] The practically unrestrained plunder of the Jewish population's property, observed throughout the towns, as well as drastic restrictions pertaining to the possession of cash and professional practice, led very quickly to serious impoverishment.[25] In addition, Wehrmacht members repeatedly engaged in arbitrary assaults, excesses, and murders, but such violence was perpetrated above all by Security Police units, which already during fall 1939 virtually exterminated a series of small Jewish communities (Kruszwica, Mogilno, Strzelno, Żnin, and others), either by shooting the Jews to death or herding them into local synagogues that were subsequently set on fire or blown up.[26]

Countless additional ordinances—not least of which was the general marking obligation for Jews in effect since 26 November 1939, introduced substantially earlier than in the Old Reich—cemented the status of Jews as pariahs. Especially in the retail but also the wholesale sector, the rapid elimination of Jewish entrepreneurs during these initial months actually led to localized disruptions in the otherwise prioritized provisioning of the German population.[27]

Though formally part of the Reich, the incorporated eastern regions retained a special status in many respects. This involved, first, the establishment of a police border in October 1939,[28] intended to stop uncontrolled migration by so-called *Fremdvölkische*—alien ethnic elements—into the Old Reich and maintained until the end of the war. An approximation with Reich law as of spring 1940 occurred only in part. The Polish and Jewish populations were subject to numerous special regulations—above all in criminal and civil law—that lacked any counterparts in Reich legislation and only became standardized for the incorporated eastern territories at the end of 1941.[29] In addition, Greiser—as did the other satraps in former Polish territories (Albert Forster in the Reichsgau Danzig-West Prussia, Hans Frank in the General Government)—distrusted the influences of the Berlin ministries and strove for as much independence as possible in all matters concerning occupation policy.[30] On the whole, however, as State Secretary Hans Pfundtner of the Interior Ministry emphasized early on, any planning developments were always supposed to ensure discrimination against the Polish and Jewish population: "Insofar as the introduction of Reich legislative stipulations in the incorporated eastern territories proves to be absolutely necessary, I request that a review be undertaken specifically in each case whether members of the German *Volk* are afforded their due preferential position, and, if necessary, that the provisions from the Reich legislation to be introduced are altered such that *fremdvölkische* [alien ethnic] *Volk* members do not become the beneficiaries of German law."[31] Significantly, even though the Police Ordinance on the Marking of the Jews of 1 September 1941 and the Ordinance on the Employment of Jews published four weeks later introduced anti-Jewish measures for the Old Reich as well as the incorporated eastern territories,[32] the final standardization of anti-Jewish legal discrimination in the annexed territories did not occur until the Ordinance on the Introduction of Regulations on the Dejudaization of the German Economy in the Incorporated Eastern Territories of 30 March 1942[33]—that is, long after the deportations of the Reich-German Jews "to the East" and the systematic mass murder began.

The incorporated eastern regions often figured in German propaganda as the "shapeless expanse of the European east," where the German *Volk* would find its developmental potential in a quasi-uninhabited territory.[34] However, Gauleiter Arthur Greiser in particular made no secret of his willingness to create such conditions using violence, if need be: "Those who want to live must fight, and if a fight is about an entire *Volk* needing to live and wanting to live, then the soil on which the *Volk* needs to live and wants to live must also belong to this *Volk*, and it is impossible for another *Volk* to also have room on it. That is actually the entire deeper significance of the structuring process being dealt with today in the eastern region."[35] The Nazis planned to settle 4 to 5 million Germans in the incorporated eastern territories over a course of approximately ten years, predominantly in the Warthegau.[36] With this in mind, Hitler had pointed out in a speech on 6 October 1939 that the most important task of German policy regarding Poland was "a new organization of the ethnographic circumstances, that is, a resettlement of nationalities so that better dividing lines result upon the completion of the development."[37] This implied, of course, the "removal" of the region's autochthonous population. Accordingly, the counterpart to settlement was a "negative population policy," namely, the Reich Security Main Office's (Reichssicherheitshauptamt) very far-reaching deportation plans regarding the Poles and Jews.[38]

The plans tied into the Nazi leadership's obsessive need to render the Reich, along with its newly incorporated territories, "free of Jews." These very extensive deportation plans coalesced with the operation to bring millions of Germans "home into the Reich"—the realization of which, however, would prove illusory during the war.[39] Already on 21 September 1939, Reinhard Heydrich had presented a program to the heads of the Reich Security Main Office group, whose major points provided for the incorporation of the "former German provinces," as well as the creation of a "foreign-language Gau," namely, the later General Government for the Occupied Polish Territories. In the territories slated for incorporation, such as the later Warthegau, the program called for the construction of Jewish ghettos in the towns "in order [to have] a better control opportunity and deportation opportunity."[40]

From the beginning of the military campaign in Poland, the Reichsführung-SS attempted to take over all fields of responsibility in occupation policy related to police and "settlement-technical" matters. On 7 October 1939, Hitler appointed Heinrich Himmler as the Reich Commissioner for the Strengthening of Germandom (Reichskommissar für die Festigung deutschen Volkstums).[41] Himmler's responsibilities included ensuring "the elimination of the harmful influence of such ethnically alien [*volksfremd*] parts of the population that signify a danger for the Reich and the German *Volksgemeinschaft*" and, finally, also developing the "settlement territories through the permanent settlement [*Seßhaftmachung*] of Reich and *Volk* Germans returning home from abroad."[42] Along with the SS and the police, Himmler also had the corresponding resources at his disposal to carry out these tasks. These settlement and deportation plans would focus on occupied Poland (see figure 7.1).

Figure 7.1. Jews in the Warthegau prior to their deportation, 1942. *Source*: United States Holocaust Memorial Museum, Photo Archives, image no: 74312B

The Period of the Occupation

A Führer decree from 8 October 1939 founded the Reichsgau Posen, thereby stipulating the territory's annexation.[43] Organized into the similarly sized Regierungsbezirke of Posen, Hohensalza, and Kalisch (renamed as Regierungsbezirk Litzmannstadt on 3 May 1940),[44] the Reichsgau encompassed a territory of just under 44,000 square kilometers and, initially, approximately 4.9 million inhabitants.[45] Thus the Warthegau included just under half of the area of the incorporated eastern territories; almost 55 percent of its territory, including the entire Regierungsbezirk of Posen, had belonged to Prussia prior to 1918. Referred to as the "granary of the Reich,"[46] the Reichsgau Wartheland's importance within the overall structure of the Greater German Reich lay above all in agriculture, which also led Nazi regional planners to focus their settlement plans on this area.

Disputes accompanied the demarcation of the border between the Warthegau and the General Government in fall 1939, primarily regarding whether the area of Łódź with its textile industry should be allocated to the incorporated regions or—taking into consideration the Polish and Jewish majority of its population—to the General Government. The fact that Łódź (renamed Litzmannstadt on 11 April 1940)[47] remained part of the Warthegau can probably be traced back essentially to the influence of Hermann Göring, who as the Commissioner for the Four-Year Plan and, as of November 1939, also the Senior Director of the newly founded Main Trustee Office East (Haupttreuhandstelle Ost), had an interest in the city's industrial potential, above all in textiles and clothing.[48]

As a result, the Reichsgaue of Danzig-West Prussia and Posen mutated into an "application area and training field for radical, *völkisch*-National Socialist master race and colonization theory."[49] This was characterized above all by the deliberate merging of state and party offices through personal unions of Reich Governor and Gauleiter positions (as with the Reichsgaue in Austria and the Sudetenland) as well as Landrat (District Administrator) and NSDAP Kreisleiter (District Leader) positions.[50] Arthur Greiser and his deputy August Jäger possessed almost unlimited power: as Reich Governor, Greiser presided over the entire administration, including the Higher SS and Police Leader (Höherer SS- und Polizeiführer) and the police; as Gauleiter he led all of the party's organizations in the Warthegau. The Germans established their administration surprisingly quickly in fall 1939, primarily by delegating Reich-German bureaucrats who created new municipal administrations, labor offices, and revenue agencies or correspondingly transformed existing Polish institutions. Within a very short time, they removed Jews from city and municipal administrations, whereas, at least initially, they tolerated Poles at the lowest hierarchical levels, even though the intended Germanization process called for their disappearance as soon as possible. The police apparatus was especially extensive: in fall 1939, the Gestapo, Criminal Police (Kriminalpolizei), Security Service, and Gendarmerie already included thousands of members, and their numbers would substantially increase by 1943.[51] To be sure, the National Socialist terror apparatus in the Reichsgau Wartheland did not consist solely of Reich Germans delegated to the region. But taking into consideration the entire occupation apparatus and the administration, ethnic Germans and new settlers were significantly underrepresented—in all three Regierungsbezirke, Reich Germans accounted for 90 percent of all of the officials.[52]

Immediately after the founding of the Reichsgau, the NSDAP's Racial Policy Office (Rassenpolitisches Amt) submitted a memorandum on the "Question of the Handling of the former Polish Territories according to Racial Policy Perspectives," specifying as a goal of German policy in the incorporated territories "the creation of a racially and therefore mentally-spiritually [*geistig-seelisch*] as well as *völkisch*-politically uniform population." This entailed the requirement that "all non-Germanizable elements [be] ruthlessly removed."[53] The first of the mass deportations from the Warthegau to the General Government—centrally planned by the Reich Security Main Office—began on 1 December 1939. By 17 December 1939, the Security Police had deported a total of almost 88,000 Jews and Poles, prioritizing wealthier persons who had to leave all of their property behind.[54] But many Jews also fled to the General Government on their own accord, hoping to find more tolerable living conditions than in the Warthegau.

As a result, by 1940 practically no Jews remained in the Regierungsbezirk of Posen. In spring 1940, a total of 1.2 million people, including 52,209 Jews (4.4 percent) lived in the Regierungsbezirk of Hohensalza, predominantly in the Stadtkreis (urban district) of Leslau (Włocławek) (6,000 Jews) and in the Landkreise (rural districts) of Warthbrücken (Koło) (9,783), Konin (7,491), Kutno (10,353), and Leslau (9,042). The overwhelming majority of the Wartheland Jews, however, lived in the Regierungsbezirk of Litzmannstadt. In spring 1940, Jews accounted for 318,306 (15.3 percent) of the Regierungsbezirk's 2.1 million inhabitants, most of them living in the Stadtkreis of Litzmannstadt (202,497) and the Landkreise of Kalisch (17,450), Łask (Lask) (22,004),

Litzmannstadt including Brzeziny (Löwenstadt) (21,152), Sieradz (16,042), and Wieluń including Radomsko (16,511).[55]

The Nazi regime obviously felt no need for special secrecy measures. Thus in October 1940, the *Neue Zürcher Zeitung* reported extensively on a lecture by Himmler on "modern settlement problems and the question of the European eastern region": "all alien ethnic-national elements [*fremdes Volkstum*] and especially Jewish elements [*Judentum*] will in future be placed in the General Government. This means that approximately 500,000 to 600,000 people will be resettled there, whereby the Jews shall be housed in a separate ghetto, namely all of the Jews from the entire Greater German Reich."[56] A dynamic between settlement and deportation set in immediately after the founding of the Reichsgau. On 15 October 1939 the German Reich signed a treaty with Estonia and on 30 October with Latvia on the resettlement of Germans living in these countries. On 16 November, the Soviet Union and the German Reich finally concluded contractual arrangements for resettling the *Volksdeutsche* from Volhynia and Galicia. The aforementioned incorporation of the Kutno/Łódź region with 700,000 inhabitants, including well over 200,000 Jews, further complicated matters.

Germany's bilateral resettlement treaties with the Baltic states and the Soviet Union were based on the financial and/or material compensation of the resettling individuals. To fulfill all of the associated responsibilities, the German Resettlement Trust Company (Deutsche Umsiedlungs-Treuhand-Gesellschaft) was founded on 3 November 1939, with offices in Posen and Litzmannstadt, among other places.[57] To minimize the burden on the state treasury, in November the German Resettlement Trust Company developed an accounting system that, right from the outset, based its calculations on the assumption that Polish and Jewish assets in the occupied territories would be available free of charge to compensate the resettlers.[58] In this way, the property of Poles and Jews contributed "to the material preconditions of the entire resettlement program."[59]

Sixty-five thousand Baltic Germans from Estonia and Latvia comprised the first resettlement group to profit from the massive plundering operation. Prior to 1939, National Socialist ideas had spread more widely among them than the Germans in Poland. The Baltic Germans were allocated substantial amounts of confiscated farmland and residential and business property and appointed in large numbers as "trustees" for confiscated companies under management by the Main Trustee Office East, which had been founded at the end of 1939 as an agency of the Four-Year Plan with offices in Posen and

Litzmannstadt.[60] Since resettlement focused on the Litzmannstadt region, where by August 1944 the German population had increased from 67,000 to 142,000, Baltic Germans also must have extensively benefited from the property of Polish Jews, although precise figures can no longer be determined.[61]

Gauleiter Greiser was very much in his element when dealing with the subject of resettlement: "For the resettlers, after dear God in heaven comes Adolf Hitler, nothing else. The Führer is, for them, the content of their lives, because, for them, the idea that there is a person who has the power to recall tens of thousands from foreign parts and give them a farm [*Hof*] where they are driven about in a wagon, where horses and cows and pigs stand in the barn, where the farm woman finds a cooking pot on the hearth and the children a doll in the doll cradle, is unimaginable."[62] Already by January 1940, however, Governor General Hans Frank came up with the idea that he wanted to be more than just the administrator of a "land of plunder" that "in its economic, social, cultural, and political structure [was to be turned into a] heap of rubble"; and even Greiser's pithy language could not conceal the problems this entailed for the deportation and displacement operations intended to create space for Germans.[63]

Over time, Frank's craving for recognition and his goal "to create an ancillary Reich of the Reich,"[64] as well as the Wehrmacht's logistical priorities and the constantly increasing number of ethnic German settlers, created a situation that historians have rightly described as a power-political deadlock, where the number of Germans that had to be taken in by the Warthegau far exceeded the Poles and Jews that could be "gotten rid of" in the General Government.[65] Quite a few settlers who had been promised a house, farm, or business found themselves in the Wartheland's transitional camps, where many would stay until the end of the war,[66] their disappointment neatly summed up by the witticism "Warthegau = Wartegau" (waiting Gau).[67] In 1940, the competent agencies began registering growing numbers of newly settled farmers who fled their allocated farms by night or refused to accept them in the first place. Along with being uncertain about the occupied territories' political future, the settlers naturally feared reprisals from the Polish resistance (which, however, rarely occurred in the Warthegau) and were also occasionally moved by a sense of injustice, noticeable above all among German small farmers from Volhynia and Romania, whom the Security Service of the SS predominantly categorized as "ethnically [*völkisch*] indifferent." On the whole, however, the autobiographical literature predominantly features the image of an overly eager ethnic

German with exaggerated National Socialist behavior, notorious for harassing and denouncing Poles and Jews.[68]

A broad consensus regarding economic objectives in the Warthegau obtained right from the outset, extending from the Reich Ministry of Economics to the larger German banks and the Gauleitung in Posen. These objectives concerned developing and rapidly integrating the incorporated territories and exploiting their industrial, agricultural, and labor potential for the benefit of Germany's war economy.[69] All things considered, we may indeed speak of a kind of "spirit of optimism" that animated how not only commercial enterprises from the Old Reich but also large numbers of ethnic German entrepreneurs set about expanding their business activities to the incorporated eastern territories.

Massive interventions in the occupied territories' ownership structures constituted the primary and essential rationale of Nazi economic policy in the Wartheland. The so-called Polish Assets Decree (Polenvermögensverordnung) of 17 September 1940, giving Nazi rulers the unrestricted right of disposal over any private property of Poles and Jews, exemplified how private assets could be requisitioned for the Reich's benefit—Polish assets *could*, and Jewish assets *had to* be confiscated "for the benefit of the Reich."[70]

This corresponded, in any event, to long-standing practice, since on 18 November 1939 the Reich Governor had already virtually legalized the state's unbounded arbitrariness with his General Decree on the Securing of Jewish Assets.[71] Moreover, many Germans (and Poles as well) viewed signs—obvious since the first days of the war—that they could virtually do anything they wanted with the Jewish population and its assets as an opportunity to personally enrich themselves, exploiting the Jews' predicament by robbing them, appropriating their apartments and other real estate (including inventories), selling foodstuffs to the Jews at excessively inflated prices, or blackmailing them for money with threats of denunciation.[72]

The government administration and private economy collaborated especially closely and smoothly when dealing with concrete expropriations of the Wartheland Jews. In turn, Litzmannstadt—where Regierungspräsident Friedrich Uebelhoer ordered the formation of a ghetto as early as December 1939—exemplifies the degree to which this expropriation was closely linked with ghettoization:[73] "The creation of the ghetto is, obviously, only an interim measure. I will decide at what points in time and by which methods the ghetto and thus the city of Lodsch shall be cleansed of Jews. The final goal, in any case, must be that we completely burn out this plague spot."[74] In spring and early summer 1940—that is, coinciding with the creation of the Litzmannstadt ghetto, initially for 160,000 Jews[75]—featured a concerted operation in which the Posen Trustee Office confiscated millions from the accounts of Jewish families, which could now be "utilized."[76] The above-average yield gained from plundering Jewish assets in the eastern part of the Warthegau, especially in Litzmannstadt, bore a direct relation to the region's aforementioned number of Jewish inhabitants.[77]

As in the General Government, the ghettoization of the Jews also constituted a complex process in the Warthegau, resulting essentially from decisions by the regional authorities and agencies and not from any previously established plan,[78] as can be demonstrated by the fact that the entire process dragged on from early 1940 to late 1941, that is, until the beginning of the systematic murder of the Jews in Warthegau. As a rule, the creation of a ghetto—the first was erected in February 1940 in Pabianice (Pabianitz) in the Regierungsbezirk of Litzmannstadt—occurred on the initiative of the respective municipal administration or security police agency, namely, in a specific part of the town that had already been inhabited by many or even predominantly by Jews prior to 1939. The extent to which authorities sealed the ghetto off from the town did not always depend on their justification for its creation (such as controlling epidemics or opposing the black market). Often, they simply lacked sufficient building materials, such as barbed wire, to separate the ghetto from the outside world by anything more than a wooden fence and/or a regular policeman at the ghetto exit.[79]

At the very least, however, the ghettos created in 1940 had one particular feature in common, namely, their erection—in terms Heydrich's aforementioned decree—as a provisional arrangement prior to deporting the Jews to the General Government. In this regard, we need to consider that the confiscation of Jewish assets ordered by the authorities for the benefit of the German *Volksgemeinschaft* stripped the Jews of the financial basis for their existence, which in turn created a central motive for their ghettoization. This fulfilled the requirements of the first stage along the path toward the systematic destruction of the Jews, all the more so because as of 1940, when the deportations failed to materialize, these provisional ghettos turned into permanent "Jewish residential districts" that were thorns in eyes of the respective municipal administrations.

Moreover, forced labor already began being used extensively in the Reichsgau Wartheland on the occupation's very first day, not only as a result of ideological hubris but because of war-related necessities.[80] Even before the invasion of Poland, on 23 May 1939 Hitler had commented on the necessity of "deploying citizens of non-German territories for work in the Reich."[81] Since Governor General Hans Frank, as of spring 1940, opposed the resumption of deportations from the incorporated territories, he suggested that, instead of deporting the Poles first to the General Government and from there to the Reich for work, they should be deported directly from the incorporated territories, which in any event "had already formed the traditional area of origin of Polish seasonal workers in Germany."[82] Himmler's objections, however, minimized or fully prevented this "'ideal combination' of resettlement and labor-deployment policy."[83]

Initially, however, the Reichsgau Wartheland lacked any systematic labor deployment policy regarding the Jews. From the first months of the occupation until well into 1940, a broad range of agencies, sometimes even private companies, randomly recruited Jews for uncompensated forced labor, and the Jewish councils dedicated some of their key efforts to curbing the arbitrary character of these measures by collaborating with the labor offices to organize the availability of Jewish workers. But when the planned deportations to the General Government did not occur, the exploitation of Jewish forced laborers in "Jewish crews," ghettos, and forced labor camps—mostly organized by local labor offices—became more radical.[84]

With the constantly growing demand for labor, authorities in Posen also centrally planned the deployment of an increasing number of Jews at large projects in the Reichsgau Wartheland. Thus, notably, several thousand Jews were involved in the construction of the Reich Autobahn between Frankfurt an der Oder and Posen. In contrast, Greiser's plans to also deploy Wartheland Jews on Reich territory failed.[85] The Jews forcibly employed specifically in the Regierungsbezirk of Posen, where they worked not only on the construction of the Autobahn but also on numerous construction projects for the Reichsbahn railway and for a range of private companies, came primarily from the Litzmannstadt ghetto and, especially in 1942, from other liquidated Wartheland ghettos. Since the end of 1940, in exchange for a "Jew rental fee" (*Judenleihgebühr*), the administration of the Litzmannstadt ghetto procured forced laborers for clients, who had to provide accommodations and food in the labor camps. In November 1941, the various forced labor camps housed a total of 7,161 Jews.[86] The number of Jews employed in the construction of the Reich Autobahn in the Regierungsbezirk of Posen alone increased from 1,689 in January 1941 to over 6,000, until in August 1942 the Gestapo in Posen ordered the liquidation of the camps. Conditions in these forced labor camps were dreadful: "Very poor housing, a lack of the most essential equipment, catastrophic sanitary conditions, insufficient allocation of food and clothing, as well as a lack of medical care: that is the existence—rather the vegetating—of the Jews in the forced labor camps."[87] Under such conditions, diseases such as typhoid and tuberculosis spread, and the death rate was extremely high. Thousands of Jewish forced laborers did not survive their sojourns in the camps.[88]

We need to distinguish labor deployments within the Litzmannstadt ghetto itself from the forced labor camps in the Regierungsbezirk of Posen. The Jewish elder Mordechai Chaim Rumkowski had already informed German authorities of the confined Jews' labor potential in spring 1940,[89] and nineteen different labor departments with 7,000 workers were operating in the ghetto by the end of the year. In 1943, more than 60,000 people were working in ninety-six departments.

The many efforts by Rumkowski and other Jewish elders to convince the National Socialists of the Jews' right to exist failed not because of the economic unsustainability of the Jewish forced labor camps and the numerous workshops and operations in the Litzmannstadt ghetto right from the outset,[90] but rather because the SS in particular showed little serious interest in wholly abandoning its ideological prerogatives for the benefit of employing Jews as forced labor (and correspondingly providing them with food). The respective city and ghetto administrations, however, had considerable interest in systematically deploying the labor of the Jewish ghetto residents. In many of the smaller ghettos, though, a comparable "productivization" occurred only in initial stages or not at all; in these cases the authorities' interest lay in liquidating the ghettos and their associated costs as quickly as possible.[91] In a few ghettos—namely, in Brzeziny, Bełchatów, Łask, and Pabianice—initiatives undertaken by the Berlin company Günter Schwarz led to the establishment of large tailor workshops with thousands of Jewish forced laborers. In practice, however, only the Wehrmacht, government bodies, and the police awarded more and less extensive contracts to the respective ghetto administration or Jewish council of elders.[92]

To be sure, the Litzmannstadt ghetto constituted an exception; as of fall 1941, its production for the Wehrmacht's army clothing depots and numerous private German companies (Rudolph Karstadt, Josef Neckermann, Felina Mannheim, the Alsterhaus in Hamburg, and others) exceeded the costs for maintaining the ghetto and feeding its inhabitants, and due to the profitable forced labor the ghetto existed until

1944. Nonetheless, as in numerous other ghettos in the Warthegau, many thousands of people died from undernourishment, epidemics, and violence. The Nazis finally liquidated the Litzmannstadt ghetto in August 1944, after deporting the last 68,000 ghetto residents to Auschwitz-Birkenau.[93]

The controversial question—still being discussed in the historiography—regarding exactly when Hitler and the Nazi leadership decided to systematically exterminate the European Jews cannot be addressed more closely here. Yet developments in the Reichsgau Wartheland undoubtedly played a central role on the path toward this decision.[94] One of the earliest documents that explicitly contemplates a violent solution is a letter by the Director of the Posen SD Section (SD-Abschnitt) Rolf-Heinz Höppner to Adolf Eichmann from 16 July 1941:

> Dear Comrade Eichmann. . . . In the appendix, I am sending you a file note that summarizes the various discussions in the local Reich Governor's Office [Reichsstatthalterei]. I would be grateful to you for a position statement on this. The things sound fantastical in part, but in my opinion could very much be implemented. . . . This winter there is a danger that the Jews can no longer all be fed. It is to be seriously considered whether the most humane solution is to finish off the Jews—insofar as they are incapable of work—through some kind of fast-acting means. In any case, this would be more agreeable than letting them starve.[95]

Considerable evidence suggests that in summer 1941 Greiser sought permission from Hitler and/or Himmler to be able to murder 100,000 Jews categorized as unfit for work in a "regional final solution of the Jewish question."[96] Perhaps the mass murder of Soviet Jews carried out by the Einsatzgruppen and Security Service after the German invasion of the Soviet Union also led Greiser to assume that his recommendation would be well received in Berlin.[97] In a subsequent letter from Greiser to Himmler in May 1942, the Gauleiter explicitly mentioned the "operation of the special treatment of around 100,000 Jews in my Gau authorized by you in agreement with the Head of Reich Security Main Office, SS-Obergruppenführer Heydrich," which proves that, in fact, the murder of the Jews in Wartheland originally resulted from Greiser's own efforts.[98] The permission to murder 100,000 Wartheland Jews thus to some extent amounted to an advanced concession or at least served in Berlin as an argument for the subsequent deportation of 20,000 German, Austrian, Czech, and Luxembourger Jews to the Litzmannstadt ghetto in fall 1941. It was no coincidence that Himmler justified his announcement on 18 September that the Litzmannstadt ghetto had to reckon with an upcoming influx of 60,000 Jews by stating that the ghetto had the "space for acceptance."[99] He could hardly have gained this impression from his visit to Litzmannstadt on 6 June 1941; despite the ultimate reduction of the planned number from 60,000 to 20,000 after protests by Greiser and Uebelhoer, Himmler's plans only make sense if he had been able to count on an impending reduction of the ghetto population from the outset. The aforementioned letter to Himmler, in which Greiser requested permission to subject some 35,000 tubercular Poles in the Warthegau to the same "special treatment" applied to the Jews, demonstrates the extent to which the Gauleiter viewed murder as contributing to the Germanization of the Warthegau.[100]

In contrast to the extermination camps (Treblinka, Bełżec, and Sobibór) set up later as part of Operation Reinhard, Wartheland's Security Police and SS-Oberführer Herbert Mehlhorn, who was ordered by Greiser to coordinate the mass murder operations, resorted to gas wagons, which had already been used to murder the sick since January 1940. From 8 December 1941 to March 1943 in Kulmhof (Chełmno), Special Detachment (Sonderkommando) Lange, numbering around eighty men, used three gas wagons to murder the Jewish population of all of the Wartheland ghettos. For the time being only the Litzmannstadt ghetto escaped liquidation completely,[101] but when Himmler and Greiser arranged for its destruction in spring 1944, the death squads put Kulmhof into "operation" for a second time, murdering an additional 7,196 Jews from Łódź. In total, at least 152,000 people were murdered in Kulmhof, including—apart from Jews—around eighty children from the Czech village of Lidice viewed by SS racial experts as not "capable of Germanization," approximately 4,300 Roma and Sinti, an unknown number of Soviet prisoners of war, and an estimated few hundred Polish civilians.[102]

Thus three aspects contributed decisively to the resolution to murder the Wartheland Jews and the implementation of this crime. First, having used the gas wagons at the end of 1941, the Nazis in the Warthegau already had one and half years of experience in mass murder—more than those in any other occupied territory. Second, whereas public awareness of the "euthanasia operation" carried out in the Old Reich led to abandonment of gassing operations there in August 1941, the "murder of defenseless inmates of institutions in the Warthegau [proceeded] virtually without a hitch."[103] In other words, mass destruction could be carried out extremely efficiently in the Warthegau and secrecy seemed to be easier to realize than in the Reich. Third, the deportation in late October/early November 1941 of 20,000 Jews from the territory of the Reich, as well as 5,000 Roma and Sinti from Burgenland, created a situation in which regional authorities, led by Greiser, pushed all the more strongly for the ability to eliminate at least those Jews in the Warthegau who were unfit for work by murdering them. The concentration of work-capable Jews in the Litzmannstadt ghetto, as well as the murder of Jews unfit for work, can be interpreted as a kind of compromise among the participating National Socialist agencies, namely, between the SS and the Reich Governor's Office, on the one hand, which pushed for a radical "solution of the Jewish question," and the municipal administration, Wehrmacht, and private businesses, on the other hand, which advocated the greatest possible exploitation of Jewish forced labor.

When in February and March 1942, in various towns in the Litzmannstadt region, large numbers of Jews were randomly removed from the ghettos, arrested, and publically executed, the local population of the eastern Warthegau quickly realized with horrible certainty that National Socialist Jewish policy had taken a decisive turn.[104] In 1942, the town of Litzmannstadt's statistical monthly reports no longer even listed the Jews. With the reference "without Jews," the numerous tables now only afforded them a virtual presence, so to speak.[105]

Numerous indications testify to the fact that knowledge of the extermination facilities in Kulmhof was more widespread than historians for a long time assumed. Barely three weeks after the extermination operation began, a letter from Koło to Izbica in the eastern General Government reported that "in a remote village named Chełmno, in special diesel trucks, thousands of Jews [were being] murdered with gas."[106] Reliable detailed information made its way to the Warsaw ghetto in February 1942 through the report of the Jewish eyewitness "Szlamek." On 19 January, "Szlamek"[107] had managed to escape first from Kulmhof and later to the General Government and to Warsaw.[108] In July 1942, an officer of a Wehrmacht sports school in Warsaw noted precise facts in his diary about the killing of Wartheland Jews in gas wagons in the immediate vicinity of Litzmannstadt.[109] Finally, a speech by Szmul Zygielbojm on 2 September 1942 at a Labour meeting in London for the first time closely described the destruction of Jews in Kulmhof to the Allies.[110] Previously, in early July 1942, a *New York Times* article had already explicitly described the gassings in Kulmhof.[111] These examples demonstrate that an individual's state of knowledge at the time was quite obviously not determined by insufficient opportunities to disseminate such reports themselves, and this applies to an even greater extent to the occupied or incorporated territories than to the Old Reich.

The flood of ordinances introduced with the goal of ensuring the supremacy of all Germans over the rest of the population required the fundamental clarification of questions regarding how to actually understand the terms *Deutscher* and *Fremdvölkischer*.[112] The National Socialists expected to accomplish this by instituting the German People's List (*Deutsche Volksliste*), but local authorities in the Reichsgaue of Danzig-West Prussia and Wartheland, as well as the Regierungsbezirke of Kattowitz and Zichenau, used it in widely different ways. Greiser viewed the People's List not so much as an instrument for immediate Germanization but rather as a means to ethnically classify the group of Germans in the Warthegau.[113] Greiser had no intention of using the list as part of a Germanization process, because, right from the start, he ruled out the possibility registering Poles in the German People's List (if this interested them at all) and subjecting them to such a process.[114]

As long as the German administration could not deport or "eradicate" all of the Poles and Jews, and furthermore relied on them for manpower during the war, it consequently had to ensure the minimization of contact between Germans and *Fremdvölkische*—that is, foreign ethnic elements. Countless memoranda and circulars from the Reich Governor's Office regulating relations between the Germans and the Poles lay at the heart of National Socialist policy. Yet this fact not only reveals the importance of this issue to the Warthegau's rulers but also suggests that such appeals arose out of a certain necessity; or in other words, that the routine interactive praxis among Poles and Germans, who often ignored these dividing lines, could look quite different, especially since they could not completely avoid such social contact anyway. It is undoubtedly true that on the part of both Germans and non-Germans, many people hardly worried about such regulations in their circle of acquaintances and friends. But it is also true that the authorities applied some very draconian measures and made various examples of people to serve as warnings, and that the Higher SS and Police Leader's situation reports meticulously recorded the sometimes quite considerable number of violations pursued by the Gestapo.[115]

The advancing ghettoization of the Wartheland Jews reduced their opportunities to maintain contact with the Polish population. To be sure, such relations among Poles and Jews were limited predominantly to trading in foodstuffs and skilled trade products or services, but at least they were possible within the context of so-called open or "village" ghettos, playing in fact a central role in the survival of many Jews. However, during the course of 1942, the Nazis liquidated all of these open, generally smaller ghettos, either transferring their inhabitants to the Litzmannstadt ghetto or murdering them in Kulmhof, depending on the criteria of their "ability to work." The comparatively high percentage of Germans in the population as a whole made hiding Jews who had escaped the ghettos much more difficult—and thus also more infrequent—than in the General Government.[116]

Apart from members of the SS and police, as well as the municipal and ghetto administrations, individual opportunities for contact between Jews and Germans were minimal. Germans occasionally maintained trade contacts with Jews, but they were subject to restrictive ordinances (notably prohibiting the selling of food to Jews), although their punishments for non-compliance were less severe than for the Poles. The few cases where individual contacts between Jews, on the one hand, and Germans or Poles, on the other, resulted in prosecutions before special courts in Posen, Litzmannstadt, and Kalisch testify more to the lack of opportunity for such encounters. Their small number with respect to Germans should not be interpreted as evidence for a particular degree of Nazification, nor should contacts between Poles and Jews be interpreted as a particular willingness to help the suffering Jewish population.[117]

Conclusion

As we view National Socialist policy in the Reichsgau Wartheland from a distance of almost seventy years, considering its plans and implemented measures, as well as its consequences and results, the term "training field" occasionally applied to the Wartheland appears fully justified. To be sure, the ideological objective of a Germanized Wartheland and a uniform Nazi *Volksgemeinschaft* remained a distant reality, but "this was above all because the interests of asserting power and war-related necessities did not allow population policy manipulations to be carried out to such a degree."[118]

In the Reichsgau Wartheland, as in the other Polish regions, the unbridled arbitrary actions and terror undertaken against Jews and Poles were characterized by their routine and public nature. Nothing more clearly symbolizes this situation than the fenced off streetcar line for Germans and Poles that traversed directly through the ghetto and could be crossed by ghetto residents only by means of wooden bridges.

In fact, the omnipresence of government and police agencies gave even local Germans little leeway for divergent behavior. However, the National Socialist authorities remained dependent on the cooperation and loyalty of the German minority in an otherwise hostile environment. If we view the occupation policy as a whole, we must assume a high level of acceptance by resident Germans in the Warthegau of the Nazi *Volkstumspolitik*—that is, national-ethnic policy—including all of its horrifying consequences for the Jewish and Polish population.

While to this day the "rupture in civilization" of the National Socialist murder of the Jews eludes rational understanding, the extensive projects involving plunder, expropriation, and deportation are less incomprehensible. The idea that the incorporated eastern territories were "German land" on which Germans had "both historical and moral property claims"[119] had been firmly anchored in the German Reich's population since the end of the First World War and all the more so during the Second.[120] In light of the Warthegau's prevailing population structure, the absurdity of this motif was exceeded only by its flexibility, which is why the "guiding principle" of consolidating German nationhood features so prominently throughout virtually all of the period's literature.[121] The murder of the Wartheland Jews formed an integral part of Nazi *Volkstumspolitik*: some of the Germans in the Warthegau participated directly in the Holocaust; many of them accepted or even welcomed the anti-Semitic policies, with their horrific consequences; all of them—including many of the Germans who had resettled in the region as a result of treaties with the Baltic states—accrued direct or indirect material benefits as a result of the Holocaust.

Of the more than 630,000 ethnic German settlers brought to the region of the incorporated eastern territories, just under 537,000—thus more than 85 percent—were allocated to the Warthegau.[122] Yet despite the massive settlement of ethnic Germans, as result of the deportation and mass murders the population in the Reichsgau Wartheland declined between September 1939 and April 1944 by almost 500,000 people, namely, from an initial 4.92 to 4.42 million people.[123] The number of Germans increased during this period from 325,000 (6.6 percent) to more than a million (22.9 percent); the number of (non-Jewish) Poles living in the Warthegau decreased from an initial 4.12 million (83.7 percent) to 3.33 million (75.3 percent).[124] Of the 435,000 Jews residing here prior to 1 September 1939, presumably only 10,000 to 15,000 survived the Holocaust.

These drastic numerical changes reflect the fate of a region and the series of unprecedented crimes that is captured only very inadequately by the term "occupation policy."[125] The Warthegau not only witnessed the realization of numerous forced resettlement and deportation projects, but also, outside the Reich, formed the initial venue and focal point for the mass killings of the murderous "euthanasia" program. Finally, the Warthegau marked the origin of the systematic, stationary destruction of Jews using gas, when on 8 December 1941 in Kulmhof am Ner, northwest of Łódź, the first National Socialist extermination camp began its killing operations. The Reichsgau Wartheland forms the key, so to speak, to understanding National Socialist occupation and *Volkstum* policies during the Second World War, especially for questions regarding the genesis of the Holocaust. Lastly, the Warthegau illustrates the major role played by regional authorities in the practices of the occupation: Gauleiter and Reich Governor Greiser, the police apparatus, and the municipal administrations were responsible first and foremost for the unprecedented radicalization in the persecution of the Jews, for which they sought approval in Berlin.

Notes

1. Adolf Hitler, *Mein Kampf*, 815th–820th ed. (Munich, 1943), 742.
2. Norbert Krekeler, *Revisionsanspruch und geheime Ostpolitik der Weimarer Republik: Die Subventionierung der deutschen Minderheit in Polen 1919–1933* (Stuttgart, 1973); Hans-Erich Volkmann, "Polen im politisch-wirtschaftlichen Kalkül des Dritten Reiches 1933–1939," in *Der Zweite Weltkrieg: Analysen, Grundzüge, Forschungsbilanz*, ed. Wolfgang Michalka (Munich, 1989), 74–92.
3. Czesław Łuczak, *"Kraj Warty" 1939–1945* (Poznań, 1972), 79f.
4. Michael Alberti, *Die Verfolgung und Vernichtung der Juden im Reichsgau Wartheland 1939–1945* (Wiesbaden, 2006) 34.
5. Thus, for example, a pogrom erupted in March 1936 in Przytyk—a village in central Poland near Radom—resulting in multiple fatalities and injuries. Regarding the context, see Yfaat Weiss, *Deutsche und polnische Juden vor dem Holocaust:Jüdische Identität zwischen Staatsbürgerschaft und Ethnizität 1933–1940* (Munich, 2000), 105–130.
6. Daniel Gerson, "Antisemitische Erfahrungen in Lodz zwischen den beiden Weltkriegen," in *Polen, Deutsche und Juden in Lodz 1820–1939: Eine schwierige Nachbarschaft*, ed. Jürgen Hensel (Osnabrück, 1999), 257–268, especially 262ff.
7. Henryk Lisiak, *Narodowa Demokracja w Wielkopolsce w latach 1918–1939* (Poznań, 2006), 248–269.
8. These figures refer to 1931, the year of the final census in Poland. See *Mały Rocznik Statystyczny* 1938 (Warsaw, 1938), 26, 41.
9. Yfaat Weiss, "Polish and German Jews Between Hitler's Rise to Power and the Outbreak of the Second World War," *Leo Baeck Institute Year Book* 64 (1999): 205–223.
10. On the problematization of the terms German, Jews, and Poles, see the editors' introduction.
11. Beate Kosmala, *Juden und Deutsche im polnischen Haus: Tomaszów Mazowiecki 1914–1939* (Berlin, 2001); Emanuel Melzer, "Relations between Poland and

Germany and Their Impact on the Jewish Problem in Poland (1935–1938)," *Yad Vashem Studies* 12 (1977): 193–229.
12. For Łódź see "Niemcy łódzcy. Po przewrocie hitlerowskim.—27 czasopism w województwie łódzkim.—Wpływ inspiracji z zewnątrz," in *Republika* [Łódź] (17 July 1938), 11; "Hitleryzm wśród Niemców łódzkich. Nastroje nazistyczne [sic] wzmogły się od chwili aneksji Austrii i Sudetów," in *Republika* (19 October 1938), 6.
13. "Protest polskich niemców-socjalistów przeciwko ekscesom antysemickim w Niemczech," in *Nasz Przegląd* [Warszawa] (25 November 1938), 11. See Ingo Loose, "'Das war einmal . . . die jüdische Glanzepoche in Deutschland': Reaktionen auf den Novemberpogrom in der jüdischen Presse in Polen 1938/39," in *"Es brennt!": Antijüdischer Terror im November 1938*, ed. Andreas Nachama et al. (Berlin, 2008), 128–135.
14. See Barbara Engelking and Helga Hirsch, eds., *Unbequeme Wahrheiten: Polen und sein Verhältnis zu den Juden* (Frankfurt, 2008); also Alberti, *Verfolgung und Vernichtung*, 29–32. Artur Eisenbach (*Hitlerowska polityka zagłady Żydów* [Warszawa 1961], 115, 128) argues that the position of Poland's Sanation government of the 1930s significantly influenced the fate of the Polish Jews after the German invasion of Poland.
15. Emmanuel [sic] Ringelblum, *Polish-Jewish Relations during the Second World War* (Jerusalem, 1974).
16. Quoted in Wolfgang Jacobmeyer, "Der Überfall auf Polen und der neue Charakter des Krieges," in *September 1939: Krieg, Besatzung, Widerstand in Polen*, ed. Christoph Kleßmann (Göttingen, 1989), 16.
17. Eisenbach, *Hitlerowska polityka zagłady Żydów*, 129ff., 268ff.; Ruta Sakowska, *Die zweite Etappe ist der Tod: NS-Ausrottungspolitik gegen die polnischen Juden, gesehen mit den Augen der Opfer* (Berlin, 1993), 10ff., 35ff. On the semantically unsatisfactory tripartite division and use of the terms "Germans, Poles, and Jews," see the editors' introduction.
18. Jochen Böhler, *Auftakt zum Vernichtungskrieg: Die Wehrmacht in Polen 1939* (Frankfurt, 2006); Alexander B. Rossino, *Hitler Strikes Poland: Blitzkrieg, Ideology, and Atrocity* (Lawrence, KS, 2003). See also, fundamentally, Jacek Andrzej Młynarczyk and Jochen Böhler, eds., *Der Judenmord in den eingegliederten polnischen Gebieten 1939–1945* (Osnabrück, 2010).
19. Hans Umbreit, *Deutsche Militärverwaltungen 1938/39: Die militärische Besetzung der Tschechoslowakei und Polens* (Stuttgart, 1977); Stanisław Nawrocki, *Hitlerowska okupacja Wielkopolski w okresie zarządu wojskowego. Wrzesień– październik 1939 r* (Poznań, 1966).
20. On Greiser as an individual, see Catherine Epstein, *Model Nazi: Arthur Greiser and the Occupation of Western Poland* (Oxford, 2010); Ian Kershaw, "Arthur Greiser— Ein Motor der 'Endlösung'," in *Die braune Elite II*, ed. Ronald Smelser et al., 2nd ed. (Darmstadt, 1999), 116–127; Czesław Łuczak, *Arthur Greiser: Hitlerowski władca w Wolnym Mieście Gdańsku i w Kraju Warty* (Poznań, 1997).
21. Michael Alberti, "'Exerzierplatz des Nationalsozialismus': Der Reichsgau Wartheland 1939–1941," in *Genesis des Genozids: Polen 1939–1941*, ed. Klaus-Michael Mallmann and Bogdan Musiał (Darmstadt, 2004), 111–126, here 120.
22. The personnel of "Operation T-4"—namely, the headquarters for the "euthanasia" murders at Tiergartenstraße 4 in Berlin—were not involved in the murder of sick persons in the Reichsgau Wartheland until September 1941. See Alberti, *Verfolgung und Vernichtung*, 333ff.; Michael Alberti, "'Niederträchtige Perfidie, gemeine, unermessliche Gier und kalte, berechnende Grausamkeit . . .': Die 'Endlösung der Judenfrage' im Reichsgau–Wartheland," in *Der Judenmord in den eingegliederten*

polnischen Gebieten, ed. Młynarczyk and Böhler, 117–142; Volker Rieß, *Die Anfänge der Vernichtung "lebensunwerten Lebens" in den Reichsgauen Danzig-Westpreußen und Wartheland 1939/40* (Frankfurt, 1995), especially 297–304.

23. Christian Jansen and Arno Weckbecker, *Der "Volksdeutsche Selbstschutz" in Polen 1939/40* (Munich, 1992).
24. Eisenbach, *Hitlerowska polityka zagłady Żydów*, 204.
25. Ingo Loose, "Die Enteignung der Juden im besetzten Polen 1939–1945," in *Vor der Vernichtung: Die staatliche Enteignung der Juden im Nationalsozialismus*, ed. Katharina Stengel (Frankfurt, 2007), 283–307. See, for example, Ordinance on Payment and Monetary Transactions of 18 September 1939 (= VOBl. der [8.] Armee, Chef der Zivilverwaltung, Lodz, no. 3 from 26 September 1939), Archiwum Państwowe w Łodzi (APŁ—Łódź State Archive), Szef Zarządu Cywilnego Okręgu Wojskowego w Łodzi, no. 1, fol. 6–8.
26. Umbreit, *Deutsche Militärverwaltungen*, 238f., 267, 270; Czesław Łuczak, *Pod niemieckim jarzmem (Kraj Warty 1939–1945)* (Poznań, 1996), 42f.; Alberti, *Verfolgung und Vernichtung*, 42–45. For Posen, see Anna Ziółkowska, "Żydzi poznańscy w pierwszych miesiącach okupacji hitlerowskiej," in *Poznańscy Żydzi* (Poznań, 2006), 378–393.
27. Friedrich Uebelhoer, "Der Aufbau im Regierungsbezirk Litzmannstadt," in *Der Osten des Warthelandes* (Litzmannstadt, 1941), 239–258, here 249.
28. Letter from the OKH from 3 October 1939 (decree no. 310/39) on residency in occupied formerly Polish territory, Bundesarchiv (BArch), R 2/5834, fol. 260.
29. "Ordinance on Criminal Justice against Poles and Jews in the Incorporated Eastern Territories," 4 December 1941, Reichsgesetzblatt (RGBl.) 1941 I, 759.
30. See also Dieter Pohl, "Die Reichsgaue Danzig-Westpreußen und Wartheland: Koloniale Verwaltung oder Modell für die zukünftige Gauverwaltung?," in *Die NS-Gaue: Regionale Mittelinstanzen im zentralistischen "Führerstaat,"* ed. Jürgen John et al. (Munich, 2007), 395–405.
31. Reich Ministry of the Interior (signed Pfundtner) to the supreme Reich authorities in the new eastern regions, BArch, R 2/5112, fol. 72.
32. Police Ordinance on the Marking of the Jews of 1 September 1941, RGBl. 1941 I, 547; Ordinance on the Employment of Jews of 3 October 1941, RGBl. 1941 I, 675.
33. Ordinance on the Introduction of Regulations on the Dejudaization of the German Economy in the Incorporated Eastern Territories of 30 March 1942, RGBl. 1942 I, 166.
34. Fritz Richter, "Der Einsatz der Volksdeutschen sowie Erfahrungen und Zukunftsaufgaben beim Postaufbau im Wartheland," *Jahrbuch des Postwesens* 5 (1941): 214–265, here 264.
35. Arthur Greiser, *Der Aufbau im Osten* (Jena, 1942), 6.
36. Czesław Łuczak, "Die Ansiedlung der deutschen Bevölkerung im besetzten Polen (1939–1945)," *Studia Historiae Oeconomicae* 13 (1978): 193–205.
37. Quoted in Philipp Bouhler, ed., *Der großdeutsche Freiheitskampf: Reden Adolf Hitlers*, vol. I/II, 3rd. ed. (Munich, 1943), 82f.
38. On this connection, see, fundamentally, Götz Aly, *"Final Solution": Nazi Population Policy and the Murder of the European Jews* (London, 1999) (German original: Frankfurt, 1995).
39. The deportation of the approximately 600,000 Jews from the eastern territories to the Generalgouvernement; the ghettoization of the resulting 2 million Jews in the Generalgouvernement; the deportation of all Jews and "gypsies" from the Reich; finally, also the deportation of all Poles from the Reich.

40. Martin Broszat, *Nationalsozialistische Polenpolitik 1939–1945* (Frankfurt, 1965), 21.
41. *Der Prozeß gegen die Hauptkriegsverbrecher vor dem Internationalen Militärgerichtshof*, vol. III (Nuremburg, 1947), 650f.
42. Ibid.
43. Second Decree of the Führer and Reichskanzler on the Amendment of the Decrees on the Organization and Administration of the Eastern Regions of 29 January 1940, RGBl. 1940 I, 251.
44. *Die Ostgebiete des Deutschen Reiches und das Generalgouvernement der besetzten polnischen Gebiete in statistischen Angaben* (Berlin, 1940), 6, 34–54.
45. On the demographic changes in Poland between 1939 and 1945, see Czesław Madajczyk, *Polityka III Rzeszy w okupowanej Polsce*, 2 vols. (Warszawa, 1970), vol. 1, 234–284.
46. Winfried Burau, "Der Reichsgau Wartheland und seine Wirtschaft," in *Die Wirtschaft der neuen großdeutschen Gebiete*, part 3: *Der Osten* (Bad Oeynhausen, 1942), 33–56.
47. Abraham Melezin, *Przyczynek do znajomości stosunków demograficznych wśród ludności żydowskiej w Łodzi, Krakowie i Lublinie podczas okupacji niemieckiej* (Łódź, 1946), 10.
48. Tadeusz Bojanowski, "Plany władz hitlerowskich wobec łódzkiego przemysłu włókienniczego w latach 1939–1945," *Rocznik Łódzki* 17 (1973), 177–193; T. Kozłowicz, "Sytuacja w przemyśle łódzkim i walka o jego utrzymania w pierwszych miesiącach okupacji niemieckiej," *Rocznik Łódzki* 7 (1963), 135–153.
49. Broszat, *Nationalsozialistische Polenpolitik*, 8. On occupation policy during the first months, see Alexander Kranz, *Reichsstatthalter Arthur Greiser und die "Zivilverwaltung" im Wartheland 1939/40: Die Bevölkerungspolitik in der ersten Phase der deutschen Besatzungsherrschaft in Polen* (Potsdam, 2010).
50. Alberti, "'Niederträchtige Perfidie,'" 121ff. See also Jörg Osterloh's contribution to this volume.
51. Wiesław Porzycki, *Posłuszni aż do śmierci. Niemieccy urzędnicy w Kraju Warty 1939–1945* (Poznań, 1997), 14ff.
52. Ibid., 96f.
53. Karol Marian Pospieszalski, *Hitlerowskie "prawo" okupacyjne w Polsce. Wybór dokumentów, część I: Ziemie "wcielone"* (Poznań, 1952), 2–28, here 15. See also Phillip Rutherford, *Prelude to the Final Solution: The Nazi Program for Deporting Ethnic Poles, 1939–1941* (Lawrence, KS, 2007).
54. Alberti, *Verfolgung und Vernichtung*, 136f., especially note 415, assumes that the majority were Jews; in contrast, for the assertion that most were Poles, see Maria Rutowska, *Wysiedlenia ludności polskiej z Kraju Warty do Generalnego Gubernatorstwa 1939–1941* (Poznań, 2003), passim, especially 49.
55. Number of inhabitants of the urban and rural districts of the Reichsgau Wartheland (June 1940), Archiwum Państwowe w Poznaniu (APP—Poznań State Archive), Reichsstatthalter im Reichsgau Wartheland, no. 594, fol. 39–42.
56. Himmler on German settlement plans in Poland (*Neue Zürcher Zeitung*, no. 296, 24 October 1940), BArch, R 2501/5526, fol. 171.
57. Ferdinand Bang, "Die Deutsche Umsiedlungs-Treuhand-Gesellschaft," *Warthegau-Wirtschaft* 1, no. 1 (1940): 9–11.
58. Reichsbank file note from 15 November 1939: "Moreover, the Reich has relief in the booty at hand in the Reichsgaue. The Reich's cash payments should substantially decrease vis-à-vis the material assets that will constitute the major portion of the compensation." BArch, R 2501/7012, fol. 7.

59. Aly, *"Final Solution,"* 78. For detail on the Deutsche Umsiedlungs-Treuhand-Gesellschaft, see Ingo Loose, *Kredite für NS-Verbrechen: Die deutschen Kreditinstitute in Polen und die Ausraubung der polnischen und jüdischen Bevölkerung 1939–1945* (Munich, 2007), 246–257.
60. Bernhard Rosenkötter, *Treuhandpolitik: Die "Haupttreuhandstelle Ost" und der Raub polnischer Vermögen 1939–1945* (Essen, 2003).
61. See Hans-Erich Volkmann, "Zur Ansiedlung der Deutschbalten im 'Warthegau,'" *Zeitschrift für Ostforschung* 30 (1981): 527–558. Volkmann emphasizes the central importance of "National Socialist activities in Estonia and Latvia" for the "relatively smooth integration into the Warthegau's National Socialist order of life." Ibid., 548.
62. Greiser, *Aufbau im Osten*, 14f.
63. Stanisław Piotrowski, ed., *Dziennik Hansa Franka* (Warsaw, 1956), 260.
64. Werner Präg and Wolfgang Jacobmeyer, eds., *Das Diensttagebuch des deutschen Generalgouverneurs in Polen 1939–1945* (Stuttgart, 1975), 129.
65. See the collected articles in Eckhart Neander, ed., *Umgesiedelt—vertrieben: Deutschbalten und Polen 1939–1945 im Warthegau* (Marburg, 2010).
66. See Markus Leniger, *Nationalsozialistische "Volkstumsarbeit" und Umsiedlungspolitik 1933–1945: Von der Minderheitenbetreuung zur Siedlerauslese* (Berlin, 2006), 91ff.
67. On this see Ingo Loose, "'Stimmungsmäßig schwierig sind die Ostgebiete überhaupt nicht': Deutsche, Polen und Juden im Kreis Kalisch (Reichsgau Wartheland) in Stimmungsberichten des SD," *Vierteljahrshefte für Zeitgeschichte* (2015, forthcoming).
68. Edmund Dmitrów, *Niemcy i okupacja hitlerowska w oczach Polaków. Poglądy i opinie z lat 1945–1948* (Warszawa, 1988); Dorota Siepracka, "Die Einstellung der christlichen Polen gegenüber der jüdischen Bevölkerung im Wartheland," in *Der Judenmord in den eingegliederten polnischen Gebieten*, ed. Młynarczyk and Böhler, 345–369, here 345ff.; on the other hand, see Jerzy Korczak, *Teodor Müller. Das Schicksal eines deutschen Polen* (Cologne, 2000). In contrast, we still do not know very much about the role of women in the incorporated territories or occupied Poland. See here the foundational work by Elizabeth Harvey, *Women and the Nazi East: Agents and Witnesses of Germanization* (New Haven, 2003).
69. Arthur Greiser, "Die Aufgaben auf dem Gebiet des Wirtschaftsaufbaues," *Warthegau-Wirtschaft* 1, no. 1 (1940): 1; see Czesław Łuczak, "Die Wirtschaftspolitik des Dritten Reiches im besetzten Polen," *Studia Historiae Oeconomicae* 14 (1979): 87–103, especially 87f.
70. RGBl. 1940 I, 1270. For more detail on this see Loose, *Kredite für NS-Verbrechen*, 112–116.
71. General Decree on the Securing of Jewish Assets and Anonymous Credit Balances and the Like, of 18 November 1939, in *Verordnungsblatt des Reichsstatthalters im Reichsgau Wartheland* 2 (1940): 22.
72. Gordon J. Horwitz, *Ghettostadt: Łódź and the Making of a Nazi City* (London, 2008), 11f.; see Andrzej Dmitrzak, *Hitlerowskie kontrybucje w okupowanej Polsce 1939–1945* (Poznań, 1983); Andrzej Dmitrzak, "Causes of Imposing Contributions and Methods of Levying them in Polish Territories under the Nazi Occupation during the Second World War," *Studia Historiae Oeconomicae* 21 (1994): 157–166.
73. Regarding the context, see Alberti, *Verfolgung und Vernichtung*, 217–227.
74. Jüdisches Historisches Institut in Warschau, ed., *Faschismus—Getto—Massenmord: Dokumentation über Ausrottung und Widerstand der Juden in Polen während des zweiten Weltkrieges* (Berlin, 1961), 81; Danuta Dąbrowska, "Zagłada

skupisk żydowskich w 'Kraju Warty' w okresie okupacji hitlerowskiej," *Biuletyn Żydowskiego Instytutu Historycznego*, nos. 13–14 (1955): 122–184.
75. Andrea Löw, *Juden im Getto Litzmannstadt: Lebensbedingungen, Selbstwahrnehmung, Verhalten* (Göttingen, 2006); Isaiah Trunk, *Łódź Ghetto: A History* (Bloomington, 2006); Icchak (Henryk) Rubin, *Żydzi w Łodzi pod niemiecką okupacją 1939–1945* (London, 1988); Julian Baranowski, *Łódzkie getto 1940–1944: Vademecum* (Łódź, 1999).
76. Loose, *Kredite für NS-Verbrechen*, 158–187.
77. Dąbrowska, "Zagłada skupisk żydowskich w 'Kraju Warty,'" 122.
78. See, generally, Christopher Browning, *The Origins of the Final Solution: The Evolution of Nazi Jewish Policy, September 1939–March 1942* (Lincoln, NE, 2007), 111–120.
79. Alberti, *Verfolgung und Vernichtung*, 193–206. For Litzmannstadt, see the associated correspondence between the ghetto administration and the Schutzpolizei in APŁ, Akta miasta Łodzi, no. 29231, passim.
80. On the following, see Ingo Loose, "Die Bedeutung der Ghettoarbeit für die nationalsozialistische Kriegswirtschaft," in *Arbeit in den nationalsozialistischen Ghettos*, ed. Stephan Lehnstaedt and Jürgen Hensel (Osnabrück, 2013), 71–90.
81. Eisenbach, *Hitlerowska polityka zagłady Żydów*, 203.
82. Broszat, *Nationalsozialistische Polenpolitik*, 100.
83. Ibid.
84. Anna Ziółkowska, *Obozy pracy przymusowej dla Żydów w Wielkopolsce w latach okupacji hitlerowskiej (1941–1943)* (Poznań, 2005); idem, "Zwangsarbeitslager für Juden im Reichsgau Wartheland," in *Der Judenmord in den eingegliederten polnischen Gebieten*, ed. Młynarczyk and Böhler, 179–202.
85. See the chapter on the Warthegau in Wolf Gruner, *Jewish Forced Labor under the Nazis: Economic Needs and Racial Aims, 1938–1944* (New York, 2006), 177–195.
86. Ziółkowska, *Obozy pracy przymusowej dla Żydów w Wielkopolsce*, 76, 82; Alberti, *Verfolgung und Vernichtung*, 283–291.
87. Ziółkowska, *Obozy pracy przymusowej dla Żydów w Wielkopolsce*, 103; see Anna Ziółkowska, "Transporty powrotne (Rücktransporte). Eliminacja więźniów niezdolnych do pracy z obozów pracy przymusowych dla Żydów w Wielkopolsce," in *Ośrodek zagłady Żydów w Chełmnie nad Nerem w świetle najnowszych badań. Materiały z sesji naukowej*, ed. Łucja Pawlicka-Nowak (Konin, 2004), 37–43.
88. Ziółkowska, *Obozy pracy przymusowej dla Żydów w Wielkopolsce*, 188–196.
89. Horwitz, *Ghettostadt*, 57–59.
90. Götz Aly, Susanne Heim, *Architects of Annihilation: Auschwitz and the Logic of Destruction* (Princeton, NJ, 2002), 198/199 (German original: Frankfurt, 1993).
91. Ulrich Herbert, "Arbeit und Vernichtung: Ökonomisches Interesse und Primat der 'Weltanschauung' im Nationalsozialismus," in *Ist der Nationalsozialismus Geschichte? Zu Historisierung und Historikerstreit*, ed. Dan Diner (Frankfurt, 1987), 209.
92. Alberti, *Verfolgung und Vernichtung*, 277–283.
93. For a detailed discussion, see Peter Klein, *Die "Gettoverwaltung Litzmannstadt" 1940–1944: Eine Dienststelle im Spannungsfeld von Kommunalbürokratie und staatlicher Verfolgungspolitik* (Hamburg, 2009).
94. Ian Kershaw, "Improvised Genocide? The Emergence of the 'Final Solution' in the 'Warthegau'," *Transactions of the Royal Historical Society*, 6th series, no. 2 (1992): 51–78. See also Christian Gerlach, "The Wannsee Conference, the Fate of German Jews, and Hitler's Decision in Principle to Exterminate All European Jews," *Journal of Modern History* (December 1998): 759–781.

95. File note of the Director of the SD-Abschnitt Posen Höppner, regarding the solution of the Jewish question with a cover letter to Adolf Eichmann from 16 July 1941 (copy), BArch, R 58/954, fol. 189–191, printed in: *Die Verfolgung und Ermordung der europäischen Juden durch das nationalsozialistische Deutschland 1933–1945 (VEJ)*, vol. 4: *Polen, September 1939—Juli 1941*, ed. Klaus-Peter Friedrich (Munich, 2011), 680f., quote on 681 (document no. 314). On Höppner, see Martin Pollack, "Jäger und Gejagter: Das Überleben der SS-Nr. 107136," in *Im blinden Winkel: Nachrichten aus Mitteleuropa*, ed. Christoph Ransmayr (Frankfurt, 1989), 169–190.
96. For a detailed discussion, see Ingo Loose, "Die Berliner Juden im Getto Litzmannstadt 1941–1944," in *Berliner Juden im Getto Litzmannstadt 1941–1944: Ein Gedenkbuch*, ed. Ingo Loose (Berlin, 2009), 44–63. Catherine Epstein has especially emphasized Greiser's leading role in this development; Epstein, *Model Nazi: Arthur Greiser and the Occupation of Western Poland*; see Jacek Andrzej Młynarczyk, "Mordinitiativen von unten: Die Rolle Arthur Greisers und Odilo Globocniks im Entscheidungsprozess zum Judenmord," in *Der Judenmord in den eingegliederten polnischen Gebieten*, ed. Młynarczyk and Böhler, 27–56.
97. Julian Baranowski, "Likwidacja Żydów z getta łódzkiego w obozie zagłady w Chełmnie nad Nerem," in *Ośrodek zagłady Żydów w Chełmnie nad Nerem w świetle najnowszych badań. Materiały z sesji naukowej* (Konin, 2004), 3–8, here 4f.
98. *Położenie ludności polskiej w tzw. Kraju Warty w okresie hitlerowskiej okupacji*, Wybór źródeł i opracowanie Czesław Łuczak (Poznań, 1990), 40–46, here 43. Alberti, *Verfolgung und Vernichtung*, 404f.
99. Reichsführer-SS to Gauleiter SS-Gruppenführer Greiser from 18 September 1941, BArch, NS 19/2655, fol. 3; printed in *VEJ*, vol. 3: *Deutsches Reich und Protektorat September 1939—September 1941*, ed. Andrea Löw (Munich, 2012), 542 (doc. no. 223). On the role of the Higher SS and Police Leader in Posen Wilhelm Koppe in selecting Litzmannstadt as deportation destination, see Alberti, *Verfolgung und Vernichtung*, 386ff.
100. *Położenie ludności polskiej w tzw. Kraju Warty*, 40–46.
101. See the foundational work by Shmuel Krakowski, *Chelmno, A Small Village in Europe: The First Nazi Mass Extermination Camp* (Jerusalem, 2009); also Patrick Montague, *Chelmno and the Holocaust: The History of Hitler's First Death Camp* (New York, 2012).
102. Alberti, *Verfolgung und Vernichtung*, 450f.; Julian Baranowski, *Zigeunerlager in Litzmannstadt 1941–1942: The Gypsy Camp in Łódź. Obóz cygański w Łodzi* (Łódź, 2003).
103. Alberti, *Verfolgung und Vernichtung*, 337.
104. These ghettos were completely liquidated by August 1942 and their inmates murdered in Kulmhof. Dąbrowska, "Zagłada skupisk żydowskich w Kraju Warty," 137–139, 164f.; Alberti, *Verfolgung und Vernichtung*, 438f.; for a description of one such execution in Poddębice in March 1942, see Alexander Hohenstein, *Wartheländisches Tagebuch aus den Jahren 1941/42* (Stuttgart, 1961), 234ff.; "The death sentences should certainly have had a strong deterrent effect. In particular, the presence of the Jews and Poles at the enforcement of the death sentence should definitely be assessed as positive. . . . An execution of this kind would not have been put on display in the Old Reich." Gau office for Volkstum policy—reports of the district office leader for March 1942 regarding the German People's List, Polish questions, Volkstum policy work, etc. [here for the Lentschütz District], Instytut Pamięci Narodowej (IPN—Institute of National

Remembrance, Warsaw), Najwyższy Trybunał Narodowy, no. 36, fol. 435–450, here fol. 439.
105. APP, Reichsstatthalter im Reichsgau Wartheland, no. 1855, passim.
106. Quoted in Thomas T. Blatt, *Nur die Schatten bleiben: Der Aufstand im Vernichtungslager Sobibór* (Berlin, 2000), 32.
107. The author's exact identity has not been established; presumably the author is Jakow Grojnowski.
108. Sakowska, *Die zweite Etappe ist der Tod*, 38–40, 159–185 ("Szlamek's" report). The "Wartheland Diary" of the mayor of the town of Poddębice, Alexander Hohenstein (the pseudonym of Franz Heinrich Bock) likewise reveals astonishing detailed knowledge about the murderous machinery in Kulmhof; Alexander Hohenstein, *Warthel̈andisches Tagebuch*, 253–262 [entries from 5 to 12 May 1942]. See the supporting documents in *VEJ*, vol. 10: *Die eingegliederten polnischen Gebiete Sommer 1941–1945*, ed. Ingo Loose (Munich, 2015).
109. Wilm Hosenfeld, *"Ich versuche jeden zu retten." Das Leben eines deutschen Offiziers in Briefen und Tagebüchern* (Munich, 2004), 626f., 653ff [entries for 23 July and 6 September 1942].
110. Speech by Szmul Zygielbojm, in *German Atrocities in Poland and Czechoslovakia: Labour's Protest*, ed. Labour Party (UK) (London, 1942), 5.
111. "Allies are Urged to Execute Nazis," *New York Times*, 2 July 1942, no. 30840 (late city edition).
112. Diemut Majer, *"Non-Germans" under the Third Reich: The Nazi Judicial and Administrative System in Germany and Occupied Eastern Europe with Special Regard to Occupied Poland, 1939–1945* (Baltimore, 2003) (German original: Boppard am Rhein, 1981).
113. Gerhard Wolf, *Ideologie und Herrschaftsrationalität. Nationalsozialistische Germanisierungspolitik in Polen* (Hamburg, 2012).
114. Łuczak, *Pod niemieckim jarzmem*, 57–65; see, in general, Isabel Heinemann, *"Rasse, Siedlung, deutsches Blut": Das Rasse- und Siedlungshauptamt der SS und die rassenpolitische Neuordnung Europas* (Göttingen, 2003); Thomas Podranski, "Gauleiter als regionale Politakteure in den eingegliederten Ostgebieten des Deutschen Reiches: Das Beispiel der 'Deutschen Volksliste'," *Zeitschrift für Genozidforschung* 9 (2008): 95–131.
115. *Położenie ludności polskiej w tzw. Kraju Warty*, 183f.
116. Siepracka, "Die Einstellung der christlichen Polen gegenüber der jüdischen Bevölkerung im Wartheland," 347f., 351ff.
117. APŁ, Sondergericht beim Landgericht in Litzmannstadt, nos. 787, 1029, 3647, 5857, 6763, 7400, 7979, 10386; Archiwum Państwowe w Kaliszu (APK—State Archive Kalisz), Sondergericht in Kalisch, nos. 23, 73.
118. Broszat, *Nationalsozialistische Polenpolitik*, 28.
119. Max Buhle, *Reichsgau Wartheland*, published by the Reichspropagandaamt Wartheland (Posen, 1943), 3.
120. Michael Burleigh, *Germany Turns Eastwards: A Study of Ostforschung in the Third Reich* (Cambridge, 1988); Wolfgang Wippermann, *Der "Deutsche Drang nach Osten": Ideologie und Wirklichkeit eines politischen Schlagwortes* (Darmstadt, 1981).
121. Georg Hansen, "'Damit wurde der Warthegau zum Exerzierplatz des praktischen Nationalsozialismus': Eine Fallstudie zur Politik der Einverleibung," in *September 1939: Krieg, Besatzung, Widerstand in Polen*, ed. Christoph Kleßmann (Göttingen, 1989), 55–72; Volkmann, "Zur Ansiedlung der Deutschbalten im 'Warthegau,'" 558.

122. Theodor Bierschenk, "Zahlen über die während des Zweiten Weltkrieges umgesiedelten deutschen Volksgruppenangehörigen," *Zeitschrift für Ostforschung* 3 (1954): 80–83, here 80f.; Madajczyk, *Polityka III Rzeszy*, vol. 1, 352; Łuczak, "Ansiedlung der deutschen Bevölkerung," 195, 201.
123. Madajczyk, *Polityka III Rzeszy*, vol. 1, 245; Łuczak, *Pod niemieckim jarzmem*, 71, 83.
124. Alberti, *Verfolgung und Vernichtung*, 34.
125. Still foundational, Czesław Łuczak, *Polityka ludnościowa i ekonomiczna hitlerowskich Niemiec w okupowanej Polsce* (Poznań, 1979).

CHAPTER 8

ZICHENAU

Andreas Schulz

Prior to the Annexation

Prior to the Second World War, approximately 1 million people, including around 80,000 Jews and only 11,000 Germans, lived in that part of the Warsaw Voivodeship annexed by the German Reich in October 1939 as the Regierungsbezirk of Zichenau (Ciechanów) (see map 8.1). The majority of the region's population consisted of 900,000 ethnic Poles. Jewish history in Northern Mazovia reaches back to the first half of the thirteenth century. The oldest documentation of a Jewish religious community in the town of Plock (Płock)—one of Poland's first Jewish communities—dates from 1237. In the early modern period, Jews increasingly settled in Northern Mazovia.[1]

The Jewish population in the predominantly agrarian region of Northern Mazovia was concentrated above all in the towns. In 1931, only 16.4 percent of the Jews lived in the countryside, whereas 83.6 percent lived in the cities. Although we can no longer reconstruct the social structure of the Jewish population in what became the Regierungsbezirk of Zichenau, we know that in 1931 for the Warsaw Voivodeship as a whole, Jews were twice as likely as the rest of the population to operate one-person businesses, and only half as likely to work as employees.[2]

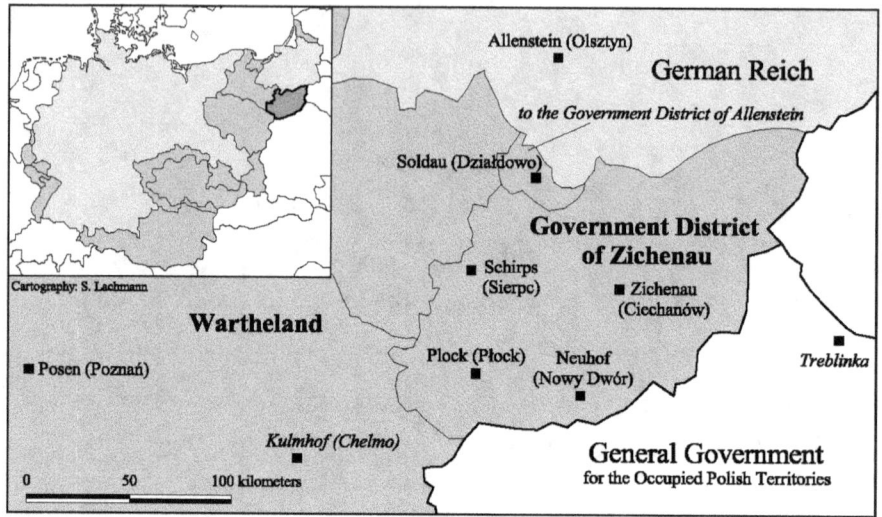

Map 8.1. Government District of Zichenau, 1939

In religious terms, Hasidic Jews dominated the region's Jewish society after the First World War. Politically, the Zionists excelled. The impoverished urban and rural Jewish population also included a few supporters of the Communist Party of Poland (Komunistyczna Partia Polski). But the Socialist-leaning General Jewish Workers Union—in short: the *Bund*—had far greater influence than the Communist Party.[3] A number of Poles of Jewish descent were also in the Polish Socialist Party (Polska Partia Socjalistyczna).[4] Comparatively little is known about the ethnic German residents in the region of the later Regierungsbezirk of Zichenau—the few "Germans" lived inconspicuously and hardly differed from the population's Polish majority. Thus the latter were all the more surprised when in the 1930s their German neighbors demonstrated their commitment to National Socialism.[5]

In contrast, Jewish-Polish relations, which were much the same as elsewhere in Poland, contained far greater potential for conflict.[6] Just a few years before the outbreak of the Second World War, for example, in Pułtusk (which later under German rule became part of the Regierungsbezirk of Zichenau as the town of Ostenburg) activists from the nationalist and anti-Semitic party National Radical Camp (Obóz Narodowo-Radykalny-Falanga[7]) organized boycotts against Jewish stores and prevented Poles from entering Jewish commercial premises. This also led in some instances to violent assaults on Jewish traders.

But most Poles repudiated such attempts to economically or even physically harm Polish citizens of Jewish descent, since they viewed such actions as echoing the anti-Semitic policies of the National Socialists in Germany. As a rule, the Polish police also intervened in boycott operations and violent eruptions to protect the Polish Jews, who had the same civic rights as ethnic Poles.[8]

The First Weeks of the War and the Annexation

Immediately upon the start of the German invasion of Poland on 1 September 1939, the territory of Northern Mazovia formed a battleground, because its northern side bordered on the "island" of East Prussia. The Third Army under General Georg von Küchler used the Reich's exclave as a deployment zone for an attack on Warsaw, only 160 kilometers away. Ciechanów (Zichenau) and Przasnysz (Praschnitz) had fallen into German hands on 3 September, followed on 6 September by Pułtusk, a mere sixty kilometers north of the Polish capital. The rapid advance of the German troops triggered a wave of flight within the Polish and Jewish population, with the Jews fleeing chiefly to Warsaw and to the larger Jewish communities in the countryside.[9]

At first, General von Küchler held executive power in occupied Northern Mazovia. SS-Brigadeführer Heinz Jost was appointed as the Head of the Civil Administration (Chef der Zivilverwaltung; CdZ); Helmuth von Wedelstädt—the Landeshauptmann of East Prussia (head of the East Prussian provincial parliament) in Königsberg since 1936 and a confidant of the East Prussian NSDAP Gauleiter and Oberpräsident (Upper President) Erich Koch—acted as his deputy.[10] The Führer decree from 8 October 1939 created the Regierungsbezirk of Zichenau and incorporated the region into the Province of East Prussia.[11] Dr. Hermann Bethke, Koch's deputy in the East Prussian Oberpräsidium (Upper Presidium), was supposed to perform the official duties of the Regierungsbezirk President.[12]

In Pułtusk, Wehrmacht soldiers began expelling some of the Jews from the town on the fourth day of the occupation. They forced Jewish males to swim across the Narew River to reach the Polish interior. Many men drowned or were shot to death.[13] With brutal violence, the soldiers herded the remaining Jewish residents into the marketplace and stole their belongings. All of this occurred in plain view of the Polish inhabitants, who were permitted to watch the cruel activities without hindrance.[14] In addition, Poles attacked and robbed the Jews who had been expelled to the other side of the river.[15] Twelve days later on 22 September, the occupiers forced the last remaining Jews to leave the city and Kreis (district) of Pułtusk; once again, people fell victim to expulsions.[16]

On 21 September 1939, Reinhard Heydrich directed the office heads of the Reich Security Main Office (Reichssicherheitshauptamt; RSHA) and the leaders of the Einsatzgruppen to concentrate Poland's Jewish population within a month's time. Heydrich's declared goal was to be able to better control and later also deport the Jews. At the same time, he ordered the formation of so-called Jewish councils, which were to ensure the implementation of orders issued by the German administration.[17]

Einsatzgruppe V under Ernst Damzog marched into Northern Mazovia behind the Wehrmacht units. The members of the RSHA Einsatzgruppen wore the grey field uniforms of the Waffen SS, which differed from those of the Wehrmacht in only a few details, such as the diamond patch on the sleeve of the Security Service (Sicherheitsdienst; SD) uniform. Thus the victims often thought they were members of the Wehrmacht.[18] The Einsatzgruppe brutalized the Polish and Jewish population, deliberately triggering a mass flight of civilians.[19] It carried out a range of operations jointly with Wehrmacht units, which thereby actively participated in the expulsions. [20]

In a number of communities, local Wehrmacht commanders ordered all Jews to leave town—for example, in Goworowo, Nowy Dwór (later renamed as Neuhof), and Ostrołęka (later Scharfenwiese).[21] An Einsatzkommando arrived in Goworowo on 6 September, only one day after the Wehrmacht. It terrorized the Jews, plundering and threatening to burn their houses and murdering many of them openly in the streets. The village's Jewish population, which had significantly increased due to the large number of refugees, was herded into the synagogue, where they were supposed to be incinerated. But a Wehrmacht officer, thinking the fate too cruel, prevented this plan; he ordered the expulsion of the Jews from the village instead.[22]

In Ostrołęka, too, Wehrmacht officers ordered the Jews to leave town within two hours; ultimately, they extended the deadline to two days. The Jews were allowed to take only hand luggage with them. Soldiers ensured that the refugees headed off in the direction of Łomża and thus into the Soviet-occupied region. A few Jews managed to settle in central Poland. Wehrmacht soldiers executed illegally returning Jews without hesitation.[23] The Einsatzkommandos "cleansed" the Kreis of Ostrołęka, which bordered directly on the German-Soviet demarcation line, with extreme brutality. In November 1939 they shot to death most of the 500 Jews still remaining in the district.[24] Within just a few weeks after the expulsions began, Jews could no longer be found anywhere in the district.[25] The murders formed part of a large-scale joint operation carried out by the Wehrmacht and the Einsatzgruppen along the line demarcating the Soviet-occupied area of Poland; the operation was supposed to prevent the return of Jews who fled into the Soviet sector.[26]

Sometimes the German military administration tried to convince the Jews to leave their hometowns on their own accord, as in Zichenau, where on 7 September the local commander summoned all of the Jews to a meeting in the synagogue and, with a reference to the Nuremberg race laws and the impending arrival of the Gestapo, encouraged them to flee. Thereupon a town resident named Lejzor Boruchowicz responded to him: "Born here and lost here." The Wehrmacht officer, incensed because of the rejection of his recommendation, threatened the Jews that the Gestapo would not just talk but rather take action.[27]

Abuses and killings of Jewish and non-Jewish Poles occurred in many localities of the later Regierungsbezirk of Zichenau. Members of the German minority participated in the attacks on their Jewish neighbors. In Neuhof, ethnic Germans (*Volksdeutsche*) collected Torah scrolls, wrapped them up with the shorn hair of Jewish women, and tried to force an elderly Jew to set the sacred scriptures on fire. Refusing to do so, he was shot. In the end, the rest of the town's Jews had to kindle the flames and dance around the burning Torah scrolls. The anti-Semitic terror in fall 1939 presumably emanated in large part from the local German residents. In Neuhof this was probably related to the fact that an ethnic German by the name of Wendt had taken over the mayoralty. Jewish libraries were burned in Ostrołęka, Mława (Mielau) and Wyszogród (Hohenburg); Polish libraries—at least in Zichenau— were not spared either.[28] The Polish-Jewish historian Michał Grynberg assumes that, despite the comparable attacks on Poles, the anti-Jewish terror of the Wehrmacht and the Einsatzgruppen of the Security Police (Sicherheitspolizei; SiPo) and Security Service basically sought to win the support of the Poles for the Nazis' anti-Semitic policies.[29]

German troops and policemen set numerous synagogues ablaze. Wehrmacht soldiers surrounded the Jewish temple in Sierpc (Schirps, later renamed Sichelberg), for example, setting it ablaze and prohibiting efforts to extinguish the flames. A young Jew who nonetheless attempted to do so paid for his efforts with his life. On the next day, the occupiers declared him to be the arsonist and imposed a 70,000 Złoty fine on the Jewish community.[30]

The Jewish population was systematically plundered. In mid September 1939, the occupiers forced the Jews of Zichenau to stand in the market square for hours with their hands raised, during which time Wehrmacht soldiers and ethnic Germans plundered their homes, stealing everything that was not nailed down, from bedding and clothing to kitchen utensils. At the same time, a number of Jews were abused outside the town borders. They had to carry boulders from the wayside to a field and back again. By the end of the day, the Jews in Zichenau had many deaths to lament. Similar excesses occurred in other communities of the region as well.

At the end of September 1939, Jewish males in Schirps and Zichenau were conscripted for forced labor, which mostly consisted of cleanup work and street sweeping. It was also accompanied by maltreatment, euphemistically referred to as "body training." On the morning before beginning their forced labor deployment, the Jews in Zichenau had to appear before the municipal administration and greet the town mayor—a certain Falke—in German. He responded, smiling, with the words: "Good morning, pigs." The Jews in Zichenau had already previously been compelled to shave and forbidden from wearing their caftans. Lending force to this order, the Gendarmerie took twenty men hostage.[31]

As one of its first measures, on 12 October 1939 the municipal administration in Schirps mandated the wearing of a yellow Star of David by all Jews, presumably one of the first such orders issued in the "incorporated Eastern regions." By the end of 1939, such decrees entered force throughout the entire Regierungsbezirk of Zichenau.[32] The Gestapo supervised the implementation of the orders, punishing Jews seized without a Star of David by taking them into so-called protective custody and transferring them to a concentration camp, which generally amounted to a death penalty.[33]

After the frenetic expropriations and plundering of the first days and weeks of the occupation, the Civil Administration already began systematically neutralizing Jewish traders and skilled tradespeople by the end of October 1939. Jewish eyewitnesses report that the authorities in Plock, Reichenfeld (Drobin), Schirps, and other towns closed all of the Jewish stores and workshops.[34] In Plock, the words "Jew—Closed" were painted in large letters on store doors. Simcha Guterman remembers that the Civil Administration posted public signs explaining these measures: "The Jews are freeloaders and usurers; their assets have been acquired through fraud and theft. Therefore the authority has resolved to confiscate their businesses and prohibit them from practicing all liberal professions. The possession of work equipment will be most severely punished."³⁵

At least some of the Poles approved of this course of action: "Hail to the German! Our Polish government never managed to eliminate the Jewish competition. He, as the true Führer, sorts out the matter in an instant!"³⁶

The municipal administration—now German—expropriated the Jewish entrepreneurs and tradespeople. Business and skilled-trade operations, along with their fixtures and goods in stock passed into German (and in a few cases Polish) hands. Even so, at least one account exists of a new Polish owner of a number of stores who allowed their previous owners to take their goods with them—something that the German authorities had expressly forbidden.³⁷ But this example nonetheless raises questions regarding the extent to which Poles, too, profited from National Socialist Jewish policies.³⁸

The Gestapo arrested any Jews who attempted to hide goods, a fate suffered by the Jewish grain dealer Abraham Mendel Forst, for example, who had hidden fifty hundredweights of corn (approximately 25 kg) in the ruins of his burned down house. The Gestapo arrested the 65-year-old on 25 May 1940 and sent him to a concentration camp.³⁹

Figure 8.1. Rounding up the Jews from the Zichenau ghetto, 1941/42. *Source:* United States Holocaust Memorial Museum photo archives, image no.: 50342.

In order to fully plunder the Jewish population and destroy its members' livelihoods, the Gestapo and municipal administrations repeatedly imposed collective and individual levies under false pretenses. Sometimes they enforced their monetary claims directly against individual families; other times they assigned this responsibility to local Jewish councils. In Plock, for example, at the end of 1939 the Jewish council managed to come up with only 200,000 Złoty instead of the demanded mandatory contribution of 1 million, whereupon the Gestapo took Jews as hostages. Ultimately, the Nazis confiscated all of the currency in the town's three remaining Jewish banks, thereby collecting an additional 500,000 Złoty. The taking of hostages almost always involved subjecting the victims to torture, referred to cynically by their tormentors as "gymnastics." When running the gauntlet, the arrested Jews were often maltreated for hours with whips and clubs.[40]

The Period of the Occupation

Compared to West Prussia and the Warthegau, the systematic expulsion and even murder of Jews and Poles in the Regierungsbezirk of Zichenau began with some delay, since Erich Koch's representative did not begin work in the area until October 1939.[41] Koch assumed direct control over the regions beyond the southern border of "his" Gau on 28 October 1939, with the end of the military administration.[42] In the 1930s, Koch for a long time had continued to display a comparatively friendly attitude toward the Poles; neither did he initially stand out as a committed supporter of Hitler's policies shaped by racial ideology.[43] But after the occupation of Poland, nothing remained of Koch's moderate position, and the Jewish population under his jurisdiction suffered just as much as did those in other parts of Poland (see figure 8.1).

As of the beginning of 1940, the mentally ill and elderly—both non-Jewish and Jewish Poles—succumbed to the murder operations of the Gestapo and the Order Police. The German authorities tried to convince local residents to accommodate old and sick relatives in specially established "hospitals" and "care homes." In Makow (Maków Mazowiecki), for example, they created such a home for around 500 people in a former school building. A short time later, however, in a nearby forest the inmates were shot to death and buried. The civilian population was no longer allowed to enter the woodland.[44] The National Socialists proceeded similarly when murdering approximately 100 people in Zichenau and a few hundred people in Schirps.[45] Meanwhile in Plock, an old-age home managed by nuns was liquidated in January 1940; the Gestapo shot the twenty-seven Polish and nine Jewish residents to death in woodlands outside the town.[46] The approximately forty residents of the Jewish old-age home succumbed to a similar operation.[47]

At the end of October 1939, Heinrich Himmler, in his new capacity as the Reich Commissioner for the Strengthening of Germandom (Reichskommissar für die Festigung deutschen Volkstums), ordered the expulsion of all Jews from the annexed parts of Poland—estimated by the Nazis to number more than half a million—into the General Government within four months. An unspecified number of Poles deemed particularly dangerous to the German occupational regime were also supposed to share their fate. The plans envisaged an operation to transfer the population that would affect a total of 1 million people. Himmler assigned the coordination of this immense operation to the Higher SS and Police Leaders (Höhere SS- und Polizeiführer).[48] The "population policy measures"—namely, the systematic *völkische Flurbereinigung* (ethnic land consolidation)—began in fall 1939 in West Prussia and the Warthegau and finally took effect in the Regierungsbezirk of Zichenau in winter 1939/40. They targeted primarily the Polish population. In the process, Nazi anti-Jewish policy receded to the background. Even so, the Gestapo, together with SS members, Order Police, and ethnic German assistants, expelled thousands of Jews from their hometowns: on 8 November 1939, approximately 2,000 persons from Schirps; on 4 December, around 4,000 persons from Nasielsk; and two days later, another 3,000 from Serock.[49] In doing so, the occupiers came to a realization: it seemed easier to murder undesired population groups than to deport them.[50]

At a conference on 4 January 1940 for high-ranking Reich Security Main Office employees and representatives from various ministries, Adolf Eichmann reported that for the time being in East Prussia, the "resettlements" affected "only" 30,000 Jews.[51] Gauleiter Koch did not view the fact that deportations had not yet occurred in his jurisdiction as a problem. On 12 February 1940 at a conference organized by Hermann Göring at his country residence Karinhall, Koch explained to Heinrich Himmler, Hans Frank, and the other Gauleiter of the annexed territories that, along with Poles, he also needed Jews as labor to develop the transport routes in the Regierungsbezirk of Zichenau. After subtracting the Polish prisoners of war from East Prussia, Koch estimated that the agricultural sector required 120,000 laborers alone.[52]

In mid November 1940, the Nazis deported almost 11,000 people from the Regierungsbezirk as part of another mandatory evacuation—the so-called Mielau Operation. One of the eleven railway transports also included Jews from Southeast Prussia, as the Regierungsbezirk of Zichenau was also called.[53] Just around one month later during another expulsion operation, the so-called Lithuanian Operation entailed the deportation of over 6,000 Poles and more than 3,000 Jews via a transit camp—the Soldau camp—to the General Government.[54] Finally, an additional 4,000 Jews from Mielau had to make the trip to the General Government in December 1940. The authorities housed Jews from Harnau (Raciąż), Schirps, and Görtzen (Żuromin), as well as Rippin (Rypin) and Dobrin (Reichsgau Danzig-West Prussia; Polish: Dobrzyn) in the apartments and houses of the Zichenau Jews. The next deportations occurred in the beginning of 1941, affecting a total of 10,000 Jews, 7,000 of them from Plock alone.[55] Thus within just a few months, in a coordinated major operation the Gestapo and police transported at least 26,000 Jews from the Regierungsbezirk of Zichenau to the General Government. At the same time, however, resettlements took place within the Regierungsbezirk itself. In parallel with the deportations, the German authorities in many places established segregated residential areas for Jews—in a word: ghettos[56]—on the basis of the abovementioned directive by Reinhard Heydrich from 21 September 1939.

We can only outline the basic structure of the tragic history of the Jewish ghettos in the Regierungsbezirk of Zichenau. We know that the Gestapo erected the Regierungsbezirk's first ghettos in the beginning of 1940, thereby at least temporarily supplanting the mass expulsions that had prevailed until that point. To establish these ghettos, the Nazis usually chose locations in outlying urban districts that even lacked paved roads and electricity. In Makow, for example, the Gestapo created the ghetto around the end of 1940 on the northern outskirts. At first, it numbered 4,500 residents; in total, 12,000 Jews passed through the ghetto, including many from the surrounding communities.[57] By 1941, German authorities had erected nineteen ghettos in the Regierungsbezirk of Zichenau.[58] Prior to the war, most of the Jewish population had still been distributed among thirty-two larger towns and communities.[59]

The Nazis already began liquidating first ghettos in early summer 1941; for example, the ghettos in Czerwinsk an der Weichsel (Czerwińsk nad Wisłą), Hohenburg, and Zakroczym, whose residents were transferred to Neuhof's "Jewish quarter"; as well as, soon thereafter, the ghettos in Lauffen (Bieżuń), Szreńsk, and Zielun (Zieluń)—the Gestapo arranged for the transfer of their populations to Striegenau (Strzegowo) and Mielau. Finally, at the end of October 1942 approximately 2,600

Jews from Czerwinsk came to Neuhof. Planned for the second half of 1942, the relocation of the Jews from Striegenau to Mielau did not take place at first, because the Jews had managed to bribe a number of German officials.[60] Authorities then dissolved the ghetto in Zichenau itself, housing up to 7,000 people, on 7 November 1942, and shipped all of its residents to Auschwitz. The Gestapo murdered all of the elderly and sick on the spot, including sixty-eight patients of a Jewish hospital.[61]

It is worth noting that the Jewish population's food and housing situation was better in the Regierungsbezirk of Zichenau than in other parts of Mazovia, especially compared to Warsaw. Perhaps the better supply situation that generally prevailed in what was now Reich territory also had an indirect, positive impact on Jewish living conditions in the Regierungsbezirk's ghettos. As a result, thousands of Jews tried to leave the General Government and come to the Regierungsbezirk of Zichenau, in part to procure provisions but also to go into hiding. Many of them paid for their attempt to cross the border with their lives,[62] since German customs and the Gestapo endeavored to stop illegal border traffic and conducted numerous checks.[63]

According to a count taken at the end of 1939, 2,800 Jews lived in the Neuhof ghetto; more than 5,000 had already fled during the combat operations, settling chiefly in Warsaw, only thirty kilometers away. In spring 1941, the Jews in the town once again numbered 4,000. Of these, however, only 750 skilled tradespeople were allowed to remain in Neuhof, while the rest were deported to the Pomiechowek (Pomiechówek) camp.[64] Authorities finally liquidated the Neuhof ghetto at the end of November 1942. First, the Gestapo forced the Jews under pain of death to deliver all of their money and jewelry to the Jewish council. Then on 20 November, the first transport, starting with approximately 2,000 elderly and sick ghetto residents, left for Auschwitz; they were followed to the extermination camp on 9 December by all families larger than four persons, and on 12 December by all of the remaining Jews.[65]

When the ghetto was created in early fall 1940, 7,000 of Plock's original 9,000 Jewish residents still lived in the small town. At first, Poles could still enter the ghetto, whereas Jews confined there were strictly forbidden to leave without a pass.[66] A labor office had already been established at the local Jewish council by the end of 1939; the office had to provide the forced laborers requisitioned by the Wehrmacht, the SS and other German agencies, and the municipality.[67] From a Jewish worker's meager wage of one RM per day, ten cents went to the Jewish council of elders, which used the money to finance general matters, and fifty cents went to the municipal administration, through which the town of Plock accumulated 100,000 RM in a special fund. The town's German residents later profited from the ghetto's liquidation: the town's Poles were forced to move into the now empty buildings of the liquidated ghetto. In turn, so-called *Volksdeutsche*—mostly people resettled from Lithuania, Latvia, and Bessarabia—moved into the apartments of the Poles. The authorities undertook similar actions in Schirps.[68]

The Regierungsbezirk of Zichenau's largest ghetto was established in September 1940 in Plöhnen.[69] Chiefly as a result of the liquidation of a number of smaller ghettos and the resettlement of their residents, the population of the Plöhnen ghetto swelled to a total of 12,000 people, who had to live crowded into a very small area. During a large-scale raid in the middle of July 1941 targeting illegal returnees from the General Government, the police brought 10 percent of Jewish quarter's residents to the Pomiechowek police prison as "undesired persons." As in the Neustadt ghetto (Nowe Miasto), the extremely cramped conditions, starvation rations, and poor sanitation led to the outbreak of epidemic typhus, which claimed sixty victims daily.[70] The Plöhnen ghetto was finally evacuated in December 1942 and all of its residents deported to Auschwitz.[71]

In Hohenburg, too, authorities fenced off a neighborhood with barbed wire to house the town's approximately 3,000 Jews. The Jewish council was responsible for organizing labor deployments. When the council dared to not fully provide the requisitioned work force contingent, the authorities had its members relocated to the Bielsk labor camp. The new Jewish council suffered a similar fate. But such open resistance against the directives of German administrations was probably an exception. In the beginning of March 1941, 700 Jews were deported from Hohenburg to an area near Radom in the General Government. In November 1941, the authorities finally completely liquidated the Hohenburg ghetto, transporting 600 Jews to Czerwinsk and another 600 to Neuhof.[72]

The concentration camp erected near the town of Soldau (Działdowo) in January 1940 was originally used primarily as a collection point and transit camp for Poles and presumably also for Jews that the Einsatzgruppen had initially detained in numerous provisional camps in East Prussia. The initiative for establishing the Soldau camp came from Otto Rasch. SS-Brigadeführer Rasch, who since November 1939 had been the Inspector of the Security Police and Security Service in East Prussia, also encouraged the Reich Security Main Office to use the Soldau camp as a place of execution. Reinhard Heydrich concurred with this recommendation, under the condition that the murders were to be carried out secretly. Thereupon the Soldau concentration camp was used as a place to murder members of Polish ruling elite and also as a transit camp for Poles and Jews, first when they were being violently deported to the General Government and later also on their way to the death camps. With a total of 30,000 prisoners, Soldau was the largest camp of its kind in the Regierungsbezirk of Zichenau. Large numbers of people in the concentration camp succumbed to malnutrition and disease. At least 1,000 political prisoners and approximately 1,600 mental patients were presumably murdered there.[73] Janusz Gumkowski estimates that the total number of fatalities in Soldau even reached as high as 10,000.[74]

The Pomiechowek police prison also spread terror. Established initially at the end of 1939 as prisoner-of-war camp near Neuhof, as of spring 1940 it was used as a transit camp for resettlement operations and finally, as of May 1941, as a concentration camp for Jews and Poles. Most of its prisoners had returned illegally to the Regierungsbezirk of Zichenau from the General Government. In large-scale raids conducted jointly with the Order Police and the Gendarmerie from May to July 1941, the agents of the Gestapo's Neuhof field office arrested thousands of people, included 6,000 Jews, bringing them to Pomiechowek. Presumably the operation was linked to Germany's invasion of the Soviet Union on 22 June 1941; the arrests were supposed to ensure security in the German rear area behind the front line. But the Gestapo also used the camp as a remand center and place of execution, where chiefly members of the Polish resistance and other unpopular Poles were put to death.[75] The prison stood on the grounds of the Modlin fortress, which had been expanded under Czar Nicholas I (who reigned from 1825 to 1855). The underground casements and bunkers were used as cells. A total of 50,000 inmates passed through the fortress, with at least 15,000 of them perishing there as a result of the prison conditions, abuse, and executions.[76]

Apart from the Soldau camp and the Pomiechowek police prison, at least fifty smaller work education and forced labor camps existed in the Regierungsbezirk of Zichenau, where more than 40,000 Jewish and non-Jewish Poles were imprisoned and exploited.[77] It is worth noting that in contrast to other regions of occupied Poland, for unknown reasons the Gestapo did not set up any segregated camps for Jewish prisoners.[78] Therefore even approximate estimates of the number of Jewish prisoners in these camps are impossible to determine reliably.

In the predominantly agrarian Regierungsbezirk of Zichenau, forced laborers were used predominantly in road construction, land improvement, stone quarries, peat production, and the agricultural economy. They were accommodated in former school buildings or barns. In Mielau, for example, the occupational authorities had no qualms about converting a Mikveh—a Jewish ritual bath—into a labor camp where they housed around 400 Jews and Poles. As in the ghettos, poor sanitation and miserable provisions led to the outbreak of epidemics. The guard units, consisting in part of local ethnic Germans (*Volksdeutsche*), brutalized the prisoners, routinely engaging torture, abuse, and murder. At least within the camps and work details, the guard personnel ensured the separation of Jews and non-Jews. Thus in one case, for example, prison personnel housed non-Jewish inmates in a building's ground-level room while forcing Jewish prisoners to live in its basement.[79]

Starting in mid 1941, the Jews remaining in the Regierungsbezirk of Zichenau were gradually concentrated in seven ghettos located along the border with the General Government: Zichenau, Makow, Mielau, Neustadt, Neuhof, Plöhnen, and Striegenau. The deportations from these towns to the Auschwitz and Treblinka extermination camps began at the end of 1942. The rail transports on 6 and 7 November 1942 from Zichenau to Auschwitz marked the anacrusis to the murder of the Jews from the Regierungsbezirk of Zichenau. Erich Koch is said to have personally attended the departure of these transports. On this occasion, he issued the order to shoot to death the resident patients of the Jewish hospital. Protection Police (Schutzpolizei) Commandant Meinert and his deputy Gotzmann were responsible for implementing the order.[80]

Work on the "final solution of the Jewish question" in the Regierungsbezirk of Zichenau resumed on 10 November 1942, when the Nazis began evacuating the ghetto in Mielau and deporting its inmates to Treblinka. Additional transports to Auschwitz on 13 and 17 November as well as on 10 December 1942 sealed the fate of Mielau's Jews. On 18 November 1942, another railway train left the Regierungsbezirk for Auschwitz—this time from Neustadt. Transports to the same destination occurred on 20 November from Neuhof and four days later from Strzegowo. Additional deportations left from Neuhof on 9 and 12 December. The last train to the death camp in East Upper Silesia left Plöhnen on 15 December 1942, finalizing the systematic and almost complete eradication of Jewish life in Northern Mazovia. In total, within just over eight weeks at the end of

1942, approximately 36,000 Jews were brought to the gas chambers of Auschwitz and Treblinka. Earlier—as already described—an estimated 40,000 Jewish men, women, and children had already been expelled to the General Government by March 1941. Only around 4,000 Jewish residents of the Regierungsbezirk of Zichenau were able to escape annihilation through either voluntary or coerced flight—the overwhelming majority of them leaving right at the beginning of the war during the course of the expulsions to the eastern Polish regions under Soviet occupation.[81]

Among the largely isolated Jews in the Regierungsbezirk of Zichenau, resistance against the terror and mass murder above all took the form of religious and cultural self-assertion: for example, in the ghettos they managed to hide Torah scrolls and Jewish books and protect them from destruction, and to organize secret religious meetings. In a number of ghettos, with the assistance of donations, self-help committees provided the poorest residents with their most essential needs. For smuggling food into the ghettos, Jews faced severe punishments that could range from consignment to a concentration camp to execution.[82] Cells of the Polish Workers' Party—which also maintained contact with non-Jewish party comrades outside the ghettos—formed in the ghettos of Plöhnen and Czerwinsk; an underground organization was created as well in Zichenau.[83] But groups of armed Jewish partisans—comparable to those in the General Government—were rare in the Regierungsbezirk, and their numbers were few. Only a small number of refugees who had escaped deportation to the extermination camps joined with Polish resistance fighters.[84]

Conclusion

Very few of the original 80,000 Jews in area of Poland designated in October 1939 as the Regierungsbezirk of Zichenau—whose ancestors had lived there since the thirteenth century[85]—escaped destruction.

The expulsions and deportations of the first months of the occupation resulted in the displacement of 40,000 Jews from the Regierungsbezirk to the neighboring Polish regions under Soviet occupation and especially to Warsaw. The Einsatzgruppen of the Security Police and Security Service, as well as the Wehrmacht, participated in the often brutal expulsions. Starting in early 1940, the German authorities herded the remaining 36,000 Jews into ghettos. The systematic discrimination, plundering, and exploitation of their labor had begun even earlier. The rampant violence against the Jews—especially during the first weeks of the war—which increased and subsided in phases, culminated in the total destruction of approximately 95 percent of the Jewish population of Northern Mazovia, that is, the so-called Regierungsbezirk of Zichenau. Within two months, starting in mid October 1942, 36,000 Jews were brought to the Auschwitz and Treblinka extermination camps, where most of them were immediately murdered. As a rule, Jews who had fled to the General Government succumbed to the "final solution" there. Presumably, only 4,000 Polish Jews from the region of the Regierungsbezirk of Zichenau survived the Holocaust.

Evidence suggests that, right from the outset, local ethnic Germans in the Regierungsbezirk of Zichenau participated in—and profited from—the anti-Jewish measures of the Wehrmacht, the Einsatzgruppen of the Security Police and Security Service, and the Civil Administration. The alignment of the interests of Reich Germans and local ethnic Germans with regard to eliminating the Poles and Jews and taking over their housing and property certainly promoted *Volkstum* (ethnic-national cultural) ideas. As has been shown, signs also indicate that, although collectively, Poles suffered severely under German occupation, individual Poles participated in—and sometimes also managed to draw material benefits from—the discrimination and persecution of the Jewish population.

Notes

1. Michał Grynberg, *Żydzi w Rejencji Ciechanowskiej 1939–1942* (Warsaw, 1984), 11.
2. Ibid., 11, 15, 20.
3. Ryszard Juszkiewicz, *Losy Żydów mławskich w okresie II-ej wojny światowej* (Mława, 1994) 24f.
4. Miron Owsiewski, *Pułtuscy Żydzi Okresu Międzywojennego* (Pułtusk, 1989), 15.
5. Interview with Edward S., conducted by the author in July 2007 (video recording).
6. For a general discussion see Paweł Machcewicz and Krzysztof Persak, eds., *Wokół Jedwabnego*, 2 vols. (Warsaw, 2002), passim; Juszkiewicz, *Losy Żydów*, 22, 33ff. This is further indicated by the fact that three of the five contemporary witnesses interviewed by the author acknowledged that they "had not liked Jews" or viewed them as an economic problem for the Polish population, although they repudiated the Nazis' subsequent policies of deportation and extermination; interviews with Aleksandr and Halina Ł., as well as Edward J., conducted by the author in July 2007 (video recordings).
7. Owsiewski, *Pułtuscy Żydzi*, 15f.; Juszkiewicz, *Losy Żydów*, 17.
8. A reference to the ideological affinity with "Falange Española," the fascist movement in Spain.
9. Ralf Meindl, *Ostpreußens Gauleiter: Erich Koch—eine politische Biographie* (Osnabrück, 2007), 250; Grynberg, *Żydzi*, 27f.

10. Meindl, *Gauleiter*, 250. In this regard, see Hans Umbreit, *Deutsche Militärverwaltungen 1938/39: Die militärische Besetzung der Tschechoslowakei und Polens* (Stuttgart, 1977), 70, 97f.; Raul Hilberg, *The Destruction of the European Jews*, 3rd ed. (New Haven, 2003), 197.
11. "Decree of the Führer and Reich Chancellor on the Organization and Administration of the Eastern Regions," of 8 October 1939, in RGBl. 1939 I, 2042.
12. Criminal trial files Erich Koch, fol. 1538, SWWW 755, Instytut Pamięci Narodowej (IPN—Institute of National Remembrance); Grynberg, *Żydzi*, 36.
13. Grynberg, *Żydzi*, 30.
14. Interview with Halina Ł. and Edward S., conducted by the author in July 2007 (video recording). The German perpetrators may also have understood the presence of spectators as approval of their operation, lending it a certain sense of normality. Harald Welzer points out this relationship between violent Nazi criminals and eyewitnesses in his book *Täter: Wie aus ganz normalen Menschen Massenmörder worden*, 3rd ed. (Frankfurt, 2005), 148.
15. Frank Golczewski, "Polen," in *Dimension des Völkermords: Die Zahl der jüdischen Opfer des Nationalsozialismus*, ed. Wolfgang Benz (Munich, 1991), 411–498, here 423; Chaim Aron Kaplan, *Buch der Agonie: Das Warschauer Tagebuch des Chaim A. Kaplan* (Frankfurt, 1967), 69.
16. Grynberg, *Żydzi*, 30.
17. Christopher Browning, *The Origins of the Final Solution: The Evolution of Nazi Jewish Policy, September 1939–March 1942* (Lincoln, NE, 2004), 111.
18. For pragmatic reasons, the following refers to Wehrmacht members if the involvement of SS and SD Einsatzkommandos cannot be substantiated and the eyewitnesses characterize them as German soldiers. On this problem, see also Jochen Böhler, *Auftakt zum Vernichtungskrieg: Die Wehrmacht in Polen 1939* (Frankfurt, 2006), 242.
19. Ibid.; Klaus-Michael Mallmann et al., eds., *Einsatzgruppen in Polen: Darstellung und Dokumentation* (Darmstadt, 2008). On the significance of the crimes of Einsatzgruppen and Wehrmacht units in Polen starting in September 1939, see in general Bogdan Musiał, "Einleitung," in *Genesis des Genozids: Polen 1939–1941*, ed. Klaus-Michael Mallmann and Bogdan Musiał (Darmstadt, 2004).
20. Böhler, *Auftakt*, 219.
21. Grynberg, *Żydzi*, 28. People who returned illegally—both Poles and Jews—were supposed to be arrested and transported to the Soldau transit camp in order to be subsequently resettled. This is evident from a letter from the Zichenau Gestapo to the district administrators of the Regierungsbezirk. It is more likely, however, that the district administrators were not supposed to be aware of the executions. Letter from the Staatspolizeistelle Zichenau from 20 March 1941 to the district administrators, Die Bundesbeauftragte für die Unterlagen des Staatssicherheitsdienstes der ehemaligen Deutschen Demokratischen Republik (BStU), MfS HA IX/11 ZUV 59, vol. 39, fol. 3.
22. Grynberg, *Żydzi*, 29. See, among other things, the sometimes pronounced conflicts between Wehrmacht members and the SS in Poland, Broszat, *Nationalsozialistische Polenpolitik*, 30.
23. Grynberg, *Żydzi*, 28. This practice was also later retained by the Gestapo. In this regard, see Jan Grabowski, "Holocaust in Northern Mazovia (Poland) in the Light of the Archive of the Ciechanów Gestapo," *Holocaust and Genocide Studies* 18, no. 3 (2004): 460–476, here 468.
24. Golczewski, "Polen," 426; Tatiana Brustin-Berenstein, "Deportacje i zagłada skupisk żydowskich w Dystrykcie Warszawskim," *Biuletyn Żydowskiego Instytutu Historycznego* 1 (1952): 83–125, here 83.

25. Grynberg, Żydzi, 30.
26. Böhler, Auftakt, 216ff.
27. Grynberg, Żydzi, 29.
28. Ibid., 30f., 33, 59f.; Criminal trial files Erich Koch, fol. 36, IPN, SWWW 742.
29. Grynberg, Żydzi, 31.
30. Ibid., 33. Somewhat later, Catholic churches were defiled in the same manner; see ibid.
31. Ibid., 34f.
32. Ibid., 38; Jan Grabowski, "Die antijüdische Politik im Regierungsbezirk Zichenau," in *Der Judenmord in den eingegliederten polnischen Gebieten 1939–1945*, ed. Jacek Andrzej Młynarczyk and Jochen Böhler (Osnabrück, 2010), 99–116, here 101.
33. IPN, Gestapo Zichenau, passim. The files of the Gestapo Zichenau contain twelve such cases. In total, of the 11,000 surviving case files of the Zichenau Gestapo, only 153 deal with "Jewish questions"; on this, see also Grabowski, "Holocaust in Northern Mazovia (Poland)." This is a result of the systematic destruction of files by the Gestapo prior to the retreat in January 1945. After his arrest by the GDR's Staatssicherheit in 1978, Herbert Helbing, a member of the Zichenau Gestapo from October 1939 to January 1945, put on record that an order was issued on 18 January 1945 to burn all processed and unprocessed files on the desks; in addition, files were taken away in trucks. Statement by Herbert Helbing, BStU, MfS HA IX/11 ZUV 59, vol. 13, fol. 124. References to such cases in the files of the Zichenau Gestapo in the holdings of the Bundesbeauftragte für die Unterlagen der Staatssicherheit: Staatspolizeistelle Zichenau/Płock daily report no. 15 from 22 April 1941, BStU, MfS HA IX/11 ZUV 59, vol. 79, fol. 161; Staatspolizeistelle Zichenau/Schröttersburg daily report no. 3 from 2 January 1942, BStU, MfS HA IX/11 ZUV 59, vol. 80, fol. 6.
34. Grynberg, Żydzi, 37.
35. Nicole Lapierre, ed., *Das gerettete Buch des Simcha Guterman*, 2nd. ed. (Hamburg, 1996), 108f.
36. Ibid.
37. Grynberg, Żydzi, 38.
38. A prominent example of this: Jan Tomasz Gross, *Sąsiedz: Historia zagłady żydowskiego miasteczka* (Sejny, 2000); published in German as *Nachbarn: Der Mord an den Juden von Jedwabne* (Munich, 2001). See also Jan Grabowski, *"Ja tego Żyda znam!" Szantażowanie Żydów w Warszawie 1939–1943* (Warsaw, 2004). Apart from the Polish-Jewish context, there is also the question regarding the extent to which Poles significantly contributed to the persecution of their fellow countrymen, for example as Gestapo informants or denunciators; in this regard, see Barbara Engelking, *"Szanowny Panie gistapo": Donosy do władz niemieckich w Warszawie i okolicach w latach 1940–1941* (Warsaw, 2003).
39. Gestapo Zichenau, daily report no. 3 from 25 May 1940, BStU, MfS HA IX/11 ZUV 59, vol. 79, fol. 7.
40. Grynberg, Żydzi, 39f.
41. Browning, Origins, 34; Umbreit, *Militärverwaltungen*, 98.
42. Criminal trial files Erich Koch, fol. 10–20, IPN, SWWW 742; Grynberg, Żydzi, 35; Martin Broszat, *Nationalsozialistische Polenpolitik 1939–1945* (Stuttgart, 1961), 29; Czesław Madajczyk, *Die Okkupationspolitik Nazideutschlands in Polen 1939–1945* (Cologne, 1988), 22f.
43. Meindl, Gauleiter, 286.
44. Grynberg, Żydzi, 41.
45. Criminal trial files Erich Koch, fol. 1540f. and fol. 750, fol. 399, IPN, SWWW 753; Grynberg, Żydzi, 41.

46. Criminal trial files Erich Koch, fol. 21, IPN, SWWW 742; Grynberg, *Żydzi*, 42.
47. Grynberg, *Żydzi*, 42.
48. Browning, *Origins*, 43f.
49. Grynberg, *Żydzi*, 42.
50. Browning, *Origins*, 35.
51. Ibid., 53.
52. Ibid., 61.
53. Ibid., 97; Gerhard Eisenblätter, *Grundlinien der Politik des Reichs gegenüber dem Generalgouvernement 1939–1945* (Frankfurt, 1969), 188.
54. Browning, *Origins*, 98.
55. Grynberg, *Żydzi*, 42.
56. Browning, *Origins*, 95–99.
57. Grynberg, *Żydzi*, 57.
58. These were located in Lauffen, Sporwitten (Bodzanów), Chorzellen (Chorzele), Czerwinsk an der Weichsel (Czerwińsk nad Wisłą), Zichenau, Reichenfeld, Makow, Mielau, Neustadt (Nowe Miasto), Neuhof, Plock, Plöhnen, Schirps, Strzegowo, Hohenburg, Radzanow (Radzanów), Szreńsk, Zakroczym, and Zielun. See Grynberg, *Żydzi*, 45ff. See also Grabowski, *Die antijüdische Politik*, 104ff.; Bożena Górczyńska-Przybyłowicz, *Życie gospodarczo-społeczne na ziemiach polskich włączonych do Prus Wschodnich w okresie okupacji Hitlerowskiej* (Ciechanów, 1989), passim.
59. Ibid., 45.
60. Ibid., 49.
61. Criminal trial files Erich Koch, fol. 407, fol. 410, fol. 413, IPN, SWWW 750; Grynberg, *Żydzi*, 53.
62. IPN, SWWW 750, fol. 143. In the trial against Erich Koch, a Jewish witness testified that on 22 June 1941, all of the Jews in Plöhnen were rounded up between 2 A.M. and 4 P.M. and had their identification papers checked in order to determine whether they were legally in the town. See also Grynberg, *Żydzi*, 52.
63. Sondergericht Ciechanów, sygn. 4, fol. 1ff., Archiwum Państwowe m. st. Warszawy [State Archive of the City of Warsaw]; Grabowski, *Die antijüdische Politik*, 101f.
64. Grynberg, *Żydzi*, 59f. As part of these partial deportations, at least twenty-nine Jews were shot to death. See ibid.
65. Ibid., 60.
66. Ibid., 61; "Do dziejów ludności żydowskiej w Płocku podczas okupacji hitlerowskiej," *Biuletyn Żydowskiego Instytutu Historycznego* 52 (1964): 72–77.
67. Lapierre, *Das gerettete Buch*, 152ff.; Grynberg, *Żydzi*, 61.
68. Grynberg, *Żydzi*, 63, 67f.; Criminal trial files Erich Koch, fol. 139, IPN, SWWW 750.
69. Grynberg, *Żydzi*, 63.
70. Ibid., 64.
71. Ibid., 65.
72. Ibid., 73.
73. Browning, *Origins*, 34. Browning refers to investigation results from the Nuremberg trials (NO-1073 and NO-1074). As demonstrated by these documents, the conditions in the camp disturbed even the SS. In any case, an internal investigation was conducted when an epidemic broke out in late summer 1941.
74. Janusz Gumkowski, "Obóz hitlerowski w Działdowie," *Biuletyn Głownej Komisji Badania Zbrodni Hitlerowskich w Polsce* 10 (1958): 57–88, here 87.
75. Gestapo Zichenau, passim, IPN; Criminal trial files Erich Koch, fol. 140, IPN, SWWW 750; BStU, MfS HA IX/11 ZUV 59, vol. 2, fol. 228; Grynberg, *Żydzi*, 80; Benz, *Dimension des Völkermords*, 437; Andrzej Sokolnicki, "Region Pułtuski w latach

okupacji hitlerowskiej 1939–1945," in *Pułtusk. Studia i materiały z dziejów miasta i region*, vol. 1, ed. Mazowiecki Ośrodek, Badań Naukowych Imienia Stanisława Herbst (Warsaw, 1969), 209–276, passim.

76. Criminal trial files Erich Koch, fol. 736, IPN, SWWW 742; Grynberg, *Żydzi*, 736.
77. Grynberg, *Żydzi*, 75; Czesław Pilichowski et al., eds., *Obozy Hitlerowskie na ziemiach polskich 1939–1945. Informator encyklopedyczny* (Warszawa, 1979), passim; Ryszard Juszkiewicz, "Obozy w rejencji ciechanowskiej," *Notatki Płockie* 1 (1968): 32–38, passim.
78. Grynberg, *Żydzi*, 75.
79. Ibid., 76ff.; Criminal trial files Erich Koch, fol. 28., IPN, SWWW 742.
80. Grynberg, *Żydzi*, 106.
81. Ibid., 107f.
82. Ibid., 109–114.
83. Ibid., 114f.
84. Ibid., 118.
85. Ibid., 11.

CHAPTER 9

EAST UPPER SILESIA
Sybille Steinbacher

Prior to the Annexation

Fueled by nationalist motivations, civil-war-like conflicts between Germans and Poles prevailed since the end of the First World War in Upper Silesia, a region that was subject to the League of Nations. The German Freikorps quelled the first Silesian uprising at the end of August 1919; two additional uprisings, answered no less violently, followed during the next two years. The referendum mandated by Article 88 of the Treaty of Versailles and conducted in March 1921 under the supervision of an Inter-Allied Administrative and Plebiscite Commission decided in favor of the German Reich, but after the decision by the Council of the League of Nations on 20 October 1921, the Allies announced the division of Upper Silesia. Large parts of the territory were awarded to Poland, including the coalfields around Dombrowa (Dąbrowa Górnicza) and along the Olsa (Olza), as well as almost the entire resource-rich industrial region around Kattowitz (Katowice) and Königshütte (Chorzów) with its valuable production facilities. Until that point, the region had been one of the German Reich's industrial centers. On 15 May 1922, the ruling was fixed by an agreement: the German-Polish Accord provided for the protection of minorities in Upper Silesia, including the Jews; it had a term of fifteen years.[1]

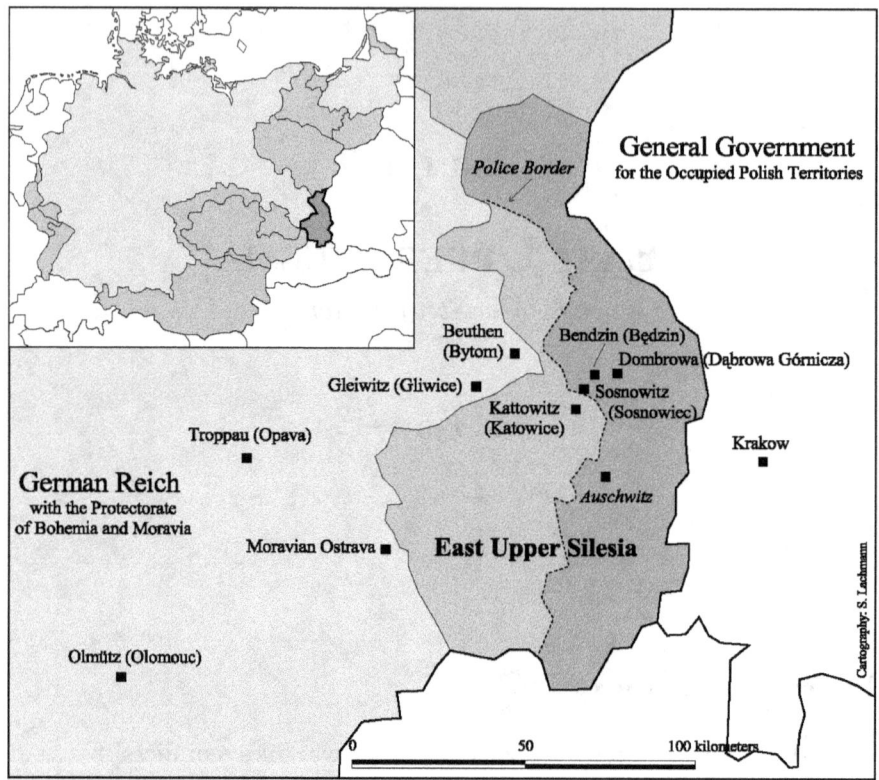

Map 9.1. East Upper Silesia, 1939

The residents in the western, German part of the region (consisting of 9,700 square kilometers) numbered 1.37 million; in the eastern, Polish part (just over 3,200 square kilometers), they numbered approximately 985,000. Poland took over the Landkreise (rural districts) of Kattowitz and Pleß (Pszczyna), large portions of the Kreise (districts) of Königshütte, Tarnowitz (Tarnowskie Góry), Rybnik, Beuthen (Bytom), Lublinitz (Lubliniec), and Hindenburg (Zabrze), and also the eastern portions of the Kreise of Gleiwitz (Gliwice) and Ratibor (Racibórz). Formerly Prussian, this severed part of Upper Silesia henceforth bore the designation "East Upper Silesia" (Ostoberschlesien) in German parlance, a term that vehemently expressed claims of territorial ownership. All of the Weimar Republic's governments made "retrieving" the region from Poland a foreign-policy objective.[2]

Relatively few Jews lived in the German part of Silesia during period between the wars; according to the results of the May 1939 census, only 17,000. Comprising even less than 1 percent of the population, they spoke German and were largely assimilated. Most of them—just over 10,000 in 1939—lived in Breslau, the city with the third-largest Jewish community in the German Reich, after Berlin and Frankfurt.[3] Just under 4,400 Jews lived in the former Upper Silesian plebiscite region in the area around Oppeln, many of them (the exact number is unknown) in the countryside. But most of the Jewish population—approximately 80,000 people—lived in Polish territory, more specifically, in the eastern part of East Upper Silesia, which even prior to 1919 had not belonged to Germany and would first be incorporated into the Province of Silesia by the National Socialists. The Jews in this region lived primarily in Sosnowiec (Sosnowitz), Będzin (Bendzin, as of 1941 Bendsburg), Chrzanów (Krenau), Dombrowa, and Oświęcim (Auschwitz), small Polish towns that had been characteristically Jewish for centuries; a number of Jewish rural communities existed as well[4] (see map 9.1). The vast majority of the region's Jews cultivated orthodox religious traditions and had been socialized by time-honored customs and traditions.

Not least because of the ethno-nationalist conflict between Germans and Poles, East Upper Silesia became a stage for vigorous anti-Jewish agitation during the interwar period.[5] This notwithstanding, by virtue of his authority the Polish Head of State Józef Piłsudski ensured that no pogroms broke out. Even so, however, nationalist Polish groups stirred up anti-Semitism in the region, as did the German minority, which according to the December 1931 census numbered around 70,000 people. After the First World War, the Germans not only lost their societal privileges but also saw themselves confronted by rigid Polonization policies, undertaken by the Polish government in reaction to German political and cultural ambitions. They combined their anti-Polish attitudes with anti-Jewish resentment. In turn, the Poles accused the Jews of making common cause with the Germans. For their part, the Germans made no effort to hide their enthusiasm for the National Socialists.[6]

The Nazi movement soon celebrated victories in the Reich's Silesian territory. The NSDAP emerged as early as 1925 from the German People's League (Volksbund) and the German National Socialist Association for Poland (Deutscher Nationalsozialistischer Verein für Polen), which later became the Young German Party (Jungdeutsche Partei). The NSDAP quickly established itself as a political force, this even though Upper Silesia was the Prussian province with the highest proportion of Catholics (88 percent of the population), who elsewhere throughout the Reich remained resistant to National Socialism for a relatively long time. During the Reichstag elections in November 1932, the Catholic Center Party still received almost 36 percent of the votes, but the NSDAP took just under 27 percent, the Communist Party almost 17 percent, the Social Democratic Party only 9 percent, and the anti-Semitic German National People's Party (Deutschnationale Volkspartei, DNVP) still took 8 percent. During the last reasonably free elections in March 1933, the NSDAP surpassed the Center Party to become the strongest political group, attaining 49 percent of the vote in Upper and Lower Silesia, which was significantly higher than the party's average for the Reich as a whole.[7]

After seizing power in 1933, the National Socialists enthusiastically set about trying to revise the eastern boundary. Particularly in Silesia (Upper and Lower Silesia were combined into a single political administrative entity in March 1938), they continued their strategy of increasing the national political strength of Germandom abroad, which had been introduced in the early 1920s and voiced above all in their propaganda. In doing so, the regime was less interested in the national cultivation of *Volkstum* (ethnic-national culture) than in instrumentalizing the German minority for the purpose of power politics. Its goal was to wage the so-called *Volkstumskampf* (ethnic-national struggle) with the utmost severity.[8]

The many forms of discrimination immediately initiated by the National Socialists against the Jewish population in the German part of the Upper Silesian plebiscite region violated the provisions for the protection of minorities agreed upon in the German-Polish Accord—and therefore became the subject of negotiations at the League of Nations. These negotiations were triggered by Franz Bernheim, who had been dismissed as a department store employee in Gleiwitz and had fled to Prague (Praha). In May 1933, he petitioned the League of Nations, which led to an investigation.[9] Meanwhile, the discrimination increased so dramatically that in August 1933 the Association of Synagogue Congregations of the Province of Upper Silesia (Synagogengemeindeverband der Provinz Oberschlesien) complained to the Foreign Office about economic discrimination and massive anti-Jewish propaganda.[10]

But when the German-Polish Accord expired in May 1937 and the German Reich obtained full sovereignty over the German part of the Silesian plebiscite area, after the end of a two-month grace period, all of the Reich's anti-Jewish laws began entering into force in Upper Silesia from one day to the next. They were rigorously implemented, often even more strictly than elsewhere. Jewish officials, salaried employees, and workers were banned from their professions; Jewish physicians, pharmacists, and lawyers were stripped of their licenses to practice. In contrast to the rest of the Reich, these restrictions also applied to Jews who had fought at the front in the First World War and so-called *Mischlinge* (hybrids).[11] While pogrom-like violence had already occurred in the Polish part of Upper Silesia after Piłsudski's death in May 1935, after the Accord's expiration Jews were also assailed—their businesses destroyed and synagogues attacked—in various localities in the German part.[12]

The First Weeks of the Annexation

Hitler and Stalin came to an agreement at the end of August 1939 on the destruction of Poland as an independent state, thereby sealing the country's fourth partitioning. After the German invasion and rapid Polish defeat, the German Reich took over approximately half of the territory with more than 20 million inhabitants; around 12 million people came under Soviet influence. By incorporating Poland, the National Socialists took over the country with Europe's largest Jewish population, suffusing it before long with unprecedented terror. Based on racism, anti-Slavism, and imperialist ambitions focused toward the East, the policy of systematic Germanization, which applied to East Upper Silesia and indeed all of the western Polish regions, sought the rigorous destruction and complete replacement of everything *fremdvölkisch,* that is, of a foreign ethnic-national character. Such was the content of the idea of *Lebensraum im Osten* (living space in in the East). The politically charged concept of "Germanization"—a term used to legitimate imperialist intentions in Eastern-Central Europe, originating in the Wilhelmine era—set the key political goal, namely, the shifting of populations in the service of "ethnic reorganization."[13]

The Einsatzgruppen of the SS acted as the advance units and most radical vehicles of Nazi policies of conquest. Behind the army's rear units, the Einsatzgruppe z.b.V. (*zur besonderen Verwendung;* for special employment), led by SS-Obergruppenführer Udo von Woyrsch, began its advance from Kattowitz. Himmler had quickly assembled the unit on the evening of 3 September 1939, after the other five Einsatzgruppen had already been formed. The Reichsführer-SS sent his good friend Woyrsch, who had led the SS Higher Administrative Section Southeast (SS-Oberabschnitt Südost) in Breslau from 1934 to 1936 before being transferred to Himmler's personal staff, purposefully into the industrial region of Upper Silesia, because the Poles were fiercely resisting the occupiers.[14] The Einsatzgruppe z.b.V. swept across the region with a wave of unprecedented violence, one that especially targeted Jews. Given the absence of orders to this effect from Berlin, the anti-Semitic operations presumably trace back to Woyrsch's own initiative. The terror erupted in the destruction of synagogues and Jewish cemeteries, in assaults and firing-squad executions. In Bendzin, for example, the occupiers forced hundreds of Jews into the synagogue and set the building on fire.[15] Non-Jewish Poles were also exposed to violent assaults.

The Silesian NSDAP Gauleiter and Oberpräsident (Upper President) of the Prussian Province of Silesia Josef Wagner served as the Head of the Civil Administration (Chef der Zivilverwaltung, CdZ) in occupied Upper Silesia.[16] The "incorporation" of the conquered western Polish region into the German Reich during the first weeks of the war was incredibly complicated. In the end, the Reich subsumed not only the former German settlement area but also regions deemed "valuable" to the war economy, military, and logistics, extending the Reich's territorial dimensions far beyond the regions Germany had been trying to reclaim since the end of the First World War. The Reich incorporated large sections of Polish terrain, with 80 percent of Polish industry and a total of approximately 10 million inhabitants. In Upper Silesia—especially East Upper Silesia—the Nazi regime pursued a special goal with its occupation: more so than in almost any other territory, the reorganization in this region focused on strengthening the war economy. The purpose was to pursue economic interests and simultaneously erase the "disgrace of Versailles." Thus the region emerged as the second most important center of the German armament industry, next to the Ruhr region.[17]

Those Jews who initially managed to escape the SS Einsatzkommandos nonetheless soon found themselves exposed to arbitrary actions and violence. At least 2,000 Jews successfully fled East Upper Silesia during the first weeks of the war,[18] while Germany's racial policies slammed those left behind with a vengeance. Already on 5 September 1939, one day after his appointment as the Head of the Civil Administration, Wagner—as his first official act—issued an ordinance "pertaining to the property of persons who have fled,"[19] thereby setting the stage for excluding the Jews from the region's economic life. Within days, official government representatives confiscated landed property, houses, immovables, companies, and factories belonging to Jews; stores were closed and sealed; security portfolio accounts, bank accounts, and safe-deposit boxes were blocked.[20]

Oberpräsident and Gauleiter Josef Wagner, who as an "old fighter" was a close confidant of Hitler, sought extensive competencies in matters pertaining to restructuring according to population policies. Together with Fritz-Dietlof Graf von Schulenburg, who as a nineteen-year-old member of the Upper Silesian Self-Defense Force (Oberschlesischer Selbstschutz) had helped suppress the third Silesian uprising in 1921 and since 1939 served as the deputy Oberpräsident in Silesia, Wagner developed ambition operations. The Germanization policy promised to win special prestige, for, shortly after the war began, Hitler had assigned his Gauleiter the task of making their terrain "German, that is, purely German" within ten years—regardless of the means.[21] Wagner and Schulenburg firmly believed in the idea of ethnic reorganization. Their faith in the superiority of German civilization and their genuine anti-Semitic and anti-Slavic mindsets shaped their administrative practices. Since initially the SS and police apparatus had not yet established itself as a powerful institution, both men at the top of the Civil Administration were openly willing to cooperate with Higher SS and Police Leader (Höherer SS und Polizeiführer; HSSPF) Erich von dem Bach-Zelewski, who led the SS Higher Administrative Section Southeast and was responsible for Upper and Lower Silesia as well as the Regierungsbezirk of Troppau (Opava) in the Sudetengau. In October 1939, Wagner assumed the control and coordination of resettlement and settlement policy. Meanwhile, in his new capacity as Reich Commissioner for the Strengthening of Germandom (Reichskommissar für die Festigung deutschen Volkstums; RKF), which he held since the beginning of October 1939, Himmler appointed his directly subordinate higher SS and police leaders as deputy RKF emissaries; as a result, Bach-Zelewski henceforth functioned as Wagner's deputy in settlement issues. Admittedly, the two men occasionally had conflicts, but never about the basic principles of Germanization policy. Wagner and Schulenburg (the latter of whom would later emerge as one of the leading figures in the nationalist conservative resistance) were far from providing any opposition. Rather, conflicts with the SS were limited to wrangling over competencies.[22] Until Wagner, pressured by Himmler, had to cede his responsibility for settlement matters to the SS around the turn of the year 1939/40, and a few months later finally had to surrender his office (as did Schulenburg as well) to Himmler's minion Fritz Bracht,[23] he ruthlessly implemented the resettlement program. The three steps of the overall *Volkstum* policy plan envisaged the liquidation of the intellectual and political elite and propertied class, the expulsion of all Jews and most non-Jewish Poles, and the strict segregation of the remaining population from newly arriving German settlers.[24]

Wagner already played a leading role in October 1939 in the first government deportation project, the "Nisko plan," which was not limited to East Upper Silesia but rather initially envisaged the deportation of the Jews from the entire German Reich to the "Reich ghetto" near Lublin.[25] Adolf Eichmann, at the time the managing director of the Central Offices for Jewish Emigration in Vienna and Prague, planned the resettlement of 70,000 to 80,000 Jews from East Upper Silesia and thousands of Jews from Vienna, Moravian Ostrava, Prague, and Brno. In the end, the deportation plans did not affect all of the Jews from East Upper Silesia, but rather those from the annexed western Polish regions, in order to quickly accelerate the "Germanization" process. On 20 and 26 October 1939, approximately 2,000 East Upper Silesian Jews were deported to Nisko. By this point, Wagner, on his own initiative, had already considered deporting the Jewish population residing chiefly in the eastern part of his province "beyond Krakow."[26] Enlisted by Eichmann, Wagner especially distinguished himself during the preparations, but he could not prevent the entire endeavor from failing

Figure 9.1. Jewish forced laborers in Bendzin marked by armbands, 1939/40. *Source:* United States Holocaust Memorial Museum photo archives, image no.: 24990.

due to logistical problems.²⁷ Himmler aborted the Nisko plan in the beginning of November 1939 and postponed the "resettlement" until February 1940.²⁸

The Period of the Occupation

Hitler decided on the demarcation of boundaries on 8 October 1939. With his decree concerning the structure and administration of the eastern regions, he first created the Regierungsbezirk of Kattowitz "with the inclusion of bordering regional parts" in the Province of Silesia, effective 1 November.²⁹ He did this not so much with the intention of permanently establishing German claims but rather to put the Germanization and exploitation policies into gear as quickly as possible.³⁰

Two newly created Regierungsbezirke—Kattowitz and Oppeln— joined the existing Regierungsbezirke of Breslau and Liegnitz. While approximately 1.7 million people lived in the Oppeln region, most of them Germans and so-called *Deutschstämmige* (persons with German origins), the spatially smaller Kattowitz, with over 2.5 million inhabitants, was the most populous Regierungsbezirk of the Prussian Province of Silesia.³¹ As a result of the boundary demarcation, Silesia was expanded to include rural districts inhabited almost exclusively by Poles and Jews. Prior to the First World War, these districts had belonged to Congress Poland, governed by Russia, and to the Habsburg monarchy's Kingdom of Galicia. The Nazi regime pursued the goal of coalescing the region's industrial companies, labor resources, and coal basins into a unified Greater Silesian Economic Region, resulting in the creation of a jagged, heterogeneous, and multinational territory. In October 1939, the inhabitants of the Regierungsbezirk Kattowitz consisted of the following: approximately 1.5 million Poles; 280,000 Germans and so-called *Deutschstämmige*; 75,000 Czechs; approximately 600,000 persons of "floating ethnicity" (*schwebenden Volkstums*), namely, Silesia's typical bilingual mixed population, which could not be assigned to any nationality; and slightly more than 80,000 Jews, the majority of whom lived in the so-called Eastern Strip (*Oststreifen*), namely, the formerly Polish region bordering directly on the middle and southern part of the shattered country of Poland, that is, the General Government. With the demarcation of borders on 8 October 1939, the Eastern Strip, too, became a part of the German Reich. As understood by the occupiers, however, hardly anyone living in the Eastern Strip could be classified as "German" according to racial principles. Because of its almost exclusively Polish and Jewish population, the Eastern Strip was almost worthless from the perspective of population policy.[32]

For anti-Jewish policy in East Upper Silesia, the administrative situation acquired fundamental importance, because the course of the new boundary oriented the reorganizational plans of population policy. The police boundary demarcated on 20 November 1939 also played a decisive role.[33] Not only did it run through the middle of the Regierungsbezirk of Kattowitz, but it also created two different regions in terms of territorial law. Although not a national boundary, the police border nonetheless effectively transformed the annexed Gaue and provinces into foreign regions with respect to police and passport laws, creating a second-class territory of the Reich; it completely separated Danzig-West Prussia and the Reichsgau Wartheland from the Old Reich, and it separated the respective eastern territorial portions of Silesia and East Prussia. In the Regierungsbezirk of Kattowitz, its purpose was to protect the economy by preventing migratory movements of *Fremdvölkische* (persons of alien national ethnicities) from the Eastern Strip into the western regions slated for Germanization. The restrictions equally affected both Jewish and non-Jewish residents. Even Auschwitz—formerly the town of Oświęcim, whose name was immediately Germanized in the first days of the war—lay in the Eastern Strip. When the war began, approximately 8,000 Jews and 6,000 Catholics lived in the town. After the demarcation of the border in October 1939, Auschwitz belonged to the German Reich.[34]

The responsibility for shifting populations in East Upper Silesia between the western portion and the region east of the police border was in the hands of the Resettler Workgroup (Arbeitsgruppe Umsiedler), directed by Deputy Oberpräsident Schulenburg in Breslau. The Kattowitz Regierungspräsident Walter Springorum (until the start of the war, a section head in the Reich Interior Ministry) played an important role here as well. At first, the workgroup's plans concentrated on the terrain west of the police border, which looked like it could be Germanized without any problems because many of its residents were already German or of German descent. On the other hand, planners considered the Eastern Strip difficult due to its *Fremdvölkische* and thus for the time being exempted the area from Germanization. In the interim, this spared the Jews living in the region from deportation. Yet all the same, the terrain played an important role in the Germanization program, for within the province the Eastern Strip was now declared to be a region used for deporting "racially undesirable" local residents from the rural districts west of the police border; thus the actions undertaken against the Jews formed a central element of German occupation policy.[35]

From the conqueror's perspective, the deportations were considered successful, for already by 1940 hardly any Jews continued to live in the western part of the Kattowitz Regierungsbezirk. The proceedings constituted a reaction to measures undertaken by Governor General Hans Frank, who at the beginning of the same year had initially reduced and finally stopped his jurisdiction's acceptance of Poles and Jews from the "annexed" eastern regions. For anti-Jewish policy, this created an explosive situation in the Eastern Strip: the Oberpräsidium (Upper Presidium) and the SS—the regional authorities responsible for Germanization—concentrated all of the Jews from East Upper Silesia in the Eastern Strip, unceremoniously turning them over to the Jewish communities to provision and accommodate. The latter's resources and funds, however, were quickly exhausted; given the minimal food rations and poor medical care, impoverishment became imminent. The largest "deportation centers" in the Eastern Strip were the towns of Bendzin, Sosnowitz, and Dombrowa, which had traditionally housed Jews. At the turn of the year 1939/40, approximately 25,000 Jews lived in Bendzin, which had a total population of 54,000. The more than 26,000 Jews in Sosnowitz constituted more than a quarter of the town's population, while in Dombrowa almost 16,000 of the town's 42,000 residents were Jewish. Closed ghettos did not yet exist, but the Jews lived separately from the rest of the population, left to themselves in city quarters with poorly developed infrastructures.[36] An ordinance issued by Higher SS and Police Leader Erich Bach-Zelewski in December 1939 stipulated the compulsory marking of Jews.[37] A month earlier in the General Government, Jews had already been forced to wear a white armband with a blue Star of Zion (see figure 9.1).

During the weeks after annexation, the Office of the Four-Year-Plan under Hermann Göring especially anticipated profiting from the redistribution of the "foreign-racial" population's assets. Geared toward strengthening and controlling the economy, the office promptly initiated efforts to build up the German greater regional economy in the annexed eastern regions. In October 1939, the Main Trustee Office East (Haupttreuhandstelle Ost) was created as an independent organization of the Office of the Four-Year-Plan, headquartered in Berlin and with branch offices in Kattowitz, Danzig, and Posen, among other places.[38] The Kattowitz Trustee Office was especially important because it was responsible for Upper Silesia's industrial region. It registered and confiscated commercial assets,[39] which included companies and landed property as well as securities, agricultural estates, precious stones, foreign currency, and even household goods. Disguised as "social restoration" and implemented through supposedly legal acts, the activities of the Kattowitz Trustee Office actually amounted to nothing more than government-organized theft. The office was initially directed by Otto Fitzner, president of the Breslau Chamber for Industry and Trade, whose responsibilities were taken over by Gauwirtschaftsberater (Gau economic advisor) Arthur Jakob in the beginning of 1940, who in turn was followed in February 1941 by Michael Graf von Matuschka, a close confidant of Schulenburg and the director of the Economics Department with the Oberpräsident and the Landrat (district administrator) of Oppeln. The provisional administrators working for the Kattowitz Trustee Office included both local ethnic Germans and Reich Germans. They formed an army of small business persons who sensed lucrative sources of income. In light of the material enticements, they were evidently more than willing to comply with the demands of the Nazi state and fulfill their intended roles. Indifference due to a greed for profits and racial-political convictions, social coldheartedness, and insensitivity spread among the German civilian population, long before the program to murder the Jews began.[40]

When Fritz Bracht assumed the offices of the Gauleiter and Oberpräsident of Upper Silesia[41]—at first provisionally, then officially in the beginning of 1941—this immediately impacted Germanization policies, because responsibility for these policies was now transferred to the SS, which separated Jewish policy and settlement policy and institutionalized them accordingly. In fall 1940, the 28-year-old Untersturmführer Fritz Arlt, an anthropology Ph.D. acting as Himmler's RKF emissary, took over the supervision of the Polish population's deportation and the settlement of ethnic Germans and Reich Germans.[42] SS-Oberführer Albrecht Schmelt, formerly the Breslau Polizeipräsident (police president), was henceforth responsible for Jewish policy. Named Organization Schmelt (Dienststelle Schmelt), his new office, established in Sosnowitz in October 1940, was a unique institution in conquered Poland. Whether Schmelt was directly subordinate to Himmler, who had pressed for the new office, or indirectly through the intermediate authority of the Higher SS and Police Leader is not entirely clear. As Himmler's Special Emissary (Sonderbeauftragter), he summoned to life a new kind of forced-labor system to "register and control the assignment of *fremdvölkisch* labor in East Upper Silesia," as stated in the designation of his office.[43] Schmelt proceeded so "effectively" that approximately 17,000 Jewish forced laborers—men and women—were soon being exploited in heavy physical work assignments for at least twelve hours a day. Their number steadily increased. Excluded from social welfare as well as unemployment benefits, old-age pensions, and health, child, and survivor benefits, the Jews had to pay a large part of their paltry wages to the Organization Schmelt. The Council of Elders of the Jewish religious communities in East Upper Silesia, led by Moshe Merin—then and now a controversial figure among the Jews—was forced to collaborate in the recruitment of workers.[44]

Economic interests determined anti-Jewish policy. With its rich deposits of zinc, iron, and lead, the gigantic smelters of the iron and steel industry, and one of Europe's largest black coal mining regions, the province became important as an "armorer of the Reich."[45] Robert Ley, the head of the Reich's NSDAP organization (Reichsorganisationsleiter), stressed this importance when on 1 February 1940 he wrote in the *Kattowitzer Zeitung*: "As one of the most powerful armorers, the Gau of Upper Silesia is called upon to strengthen the German arms industry and thereby contribute to the attainment of our forces' final victory." By means of the "Jewish deployment" (*Judeneinsatz*) specifically in the center of the arms industry, Himmler wanted to secure additional influence for the SS. The construction of the strategically important Autobahn—for which Schmelt procured the Jews—also served this purpose especially well.[46] Schmelt's activities pursued the intention of increasing the war economy's performance by recruiting Jewish workers and exploiting them as much as possible. Therefore, after fall 1940, the rigorous deportations organized by Arlt excluded the Jews; this is why the victims of the "Saybusch action"—the first systematic deportation of "foreign ethnic elements" from East Upper Silesia to the General Government—consisted exclusively of Poles, a total of approximately 18,000 persons. Between September 1940 and January 1941, more than 4,000 Galician-German peasants were settled in the deportees' houses, apartments, and farmsteads.[47] With respect to the approximately 560 Jews in the Landkreis of Saybusch, a directive from the Kattowitz Gestapo, composed of members of the former Einsatzgruppe z.b.V., stated: "Jews may not be evacuated."[48]

Under the direction and supervision of Organization Schmelt, Jews were henceforth obligated to perform forced labor in three different ways: in specially established camps at construction sites along the Silesian section of the Reich Autobahn from Berlin to Krakow; in factory-specific forced-labor camps on the grounds or in the vicinity of large industrial companies; and in factories for Wehrmacht production, the so-called *Shops* that were created in large numbers under

German control in the towns of the Eastern Strip. Whereas the Autobahn construction camps forcibly employed almost exclusively Jewish men, enlisting only a few women for kitchen and cleanup work, the *Shops* and industrial companies employed chiefly women. The largest Wehrmacht production centers in the Eastern Strip were the *Shops* operated by Rudolf Braune and Alfred Rossner.

Enlisting Jews for forced labor in guarded camps had already been common practice in the Old Reich since the end of 1938; in annexed Austria, the practice even began a few weeks earlier.[49] After the war started, forced labor was also at the core of anti-Jewish policy in conquered Poland,[50] where labor market interests likewise played a role. In East Upper Silesia, the forced-labor measures were undertaken strictly in the name of increasing efficiency in the armaments sector. The labor assignment scheme, monopolized by Schmelt, became a systematic method for pursuing anti-Jewish policy. Himmler's Special Emissary hereby anticipated the principle of leasing out prison laborers, which was later adopted for the first time by a private company—namely, in Auschwitz by IG Farben—in spring 1941;[51] after the founding of the SS Economic and Administrative Main Office (SS-Wirtschafts-Verwaltungshauptamt; WVHA) in February 1942, the principle was ultimately adopted throughout the Reich.

Schmelt established an extensive network—independent from the Concentration Camps Inspectorate—of more than two hundred individual camps with exclusively Jewish prisoners, spanning from Upper Silesia all the way to Lower Silesia and the Sudetengau. Even though he subjected the Jews to a strict system of control, repression, and exploitation, Schmelt nonetheless sought to preserve their capacity for work. Thus, for a certain period, pragmatic economic considerations slowed down the dynamics of the dogmatic interpretation of "racist" principles. Even so, due to the catastrophic living conditions that prevailed above all in the forced-labor camps along the Reich Autobahn, many Jews did not survive the coercive measures. As a result of their relentless physical exploitation, the number of Jews who became unable to work soon grew immensely.[52] As of fall 1941, they were all brought to the Auschwitz camp and murdered. In the context of the strict labor assignment policy, Auschwitz assumed a critical role, serving as a "solution" to the regional "Jewish question" even before the deportation trains begin arriving at the camp with Jews from throughout Europe. The East Upper Silesian Jews were exposed to miserable living conditions in Sosnowitz, Bendzin, Dombrowa, and other places, although they were better than those in the Autobahn camps. The efforts of the Jewish Council of Elders to improve the provisioning situation in the collection points admittedly led to the creation of relief facilities such as soup kitchens and outpatient clinics for the sick, but over time the available funds and resources became too depleted to sustain Jewish self-help efforts.[53]

Hardly anything is known about the productivity of Jewish forced laborers in the Schmelt system. Regardless of the system's "efficiency," Schmelt collected fees from companies in return for leasing Jews to them. His office thereby attained a sufficient flow of income to finance Gauleiter and Oberpräsident Bracht's special fund for settlement projects involving ethnic German settlers.[54] The revenue also served to subsidize the families of fallen SS members; in addition, Organization Schmelt participated in the government-financed purchase of the Gau model estate (*Gaumustergut*) Parzymiechy, used to settle ethnic German peasants. Promoted in 1942 to SS-Brigadeführer, Schmelt also made personal use of monies from the "Jewish deployment," financing his house in an idyllic location on the Parzymiechy estate and directing a further 100,000 RM into his private account.[55]

For the purpose of attaining the complete bureaucratic registration and control of the Jewish population, in 1941 the authorities finally established a legal environment in East Upper Silesia that was congruent with the Old Reich. An important step in this direction was the introduction of the Nuremberg Laws in June 1941. Enacted in the Old Reich already in 1938, the ordinance compelling Jews to assume the common first names of "Israel" and "Sara" followed in the same month.[56] Starting in September 1941, the ordinance stipulating the wearing of the "Jewish star" applied as it did in the Old Reich; the previously typical armbands were no longer used.[57] There were countless routine chicaneries as well. As early as December 1940, Jews were prohibited from shopping in or trading with non-Jewish grocery stores. As of February 1941, they were no longer allowed to use public transportation. Exceptions were made for Jews who needed to travel long distances to reach their workplaces in the factories of Organization Schmelt in the Eastern Strip. For a while, a streetcar marked with a blue Star of David and the inscription: "only for Jews" traveled between Sosnowitz and Bendzin for this purpose. As of April 1941, the Jewish population was also denied access to authorities; anyone who had to visit an office required special approval, which in turn required a separate time-consuming application. In Sosnowitz, a post office opened solely for Jews. The measures came from the Kattowitz Regierungspräsidium (Government Presidium), the Kattowitz Gestapo, and the police headquarters in Sosnowitz. The commander of the Protection Police (Schutzpolizei) in Sosnowitz also issued a regulation in May 1941 prohibiting Jews from keeping any cows or other animals for commercial use. As of December 1941, they were also prohibited from giving or attending concert performances; even their bicycles were taken away. The identity card requirement, introduced the previous month, stipulated photo identification for all Jews above the age of six. The paper was yellow like the "Jewish star," printed with word "Jew" in stylized Hebrew letters. The Gestapo kept carbon copies of the IDs, and the Jewish Council of Elders had to pay for and distribute them.[58]

When in March 1941 preparations for the invasion of the Soviet Union disrupted the resettlements to the General Government due to logistical reasons, the situation in the Eastern Strip once again became serious. The concentration of Jews in this region now conflicted directly with other resettlement measures. Thousands of Poles had to be housed east of the police border in mass accommodations in so-called Polish camps; at the same time, ethnic Germans from Romania's Bukovina region had to be settled as well. In the dramatically intensifying conflict for residential space, municipal politicians, settlement strategists, architects, and spatial planners soon viewed the Jews as an impediment for the settlement program.[59] Since the resettlement and settlement programs were coordinated in theory but never balanced in practice, the conflict served as a pretext for excluding the Jews from future planning right from outset. In light of the impasse, lack of restraint and latent murderous inclinations increased immensely. During the shift from a policy of deportation to mass murder, the logistical conundrum in the Eastern Strip provided local planners with the ostensibly rational legitimation to simply arrange for the Jews to disappear.

The activities in East Upper Silesia clearly demonstrate that, against the background of the concept of Germanization, plans for long-term structural changes to the economy and society played a central role, and that a functional relationship obtained between Germanization and genocide. Wagner and Schulenburg already laid the logistical foundations for the mass murder in October 1940, when during their last official actions they arranged for the addition of the Eastern Strip (which had originally been excluded from the Germanization program) to the regions undergoing ethnic reorganization. Himmler viewed the measure as increasing the territory's value, granting his approval in his capacity as the Reich Commissioner for the Strengthening of Germandom in the middle of January 1941.[60]

At the same time, the number of Jews living in Sosnowitz and Bendzin steadily increased, for in the course of recruiting forced laborers, Schmelt had small Jewish communities dissolved and their inhabitants brought to the large ghettos for forced labor.[61] The uninterrupted flow of incoming Jews evoked massive criticism from the municipal leaders of Sosnowitz and Bendzin. Both Oberbürgermeister Schönwälder and his colleague Kowohl felt that it significantly jeopardized plans for the Germanization of their cities. They only supported Schmelt's forced-labor policy when Jews were shipped off to the camps serving the Reich Autobahn and industry.[62] If Jews were brought to Eastern Strip's Wehrmacht production centers instead, the mayors would protest. Responsible for Bendzin and Sosnowitz, Polizeipräsident Alexander von Woedtke concurred with them, likewise looking for a way to get rid of the Jews. The German population, said Kowohl emphatically, can no longer be "reasonably expected" to live together "with the Jewish parasites."[63]

The pressure from the Civil Administration to make the Jews quickly disappear conflicted with Organization Schmelt's work assignment policies. The worse the military situation became after the Wehrmacht's failure near Moscow in December 1941, the more intensely Schmelt pushed ahead with the exploitation of Jewish forced laborers deployed in the arms industry. A serious conflict regarding the "Jewish deployment" erupted between him and the Civil Administration's authorities. The fact that the conflict arose indicates that local functionaries had plenty of room to maneuver. In conjunction with the program to massively stimulate the arms industry introduced by Albert Speer as the new Reich Minister for Armaments and Munitions, Schmelt intensified the employment of Jews. From spring 1942 onward, he had Jewish forced laborers trained for war production and as specialists in construction and concrete production.[64] A total of 6,500 Jews were now deployed in forty major arms industry installations deemed critical for the war effort. In addition, numerous Schmelt camps were established near submarine and airplane construction firms, munitions and clay pipe factories, wagon and machinery construction plants, brick works, light-bulb and sugar factories, and road and underground construction sites.[65]

The integration of the Jews into armaments production slowed down the murder process in the region. Contrary to what might be assumed based of the proximity of the Auschwitz-Birkenau death camp, the Jews of East Upper Silesia were not the first to be sent to the machinery of death. Rather, here of all places, most of them were still alive even as the Jewish populations of entire cities and districts in the conquered East had already been exterminated. All appearances suggest that Schmelt had extensive powers: in Groß Kosel (Koźle) in Lower Silesia, he had approximately 10,000 work-capable Jews "pre-selected" from transports from the Netherlands and France before they continued to Auschwitz-Birkenau, having them brought to his camps.[66] According to the figures of Richard Korherr, the Inspector for Statistics with the Reichsführer-SS (Inspekteur für Statistik beim Reichsführer SS), as late as the beginning of 1943, Schmelt still presided over 50,570 Jews,[67] amounting to approximately one-third of the Jewish forced laborers still employed in the German Reich at this time.

The mass murder of the Jews in East Upper Silesia took place in multiple phases. The deportation of so-called work-incapable Jews from the cities in the Eastern Strip to the Auschwitz camp began in May 1942; approximately 38,000 of these Jews had died there by August 1942, when operations reached an interim peak. The "action" on 12 August 1942 formed the climax of this deportation phase. In Sosnowitz, Bendzin, and Dombrowa, the Jews had to assemble in the large town squares, supposedly to update their work identification cards, but this served only as a pretext to round them up. In actual fact, the purpose was to "select" them—work-capable persons were to be brought to the Schmelt camps and the rest shipped to the Auschwitz extermination camp. Approximately 15,000 Jews remained behind to continue working in the *Shops* for the Wehrmacht. The next phase began in October 1942. In the months leading to March 1943, the SS sealed the Jewish quarters in Sosnowitz and Bendzin, turning them into closed ghettos.[68] The Reich Security Main Office (Reichssicherheitshauptamt) ordered that all Jewish workers outside the forced-labor camps be transported by the middle of February 1943. Since this jeopardized manufacturing in the *Shops*, however, Wehrmacht offices—specifically from the Armaments Command (Rüstungskommando) Kattowitz—pressed to have the Jews remain in the workshops and for the time being they were successful.[69] By the end of May, most of the Jews were still alive. In June 1943, however, the Jewish elder Moshe Merin was transported to Auschwitz-Birkenau, which marked the beginning of the mass murder's third and final phase in the region. In the middle of August 1943, the German occupiers finally liquidated the ghettos. In one large operation, the SS and the police quickly rendered the towns in the Eastern Strip "Jew-free." [70]

Schmelt now moved his office to Annaberg, where he took over the state government administration as Regierungspräsident of the Oppeln Regierungsbezirk in September 1943. Upon Himmler's instructions, his largest camps were absorbed by the concentration camp system, with the Groß-Rosen concentration camp taking over twenty-eight Schmelt camps and Auschwitz-Birkenau at least fifteen; smaller Schmelt camps with fewer than 800 forced laborers were dissolved.[71] How many Jews survived is unknown.[72] The last transport from an East Upper Silesian forced-labor camp arrived in Auschwitz-Birkenau at the end of July 1944 with twelve Jews.[73] Schmelt retained both his function as Himmler's Special Emissary and his forced-labor system—albeit substantially reduced in size—which he now continued to operate primarily with Christian Polish workers. Toward the end of the war, however, when his misappropriation of funds came to light, he fell out of favor with Himmler and was brought before an SS and police court for exploiting his office for personal gain. The verdict has not survived; in the beginning of May 1945, he committed suicide.[74]

The deportations of the Jews of East Upper Silesia to Auschwitz by no means occurred in secret. Rather, in the Eastern Strip, increasingly inhabited by Germans, the violent evacuation of the Jewish collection sites took place so openly that in April 1944, under the headline: "How Bendzin became Bendsburg," the *Oberschlesische Zeitung* published a richly illustrated article about the town's transformation from an ugly "Jewish nest" to an up-and-coming small German city. The town of Bendzin, formerly "almost completely jewified," the article stated, where "the most degenerate phlegm of this race" once lived, was "now German and clean."[75] In a letter to the NSDAP Party Chancellery in September 1944, the Kattowitz Oberpräsidium under Fritz Bracht presented a balance sheet indicating that the "Jewish element" had now been "resettled or removed." Vivid statistics, consisting of two rows of numbers under the succinct headings "before and now," encapsulates what had transpired. According to Bracht's balance sheet, a total of 79,041 Jews from East Upper Silesia had perished. In Sosnowitz the number of residents fell from 130,000 to 101,783; in Bendzin from 54,739 to 25,595; in Dombrowa from 41,491 to 29,018; in Czeladź from 23,000 to 20,571; and in Zagórze from 16,400 to 12,556.[76] This demonstrates that the murder of the Jews took place in full public view, such that one could even read about it in the newspaper.

Meanwhile, large-scale construction projects had been developed for all of these cities. The activist planning in East Upper Silesia virtually knew no bounds. The projected city of "Oststadt" intended for 200,000 to 250,000 inhabitants was supposed to be created in the open countryside during a construction period of ten to fifteen years. Chosen to replace Kattowitz as the Gau's future capital, Tichau (Tychy) was supposed to grow from 30,000 to 150,000 inhabitants. Auschwitz featured especially prominently in the Germanization program, for after the founding of IG Auschwitz in spring 1941, thousands of Reich Germans settled in the town, most of them as employees of the factory. The founding of the IG Farben corporation's factory promptly resulted in the introduction of an industry-led urban development policy and the city of Auschwitz advanced to become the "bulwark of Germandom."[77] The program had its own architect, Hans Stosberg, who was responsible for its development. He designed residential space in the city of Auschwitz for up to 80,000 Reich Germans. In fact, Stosberg also realized a number of his large urban developmental projects, while others at least existed on the drawing board. Stosberg and the other strategists refused to be intimidated by war-induced austerity measures. Rather, in summer 1943 they developed yet another far-reaching futuristic plan that looked ahead to 1980.[78]

Conclusion

The ethnic-nationalistically motivated conflicts between Germans and Poles fueled the anti-Jewish atmosphere in Silesia after the First World War. Although Jews enjoyed legal protections under the May 1922 German-Polish Accord, pogrom-like excesses began immediately after its expiration in summer 1937 in both the German and Polish (named "East Upper Silesia") parts of the region. The majority of the Jewish population—approximately 80,000 persons—lived in Polish districts that were first incorporated into Silesia by the National Socialists in the course of forming the Regierungsbezirk of Kattowitz in October 1939. Within just over a year, the Jewish population was deported and concentrated in the area referred to in Nazi administrative language as the Eastern Strip—namely, the region east of the police border, delineated in November 1939—which soon functioned as a provincially internal deportation zone for *Fremdvölkische*. Responsibility for the racial program of "ethnic reorganization" fell to the Civil Administration and the SS. Gauleiter and Oberpräsident Josef Wagner and his deputy as Oberpräsident Fritz-Dietlof Graf von der Schulenburg closely cooperated in this matter with Erich von dem Bach-Zelewski, the Higher SS and Police Leader in the SS-Oberabschnitt Südost, who later during the war against the Soviet Union was responsible for countless mass executions of Jews in the Baltic and Belarus.

East Upper Silesia's exceptional economic status as the "armorer of the Reich" led to the founding of a regionally specific special authority—the Organization Schmelt—in October 1940. On Himmler's orders, SS-Oberführer Albrecht Schmelt, formerly the Breslau Polizeipräsident, systematized the use of Jewish forced labor in various forms, including for the construction of the Reich Autobahn and the armaments industry. He created a separate network of around two hundred labor camps under his control. Economically determined pragmatism was the reason for the comparatively long survival of the majority of Jews in East Upper Silesia. Schmelt's labor deployment policy had a restraining effect on the "final solution" and, within the province, dampened the dynamics of the extermination program. But the labor deployments did not provide permanent protection; rather, they only delayed the murders. The ambivalence of Schmelt's coercive system lay in the fact that even though it protected the Jews for a certain period from being deported to the extermination camps, at the same time it cleared the path toward their murder, for the systematized labor deployments transitioned smoothly to the subsequent mechanical practices of extermination. Starting in fall 1941, Schmelt arranged for old and sick Jews to be removed from the camps along the Reich Autobahn and brought to Auschwitz, where they were immediately killed. Thus, the Auschwitz-Birkenau concentration and extermination camp first played an important regional role in connection with the "solution of the Jewish question," before being expanded by the National Socialists in 1942/43 to become Europe's center for the murder of the Jews. By all appearances, Schmelt oriented himself according to practice of "euthanasia" murder, applying the selection principle in accordance with criteria of economic utility even before this procedure become the principle for deciding on life and death in Auschwitz-Birkenau.

The radicalizing impulses of anti-Jewish policy came from the large-scale urban development program, which in East Upper Silesia formed a core element of the Germanization policy and was advanced by functionaries on all administrative levels. This decisively shaped the situation of the Jews. Their situation already dramatically deteriorated as a result of the deportations to the Eastern Strip, for their funds to procure food and medication quickly dwindled. When in 1941 Wagner and Schulenburg declared that the Eastern Strip would also be Germanized, the Jews in that region no longer had much of a future. The large ghettos in Sosnowitz, Bendzin, and Dombrowa, where Schmelt set up workshops for Wehrmacht production and employed Jews as forced laborers, sank deeper into poverty. Catastrophic living conditions prevailed in the camps along the Reich Autobahn; many Jews died of starvation and exhaustion. In August 1943, the now closed ghettos in the Eastern Strip were dissolved, their inmates deported to Auschwitz-Birkenau and murdered. Tens of thousands of Jews remained as forced laborers in the former Schmelt camps, which since 1943/44 were subordinate to the concentration camp system. When the Red Army approached, they escaped the death marches. The camps were liberated in the beginning of May 1945; despite the devastating living conditions, and despite the proximity of the Auschwitz-Birkenau extermination camp, some Jews in the Schmelt camps survived the Holocaust, but their number is unknown.

Notes

The preparation of this chapter for the English translation was made possible thanks to my tenure as an Ina Levine Invitational Scholar at the Center for Advanced Holocaust Studies, United States Holocaust Memorial Museum.

1. On the minority rights in the law, see RGBl. 1922 II, 270–304; Adelheid Weiser, "Der Schutz der jüdischen Rechte in Oberschlesien unter dem Mandat des Völkerbundes 1933–1945," in *Geschichte der Juden in Schlesien im 19. und 20. Jahrhundert: Dokumentation einer Tagung in Breslau*, ed. Friedrich Carl Schultze-Rhonhof (Hannover, 1995), 37–53.
2. Ralph Schattkowsky, *Deutschland und Polen von 1918/19 bis 1925: Deutsch-polnische Beziehungen zwischen Versailles und Locarno* (Frankfurt, 1994), 85–94; Konrad Fuchs, "Die wirtschaftlichen und sozialen Rahmenbedingungen der schlesischen Verwaltung 1815–1945," in *Verwaltungsgeschichte Ostdeutschlands 1815–1945: Organisation—Aufgaben—Leistungen der Verwaltung*, ed. Gerd Heinrich et al. (Stuttgart, 1993), 943–1005, here 973ff.; Klaus Hildebrand, *Das vergangene Reich: Deutsche Außenpolitik von Bismarck bis Hitler 1871–1945* (Stuttgart, 1995); Gottfried Niedhart, *Die Außenpolitik der Weimarer Republik* (Munich, 1999).
3. Statistisches Reichsamt, ed., *Statistik des Deutschen Reichs*, vol. 552, no. 4 (Berlin, 1944), 14. On the Breslau Jews in the Wilhelmine Empire and the early Weimar Republic see Till van Rahden, *Juden und andere Breslauer: Die Beziehungen zwischen Juden, Protestanten und Katholiken in einer deutschen Großstadt von 1860 bis 1925* (Göttingen, 2000). On the Nazi period, see Abraham Ascher, *A Community under Siege: The Jews of Breslau under Nazism* (Stanford, CA, 2007).
4. Sybille Steinbacher, *"Musterstadt"Auschwitz: Germanisierungspolitik und Judenmord in Ostoberschlesien* (Munich, 2000), 41, note 110.
5. Adelheid Weiser, "Juden in Oberschlesien: Ein historischer Überblick," in *Juden in Oberschlesien Teil 1: Historischer Überblick: Jüdische Gemeinden (I.)*, ed. Peter Maser and Adelheid Weiser (Berlin, 1992), 13–63, here 47ff.
6. Joachim Bahlcke, *Schlesien und die Schlesier* (Munich, 2000), 136f.
7. Lothar Bossle et al., eds., *Nationalsozialismus und Widerstand in Schlesien* (Sigmaringen, 1989); Helmut Neubach, *Parteien und Politiker in Schlesien* (Dortmund, 1988).

8. Rudolf Jaworski and Marian Wojciechowski, eds., *Deutsche und Polen zwischen den Kriegen: Minderheitenstatus und "Volkstumskampf" im Grenzgebiet; Amtliche Berichterstattung aus beiden Ländern 1920–1939* (Munich, 1997).
9. On the Bernheim case, see Philipp Graf, "Die 'Bernheim-Petition' 1933—Ein Fall jüdischer Diplomatiegeschichte," *Leipziger Beiträge zur jüdischen Geschichte und Kultur* 2 (2004): 283–306. On the German reaction, see *Die Verfolgung und Ermordung der europäischen Juden durch das nationalsozialistische Deutschland 1933–1945*, vol. 1: *Deutsches Reich 1933 bis 1937*, ed. Wolf Gruner (Munich, 2008), doc. 46, 162f.
10. Ibid., doc. 67 dated 4 August 1933, 223–227.
11. Law on measures in the former Upper Silesian plebiscite region of 30 June 1937, RGBl. 1937 I, 717–720. See Eliahu Ben Elissar, *La diplomatie du IIIe Reich et les Juifs (1933–1939)* (Paris, 1969), 112–132. Karol Jonca, "Judenverfolgung und Kirche in Schlesien (1933–1945)," in *Deutsche—Polen—Juden: Ihre Beziehungen von den Anfängen bis ins 20. Jahrhundert*, ed. Stefi Jersch-Wenzel (Berlin, 1987), 211–227. Steinbacher, *"Musterstadt" Auschwitz*, 76, note 318.
12. Report of the Jewish Central Information Office from 11 August 1937 about anti-Jewish excesses in Upper Silesia after the expiration of the agreement regarding minorities, in Gruner *Verfolgung und Ermordung*, vol. 1, doc. 292, pp. 691–695.
13. On the concept of Germanization, see Gerhard Wolf, *Ideologie und Herrschaftsrationalität: Nationalsozialistische Germanisierungspolitik in Polen* (Hamburg, 2012), 10ff. Hitler had already addressed the "Germanization" of the East in *Mein Kampf*; on the political practices in the Wilhelmine Empire, which provided the experiential background for the actions of the National Socialists, see ibid., 41–52.
14. Jochen Böhler, *Auftakt zum Vernichtungskrieg: Die Wehrmacht in Polen 1939* (Frankfurt, 2006), 210ff., 216; Wolf, *Ideologie und Herrschaftsrationalität*, 76–79, 83f.; Helmut Krausnick and Hans-Heinrich Wilhelm, *Die Truppe des Weltanschauungskrieges: Die Einsatzgruppen der Sicherheitspolizei und des SD* (Stuttgart, 1981), 36, 54.
15. On the examples, see Czesław Madajczyk, *Die Okkupationspolitik Nazideutschlands in Polen 1939–1945* (East Berlin, 1987), 17; Jochen Böhler, "Die Judenverfolgung im deutsch besetzten Polen zur Zeit der Militärverwaltung (1. September bis 25. Oktober 1939)," in *Der Judenmord in den eingegliederten polnischen Gebieten*, ed. Jacek Andrzej Młynarczyk and Jochen Böhler (Osnabrück, 2010), 79–98, on East Upper Silesia, 88ff. On the actions in Bendzin, see Mary Fulbrook, *A Small Town near Auschwitz: Ordinary Nazis and the Holocaust* (Oxford, 2012), 1, 46–58.
16. Steinbacher, *"Musterstadt" Auschwitz*, 106f.
17. On the region's economic importance, see Alfred Sulik, "Die Bedeutung der Großindustrie Oberschlesiens in der Kriegswirtschaft des Dritten Reiches (1939–1945)," *Studia Historiae Oeconomicae* 20 (1993): 203–226; Alfred Sulik, "Volkstumspolitik und Arbeitseinsatz: Zwangsarbeiter in der Großindustrie Oberschlesiens," in *Europa und der "Reichseinsatz": Ausländische Zivilarbeiter, Kriegsgefangene und KZ-Häftlinge in Deutschland 1938–1945*, ed. Ulrich Herbert (Essen, 1991), 106–126; Werner Röhr, "Zur Rolle der Schwerindustrie im annektierten polnischen Oberschlesien für die Kriegswirtschaft Deutschlands von 1939 bis 1949," *Jahrbuch für Wirtschaftsgeschichte* 4 (1991): 9–58.
18. War diary of Armaments Inspectorate VIII Breslau, 12 September 1939, Bundesarchiv-Militärarchiv (BA-MA), RW 20–8/1, fol. 98.
19. CdZ ordinance, 5 September 1939, Geheimes Staatsarchiv Preußischer Kulturbesitz (GStAPK), HA XVII, BA Ost, Reg. Kat./3, fol. 116.
20. Steinbacher, *"Musterstadt" Auschwitz*, 170–178.

21. Hitler's verbal instructions dated from 25 September 1939. Bormann to Lammers, 20 November 1940, Bundesarchiv (BArch), R 43 II/1549, Bl. 47ff.; also in Institut für Zeitgeschichte (IfZ), Fa 199/51, fol. 47ff.
22. The postwar myth surrounding Schulenburg also contributed to the glorification of Wagner, whom the scholarship—which is surprising uncritical—has deemed to be a "prudent statesman." But his position in the settlement issue was by no means mild. By no means can we speak about any humanely motivated defiance of the Germanization program; at best, Wagner may appear relatively "restrained" in comparison to Arthur Greiser in the Warthegau, who was a fanatic with regard to Volkstum policies. On Wagner's biography, see Peter Hüttenberger, *Die Gauleiter: Studie zum Wandel des Machtgefüges in der NSDAP* (Stuttgart, 1969), 219; Karl Höffkes, *Hitlers politische Generale: Die Gauleiter des Dritten Reiches; Ein biographisches Nachschlagewerk* (Tübingen, 1986), 367ff. On Schulenburg, see the apologetic biography by Albert Krebs, *Fritz-Dietlof Graf von der Schulenburg: Zwischen Staatsraison und Hochverrat* (Hamburg, 1964) and the critical study by Ulrich Heinemann, *Ein konservativer Rebell: Fritz-Dietlof Graf von der Schulenburg und der 20. Juli* (Berlin, 1990).
23. The background cannot be precisely reconstructed. Perhaps Himmler was engaging in intrigue; but perhaps the fact that Wagner opposed a new division of Silesia—desired by the regime—into the Gaus of Upper and Lower Silesia also played a role. Hitler presumably recalled him from Breslau in order to implement the territorial plans.
24. On the connections between Jewish and settlement policy in terms of functions and personnel (particularly in the case of the Warthegau), see Götz Aly, *"Final Solution": Nazi Population Policy and the Murder of the European Jews* (London, 1999) (German original: Frankfurt, 1995); Götz Aly, "'Judenumsiedlung'—Überlegungen zur politischen Vorgeschichte des Holocaust," in *Nationalsozialistische Vernichtungspolitik 1939–1945: Neue Forschungen und Kontroversen*, ed. Ulrich Herbert (Frankfurt, 1998), 67–97.
25. Aly, *"Final Solution"*, 35–38, 76–77; Peter Longerich, *Holocaust: The Nazi Persecution and Murder of the Jews* (New York, 2010), 151–155 (German original: Munich, 1998). Also Wolf, *Ideologie und Herrschaftsrationalität*, 108–120, which clarifies some of the contradictions in the scholarship.
26. Notes on the discussion between Eichmann and Wagner on 11 October 1939, printed in *Nazi-Dokumente sprechen*, edited by the Rat der jüdischen Gemeinden in den böhmischen Ländern (Praha) and by the Zentralverband der jüdischen Gemeinden in der Slowakei (Bratislava) (Prague, n.d.), no pagination.
27. On the interruption of the deportations, see Hans Safrian, *Die Eichmann-Männer* (Vienna, 1993), 78ff.
28. Wolf Gruner, "Von der Kollektivausweisung zur Deportation der Juden aus Deutschland (1938–1945): Neue Perspektiven und Dokumente," in *Die Deportation der Juden aus Deutschland: Pläne, Praxis, Reaktionen 1938–1945*, Beiträge zur Geschichte des Nationalsozialismus, vol. 20, ed. Birthe Kundrus and Beate Meyer (Göttingen, 2004), 21–62, especially 32–35.
29. RGBl. 1939 I, 2042.
30. The newly stipulated boundary entered into force on 26 October 1939, when Hitler prematurely ended the military administration. On the issue of the border, see Steinbacher, *"Musterstadt" Auschwitz*, 69–78. On the "new order of the ethnographic circumstances," announced by Hitler in a speech to the Reichstag on 6 October 1939, see Wolf, *Ideologie und Herrschaftsrationalität*, 89f. On the new

demarcation of the boundary in connection with the annexation of all of western Poland, see ibid., 93–97.
31. Walther Hubatsch, ed., *Grundriß zur deutschen Verwaltungsgeschichte 1815–1945*, Series A: *Preußen,* vol. 4: *Schlesien* (Marburg , 1976), 285–313; Dieter Rebentisch, *Führerstaat und Verwaltung im Zweiten Weltkrieg: Verfassungsentwicklung und Verwaltungspolitik 1939–1945* (Stuttgart, 1989), 196f.
32. Christian Jansen and Arno Weckbecker, *Der "Volksdeutsche Selbstschutz" in Polen 1939/40* (Munich, 1992), 40, note 91.
33. Report to the district administrators in the Regierungsbezirk of Kattowitz regarding the demarcation of the police boundary, 4 December 1939, Archiwum Państwowe w Katowicach (APKa—State Archive Katowice), RK 10, fol. 5, also RK 4507, fol. 35; see Steinbacher, *"Musterstadt" Auschwitz,* 109ff.
34. Steinbacher, *"Musterstadt" Auschwitz,* 69–78.
35. Confidential circular from the Gestapo Kattowitz to the Landräte, Oberbürgermeister, Regierungspräsidenten, Polizeipräsidenten, the Inspekteur of the Sicherheitspolizei and all Gestapo field offices in the Regierungsbezirk, 23 February 1940, APKa, RK 2833, fol. 21; also APKa, HTO 62, fol. 225. See Steinbacher, *"Musterstadt" Auschwitz,* 110–115; Wolf, *Ideologie und Herrschaftsrationalität,* 137ff.
36. On Oświęcim, see Chaim Volnerman, Aviezer Burshtein, and Meir Shimon Gashuri, eds., *The Book of Oshpitsin* (Jerusalem, 1977). Regarding the size of the Jewish population in the Eastern Strip, see Wacław Długoborski, "Die Juden aus den eingegliederten Gebieten im Vernichtungslager Auschwitz-Birkenau," in *Der Judenmord in den eingegliederten polnischen Gebieten,* ed. Jacek Andrzej Młynarczyk and Jochen Böhler (Osnabrück, 2010), 219–250, 221f., 223, note 25. Generally on Bendzin, see Fulbrook, *A Small Town near Auschwitz,* on the number of residents, 127.
37. Woedtke to Gestapo Kattowitz, 9 June 1942, which includes a reference to the order from 21 December 1939, APKa, RK 2780, fol. 149f. In May 1941, Ernst-Heinrich Schmauser became Bach-Zelewski's successor in the office of the HSSPF. As part of the preparations for the military campaign against the Soviet Union, Himmler appointed Bach-Zelewski—who removed the Slavic-sounding part of his hyphenated name in fall 1940—as HSSPF Russland-Mitte (Central Russia). The following year, Bach became Himmler's Bevollmächtigter für die Bandenbekämpfung (Authorized Representative for Anti-partisan Warfare); a year after that he became the Chef der Bandenkampfverbände (Head of the Anti-Partisan Warfare Formations), in which capacity he was responsible for countless mass executions of Jews in the Baltic and Belarus. On Bach-Zelewski, see Tom Lampert, *Ein einziges Leben: Acht Geschichten aus dem Krieg* (Munich, 2001), 201–238.
38. Bernhard Rosenkötter, *Treuhandpolitik: Die "Haupttreuhandstelle Ost" und der Raub polnischer Vermögen 1939–1945* (Essen, 2003); Ingo Loose, *Kredite für NS-Verbrechen: Die deutschen Kreditinstitute in Polen und die Ausraubung der polnischen und jüdischen Bevölkerung 1939–1945* (Munich, 2007), 98–112.
39. Ordinance on Securing the Assets of the Former Polish State, of 15 January 1940, RGBl., 1940 I, 174; Ordinance on the Handling of Assets of Citizens of the Former Polish State, of 17 September 1940, RGBl. 1940 I, 1270.
40. Steinbacher, *"Musterstadt" Auschwitz,* 170–178.
41. In spring 1941, Silesia was divided into Upper and Lower Silesia. Karl Hanke directed the newly created Gau of Lower Silesia (with Breslau as its administrative center).
42. On Arlt, see Götz Aly and Susanne Heim, *Architects of Annihilation: Auschwitz and the Logic of Destruction* (Princeton, 2002), 102–112 (German original: Frankfurt,

1991); Götz Aly and Karl Heinz Roth, *Die restlose Erfassung: Volkszählen, Identifizieren, Aussondern im Nationalsozialismus* (Berlin, 1984), 71–74, 84f.
43. Personnel file Albrecht Schmelt, BArch.
44. On Organization Schmelt, see Steinbacher, *"Musterstadt" Auschwitz*, 138–153; Wolf Gruner, *Jewish Forced Labor under the Nazis: Economic Needs and Racial Aims (1938–1944)* (New York, 2006), 214–229; Andrea Rudorff, "Arbeit und Vernichtung *reconsidered*: Die Lager der Organisation Schmelt für polnische Jüdinnen und Juden aus dem annektierten Teil Schlesiens," *Sozial.Geschichte Online* 7 (2012): 10–39; Stephan Lehnstaedt, "Coercion and Incentive: Jewish Ghetto Labor in East Upper Silesia," *Holocaust and Genocide Studies* 24 (2010): 400–430; Loose, *Kredite*, 143–158; Alfred Konieczny, "Die Zwangsarbeit der Juden in Schlesien im Rahmen der 'Organisation Schmelt'," *Beiträge zur nationalsozialistischen Gesundheits- und Sozialpolitik* 5 (1987): 91–110. On Merin, his actions as a Jewish elder, and how he was perceived by contemporaries, see Aleksandra Namyslo, "Der Einfluss der Zentrale der Jüdischen Ältestenräte in Ostoberschlesien auf das Verhalten der Juden," in *Der Judenmord in den eingegliederten polnischen Gebieten*, ed. Jacek Andrzej Młynarczyk and Jochen Böhler (Osnabrück, 2010), 311–327. On Merin, see also Fulbrook, *A Small Town near Auschwitz*, 62ff., 143f., 186ff., 233.
45. "Ein Jahr Gau Oberschlesien," *Kattowitzer Zeitung*, 1 February 1942.
46. See Gruner, *Jewish Forced Labor*, 196–222.
47. Directives from Himmler, 1 August 1940, BArch, R 17.02/428, no fol.
48. Directive for the implementation of the evacuation action in the district of Saybusch, 14 September 1940, printed in Instytut Zachodni, ed. *Documenta Occupationis Teutonicae*, vol. 11 (Poznań, 1983), 166–171.
49. Wolf Gruner, *Der Geschlossene Arbeitseinsatz deutscher Juden: Zur Zwangsarbeit als Element der Verfolgung 1938–1943* (Berlin, 1997).
50. In the Generalgouvernement, the SS had already been organizing forced-labor assignments of Jews since October 1939; the Arbeitsverwaltung (work administration) systematized the measures starting in summer 1940; see Christopher R. Browning, "Nazi Germany's Initial Attempt to Exploit Jewish Labor in the Generalgouvernement: The Early Jewish Work Camps 1940–1941," in *Die Normalität des Verbrechens: Bilanz und Perspektiven der Forschung zu den nationalsozialistischen Gewaltverbrechen*, ed. Helge Grabitz et al. (Berlin, 1994), 171–185; Christopher R. Browning, "Jewish Workers in Poland: Self-Maintenance, Exploitation, Destruction," in *Nazi Policy, Jewish Workers, German Killers*, ed. Christopher R. Browning (Cambridge, 2000), 58–88; Christopher R. Browning, *The Origins of the Final Solution: The Evolution of Nazi Jewish Policy, September 1939–March 1942* (Lincoln, NE, 2004), 141–151 (German original: Berlin, 2003).
51. Bernd C. Wagner, *IG Auschwitz: Zwangsarbeit und Vernichtung von Häftlingen des Lagers Monowitz 1941–1945* (Munich, 2000).
52. Admittedly, statistics are unavailable, but according to reports from survivors, at least twelve people died each day in the Faulbrück and Markstädt Reich Autobahn camps. Witness report by Rudolf Schönberg, 21 July 1946, IfZ, Nürnberger Dokumente PS-4071.
53. On the situation of the Jews, see Natan Eliasz Szternfinkiel, "Zagłada Żydów sosnowieckiego getta," in *Żydzi w Zagłębie (Śląskim): Żyli wśród nas, mieszkali i zginęli*, (Sosnowice, 1993); Steinbacher, *"Musterstadt" Auschwitz*, 153–157, Rudorff, "Arbeit und Vernichtung *reconsidered*," 24–30, on Bendzin, see Fulbrook, *A Small Town near Auschwitz*, 167–171.
54. Notes by Commandant of Auschwitz Rudolf Höß, IfZ, F 13/1–8, fol. 31f., excerpts printed in *Faschismus—Ghetto—Massenmord: Dokumentation über Ausrottung*

und Widerstand der Juden in Polen während des Zweiten Weltkriegs, ed. Jüdisches Historisches Institut Warschau (East Berlin, 1962), 226. War diary of the Armaments Inspectorate of Wehrkreis VIII Breslau, 1 January–31 March 1941, comments on the deployment of "Schmelt Jews" in the clothing industry, BA-MA, RW 20/8–6, fol. 87.

55. Correspondence between the Hauptamt für Verwaltung und Wirtschaft (later WVHA) and HSSPF Schmauser, the NSDAP-Reichsleitung, and Himmler, 17 November 1941–26 January 1944, IfZ, MA 303, fol. 2589715–25898758. Greifelt to Brandt (Personal staff of the RFSS), comments on a presentation by Himmler on 28 May 1942, IfZ, Nürnberger Dokumente, NO 3182.
56. Ordinance on the introduction of the Nuremburg race law in the incorporated territories, from 31 May 1941, RGBl. 1941 I, 297; Regierungspolizeiverordnung of 15 April 1941, Amtsblatt des Regierungspräsidenten in Kattowitz, 26 April 1941; Regierungspolizeiverordnung of 9 May 1941, ibid., 17 May 1941.
57. Notifications from 20 September 1941 and 2 October 194, Archiwum Żydowskiego Instytutu Historycznego Warszawa (AŻIH—Jewish Historical Institute Warsaw), Judenrat Bendzin 212/1, fol. 48 and fol. 52.
58. Police Ordinance on Economic Transactions with Jews from 23 November 1940, *Kattowitzer Zeitung*, 30 November 1940; Commander of the Schutzpolizei Sosnowitz to Gestapo Kattowitz, 17 December 1941APKa, Polizeipräsident Sosnowitz 315, fol. 1; Situation report by the NSDAP-Kreisleitung Bendzin to NSDAP-Gauleitung, October 1941, Archiwum Państwowe w Opolu (APO—State Archive Oppeln), NSDAP-Gauleitung 207, fol. 22; Notification by the jüdische Interessenvertretung Bendzin (Bendzin Jewish Lobby) from 30 May 1941, AŻIH, Judenrat Bendzin 212/1, fol. 3; Steinbacher, *"Musterstadt" Auschwitz*, 261.
59. Comments by Hans Butschek, an employee with the RKF-Ansiedlungsstab (RKF settlement staff) of the Kattowitz office, dated 20 March 1941, regarding a conference the previous day in Berlin on solutions to the settlement problems, BArch, Film 16786, Deutsches Auslandsinstitut (no pagination).
60. Schulenburg to Himmler via Reichsstelle für Raumordnung (Reich Office for Regional Planning), 20 May 1940, BArch, R 49/902 (no pagination); Himmler's order as RKF no. 10/II, 16 January 1941, IfZ, MA 125/13, no. 387178 (no pagination); "Raumplanung in den Ostgebieten," *Kattowitzer Zeitung*, 10 November 1940.
61. File notes regarding a conference in the Sosnowitz police presidium, 12 November 1941, APKa, RK 2780, Bl. 97; Woedtke's notes from 25 November 1941 regarding the resettlement of the Jews according to the conference on 19 November 1941, APKa, Polizeipräsident Sosnowitz 316, fol. 78.
62. Schönwälder to Walter Springorum, the Regierungsbezirk President in Kattowitz, situation report for November 1940, 30 November 1940, GStAPK, HA XVII, BA Ost, Reg. Kat./13, fol. 116. Schönwälder appeared satisfied that the "unemployed, loitering, and profiteering" Jews were "finally" out of sight.
63. Kowohl to Udo Klausa, the district administrator of Bendzin, 24 June 1941, APKa, RK 2785, fol. 18. On Udo Klausa's role in the Holocaust and his conduct after the end of the war, see Fulbrook, *A Small Town near Auschwitz*.
64. Notes by Commandant of Auschwitz Rudolf Höß, IfZ, F 13/1–8, fol. 31f., excerpts printed in *Faschismus—Ghetto—Massenmord*, 226. In contrast to Höß's representations, however, efforts did not yet exist in 1941 to dissolve the Schmelt camps.
65. Steinbacher, *"Musterstadt" Auschwitz*, 275f., Rudorff, "Arbeit und Vernichtung reconsidered," 19–24.
66. See the witness reports by those affected: Hans-Werner Wollenberg, . . . *und der Alptraum wurde zum Alltag: Autobiographischer Bericht eines jüdischen Arztes*

über NS-Zwangsarbeiterlager in Schlesien (1942–1945) (Pfaffenweiler, 1992); Coen Rood, *"Wenn ich es nicht erzählen kann, muß ich weinen": Als Zwangsarbeiter in der Rüstungsindustrie* (Frankfurt, 2002).

67. The Final Solution of the European Jewish Question, Statistical Report of the Inspector for Statistics with the Reichsführer SS, Secret Reich Matters, 1 January 1943, BArch, NS 19/1570, fol. 8, fol. 25.
68. On Nazi ghettoization policies, see Dan Michman, *The Emergence of Jewish Ghettos during the Holocaust* (Cambridge, 2011), Sybille Steinbacher, Leben und Überleben in Lagern und Ghettos, in *Was hat der Holocaust mit mir zu tun? 37 Antworten*, ed. Harald Roth (Munich, 2014), 65–73.
69. Inspector of the Ordnungspolizei by teletype to the headquarters of the Schutzpolizei in Kattowitz and Gleiwitz and to the Regierungsbezirk presidents in Kattowitz und Oppeln, 19 August 1943, APKa, RK 3920, fol. 28. See Steinbacher, *"Musterstadt" Auschwitz*, 285–306. On the actions undertaken in the Bendzin ghetto, see Fulbrook, *A Small Town near Auschwitz*, 123ff., 132f., 136f., 141–150, 197–213, 217–226, 236–254, 276–300.
70. War diary of the Kattowitz Armaments Command, first quarter of 1943, BArch-MA, RW 21–31, fol. 4, fol. 48; see Steinbacher, *"Musterstadt" Auschwitz*, 299–304, Rudorff, "Arbeit und Vernichtung *reconsidered*," 32f.
71. Quarterly report of the Armaments Inspectorate in Wehrkreis VIII, October–December 1943, here: employment of Jews, undated, presumably January 1944, BA-MA, RW 20–8/32, fol. 49; notes by Commandant of Auschwitz Rudolf Höß, IfZ, F 13/1–8, fol. 31f., excerpts printed in *Faschismus—Ghetto—Massenmord*, 226. Höß is mistaken when he dates the integration of the Schmelt camps into the concentration camp administrations as spring 1943 and declares that it was already "completely implemented." On the dissolution of Schmelt's camp system, see also Steinbacher, *"Musterstadt" Auschwitz*, 305f, Rudorff, "Arbeit und Vernichtung *reconsidered*," 34–38.
72. Bella Gutterman, *A Narrow Bridge to Life: Jewish Forced Labor and Survival in the Gross-Rosen Camp System, 1940–1945* (New York and Oxford, 2008).
73. See Franciszek Piper, *Die Zahl der Opfer von Auschwitz: Aufgrund der Quellen und der Erträge der Forschung 1945 bis 1990* (Oświęcim, 1993), 183–186, table 15. Briefly on the number of victims in East Upper Silesia, see Frank Golczewski, "Polen," in *Dimension des Völkermords: Die Zahl der jüdischen Opfer des Nationalsozialismus*, ed. Wolfgang Benz (Munich, 1996) (first published in 1991), 412, 422, 450, 457, 460, 468f.
74. Steinbacher, *"Musterstadt" Auschwitz*, 306.
75. "Wie aus Bendzin Bendsburg wurde: Ein Bildarchiv erzählt von der Wandlung einer Stadt," *Oberschlesische Zeitung* (formerly *Kattowitzer Zeitung*), 4 April 1944, see Steinbacher, *"Musterstadt" Auschwitz*, 318.
76. Gau office for municipal policy at the Kattowitz Oberpräsidium to the NSDAP party office, 6 September 1944, APKa, RK 1654, fol. 104; Reich Ministry of the Interior to Main Office of the Ordnungspolizei, 10 October 1944, IfZ, Nürnberger Dokumente NG-2660, Steinbacher, *"Musterstadt" Auschwitz*, 302, note 248.
77. Steinbacher, *"Musterstadt" Auschwitz*.
78. Presumable development of the number of inhabitants in Upper Silesia by 1980, current and future cities, 26 August 1943; see Steinbacher, *"Musterstadt" Auschwitz*, 272.

CHAPTER 10

EUPEN-MALMEDY
Christoph Brüll

Prior to the Annexation

The League of Nations awarded the territory of Eupen-Malmedy—composed of the former Prussian-German Kreise (districts) of Eupen and Malmedy—to Belgium in September 1920.¹ While Kreis Eupen was German-speaking, the predominant population of the district town and its neighboring municipalities in the Kreis Malmedy spoke French and Walloon. In the southern part of the region, around the small town of St. Vith, which formed its own canton after the territories were integrated with Belgium, the population spoke German.

In spring 1938 Hans Joachim Beyer, the director of the Arbeitsstelle für Auslandsdeutsche Volksforschung (special department for ethnic research into Germans living abroad) in Stuttgart,² submitted plans for intensifying the National Socialist impact of *Westforschung*. They also included an Eupen-Malmedy program, which suggested creating a "list of all Jews living in the territory and their occupations" in the "event of a reintegration" with Germany.³ Even though the sources for the post-annexation period fail to provide evidence of such a list, Beyer's plans at the very least document the interest of *Westforschung* in the area's Jewish population. In any event, creating such a list would have proved difficult, since no quantitatively significant Jewish

Figure 10.1. Parade by the Segelfliegerverein (glider pilot association) in Eupen, 1938/39. *Source:* Archive Herbert Ruland.

population lived in that small region. Neither in the Middle Ages nor in modern times did the area have a significant Jewish presence. To be sure, street names like "Judenstraße" in Eupen and "Judengasse" in St. Vith suggest the presence of Jewish merchants in these localities. But a larger community, like those that, due to particular historical circumstances, existed in the Kreis Schleiden on the German side of the border, never developed here. The population census of the German Reich in 1890 for the Kreise of Eupen and Malmedy registered thirteen Jews in each—this out of a total population of approximately 60,000 inhabitants.[4]

Due to the small size of the Eupen-Malmedy region and the almost complete absence of Jews, the area did not witness any large-scale deportation operations during the Second World War. Nonetheless, after the National Socialists assumed power, the region played an important role because of its border location. Until the war, for many German, Austrian, or eastern European Jews, reaching Eupen-Malmedy meant an initial successful escape from terror and persecution.[5] During the war, the border—impossible to monitor continuously along its entire length, but certainly very well guarded—was the last obstacle before arriving in Belgium. To be sure, after the occupation, reaching Belgium did not guaranty safety, particularly after the deportations began there in June 1942; nevertheless, it could open up certain opportunities for further flight for those threatened by death and destruction.

Thus the history of the Jews in Eupen-Malmedy is in the first instance a history of refugees, but it is also about the non-Jewish population's attitudes toward them. The following will demonstrate how a constellation of perpetrators, rescuers, and bystanders developed in this region and investigate the motivations that guided the actors. To do so, however, we must first turn our attention to the political and social conditions in the period between the two world wars.[6] The integration of Eupen-Malmedy into the Belgian state was accompanied by great difficulties from the outset. The referendum stipulated by the Versailles Treaty and held by the Belgian administration in the first half of 1920 was conducted neither in secret nor neutrally. Many inhabitants perceived General Herman Baltia's transitional government, which for five years determined the region's administrative and political fate, as a paternalistic colonial regime. Press censorship did the rest. The region's final integration into the Belgian state did not occur until 1925, with its first involvement in the parliamentary elections ending in disappointment. The candidate for the Catholic Union, which managed to unite two-thirds of the votes in the three cantons, was not elected for the chamber at the Verviers district level. The refusal to confirm an Eupen mayoral candidate because of doubts about his pro-Belgian attitudes conveyed to many residents once and for all the feeling of being second-class Belgians.

The division within the population appeared at the latest during the 1929 elections. While the Catholic Union belonged to the traditional Belgian political parties and naturally advocated the continued existence of the Belgian state, the Christian People's Party (Christliche Volkspartei) gave voice to the pro-German bloc, whereby in this deeply Catholic region the commitment to the former fatherland explicitly included the requisite reference to religion.[7] The Belgian Labour Party, which since 1925 had sent to Brussels the delegate Marc Somerhausen, a resolute proponent of the new Belgians' interests, demanded the opportunity for the population to vote in a new referendum that ensured secret ballots and neutrality. The Socialists maintained this demand until Hitler's takeover of power and the banning of the Social Democratic Party in Germany.

Strongly diverging opinions on how to achieve the goal of returning the region to the Reich plunged the Christian People's Party into serious crisis in the mid 1930s. In addition, in 1935 four leaders of the *heimattreue* (faithful-to-the-homeland) movement lost their citizenship on the basis of a new law that punished breaches of state civic duty with the revocation of citizenship. The Christian People's Party ultimately merged into a new pro-German movement called the Heimattreue Front (patriotic front). The Heimattreue Front, however, had formed under very different auspices, and its leadership clearly operated under the influence of National Socialism. Not only did it receive—as had earlier the Christian People's Party—substantial financial support from Germany, but it also organized its operations according to the directives of the NSDAP Gauleitung in Cologne.⁸ Over time, the pro-German movement established front organizations like the Segelfliegerverein (glider pilot club) in Eupen (see figure 10.1), the Bogenschützenverein (archery club) in St. Vith, and the Saalschutz (venue security) in Malmedy, which were supposed to make preparations for the region's return to the German Reich. All of these groups were basically gangs of thugs that emulated the SA and chiefly served to intimidate political opponents.⁹

In Eupen-Malmedy since the end of the 1920s, pro-Belgians and pro-Germans opposed each other with such irreconcilable severity that social communication had become impossible.¹⁰ The spring election campaign for the 2 April 1939 parliamentary election—the last before the start of the war and thus the region's reintegration with Germany—took place in an extremely inflamed atmosphere. The pro-Belgian Catholic Party confronted the Eupen-Malmedy electorate with an extreme alternative: "Christian cross or crooked cross." The Catholic Party's opponent was the Heimattreue Front, which served as a "reservoir for National Socialists, revanchists, national-conservative Catholics, and German nationals."¹¹

In the end, the elections gave the Heimattreue Front 45.7 percent of the votes in the three cantons of Eupen, Malmedy, and St. Vith. As a result, it admittedly remained the second strongest party, but for the first time since participating in elections, the revanchist camp had lost the absolute majority. This election result has been interpreted repeatedly as a vote for Belgium.¹² Yet it is perhaps more appropriate to seek an explanation in the growing skepticism toward National Socialist Germany on the part of many Catholics, who were further stirred up by a pastoral letter from the Bishop of Liège Kerkhofs, and likewise in the fact that these elections featured the first-time participation of a generation that had lived and gone to school exclusively in the Belgian state. Also significant was the fact the Heimattreue Front had indeed not brought about the region's return to Germany and, furthermore, that the Third Reich appeared to show little interest in the small border region.

The Belgian state reacted to the increasing radicalization with legal, police, and military measures. Thus in 1939/40, during the mobilization period, new-Belgian soldiers in the Belgian army were removed in many cases from their regular units and transferred to logistics and support units behind the frontline troops. This measure was one of the major reasons why approximately 10 percent of new-Belgian soldiers deserted to Germany; during the Wehrmacht's march into Belgium on 10 May 1940, they would return, together with a few other eastern Belgians, as actively involved "locally informed *Volksdeutsche* [ethnic Germans]" in the Brandenburg Battalion's Special-Purpose Training and Construction Company No. 800.[13]

The desertions provide insights, on the one hand, into the polycratic structures of National Socialist rule and, on the other hand, into the *Volkstum* work carried out for Eupen-Malmedy, which, apart from the all-important People's Federation for Germandom Abroad (Volksbund für das Deutschtum im Ausland), involved the participation of seventeen other institutions. While German agencies near the border encouraged and helped organize the desertions, the authorities in Berlin viewed this matter quite differently. Thus the Foreign Office warned the Nazi Reich Warriors League (Reichskriegerbund) that the flight of Eupen-Malmedy residents into the German Reich could "cause a significant weakening of local German *völkisch* elements."[14] The scope of this article does not allow for a detailed description of the *Volkstum* work of Germany's *Westforschung*. But it should be noted that participants in this conflict of nationalities thought in *völkisch* categories; that is, they distinguished primarily between Germans and Walloons (or Belgians), but racist attributions hardly played a role.[15]

This does not mean that the conflicts of the 1930s were free of anti-Semitism, as came to light most clearly in the context of the 1938 November pogroms. While increased refugee activity had already been registered at the German-Belgian border ever since the National Socialists had assumed power, now hundreds of Jewish families attempted to reach Belgium. In this regard, however, Eupen-Malmedy was not a preferred haven, since it was part of a border zone from which the Belgian gendarmerie could immediately deport illegals to Germany—and it did so.[16]

Reports about the deplorable fates of refugees multiplied.[17] The Catholic, pro-Belgian newspaper *Grenz-Echo* (border echo) played a major role in this regard. Its editor Henri Michel had denounced

Germany's racial policies since 1933, and the archeologist Otto Eugen Mayer and Socialist Jewish journalist Kurt Grünebaum, both of whom had been persecuted by the National Socialists, worked on the newspaper's editorial board.[18] Of the articles covering events at the border, one from December 1938 stands out in particular, stating:

> On the other hand, one repeatedly encounters cases of true humanity. As we learned this morning, a local resident, who supposedly is even a member of the Heimattreue Front, went over to Germany in order to pick up a child there and bring it via Eupen on to Brussels where relatives are accepting the abandoned child, whose father and grandfather find themselves in a German concentration camp. Although the resident in question may not be pleased to have his local friends in the Heimattreue Front made aware of his noble-minded conduct, we cannot help but issue a fine testimony to his human decency, which naturally stands in blatant contradiction to the political principles of the Heimattreue Front.[19]

As well as taking an understandable jab at the pro-German movement, the article made it clear that supporters of the Heimattreue Front were not invariably radical anti-Semites, but that, even here, anti-Semitism clearly competed with Christian and humanist precepts of charity. In the harsh words of the Reich Commissioner (Reichsbeauftragter) for Eupen-Malmedy Franz Thedieck (1900–1995), who had been employed in the Prussian Interior Ministry as early as 1923 and, among other things, had acted as the region's Special Administrator (Sonderbeauftragter): "The leadership level of the *heimattreue* movement is decayed and spent, because it cannot detach itself from Catholicism."[20] This statement by the future State Secretary for the Ministry of All-German Affairs of the German Federal Republic (1949–1964) is all the more remarkable, since in 1943 he himself was relieved of his responsibilities as an Oberkriegsverwaltungsrat (Chief Military Administrator) in Brussels for "favoring Catholic interests" and assigned to front-line duties.[21]

Likewise in the context of the November pogroms, an article from newspaper *Die fliegende Taube* (The Flying Dove)—the Catholic's Union's mouthpiece in the old Belgian/Low German region—illustrates the competition between an evidently widespread Christian anti-Semitism and human compassion:

> What has happened and is still happening to the Jews these days in Germany is a disgrace for the entire country. To millions of Germans, this dishonoring of their good name and the responsibility that they thereby have

to bear must be repugnant in the depths of the soul. Their influence today is undoubtedly vanishingly small, and we know well enough that the indignation abroad likewise no longer plays a role. Incidentally, perhaps nothing reveals with greater brutal clarity than these events how frighteningly far European humanity has fallen and how thoroughly European thought has already lost even its merely humane character. *One need not for this reason absolve Jewry of all economic and cultural guilt and may even be in agreement with the limitation of a certain overgrowth.* But what is happening at the moment can only be described as inhuman, and even the Jews themselves would probably concede that their much-maligned fate under the Christian solution to this question was one almost worth envying. . . . The totalitarian countries, especially Germany, are making life on their soil practically impossible for the Jews. . . . The other states, which for normal circumstances are themselves already pervaded by foreign influences [*überfremdet*] and in large part also pervaded by Jewish influences [*überjudet*], often refuse to accept them; accordingly the only choice remaining to the Jews, therefore, is to emigrate to the moon or allow themselves to be slaughtered, if they do not prefer to commit suicide.[22]

The positions represented here can also easily be found in the Belgian refugee policies of those years.[23] Belgian gendarmes, for instance, were practically trained to be able to detect the escape organizations that regularly operated in the border region beginning in 1936. It would be a mistake to ascribe exclusively altruistic motives to those who helped refugees escape. In any case, according to Hans-Dieter Arntz, one can observe a shift, starting in 1938, from helping escaping refugees to systematic people smuggling. Such activity was widespread above all among the workers engaged in the construction of the West Wall in the South Eifel. They often coldly exploited the plight of the refugees out of a greed for profit, whereby prices of approximately 1,000 RM per refugee were the rule. In very extreme cases, after they had paid, refugees were driven back into the arms of their German persecutors.[24] Such motives and the necessary precautionary measures explain the statement today of a witness who at the time was still a youth: "Everyone knew that Jews were fleeing through our village. I believe that the adults also knew why they fled. But this topic was simply not talked about."[25]

In terms of their attitude toward the November pogrom, however, a few of the leading members of the Heimattreue Front, directed by the "especially anti-Semitic minded"[26] Cologne Gauleiter Josef Grohé, completely followed the National Socialist line,[27] as demonstrated even just by the reporting in the so-called revisionist newspapers, which were controlled by the pro-German movement. The report about the attack on the diplomat Ernst vom Rath stated that a "Jew" had "taken up arms. . . . International Jewry, which is conspiring against Germany, does not shy away from leading the campaign against Berlin from French soil, as if its intention were to provoke difficulties between Germany and France."[28] This was followed by warnings addressed to France regarding Jewish emigrants who "show no consideration whatsoever, but rather apply the same parasitical methods as in other countries."[29] A report on the burning of the synagogue in the neighboring city of Aachen lacked any references to perpetrators, not even to the "spontaneous people's rage [*Volkszorn*]" that was mentioned with respect to other cities.[30] The left-wing Dutch writer and journalist Nico Rost, who toured Eupen-Malmedy in 1938, also reported on the region's anti-Semitism, mentioning, for example, that a Jewish store in Eupen was smeared with the slogan "Juda die!"[31] But there is no knowledge of any physical violence against Jewish residents.

Yet for most Jewish refugees, the border region by no means constituted a desirable haven, and the social climate did nothing to alter this fact. Almost no Jews at all seem to have been in the Belgian Eifel—the southern part of Eupen-Malmedy—shortly before the beginning of the Second World War. A number of Jewish families fleeing from Poland had settled in the Eupen region in the 1930s, where they primarily engaged in retail commerce. Because of their small numbers, they did not support a community life, apparently celebrating religious festivals in Liège, 35 kilometers away.[32] During the course of 1939, approximately forty Jews presumably settled in the Eupen region,[33] but they were by no means safe in the border zone.

The First Weeks after Annexation

The German invasion on 10 May 1940 hardly took anyone in Belgium by surprise. Government and military circles in Brussels had been expecting the Wehrmacht's attack since fall 1939.[34] In spring 1940, the families of a number of exposed members of the pro-Belgian milieu, as well as high officials in Eupen-Malmedy, had even been evacuated into the country's interior. Many of those less fortunate were among the victims of the German persecutions—often based on local denunciations—during the first weeks after the Germans entered Belgium. They included, for example, the journalist Henri Michel, who would spend almost five years in the Oranienburg-Sachsenhausen concentration camp, as well as the Eupen Police Commissioner Fritz Hennes and the Malmedy's Socialist mayor Joseph Werson, who both died in the concentration camps.[35]

There is no dispute in the scholarship today: 10 May 1940 constituted a day of celebration for the substantial majority of Eupen-Malmedy's population.[36] The territory's reintegration into the German Reich occurred by means of a Führer decree issued on 18 May 1940, thus even before combat operations against the Belgian army came to an end on 28 May 1940.[37] Judging by the ample volume of *Heimkehr* (homecoming; repatriation) literature, anti-Semitism probably did not play any role in the celebratory announcements.[38] But the Germans went beyond annexing merely the formerly Prussian-German region of Eupen-Malmedy. A circular decree from the Reich Interior Ministry from 29 May 1940 also incorporated into the Reich ten municipalities that had never belonged to Prussia or Germany,[39] justifying this move by referring to the German mother tongue of a portion of the population of these municipalities. The German Reich thereby gained a total of 87,000 inhabitants (see map 10.1).[40]

After a one-week military administration, the Reich administration took over the territory of Eupen-Malmedy. The responsibility was assigned to the Prussian Regierungspräsidium (government presidium) Aachen, which formally received authority over Eupen-Malmedy, but was never at any point provided with additional officials in order to fulfill this duty. As with other integrations, essential decrees for the region needed to be approved by the Reich Interior Ministry in its capacity as the Central Office for Reunification (Zentralstelle für die Wiedervereinigung). Section I/1, headed by Ministerialdirigent (Ministerial Director) Dr. Medicus, reviewed them "to ensure a standard procedure for carrying out the reunification."[41]

At the municipal level, after the Belgian mayors either departed or were deposed, their offices were initially taken over by members of Heimattreue Front: for Eupen, Ortsgruppenleiter (local group leader) Walther Rexroth; for Malmedy, Bezirksleiter (district leader) Wilhelm Buhrke; and for St. Vith, Bezirksleiter Franz Genten (the two latter men held office only until fall 1940). However, no significant personnel changes took place in the lower administrative ranks.[42]

The administrative boundaries were readjusted in accordance with the given realities of the German Reich, which entailed rescinding the Belgian divisions. Thus between May and November 1940, the Germans instituted Rhineland-Westphalia's District Code (Amtsordnung),[43] and Eupen-Malmedy once again consisted of two German Kreise instead of three Belgian cantons. The two Landräte (district administrators)—Felix Seulen in Eupen and Heinz Ehmke in Malmedy—and the NSDAP Kreisleiter (district leader), Gabriel Saal, stemmed from the Old Reich. Such appointments would prove to be a trend; soon almost all of the Amtsbürgermeister (district mayors) and officials came from the Old Reich. Uncertainty about the loyalties of the locals, but also very urgent practical reasons, explain this staffing policy, which the people in Eupen-Malmedy experienced as a harsh disappointment. Only the Eupen Kreisleiter Stefan Gierets, in office until his death in 1941, came from the leadership of the Heimattreue Front; in contrast, his successor Karl Herwanger did not.[44]

The NSDAP officially assimilated the Heimattreue Front as early as May 1940, although it did not automatically accept the Heimattreue Front's members, much to the latter's disappointment. The mission of the Heimattreue Front had been accomplished. The (self-imposed) *Gleichschaltung* (synchronization) of the population relentlessly advanced during the next months and years. Martin Schärer estimates the number of NSDAP members in Eupen-Malmedy as approximately 7,000 during the period shortly before the region's liberation by the Allies in 1944.[45] Similar membership figures obtained for party organizations like the Hitler Youth and the Nazi Women's League. Even the SA enjoyed great popularity, and on 18 May 1941 the 1,240 men (some sources mention 1,500) of Standarte (regiment) 174 were able to welcome SA Stabschef (chief of staff) Viktor Lutze to Eupen for the oath-taking ceremony. Despite strong promotional efforts, the SS did not achieve the same success. Nonetheless, a few of the 800 military volunteers from Eupen-Malmedy were assigned to the Waffen SS.[46]

With respect to the subject of anti-Jewish policies, to date we have only been able to identify a single directive from any of the Reich agencies. In this May 1940 directive, the director of the Section IV A5 Emigration in the Reich Security Main Office (Reichssicherheitshauptamt) and officer responsible for "Jewish matters," Walter Jagusch, stipulated that the Reich Association of the Jews in Germany "itself or the Bezirksstelle [regional office] Cologne could take care of the (in any case few) Jews in Eupen-Malmedy."[47]

The few scattered Jews who had remained in the region had only two options. They could either attempt to relocate to Belgium's interior or go underground.[48] In order to hide, they had to rely on the help of the local population.[49] Otherwise they faced the danger of being taken into custody. Meanwhile, efforts to flee from the Old Reich to Belgium apparently continued without interruption. A 1916 emergency law put into force by the Belgian government on 10 May 1940 proved fateful for

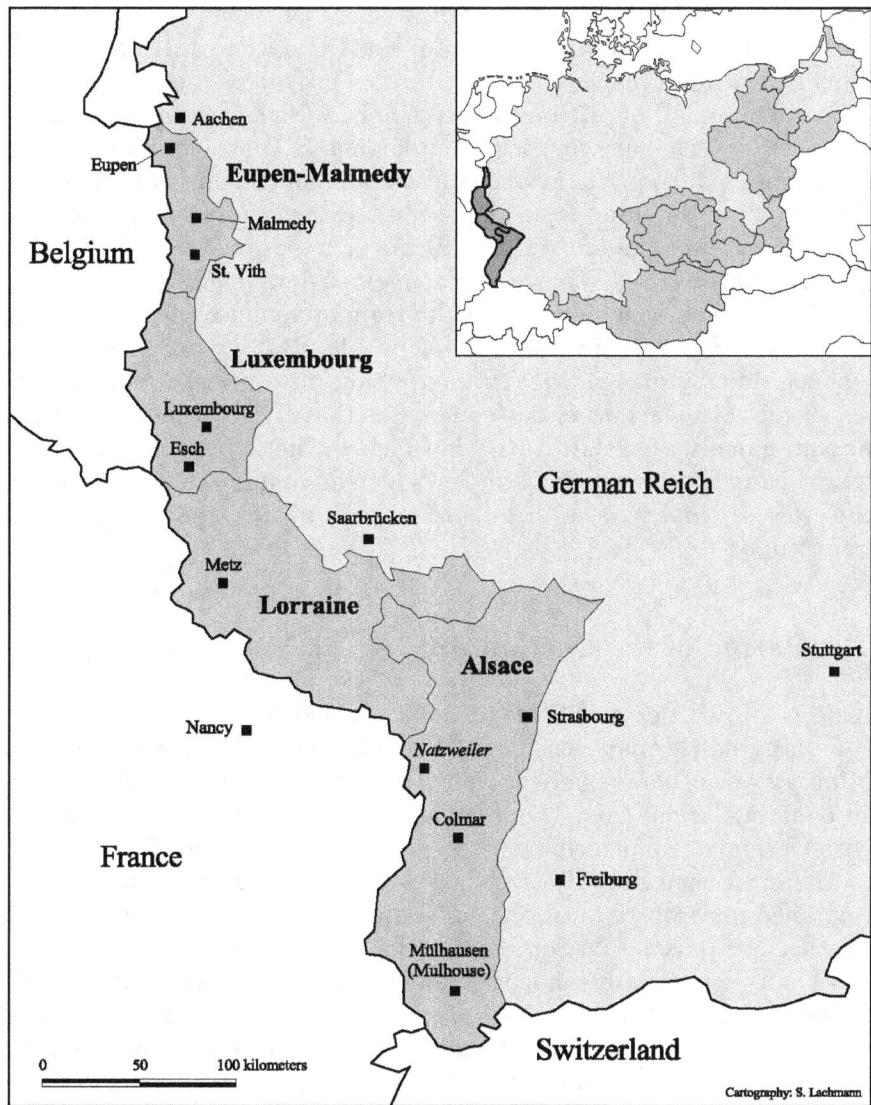

Map 10.1. Eupen-Malmedy, Luxembourg, and Alsace-Lorraine, 1940

at least 6,000 Jewish refugees who had reached Belgium since 1938, declaring them at the onset of the war to be enemies of the state. For many this meant being arrested by the Belgian gendarmerie and deported to France.[50]

The arrests during the war's first weeks mentioned earlier were often preceded by denunciations. In at least one case, anti-Semitism—namely, in its typical Christian form—provided the justification. Einsatzkommando 5 of the Security Police (Sicherheitspolizei; SiPo) and the Security Service (Sicherheitsdienst; SD), which, like the Einsatzgruppen during the invasion of Poland, had evidently also followed the army into Belgium, reported a complaint from an Ortsgruppenführer of the Heimattreue Front to the government in Aachen. The Ortgruppenführer's village pastor—a converted Jew—had denied paschal absolution to those who voted for the Heimattreue Front and also performed indecent acts involving young people: "But my mind has almost stopped due to outrage, that it is possible that a priest who takes the savior into his heart every day can lie like that. There is only one explanation, namely this, that it was Jews whom the savior drove from the temple, and that it was, in turn, Jews who hammered the Most High to the cross . . . and that, after all, our current pastor emerged from this unfortunate *Volk*."[51]

The Period of the Occupation

A decree by Hitler on 23 May 1940 provided for the introduction of Prussian and German laws on 1 September 1940.[52] The Reich Interior Ministry was in charge here as well. An ordinance on the civil-legal transitional regulations from 3 September 1940 sought to achieve conformity with German legal principles with as few problems as possible.[53]

The most complicated issue, however, was state citizenship, which remained unresolved until settled by an ordinance issued by the Reich Interior Ministry on 23 September 1941. Hitler's decree from 23 May 1940 had provisionally made the residents of Eupen-Malmedy German citizens, but only "in accordance with more specific provisions."[54] Notably, the new ordinance did not explicitly annul Belgian nationality, resulting in a kind of "double state citizenship" in terms of international law (fully ignored by those affected).[55]

The new state citizenship laws distinguished between two groups in the annexed region. Most of the population obtained Reich-German citizenship, while those deemed to be Jews as per the First Decree to the Reich Citizenship Law from 14 November 1935[56] or gypsies were excluded.[57] Because they had already been Belgians prior to the Treaty of Versailles, approximately 20,000 residents of the Kreise who spoke Low German received the status "German until revoked." Revocation was supposed to be possible for a period of ten years. Here, too, Jews and "gypsies" were excluded, but *Mischlinge* (people of mixed race) were not, as long as "they had committed themselves to Germandom before 18 May 1940."[58] Even the SS Race and Settlement Main Office (Rasse- und Siedlungshauptamt) held that its duty was less to emphasize restrictions than to keep "valuable German blood [from] being lost" by means of a generous interpretation of the state citizenship law.[59]

In spring 1941, a controversy regarding the question of so-called *Mischlinge* erupted between the NSDAP Kreisleiter Gierets and the Eupen Bürgermeister Rexroth—notably two former members of the Heimattreue Front. It involved two brothers with the status of "Half-Jew," born in Berlin and Dresden, who attended the city school. It is striking that Gierets, who as a faithful Catholic operated a shop for devotional items, had no qualms whatsoever with the National Socialist dictum: "The Half-Jew is to be equated to the widest extent with the Jew. Therefore it can hardly be reasonably expected that parents of German children send children to a class where, at the same time, a Half-Jew sits. Beyond that, there can probably be no interest whatsoever in still making a special school education in the German Reich available to Half-Jews." In a letter with an emphatically sober tone, Bürgermeister Rexroth invoked—as did Landrat Seulen—the applicable legislation, according to which the Reich Citizenship Law did not prohibit school attendance by *Mischlinge*. The Rhine province's Oberpräsidium (Upper Presidium) in Koblenz likewise saw no legal basis to forbid school attendance "even though it is unpleasant and undesired."[60]

This kind of anticipatory self-conformity can also be observed in a contemporaneous exchange of letters about renaming streets in the Eupen area. Since 1940, the new city leaders and German officials had renamed a fair number of the major streets after National Socialist politicians. It hardly seems surprising that the "Judenstraße" especially riled up anti-Semitic temperaments. The leadership of the Heimattreue Front had already conducted research into the street name's origins in the 1930s, but could never rule out the presumption that the name actually stemmed from a dialectal mutation of the name "Johannes." Nonetheless, from the perspective of the authorities in summer 1941, the matter seemed clear: "The inhabitants . . . have long been offended by the retention of the previous designation."[61] The new name, "Rötgener Straße," now referred to the next-closest village in the German Reich. The city's open-air swimming pool, which bore the name of Prussian Commercial Councilor Robert Wetzlar, an industrialist with Jewish origins, was also renamed "Waldbad" (literally, forest swimming pool).[62]

It would probably be a mistake to interpret such measures in terms of their intent and effect as manifestations of a pronounced anti-Semitism. Rather, they appear to be attempts on the part of the few persons from Eupen-Malmedy still holding senior positions to accommodate the conceptions of the Reich-German agencies. After all, even though the term never shows up in the associated sources, these players considered themselves members of the *Volksgemeinschaft*. This interpretation is also suggested by the fact that prior to taking action, at least with respect to the renaming of roads, the city had been pressured by articles in the NSDAP party newspaper *Westdeutscher Beobachter*.[63] Whether the insufficient radicalism also had something to do with a lack of material incentives—the opportunity for systematic "Aryanization" obviously did not exist—must remain a matter for speculation.[64]

To prepare for the deportations from the Reich's territory, on 1 September 1941 the Reich Interior Ministry issued the Police Decree on the Identification of the Jews, which also restricted their mobility and freedom of movement.[65] Shortly thereafter, the ministry refined the decree to the effect that "until ruled otherwise, Jews of foreign origin are not subject to the provisions of the decree, with the exception of the Jews living in the territories of Eupen/Malmedy and Moresnet . . . who hold Belgian state citizenship."[66]

Since an emigration ban was also issued in October 1941 for Germany and the annexed and occupied territories, the only chance to escape the incipient deportations was to flee. The available sources do not allow us to determine whether any raids or deportations subsequently occurred in Eupen-Malmedy. But in any event, surveillance of the German-Belgian border would once again intensify. The fact that German authorities had compelling reasons for such measures seems beyond dispute. A number of escape networks remained active in the border region as late as 1943 and in many cases successful—as we can assume based on the Germans' inability to maintain constant surveillance along the entire border.[67] The refugees during this phase consisted mostly of French prisoners of war. Naturally, precise figures are impossible to establish. Yet recent research on the deportation of Jews living on Belgian soil during the war years suggests that the number of successful escape efforts was quite high. Insa Meinen has argued that a substantial portion of the Jews deported from Mechelen and Drancy were picked up individually or in small groups, and not during raids in Antwerp or Brussels. This leads her to conclude that these Jews, escaping from the Old Reich, Austria, Eastern European countries, and the Netherlands, did not reach Belgian territory until after 1938 and during the first years of the war.[68]

An example of a failed escape attempt in fall 1942—one that has already been discussed a number of times in the scholarly literature—illustrates both how the escape was organized as well as the mechanisms of persecution in the German-Belgian border region.[69] On 3 September 1942, two Berlin Jews, Jacques Bar (born in 1886) and Dr. Emil Hirsch (born in 1875) were taken into custody near the border in Eupen; Rywa Löwinsohn (born in 1886 in Warsaw), who had stayed behind in Aachen, was arrested as well. Of the group of refugees, only a single Jewish married couple with a child successfully reached Belgium. Two people who facilitated the escape, Hubert K. and Hedwig R. (who gave the escape organization "Hedwig" its name), were also arrested.

The Aachen Gestapo's interrogation records provide more precise information not only on how the Jews contacted the escape agents while still in Berlin and the horrendous amounts of money paid for the escape, but also about the despair that drove them to flee as a last resort to avoid deportation to the East. The refugees were not held in custody in Eupen very long, but were quickly transferred to prison in Aachen. In Aachen, a court sentenced them to prison terms of between eighteen months and two years. After the verdict, any traces of them disappear, and their names are not found on any lists. We know, however, that other Jewish refugees arrested in connection with the trial against Hedwig R. were deported.[70]

The origins of these refugees were by no means unusual. Those fleeing in the 1930s predominantly came from the eastern part of Germany and Austria. From the Old Reich, however, the geographically nearest group was the Jews from Cologne, which has led Arntz to note: "But the phenomenon—which to this day the author finds incomprehensible—was that refugees arrived from afar, often without any knowledge of what this 'green border'[71] looked like, while many Jews from the Eifel, who knew every stick and stone in the old German-Belgian border zone, all too rarely took their chances."[72]

The inmate registry of the Eupen jail, which briefly held a number of refugees, also suggests the latter's distant origins, although, admittedly, the 1,000 inmates registered between 1941 and the end of the German occupation in September 1944 included only ninety-three captured refugees.[73]

Escape agents faced the threat of punishment. While a few got off with prison terms, others were sent to concentration camps.[74] It appears as if a number of families incurred immense risks and hid Jewish families in Eupen-Malmedy. Contemporary witnesses have also referred to the sudden disappearance of a Jewish family, but also, for example, to people with disabilities being seized from their hiding places by the Gestapo,[75] although documents pertaining to such incidents have not yet been found. In light of the small number of Jews, estimates of the number of rescuers should not be set too high. A few rescuers from the core region of Belgium, however, operated specifically along the border between Eupen-Malmedy and occupied Belgium. At the local border railway station at Montzen, for example, which belonged to the annexed territory, a number of locomotive engineers are said to have attempted to free prisoners as the locomotives shunted the deportation trains.[76]

Who exactly informed authorities about the refugees and escape organizations can no longer be determined, although presumably they came from Eupen-Malmedy. However, they probably numbered no higher than the rescuers. Evidence of perpetrators is scarce. In 1947, a court in Liège sentenced the Eupen resident August Voss, who had volunteered for service with the Gestapo and worked in occupied Belgium, to a twenty-year prison term. He was said to have participated in the arrest and deportation of 1,000 Jews in this area.[77]

Conclusion

Because of Eupen-Malmedy's particular geographical situation, Nazi Jewish policy amounted in the first instance to a policy of border control, developed after the start of the war by the Reich Interior Ministry and implemented by the Gestapo. Actors from the annexed region were few. A decisive factor in this respect was the region's integration into the Aachen Regierungsbezirk and the appointment of Germans from the Old Reich to the most important offices.

While to some extent, Christian anti-Semitism in Eupen-Malmedy provided a bridge for anti-Jewish Nazi policies, racial anti-Semitism did not play a major role in the population. Consequently, with respect to reintegration, anti-Semitism could hardly have functioned to establish a bond between the Old Reich and what had been separated from Germany twenty years earlier; the conflicts between nationalities and national traditions and practices were too virulent. Yet it should also be said that, for most people, what they knew or could have known— whether from newspapers, relatives, or even refugee activities at the border—since the 1930s about the treatment of Jews in the German Reich did not prevent them from dreaming about, or actively striving toward, their region's return to Germany.

Due to the very small numbers of Jews in Eupen-Malmedy, their fate came to the fore only as a result of refugee movements triggered by National Socialist policies of persecution. Because of the border situation of the Kreise, as well as the region's Christian anti-Semitism, none of the refugees could imagine permanent settlement. Many residents, however, became either members or accessories of organizations that helped escaping refugees. Apart from humanitarian motives, the basis for such involvement was chiefly the pursuit of profit, which probably explains why any discussion of these activities was later suppressed. Once the war began, the few Jews still living in Eupen-Malmedy were left with only the choice of fleeing into occupied Belgium or hoping that they could survive the war in hiding. In both instances, opportunities to do so were created above all by residents of the ten old-Belgian municipalities that were annexed by Germany in addition to the actual territory of Eupen-Malmedy; their willingness to engage in resistance was significantly more pronounced than their counterparts in the old-German districts.

Looking back on a project involving interviews with contemporary witnesses, the eastern Belgian historians Carlo Lejeune and Klaus-Dieter Klauser have stated that the twentieth century "did not even leave [German-speaking Belgians] with any heroes."[78] This is certainly also applicable with regard to the subject of the persecution of Jews during the Second World War and the preceding refugee movements of the 1930s.

For a number of important reasons, eastern Belgian efforts to deal with the past—even scholarly efforts—have included few attempts to analyze this aspect of the war years. For a public chiefly interested in the conflict between Belgian and German nationalism and its consequences, the issue has seemed marginal,[79] all the more so because very few Jews settled in this area after 1945.[80] A growing number of recent publications and Dietrich Schubert movie *Nicht verzeichnete Fluchtbewegungen—oder: Wie die Juden in der West-Eifel in die Freiheit kamen* (1990)[81] have not yet ended the subject's suppression, perhaps also because a widespread "anti-Semitism without Jews" continues to exist.

Notes

1. The territory of Neutral Moresnet (today Kelmnis) was an exception. Starting in 1815, it was initially governed by the Netherlands and later (as of 1830) jointly by Belgium and Prussia; it was assigned directly to Belgium by the Treaty of Versailles—the relevant articles 32, 33, and 34 of the Treaty of Versailles are printed

in Freddy Cremer and Werner Mießen, *Spuren: Materialien zur Geschichte der Deutschsprachigen Gemeinschaft Belgiens. Einführung* (Eupen, 1996), 10.
2. The *Arbeitsstelle* was created in 1936 under the direction of the Deutschen Auslandsinstituts in Stuttgart as a *Mittelstelle* (intermediate position); it was renamed in 1937. Karl Heinz Roth, "Heydrichs Professor: Historiographie des 'Volkstum' und der Massenvernichtungen: Der Fall Hans Joachim Beyer," in *Geschichtsschreibung als Legitimationswissenschaft 1918–1945*, ed. Peter Schöttler (Frankfurt, 1997), 262–342.
3. Archiv des Landschaftsverbandes Rheinland (Pulheim), no. 4585, Forschungsbereich Eupen-Malmedy, Anlage zu: Niederschrift über Besprechung am 8. April 1938, quoted in Thomas Müller, "Die Formierung des 'Grenzraums': Die 'Abteilung G' des Reichsinspekteurs und Landeshauptmanns Haake," in *Griff nach dem Westen: Die 'Westforschung' der völkisch-nationalen Wissenschaften zum nordwesteuropäischen Raum (1919–1960)*, vol. 2, ed. Burkhard Dietz, Helmut Gabel, and Ulrich Tiedau (Münster, 2003), 763–790, quote on 788.
4. Figures from http://www.verwaltungsgeschichte.de/eupen.html and http://www.verwaltungsgeschichte.de/malmedy.html (accessed 26 December 2012). This information is based on the German Reich's statistics at the time.
5. See Herbert Ruland, "Fluchtbewegungen an der deutsch-belgischen Grenze und in Innerbelgien vor dem Hintergrund der zeitgeschichtlichen Entwicklung 1914–1945," http://www.grenzgeschichte.eu/archiv/FLUCHT1.pdf (accessed 26 December 2012); Herbert Ruland, "Belgien: Zeitgeschichte und Erinnerung an zwei Weltkriege in einem komplizierten Land; Beobachtungen aus der Randposition des deutsch-belgischen Grenzraums," in *Gemeinsames Erinnern an den Nationalsozialismus? Gedenkorte und Geschichtsprojekte in den Niederlanden, Belgien und Nordrhein-Westfalen*, ed. Bildungswerk der Humanistischen Union NRW (Recklinghausen, 2000), 22–38.
6. Since 1990, an increasing number of publications have dealt with the history of Eupen-Malmedy and Belgium's German-speaking community. The references here are to a few recent overviews that largely provide the basis for the following paragraphs: Carlo Lejeune, *Die Säuberung*, vol. 1: *Ernüchterung, Befreiung, Ungewissheit (1920–1944)* (Büllingen, 2005), 25–59; Christoph Brüll, "Un passé mouvementé: L'histoire de la Communauté germanophone de Belgique," in *La Communauté germanophone de Belgique–Die Deutschsprachige Gemeinschaft Belgiens*, ed. Katrin Stangherlin (Brussels, 2005), 17–47; Ulrich Tiedau, "Die Rechtslage der deutschsprachigen Bevölkerung in Belgien nach dem Zweiten Weltkrieg,"in *Deutschsprachige Minderheiten 1945: Ein europäischer Vergleich*, ed. Manfred Kittel et al. (Munich, 2007), 435–522; Peter M. Quadflieg, *"Zwangssoldaten" und "Ons Jongen": Eupen-Malmedy und Luxemburg als Rekrutierungsgebiet der deutschen Wehrmacht im Zweiten Weltkrieg* (Aachen, 2008), 20–41.
7. The population voted predominantly for the Zentrum (Catholic Center Party) during the Prussian-German period as well. See Benedikt Jonas, "Die Wahlen zum preußischen Abgeordnetenhaus in der Stadt Eupen zur Zeit des Deutschen Kaiserreichs (1871–1918)," in *Geschichtliches Eupen* 35 (Eupen, 2001): 119–137.
8. See Bruno Kartheuser, *Die 30er Jahre in Eupen-Malmedy: Einblick in das Netzwerk der reichsdeutschen Subversion* (Neundorf, 2001). The study, however, has a predominantly documentary character, since the author engages in a questionable selection of sources. He organizes them in a very one-sided manner, therefore significantly narrowing the work's interpretive content.
9. Ibid., 121–124; Cremer and Mießen, *Spuren*, 12.
10. See Heidi Christmann, *Presse und gesellschaftliche Kommunikation in Eupen-Malmedy zwischen den beiden Weltkriegen* (Munich, 1974).

11. Quadflieg, *Zwangssoldaten*, 28.
12. On the elections in Eupen-Malmedy between 1925 and 1939, see Jochen Lentz, *Das Wahlverhalten in den Kantonen Eupen, Malmedy und St. Vith bei den Parlamentswahlen von 1925 bis 1939*, 2 vols. (Eupen, 2000).
13. See Christoph Brüll, "Entre méfiance et intégration. Les germanophones dans l'armée belge (1920–1955)," *Cahiers Belge d'Histoire Militaire* 4 (December 2006): 135–166, here in particular 151–158; Christoph Brüll, *Die deutschsprachigen Einheiten in der belgischen Armee zwischen den beiden Weltkriegen* (St. Vith, 2004), 76–96; Quadflieg, *Zwangssoldaten*, 29–31.
14. Luther to Major (ret.) von Rechenberg, 21 February 1940, in *Documents on German Foreign Policy, 1918–1945*, ed. Paul R. Sweet et al., series D, vol. 8 (4 April 1939–18 April 1940) (London, 1954), no. 632, 807–808. See Brüll, *Einheiten*, 94.
15. Carlo Lejeune, "'Des Deutschtums fernster Westen' Eupen-Malmedy, die deutschen Dialekt redenden Gemeinden um Arlon und Montzen und die 'Westforschung,'" in *Griff nach dem Westen*, vol. 1, ed. Dietz, Gabel, and Tiedau, 493–538.
16. See Hans-Dieter Arntz, *Judenverfolgung und Fluchthilfe im deutsch-belgischen Grenzgebiet: Kreisgebiet Schleiden; Euskirchen–Monschau–Aachen–Eupen/Malmedy* (Euskirchen, 1990), 269. See also the documentation in Günther Bernd Ginzel, ed., " . . . *das durfte keiner wissen!": Hilfe für Verfolgte im Rheinland von 1933 bis 1945; Gespräche, Dokumente Texte* (Cologne, 1995); Stefan Kirschgens, *Wege durch das Niemandsland: Dokumentation und Analyse der Hilfe für Flüchtlinge im deutsch-belgisch-niederländischen Grenzland in den Jahren 1933 bis 1945* (Cologne, 1998).
17. Arntz, *Judenverfolgung*, 493–498.
18. Ibid., 247–255. On Grünebaum see Roland Baumann, "Kurt Grünebaum, entre l'Allemagne et la Belgique," in *Carl Einstein in Brüssel: Dialoge über Grenzen; Carl-Einstein-Kolloquium 1998*, ed. Roland Baumann and Hubert Roland (Frankfurt, 2001), 277–292. On Mayer see Heinrich Toussaint, *Die drei Leben des Otto Eugen Mayer* (Eupen, 1989).
19. *Grenz-Echo*, 2 December 1938.
20. Quoted in Carlo Lejeune, *Die Säuberung*, vol. 2: *Hysterie, Wiedereingliederung, Assimilierung (1945–1952)* (Büllingen, 2007), 179.
21. Martin R. Schärer, *Deutsche Annexionspolitik im Westen: Die Wiedereingliederung Eupen-Malmedys im Zweiten Weltkrieg*, 2nd ed. (Frankfurt, 1978), 108. Regarding Thedieck's later career, see Stefan Creuzberger, *Kampf für die Einheit: Das gesamtdeutsche Ministerium und die politische Kultur des Kalten Krieges 1949–1969* (Düsseldorf, 2008), 65ff.
22. Emphasis in the original; quoted in Herbert Ruland, "Faschistische Bewegungen, Widerstand und Flüchtlingsschicksale in Neu-Belgien in der Zwischenkriegszeit," http://www.grenzgeschichte.eu/archiv/faschNeu-Belgien.pdf, 8–9 (accessed 26 December 2012), emphasis by the author.
23. See Rudi Van Doorslaer et al., *La Belgique docile: Les autorités belges et la persécution des Juifs en Belgique durant la Seconde Guerre mondiale*, vol. 1 (Brussels, 2007), 59–117; Frank Caestecker, "Onverbiddelijk, maar ook clement: Het Belgische immigratiebeleid en de Joodse Vlucht uit nazi-Duitsland, maart 1938-augustus 1939," *Bijdragen tot de Eigentijdse Geschiedenis* 13–14 (2004): 99–139.
24. Arntz, *Judenverfolgung*, 510–511.
25. Quoted in Carlo Lejeune and Klaus-Dieter Klauser, *Die Säuberung*, vol. 3: *Verdrängte Erinnerungen–340 Zeitzeugen berichten* (Büllingen, 2008), 52.
26. Peter Longerich, *Heinrich Himmler* (Oxford, 2012), 216 (German original: Munich, 2008).

27. The gardener Josef Kerres, shot by Belgian soldiers on 10 May 1940, serves as prototypical National Socialist fanatic in the Heimattreue Front; he was posthumously appointed to the rank of SS-Sturmbannführer and stylized as a "martyr of the movement." See Schärer, *Annexionspolitik*, 47–49.
28. "Mordanschlag auf den deutschen Legationssekretär in Paris," *Eupener Nachrichten*, 8 November 1938.
29. "Die französische Öffentlichkeit gegen jüdische Parasiten," *Eupener Nachrichten*, 9 November 1938.
30. "Antijüdische Kundgebungen im Reich," *Eupener Zeitung*, 10 November 1938.
31. Nico Rost, "In Eupen 3, " *Die neue Weltbühne* 35, no. 44 (1939), quoted in Herbert Ruland, "Faschistische Bewegungen," in *Ostbelgien und der 10. Mai 1940: Zeitgeschichte, Verdrängung und Aktualität; Kolloquium in Büllingen am 12. Mai 1990*, ed. Volkshochschule der Ostkantone (n.p., 1990), 37–41.
32. Herbert Ruland, "Spuren jüdischen Lebens in Eupen 1930–1949: Rosa Schalit-Mendelzwaig; eine gebürtige Eupenerin überlebt den Holocaust," *GrenzGeschichte DG: Rundbrief* (February 2011): 2–7, here 2–3, http://www.grenzgeschichte.eu/rundbriefe/Rundbrief-Nr.-11_kl.pdf (accessed 26 December 2012).
33. Lejeune and Klauser, *Säuberung*, vol. 3, 53.
34. See Jean Vanwelkenhuyzen, *Les avertissements qui venaient de Berlin* (Paris, 1982).
35. See Heinrich Toussaint, "Kollaboration und Widerstand," *Grenzland seit Menschengedenken*, cassette 2: *Abhängigkeit*, no. 71, ed. Groupe de Recherche et d'Etudes sur la Communication Culturelle (Eupen, 1990).
36. See the very balanced discussion in Quadflieg, *Zwangssoldaten*, 40. The enthusiasm also applied in particular for the French- and Walloon-speaking canton of Malmedy.
37. The Führer decree dated 18 May 1940, complemented by the enforcement decree dated 23 May 1940; Reichsgesetzblatt (RGBl.), 1940 I, 777 and 803. On the historical and international-legal assessment of this annexation, see Lejeune, *Säuberung*, vol. 1, 63–75; Lejeuene, *Säuberung*, vol. 2, 41–43; Jacques Wynants, "Les autorités belges et la situation des Cantons de l'Est 1940–1944," *Bulletin d'information du Centre liégeois d'Histoire et d'Archéologie Militaires* 9 no. 1 (March 2004): 15–26.
38. See, for example, Julius Boehmer, *Eupen-Malmedi bleibt deutsch!* (Eupen, 1941); Peter Dehottay, *Die Fremdherrschaft in Eupen-Malmedy* (Cologne, 1940); Karl Pütz, ed., *Volksdeutsche Jugend zwischen den Fronten* (Aachen, 1942); Anonymous, *Eupen-Malmedy ist frei! Tatsachenberichte* (Aachen, 1940).
39. Circular decree from the Reich Interior Minister, signed by Frick, dated 29 May 1940, Bundesarchiv (BArch) Koblenz, R43 II/1404a, I 440/40–1933; quoted in Schärer, *Annexionspolitik*, 283.
40. Ibid., 79–80.
41. Circular decree from the Reich Interior Ministers, dated 20 May 1940, BArch, R18/359, and Circular decree from the Reich Interior Minister, dated 31 May 1940, ibid., R18 (Rep. 320)/380; quoted in Schärer, *Annexionspolitik*, 108. The first circular decree also affected other annexed territories.
42. Ibid., 56ff., 146.
43. Ibid., 113.
44. Ibid., 125.
45. In any event, prior to 1942, non-Heimattreue Front members were not yet allowed to apply for NSDAP membership. Supposedly, however, party authorities interpreted the *Ariernachweis* (proof of Aryan ancestry) back to 1800 very broadly. See ibid., 170. So-called *Sippenforscher* (clan researchers) began operating in the area in 1940: Notes from summer 1940, Staatsarchiv (StA) Eupen, Eupen–Neuzeit, no. 456/45.

46. Schärer, *Annexionspolitik*, 170–173; Lejeune, *Säuberung*, vol. 2, 181–189.
47. Esriel Hildesheimer, *Jüdische Selbstverwaltung unter dem NS-Regime: Der Existenzkampf der Reichsvertretung und Reichsvereinigung der Juden in Deutschland* (Tübingen, 1994), 136. Unfortunately, Hildesheimer does not provide any verifiable source references. On the context, see Christopher R. Browning, *The Origins of the Final Solution: The Evolution of Nazi Jewish Policy, September 1939–March 1942* (Lincoln, NE, 2004), 197–205.
48. Rosa Schalit-Mendelzwaig, who grew up in Eupen, reported on how the local victory celebrations in May 1940 frightened the family. Since it was not yet possible to reach the Belgian interior from annexed Eupen-Malmedy, the family moved to Liège. In summer 1942, most of the family members were deported to Auschwitz and murdered in the gas chambers. Ruland, "Spuren," 4–5.
49. See Lejeune and Klauser, *Säuberung*, vol. 3, 51–54.
50. See Ruland, "Fluchtbewegungen," 11; Van Doorslaer et al., *Belgique*, vol. 1, 177–261.
51. Einsatzkommando 5 of the SiPo and the SD, Eupen-Malmedy to Gauleiter Grohé, Cologne, and Regierungspräsident Vogelsang, Aachen, dated 22 June 1940, quoted in Schärer, *Annexionspolitik*, 295. See Lejeune, *Säuberung*, vol. 1, 44–45.
52. Schärer, *Annexionspolitik*, 133ff.
53. RGBl. I 1940, 1222ff., and Durchführungsverordnung (enforcement order) dated 7 August 1941, RGBl. I 1941, 376f.
54. RGBl. I 1940, 803.
55. Ordinance on the state citizenship of the residents of Eupen, Malmedy, and Moresnet, dated 23 September 1941, RGBl. I 1942, 584; see Schärer, *Annexionspolitik*, 143–158.
56. RGBl. I 1935, 1333.
57. Ordinance on the state citizenship of the residents of Eupen, Malmedy, and Moresnet, dated 23 September 1941, RGBl. I 1942, 584.
58. Quoted in Schärer, *Annexionspolitik*, 150. References to the relevant ordinances from the various German authorities can also be found here.
59. BArch Berlin, NS 2, no. 89, vol. . 4/1, Aufgaben des Rasse- und Siedlungshauptamtes-SS im Westen–Elsass, Lothringen, Luxemburg, Eupen, Malmedy und Moresnet, Aktenvermerk, 28 September 1942.
60. Gierets to Rexroth, 10 February 1941; Rexroth to Gierets, 14 February 1941; Oberpräsident der Rheinprovinz, Abteilung für Höheres Schulwesen, to Landrat Seulen, 6 March 1941, StA Eupen, Eupen–Neuzeit, no. 314/126. The entire exchange of letters is also found in Cremer and Mießen, eds., *Spuren*, folder 2: 1939–1944, Spur (trace), 17.
61. StA Eupen, Eupen–Neuzeit, no. 330/201, Vermerk Rexroth, 5 August 1941. See also Hubert Keutgen, "Eupener und Kettenisier Straßennamen und ihre Bedeutung," in *Geschichtliches Eupen* 40 (Eupen, 2006): 31–49, here 40.
62. Sabine Haring, "Wer war Robert Wetzlar?" in *Geschichtliches Eupen* 40 (Eupen, 2006): 51–53.
63. StA Eupen, Eupen–Neuzeit, no. 330/201, Vermerk für Bürgermeister Rexroth, 9 April 1941.
64. The limited sources only permit conjectures. Consequently, the fate of the few Jewish businesses that existed prior to the war remains obscure. One suspects "Aryanization" in these cases, but there is no evidence. In addition, during the last two years of the war, forced laborers worked in the Eupen-Malmedy region. However, nothing suggests the presence of Jewish forced laborers. See Els Herrebout, "Von der osteuropäischen Scholle zum Eifeler Acker: Einsatz von ausländischen Arbeitern in der hiesigen Landwirtschaft im Zweiten Weltkrieg," *Zwischen Venn und Schneifel*, vol. 5 (2001): 89–82.

65. RGBl. 1941 I, 547.
66. Express letter from the Reich Minister of the Interior to all State Police headquarters, 15 September 1941, 12, quoted in Arntz, *Judenverfolgung*, 656–657.
67. Ibid., 663–666. See also Leo Wintgens, *Honneurs aux passeurs, Commémoration de la Résistance au nazisme dans la région de Montzen* (Montzen, 1990); Leo Wintgens, ed., *Le journal de Germaine Demoulin. Montzen 18.01.1941–15.09.1944: Chronique d'une famille de passeurs* (Montzen, 2006).
68. See now Insa Meinen and Ahlrich Meyer, *Verfolgt von Land zu Land: Jüdische Flüchtlinge in Westeuropa 1938–1944* (Paderborn, 2013). Arntz (*Judenverfolgung*, 668) also notes: "Basically one can say that in 1942 there were still many Jewish refugees whose path led them over the *'grüne Grenze'* [see note 72 below] to Belgium and old Belgium."
69. On this and the following, see Arntz, *Judenverfolgung*, 663–678, as well as Insa Meinen and Ahlrich Meyer, "La Belgique–pays de transit: Juifs fugitifs en Europe occidentale au temps des déportations de 1942," *Cahiers d'Histoire du Temps Présent* 20 (2008): 145–194, here 151–155, first printed in German: "Transitland Belgien: Jüdische Flüchtlinge in Westeuropa während der Zeit der Deportationen 1942," *Theresienstädter Studien und Dokumente* 14 (2007): 378–431.
70. Meinen and Meyer, "Belgique," 155.
71. Green border—*Grüne Grenze*—refers to the course of an international boundary between official border crossings.
72. Arntz, *Judenverfolgung*, 656.
73. See Manfred Müller, *Die Kommunalverwaltung der Stadt Eupen und des Amtes Eupen-Land während des Zweiten Weltkriegs* (unpublished thesis, Katholische Universität Neu-Löwen, 1997), 209ff. Due to imprecise references, this information is based on speculation; in addition, figures are lacking for 1942, the year that the deportations from the West began.
74. Lejeune, Klauser, *Säuberung*, vol. 3, 54.
75. Ibid., 52, 112, 150.
76. See Marion Schreiber, *Stille Rebellen: Der Überfall auf den 20. Deportationszug nach Auschwitz* (Berlin, 2000).
77. "Vor dem Lütticher Kriegsgericht," *Grenz-Echo*, 4 June 1947; "Vor dem Lütticher Kriegsgericht," *Grenz-Echo*, 26 June 1947.
78. Lejeune, Klauser, *Säuberung*, vol. 3, 328.
79. Freddy Cremer, "'Verschlusssache Geschichte': Über den Umgang mit der eigenen Vergangenheit," in *Spuren in die Zukunft: Anmerkungen zu einem bewegten Jahrhundert*, ed. Freddy Cremer, Andreas Fickers, and Carlo Lejeune (Büllingen, 2001), 9–26.
80. See Herbert Ruland, "Horst Naftaniel–ein Überlebender des Konzentrationslagers Auschwitz-Monowitz," in *Zwischen Hammer und Amboß. Eupen, Malmedy, St. Vith und die "zehn Gemeinden" von 1939–1945*, ed. Herbert Ruland et al. (Eupen, 1996), 91–100.
81. Translation: "Unrecorded Refugee Movements—or How the Jews in the West Eifel Made It to Freedom."

Chapter 11

Luxembourg
Marc Schoentgen

Prior to the Annexation

From the Middle Ages to the end of the eighteenth century, Jewish families and individuals settled only sporadically in Luxembourg (German: Luxemburg; Luxembourgish: Lëtzebuerg). A permanent Jewish presence developed only after the French Revolution and the region's annexation in 1795 by French troops, when the foundations for the emancipation of the Jews were laid in the newly created Département des Forêts. After the Congress of Vienna, Luxembourg was linked through personal union with the kingdom of the Netherlands. The Grand Duchy became an independent state in 1839, even though it belonged to the German Confederation from 1815 to 1867.

These political changes only marginally affected the lives of the Jewish inhabitants. The Napoleonic decree from 17 March 1808 regulating the organization of the Jewish religion remained partially in effect. Full equality between Jews and non-Jews, however, had yet to materialize, as reflected above all in the discrimination by the state administration. Special Jewish censuses (1808, 1815, 1818), the lack of any legal right to state subsidies, and protracted disputes regarding the founding of an Israelite elementary school exacerbated the Jewish minority's situation. The foundations for permanent legal security and real legal equality were first established in the Grand Duchy by the constitutions of 1842 and 1848. In the second half of the nineteenth century, the introduction of the concordat principle and the financing of Jewish religious institutions by the state treasury further normalized relations between the state and Luxembourg's Jewish Consistory, which represented the interests of the Israelite religious community vis-à-vis municipal and state authorities.[1]

As a result of immigration and marriage, the small Jewish community steadily grew. Whereas only seventy-five Jews lived in Luxembourg in 1808, by 1871 that number had increased to approximately 500; just before the turn of the twentieth century, it exceeded 1,000 for the first time. Within the predominantly Catholic Grand Duchy, citizens of the Jewish faith formed a very small minority, accounting for just under 0.5 percent of the total population around 1900. A substantial influx of Eastern European Jews occurred before and after the First World War, but it was not statistically registered. Their integration evidently proved to be more difficult than that of the German and French Jews who emigrated from Luxembourg's neighboring countries. The so-called Galician Jews were often viewed as undesirable competition, accused of "dishonest scheming" and usury, whereas the old-established Jewish families of merchants and business people had already long been integrated into local commerce.[2]

Jewish institutionalized religion remained organized on the basis of the 1808 Napoleonic decree until 1998. The state paid the salary of a grand rabbi, who was responsible for all of the country's Jewish communities. The country's largest Jewish communities established themselves in the capital and in the industrial town of Esch-sur-Alzette (German: Esch-an-der-Alzette; Luxembourgish: Esch-Uelzecht). Smaller Jewish communities—for example in Ettelbrück (Ettelbréck), Grevenmacher (Gréiwemaacher), Medernach (Miedernach), and Mondorf (Munneref)—formed in the rural regions. Jewish associations for women, men, and youth, as well as a Zionist association and a number of charitable organizations, had developed by the beginning of the twentieth century. The religious communities also had the legal status of an association. The Jewish community valued its good relations with state authorities and always emphasized its loyalty to the state and monarchy. Like the other religious communities, on the occasion of the national holiday celebrating the birthday of the ruling Grand Duke, it organized a festive service in the capital's synagogue.[3]

The large majority of the Jews in Luxembourg were assimilated into the broader society. The Zionist and Orthodox Jews usually had

Eastern European origins, but they generally exercised very little influence on the life of the Jewish community. Traditionally, the Catholic Party of the Right had dominated politics since its foundation in 1914, which meant that few Jews became publicly involved in politics. Most Jews probably leaned toward the bourgeois-liberal camp, and some toward to the Socialist Party, which as of 1937 formed part of a coalition government with the Party of the Right. But the Jews as an identifiable interest group did not play a major role in political life. The prewar parliament only included a single delegate of the Jewish faith; he belonged to the Liberal Party.[4]

The 1930s constituted an important break in the demographic development of Luxembourg's Jewish community. As of 1933, Luxembourg became a country of refuge and transit for German and later also Austrian Jews seeking to escape the reach of National Socialist rule and racial persecution. According to official statistics, a total of 3,144 Jews lived in Luxembourg in 1935, a very high proportion of whom—75 percent—were foreigners. On 31 December 1938, German and Austrian refugees alone numbered 901. We can no longer determine the precise number of Jews living in Luxembourg prior to the occupation on 10 May 1940, but new research estimates a total Jewish population of 4,000 individuals, with just under 25 percent of them holding Luxembourg citizenship. Therefore, Jews accounted for just over 1 percent of Luxembourg's total population of approximately 300,000.[5]

Little research has been done into the social composition of Luxembourg's Jewish community. However, most Luxembourg Jews probably belonged to the middle class and petty bourgeoisie. The large proportion of merchants is striking. Prior to the Second World War, the country had an estimated 350 Jewish stores and enterprises, 40 percent of which were small family-owned retail operations, such as stores selling colonial goods, textiles, or hats. Many Jews also worked as sales agents or wholesalers. In many regions, Jews firmly controlled the trade of livestock. In contrast, Jewish workers and employees played a negligible role in other areas, such as agriculture, skilled trades, and government service. Prior to 1940 the country only had a single Jewish teacher, while Jewish medical doctors and lawyers were also rare. In contrast to other European states, Luxembourg lacked a Jewish patrician class. The country featured only a single Jewish-owned bank, and although Luxembourg was also home to a number of Jewish department store owners and industrialists, they did not cultivate a flamboyant lifestyle. In larger economic terms, only a tobacco factory, a large leather factory, and a few textile factories played a significant industrial role, jointly employing a few hundred workers.[6]

Luxembourg's population was predominantly Catholic. The Church's strong position in everyday life and in the schools accounts for anti-Jewish prejudice and resentment. Nonetheless, pogroms or other acts of severe violence had been unknown since the Jewish emancipation. Despite the existence of sporadic threats and insults, the two faiths lived peacefully side by side. Admittedly, anti-Semitism grew stronger in the second half of the nineteenth century in reaction to the economic success of a number of Jews. Above all, the newspaper *Luxemburger Wort*—the main organ of the Catholic press—regularly printed articles that, while not usually explicitly targeting Luxembourg's Jewish residents, generally decried the "Jewish problem" and the supposed Jewish influence on economic, cultural, and political life.[7] It frequently adopted and disseminated anti-Semitic texts from foreign parts of Europe. The influence of this propaganda on public opinion is difficult to assess. The everyday use of anti-Jewish slogans, mocking verse, and idioms proved to be resilient. Times of economic distress—for example, during the First World War or in the years of crisis during the interwar period—witnessed the repeated emergence of dangerous mixtures of nationalist, xenophobic, and anti-Jewish prejudices, directed predominantly against Jewish business people.[8]

Starting in 1933, thousands of Germans fled to Luxembourg to escape National Socialist persecution. While the Grand Duchy merely constituted a land of transit for most of these Jews, some remained longer. Between 1935 and 1940, the number of foreign Jews rose from 2,274 to 2,902. Nationalist and extreme right-wing groups fueled fears of foreign inundation, yet they enjoyed little success at the polls.[9] The Luxembourg government tried to master the refugee crisis, initially during the first phase by issuing generous residence permits but then, starting in 1938, by taking a more restrictive approach in an effort to discourage prospective emigrants. On occasion, authorities also deported refugees without valid documents back to Germany, as in May 1938 when approximately fifty Jewish persons who had been transported by German officials to Luxembourg had to go back across the border.[10]

Luxembourg's historical, political, and economic relationship with its German neighbor had grown especially important for Luxembourg, particularly since the nineteenth century. Upon the dissolution of the German Confederation, the Grand Duchy pursued a strict policy of neutrality, yet the country remained closely linked to the German Reich until 1918 through its membership in the Customs Union. After being occupied by Germany during the First World War, Luxembourg admittedly still based its foreign policy on a position of neutrality but also began aligning itself more strongly with France and Belgium. Even though cooperation between the two nations became increasingly difficult as of 1933, bilateral relations with Germany never completely broke down.[11]

The political and public spheres in Luxembourg followed the political changes in Germany with growing concern. The second half of the 1930s witnessed the formation of various extreme right-wing groups and parties, influenced in part by the German model and supported by Reich Germans living in Luxembourg, but they failed to gain any influence on public opinion and political life. Within the circles of political Catholicism, ideas of a Christian corporatist state acquired a certain level of importance. In the right-wing spectrum, political splinter groups engaged in nationalist propaganda and developed a Luxembourger variation of so-called blood-and-soil ideology.[12] But even in pro-German circles, prior to 1940 hardly anyone could imagine the integration of Luxembourg into the German Reich or a "return" to the German *Volksgemeinschaft*, as suggested by the Koblenz Gauleiter Gustav Simon in a speech in 1933. To be sure, the NSDAP operated in Luxembourg, but it recruited its members exclusively from the country's Reich-German residents (the party had 850 members in 1934). The Luxembourgers themselves were not very susceptible to anti-democratic or totalitarian ideologies. The centennial celebrations organized in 1939 to honor the 100th anniversary of Luxembourg's independence patriotically demonstrated national autonomy and the country's unique cultural identity, which of course also included contributions by Luxembourg's Jews. Most of Luxembourg's population also understood these celebrations as a clear rejection of the craving for annexation found in the territory of the Reich. In 1939, the German envoy in Luxembourg Otto von Radowitz noted in a report: "The national sentiment that has been developing more and more in recent years found expression in powerful rallies and demonstrated all the features of a small nation [*Volk*] that is proud of its independence and determined to remain the way it is."[13]

The First Weeks of the Annexation

When the Wehrmacht advanced into the Grand Duchy on 10 May 1940, the government and head of state hastily fled the country. The government in exile later established itself in London and joined the Allies. The German military occupied Luxembourg within just a few hours and the administration of the German military commander of Belgium and northern France, General Alexander von Falkenhausen, took control of the country. An Administrative Commission led by senior Luxembourg ministry officials tried to manage ongoing affairs as well as possible.[14]

During the beginning of the occupation, the government had evacuated over 40,000 civilians from the southern part of Luxembourg to France. These refugees included approximately 1,500 Jews, most of whom decided not to return to occupied Luxembourg after France's defeat. Approximately 2,500 Jews of various nationalities still remained in Luxembourg after 10 May 1940. During the phase of the military administration, which lasted several weeks, the Wehrmacht by and large conducted itself decently in its relations with the civilian population. In a parley with Grand Rabbi Dr. Robert Serebrenik, the German military agreed not to infringe upon the rights of the Jews. Isolated anti-Jewish actions were committed not by the invaders but by collaborators and the country's Reich-German residents, who distributed anti-Semitic pamphlets and signs, for example, while unknown perpetrators repeatedly smashed the windows of the capital's synagogue. By order of the military commander, the signs had to be removed and the synagogue placed under police protection. In the southern part of the country, vacant Jewish stores were looted in Esch-sur-Alzette while in another town pro-German Luxembourgers distributed stolen goods to Reich Germans.[15] Notwithstanding such individual incidents, however, most of the Jews still living in Luxembourg remained largely unmolested from May until the end of July 1940.[16]

In the first weeks after the occupation and prior to the appointment of a Head of the Civil Administration (Chef der Zivilverwaltung; CdZ), various pro-German groups sought to gain the political initiative, yet only with moderate success. In early June 1940, the Ethnic German Movement (Volksdeutsche Bewegung) drew public attention with the appeal: "Luxembourgers, hear the voice of blood! It is telling you that, according to race and language, you are a German." Under the leadership of the movement's "Führer" Damian Kratzenberg, the Volksdeutsche Bewegung strongly advocated Luxembourg's integration into the German Reich. A *Heim-ins-Reich* (back home to the Reich) manifesto, signed by thirty-two Luxembourgers, appeared on 31 August 1940, leaving no doubt as to the thrust of the Nazi administration's policy: "The Luxembourger is a German, a German in his entire nature, according to history, according to lineage, language, and the region in which he is born . . . Now he is left with two options: either he finds his way home into the Reich . . . as an equal-in-birth and fully entitled *Volksgenosse* [national-ethnic comrade] . . . or he lets himself be driven into the new order as a second-grade citizen. . . ."[17]

The manifesto was not very successful. The Ethnic German Movement failed by far to attract the throngs of members hoped for by the Germans and their supporters. Only after the National Socialists reacted with coercive measures and threats, such as dismissing civil servants and employees, did the movement's membership begin to climb, whereupon it quickly reached over 70,000. Thus just under a quarter of Luxemburg's 300,000 inhabitants now belonged to the Ethnic German Movement. Many only signed their membership applications "to avoid the constant pressure and not to suffer any material disadvantages," presumes Paul Dostert. Probably only a few thousand Luxembourgers identified with the slogan printed on the Ethnic German Movement's green applicant card, which read like a definition of the term *Volksgemeinschaft*: "The German Reich is the homeland of all Germans. The general good is the supreme law. Gaining the soul of the *Volk* can succeed only if, along with conducting the positive struggle for one's own goals, one destroys the goals of the opponent."[18] The card also unmistakably identified the main opponent in the pursuit of these goals: the Jews.

Figure 11.1. Postcard with portraits of Josef Bürckel (Head of the Civil Administration in Lorraine) and Gustav Simon (Head of the Civil Administration in Luxembourg), 1940. *Source*: sz-photo, image no.: 24267.

The Period of the Occupation

The situation for Luxembourg's civilian population and the remaining Jews deteriorated when, upon Hitler's order, the direct military administration departed and the Gauleiter of Koblenz-Trier, Gustav Simon, was appointed the Head of the Civil Administration in Luxembourg on 2 August 1940 (see figure 11.1). Directly subordinate to Hitler,[19] Simon quickly implemented measures that sought the *Gleichschaltung* (synchronization) of Luxembourg and resulted in major changes for all of the occupied country's inhabitants. The goal of the Germanization policy, according to the "Führer's commission" issued to Gustav Simon, was to win the "hearts of the Luxembourgers for Germandom," and the Gauleiter was convinced that the Germans could wear away the "French varnish" and win over the majority of Luxembourgers to National Socialism. As *Volksdeutsche*—ethnic Germans—they were to supposed to be brought "home into the Reich."[20]

Step by step, the Civil Administration dissolved all state institutions (the Chamber of Delegates, the Administrative Commission) by the end of 1940, and the country of Luxembourg was gradually bound to the Gau of Koblenz-Trier. As a result, Luxembourg was de facto annexed by the Reich, even though this step was never taken in terms of international law. Appointed by Hitler, the Head of the Civil Administration also had an interest—at least during the initial phase—in postponing Luxembourg's formal annexation by the Reich, because he could thus ensure himself a large degree of freedom when resolving political and economic issues. Simon justifiably hoped that he could operate more or less independently in the integrated region without regard to Reich authorities. This independence was reflected, for example, not only in economic policy, which primarily asserted the interests of the Gau, but also clearly in Jewish policy. In early September 1940, when Gustav Simon wanted to issue his first anti-Jewish ordinances, he circumvented the Reich Interior Ministry and approached Hitler directly, who approved the implementation of such measures in Luxembourg. Thus Simon had free rein.[21]

While the new political leadership during the first weeks of the Civil Administration largely limited itself to the goal of winning over the Luxembourgers to National Socialism through a major propaganda campaign, at the same time its treatment of opponents and Jews demonstrated that the Germans would not shrink from using violence and repression when pursuing their political objectives. With the Einsatzkommando of the Security Police (Sicherheitspolizei; SiPo) and Security Service (Sicherheitsdienst; SD) along with his devoted officials, the Head of the Civil Administration had the necessary administrative and terror apparatus at his disposal. This Einsatzkommando moved into its offices in the Villa Pauly in Luxembourg City in August 1940, which became the control center for all of the German administration's illegal measures. The Security Service had been writing reports on the development of the political situation in the occupied country since May 1940. The ideologically tinted situation reports undoubtedly influenced the further course of illegal measures undertaken against the remaining Jewish population. SS-Sturmbannführer Wilhelm Nölle, ordered to Luxembourg from Trier, assumed command of the Einsatzkommando in the middle of August. His successor was SS-Obersturmbannführer Dr. Fritz Hartmann, whose term in office (1941–1943) coincided with most of the expulsions and deportations.[22]

Right from the outset, one of Simon's declared objectives was to form the *Volksgemeinschaft*. With numerous measures, he tried to win over the Luxembourgers to the National Socialist cause and this way cement the de facto annexation. At the same time, Jews could not be a part of this *Volksgemeinschaft*. They were excluded by the new social welfare measures, like the subsidies introduced for families with many children.[23] Already on 23 August 1940, Jewish livestock traders and butchers were expelled from the capital's slaughterhouse. On 24 August, Simon called upon the Administrative Commission to dismiss all Jews from Luxembourg's government apparatus and ensure that Jewish medical doctors and lawyers ceased their activities. On 12 September 1940, the Commission had to see to the dismissal of any Jewish employees. Until the end of 1940, the Administrative Commission functioned as a transmission channel through which the Head of the Civil Administration transferred its orders to the remaining subordinate authorities.[24]

Two groups of Jews, each with over 100 individuals—many of them German and Austrian Jews who were now fleeing for the second as a result of the expanding sphere of German influence—had already left Luxembourg for Portugal in the summer, furnished with documents from the German Pass Certificate Office (Passierscheinstelle).

Meanwhile, in the Villa Pauly, the "Jews Section" (*Judenreferat*) had started producing a *Judenkartei* (Jewish card index) using names provided by the Administrative Commission and/or the Luxembourg police upon the instructions of the Head of the Civil Administration. In November 1940, for example, the Luxembourg police sent a list that included the names of 480 Polish Jews. This list had been compiled "on the basis of the names and first names of the parties concerned" with the aid of documents used for policing foreigners, since registration papers from interwar period contained no information whatsoever regarding religion or "racial membership." The Jewish Consistory had to provide additional names, so that within a short time the Germans had registered hundreds of Jews.[25] Thus the Luxembourg authorities were coerced to become accessories in the Nazis' illegal undertakings. As a rule, Kriminalsekretär (criminal secretary) Oskar Schmalz, an employee of the Jews Section, delivered instructions verbally to the Consistory (as of 1942, the Council of Jewish Elders), which then had to ensure their implementation.

On 5 September 1940, one month after Simon's appointment as the Head of the Civil Administration, the measures for excluding the Jews and depriving them of their rights received a pseudo-legal basis with the Ordinance on the Measures in the Area of Jewish Legislation, which introduced the Nazi race laws and thereby abolished the basic constitutional rights of the Jewish population. Meanwhile the Ordinance on the Jewish Assets in Luxembourg, enacted on the very same day, cleared the way for plundering the Jews.[26]

The "synchronized" press highlighted the ordinances on its front pages, commenting extensively on the "neutralization [Ausschaltung] of Jewry." Making reference to the immigration of Jews during the period before the war, the press blatantly pandered to xenophobia and jealousy: "Luxembourg, which countless Jews in recent years have fraudently made their homestead, never saw them as dear guests." The Jews "in the background," the press reported, were responsible for the current political situation and the widespread rejection of Nazi Germany; now was the time to "extinguish" the powers that made Luxembourg dependent on Belgium and France. The Jews were "vermin" who made illegal "unprecedented profits." The anti-Semitic propaganda culminated in an appeal to boycott Jewish stores.[27] In fact, shock troops from the Ethnic German Movement roamed through the streets, pasting notices with the words "Jewish Store" on display windows. The Luxembourgers reacted in different ways: some welcomed the measures, while others deliberately sought out Jewish stores in the hope of quickly making a bargain purchase before the stores were shut down—this according to a Security Service report. Usually, however, the non-Jews were making a point of signaling their rejection of "Prussianism."[28]

On 12 September 1940, the Gestapo ordered that all Jews living in Luxembourg had to leave the country. Their expulsion was scheduled to take place a month later on Yom Kippur, the most important Jewish holiday. In a memorandum describing the prevailing situation, the Chair of the Consistory Alex Nussbaum turned to the German authorities and Luxembourg's Administrative Commission. In principle, he noted, a large portion of the Jews still living in Luxembourg were willing to emigrate via Portugal. Arguing against the deportation, Nussbaum pointed out that, as a result of the ordinance from 5 September, Luxembourg Jews had a status equal to that of German Jews and therefore should receive the same treatment; thus they should be permitted to remain in the country until they voluntarily emigrated. Also, he noted, the situation could not be compared to that in Alsace-Lorraine, since that region belonged to a conquered state, whereas Luxembourg, as a neutral state, was subject to different conditions.[29]

Ultimately, for unknown reasons, the order issued by the Gauleiter and Head of the Civil Administration was not implemented, yet the threat made an impact, for the Jews frantically tried to obtain the papers they needed to emigrate. Some of the people now left the territory "voluntarily," while others were forced to emigrate by German authorities. A wave of transports began in October 1940. In hastily arranged buses, around fifteen convoys left the country, bringing refugees to France (both to the occupied and unoccupied regions), Portugal, and Spain. Hundreds of Jews still managed in this way to reach safe countries outside of Europe. Some later joined resistance movements, such as the French Résistance, while others volunteered to serve in the Allied armies to fight against Germany.[30]

Had the planned mass deportation materialized, Gustav Simon would by means of this measure have preempted the so-called Wagner-Bürckel operation and been able to declare the region under his control "Jew free." Unprecedented in the West, the Wagner-Bürckel operation involved the deportation of more than 6,000 Jews on 22 October 1940 from Baden and the Saar-Palatinate to France. Earlier in July, Robert Wagner and Josef Bürckel—as the Heads of the Civil Administrations in Alsace and Lorraine—had already deported over 22,000 Jews and other undesired persons from the occupied and integrated territories across the demarcation line into unoccupied France.[31] The extent to which the deportations carried out by Simon were linked to the Wagner-Bürckel operation remains unclear to this day. The Head of the Civil Administration in Luxembourg, however, found himself in direct competition with the other two Heads of the Civil Administration.[32]

The German administration registered the assets of the Jews, both those who had fled as well as those still living in Luxembourg after 10 May 1940. The Head of the Civil Administration had laid the foundation for their expropriation with the Ordinance on Jewish Assets in Luxembourg in September 1940. The ordinance required the reporting of all assets and stipulated that Jews could be compelled to close, liquidate, and sell their factories and stores, and that legal transactions were subject to approval by the Civil Administration. By the end of 1940, the registration of Jewish assets had been completed, after which the systematic plundering began. Further ordinances regarding "Jewish assets" (issued on 7 February 1941), as well as executive orders (issued between April 1941 and April 1942) enabled the Head of the Civil Administration to take over the management of the assets of all Jews who had emigrated, died, or "still had their residence in the region of the Head of the Civil Administration in Luxembourg" and to assign those assets to third parties.[33]

Whereas in May 1941 most of the Jewish companies had already been liquidated, according to official figures the Civil Administration had "Aryanized" seventy-five companies. The furnishings that emigrants and deportees had to leave behind were given to "needy" families, while most of the real estate went to party organizations, municipalities, and government agencies. Administratively, these threads came together in the offices of the Civil Administration, where the notorious Section IV A organized the plundering of the Jews. Created on 12 December 1940, it dealt with the "management of Jewish and other assets." This section was headed by a member of Gustav Simon's innermost circle, namely, the Reich German Josef Ackermann, an NSDAP member since 1925 and a "Gau Inspector" as of 1936. Operating in parallel, the Stillhaltekommissar (Liquidation Commissar) Franz Schmidt, appointed in October 1940, was dissolving the Jewish associations, the assets of which flowed into the Head of the Civil Administration's coffers.[34]

In April 1941, a noteworthy encounter took place at the Reich Security Main Office (Reichssicherheitshauptamt) in Berlin. Judenreferent (Jewish Affairs Officer) Eichmann, the rigorous "instigator of emigration,"[35] had summoned the representatives of Luxembourg's Jewish communities to discuss emigration. Escorted by Gestapo officials, Chief Rabbi Robert Serebrenik and the Chair of the Consistory Louis Sternberg came to Berlin on 24 April 1941, where they were received in Eichmann's office at around 11:00 A.M. Eichmann suggested that Serebrenik make use of his good contacts in Portugal to acquire additional visas for a few thousand German Jews waiting to depart in Berlin. Eichmann seemed very well informed about a number of Nussbaum's and Serebrenik's trips to Lisbon, for agents from the German consulate had followed them at every turn. He made it clear that the time for legal emigration would soon be gone, because the borders would be closed. Luxembourg needed to be "clean of Jews" as soon as possible, a requirement for which there were only two solutions: either emigration toward the West or deportation to the East. At a second meeting in the afternoon, Eichmann informed the Luxembourgers and the now also present representatives of the Reich Association of the Jews in Germany that, until further notice, the Jews would still be permitted to emigrate from Luxembourg, subject to the generally applicable provisions. Approximately 100 individuals who already held the visa required for the United States were able to leave Europe immediately. In addition, he stipulated that henceforth Jews from Luxembourg were supposed to emigrate only in a ratio of one to ten with respect to Jews from the Old Reich.[36]

The extent to which this meeting on 24 April 1941 influenced Eichmann's later decisions cannot be determined. On 20 May, the Reich Security Main Office ordered the prevention of Jewish emigration from France and Belgium "in view of the doubtlessly forthcoming final solution of the Jewish question." This confirmed what had been intimated to Rabbi Serebrenik at the Reich Security Main Office, namely, that there could also be another solution to the "Jewish questions" apart from emigration.[37]

Until mid October 1941, however, Jews still had the opportunity to leave Luxembourg for other countries; an estimated 1,450 Jews managed in this way to escape the influence of the Nazi state. The last convoy with 120 people left the Luxembourg on 15 October for Portugal, one day before the first major deportation to the East—to occupied Poland—took place, after which German authorities banned emigration, without, however, publicly announcing the prohibition. Many unsuspecting Jews continued to prepare for their emigration even as the deportations were getting underway.[38]

In Luxembourg, living conditions became increasingly more difficult for the shrunken Jewish community. Alongside the anti-Semitic ordinances, organized "spontaneous" actions intended to inflame the atmosphere and intimidate the Jews resumed. In November 1940, collaborators had abused Jews in Mersch (Miersch). In February 1941, arsonists attacked the synagogue in Luxembourg City. In early May 1941, Nazi collaborators stormed the building during the religious service and threatened the attending believers. A few days later, all of the synagogues in Luxembourg had to close. By order of the Civil Administration, the Jewish houses of worship in Luxembourg City and Esch-sur-Alzette were completely torn down. Yet not everyone allowed themselves to be intimidated. As late as July 1941, the Security Service of the SS complained about the "provoking behavior" of Jews. Furthermore, the Gestapo discovered that Jews were shopping unhindered in stores and marketplaces. The daily press once again informed the public that, under threat of punishment, Jews could now only buy in certain stores. Spies had also heard about the "noticeable approach of the Jews to the anti-German minded clergy."[39]

Already in July 1941, Head of the Civil Administration Gustav Simon ordered Luxembourg Jews to wear yellow armbands, a measure that had previously only been instituted in the occupied and annexed regions of Poland.[40] The policies of exclusion in Luxembourg in early summer 1941, however, did not portend the subsequent mass murder. If one believes the Security Service reports, there were plans to consign approximately 300 infirm and sick Jews to a Jewish "lunatic asylum." Unfit for long-range transport, these people were supposed to be housed in the two Jewish old-age homes in Luxembourg until their final transfer to the asylum, which was not yet possible due to lack of space. The Nazis planned to use the work-capable Jews—approximately 425—for forced labor; around one-quarter of them were already on work assignments. Later in fall 1941, for example, thirty-five Luxembourg Jews consigned to a camp in Greimerath near Wittlich (in the Bezirk [district] of Trier) provided forced labor for the Chief Construction Directorate of Cologne, building the Autobahn.[41] Until "another evacuation or emigration opportunity" opened up, the work-capable Jews and their families were supposed to be transported to SS camp Hinzert in Hunsrück and deployed in segregated work details (*geschlossener Arbeitseinsatz*). Thus, for the Germans the "Jewish question in Luxembourg" seemed to have already been solved in July 1941, less than a year after Simon assumed his post as the Head of the Civil Administration.[42]

The measures outlined in the Security Service's July report, however, were only partially implemented. In Berlin, the Nazi leadership had decided in summer 1941 to conduct deportations from the German Reich, starting with the large cities in the Greater German Reich and the western border regions. The deportations began in Vienna on 15 October, followed by transports from Prague and Luxembourg on 16 October and Berlin on 18 October. In what was the first deportation of Jews from an occupied Western European country to Eastern Europe, the Gestapo deported approximately 300 Jews of various nationalities from Luxembourg to the Litzmannstadt (Łódź) ghetto in the Warthegau.⁴³ At the time, the "synchronized" daily press informed the population that Luxembourg was now "Jew free" and that "only a few, mostly sick and infirm persons" had stayed behind. "But they too will be segregated from the German *Volksgenossen* [national-ethnic comrades] and housed in a remote shared home, so that Luxembourg can be considered to be Jew free."⁴⁴ The transport on 16 October did not affect the majority of non-Jewish Luxembourgers, although members of the clergy, who appeared at the freight train station to make a point of seeing off their Jewish fellow citizens, spontaneously expressed their solidarity.⁴⁵

October 1941 marked a turning point in multiple ways. First, the final opportunities for "legal" departures lasted until the middle of the month; then on 23 October Himmler prohibited any emigration for the duration of the war. The mass murder of the Jewish population had already started during the military campaign against the Soviet Union, conducted behind the front. The Nazi leadership began pursuing its "total solution of the Jewish question" in Europe at the end of July, and this radicalization of anti-Semitic policy also affected Luxembourg. The second Ordinance Regarding the Regulation of Jewish Life in Luxembourg tightened the "Jewish Ordinance" of September 1940, restricting the freedom of movement of the remaining Jews to expedite their segregation from the Nazi *Volksgemeinschaft*. The ordinance drastically reduced their permitted shopping times, banned them from using streetcars, and prohibited them from leaving their residential communities without local police authorization. Around one month later than in the German Reich, the occupiers also introduced to Luxembourg the ignominious "Jewish Star," which replaced the yellow armband mandated for Jews since July 1941.⁴⁶

In Luxembourg, the compulsory marking of the Jews did not produce the desired effect. In isolated cases, Jews refused to wear the star, and parts of the non-Jewish population reacted with compassion and criticism to the visible exclusion. Eyewitnesses reported that Jews entering businesses while wearing the star on their clothing were even given preferential treatment.⁴⁷ By order of the Security Police's Einsatzkommando, a consistory announcement from 17 November 1941 went to all members of the Jewish community, warning them against dealing with non-Jews: "It still happens that Jews cultivate friendly relations with Aryans and even converse with them on the street." In the event of violations, the announcement warned, Jews and non-Jews faced the threat of being conveyed to a concentration camp.[48] Even in the following year, in March 1942, the Israelite religious community had to announce once again that all Jews had to wear a clearly visible "Jewish Star" and that violations had already been punished with the "heaviest penalties." In April, the Consistory beseeched community members to avoid "the streets if at all possible." Since 12 May 1942 all Jewish residences were to be marked with a clearly visible "Jewish Star in black print on white paper," a measure that already been mandated in the Reich since 26 March.[49] In June 1942, Jewish schools had to close as well. The Head of the Civil Administration had already issued an ordinance on 29 October 1940 that excluded Jewish children from classes at public schools, whereupon a private Jewish elementary school was founded in December 1940, attended at times by up to 100 children.[50]

Since the start of the mass deportations, the systemic plundering of Jewish families also intensified in Luxembourg. In November 1941, they—like all Jews in the Reich—had to surrender, among other things, their cameras, typewriters, and bicycles; in January 1942, they had to turn in their furs and all wool products of any kind, with the sole exception of clothing for personal use. At the same time a "soap action" demanded the contribution of all toilet soaps; in May, Jews were ordered to hand over all of their all silverware. In June, as throughout the Reich, the "Council of Elders" also collected gramophones as well as any electrical devices.[51] Finally, Jews had to deliver all "superfluous old woven material," although the Gestapo emphasized that the textiles should not contain any signs or references that might allow people to deduce their origins.

Recent research has revealed that Luxembourgers did not generally profit from the "Aryanizations." A file memorandum from 29 October 1941 states: "Gauleiter Simon at first proceeded from the idea of chiefly taking Luxembourgers into consideration in 'Aryanizations.' But for all possible political reasons, the Luxembourgers had displayed reluctance in the 'Aryanizations,' since involvement in such transactions appeared risky to them. For this reason, many land parcels, retail stores, and the few industrial firms have meanwhile gone to Old-Reich Germans, whereby interested parties from the Koblenz Gau were again given preference."[52]

On the other hand, however, we know of individual cases in which Luxembourgers willingly participated in the administrative processes of expropriation and "Aryanization." In the Revisions- und

Treuhandgesellschaft Luxembourg (auditing and trustee company), founded at the instigation of the Civil Administration, Luxembourger accountants registered and assessed countless Jewish firms for the Civil Administration, thereby facilitating their expropriation. Luxembourger notaries also issued the acts of donation and sale through which Jewish owners of real estate and companies lost everything.[53]

While the Nazis once again tightened the anti-Jewish provisions in October 1941 and prepared for the first deportation, the conflict regarding the Personal Status Registration (*Personenstandsaufnahme*) came to head. Scheduled for 10 October 1941 and prepared manually by the Civil Administration, this special census marked a preliminary high point in Nazi ethnic policy in Luxembourg. After Gustav Simon's appointment as the Administrator for the Tasks of the Reich Commissioner for the Strengthening of Germandom in the Gau Koblenz-Trier and in Luxembourg (Beauftragter für die Aufgaben des Reichskommissars für die Festigung deutschen Volkstums im Gau Koblenz-Trier und in Luxemburg) on 20 December 1940, initial efforts to individually register the ethnic-national affiliation (*Volkstumszugehörigkeit*) of Luxembourg's inhabitants had made little progress. Then in a secret letter on 1 September 1941, the Ethnic German Liaison Office (Volksdeutsche Mittelstelle) stipulated how to handle the "Volkstum question" in Luxembourg: "The foreign *Volkstum* is to be neutralized [*ausschalten*] as soon the political and economic circumstances allow." According to the letter, the Personal Status Registration—which took place on 10 October 1941—was supposed to contribute to the production of a *Volkstum* card index, and, if appropriate, inhabitants were to answer the three questions regarding citizenship, mother tongue, and ethnic affiliation with "German." Yet despite extensive propaganda and threats, the census ended in defeat. Random sampling indicated that over 90 percent of Luxembourgers had filled out the census cards with "Luxembourgish." The status registration therefore ended in a "large-scale political failure," since the Luxembourgers had unexpectedly "turned the administrative measure into a political referendum."[54]

The ethnic policy ultimately culminated in the granting of German citizenship. With the Ordinance on State Citizenship in Alsace, Lorraine, and Luxembourg from 23 August 1942,[55] members of Wehrmacht and the SS, as well as those "recognized as proven Germans," were granted German citizenship. In an order issued a few days later, the Head of the Civil Administration determined who in Luxembourg would be granted citizenship under the ordinance. In the first instance, this included members of the Ethnic German Movement, who obtained citizenship subject to revocation. In contrast, opponents such as members of the resistance, draft dodgers, and deserters faced the threat of resettlement, which especially after the strike movement in 1942 was implemented as an instrument of repression and terror.[56]

The former monastery of Fünfbrunnen (Cinqfontaines), converted by the Nazis into the Fünfbrunnen Jewish Old-Age Home in August 1941, played a central role in anti-Jewish policy in Luxembourg. Most of the Jews who remained in the country after the expulsion operation and the first deportation were brought here by order of the Gestapo. By and by, the people gradually arrived at the vacant monastery in small groups by bus or train. The Jewish Consistory hoped that they could wait for the end of the war or an opportunity to emigrate overseas, protected from further excesses and deportations. In fact, the Jewish old-age home became a kind of collection point for approximately 300 people, most of them foreign Jews who had fled to Luxembourg before the war began. The residents were predominantly elderly and sick—supervised by younger members of the Jewish community—living in degrading conditions, their everyday lives marked by insufficient space, hunger, and disease. Although the home was somewhat removed from the nearest sizeable town, its existence was by no means kept secret. In principle, anybody could freely access the old-age home since it was completely unguarded. The Gestapo and local Nazi collaborators conducted verification visits, which were feared by the home's residents and frequently ended in harassment. But regular encounters between the residents and their visiting friends and acquaintances as well as contacts with non-Jewish individuals from the surrounding communities are also documented.[57]

After the first deportation in October 1941, the Gestapo resumed the transports in April 1942, and it quickly became clear that Fünfbrunnen, too, was merely a way station on the route to Theresienstadt and Auschwitz. After each deportation, new groups were brought to Fünfbrunnen. In June 1943, the last of the total of seven transports that deported Jews from Luxembourg also included the Jewish Elder Alfred Oppenheimer and ten other individuals, bringing them from Fünfbrunnen to Theresienstadt. The old-age home was closed and the Jewish community ceased to exist. Only a few Jews living in "mixed marriages" remained in Luxembourg; grouped into the Residual Association of Jewish Mixed-Marriage Partners (Restvereinigung der jüdischen Mischehepartner), they survived the war.[58]

Due to the poor quality of the source material, it is difficult to appropriately assess the attitude of Luxembourgers with respect to the persecuted Jews. Most non-Jews passively followed the deprivation of rights, plundering, and expulsions without approving of these illegal measures.[59] At times the anti-Semitic propaganda during the first months of the Civil Administration probably fell on fertile soil, as indicated by the example of the Nazi propaganda film *Jud Süss*. The film ran only briefly, but the Security Service considered its screenings a success: "The film is very well attended by all circles. During the showing, on several occasions there were statements against Jewry."[60] On the other hand, with a certain sense of bewilderment, the Gestapo repeatedly had to concede that the anti-Semitic propaganda bore little fruit. Even punishments could not prevent brave accomplices from safeguarding the valuables and personal possessions of those who had already left the country or been deported. Others helped with foodstuffs or demonstrated their willingness to help in other ways. In a number of individual cases, people even hid Jews from their persecutors, thus enabling them to survive.[61]

The example of the Cahen cigarette factory, which belonged to the liberal member of Parliament Marcel Cahen, suggests that Luxembourg Jews may have been more likely to receive help than their counterparts in other countries. Cahen fled in May 1940 and his factory was placed under provisional management. To remove the company from German influence, the competing firm Heintz van Landewyck, whose director was a long-time business associate of Cahen, decided to take over the factory and manage it in the interests of its Jewish owner. This fact evidently escaped the competent German authority, which in this case had chosen a local company over a Reich German company from outside the Gau. After Luxembourg's liberation, the company was returned immediately and unscathed to Cahen.[62]

The resilience of anti-Jewish and xenophobic currents, however, appears in areas where one might least expect it. A number of political programs formulated by resistance organizations bore anti-Semitic features whose deeper origins lay in the widespread hostility toward foreigners prior to 1940. These programs sought above all to prevent the return of foreign Jews after the end of war and curtail their supposed economic influence.[63] However, most of the staunch anti-Semites who unscrupulously approved of the Civil Administration's measures belonged to the circle of collaborators. They did not hesitate to personally enrich themselves with the property of deported Jews, participate in the lootings, or take part in the brutal attacks on synagogues and private homes. The controversy surrounding Reserve Police Battalion 101 revealed that Luxembourgers also participated in the murder of the Jews. However, the men and women of Luxembourg were not involved in any decision-making processes. Even the Ethnic German Movement, led by Luxembourgish collaborators, did not exercise any significant influence on the measures undertaken by the Head of the Civil Administration. Hardline Reich Germans held all of the leadership positions in the police, administration, and economy. Nazi decision makers in Luxembourg and Berlin determined the anti-Jewish policy directives.[64] As far as we know, the municipal administration of Luxembourg City did not play an active role in the illegal measures undertaken against the Jews. In 1940, the city had fewer than 100,000 inhabitants, while the population of the entire country numbered only approximately 300,000, enabling the Gestapo, Security Service, and Security Police—with branch offices in larger communities in the southern and northern parts of the country—to implement their anti-Semitic measures without much difficulty. Only in smaller villages, such as Medernach, for example, which had a small Jewish community, did the Germans have difficulty exercising effective supervision.[65]

The ideas of most Luxembourgers with respect to community clashed with the image of the *Volksgemeinschaft* preached by the Nazis. For constitutionally loyal Luxembourgers, the *Volksgemeinschaft* remained a purely propagandistic notion, and they barely responded to party assemblies and mass rallies unless ordered to participate. Coercive measures, however, did not thrill anyone and they certainly could not win anybody over. Instead, in Luxembourg between 1940 and 1944 the repudiation of the "Prussian" occupiers grew increasingly apparent. Most Luxembourgers rallied around Grand Duchess Charlotte, who in exile became a symbol of independence.

To the extent that the desired Nazi *Volksgemeinschaft* was based primarily on the exclusion of certain population groups, we can cautiously maintain that the new rulers' ethnic-national policies enjoyed a modicum of success, for at no point in time did the Luxembourgers develop any widespread solidarity with the country's victims of Nazi anti-Jewish policies. But neither did most of them participate in the illegal measures. In 1942, reacting to the introduction of compulsory military service and the conscription of Luxembourgers into the German Wehrmacht, tens of thousands of Luxembourgers clearly expressed their opposition to the regime with a spontaneous strike movement. The "non-compliance movement" against compulsory military service had a considerable scope: many Luxembourgers evaded military service and were hidden by the civilian population. The Germans initiated a considerable number of courts-martial against Luxembourgers for desertion or undermining the war effort.[66]

The reason for the lack of solidarity, however, lay not so much in any hatred toward Jews but rather in the social structure of the Jewish community. Three-quarters of the Jews living in Luxembourg were foreigners; many did not arrive in the country as refugees until the 1930s and had difficulty integrating into established society. Moreover, after the Head of the Civil Administration had assumed power, non-Jewish Luxembourgers were exposed to a barrage of propaganda and thousands of them were forced into Nazi organizations. In May 1941, Rabbi Serebrenik wrote a report for the government in exile on the situation in occupied Luxembourg, which demonstrated the pressure imposed on both Jews and non-Jews: "It is important to be aware that the Catholic population suffers more psychologically and physically than the Jews in the country. The latter are only supposed to be expelled in their entirety, and this expulsion is being pursued with the most frightening methods of intimidation. But with the former they want to fulfill a mission and, keeping them in the country, make them into 'Germans.'"[67] Although Serebrenik accurately assessed the scope of the National Socialist's ethnic-national policies in Luxembourg, at the same time his report also reveals the extent to which Jews themselves falsely assessed their situation in occupied Europe.

Conclusion

At first glance, anti-Jewish policy in occupied Luxembourg hardly differed from that in other occupied regions in the West, but at times it had a dynamic of its own. In the first weeks after 10 May 1940, it still looked as if the country would only be subject to a military administration, as had been the case in the First World War. From 1914 to 1918, the government and head of state were able to stay in office and the country's political and social order remained intact. But the creation of a Civil Administration by Hitler's order quickly shattered any hope that this model would be repeated.

With the appointment of Gustav Simon as the Head of the Civil Administration, Luxembourg was supposed to be brought "home into the Reich"; in many respects, it became subject to the Reich's regulations. On the other hand, the Gauleiter of Koblenz-Trier developed his own initiatives in all administrative areas in order to govern his "Moselland" according to the Führer principle while relying on Berlin no more than necessary. "Führer decisions" in critical questions regarding economic and Jewish policy backed up Simon's centrifugal aspirations for power. There were hardly any interactions between Luxembourg as a territory under the Head of the Civil Administration and the Old Reich, apart from the marking of the Jews, which was introduced in Luxembourg earlier than in the Old Reich. In this respect, according to Raul Hilberg's assessment, after just one year of the Civil Administration, Simon was ahead of the Reich with the implementation of his anti-Jewish measures.[68]

Between May and the end of 1940, the Administrative Commission functioned as a communication channel that forwarded the orders of the Head of the Civil Administration to the remaining subordinate authorities. Before their introduction, measures developed on the Civil Administration's own initiative—above all during the first period of the occupation—that discriminated against the Jews and deprived them of their rights were discussed with the Reichssicherheitshauptamt in Berlin; on the other hand, some orders—for example, the deportation orders starting in 1941—came directly from the Reich Security Main Office. Other illegal orders by the Gestapo—for instance, the prohibition against Jews buying newspapers (March 1942) or owning electrical devices (June 1942)—were enacted in Luxembourg and the territory of the Reich almost at the same time.[69] Only in exceptional cases did the Head of the Civil Administration introduce measures earlier than in the territory of the Reich. Reich laws and ordinances, however, did not automatically apply to Luxembourg; in contrast to the Protectorate, they only took effect later on.

Overall, the four years of German occupation left wounds that failed to heal even after decades; the trench between the "good Luxembourgers" and the many minor fellow travelers and major collaborators was too deep. The Germanization measures themselves hardly left any traces, though, in Luxembourg in regard to the population. But the occupation period resulted in a catastrophe for the Jewish community, even if drawing up a conclusive balance sheet for the National Socialist reign of terror is impossible.

Most recent estimates calculate the total number of Jews living in Luxembourg at the time of the German invasion as approximately 3,900. Over 3,000 fled immediately after the beginning of the military campaign in the West or left the Grand Duchy's territory by October 1941 for France or Belgium. Meanwhile, 816 people remained in Luxembourg itself, of whom 664 were deported in a total of seven transports. At 92 percent, the death rate was extremely high; only fifty-three Jews survived the deportations. Some of the aforementioned 3,000 refugees (at least 890 individuals) managed to flee to countries beyond the Nazi sphere of influence. Most of them, however, settled in France or Belgium, where at least 565 Jews (475 of them in France alone) were captured and deported to the extermination camps, where a great majority were killed (approximately 95 percent). Assuming a prewar Jewish population of 3,900 people (Luxembourg nationals, foreign residents, and refugees), the number of dead must be calculated as over 1,400. After the war, approximately 1,600 individuals managed to return to Luxembourg or their homelands, or immigrate to Israel or other countries overseas. The fate of 900 Jews still remains unknown.[70]

Notes

1. There are only a few well-founded accounts of the history of Jews in Luxembourg. A good overview is provided by Laurent Moyse, *Du rejet à l'intégration: Histoire des Juifs du Luxembourg des origines à nos jours* (Luxembourg, 2011). Individual studies can be found in the anthology by Laurent Moyse and Marc Schoentgen, eds., *La présence juive au Luxembourg: du Moyen Âge au XXe siècle* (Luxembourg, 2001). On anti-Semitism in Luxembourg, see Marc Schoentgen, "Luxemburg," in *Handbuch des Antisemitismus: Judenfeindschaft in Geschichte und Gegenwart*, vol. 1: *Länder und Regionen*, ed. Wolfgang Benz (Munich, 2008), 222–226.
2. Letter from the police commissioner to the mayor of the town of Esch from 29 April 1916, Archives Nationales Luxembourg, Affaires Étrangères AE 581, Juifs galiciens établis dans le Grand-Duché. Expulsions (1916–1918).
3. See the speech of Grand Rabbi Dr. Robert Serebrenik, *Die Luxemburger Judenschaft und der 23. Januar: Festrede gehalten anlässlich des Geburtstages I.K.H. der Grossherzogin Charlotte* (Luxembourg, 1935).
4. Marcel Cahen (1887–1949) served as a member of parliament from 1922 to 1940. In addition, he was a city councilman in Luxembourg from 1921 to 1940.
5. See the report of the state commission for the investigation of the expropriation of Jews in Luxembourg during the German occupation. The government commission was created through the initiative of the Socialist delegate Ben Fayot, beginning its activities in 2002. An interim reported was submitted in 2007; the work was completed in July 2009. See Commission spéciale pour l'étude des spoliations des biens juifs au Luxembourg pendant les années de guerre 1940–1945, ed., *La spoliation des biens juifs au Luxembourg 1940–1945* (Luxembourg, 2009), published only on the Internet, http://www.gouvernement.lu/salle_presse/communiques/2009/07-juillet/06-biens-juifs/rapport_final.pdf (accessed 18 October 2009). On the number of Jewish refugees, see Serge Hoffmann, "Die Reichskristallnacht im Spiegel der Presse. Auswirkungen auf Luxemburg und dessen Nachbarregionen," *Galerie: Revue culturelle et pédagogique* 6 (1988): 379–390.
6. *La spoliation des biens juifs au Luxembourg 1940–1945*, 42ff.
7. Tanja Muller, "'Nichts gegen Juden als solche . . . ' Das 'Judenproblem' im Luxemburger Wort und in der katholischen Kirche im 19. Jahrhundert," *Forum für Politik, Gesellschaft und Kultur* 312 (November, 2011), 54–57. See also Marc Schoentgen, "Luxemburger Wort," in *Handbuch des Antisemitismus: Judenfeindschaft in Geschichte und Gegenwart*, vol. 6, *Publikationen*, ed. Wolfgang Benz (Munich, 2013), 439–441.

8. Schoentgen, "Luxemburg," 223f.
9. On the role of anti-Semitic groups in the prewar period, see Marc Schoentgen, "Mouvement Antisémitique Luxembourgeois," in *Handbuch des Antisemitismus. Judenfeindschaft in Geschichte und Gegenwart*, vol. 5: *Organisationen, Institutionen, Bewegungen*, ed.Wolfgang Benz (Munich, 2012), 408–410.
10. See "Ein Wort zum Problem der Flüchtlingsfrage," *Escher Tageblatt* 124 (28 May 1938). Serge Hoffmann, "Asyl und Gastfreundschaft in einem kleinen Land," in *Solidarität und Hilfe für Juden während der NS-Zeit: Regionalstudien I. Griechenland, Luxemburg, Norwegen, Polen, Rumänien, Schweiz*, ed. Wolfgang Benz and Juliane Wetzel (Berlin, 1996), 187–204. See also the exhibition catalog, Germaine Goetzinger et al., eds., *Exilland Luxemburg 1933–1947: Schreiben—Auftreten—Musizieren—Agitieren—Überleben* (Mersch, 2007).
11. Paul Dostert, *Luxemburg zwischen Selbstbehauptung und nationaler Selbstaufgabe: Die deutsche Besatzungspolitik und die Volksdeutsche Bewegung 1940–1945* (Luxembourg, 1985), 23–28.
12. Lucien Blau, *Histoire de l'extrême-droite au Grand-Duché de Luxembourg au XXe siècle* (Esch-sur-Alzette, 1998); see also idem "L'antisémitisme au Grand-Duché de Luxembourg pendant l'entre-deux-guerres," *Galerie* 10 (1992): 48–71.
13. Quoted in Dostert, *Luxemburg zwischen Selbstbehauptung und nationaler Selbstaufgabe*, 28.
14. On German occupation policy and the political reorganization of Luxembourg, see ibid., 39ff.
15. Thus in Esch-sur-Alzette, Luxembourg's second largest city, various shoe stores were looted. In Ettelbrück, which had the third largest Jewish community after Luxembourg and Esch-sur-Alzette, goods from Jewish stores were distributed. Cerf, *L'étoile juive au Luxembourg* (Luxembourg, 1986), 40.
16. For a detailed study of the weeks of the military administration, the establishment of the Civil Administration, and Nazi policies in Luxembourg during the Second World War, see Dostert, *Luxemburg zwischen Selbstbehauptung und nationaler Selbstaufgabe*. See also Emile Krier, "Die deutsche Volkstumspolitik in Luxemburg und ihre sozialen Folgen," in *Zweiter Weltkrieg und sozialer Wandel: Achsenmächte und besetzte Länder*, ed. Wacław Długoborski (Göttingen, 1981), 224–241. The anti-Semitic action during the first weeks after the occupation are described in an important account by Paul Cerf, *Longtemps j'aurai mémoire: Documents et témoignages sur les Juifs du Grand-Duché de Luxembourg durant la seconde guerre mondiale* (Luxembourg, 1974); idem, *L'étoile juive au Luxembourg* (Luxembourg, 1986). A very readable summary is provided by André Hohengarten, *Die nationalsozialistische Judenpolitik in Luxemburg*, 2nd ed. (Luxembourg, 2004). See also the following lexicon entries: Benoît Majerus, "Luxemburg," in *Lexikon des Holocaust*, ed. Wolfgang Benz (Munich, 2002), 145f.; Ruth Zariz, "Luxemburg," in *Enzyklopädie des Holocaust*, vol. 2, ed. Israel Gutman (Munich, 1995), 911–913. See also Willard Allen Fletcher and Jean Tucker Fletcher, eds., *Defiant Diplomat: George Platt Waller; American Consul in Nazi-Occupied Luxembourg, 1939–1941* (Newark, 2012). Waller is a witness of Nazi measures against Luxembourgers and Jews living in the Grand Duchy. In September 1940 he had a first meeting with Grand Rabbi Dr. Serebrenik. Later, the U.S. Legation issued visas for Jews legally entitled to them (cf. Waller, 101–110).
17. Both quotes are from the propagandistic article by Eduard Gerlach, "Wesen und Werden der Volksdeutschen Bewegung," in *Luxemburg*, ed. Paul Hermann Ruth (Breslau, 1942), 58f.

18. Quoted in Dostert, *Luxemburg zwischen Selbstbehauptung und nationaler Selbstaufgabe*, 234, note 38.
19. Decree of the Führer on the preliminary administration Luxembourg (2 August 1940), printed in Martin Moll, ed., *"Führer-Erlasse" 1939–1945: Edition sämtlicher überlieferter, nicht im Reichsgesetzblatt abgedruckter, von Hitler während des Zweiten Weltkrieges schriftlich erteilter Direktiven aus den Bereichen Staat, Partei, Wirtschaft, Besatzungspolitik und Militärverwaltung* (Stuttgart, 1997), 132f.
20. Second decree of the Führer on the preliminary administration in Luxembourg (18 October 1940), printed in Moll, ed., *"Führer-Erlasse" 1939–1945*, 147f. There were similar Führer decrees for Alsace and Lorraine.
21. Raul Hilberg, *The Destruction of the European Jews* (New Haven, Conn., 2003), vol. 2, 632. On the introduction of the first anti-Semitic ordinances, see Dostert, *Luxemburg zwischen Selbstbehauptung und nationaler Selbstaufgabe*, 161. On the role of the Security Service between May and December 1940, see Marc Schoentgen, "Das Einsatzkommando der Sicherheitspolizei und des Sicherheitsdienstes in Luxemburg und die Judenverfolgung im Jahre 1940," in *Du Luxembourg à l'Europe: Hommages à Gilbert Trausch à l'occasion de son 80e anniversaire*, ed. Jacques P. Leider. (Luxembourg, 2011), 301–326.
22. Cerf, *L'étoile juive au Luxembourg*, 169–174.
23. Ordinance on the Granting of Educational Aid to Families with Many Children and Ordinance on the Granting of Child Support to Families with Many in Children in Luxembourg of 23 December 1940, in *Verordnungsblatt für Luxemburg* (1940), 439f. All ordinances issued for occupied Luxembourg were published in the *Verordnungsblatt für Luxemburg*, published by the CdZ from 1940 to 1944. In addition, the full texts were also published in the daily press. The wording of the anti-Semitic ordinances issued in the CdZ's Luxembourg territory is printed in Cerf, *Longtemps j'aurai mémoire*, 153–177.
24. On the role of *Landesverwaltungskommission* (State Administrative Commission)—later renamed the *Verwaltungskommission* (Administrative Commission) by the Civil Administration as part of its Germanization policy—see also *La spoliation de biens juifs au Luxembourg 1940–1945*, 45–48; Archives Nationales Luxembourg, Affaires Étrangères AE 3834, Ausländerwesen. Ausweispolizeiliche Behandlung der Ausländer in Luxemburg, Schriftwechsel Verwaltungskommission mit Zivilverwaltung und Luxemburger Verwaltungen, 1940.
25. *La spoliation des biens juifs au Luxembourg 1940–1945*, 9.
26. *Verordnungsblatt für Luxemburg* (1940), 10f.
27. "Ausschaltung des Judentums," in *Luxemburger Wort*, 7 and 8 September 1940.
28. Ino Arndt, "Luxemburg: Deutsche Besetzung und Ausgrenzung der Juden," in *Dimension des Völkermords: Die Zahl der jüdischen Opfer des Nationalsozialismus*, ed. Wolfgang Benz (Munich, 1991), 95–104. See also Cerf, *L'étoile juive au Luxembourg*, 35–40.
29. See Cerf, *L'étoile juive au Luxembourg*, 53–69.
30. See Moyse, *Du rejet à l'intégration*, 212–216.
31. See the chapter on Alsace-Lorraine in this volume.
32. See Dostert, *Luxemburg zwischen Selbstbehauptung und nationaler Selbstaufgabe*, 65–74.
33. *Verordnungsblatt für Luxemburg* (1941), 90; first and second executive order, in *Verordnungsblatt für Luxemburg* (1941), 208, 298; as well as the third executive order in *Verordnungsblatt für Luxemburg* (1942), 134.
34. *La spoliation des biens juifs au Luxembourg 1940–1945*, 21–36, 40ff.

35. Juliane Wetzel, "Auswanderung aus Deutschland," in *Die Juden in Deutschland 1933–1945: Leben unter nationalsozialistischer Herrschaft*, ed. Wolfgang Benz (Munich, 1988), 429.
36. Cerf, *L'étoile juive au Luxembourg*, 251f. See also Moyse, *Du rejet à l'intégration*, 184–188.
37. Wetzel, "Auswanderung aus Deutschland," 425–431.
38. For the example of the Gottlieb family, see Marc Schoentgen, "Furcht vor der Fahrt nach Polen: Das Jüdische Altersheim in Fünfbrunnen (1941–1943)," *De Cliärrwer Kanton* 17, no. 2 (1995): 31f.
39. "Meldungen aus dem Reich," 14 July 1941, printed in *Rappel* 55 (2000): 88–104, quote on 103.
40. Ordinance regarding the organization of Jewish life in Luxembourg of 29 July 1941, in *Verordnungsblatt für Luxemburg* (1941), 325.
41. Wolf Gruner, *Jewish Forced Labor under the Nazis: Economic Needs and Racial Aims (1938–1944)* (New York, 2006), 205.
42. "Meldungen aus dem Reich," 14 July 1941, printed in *Rappel* 55 (2000): 88–104, quotes on 103.
43. Alfred Gottwaldt and Diana Schulle, *Die "Judendeportationen" aus dem Deutschen Reich 1941–1945: Eine kommentierte Chronologie* (Wiesbaden, 2005), 52ff. In 2011, an exhibit commemorated the fate of over 500 Jewish citizens from Luxembourg and the Trier region who had been transported to Litzmannstadt. A catalog in three languages (German, French, and English) was published in 2012. Pascale Eberhard, ed., *Der Überlebenskampf jüdischer Deportierter aus Luxemburg und der Trier Region im Getto Litzmannstadt: Briefe Mai 1942* (Saarbrücken, 2012).
44. "Ausschaltung des Judentums," *Luxemburger Wort*, 17 October 1941.
45. See Marc Schoentgen, "Luxemburger und Juden im Zweiten Weltkrieg: zwischen Solidarität und Schweigen," in *. . . et wor alles net esou einfach: Questions sur le Luxembourg et la Deuxième Guerre mondiale. Contributions historiques accompagnant l'exposition/Fragen an die Geschichte Luxemburgs im Zweiten Weltkrieg: ein Lesebuch zur Ausstellung*, ed. Musée d'histoire de la Ville de Luxembourg (Luxembourg, 2002), 150–163.
46. Ordinance Regarding the Organization of Jewish life in Luxembourg of 14 October 1941, in *Verordnungsblatt für Luxemburg* (1941), 420f.
47. See the eyewitness account by Hugo Heumann, *Erlebtes—Erlittenes: Von Mönchengladbach über Luxemburg nach Theresienstadt: Tagebuch eines deutsch-jüdischen Emigranten*, ed. Germaine Goetzinger and Marc Schoentgen (Mersch 2007), 102.
48. Consistory announcement, printed in Cerf, *Longtemps j'aurai mémoire*, 179.
49. Reports from the Consistory and/or Council of Elders, printed in Cerf, *Longtemps j'aurai mémoire*, 178–196.
50. The school was directed by a German emigrant, Ernst Ising. See Germaine Goetzinger, "Ernst Ising: Lehrer an der Jüdischen Schule in Luxemburg," in *Savoirs et engagement: Hommage à Georges Wirtgen*, ed. Charles Berg et al. (Differdingen, 2009), 15–28.
51. By order of the Gestapo, the Jewish Consistory was renamed as the "Council of Jewish Elders" in April 1942. The "Jewish Elder" was Alfred Oppenheimer (Chair of the Consistory since October 1941).
52. File memorandum by R. Reschl from 29 October 1941, Centre de documentation juive contemporaine (Paris), CLIV 78 (NI-2870).
53. "Verwaltung und Verwendung des Judenvermögens in Luxemburg," *Die Judenfrage* (31 May 1941): 97. See also *La spoliation des biens juifs au Luxembourg 1940–1945*, 51f.

54. Dostert, *Luxemburg zwischen Selbstbehauptung und nationaler Selbstaufgabe*, 158; on ethnic-national and racial policies during the Nazi occupation, see ibid., 152ff.
55. RGBl. 1942 I, 533.
56. Dostert, *Luxemburg zwischen Selbstbehauptung und nationaler Selbstaufgabe*, 182–188.
57. Schoentgen, "Luxemburger und Juden im Zweiten Weltkrieg," 159f.
58. Marc Schoentgen, "Das 'Jüdische Altersheim' in Fünfbrunnen," in *Terror im Westen: Nationalsozialistische Lager in den Niederlanden, Belgien und Luxemburg 1940–1945*, ed. Wolfgang Benz and Barbara Distel (Berlin, 2004), 49–71. The perception of the Fünfbrunnen monastery in Luxembourg society's culture of commemoration is dealt with in Jürgen Michael Schulz, "Fünfbrunnen," in *Lieux de Mémoire au Luxembourg: Usages du passé et construction nationale / Erinnerungsorte in Luxemburg: Umgang mit der Vergangenheit und Konstruktion der Nation*, ed. Sonja Kmec et al. (Luxembourg, 2007), 203–208.
59. Schoentgen, "Luxemburger und Juden im Zweiten Weltkrieg," 159f.
60. Quoted in Paul Lesch, "Le cinéma au Luxembourg sous l'Occupation," in *. . . et wor alles net esou einfach*, ed. Musée d'histoire de la Ville de Luxembourg, 86–95, here 91.
61. Schoentgen, "Luxemburger und Juden im Zweiten Weltkrieg," 159f.; Heumann, *Erlebtes—Erlittenes*, 102. See also Arno Lustiger, *Rettungswiderstand: Über die Judenretter in Europa während der NS-Zeit* (Göttingen, 2011), 247–249.
62. Paul Dostert, "Solidarität und Hilfe für Juden während der NS-Zeit," *Die Warte* 34 (1996): 1f.
63. Schoentgen, "Luxemburger und Juden im Zweiten Weltkrieg," 160. See the anti-Semitic statements in Franz Delvaux, *Luxemburg im Zweiten Weltkrieg: Ein Kriegstagebuch* (Luxembourg, 1945) 23. The second edition of the book appeared in 1946 and was reprinted in 1989.
64. The extent of collaboration can be illustrated by a number of figures. After 1945, investigations were launched into more than 10,000 cases; by 1947, approximately one quarter of these investigations had already been called off due to a lack of evidence or the case's negligibility. In 2,260 cases, judges imposed prison sentences on collaborators, while twelve individuals received death sentences. At the time, Luxembourg had slightly fewer than 300,000 residents (including foreigners). See Paul Cerf, *De l'épuration au Grand-Duché de Luxembourg après la seconde guerre mondiale* (Luxembourg, 1980); Paul Dostert, "Die Luxemburger im Reserve-Polizei-Bataillon 101 und der Judenmord in Polen," *Hémecht: Zeitschrift für Luxemburger Geschichte* 52 no. 1 (2000): 81–99; and recently Vincent Artuso, *La collaboration au Luxembourg durant la Seconde Guerre mondiale (1940–1945): Accommodation, adaptation, assimilation* (Luxembourg, 2013).
65. See Marc Schoentgen, "Die jüdische Gemeinde in Medernach: Einwanderung, Integration und Verfolgung," in *Fanfare Miedernach 1930–2005* (Medernach, 2005), 299–366.
66. In 1943, for example, there were 221 trials against Luxembourgers. See Michael Eberlein and Norbert Haase, *Luxemburger Zwangsrekrutierte im Wehrmachtsgefängnis Torgau-Fort Zinna 1943–1945* (Dresden, 1996), 11–20.
67. Report dated 3 June 1941, Archives Nationales Luxembourg, ANL Gouvernement en exil 380.
68. Hilberg, *Destruction*, vol. 2, 633.
69. Benz, *Die Juden in Deutschland*, 751f.
70. *La spoliation des biens juifs au Luxembourg 1940–1945*, 11–15.

CHAPTER 12

ALSACE-LORRAINE
Jean-Marc Dreyfus

Prior to the Annexation

Viewed in the context of the history of French Jews, the history of the Jews living in Alsace is both long and atypical. Archeological traces of Jewish life in this region reach back to the ninth century,[1] and the presence of Alsatian Jews persisted virtually uninterrupted over the course of centuries. At the time of the last expulsion of the Jews from the French kingdom in 1394, Alsace belonged to the Holy Roman Empire of the German Nation. After the Peace of Westphalia in 1648, Alsace became French (with the exception of the Free Imperial City of Strasbourg), yet Jews were allowed to continue to live in the region, except in the large towns. During its very complicated history prior to 1789, Lorraine shifted between the French kingdom, the Holy Roman Empire, and the Duchy of Lorraine. The Kingdom of France, however, already controlled the Three Bishoprics of Metz, Toul, and Verdun by 1552, all of which had Jewish communities.[2] During the period of the French Revolution, Alsatian Jews accounted for half of the new regime's Jews. From one day to the next in September 1791, they gained full equality before the law, which facilitated the process of their integration into the French nation.[3]

The annexation by the German Reich in 1871 caused a demographic upheaval in Alsace-Lorraine. Twenty percent of the Jews residing in the region, many of them members of the bourgeoisie, decided in favor of France and left their homeland. The new "imperial state" (Reichsland) consisted of what prior to 1871 had been two departments in Alsace and one (namely, the former Moselle) department in Lorraine. On the other hand, a German-Jewish bourgeoisie grew rapidly with the economic success of the Reichsland,[4] primarily in Strasbourg and Metz.[5] In 1911, after years of debate and conflict, Alsace and Lorraine were granted a "constitution" as a Reichsland and a legislative assembly with limited powers, located in Strasbourg.[6]

After regaining Alsace-Lorraine as a result of its victory over the German Empire during the First World War, France deported the Germans, including the German Jews.[7] In the beginning of the 1920s, the people in Alsace and Lorraine hardly questioned the region's repatriation with France; all political orientations took it for granted, all the more so because any politicians who might have campaigned for remaining with the German Reich had either voluntarily left the region or been deported by the French authorities. Only those Alsatians and Lorrainians now living in Germany (who incidentally received compensation from the Weimar Republic) mourned the loss of the German Reichsland. Joining together to form associations, they established their intellectual center at Frankfurt, which featured the founding of the Scientific Institute of Alsace-Lorrainians in the Reich at the university in 1921.[8] In its publications, this scientific society increasingly advocated German nationalist and irredentist positions. Using the period prior to the Peace of Westphalia as its point of reference, the institute moved from mourning the loss of a German Alsace to once again legitimizing it.

In Alsace and Lorraine themselves, the pro-French enthusiasm that prevailed within a large part of the population between 1918 and 1921 soon gave way to what the Parisian press henceforth referred to as "Alsatian discontent." Economic problems and people's desire to retain what little had been achieved in 1911 soon generated reasons to oppose Jacobinism, namely, that republican centralism which negated particularism in Alsace and the reconstituted department of Moselle.[9] Many Alsatians—supported by local political parties—feared their province's complete "assimilation," both at the level of language (the issue regarding German classes in what were now francophone schools quickly moved to the forefront) as well as in the area of religion. Since the Napoleonic Concordat of 1801 had not been repealed in 1905 in the departments of Alsace and Moselle and was still enforced after 1918, the separation of church and state did not apply in these regions, allowing churches to retain special rights. Thus state-appointed teachers taught religion in the public schools; pastors and rabbis received their salaries from the state. At the same time, discontent grew because the Alsace found itself in a difficult economic situation as industries tried to reorient their production toward the French market. The left-wing coalition, governing the country since 1924, undertook a number of measures to equalize the status of officials in the provinces with those of their counterparts in the rest of France. These "threats" to particularism led to the creation of the so-called autonomist movement.[10]

On 9 May 1925, the first issue of the newspaper *Die Zukunft* appeared in Strasbourg, and the paper quickly reached a circulation of 20,000 copies. The Homeland Federation (Heimatbund) formed immediately thereafter under the leadership of the former Catholic Reichstag delegate Dr. Eugène Ricklin and soon registered a strong growth in popularity.[11] Did this autonomist movement, which during the elections played no role in the Haut-Rhin department yet in the Protestant cantons of northern Alsace obtained 45 percent of the vote, prepare the way with its ideas for the forced Germanization of the Alsace initiated in summer 1940? Considering the movement's ideological background, this seems unlikely. Heterogeneously composed, the movement drew its leadership from both the Socialist Party and the former Catholic Center, which had been especially influential in Alsace prior to 1918 and reestablished itself as the Republican People's Union of Alsace (Union populaire républicaine d'Alsace), dominating elections throughout the 1920s. Camille Dahlet, for example, was a pro-French democrat[12] and member of the radical party. The German-speaking writer René Schickelé, who supported the movement despite having already left the Alsace at this point in time (he lived both in Badenweiler in the Black Forest and also in Berlin), followed Socialist ideas.[13] And someone like Jacques Peirotes, a mayor of Strasbourg and parliamentarian whose political career combined Catholic ideas with moderate socialism, took a firm stand against banning the movement in 1929 with a famous speech in the Chamber of Deputies.[14]

The autonomist movement called for the preservation of "religious and cultural freedoms," albeit within the framework of the French Republic. The Homeland Front demanded a regional parliament and a local executive. Its program lacked any racist or anti-Semitic tones. Some elected autonomists were Jews, like the Mayor of Barr, Dr. Moïse. How can we interpret this movement, which dominated Alsatian politics until the elections of 1931? In a famous newspaper article, the Germanist Edmond Vermeil compared Alsatian autonomism with Rhenish Catholic federalism as represented by Constantin Frantz.[15] The Alsatian autonomists struggled for homeland rights, for the regional customs and practices of what they understood as their traditional community, and against the *Herrenvolk* (master race), a role the French took over from the Germans in 1918. This was why the French government doggedly combatted the movement, conducting a major trial, for example, against autonomist leaders in Colmar (Kolmar) from 30 April to the end of December 1927.[16] It must be emphasized that the autonomist movement had shallower roots in Lorraine, probably due to many factors, such as the high percentage of foreigners in an industrial region dominated by the steel industry, the French-speaking nature of the southern part of the department, and the prominent influence of French culture in the reunified region. Nonetheless, the Lorraine produced a number of autonomist leaders, such as Catholic priest François Goldschmidt, who in his small village of Dieuze actively maintained links with Alsatian autonomist leaders.[17]

Even though the movement at this point in time can hardly be described as *völkisch* (ethnic-nationalist), its opposition to the vision of a nation based on a social contract and its insistence on preserving an "authentic" regional community nonetheless cleared the way for a second more radical autonomist movement. This subsequent movement, which as of 1935 drifted toward fascism and even Nazism, found greater support on the opposite side of the Rhine in the milieu of the Alsatians and Lorrainians deported to Germany in 1919. One of its figure heads was Robert Ernst, the son of an Alsatian pastor born in 1897. Ernst and his family had opted for Germany to avoid becoming French and had benefited from the funds made available by the German Foreign Office for pro-German propaganda in Alsace.[18]

The leaders of the autonomists—most of whom held political offices (Alsace sent up to twelve autonomist delegates to the French National Assembly)—came from totally different political camps. Thus in 1930 the French Communist Party (Parti communiste français) had expelled Charles Huber—Strasbourg's mayor in 1932—because of his "alliance with the bourgeoisie," even though the Communist Party itself, in the statements of Maurice Thorez, espoused autonomism. Nonetheless, a small number of autonomist leaders converted to National Socialism, most importantly Armand (Hermann) Bickler[19] and Friedrich Spieser.[20] In 1933, after Hitler seized power, Bickler founded both a journal and an action group named *Jungmannschaft* (youth team), structured along the lines of the Hitler Youth. Adopting the Führer principle and organized into cells and local groups, the Jungmannschaft flew a black flag with a red wolf's hook (a runic character).[21] Spieser occupied himself above all with "cultural politics," maintaining connections with every site of German expatriate agitation, as well as with the German Foreign Institute (Deutsches Ausland-Institut) in Stuttgart. He did not join the NSDAP until 1942, but he had earlier already staged National Socialist ceremonies at his castle, the Hüneburg in the Vosges. In his writings, he delivered panegyrics about the Führer.[22] In Lorraine, fewer politicians—none of them prominent—embraced autonomism. The most active was Victor Antoni, born in Fénétrange (German: Finstingen), a small city in the mining region. A cantonal advisor and member of the departmental assembly, Antoni failed to be elected at the French National Assembly in 1936.[23]

How strongly did anti-Semitism feature in all of these Alsatian and Lorrainian movements and parties? The emigrations as a result of the region's changing nationality had significantly weakened the Jewish bourgeoisie in Alsace and Lorraine, compared to the Jewish middle class in Germany. During the interwar period, the Jewish livestock dealer, acting as an intermediary between farmers and butchers, figured more prominently in Alsace than did the Jewish banker.[24] A popular anti-Semitism, latent since the nineteenth century, needed only to be aroused. Even so, in his dissertation Eric Kurlander has shown that political anti-Semitism held little attraction in Alsace at the end of the nineteenth century.[25] In fact, anti-Semitism was neither absent (especially after 1933), but nor did it strongly express itself. This is exemplified, for instance, by the first volume from the *Kleine Reihe der Jungmannschaftsbücherei* (small series of the Jungmannschaft library) published in Strasbourg in 1938 by Hermann Bickler. The booklet *Die Hintergründe der kommunistischen Politik* (the background of Communist politics) makes no mention of Jews and so-called Jewish Bolshevism. Indeed, the large French anti-Jewish newspapers such as *Je suis partout* propagated anti-Semitism far more fiercely than did the local press in Alsace and Lorraine.

The one autonomist and pro-German organization that especially advanced anti-Semitism in Alsace prior to the Second World War was Joseph Bilger's Farmer's League (Bauernbund),[26] which unified German-speaking farmers and cultivated a blood-and-soil rhetoric. Apart from engaging in apologetics for Hitler, Bilger revived the traditional anti-Semitism of rural Alsace, home to a particularly large number of Jews who traded livestock, agricultural equipment, grain, and hops. At the same time—and this further complicated the situation—the Farmers' League formed part of the "Greenshirts" (*chemises vertes*) fascist movement, which under the leadership of Roland Dorgères, advocated an extreme French patriotism. The movement numbered up to 6,000 members, predominantly in the Haut-Rhin department. As of 1938, Bilger drew increasingly closer to Germany, whereupon, however, the membership of the Farmer's League shrank. As the war approached, the Alsatians reverted back into pro-French legitimists. Starting in 1938, however, the massive agitation motivated a number of Jewish families to begin getting ready to move out of Alsace and Lorraine. The tense atmosphere and expressive anti-Semitism led those with the means to do so to purchase homes far from Alsace.[27] In 1938, approximately 20,000 Jews lived in Alsace, mostly residing in Strasbourg, Colmar, and Mulhouse (Mülhausen).[28] The Jewish community in Moselle was substantial for such a small region; in 1936, a general population census registered 8,513 Jews, 4,200 of them living in Metz.

In Alsace and Lorraine, however, the republic's law and order still applied. The police and the General Intelligence (Renseignements Généraux—the French service for domestic intelligence) monitored the autonomist movement and, while not taking action against anti-Semitic propaganda, prosecuted all operations against Jews. Yet this failed to prevent a number of restaurants in the town center of Strasbourg from posting signs labeled "forbidden for Jews." Nonetheless, Eric Kurlander has maintained that most Alsatians adhered to the kind of moderate liberalism that prevailed in France in the 1930s and at the same time rejected National Socialism.[29]

The autonomist organizations and parties strongly relied on financing from German sources; funding came either directly from the German Foreign Office or from various institutions that supported German expatriates. Strasbourg functioned, moreover, as a distribution center for pro-German propaganda, produced in Paris in the workplace of Otto Abetz, for example, the representative of the Franco-German Committee. In summer 1940 he would take over the position of German ambassador in Paris. Moreover, experts in the German *Westforschung* program, especially the historians, worked diligently to highlight the Germanic characteristics of Alsace-Lorraine.[30]

When France declared war on the German Reich on 3 September 1939, French police arrested fourteen leading autonomists in Nancy.[31] The former chair of the Homeland Federation and member of the

Strasbourg city council, Karl Roos, who in the 1930s enthusiastically supported a German-oriented autonomism, had already been arrested in February 1939. A court sentenced him to death in October 1939 for espionage against France, and he was executed on 7 February 1940. The remaining *Nanziger* ("the ones from Nancy"), as they were called in Alsace, were released in July 1940 upon the Hitler's explicit request.[32]

In addition, the French state arranged for the orderly evacuation of 175 communes along the German border.[33] Government offices, schools, and consistories were closed and 430,000 people evacuated to the Massif Central, Périgord, and Limousin. The town of Strasbourg now only housed an army garrison. The town's many Jewish residents were also evacuated. Jewish residents in the smaller rural communities located further from the border were allowed to remain. Later, in the wake of the French defeat, many of them fled to the Vosges.[34]

The First Weeks of the Annexation

The German army had advanced across the border into France on 10 May 1940. On 19 June 1940, it marched into Strasbourg. Shortly after twelve noon, the swastika flew over the Strasbourg cathedral. Two days before the cease-fire on 22 June, Hitler decided that Alsace would be governed by the Reich and not be dependent on the military commander in France, headquartered on Avenue Kléber in Paris.[35] As of 24 June, the Badenese Reich Governor (Reichsstatthalter) and Gauleiter Robert Wagner took over Alsace while the Saarland Reich Commissioner (Reichskommissar) and Gauleiter Joseph Bürckel assumed control of Lorraine, both as the respective Heads of the Civil Administrations (Chef der Zivilverwaltung; CdZ); the annexed territories were also de facto integrated into their NSDAP Gaue.[36]

In their euphoria in light of the German victory, the still detained *Nanziger* envisioned an independent state of Alsace-Lorraine, modeled on Slovakia and naturally aligned with the German Reich. In his memoirs, Robert Ernst referred to the idea of creating a confederation of autonomous states under a German protectorate with borders corresponding to the fifteenth-century states of Lorraine or even Burgundy. But the Nanziger remained imprisoned until they declared their willingness to sign a declaration of submission vis-à-vis the German Reich.[37] They were not released until 14 July 1940, when the decision to deport the Jews and other "undesirables" from Alsace-Lorraine had already been made.

Hitler had given the order to Germanize Alsace and Lorraine within ten years. Robert Wager attempted to radically accelerate this process. One of the most important measures in this regard constituted the mass deportation of persons "hostile to the *Volk* and Reich," a category intended to include non-German-speaking Alsatians, pro-French activists, members of left-wing political parties, senior French officials, and Jews. Wagner wanted to extend his power as the Reich Governor and Gauleiter of Baden by using the annexation of Alsace to also further expand the administration of the state of Baden. When setting up the region's administration and the newly created NSDAP Gau of Baden-Alsace in Strasbourg, however, he only gave minor posts to the leading Alsatian autonomists. They were mostly assigned to the Auxiliary Service (Hilfsdienst), an organization that was supposed to convince Alsatians that the Germans cared for their well-being by providing social support. Bickler obtained the highest position, advancing to the post of NSDAP Kreisleiter (district leader) for Strasbourg.[38] Victor Antoni was appointed mayor of his hometown Fénétrange.[39] Further west, the Nazis created the Gau Westmark on 30 November 1940, consisting of the Saar Region, the Palatinate to Ludwigshafen, and the former Moselle department. The region's Gauleiter Josef Bürckel, a former school teacher and a member of the Nazi Party as early as 1925, had been in charge of integrating Austria into the Reich from April 1938 to March 1940. Since he did not choose Metz as the capital city for the new Gau, the Civil Administration remained in Saarbrücken. However, the creation of the new Gau was celebrated by a visit from Hitler himself in Metz on 26 December 1940.[40]

The National Socialist *Gleichschaltung* (synchronization) took place above all through the regulation requiring the use of the German language. Greeting people with "bonjour" in a public place was forbidden under the threat of a prison sentence. Lower- and mid-level French officials, however, retained their posts. Alsatian primary school teachers had to undergo retraining on the opposite side of the Rhine. Because of the traditional distrust toward the Alsatians, who were always suspected of being autonomists or too "French," the population was increasingly oppressed.[41]

Today, the Germanization of Lorraine is considered to have been less violent and ruthless than in Alsace. In fact, Bürckel wanted to proceed more slowly. He was confronted with the necessity of keeping industry running, for the new Gau had become an important center of steel production. Nonetheless, he expelled the Bishop of Metz Monsignor

Figure 12.1. "Jews not wanted"—notice at a Strasbourg tavern, 1940. *Source:* sz-photo, image no.: 74004.

Heinz, together with 200 Catholic priests.[42] In a rare example among the numerous memoirs published after the war by non-Jewish citizens describing their tribulations in the annexed regions, Léon Sidot discusses the meeting on the "Jewish question" that he had to attend, along with other young men, on 2 December 1940 during a reeducation sojourn in the Saarland town of Annweiler.[43]

The first weeks of the annexation also witnessed the eruption of anti-Semitic violence. Surviving Jews chiefly recalled the abuses perpetrated in Mulhouse. On 1 July 1940, the occupying Germans had forced twenty-five local Jews to clean a villa that presumably was going to be used by a senior German official. While taking photographs, the tormentors also abused them in public, forcing them to crawl on the ground and cut each other's hair, among other things. With the help of Alsatians, German soldiers plundered the synagogues and the premises of the Jewish communities, completely devastating everything.[44] In the Lorraine village of Lisheim, the cantor of the synagogue committed suicide, cutting his throat; German soldiers forced his daughter to clean the blood and walk in front of the funeral procession, holding the stained rag and finally throwing it into the grave. In Phalsbourg (Pfalzburg), a 93-year-old man died as a result of abuse, and another elderly man lost his mind.[45]

The Period of the Occupation

On 14 July 1940, the Head of the Civil Administration in Alsace, Robert Wagner, announced the intention to deport political opponents, "Francophiles," members of the prewar political parties, and Jews within twenty-four hours—one of his first official acts after arriving in Strasbourg. The previous day he had already signed an order stipulating the confiscation of all property belonging to persons falling within these categories.[46] The victims later reported receiving very little time to pack their permitted twenty kilograms of luggage. From the collection point—a public building in their home village or town—they were transported to the newly demarcated border between the de facto annexed Alsace and occupied, so-called inner France, to the Vosges, or even to Belfort. Only an unknown—presumably small—number of "half-Jews" and Jews living in "mixed marriages" remained in Alsace. As early as 15 August 1940, Wagner announced in the regional newspaper—the recently "synchronized" *Strasburger Neuesten Nachrichten*—that "Alsace is cleansed of Jews"[47] (see figure 12.1).

In many small rural Jewish communities, the deportations probably proceeded as follows. In Hirsingue (Hirsingen) in the Sundgau (Haut-Rhin) on 15 July 1940, German soldiers visited every Jewish home in order to summon all of the Jews. At the town hall, the summoned individuals learned that they had one hour to pack. Soon thereafter, the Jews were shipped off in a truck. The deportees spent the night in the Altkirch barracks, which evidently constituted a collection point. On the next day, the Germans transported them to Dole in the French department of Jura. The conditions of the deportation were severe, especially since most of the deported Jews consisted of elderly and sick individuals. In the district of the Lower Rhine (Bas-Rhin), the town mayors often informed the Jews twenty-four hours in advance of what awaited them the following day. They were allowed to bring 5,000 francs with them and were brought to Schirmeck by bus. All of this occurred very chaotically.[48]

After the announcement of the deportation, a few families who were in a position to do so had left the area immediately with as many of their possessions as possible. But this required a vehicle. Léon Dreyfus, fourteen years old at the time, lived with his mother in Benfeld. He recalled that the chairman of the town's small Jewish community came and informed the handful of Jews still remaining in Benfeld about the deportation. Mrs. Dreyfus managed to rent a small truck and, on 14 July, move with her son and a small portion of her household goods to Saint-Dié-des-Vosges (Sankt Didel) in the Vosges.[49] The French administration recognized the Jews as Alsatian refugees, granting them a subsistence allowance that was not repealed until summer 1943. A few hundred were transferred to Lons-le-Saunier in a convoy of freight trucks.[50]

The deportation on 15 July 1940 directly resulted in Bürckel's decision one month later to deport the Jews from annexed Lorraine as well. However, not very many Jews still lived in this region, either. Almost no witness reports are available for this operation, which was supposedly even more brutal than the one in Alsace in July. Along with more than 40,000 French persons, at least a few hundred Jews were exiled to "inner" France, controlled by the military administration.[51] Gauleiter Bürckel organized four deportation waves. The first one indeed took place in mid July, the second on 16 August, the third in mid September, and the last one, symbolically, on 11 November. The Jews were expelled in the second wave, on 16 August.[52] One victim of expulsion was Marcel Halphen, who had lived in Bionville.[53]

Against the background of Hitler's approval, the "successful" deportation of the Jews from Alsace and Lorraine, and the absence of any international protests, Wagner and Bürckel now also recommended deporting those Jews living in the German parts of their NSDAP Gaue, namely, Baden and the Saar-Palatinate. The deportation of the Jews from Baden, Saarland, and the Palatinate was controlled and carefully prepared by the Reich Security Main Office (Reichssicherheitshauptamt). On the morning of 22 October 1940, German police arrested all of the Jews in this border region. On 22 and 23 October, the authorities deported them in nine trains to the non-occupied zone of France.[54]

Nonetheless, this deportation did not run as smoothly as those in the annexed territories. Adolf Eichmann, the Reich Security Main Office's deportation specialist, waited in Chalon-sur-Saône at the demarcation line marking the border between occupied and unoccupied France to ensure that the trains were not stopped by the French police. Believing that these convoys carried more deported Alsatians, the French authorities allowed them to pass. When they became aware of their mistake, they ordered the internment of the Jews from Baden, Saarland, the Palatinate in camps in southwestern France that had been erected in order to confine republican Spanish fighters and—after the declaration of war in 1939—Germans and Austrians.[55] These measures brought large numbers of German Jews—6,500 from Baden, Saarland, and the Palatinate—to the Gurs internment camp in the Pyrenees, near the small town of Oloron-Sainte-Marie.[56] In January 1941, French authorities transferred more than 3,000 to the Rivesaltes camp in the western Pyrenees, near Perpignan.[57]

The Vichy government energetically protested the deception in the Jewish matter, but not through the official channels typically used throughout the occupation period. Rather, it conveyed its protests through the delegation of the German-French cease-fire commission, headquartered in Wiesbaden.[58] In addition, French police at the demarcation line now refused to allow trains carrying deported Jews to pass, such as a transport from Luxemburg on 14 November 1940.[59] According to an anonymous report sent to the German Foreign Office, preparations had also been made to deport the Hessian Jews to the West, but Vichy's determined opposition on the matter of deported Jews prevented this plan from being realized.[60]

The German Jews remained in the camps until August 1942. Numerous children were handed over to Jewish organizations such as the Œuvre de secours aux enfants (a Jewish children's aid organization; OSE) and in this way liberated. In August 1942, the French facilities served as "collection camps" for the "Final Solution." Pierre Laval's government surrendered all of the interned foreign Jews. The Gestapo brought them to Drancy and from there deported them to Auschwitz.[61]

According to German sources, from a total of 23,790 persons deported from Alsace and Lorraine in summer 1940, 3,259 were Jews. The same source states more precisely that 71,537 were evacuated into the interior of France and that Alsatians who fled during the French collapse—among them 17,875 Jews—were not permitted to return, since they fell into one of the categories of persecuted persons. Together with the abovementioned Jews, 2,381 persons living in "mixed marriages" were deported, although the sources do not reveal whether they were Jews or "Frenchmen." The evacuees also included 1,797 citizens of hostile countries, 672 "gypsies," 738 alcoholics and prostitutes, 171 "professional criminals," and 161 homosexuals.[62]

By February 1941, 95,327 individuals from all categories of persecuted persons had been expelled from Alsace and at least 200,000 from Moselle, emptying this latter region of almost half of its inhabitants. In fact, the southern part of Moselle, formerly French-speaking, became a region for German colonization. The Ostland organization (Ostdeutsche Landbewirtschaftungsgesellschaft)[63] began actively developing German settlements in Lorraine as well as in parts of the neighboring, occupied departments (especially in the Ardennes). The deportations continued until at least 1943, though with diminishing frequency. Many of the Alsatians threatened by Nazi policies or increasingly hostile toward Germanization attempted to flee the region by way of Switzerland or France.[64]

The confiscation of all the deportees' property enabled Robert Wagner and his administration to expand their authority to the entire Alsace. As indicated clearly by an ordinance from 13 July 1940,[65] they took a radical approach, unrestricted by any contingencies, one that only depended on deporting the owners, regardless of whether they were Jews or non-Jews.[66] A number of offices in the Civil Administration organized the transfer of possessions: the Plenipotentiary for Assets Hostile to the People and Reich (Generalbevollmächtigter für das volks- und reichsfeindliche Vermögen), an office held by Regierungsrat (Government Councilor) Späth; the War Damages Office at the Reich Governor's Office (Kriegsschadensamt bei der Reichsstatthalterei), run by Oberbaurat (Senior Building Officer) Feldmann. The NSDAP Kreisleiter (district leaders) also played a role here.[67] The Civil Administration appointed temporary administrators for companies and real estate that were declared to be assets hostile to the *Volk* and the Reich. Furnishings were removed from residences and distributed to German and National Socialist establishments setting themselves up in Alsace and to people who had suffered damages in the war. Some of the furnishings were sold at auctions, which frequently took place directly on the sidewalk in front of the emptied buildings, similar to what later happened in some parts of Germany after the Nazis deported the Jews to the East. Stores were sold off, but important companies were simply placed at the disposal of large German companies, whereby the Head of the Civil Administration made an effort to favor companies from Baden. Only rarely were companies sold or liquidated.[68]

During the course of 1942, the fate of the confiscated possessions drew the attention of the Reich Finance Ministry, which wanted to unify the management of these assets for Alsace, Lorraine, and Luxemburg and above all to organize their transfer to the Old Reich. For this purpose, the ministry held a conference in Berlin on 16 February 1942, where representatives of the three Heads of the Civil Administrations explained to those responsible in the finance ministry that the plunder in each region was organized differently.[69] In Lorraine, for example, the Civil Administrations did not have any actual power of disposition over the possessions; rather, the assets were simply placed under receivership administration for the benefit of the Gauleitung. Whereas the authorities in Lorraine treated the possessions plundered from the Jews as enemy assets, Luxemburg and Alsace had new laws that stipulated the expropriation of all Jews and the liquidation of their property.[70] Thus significant legal differences prevailed between the treatment of Jewish properties in Alsace and in Lorraine. But in actual fact, the practical differences turned out to be only minimal, for in both Alsace and Lorraine the Civil Administrations retained control of the looted properties and did not sell them to new owners.[71]

The deportation of the Alsatian Jews on 15 and 16 July 1940 involved a radical and brutal operation. As evident from the files of the Stillhaltekommissar (Liquidation Commissar), the authorities confiscated their property without major complications, quickly and unhampered by any cumbersome administrative procedures. Subsequently, they sought to eliminate all traces of Jewish life in the region. The names of Jewish soldiers in German uniforms who fell in the First World War were removed from war memorials. Dozens of small rural cemeteries also bore witness to the roots of Jewish communities in the area. But even though the Civil Administration opened a file on this matter, it strangely decided not to take any action because of a French law from the revolutionary period that prohibited any infringement of cemeteries for twenty years following their decommissioning.[72] An important symbol of Jewish life succumbed to an act of arson perpetrated by a squad of Hitler Youth in the night from 30 September to 1 October, namely, the large Synagogue of Quai Kléber in Strasbourg, which had been constructed at the end of the nineteenth century according to plans drawn by Ludwig Levy, an architect from Baden Baden.[73] The Head of the Civil Administration negotiated an arrangement with Strasbourg's municipal administration to tear down the destroyed building; a local company received the contract for job.[74] The synagogues of Wissembourg (Weißenburg), Grussenheim (Grüssa), Biesheim, Hastatt, and Thionville (Diedenhofen) in Lorraine were also completely destroyed. Overall, this wave of destruction struck the annexed parts of Lorraine far more severely. Of the forty-two synagogues that existed in Lorraine before the war, twelve were systematically destroyed,[75] including the synagogues of Bionville (Bingen), set ablaze in October 1940, Niedervisse,[76] and Boulay (Bolchen). Delme's synagogue, built in an oriental style, was also destroyed, along with numerous Jewish cemeteries.[77] In contrast, dozens of smaller rural synagogues were admittedly desecrated but not torn down.[78]

The extent to which the National Socialist *Gleichschaltung* gripped the population of Alsace and Lorraine is difficult to determine. Hitler's decision—upon Wagner's request in August 1942—to conscript Alsatian men into the Wehrmacht came as a shock to most of these men, many of whom faced severe punishments for their efforts to escape this coercive measure, some condemned to death. On the other hand, the brutal practices of Germanization and ethnic cleansing undertaken in the region—which was deemed recalcitrant—since June 1940 helped develop the policies of the National Socialist *Volksgemeinschaft*. Two events symbolized this German success: the construction of the Natzweiler-Struthof concentration camp in the Alsatian part of the Vosges, and the founding of a skeleton collection in the Reich University of Strasbourg, reopened in 1941 with German professors.[79] One of the Germans appointed to the Reich University, Professor August Hirt, is gruesomely remembered for the human skeleton collection he started. Eighty-six Jews, including thirty women, had been selected for him in Auschwitz and sent to Struthof in August 1943. They had all been murdered in the small gas chamber located outside the camp and their bodies sent to the anatomical institute of the university in Strasbourg.[80] The SS brought a total of 46,000 prisoners—predominantly non-Jewish men—to the Natzweiler concentration camp, officially opened on 1 May 1941.[81] Later, the camp had more than eighty satellite camps, which also held Jewish prisoners, on both sides of the Rhine.[82]

Main sites of martyrdom in Lorraine included the camps of Ecrouves[83] near Nancy as well the Fort de Queuleu in Metz.[84] Few Jews were arrested in Moselle itself, as most of them had been expelled in 1940; they were arrested in other regions of France. Only eight Jews are said to have been arrested in Moselle, from where they were transferred to Drancy, then to Auschwitz.

Once deported, the Jews from Alsace-Lorraine suffered the same fate as the other Jews in occupied France. However, representing 15 percent of the total Jewish population of Alsace and Lorraine, the number of these deportees was proportionally smaller than for France as a whole, where the deportees represented 25 percent of the Jewish population.[85] Fifteen percent of the Alsatian Jews were presumably murdered (2,464 deportees came from the Bas-Rhin[86] and 1,100 from the Haut-Rhin[87]). Deportees constituted a much higher percentage of the Jews from Moselle. Recent research indicates that 2,783 Jews were deported from Moselle,[88] corresponding to approximately 30 percent, but we cannot rely on the 1936 census figure of 8,513 for the region's Jewish population as a whole because many foreign Jews had emigrated to Metz in the years just before the war. Indeed, this discrepancy regarding the proportion of the Jewish population that was deported can be explained by the higher percentage of foreign Jews among the Jewish population of Lorraine (compared to Alsace). Older research provides some statistics: 42 percent of these Jews were born in Moselle, 9 percent in Alsace, 10 percent in Germany, and 33 percent in another country. Those Jews originally from Moselle and dispersed throughout France by the successive expulsions were arrested in their respective places of exile—such arrests occurred in 55 different French departments.[89]

A number of reasons explain why the percentage of deportees in Alsace and Lorraine was comparatively low. First, the Jews from these regions had fewer illusions about Nazi anti-Semitism than did Jews in the rest of France—the three departments had already been exposed to National Socialist propaganda in the 1930s. As French citizens, the Jews from Alsace and Lorraine also largely escaped the arrests of the Vichy regime, which primarily surrendered foreign Jews to the Germans.[90]

Conclusion

The example of Alsace (and to a lesser extent Lorraine) demonstrates how quickly the Nazis could introduce and intensify anti-Jewish policies after annexing a territory. Shocked by defeat and expulsions, the region's population was incapable of reacting. In addition, this example illustrates how new radical policy directives—in this case the deportation of the Jews to the West—were transferred by Head of the Civil Administration Wager (who also served simultaneously as the Reich Governor and Gauleiter of Baden) to the territory of the Old Reich. We can also see how other Heads of the Civil Administrations—Bürckel in Lorraine and Gustav Simon in Luxemburg—followed Wagner's initiatives.

As a result of the expulsions, the authorities in Alsace encountered no obstacles when ruthlessly confiscating Jewish assets. The German administrations were able to redistribute the assets locally themselves, much more easily than in the Reich or France, where countless ordinances and competing bureaucrats complicated the "Aryanization" process. After the Nazis either expelled or deported the Jews, they intended to Germanize the region according to the criteria of the *Volksgemeinschaft*. Based on historical experience and a view of the Alsatians shaped by racist reservations, their efforts, however, were informed by an intense suspicion toward the population; the Alsatians were not deemed to be fully German and therefore had to be "reeducated." The Wehrmacht's massive losses on the Eastern Front accelerated this policy. All Alsatians remaining in the region were forced to accept German citizenship on 25 August 1942, which resulted in their conscription to provide military service in the Wehrmacht.

An overall assessment of the annexation and Germanization is difficult to make. Commemorative reconstructions during the postwar period have impeded an objective analysis of the successes and failures of Nazi policy in Alsace and Lorraine—and, in part, they still do so today. For French governments, the three departments had formed symbolic *Remparts français sur le Rhin* (French ramparts on the Rhine), to cite the title of an Alsatian publication from the postwar period,[91] and the Germanized population has been viewed as a victim of Hitler's Germany. Meanwhile, nostalgic voices surfaced among the Germans as, one after another, the leading autonomist politicians who had fled to Germany published books with their view of history.[92] Yet they failed to describe the reality of *Volkstum* (ethnic-nationalist) policies, ethnic cleansing, and the persecution of the Jews.

After the end of the war, the French administration was unable to conduct an ideological purge, since the Alsatians were deemed to be loyal Frenchmen. The purge in Alsace-Lorraine occurred on the same basis as it did throughout the rest of the country, remaining purely political in nature. It seems somewhat paradoxical that Jews who had survived outside the region returned again to Alsace and Lorraine to the towns and villages that they were forced to leave in 1939 and 1940. Yet they re-created their rural religious communities in the region, almost the only ones of their kind in Europe after the Shoah. These communities continued to exist into the 1970s, when an exodus to the cities finally made them obsolete.

The lack of discussion of the Alsatians' behavior at the end of the 1930s and above all in 1940 during the period of the expulsions and plundering of assets in France fostered a latent and suppressed unease. Today, Jewish families still recall finding their furniture and their children's toys in the homes of their non-Jewish neighbors. The fact that official commemorations of the Holocaust and the construction of Holocaust memorials began even later in Alsace than on the German side of the Rhine did not diminish this problem. Quite the opposite.[93]

Notes

1. Elie Scheid, *Histoire des Juifs d'Alsace* (Paris, 1887).
2. Nathan Netter, *Vingt siècles d'histoire d'une communauté juive (Metz et son grand passé)* (Paris, 1938) (Nathan Netter was the Lorraine Chief Rabbi before the Second World War); Pierre-André Meyer, *La Communauté juive de Metz au XVIIIe siècle* (Metz, 1993).
3. Paula Hyman, *The Emancipation of the Jews of Alsace: Acculturation and Tradition in the Nineteenth Century* (London, 1991).
4. On the Jews during the period when the region belonged to the German Reich, see Vicki Caron, *Between France and Germany: The Jews of Alsace-Lorraine, 1871–1918* (Stanford, CA, 1988).
5. Netter, *Vingt siècles d'histoire d'une communauté juive*.
6. See Jean-Marie Mayeur, *Autonomie et politique en Alsace: La Constitution de 1911* (Paris, 1970).
7. On the expulsion between 1918 and 1921 of 75 percent of the Germans living in Alsace and Lorraine, see François Überfill, *La société strasbourgeoise entre France et Allemagne (1871–1924)* (Strasbourg, 2001); Christiane Kohser-Spohn, "Die Vertreibung der Deutschen aus dem Elsass 1918–1920," in *Die "Volksdeutschen" in Polen, Frankreich, Ungarn und der Tschechoslowakei. Mythos und Realität*, ed. Jerzy Kochanowski and Maike Sach (Osnabrück, 2006), 79–94.
8. On these associations, see Irmgard Grünewald, *Die Elsass-Lothringer im Reich, 1918–1933: Ihre Organisationen zwischen Integration und "Kampf um die Seele der Heimat,"* (Frankfurt, 1984); on the whereabouts of the its library after 1945, see Jean-Marc Dreyfus, "Un symbole disputé: la bibliothèque de l'Institut scientifique des Alsaciens-Lorrains à Francfort après la Seconde Guerre mondiale," *Revue d'Allemagne et des pays de langue allemande* 36, no. 3/4 (2004): 384–389.
9. Mayeur, *Autonomie et politique*.
10. François-Georges Dreyfus, *La vie politique en Alsace 1919–1936* (Paris, 1969), 90ff.

11. Christian Baechler, "Ricklin, Eugène," in *Dictionnaire du monde religieux dans la France contemporaine*, vol. 2: *L'Alsace*, ed. Jean-Marie Mayeur and Yves-Marie Hilaire (Paris, 1987), 360f.
12. On the long career of Camille Dahlet (1883–1963), see Pierre Klein, *Camille Dahlet: Une vie au service de l'Alsace* (Strasbourg, 1983).
13. On René Schickelé, see for example Adrien Finck, *René Schickelé* (Strasbourg, 1999).
14. He gave his speech on 7 February 1929; see Stefan Fisch, "Goethe, Bebel und Zola: Lehr- und Wanderjahre des Straßburger Sozialisten Jacques Peirotes (1869–1935) im katholischen Europa," in *Grenzregionen im Zeitalter der Nationalismen. Elsaß-Lothringen/Trient-Triest, 1870–1914*, ed. Angelo Ara and Eberhard Kolb (Berlin, 1998), 201–226, here 204.
15. Edmond Vermeil, "L'autonomisme alsacien et ses horizons européens," *L'Alsace Française*, 27 March 1926.
16. F.-G. Dreyfus, *Vie politique*, 133.
17. On this, see Chantal Metzger, "Relations entre autonomistes lorrains et alsaciens de 1919 à 1932," in *La Lorraine de 1610 à nos jours*, vol. 2: *Questions diverses, Congrès National des sociétés savantes*, (Nancy, 1979), 156–170.
18. In 1928/29, this method was used to distribute 280,000 RM to the Alsace's various autonomist movements; Philip Charles Bankwitz, *Alsatian Autonomist Leaders, 1919–1947* (Lawrence, KS, 1978), 29.
19. Ibid., 52.
20. On Spieser, see Leo Strauss, "Fritz Spieser, le reconstructeur de la Burg," in *Hunebourg, un rocher chargé d'histoire: Du Moyen Âge à l'époque contemporaine*, ed. G. Barnagaud (Strasbourg, 1997), 121–154; Heinz-Dietrich Loock, "Der Hüneburg-Verlag: Friedrich Spieser und der Nationalsozialismus," in *Gutachten des Instituts für Zeitgeschichte*, vol. 2, (Stuttgart, 1966), 399–447.
21. Francis Arzalier, *Les perdants: La dérive fasciste des mouvements autonomistes et indépendantistes au XXe siècle* (Paris, 1990), 57.
22. See, for example, Friedrich Spieser, *Das Elsass: Schönes deutsches Land am Oberrhein*, with a preface by Dr. Robert Ernst, published by the Deutschens Ausland-Institut (Stuttgart, 1942), 10:

    > When the distress of the pressured *Volkstum* had reached its highest level and the French were turning the Alsace into a military glacis, interspersing the lovely meadows with bunkers, hassling the peaceful Alsatian population with spies, and finally deporting hundreds of thousands to southern European [*welsche*] desolation, jailing, expelling, or as with Karl Roos, shooting their leaders, economically and spiritually reducing the land and finally leading it to war against the German brothers, then the incomparable German Wehrmacht under Adolf Hitler's ingenious leadership became Alsace's savior in the hour of need. On 19 June 1940, the swastika flag flew over the over the miraculously preserved, old, and now free again German imperial city for the first time.

23. Jean-Claure Bonnefont, *Histoire de la Lorraine de 1900 à nos jours* (Toulouse, 1979), 128.
24. On the minor role of small Jewish banks in Alsace, see Jean-Marc Dreyfus, *Pillages sur ordonnances: Aryanisation et restitution des banques en France 1940–1953* (Paris, 2003), 34ff.
25. Eric Kurlander, *The Price of Exclusion: Ethnicity, National Identity, and the Decline of German Liberalism, 1898–1933* (Oxford, 2006), 137ff.

26. Samuel Huston Goodfellow, *Between the Swastika and the Cross of Lorraine: Fascisms in Interwar Alsace* (DeKalb, IL, 1998), 86ff. This book provide the most complete description of the populist, pro-French, or pro-German movement in Alsace between the wars, yet the author's use of term "fascist" should be viewed cautiously.
27. See the example of the Weill-Samuel family from Wasselone (Wasselnheim), in Jean Samuel and Jean-Marc Dreyfus, *Il m'appelait Pikolo: Un compagnon de Primo Levi raconte* (Paris, 2007), 45.
28. The census of 1936 resulted in the figure of 20,684, but reporting one's religious affiliation was voluntary. See Léo Strauss, "Exil, exclusion, extermination. Les juifs alsaciens en zone sud," in "La Guerre totale, 1943," special issue, *Saisons d'Alsace* 121 (Fall 1993): 183ff.
29. Kurlander, *The Price of Exclusion*, 291ff.
30. Lothar Kettenacker, *Nationalsozialistische Volkstumspolitik im Elsass* (Stuttgart, 1973), 45ff.
31. They were Bickler, Mourrer, Huber, Rossé, Stürmel, Bieber, Brauner, Hauss, Keppi, Lang, Lefftz, Meyer, Schall and Schlegel. Victor Antoni was also interned in Nancy.
32. Bankwitz, *Autonomist Leaders*, 68.
33. François-Georges Dreyfus, *Histoire de l'Alsace* (Toulouse, 1984), 332.
34. For example, the Weill-Samuel family from Wasselone; see Samuel and J.-M. Dreyfus, *Il m'appelait Pikolo*, 123ff.
35. The decree is published neither in the Reichsgesetzblatt nor in *"Führer-Erlasse" 1939–1945: Edition sämtlicher überlieferter, nicht im Reichsgesetzblatt abgedruckter, von Hitler während des Zweiten Weltkriegs schriftlich erteilter Direktiven aus den Bereichen Staat, Partei, Wirtschaft, Besatzungspolitik und Militärverwaltung*, compiled and introduced by Martin Moll (Stuttgart, 1997). The latter, however, includes Hitler's decree of 2 August 1940 "on the provisional administration in Alsace and Lorraine," which designates Wagner and Bürckel as the persons responsible for the entire administration in the civil sector. They received their orders directly from Hitler. Accordingly, the army's supreme commanders now exercised only military authority. Their ordinances, however, took precedence over the directives of the Reich's supreme state authorities, provided they were necessary to carry out military assignments. *"Führer-Erlasse" 1939–1945*, 131f. (doc. 44).
36. Kettenacker, *Volkstumspolitik*, 53.
37. Robert Ernst, *Rechenschaftsbericht eines Elsässers* (Berlin, 1954).
38. Arzalier, *Les perdants*, 101. Bickler came to France in 1943, after he had joined the SS and the SD. He directed the SD's Office VI (counter espionage) in France and created a training center for National Socialist cadres in Vaucelles, in Normandy. He escaped punishment after the war, dying in Italy in 1984 as a wealthy businessman.
39. See the very long memoir he published in 1957 (self-published), in German, *Grenzlandschicksal, Grenzlandtragik: Lebenserinnerungen und menschliche Betrachtungen eines Lothringers zu den politischen Irrungen und Wirrungen seiner Zeit* (Fénétrange, 1957).
40. Marcel Neigert, *Internement et déportation en Moselle, 1940–1945* (Metz, 1978), 9.
41. The best description of Germanization policies in Alsace is still Kettenacker, *Volkstumspolitik*.
42. On the Germanization of Loraine, see Dieter Wolfanger, "Die nationalsozialistische Politik in Lothringen, 1940–1945," (diss., Universität des Saarlandes, Saarbrücken, 1977). See also Eugène Heiser, *La tragédie Lorraine*, vol. 1:

Sarreguemines-Saargmünd, vol. 2: *Ecartelés au quatre vents: Documents et témoignages* (Sarreguemines, 1978–1979).

43. Léon Sidot, *L'identité française dans la Lorraine annexée et nazifiée: Une logique de l'être* (Gourdon, 1996), 125. As opponents to Germanization, the members of Sidot family were ultimately resettled in the Sudeten region. They were among the 9,337 people from Lorraine who were transported to Silesia or the Sudeten region.
44. Simon Schwarzfuchs, *Le 15 juillet 1940: La dernière expulsion des Juifs d'Alsace*, webpage of *judaïsme alsacien* (Judaism of Alsace), http://judaisme.sdv.fr/histoire/shh/expuls/exp1.htm (accessed 17 March 2010).
45. Bernard Le Marec and Gérard Le Marec, *Les années noires; la Moselle annexée par Hitler: documents et témoignages* (Metz, 1990), 96.
46. The ordinance was not published in the Civil Administration's regulatory gazette. It stated:

> I) To deprive assets serving endeavors hostile to the Volk and Reich of any use for these purposes, these assets shall be confiscated for the benefit of the Reich. Assets hostile to the Volk and the Reich can therefore no longer legally be used. II) Assets hostile to the Volk and the Reich are all things and rights of any kind, without regard to conditions of ownership, which are used and intended to support endeavors hostile to the Volk and the Reich. This includes the total assets of: a) all political parties as well as their auxiliary, relief and substitute organizations, b) the lodges and associations similar to lodges, c) the Jews, d) the French who acquired assets in Alsace after 11 November 1918, e) the members of the other hostile states . . .

47. Announcement: "Elsass ist judenrein," *Straßburger Neueste Nachrichten*, 15 August 1940.
48. The most comprehensive account thus far appears to be the work by Simon Schwarzfuchs, published on the Internet. The text was composed on the basis of accounts by contemporary witnesses that were collected after an invitation issued on the webpage, *Le 15 juillet 1940*.
49. Author's interview with Léon Dreyfus, La Baule, 4 August 2008.
50. Schwarzfuchs, *Le 15 juillet 1940*.
51. Ibid.
52. Neigert, *Internement*, 13.
53. Marcel Halphen survived the war and returned to Bionville. He was then elected mayor of the village.
54. On these deportations, see *Dokumente über die Verfolgung der jüdischen Bürger in Baden-Württemberg durch das nationalsozialistische Regime 1933–1945*, vol. 2, ed. Paul Sauer (Stuttgart, 1966); Gerhard J. Teschner, *Die Deportation der badischen und saarpfälzischen Juden am 22. Oktober 1940: Vorgeschichte und Durchführung der Deportation und das weitere Schicksal der Deportierten bis zum Kriegsende im Kontext der deutschen und französischen Judenpolitik* (Frankfurt, 2002); Wolf Gruner, "Von der Kollektivausweisung zur Deportation der Juden aus Deutschland (1938–1945): Neue Perspektiven und Dokumente," in *Die Deportation der Juden aus Deutschland. Pläne, Praxis, Reaktionen 1938–1945*, ed. Birthe Kundrus and Beate Meyer, Beiträge zur Geschichte des Nationalsozialismus, vol. 20 (Göttingen, 2004), 21–62.
55. On the French internment camps, see Anne Grynberg, *Les camps de la honte: Les internés juifs des camps français 1939–1944* (Paris, 1991); Denis Peschanski, *La France des camps: L'internement, 1938–1946* (Paris, 2002).

56. On the Gurs internment camp, see Claude Laharie, *Le camp de Gurs: Un aspect méconnu de l'histoire du Béarn* (Pau, 1985); and on the arrival of the Jews from Baden, Saarland and the Palatinate, see Laharie, *Le camp de Gurs*, 122ff.
57. On Rivesaltes, see Anne Boitel, *Le camp de Rivesaltes 1941–1942: Du centre d'hébergement au "Drancy de la zone libre"* (Perpignan, 2000).
58. See the German edition in *Dokumente über die Verfolgung der jüdischen Bürger in Baden-Württemberg*, 241.
59. Christopher R. Browning, *The Origins of the Final Solution: The Evolution of Nazi Jewish Policy, September 1939–March 1942* (Lincoln, NE, 2004), 92.
60. Ibid., 91.
61. Serge Klarsfeld, *Les transferts de Juifs du camp de Rivesaltes et de la région de Montpellier vers le camp de Drancy en vue de leur déportation, 10 août 1942–6 août 1944* (Paris, 1993).
62. Browning provides the only exact figures regarding the deportation of Jews from Alsace-Lorraine. For Lorraine he cites the Nuremberg document NO-5150, for Alsace the files of NSDAP Party Chancellery, microfilm 101 23 821f.; Browning, *Origins*, 90.
63. Cf. Jacques Mièvre, "L' 'Ostland' en France durant la Seconde Guerre mondiale: une tentative de colonisation agraire allemande en zone interdite," *Annales de l'Est*, no. 46 (1973): 163.
64. Report of the CdZ in Alsace to the deputy of the Führers, Reichsleiter Martin Bormann, 22 April 1941, cited in Bankwitz, *Autonomist Leaders*, 77.
65. See the text of the ordinance in note 46.
66. On the policy of plunder in annexed Alsace, see J.-M. Dreyfus, *Pillages sur ordonnances*, 42ff. Expropriating the assets of deported Jews according to the eleventh ordinance on the Reich Citizenship Law only became possible as of 25 November 1941; RGBl. 1941 I, 722.
67. The files have survived and were turned over to the Service francais de Restitution. They are kept in series AD63 of Archives départementales du Bas-Rhin, Strasbourg (AdBR).
68. For the banks, see J.-M. Dreyfus, *Pillages*, 40ff.
69. Copy of the protocol of the meeting from 16 February 1942, cited in *La spoliation des biens Juifs au Luxembourg 1940–1945*, Rapport final, Commission spéciale pour l'étude des spoliations des biens juifs au Luxembourg pendant les années de guerre 1940–1945 (Luxemburg, 19 June 2009), 28; published only on the Internet at http://www.gouvernement.lu/salle_presse/communiques/2009/07-juillet/06-biens-juifs/rapport_final.pdf (accessed 18 October 2009); Nationalarchiv, Großherzogtum Luxemburg, CdZ, A-0-1/593:0001–0002.
70. The most important ordinances in Luxemburg were: Ordinance Regarding Jewish Assets in Luxembourg of 5 September 1940, *Verordnungsblatt für Luxemburg*, published by the CdZ in Luxemburg (VOBl. L.), (1940), 11–13; Ordinance Concerning Measures Pertaining to Emigrant and Jewish Assets of 7 February 1941, VOBl. L. (1941), 90. In Alsace, a range of ordinances determined the various confiscation measures, most importantly the Fourth Order Regarding the Implementation and Supplementation of the Order Regarding Assets Hostile to the People and Reich of 4 April 1941, *Verordnungsblatt für das Elsass*, published by the CdZ im Elsass (VOBl. E.), no. 26, (6 August 1941), 493f.; Ordinance regarding the Assumption and Utilization of French Assets in Alsace of 1 December 1941, VOBl. E., no. 41 (3 December 1941), 711; Ordinance on the Return of Refugees to Alsace of 20 April 1942, VOBl. E., no. 15, (22 May 1942), 166. In Lorraine, the specific ordinances were published in the Bulletin for Lorraine (Verordnungsblatt für Lothringen, VBL):

Ordinance on the Registration of Assets Hostile to the People and Reich in Lorraine of 6 November 1940, VBL (18 November 1940), 200; Second Ordinance regarding the Registration of Assets Hostile to the People and Reich in Lorraine of 17 August 1941, VBL (3 September 1931), 763; Ordinance on the Assumption and Utilization of French Assets in Lorraine of 1 December 1941, VBL (8 December 1941), 1043. After the war, all of the texts were translated into French and published in Paris: *Recueil des principaux textes allemands appliqués en Alsace et en Lorraine pendant l'occupation (1940–1944)*, 2 vols. (Paris, n.d.).

71. On this topic, see Joanna Linsler, "La spécificité de l'Alsace-Moselle sous occupation allemande," in "Spoliations: Nouvelles recherches," special issue, *Les Cahiers du Judaïsme* 27 (December 2009): 80–95.
72. "Jüdische Friedhöfe im Elsass," AdBR, 126 AL 121.
73. On Strasbourg's large synagogue and its destruction, see Jean Daltroff, *1898–1940: La synagogue consistoriale de Strasbourg* (Strasbourg, 1996).
74. Letter from the Strasbourg city commissioner to the CdZ, administration and police division, Strasbourg, from 2 October 1940, regarding the demolition of the synagogue in Strasbourg, AdBR, 126AL 2844.
75. See *Le Martyrologe des Juifs de la Moselle 1939–1945*, ed. Consistoire israélite de la Moselle, prefaces by Armand Roseneck and Robert Hayem, notes by Jacques Bloch (Metz, 1999).
76. Jean Daltroff, *Les Juifs de Niedervisse. Naissance, épanouissement et déclin d'une communauté*, self-published, (Strasbourg, 1992), 85–97.
77. Gilbert Cahen, "Pour un martyrologue des Juifs mosellans," in "Moselle et Mosellans dans la Seconde Guerre mondiale," ed. François–Yves Lemoigne, special issue, *Les Cahiers Lorrains* 4 (1983): 265–272.
78. Max Warschawski, "Histoire récente et histoire à venir: l'entre-deux guerres, la guerre, la reconstruction de la communauté, les Juifs d'Europe," in *Regards sur la culture judéo-alsacienne: Des identités en partage*, ed. Freddy Raphaël (Strasbourg, 2001), 175.
79. Robert Steegmann, *Das KZ Natzweiler-Struthof und seine Außenkommandos an Rhein und Neckar 1941–1945* (Berlin, 2010) (original edition: Strasbourg, 2005).
80. Frederik Kasten, "Unethical Nazi Medicine in Annexed Alsace-Lorraine: The Strange Case of Nazi Anatomist Professor Dr. August Hirt," in *Historian and Archivists: Essays in Modern German History and Archival Policy*, ed. George O. Kent (Fairfax, 1991), 170–208; Hans-Joachim Lang, *Die Namen der Nummern: Wie es gelang, die 86 Opfer eines NS-Verbrechens zu identifizieren* (Hamburg, 2004); *Le camp de concentration de Struthof (Bas-Rhin) et l'activité de l'Institut d'Anatomie de Strasbourg pendant l'occupation*, Notes et études documentaires, vol. 140 (Paris, 1950).
81. Kristian Ottosen, *Nuit et brouillard: Histoire des prisonniers du camp de Natzweiler-Struthof* (Brussels, 1994), 56.
82. Steegmann, *Struthof*.
83. On Ecrouves, see Françoise Job, *La déportation des Juifs de Lorraine: Le camp d'internement d'Ecrouves* (Paris, 2004).
84. Philippe Wilmouth and Cédric Neveu, *Les camps d'internement du Fort de Metz-Queuleu, 1943–1946* (Saint-Cyr-sur-Loire, 2011).
85. Jacky Dreyfus and Daniel Fuks, *Le mémorial des Juifs du Haut-Rhin: Martyrs de la Shoah* (Colmar, 2006); René Gutman, *Le Memorbuch: Mémorial de la déportation et de la Résistance des Juifs du Bas-Rhin* (Strasbourg, 2005).
86. Gutman, *Memorbuch*, 15.
87. Dreyfus and Fuks, *Le mémorial*, 12.

88. See the work by Jacques Bloch, *Le martyrologue des Juifs de Moselle* (1998), 75–84, 84: http://documents.irevues.inist.fr/bitstream/handle/2042/33781/ANM_1998_75.pdf?sequence=1, (accessed 31 August 2014). I thank Mr. Bloch for his help in dealing with those figures.
89. Neigert, *Internement*, 49–50.
90. On the statistical difference between the deportation of the French and foreign Jews, see Serge Klarsfeld, *Le calendrier de la persécution des Juifs de France* (Paris, 1993), 1250.
91. Walter Rinckenberger, *L'Alsace, rempart français sur le Rhin* (Paris, 1946).
92. See, for example, Hermann Bickler, *Ein besonderes Land: Erinnerungen und Betrachtungen eines Lothringers* (Lindhorst, 1978).
93. Christiane Kohser-Spohn, "Der Staat in Stein: Die Kriegsdenkmäler im Elsass 1918–1945," in *Wiedergewonnene Geschichte: Zur Aneignung von Vergangenheit in den Zwischenräumen Mitteleuropas*, ed. Peter Oliver Loew et al. (Wiesbaden, 2006), 382–398, here 397. A monument at the site of the destroyed synagogue in Strasbourg was not erected until 1976.

Conclusion
Wolf Gruner and Jörg Osterloh

In his analysis *Lingua Tertii Imperii* published in 1947, the German-Jewish professor for Romanic languages Victor Klemperer—today mostly known for his impressive diary detailing his experiences in the Third Reich—wrote about the propaganda that accompanied the German annexations: "At solemn moments, both positive and negative, blood must of course be called upon. . . . [W]hen Hitler's troops subsequently march into Austria the 'hour of the blood' has finally come. At which point the old Ostmark 'has found its way home to everlasting Germany.'"[1] Behind this supposed voice of the blood, however, stood the tangible interests of power politics and economic policy. As early as 1932, the NSDAP's leadership internally discussed a future *Ostraum*—Eastern Region—policy, the core of which was the vision of a confederation of states in Central Europe. Its heart would beat in a future "Greater Germany," consisting of Germany, Austria, Bohemia and Moravia, as well as western Poland, surrounded by a wreath woven of dependent state-like formations—that is, *Hilfsvölker* (auxiliary nations). But as first became apparent when the Nazis established the Protectorate of Bohemia and Moravia, where only 0.5 percent of the inhabitants considered themselves German, these grand spatial ideas were not so much motivated by population policy but rather primarily based on power politics. The Protectorate revealed what the *Ostraum* policy was all about: the appropriation of land with the goal of "(re)Germanizing" territories proclaimed to be German "linguistic and cultural land."[2]

To be sure, as late as 12 December 1944, Hitler still announced to his Wehrmacht generals that they were fighting for a final solution of the German question in Europe, telling them that the war had the same objective as the wars of unification in the second half of the nineteenth century, namely, the "complete unification of all Germans."[3] The Nazi state, however, went well beyond bringing the so-called Germanic regions "home into the Reich," pursuing a policy of expansion very much intent on conquering "settlement space" for the "German *Volk*." The Nazi regime basically distinguished between settlement areas, on the one hand, and colonial territories slated for economic exploitation—for example, in the occupied Soviet Union—on the other.[4] With regard to the latter, Hitler's interest focused primarily on raw materials and labor.[5] In contrast, for the "Germanization" of the "settlement region," the architects of population and racial policies planned nothing less than the "total displacement" of the endemic "non-German" population and settling the region with Germans. According to their logic, "blood" decided who would be expelled, resettled, or destroyed—a logic that was especially brutally reflected in the *Generalplan Ost* (master plan for the East).[6]

Prior to each annexation, the populations in the Reich's new border regions usually consisted of multiple ethnic groups. The chapters in this volume register a growth in anti-Semitic currents in the various regional populations after 1933, albeit in widely varied forms in the different countries—relatively little in Alsace and Czechoslovakia, but quite substantial in the Sudetenland and the Polish territories. National Socialism strongly shaped the political conditions prior to annexation in the Saarland, Danzig-West Prussia, the Sudetenland, the Memel Territory, and East Upper Silesia. In a few areas—for example, Eupen-Malmedy—the influence of National Socialism helped polarize the population. In other regions, such as Luxembourg, the Nazi movement barely gained a foothold before the annexation. The Warthegau featured numerous individuals who sympathized with the Nazi movement and its anti-Semitism, but most of the region's ethnic Germans—Polish citizens who considered themselves ethnically German—were loyal to the Second Polish Republic. In a few regions, home-grown fascist movements emerged after the First World War, like the Greenshirts (*chemises vertes*) in Alsace and the Aryan Union in the ČSR.[7]

The majority of the German inhabitants ignored the obviously criminal character of the Nazi regime. In Austria as well as Bohemia and Moravia, the desire to "return home into the Reich" eclipsed the worrisome news from Germany. In contrast, the Jews—especially after the

Anschluss of Austria—took the signals from Nazi Germany very seriously, which saved many of their lives. Indeed, each annexation of a neighboring territory taught them that, regardless of their proclaimed national affiliation, the Jews had no place in the emerging *Volksgemeinschaft*. Militias formed—often modeled on the SA and SS—even before each respective *Anschluss* occurred; nothing other than groups of thugs, they terrorized political opponents and the Jewish minority. This mortified Jews all the more, since they had often professed to be nationally German and felt like Germans.[8]

As the chapters in this volume demonstrate, most Jews from territories annexed at later stages therefore fled even before the occupation took place, for example from the Saarland, the Memel Territory, Danzig-West Prussia, Alsace, Luxembourg, and Eupen-Malmedy. They also had directly adjacent escape routes, namely, into France, Czechoslovakia, Poland, or Lithuania. Thus only a few thousand Jews still lived in these aforementioned annexed territories when these territories were integrated into the German Reich. From the Sudetenland, too, many Jewish residents fled along with the Nazis' political opponents. In contrast, only small portions of the extensive Jewish populations in Austria, Bohemia, and Moravia managed to flee, while the 600,000 Jews in the later annexed parts of western Poland had even fewer flight opportunities; surprised by the German invasion, they could not escape to any bordering territories. Thus whereas 90 percent of Saarland's Jewish inhabitants managed to save themselves, 95 percent of the Jews in the later Regierungsbezirk (government district) of Zichenau lost their lives under the Nazi tyranny.[9]

In this connection, the oscillating web of relationships between Reich Germans, Jews, ethnic Germans, and the rest of the population in each respective annexed territory deserves attention. In this regard—with the exception of Saarland and Austria—the respective minority status of the indigenous German ethnic groups prior to the annexation played a crucial role. Against the background of real or in many cases merely perceived oppression, they developed a "circle-the-wagons mentality," and the concept of the *Volksgemeinschaft* gained importance early on.[10] This becomes very clear in the behavior of the Germans after the First World War in the city of Danzig (Gdańsk), the Sudetenland, and Alsace.[11] National Socialism seized on numerous demands of broad parts the German population, such as the revision of the Versailles Treaty and repression of "Jewish influence" in the economy. This allowed conservatives to close ranks with the National Socialists. With regard to an individual's national classification, ethnic Germans everywhere in Europe had increasingly shifted from the principle of personal identification to one of personal lineage[12]—which simultaneously entailed an exclusion of the Jews, who indeed often affirmed their own German nationality.[13] Thus, since Czechs and Poles—among others—frequently perceived the Jews as German, the latter were treated as Germans when fleeing Sudetenland in search of refuge in Czechoslovakia, for example.[14]

The establishment of the Nazi government and its apparent successes after 1933 increased the attraction of National Socialist ideas and the vision of uniting all Germans in a *Volksgemeinschaft*. This concept does not refer here to a "natural" entity but rather to a mental image constructed through processes of inclusion and exclusion.[15] Michael Wildt has pointed out that violence formed a fundamental element of this process. By exercising violence against the group to be excluded, the *Volksgemeinschaft* constituted itself as a community of ostracizing persons.[16] Like the "Greater German Reich," the *Volksgemeinschaft* was imagined as a "racially" homogeneous community of "Aryans."[17] This was reflected in the violent attacks against Jews that occurred after annexation in almost every region—thus in Austria, the Sudetenland, the Protectorate, Alsace, and in the Polish regions—and which always involved the active participation of indigenous Germans—albeit non-Germans as well, to varying degrees. This was compounded by the early mass expulsions carried out by the annexing power, for example in Burgenland (Austria), Alsace, Luxembourg, and the Zichenau (Ciechanów) region.[18]

In order to carry out the targeted expulsions in the annexed territories, above all in the eastern regions, the so-called Einsatzgruppen consisting of Security Police (Sicherheitspolizei) and Security Service (Sicherheitsdienst) personnel moved in immediately behind the Wehrmacht—in 1938 in Austria and the Sudetenland, in 1939 in Bohemia and Moravia, the Memel Territory, and naturally everywhere in Poland, but also in 1940 in the West, for example in Eupen-Malmedy and Luxembourg.[19] Their respective functions and activities—apart from events in Poland—have not yet been sufficiently analyzed.[20]

Thus when examining the first phase of the annexations, the chapters collected here focus on the Security Police and the Security Service, as well as on the previously largely unexamined Heads of the Civil Administration (Chef of the Zivilverwaltung; CdZ) and their roles in the policies of persecution. For the phase of the occupation, the authors investigate the establishment of the Zivilverwaltung, thus also the newly created regionally specific government bodies and institutions, such as the Liquidation Commissar for Associations, Organizations and Societies (Stillhaltekommissar für Vereine, Organisationen und Verbände). They analyze the development of independent persecution policies as well as the introduction (or non-introduction) of laws already in effect in the Reich. The chapters also illustrate that in certain regions and in many sectors the agents of expulsion acted on the basis of specialized knowledge and qualifications.

Incrementally accumulating experience in how to structure persecution policies, some of them transferred their growing expertise from one region to the next. These "specialists" included Josef Bürckel, for example, the Reich Commissioner (Reichskommissar) in the Saarland and Austria, Head of the Civil Administration in both Moravia and Lorraine, and later the Reich Governor (Reichsstatthalter) of the Westmark. This accumulation of persecutory experience by such actors and their concomitant accrual of regional competencies played an essential role in the independent development of Jewish policy in most annexed regions, alongside initiatives of a few non-German protagonists, such as the Czech government in the Protectorate.

In any event, the formal integration of the annexed territories into the Reich by no means followed a standardized scheme: the Saarland's reintegration occurred on the basis of a plebiscite after the expiration of the period stipulated by the Versailles Treaty; the annexations of Austria and the Sudetenland were made legitimate by laws. Berlin created the Protectorate of Bohemia and Moravia as part of the Reich by means of a "Führer decree," but granted the region an autonomous status.[21] The (Czech) government of the Protectorate could enact "its own laws in all fields of law not taken over by the Reich for direct administration"—thus in particular also in Jewish policy. At the same time, the (German) Reich Protector (Reichsprotektor) was given immense flexibility, for he answered directly to Hitler and was not subject to the directives of the Reich authorities. The region's ethnic Germans all became Reich citizens, while non-Germans became *Protektoratsangehörige* (protectorate subjects) with inferior rights.[22] The first signs of the end of the Protectorate's ambiguous constitutional status and its complete assimilation by Reich appeared in 1942, when all Protectorate residents were required to possess a *Kennkarte*, that is, the ID card introduced for general domestic use in the German Reich in 1938.[23]

While the inhabitants of Austria and the Sudetenland obtained *Reichsbürgerschaft* (Reich citizenship) in accordance with the Nuremberg Laws—already applicable in the Reich—shortly after annexation, the inhabitants of Danzig-West Prussia did not receive Reich citizenship until two years later "in accordance with more detailed provisions"; the Reich acted similarly in 1941 in the case of Eupen-Malmedy. The greater part of the population obtained Reich citizenship, while the Jews, Sinti, and Roma, as well as the French, were excluded as they were entitled only to become *Staatsangehörige* (state subjects). Consequently, a two-class citizenship applied here as in the Reich and the Protectorate. In Alsace, Lorraine, and Luxemburg, most people did not receive German citizenship until August 1942.[24]

The racist population hierarchy in the incorporated territories was reflected not only in the discrimination against non-Germans in the economy, labor markets, and social policy, but also in their lack of political rights. During the occupation of the Polish territories, the Einsatzgruppen murdered thousands of members of the Polish intelligentsia and—even at that point—numerous Jews. In addition, the demarcation of a police border in October 1939 in this region was supposed to prevent the uncontrolled migration of *Fremdvölkische*—ethnically foreign elements—into the Old Reich.[25] It existed until the end of the war. The police border deviated significantly from the new state administrative boundaries, and thus expanded the influence of the Reichsführer-SS Heinrich Himmler and created "a second-class Reich territory" (Steinbacher) in the eastern part of East Upper Silesia.

The Warthegau, East Upper Silesia, Danzig-West Prussia, and Northern Mazovia were incorporated into the Reich by means of "Führer decrees" in 1939, as was Eupen-Malmedy in the West one year later. In contrast, Alsace-Lorraine and Luxembourg belonged de facto to the German Reich, but not formally.[26] For example, in November 1940 the Head of the Civil Administration introduced the German municipal code and other parts of Reich legislation to Luxembourg and dissolved all of the endemic institutions.[27] De jure, however, the Heads of the Civil Administrations continued to govern—this in contrast to other integrated and occupied territories, where the Heads of the Civil Administrations had only directed the reorganization of the indigenous institutions and the establishment of occupational authorities during the first weeks of military rule, after which they were replaced by actual German administrations, such as Reich Commissioners or— for regions integrated into Prussia—Regierungspräsidenten (government district presidents). Until the end of the war, Luxembourg, as well as Lower Styria, remained frozen, so to speak, in the first annexation phase, which was usually controlled by the Head of the Civil Administration only until German (occupation) institutions had been established; but this neither halted nor slowed down the Germanization process in these territories.[28]

In both the East and West, the Heads of the Civil Administrations usually came from an adjacent Reich territory, where they often acted as a Reich Governor and/or NSDAP Gauleiter—for instance, Robert Wagner in Baden took over Alsace and Sigfried Uiberreither from the Reichsgau Styria assumed control of Lower Styria. Thus far, fundamental accounts of the Holocaust[29] have not thematized the role of the Heads of the Civil Administrations in developing governments, securing power, and, last but not least, establishing anti-Jewish policy, even though Hans Umbreit had already stressed their importance in 1977.[30] Subordinate to Hitler and/or the Wehrmacht,[31] they were not subject to the directives of the Reich ministries, yet they operated in accordance with the Reich's budget law.[32]

The texts provided here show that the Heads of the Civil Administrations established important personal networks in the process of the annexations. The staff of Josef Bürckel—the Reich Commissioner in the Saarland and Austria and subsequently the Head of the Civil Administration in Moravia—wandered with him from one annexed region to the next, in large part so that they could put the lessons learned in occupation and persecution policy to effective use. The same applied to other institutions of the German occupation, as with Stillhaltekommissar Albert Hoffmann and his personnel, and in part with the Security Police and the Security Service, which sent their most effective officials—Franz Walter Stahlecker and Adolf Eichmann—from the Reich to Vienna and from there to Prague. At the same time, in a number of cases, players changed their positions and functions in the process of the Reich's expansion. Reich Student Leader Gustav Adolf Scheel initially acted as the NSDAP Gauleiter of Salzburg and later as the Inspector for the Security Police and Security Service in Alsace.[33]

With the supersession of the Heads of the Civil Administrations (which were technically part of the military administration), control of the German administrations in the annexed regions was initially—as in Saarland and Austria—assigned to Reich Commissioners, and later to the Reich Governor, or, in the case of the territories allocated to the Prussian provinces, to Regierungspräsidenten; although the Protectorate, under the dual leadership of the Reich Protector and the Czech government, and Luxembourg, which retained an active Head of the Civil Administration until the end of the war, constituted notable exceptions.

On 14 April 1939, Hitler had legislatively granted Reichsgau status to the Sudeten region and the Austrian lands.[34] Simultaneously an administrative district of the Reich and a self-regulating body, each Reichsgau was led by a Reich Governor who directed the state apparatus under the supervision of the Reich Interior Ministry. The Reichsgaue were supposed to symbolize the unity of the party and the state.[35] Reich Governors such as Konrad Henlein in the Sudetenland, Josef Bürckel and later Baldur von Schirach in Austria, and Arthur Greiser in the Warthegau,[36] as well as Oberpräsidenten (upper presidents) such as Fritz Bracht in East Upper Silesia, merged their government offices with their party functions as NSDAP Gauleiter. And this despite the fact that Deputy Führer Rudolf Heß had dissolved the couplings of state and party offices (viewed as impractical for government) in the Old Reich in 1937.[37] Even at lower administrative levels, the occupying authorities frequently installed suitable persons in dual capacities as Landräte (district administrators) and NSDAP Kreisleiter (district leaders).[38] In reaction to such developments in the annexed territories, on 28 December 1939 Reich Interior Minister Frick, Göring, and Heß ordered the strict separation of state-office and party-office responsibilities.[39]

On the other hand, NSDAP leaders had long wanted to expand the Gauleitungen into regional self-governments based on the municipal model and to limit the Reich Interior Ministry to administrative supervision. They now appeared to have their chance to do so, since, as Hans Mommsen noted early on, "the incorporation of the *Ostmark*, the Sudeten regions, and in particular the newly created Reichsgaue of Danzig-West Prussia and Wartheland . . . gave the newly appointed Reich Governor much more room to maneuver than would have been possible within the previous Reich territory."[40] Significantly, as the chapters in this volume demonstrate, this flexibility also applied to their often very independent anti-Jewish policies.

Despite often being attributed to their role as Gauleiter, the strength of the Reich Governors' positions in the integrated territories owed more to their state function. To be sure, they acted as executive organs of the Reich administration, but in actual practice they simultaneously directed a semi-autonomous central authority, for they often governed more by decree than through ordinances, for only the latter depended on the Reich Interior Ministry's approval.[41] Thus the situation was reversed: it was not the NSDAP that dominated the administration by means of personal unions; rather such personal unions led to what the Hauptamtsleiter (main department leader) in the Deputy Führer's staff criticized in retrospect as a "floating-off into the state sphere" that eliminated the party's influence on the office.[42]

Moreover, this configuration of power in the annexed territories drew its energy not merely from local sources but rather originated in part in Berlin itself. The Reich Interior Ministry, namely, controlled the administrative takeover and legal approximation in each annexed region. As late as March 1938, Hitler had personally appointed State Secretary Wilhelm Stuckart as the director of the Central Office for the Implementation of Austria's Reunification with the German Reich (Zentralstelle zur Durchführung der Wiedervereinigung Österreichs mit dem Deutschen Reich). On 1 October, the latter also took over the new Central Office for the Transfer of the Sudetenland Regions (Zentralstelle für die Überleitung der sudetendeutschen Gebiete) and on 22 March 1939 the Central Office of the Implementation of the Decree for the Protectorate of Bohemia and Moravia (Zentralstelle zur Durchführung des Erlasses für das Protektorat Böhmen und Mähren). After the conquest of France, on 9 August 1940 Hitler appointed Stuckart as the director for the Central Office for Alsace, Lorraine, and Luxembourg (Zentralstelle für das Elsass, Lothringen und Luxemburg). In 1941, Stuckart subsequently became the director of the Central Office for the Occupied South-East Regions (Zentralstelle für die besetzten Südostgebiete), in which capacity he then negotiated with Himmler and the authorities responsible for the adjacent territories for the incorporation of the Yugoslavian regions; finally, he was appointed as the Central Office Director (Zentralstellenleiter) for the Bezirk [district] Byalistok. State Secretary Stuckart in Berlin therefore held all of the strings to the annexed territories in his hands. He was responsible for coordinating between the Reich administration and the regional administrations. To do so, he traveled to the annexed regions, where he received reports about occupation policy and the integration of the indigenous government bodies. In addition, the Reich Interior Ministry controlled the selection of administrative personnel for the occupied regions.[43]

This casts serious doubt on the assumption of Diemut Majer and other researchers that, in the annexed territories, the dominance of Party policy produced a "natural" opposition to the Reich administration and its interest in providing continuity and legal security also for foreign ethnic groups.[44] To begin with, the Reich administration had changed enormously since 1933, especially with regard to the issue of discriminating against "non-Aryans"; moreover, recent research into individual administrative branches has refuted the legend of an unchallenged Party rule, even in the field of anti-Jewish policy.[45] In addition, the chapters presented here on the annexed territories indicate the existence of a division of labor in anti-Jewish policy between various state institutions, one that prevailed in Austria, the Sudetenland, the Protectorate, and even in the Polish territories until—and often even after—the mass deportations in fall 1941.

While recent research into perpetrators has intensively dealt with the crimes in occupied Poland and the Soviet Union, the institutions and responsible individuals in the territories annexed by Germany have hardly received any attention. Significantly, it was not the SS that generally took over persecution policy with the annexations of 1938; rather, as forcefully demonstrated in this volume, in most of the integrated regions, multiple institutions and their respective personnel were responsible for inventing, introducing, and shaping anti-Jewish policy. These included not only the occupation agencies, Wehrmacht, Gestapo, police, NSDAP, and municipalities, but also indigenous administrations and organizations.

The "Germanization" of institutions formed an important part of Nazi annexation policy.[46] This meant not only the introduction of German governmental structures, but also the utilization and/or transformation of indigenous administrative apparatuses. The new rulers regularly installed labor offices, police agencies, and administrations based on German models. Municipal administrations were retained, but sooner or later reconfigured according to the German municipal code of 1935. After the annexations, National Socialists quickly occupied key positions above all in large cities governments—Vienna, Linz, Prague, and Łódź (later Litzmannstadt).[47] At the same time, however, municipalities remained dependent on indigenous personnel. Since, as in the Old Reich, the Jewish inhabitants in the various incorporated territories lived mostly in large urban centers, the parameters of their daily lives were thus substantially determined by the municipal governments in these cities. This likewise applies for the annexed Polish regions, where in Łódź, for example, the city administration both supported and organized the ghetto.[48]

As the central coordinating body for the municipalities in the Reich—and significantly also for their anti-Jewish policies[49]—the German Council of Municipalities (Deutscher Gemeindetag) established branches in all of the annexed regions, which strengthened the ties between local and national policies.[50] The German Council of Municipalities even extended its influence into territories that were not yet fully integrated. Under the supervision and guidance of the East Prussian provincial office, the mayors of the district towns in the Head of the Civil Administration jurisdiction of Białystok discussed sanitary conditions in their region's ghettos.[51]

In fact, the municipal administrations were responsible for and actively collaborated in the concentration of Jewish residents in the annexed regions—namely, their resettlement from rural locations into certain cities such as Vienna in Austria, Theresienstadt (Terezín) in the Protectorate, Będzin (Bendzin) and Sosnowiec (Sosnowitz) in East Upper Silesia, and Łódź in the Warthegau; and within metropolises, for example in Vienna, Prague, or Łódź. As a result of the mass relocations, hundreds of thousands of Jews had to give up their homes and leave behind other property. The significance of the "Aryanization" of Jewish property can hardly be overestimated. Established after each respective occupation, this policy led to private enrichment, especially of local populations, as exemplified by the plundering that occurred in the Regierungsbezirk of Zichenau. But it also led to plundering operations by the municipal authorities themselves. In East Upper Silesia, the German municipal governments expropriated Jewish businesspeople and trade workers, whose stores and operations passed into German and—in a few instances—Polish hands.[52]

As a number of our chapters clearly show, Göring in particular, in his capacity as the head of the Reich government's Four-Year-Plan, intervened to ensure that annexations ran smoothly and profitably in economic terms, whether in Austria, the Protectorate, or East Upper Silesia. Arising due to Germany's ever more extensive rearmament program, the Third Reich's glaring shortage of cash and foreign currency had of course played a major role in the decision to rapidly subjugate Austria and Czechoslovakia. The case of Austria in particular vividly demonstrates the repercussions of the annexations on the Nazi regime's persecution policies. Reacting to the blatant acts of personal enrichment during the "wild Aryanizations" in Vienna and on the basis of groundwork conducted there, Göring and Frick ordered that as of April 1938, all Jews living in the German Reich had to register their assets if they were worth more than 5,000 RM. This was supposed to guarantee central control over future transfers of property.[53]

To avoid the recurrence of this "wild" situation, the "Aryanization" of Jewish property not only in the Sudetenland, the Protectorate, and the Memel Territory but also in occupied Poland and in the western regions became a priority of the Reich government, which monitored and controlled important cases from Berlin. Just one day after being appointed the Head of the Civil Administration in East Upper Silesia, Josef Wagner issued an ordinance on the "property of persons who have fled." Shortly thereafter, state agents confiscated Jewish-owned buildings, real estate, stores, companies, and bank accounts. In Luxembourg, the furniture forcibly left behind by emigrants and deportees went to "needy" families, while NSDAP organizations, municipalities, and government agencies appropriated their real estate. While the German administration in Lorraine treated the possessions plundered from the Jews as enemy assets, the expropriation of the Jews in Luxemburg and Alsace occurred on the basis of special laws.[54]

Each annexation brought the German Reich gains in territory and resources, whether labor, natural resources, agricultural products, industry, and/or capital. The *Anschluss* of Austria alone increased German industrial potential by 8 percent and proved to be a "useful fillip" (Adam Tooze) for the Nazi regime. To be sure, the heavy industrial capacities contributed only marginally to the Reich's armaments industry, yet the high unemployment in the Reich's new "Ostmark" made available a substantial pool of manpower. In addition, ever since the Wilhelmine period, Vienna was viewed as the gateway to the regions of southern Europe.[55] But the annexations did not solely benefit the Reich; rather, most public and many private institutions also profited.

The German savings banks (*Sparkassen*) took over 147 municipal financial institutions in the "Ostmark" alone and another 155 in the Sudetenland, along with dozens of private lending institutions.[56] With the "home coming" of Austria, the Sudetenland, the Memel Territory, and Danzig-West Prussia, German savings banks increased their savings deposits from 18 billion RM to 19.87 billion RM, thus by more than 10 percent, which the Reich Statistical Office rightly saw as strengthening the municipal monetary economy.[57] As in the case of the savings banks, the expanded spheres of activity generated unprecedented advancement opportunities for employees of German institutions, while local residents working for acquired establishments lost their jobs. During the annexation of the Sudetenland—the "prelude to eastern expansion" (Harald Wixforth)—the Dresdner Bank assumed the responsibility of gaining control of the Bohemian Escompte Bank's industrial holdings and "Aryanizing" the large coal mining companies for the industrial conglomerate Reichswerke "Hermann Göring" AG. Not only German banks and state-owned enterprises but also large corporations and conglomerates such as IG Farben and Flick KG profited from the takeover of companies proclaimed to be "Jewish" in the annexed regions.[58]

The legal approximation and administration of the annexed regions required an enormous bureaucratic effort; the corresponding laws and ordinances filled the *Reichsgesetzblatt* (Reich Law Gazette) in the months following each annexation. As noted above, central offices were established for each annexed territory in the Reich Interior Ministry, directed through personal union by State Secretary Stuckart. Even though these offices were supposed to ensure legal approximation at the domestic level, the timing and form of each territory's anti-Jewish policy varied enormously. The reasons lay in the dissimilar local conditions and external circumstances, as well as in divergent national and regional interests.

Thus not all of the "Jewish laws" enacted in the "Old Reich" came to be applied everywhere or immediately. In the Saarland, Jewish residents remained protected for an entire year due to the intervention of the League of Nations, until on 1 March 1936 they were placed on an equal footing with the Jews in the rest of the Reich and the laws already enacted in the Reich gradually took effect in the Saarland as well. An ordinance issued in the Reich in March 1938 revoked the status of Jewish religious communities as corporations under public law, placing them instead under the control of the Reich Interior Ministry as associations; but because of the particular need to fund emigration, Eichmann prevented the ordinance from entering into force in Austria, so as to avoid the financial collapse of Vienna's religious communities as a result of such a measure.[59] In the Sudetenland, the Nazi regime introduced the Old Reich's anti-Jewish laws within just a few weeks. After the occupation of the Polish territories and the creation of Danzig-West Prussia, the laws of the Reich in their entirety went into effect in Danzig-West Prussia as of 1 January 1940. The Warthegau, on the other hand, implemented a (partial) legal approximation as of spring 1940, and in East Upper Silesia, the Nuremburg Laws did not enter into force until summer 1941, two years after the annexation. In Luxembourg, the Head of the Civil Administration, which continued to function as the region's supreme administrative authority, issued the Ordinance regarding Measures in the Area of Laws for Jews on 5 September 1940, which included the introduction of the Nazi race laws. The Second Ordinance regarding the Regulation of Jewish Life in Luxembourg on 14 October 1941 further restricted the freedom of movement of the still-remaining Jews and introduced the wearing of the "Jewish Star"—compulsory in the Reich since September—to Luxembourg as well.[60]

In the Old Reich, the Reich Association of the Jews in Germany (Reichsvereinigung der Juden in Deutschland), an organization under Gestapo supervision with compulsory membership for all Jews, had to organize the Jewish school and welfare systems and Jewish emigration after the November pogrom in 1938;[61] but in Austria, the Vienna Israelite Community functioned as the representative agency for all the Jews. By contrast, the Sudetenland received its own regional office of the Reich Association. In the Protectorate, the religious community of Prague—much like the situation in Vienna—bore responsibility for all of the Jewish communities as of 1940, whereas in East Upper Silesia the Central Office of the Jewish Councils of Elders of East Upper Silesia assumed this role.[62]

Let us return, however, to institutional and personal continuities, as well as the accumulation and transfer of persecutory experience from various annexed territories: these are particularly evident in a new type institution, namely, the Central Office for Jewish Immigration (Zentralstelle für jüdische Auswanderung). Established in Vienna under Stahlecker in August 1938, the Central Office developed new procedures and approaches under its managing director Eichmann. They included, for instance, the centralized processing of potential emigrants, conducted in an assembly-line manner; the Security Service's tight-knit and smooth collaboration with municipal and state officials delegated to the Central Office; and the plundering of wealthy Jews by means of an "emigration fund" to finance the expulsion of destitute Jews. The Security Service had brought along the idea of the Central Office and parts of its apparatus, but both in Vienna as well as in Prague—where the same Stahlecker and Eichmann founded another Central Office in July 1939—Reich Commissioner Josef Bürckel and respectively Reich Protector Konstantin von Neurath reserved the institution's formal installation for the regional government—in the case of Prague, even in coordination with the Protectorate's Czech government. In Berlin, Göring himself founded the Reich Central Office for Jewish Emigration as part of the Reich Interior Ministry.[63] Initially responsible only for efficiently organizing the expulsions, the Central Offices attempted to appropriate more and more areas of Jewish policy, albeit with only moderate success until 1941. In Vienna, apart from supervising and dissolving the Jewish communities and directing the expulsions, Stahlecker and Eichmann failed to gain control of any additional operational sectors. They enjoyed more success in Prague, at least in the sector of residential concentration in 1940 and partially with respect to monitoring forced labor deployments from Prague to other areas of the Protectorate in 1941.[64]

In a number of specialized fields, such as the acceleration of emigration and "Aryanization," the experts "wandering" from one annexed region to the next carried their newly won experiential knowledge in their luggage like persecutory technology, so to speak, applying and further developing this technology within the situations they discovered in the territory currently undergoing integration. The Viennese techniques used to plunder the Jews and force Jewish organizations to collaborate were refined in Berlin and Prague. In the context of the deportations directed by Eichmann in the Reich Security Main Office (Reichssicherheitshauptamt), they were ultimately also applied in the territories occupied by Germany and in allied states. In the various European theaters, the Reich Security Main Office frequently delegated men who received their "basic training" in the implementation of anti-Jewish measures at the Central Offices for Jewish Emigration in Vienna, Prague, or Berlin, or at Eichmann's section in the Reich Security Main Office. After the Germans occupied the Netherlands, for example, the country received a Central Office for Jewish Emigration and an emigration fund.[65]

German financial institutes also played a key role in plundering the Jewish population. They financed numerous "Aryanizations," especially in Austria, the Sudetenland, and the Protectorate. They brought their knowledge on how to smoothly settle such "transactions" into each new territory and profited from the information they collected in their headquarters about businesses and companies targeted for "Aryanization." Primarily because of their client networks, which generated numerous prospective "Aryanizers," and because of the immense need for capital, German financial institutions developed into the major hubs in the "dejudaization" process. For example, as early as October 1938 the Reich Economics Ministry conveyed a list of large-scale operations in the Sudetenland that were scheduled or being considered for "Aryanization."[66] The banks' involvement, however, pertained not solely to the acquisition of large companies by the state, the SS, or conglomerates from the Old Reich but also to transactions involving the sale of smaller and mid-sized firms, which were supposed to establish new client relationships in the annexed regions themselves.[67]

The successful transfer of persecution techniques is further exemplified by the Stillhaltekommissar for Organizations, an office established for the first time in Vienna after the annexation of Austria. It was supposed to register all associations, federations, and organizations in the new Reich territories, convert them into Nazi structures, or—especially if they were Communist, Social Democratic, Masonic, or Jewish institutions—dissolve them, and confiscate their assets. In the Old Reich, the Nazi regime had "merely" synchronized most of the organizations, taking more radical measures only in isolated cases, as when dealing with the Jewish lodge B'nai B'rith in April 1937.[68] In the following period, the Nazis deployed the Viennese model and to a large extent the staff around Stillhaltekommissar Albert Hoffmann in the Sudetenland,[69] the Protectorate of Bohemia and Moravia, Alsace, Luxembourg, and the occupied Netherlands. Hoffmann himself directed the offices in Vienna, Reichenberg (Liberec), and Prague. When the Reich Interior Minister assigned the restructuring of the organizations and associations to the Reich Protector in Prague in June 1939, the latter created a new office, namely, the Commissioner for the Organizations (Beauftragter für die Organisationen) and appointed Hoffmann to the post. The Nazis also drew upon experienced personnel from Austria when using the Viennese model during the annexations in the West. Franz Schmidt, previously Hoffmann's deputy in Vienna, was later appointed as the Stillhaltekommissar West. The competent Heads of the Civil Administrations entrusted him with Stillhaltekommissar responsibilities on 22 August 1940 for Lorraine, on 2 September for Alsace, and on 6 September for Luxembourg; later he also fulfilled these duties in the Netherlands.[70] In all of the territorial integrations, this fundamental restructuring of the entire system of social and cultural organizations, which affected both Jewish and non-Jewish associations, sought to neutralize political opponents and the racially persecuted, realign organizational structures, plunder assets, and safeguard Nazi rule.[71] In spring 1939, Nazi leadership discussed the creation of a Reichsstillhaltekommissar—that is, a Stillhaltekommissar at the level of Reich itself—but the office was never established. Later in Poland, however, a Main Trustee Office East and its personnel carried out the expropriation of Poles and Jews.[72] Especially here, as in Danzig-West Prussia and the Warthegau, "Jewish policy," "Polish policy," and "*Volkstum* policy" intertwined.

Depopulation and the introduction of new settlements already played a central role in German occupation policy in the plans for the Czech territories, but it would take on far greater importance in Poland. Whereas the murders during the occupation of Austria, the Sudetenland, and the Protectorate still consisted of numerous isolated cases, the Einsatzgruppen of the Security Police and the Security Service that followed the German military's advance into Poland systematically killed thousands of people, at first primarily members of the Polish elite but also, right from the outset, Jews. Wehrmacht soldiers participated en masse in the excesses and murders.[73] The Nazis viewed western Poland as the key region for the Reich's expansion. After thirty years, Hitler stated, one should no longer notice that the land had ever been contested by Germans and the Poles. He and his advisers needed a month to determine how far the new border should extend beyond the former Prussian territories. His decision, which brought many Poles into the country of Germany itself, troubled even members of the regime. For strategic reasons, however, the further east they drew the boundary, the better it was for the German Reich. As a result, the Reich's new territories included more than 8.9 million Poles, 603,000 Jews, and only 600,000 Germans.[74]

Soon after the invasion began in September 1939, the Nazi leadership decided to remove the Jews from the entire "Greater German Reich"—thus also from the annexed western Polish regions—and resettle them in the General Government (Generalgouvernement).[75] The decision substantially shaped short- and mid-term Jewish policy not only in the former Polish regions—that is, the Warthegau, East Upper Silesia, and Danzig-West Prussia—but also in the Protectorate. Since authorities in all these regions fully anticipated the mass removal of Jews within months, when dealing with the Jews they focused on interim solutions: forced labor was not broadly introduced, in contrast to the General Government;[76] for the moment, ghettos were supposed to temporarily concentrate the population at certain points.[77] The authorities changed their approach only once they realized that the complete removal of the Jewish population could no longer be expected, even in the mid term. As a result, the respective regions shifted to a more systematic Jewish policy, but at the same time—as the individual chapters show—substantial regional differences prevailed with respect to processes, the formulation of measures, and the responsible institutions.[78]

"Regional planners" everywhere, however, soon faced what proved to be a fundamental problem, namely, the lack of enough Germans to Germanize the occupied Polish land.[79] More so than any other territory conquered during the Second World War, the Reichsgau Wartheland developed into a testing ground where National Socialists interlinked the settlement of ethnic German settlers from Eastern Europe with the deportation of large parts of the Polish populations and the destruction of the Jews, proceeding in the process with an unprecedented ruthlessness and cruelty.[80] In East Upper Silesia, Auschwitz (Oświęcim)—belonging to the German Reich since October 1939 and later the site of the extermination camp—constituted one such Germanization nucleus; since Oświęcim was to be replaced by a German model town, the Nazis resettled its Jewish residents in the ghettos of East Upper Silesia.[81]

Indigenous ethnic Germans living in the annexed territories benefited in numerous ways. First, the Nazi regime fulfilled its long-held desire for a "homecoming to the Reich"; second, the regime often satisfied its material needs, albeit generally at the expense of non-Germans—especially the Jewish population, which was segregated and/or deported. The course of the "Aryanization" and Germanization processes influenced the behavior of ethnic Germans and the ruthlessness of policies in the respective territories. In their supposed debt of gratitude to the "Führer" and the regime, these Germans often exhibited their willingness to not only accept but also actively support the Third Reich's racial policies. In conjunction with the generally widespread endemic anti-Semitism, this led to what for the Jews was a fatal radicalization of the German populations, chiefly in the weeks immediately before and after each respective *Anschluss*. Later, as they increasingly found themselves competing with Reich Germans delegated to the annexed regions, ethnic Germans often thought that Berlin eyed them suspiciously as second-class Reich citizens and thus felt all the more pressured to prove themselves as loyal and committed National Socialists.[82]

Especially important posts were regularly assigned to Reich Germans. Already in the Saarland, Bürckel entrusted the best positions in his commissariat to numerous confidants from the Palatinate, which did not go over very well with the locals. He subsequently also brought his staff with him to Austria. In the Sudetenland, all institutions relevant to security matters were in the hands of officials from the Reich. Admittedly, Berlin filled the Regierungspräsident positions with three Sudeten Germans, but also appointed Reich Germans to serve as deputies at their side. Even the "Aryanizations" generated displeasure among the Sudeten Germans. The authorities and the population both complained that the local economy was being "taken over by the Old Reich." Ethnic Germans and new settlers in the Warthegau did not receive many opportunities either, for Reich Germans accounted for 90 percent of the occupation administration's officials. In Eupen-Malmedy, too, players from the incorporated region rarely retained their positions, for the region was directly integrated in the Regierungsbezirk of Aachen. Alsatians obtained only modest positions in the German administration in Strasbourg. Local ethnic Germans and Reich Germans also evidently competed economically. Even so, their interests converged when it came to neutralizing Poles and Jews and taking over their housing and property.[83]

Michael Mann has argued that the persecutors in the border regions were especially radical, referring to the Freikorps' wealth of experience with violence after the First World War in the eastern part of the Reich, the struggle against the Left in Austria, and the militias in the

West.⁸⁴ However, the annexations did not everywhere entail a radicalization of Jewish policy, particularly in the western regions. After the terror of the first weeks of the annexation, the situation sometimes calmed down once the occupation government was in place and took over the policies of persecution. To be sure, the administrative pressure on the Jewish population continued, but the authorities in the West and in the Protectorate had no interest in constant "wild" terror, which would only fuel the resistance of the non-German population.⁸⁵

Many of the chapters in this volume reveal the important role of local initiatives in the development and radicalization of Jewish policy. After the wild "Aryanizations" in March/April 1938, the Ostmark generated the first recommendations for the registration of Jewish property. In the Sudetenland, on the other hand, party and state authorities abruptly confiscated the property of Jews, especially housing, to meet their needs when establishing the administration in the new region. Even more explicitly than earlier in Austria, the "Aryanization" of Jewish businesses and companies supported economic structural policy measures.⁸⁶ When occupying Bohemia and Moravia, the Heads of the Civil Administrations—the Sudeten-German Gauleiter Henlein and the Reich Commissioner for Austria Bürckel—already issued the first ordinances restricting the ability of Jews to dispose over their property in March 1939. In a parallel move, the Czech Ministry of Finance under Josef Kalfus froze all of the bank deposits of Jews in the Protectorate. In summer 1939, the Reich Economics Ministry applied this measure to all Jews in the Reich.⁸⁷ After the occupation of Poland, the German Resettlement Trustee Company (Deutsche Umsiedlungs-Treuhand-Gesellschaft), tasked in actual fact with deploying Polish and Jewish property for the benefit of ethnic German settlers, was established in the Warthegau.⁸⁸

The interactions between the new and old parts of the Reich can be illustrated even more precisely with the example of the forced labor deployments. The Austrian labor administration presented the idea of using (at first) Jews who were registered as unemployed and receiving unemployment benefits for forced labor to Reich Commissioner Bürckel, who approved the project in fall 1938. Adopting the Viennese model, the Reich's labor administration introduced forced labor for these Jews on 20 December 1938 throughout Greater Germany, informally extending the policy to include all Jews as of 1940. The labor offices compelled tens of thousands of men and women to labor in construction, agriculture, and forestry, as well as—with some delay—in industry. In a few regions annexed at a later stage, all Jews had to perform forced labor from the moment the authorities realized that the plans formulated early in the war to "resettle" the Jews in the General Government could no longer be realized in the short term. After this point, the forced labor assignments were organized by labor offices in the Protectorate, by an SS Special Emissary (Sonderbeauftragter) in East Upper Silesia, and by various authorities—including for example, the labor administration but also the city administration responsible for the Litzmannstadt ghetto—in the Warthegau. While forced Jewish labor deployments in the incorporated regions initially followed the model provided by such deployments in the Reich, they often involved more brutal practices, which in turn influenced the Reich and the development of Reich law. Jews in East Upper Silesia, for instance, received minimal wages and had to pay a portion of them to the SS Organization Schmelt; payments to Litzmannstadt ghetto inmates working on the Reich Autobahn followed similar patterns.[89] In early 1941, the Reich Labor Ministry aligned the practical conditions of forced labor in Reich with those in the incorporated eastern territories. All Jews in the Reich (except in Warthegau, the Regierungsbezirk of Zichenau, and the specific districts of East Upper Silesia that contained ghettos) had to pay a special 15 percent levy on their wages.[90] When discussions simultaneously began in the Reich about introducing the general conscription of Jews for labor, representatives from the incorporated eastern territories pointed out that they were already using compulsory labor "in specific forms deviating from the rest of the Reich's territory."[91] In an ordinance from 3 October 1941, the Reich Labor Administration legalized Jewish forced labor in the Old Reich, Austria, and the annexed eastern regions.[92]

The same applied to the repression of the Jewish religious communities. In Germany, the Gestapo had set up a system for completely monitoring the Jewish communities by 1937. In Austria, Eichmann and his Central Office had already forced the collaboration of the Vienna Israelite Community (after it had initially been banned). Much the same occurred in Prague, whereas the authorities in the occupied Polish territories—upon Heydrich's instructions in September 1939—formed the so-called Jewish Councils, whose role was often only to carry out instructions from the German administration. In turn, these procedures then exacerbated relations between Nazi authorities and the Reich Association of the Jews in Germany and the religious communities in Vienna and Prague.[93]

The first initiative with respect to the marking of the Jews came from the municipal administration in Schirps (Sierpc) in the annexed Polish region of Zichenau, which ordered Jews to wear a yellow Star of David. By the end of 1939, such decrees entered into force throughout the Regierungsbezirk of Zichenau, while developments in the Warthegau followed similar lines. Meanwhile, for the entire region of East Upper Silesia, the Higher SS and Police Leader (Höherer SS- und Polizeiführer) Erich von dem Bach-Zelewski ordered the marking of the Jews with armbands in December 1939. Hitler initially prevented similar plans for the rest of the territories of the Greater German Reich. Then in 1940, Jewish forced laborers began being marked in Austrian labor camps, and in July 1941, the Head of the Civil Administration in Luxembourg compelled all Jews to wear an armband. At the same time, a new initiative to introduce an identifying mark for all Jews in the "Greater German Reich" reached Berlin from Prague, leading in September 1941 to the labeling of Jews with the "Jewish Star" during the preparations for the new mass deportations. Thereupon all of the various identifying marks previously used in the integrated eastern regions were replaced by the notorious yellow star, affixed to the wearer's clothing.[94]

The reciprocal effects between the regional and Reich-wide persecutory measures persistently influenced the development of anti-Jewish policy in the Third Reich. The authorities in the annexed regions only began losing their opportunities to independently shape the contours of Jewish persecution in the wake of the final decision to murder the European Jews and the resulting exertion of central influence by the Reich Security Main Office. Yet this by no means ruled out new regional initiatives. In East Upper Silesia and the Warthegau, for example, economic interests continued to shape anti-Jewish policy even during the mass extermination phase, for a long time exempting hundreds of thousands of forced laborers from deportation and delaying the liquidation of the Litzmannstadt ghetto until 1944—this even though Nazi aims explicitly called first and foremost for the annexed regions in particular to be rendered "Jew-free."[95]

Throughout the entire period, the number of remaining Jews—both regionally and in the Reich as a whole—influenced specific developments of Jewish policy within the annexed regions and also Jewish opportunities for emigration and flight and Nazi plans for concentration and deportation. Thus the Gestapo's policies oscillated between promoting and preventing emigration, since Berlin assigned absolute priority to the expulsion of the Jews from the "Old Reich." Whereas some authorities in the annexed regions wanted to be rid of "their" Jews, others in turn wanted to keep them for labor. Thus anti-Jewish measures—in large part, during long periods, and in various forms in different annexed regions—were influenced by: local conditions; specific political, economic, demographic, and social factors; external temporal circumstances; the collaboration of a wide range of institutions; and German and non-German players and their initiatives. The diverging interests of central, regional, and local institutions could trigger radicalizing impulses or bring certain measures to a halt. And the differing objectives in the annexed regions explain both the radical dynamics as well as the diverse configurations of many aspects of anti-Jewish policy.

Prospective Fields of Research

Five years after the annexation of Austria, in summer 1943, Hitler ordered that all diplomatic correspondence should henceforth refer to him as the "Führer of the Greater German Reich." Only after this point did the Nazi state officially adopt the term, using it in international agreements and on postage stamps. It was probably no coincidence that this occurred at the moment when Hitler and Himmler regarded the mass deportations from Germany, Austria, and the Protectorate as having largely been completed—without however taking the Warthegau and East Upper Silesia into account, where more than 100,000 Jews languished, most of them as forced laborers.[96]

To render the Reich's territory "Jew-free," the Gestapo began with early mass transports in October 1939, deporting thousands of Austrian, Czech, and Polish Jews to Nisko near Lublin. Next, in spring and fall 1940 it deported several thousand German Jews to Poland and France, followed in February and March 1941 by several thousand Austrian Jews to the Generalgouvernement and in October 1941 by 20,000 German, Austrian, Czech, and Luxembourg Jews to Litzmannstadt in the Warthegau. This last operation marked the prelude to deportations from occupied Western Europe. In December 1941, the German death squads in the Warthegau began systematically murdering Polish Jews; mass transports from the Old Reich, Austria, and the Protectorate now headed for Riga or Minsk, and—in spring and summer 1942—to the General Government. In May 1942, the Gestapo finally began deporting the Jews within the Reich's territory to Auschwitz, first from Upper Silesia, later from the rest of the Reich and the Protectorate. As of this time, elderly people were being deported from Germany, Austria, and the Sudeten region to the Theresienstadt ghetto in the Protectorate, followed much later also by Jews from "mixed marriages" (as well as Jews from Bohemia and Moravia since December 1941); however, such deportations to the Protectorate did not occur in the former Polish western regions, with the exception of few German Jews from Danzig.[97] Against the background of the systematic murder of the Jews from Germany and the annexed regions, the regional and central competencies with respect to Jewish policy changed.

Numerous questions could only be addressed briefly in this volume; many subjects invite further research. Almost all of the chapters in this volume reveal how little we know about the political, social, and cultural life of the Jewish populations prior to the annexations, and that we know even less about the reactions of the Jewish communities, Jewish organizations, and individual Jews to the occupation and persecution. Were there instances of individual or even organized resistance and if so what form did they take? What similarities and differences can be discerned in this regard in the various annexed regions, and to what degree did they result from each specific form of regional annexation and rule?

Surprisingly few studies are available that deal particularly with the Nazi government's domination techniques in the individual annexed territories. Research into the Memel Territory and Alsace remains in its very early stages. But even the other annexed regions have not been sufficiently researched. In particular, we still lack in-depth local and regional studies as well as biographies of important players such as Bürckel, Stahlecker, and Hoffmann, who gathered the accumulated experience of a multifaceted anti-Jewish policy and transported their expertise from region to region while developing it further.[98] Institutional histories and prosopographical studies of the members of the abovementioned staffs would promise to provide insight into their influence on policy developments in the annexed regions. In this regard, questions about the origins of the other personnel in the annexed regions—working for the authorities, the NSDAP, and above all the persecuting agencies—also seem critical. As a rule, these regions lacked suitable and—as seen from the perspective of the Nazi center of power in Berlin—reliable officials and functionaries. In examining the governmental bodies responsible for the occupation and persecution, more detailed research should be conducted into which principles guided the selection, composition, and deployment of personnel from both the Reich and these regions themselves. Did regional origins, expertise, or party loyalty dominate delegations when establishing the authorities and offices in the annexed regions?

Comparative studies of the activities of important institutions would also promise to provide special insights. Thus the central role of the

Heads of the Civil Administrations in implementing initial measures against the Jewish populations in the occupied regions—for instance regarding the registration and confiscation of their assets—should be investigated. Since the Heads of the Civil Administrations in Bohemia and Moravia, as well as in Poland, adopted similar procedures, perhaps their actions were based on instructions from central authorities. If such instructions in fact existed, it would be interesting to know whether they came from the Wehrmacht, which formally commanded the Heads of the Civil Administrations, or from Hitler himself. Nor do we know very much about the function of the Heads of the Civil Administrations as institutions and as persons in the various regions, or about their administrative staffs.

Comparative studies into the consequences of specific anti-Jewish polices for the respective Jewish populations deserve special attention in the future. This is the only way to better understand the reactions of individuals and the actions of the Jewish communities. The exchange of information between the various annexed regions—whether through Jewish institutions or individual people—should also be illuminated. As we can presume from the fact that refugees who managed to reach Czechoslovakia from Austria and the Sudeten region, or who arrived in Belgium, Luxembourg, or France from Germany also conveyed useful knowledge about the Nazi regime's persecutory practices, the transfer of experiences of persecution among the people living in the various annexed regions probably significantly influenced their conduct and later also their post-deportation survival in new conditions in Poland.

As the chapter about the Warthegau demonstrates, especially in the annexed regions, National Socialist policies toward the rest of the Polish and Czech populations must be examined more closely, because initially these could hardly be distinguished from anti-Jewish policy; furthermore, they provided the backdrop for the measures undertaken against the Jews living in these regions. For the future, research into the relations between Germans, Jews, and—for example—the French in Alsace-Lorraine appears equally important. A crucial question is whether interests in the property of the Jewish population and opportunities to benefit from better careers and dealings as a result of the expulsions—as we see in several of the chapters—can help explain why certain non-Jewish inhabitants in the East and the West were motivated to cooperate with the Nazi regime or even radicalize the persecution through their own initiatives.

The ghettoization and/or deportation of the Jews and the settlement of ethnic Germans formed two sides of the same coin, namely, the

Germanization of the regions annexed by the German Reich. Whether and to what extent the autochthonous ethnic Germans and the settlers from Eastern Europe directly or indirectly affected these developments needs to be more carefully explored. What influence did they exert specifically on National Socialist Jewish policy, namely, on discrimination, plundering, ghettoization, forced labor, and mass murder? Did they form a pressure group pushing for a more radical occupation policy, or did they merely provide the Nazi leadership—particularly in the annexed Polish regions—with a pretext to press ahead with the murder of the Jews as a stage in the territory's Germanization?

The volume presented here reveals not only the lack of more in-depth comparative analyses of anti-Jewish policy, but also the absence of comprehensive accounts about the behavior of long-established or newly settled German minorities and their interactions in various parts of Europe. Only such studies could enable a systematic analysis of how such minorities were influenced by the Reich, their reactions to such influences, as well as of their participation in the crimes of National Socialism; on this basis, it would also become possible to scrutinize the image of ethnic Germans that has hitherto been shaped by homeland and expellee associations. In this context, urgent questions arise regarding the extent and significance of postwar compensation benefits for Germans expelled from their homelands. We can assume that some of them received compensation payments in the Federal Republic of Germany for Jewish enterprises they had "Aryanized" and then subsequently left behind. Did the Lastenausgleichsgesetz—the "burden sharing act" enacted in 1952—ultimately ensure that "Aryanizers" once again profited from the "dejudaization" of the economy during the Third Reich?

The inconsistencies of the persecution of Jews in the Reich and the annexed regions can thus be explained—as shown—by the differing initiatives and interests of various actors, whether they were German or indigenous institutions or persons, as well as by the local economic, social, political, and demographic conditions and constellations, and last but not least from the conflicts and interactions between regional and central policies.

We conclude by returning to our example from the introduction: only the geographical location of the Auschwitz extermination camp explains why tens of thousands of Jews since summer 1942 had to be individually expropriated as "Communists" or "enemies of the state" according to two laws from 1933, prior to being transported to the camp.[99] The Eleventh Ordinance on the Reich Citizen Law of 25 November 1941, created specifically for the mass deportations to the East, stipulated that all Jews "ordinarily domiciled" in a foreign country lost their German state membership, and thus forfeited all of their assets automatically to the state.[100] However, Auschwitz at this point in time no longer happened to be located in a foreign country, but rather in East Upper Silesia, which had been annexed by Germany. Thus, ironically, the tens of thousands of Jews deported to the Auschwitz camp could not be expropriated by means of this special new ordinance precisely because the camp lay within the territory of the Reich.

Notes

1. Victor Klemperer, *The Language of the Third Reich?: LTI, Lingua Tertii Imperii?: A Philologist's Notebook* (London, 2000), 263. (German original: Berlin, 1947).
2. Majer, *"Fremdvölkische" im Dritten Reich*, 188ff.
3. Quoted in Mazower, *Hitler's Empire*, 5.
4. On this see Mazower, *Hitler's Empire*, 2–4.
5. On this see Wolfgang Benz, "Typologie der Herrschaftsformen in Gebieten unter deutschem Einfluß," in *Die Bürokratie der Okkupation. Strukturen der Herrschaft und Verwaltung im besetzten Europa*, ed. Wolfgang Benz et al., (Berlin, 1998), 11–25, here 12f.
6. See here the concise account by Christoph Dieckmann, "Plan und Praxis: Deutsche Siedlungspolitik im besetzten Litauen 1941–1944," in *Wissenschaft, Planung, Vertreibung. Neuordnungskonzepte und Umsiedlungspolitik im 20. Jahrhundert*, ed. Isabel Heinemann and Patrick Wagner (Stuttgart, 2006), 93–118, here 94f. On the *Generalplan Ost*, see, among others, Bruno Wasser, *Himmlers Raumplanung im Osten: Der Generalplan Ost in Polen 1940–1944* (Basel, 1993); Mechthild Rössler and Sabine Schleiermacher, ed., *Der "Generalplan Ost": Hauptlinien der nationalsozialistischen Planungs- und Vernichtungspolitik* (Berlin, 1993); Czesław Madajczyk, ed., *Vom Generalplan Ost zum Generalsiedlungsplan: Dokumente* (Munich, 1994).
7. On this and the following section, see the corresponding chapters in this volume.
8. See, for example, the chapter by Wolfgang Gippert in this volume.
9. For this and the following section, see the corresponding chapters in this volume.
10. Jörg K. Hoensch, "Hitlers 'Neue Ordnung Europas': Grenzveränderungen, Staatsneugründungen, nationale Diskriminierungen," in *Der nationalsozialistische Krieg*, eds. Norbert Frei and Hermann Kling (Frankfurt, 1990), 238–254.
11. See the contributions by Wolfgang Gippert, Jörg Osterloh, and Jean-Marc Dreyfus in this volume.
12. Gerhard Wolf, "Deutsche Volksliste," in *Handbuch der völkischen Wissenschaft*, ed. Ingo Haar and Michael Fahlbusch (Munich, 2008), 129–135.
13. On this, see for example Jörg Osterloh, *Nationalsozialistische Judenverfolgung im Reichsgau Sudetenland* (Munich, 2006), 66–80, 165–170. On the development of the German ethnic group in Romania, see Hildrun Glass, *Zerbrochene Nachbarschaft: Das deutsch-jüdische Verhältnis in Rumänien (1918–1938)* (Munich, 1996).
14. See, for example, the chapter by Jörg Osterloh in this volume.
15. See the foundational work by Benedict Anderson, *Imagined Communities: Reflections on the Origin and Spread of Nationalism* (London, 1991).

16. Michael Wildt, *Hitler's Volksgemeinschaft and the Dynamics of Racial Exclusion: Violence against Jews in Provincial Germany, 1919–1939* (New York, 2011) (German original: 2007). See also Frank Bajohr and Michael Wildt, eds., *Volksgemeinschaft: Neue Forschungen zur Gesellschaft des Nationalsozialismus* (Frankfurt, 2009).
17. Majer, *"Fremdvölkische" im Dritten Reich*, 36ff.
18. On this, see the corresponding chapters in this volume.
19. On this, see the corresponding chapters in this volume.
20. See the brief overview in Klaus-Michael Mallmann, "Menschenjagd und Massenmord: Das neue Instrument der Einsatztruppen und -kommandos 1938–1945," in *Die Gestapo im Zweiten Weltkrieg: "Heimatfront" und besetztes Europa*, ed. Gerhard Paul and Klaus-Michael Mallmann (Darmstadt, 2000), 291–316; as well sections on individual regions in Michael Wildt, *An Uncompromising Generation? The Nazi Leadership of the Reich Security Main Office* (Madison, 2009) (German original: 2002). On Poland, see Klaus-Michael Mallmann et al., *Einsatzgruppen in Polen. Darstellung und Dokumentation* (Darmstadt, 2008).
21. On the following section, see the corresponding chapters in this volume, as well as Benz, "Typologie der Herrschaftsformen," 11–26.
22. Minutes of the state secretary conference on 25 March 1939 and appendix in Andrea Löw, ed., *Die Verfolgung und Ermordung der europäischen Juden durch das nationalsozialistische Deutschland 1933–1945*, vol. 3: *Deutsches Reich und Protektorat September 1939—September 1941* (Munich, 2012), doc. no. 240, 574–580, here 579; appendix only printed in *Europa unterm Hakenkreuz: Die faschistische Okkupationspolitik in Österreich und der Tschechoslowakei (1938–1945)*, document selection and introduction by Helma Kaden with the collaboration of Ludwig Nestler, et al. (East Berlin, 1988), doc. no. 36, 110–112.
23. Notification of the Ordinance regarding ID cards [*Kennkarten*] of 3 March 1942, Reichsgesetzblatt (RGBl.) 1942 I, 100.
24. On this and the following section, see the corresponding chapters in this volume.
25. Letter from the Oberkommando des Heeres (Army High Command) from 3 October 1939 (Erlass no. 310/39) regarding sojourns in occupied former Polish territory Bundesarchiv (BArch), R 2/5834, fol. 260.
26. New Reichstag electoral districts were created for Saarland in 1935, Austria and the Sudetenland in 1938, Bohemia/Moravia and the Memel Territory in 1939, and Danzig-West Prussia, Wartheland, East Prussia (Zichenau), Silesia (Regierungsbezirk of Kattowitz, which included parts of East Upper Silesia), and Eupen-Malmedy in 1941; Joachim Lilla, ed., *Statisten in Uniform: Die Mitglieder des Reichstags 1933–1945: Ein biographisches Handbuch: Unter Einbeziehung der völkischen und nationalsozialistischen Reichstagsabgeordneten ab Mai 1924* (Düsseldorf, 2004), 770.
27. Emile Krier, "Deutsche Besatzung in Luxemburg 1940–1944," in *Die Bürokratie der Okkupation*, ed. Benz et al., 27–48, here 47.
28. Krier also points to the intended temporary character of CdZ rule with respect to Luxembourg; Krier, "Deutsche Besatzung in Luxemburg," 42.
29. For example Peter Longerich, *Holocaust: The Nazi Persecution and Murder of the Jews* (Oxford, 2010) (German original: Munich 1998); Leni Yahil, *Die Shoah: Überlebenskampf und Vernichtung der europäischen Juden* (Munich, 1998).
30. Hans Umbreit, *Deutsche Militärverwaltungen 1938/39: Die militärische Besetzung der Tschechoslowakei und Polens* (Stuttgart, 1977).
31. Thus even Reinhard Heydrich failed in his efforts in fall 1941 to acquire directorial authority for the SS-Reichsführer over the CdZs; Majer, *"Fremdvölkische" im Dritten Reich*, 697, fn 65; Krier, "Deutsche Besatzung in Luxemburg," 40.

32. Krier, "Deutsche Besatzung in Luxemburg," 35.
33. Bernhard Gotto, "Dem Gauleiter entgegen arbeiten? Überlegungen zur Reichweite eines Deutungsmusters," in *Die NS-Gaue. Regionale Mittelinstanzen im zentralistischen "Führerstaat,"* ed. Jürgen John et al., (Munich, 2007), 80–99, here 88f. On this and the following paragraph, see the corresponding chapters in this volume.
34. RGBl. 1939 I, 777–782.
35. On this, see Jörg Osterloh's contribution in this volume.
36. Catherine Epstein, *Model Nazi: Arthur Greiser and the Occupation of Western Poland* (Oxford, 2010).
37. Hans Mommsen, *Beamtentum im Dritten Reich: Mit ausgewählten Quellen zur nationalsozialistischen Beamtenpolitik* (Stuttgart, 1966), 108.
38. Majer, *"Fremdvölkische" im Dritten Reich,* 199–204.
39. RGBl. 1940 I, 45; see also Mommsen, *Beamtentum,* 112–120.
40. Mommsen, *Beamtentum,* 99 f.
41. Majer, *"Fremdvölkische" im Dritten Reich,* 203f.
42. Helmuth Friedrich (StdF) cited in Mommsen, *Beamtentum,* 114.
43. Hans-Christian Jasch, *Staatssekretär Wilhelm Stuckart und die Judenpolitik: Der Mythos von der sauberen Verwaltung* (Munich, 2012), 140–144.
44. See, for example, Majer, *"Fremdvölkische" im Dritten Reich,* 198.
45. This is vividly demonstrated with respect to the area of public welfare by Gruner, *Öffentliche Wohlfahrt und Judenverfolgung.* For Austria, see Wolf Gruner, *Zwangsarbeit und Verfolgung: Österreichische Juden im NS-Staat 1938–45* (Innsbruck, 2000). For the Sudetenland, see Osterloh, *Judenverfolgung.*
46. Raphael Lemkin already pointed this out; Lemkin, *Axis Rule,* 8f.
47. On this, see Wolf Gruner, "Die Kommunen im Nationalsozialismus: Innenpolitische Akteure und ihre wirkungsmächtige Vernetzung," in *Der prekäre Staat: Herrschen und Verwalten im Nationalsozialismus,* ed. Wolfgang Seibel and Sven Reichardt (Frankfurt, 2011), 167–212.
48. See the detailed account in Peter Klein, *Die "Gettoverwaltung Litzmannstadt" 1940–1944: Eine Dienststelle im Spannungsfeld von Kommunalbürokratie und staatlicher Verfolgungspolitik* (Hamburg, 2009).
49. On this, see Wolf Gruner, "Die NS-Judenverfolgung und die Kommunen: Zur wechselseitigen Dynamisierung von zentraler und lokaler Politik 1933–1941," *Vierteljahrshefte für Zeitgeschichte* 48 (2000): 75–126; idem, "Local Initiatives, Central Coordination: German Municipal Administration and the Holocaust," in *Networks of Nazi Persecution: Bureaucracy, Business, and the Organization of the Holocaust,* ed. Gerald D. Feldman and Wolfgang Seibel (New York, 2005) 269–294.
50. Report of the Supreme Directorate of the NSDAP Party Organization/Municipal Policy Section to the Organization Office (September 1933), BArch, R 2 Pers. (formerly BDC), file 850, fol. 10; DGT business allocation plan May 1938, ibid. 58–60; DGT office register from 7 February 1944, pp. 1–3, Landesarchiv (LA) Berlin, B Rep. 142-07, 0-1-13/no. 2, vol. 2, no fol.; DGT to DGT Reichgau office Sudetenland on 11/ May 1942, BArch, R 36/589, fol. 40.
51. DGT Provincial Office East Prussia to the mayors of the district towns in the district [Bezirk] of the CdZ of Bialystok with minutes of the meeting on 25 October 1942, pp. 1–6, LA Berlin, B Rep. 142-07, 0-1-16/no. 316, no fol.
52. On this, see the corresponding chapters in this volume.
53. Ordinance on the Registration of the Assets of Jews of 26 April 1938, RGBl. 1938 I, 414. On the creation of this ordinance see Hans Safrian, "Expediting Expropriation and Expulsion: The Impact of the 'Vienna Model' on Anti-Jewish Policies in Nazi Germany 1938," *Holocaust and Genocide Studies* 14, no. 3 (2000): 390–414, also

idem, "Kein Recht auf Eigentum: Zur Genese antijüdischer Gesetze im Frühjahr 1938 im Spannungsfeld von Peripherie und Zentrum," in *Vor der Vernichtung: Die staatliche Enteignung der Juden im Nationalsozialismus*, ed. Katharina Stengel (Frankfurt, 2007), 245–262.
54. On this, see the corresponding chapters in this volume.
55. J. Adam Tooze, *The Wages of Destruction: The Making and Breaking of the Nazi Economy* (New York, 2007), 245ff., quote on 245.
56. Features in the status and development of the Sparkassen in the repatriated regions. Results of the annual statistics of the Sparkassen for 1938 and 1939. Prepared in the Reich Statistical Office. Reporting secretary Dr. Dr. Winkler. Concluded 3 July 1941, [MS Berlin 1941], 5ff., LA Berlin, A Rep. 219 Sparkasse der Stadt Berlin, no. 140, no fol.
57. Ibid., 1.
58. Klaus-Dietmar Henke, *Die Dresdner Bank 1933–1945: Ökonomische Rationalität, Regimenähe, Mittäterschaft* (Munich, 2006), 109; Norbert Frei et al., *Flick: Der Konzern, die Familie, die Macht* (Munich, 2009), 225–254. On the plunder of precious metals in the annexed and occupied regions, see Ralf Banken, *Edelmetallmangel und Großraubwirtschaft: Die Entwicklung des deutschen Edelmetallsektors im "Dritten Reich" 1933–1945* (Berlin, 2009) 286–364, 397–475.
59. Gruner, *Zwangsarbeit und Verfolgung*, 103f.
60. On this, see the corresponding chapter in this volume.
61. On the Reich Association, see Esriel Hildesheimer, *Die Jüdische Selbstverwaltung unter dem NS-Regime. Der Existenzkampf der Reichsvertretung und Reichsvereinigung der Juden in Deutschland* (Tübingen,1994); Beate Meyer, *Tödliche Gratwanderung: die Reichsvereinigung der Juden in Deutschland zwischen Hoffnung, Zwang, Selbstbehauptung und Verstrickung (1939–1945)* (Göttingen, 2011); Wolf Gruner, "Poverty and Persecution: The Reichsvereinigung, the Jewish Population, and the Anti-Jewish Policy in the Nazi-State, 1939–1945," *Yad Vashem Studies* 27 (1999), 23–60.
62. On this, see the contributions by Albert Lichtblau, Jörg Osterloh, Wolf Gruner, and Sybille Steinbacher in this volume.
63. The founding of the Reich Central Office by Göring as well as its status as part of the Reich Interior Ministry contradicts the claim, reiterated most recently by Jasch, that the SS assumed control of Jewish policy as a result of this founding; Jasch, *Staatssekretär Wilhelm Stuckart*, 271 and 282; in contrast, see Jasch himself regarding the further leading role of Reich Interior Ministry in important measures to strip Jews of their rights, ibid., 293.
64. See here the chapters by Albert Lichtblau and Wolf Gruner in this volume.
65. Hans Safrian, *Eichmann's Men* (Cambridge, 2009) (German original: 1993); Gabriele Anderl, "Die 'Zentralstellen für jüdische Auswanderung' in Wien, Berlin und Prag—ein Vergleich," *Tel Aviver Jahrbuch für deutsche Geschichte* 23 (1994): 276–299; Gabriele Anderl, and Dirk Rupnow, *Die Zentralstelle für jüdische Auswanderung als Beraubungsinstitution*, (Vienna, 2004); Anna Hájková, "The Making of a Zentralstelle: Die Eichmann-Männer in Amsterdam," *Theresienstädter Studien und Dokumente* (2003): 353–382.
66. Harold James, *Die Deutsche Bank und die "Arisierung"* (Munich, 2001), 141.
67. On this, see also Bernhard Lorentz, "Die Commerzbank und die 'Arisierung' im 'Altreich': Ein Vergleich der Netzwerkstrukturen und Handlungsspielräume von Großbanken in der NS-Zeit," *Vierteljahrshefte für Zeitgeschichte* 50 (2002): 237–268, here 239.
68. Wolf Gruner, ed., *Die Verfolgung und Ermordung der europäischen Juden durch das nationalsozialistische Deutschland 1933–1945*, vol. 1: *Deutsches Reich 1933 bis 1937* (Munich, 2008), doc. 274, 649–656.

69. On this, see Osterloh, *Judenverfolgung*, 263–299, as well as his contribution to this volume.
70. For details on the Protectorate of Bohemia and Moravia, Alsace, and Luxembourg, see the corresponding chapters in this volume.
71. Verena Pawlowsky et al., *Vereine im Nationalsozialismus: Vermögensentzug durch den Stillhaltekommissar für Vereine, Organisationen und Verbände und Aspekte der Restitution in Österreich nach 1945* (Vienna, 2004), 43ff., 79f., 97ff.
72. Jeanne Dingell, *Zur Tätigkeit der Haupttreuhandstelle Ost, Treuhandstelle Posen 1939 bis 1945* (Frankfurt, 2003); Ingo Loose, *Kredite für NS-Verbrechen: Die deutschen Kreditinstitute in Polen und die Ausraubung der polnischen und jüdischen Bevölkerung 1939–1945* (Munich, 2007); Bernhard Rosenkötter, *Treuhandpolitik: Die "Haupttreuhandstelle Ost" und der Raub polnischer Vermögen 1939–1945* (Essen, 2003).
73. Alexander B. Rossino, *Hitler Strikes Poland: Blitzkrieg, Ideology, and Atrocity* (Lawrence, KS, 2003); Jochen Böhler, *Auftakt zum Vernichtungskrieg: Die Wehrmacht in Polen 1939* (Frankfurt, 2006).
74. Mazower, *Hitler's Empire*, 79, 84 See also the recent work by Gerhard Wolf, *Ideologie und Herrschaftsrationalität: Nationalsozialistische Germanisierungspolitik in Polen* (Hamburg, 2012).
75. On the following, see the detailed account by Longerich, *Holocaust*, 150–155. On the planning of the deportations see Wolf Gruner, "Von der Kollektivausweisung zur Deportation der Juden aus Deutschland (1938–1945): Neue Perspektiven und Dokumente," in *Die Deportation der Juden aus Deutschland. Pläne, Praxis, Reaktionen 1938–1945*, ed. Birthe Kundrus and Beate Meyer, Beiträge zur Geschichte des Nationalsozialismus, vol. 20 (Göttingen, 2004), 21–62.
76. See chapters 5, 6, 8, and 9 in Wolf Gruner, *Jewish Forced Labor under the Nazis: Economic Needs and Racial Aims, 1938–1944* (New York, 2006).
77. Using the Litzmannstadt ghetto as an example, Christopher Browning, *Die Entfesselung der "Endlösung": Nationalsozialistische Judenpolitik 1939–1942*, with an article by Jürgen Matthäus (Munich, 2003), 173–183.
78. See the contributions by Wolfgang Gippert, Ingo Loose, Sybille Steinbacher, and Wolf Gruner to this volume.
79. Mazower, *Hitler's Empire*, 79, 84.
80. See most recently Michael Alberti, *Die Verfolgung und Vernichtung der Juden im Reichsgau Wartheland 1939–1945* (Wiesbaden, 2006); also Ingo Loose's contribution to this volume.
81. On this, see Sybille Steinbacher's contribution to volume, as well as idem., *"Musterstadt" Auschwitz: Germanisierungspolitik und Judenmord in Ostoberschlesien* (Munich, 2000).
82. See the chapters by Jörg Osterloh and Jean-Marc Dreyfus in this volume.
83. See the corresponding chapters in this volume.
84. Michael Mann, *The Dark Side of Democracy: Explaining Ethnic Cleansing* (New York, 2005), 195f.
85. On this, see the corresponding chapters in this volume.
86. See Jörg Osterloh's contribution to this volume, as well as Osterloh, *Judenverfolgung*, especially 302–313.
87. See Wolf Gruner's contribution to this volume, as well as Martin Dean, *Robbing the Jews: The Confiscation of Jewish Property in the Holocaust, 1933–1945* (Cambridge, 2008), 136ff.
88. On this, see the chapter by Ingo Loose in this volume.
89. Gruner, *Jewish Forced Labor*; also ibid., *Der Geschlossene Arbeitseinsatz deutscher Juden: Zur Zwangsarbeit als Element der Verfolgung 1938–1943* (Berlin, 1996). On

East Upper Silesia, see Sybille Steinbacher's contribution to this in volume, as well as Steinbacher, *"Musterstadt" Auschwitz*. On the Litzmannstadt ghetto, see Andrea Löw, *Juden im Getto Litzmannstadt: Lebensbedingungen, Selbstwahrnehmung, Verhalten*, (Göttingen, 2006); Klein, *Die "Gettoverwaltung Litzmannstadt."*

90. Second Ordinance on the Enactment of the Ordinance on the Levy of a Social Equalization Tax of 24 December 1940, RGBl. 1940 I, 1666.
91. On this discussion see the detailed account in Gruner, *Geschlossener Arbeitseinsatz*, 194–204. On the situation in the Warthegau and East Upper Silesia, see the chapters by Ingo Loose and Sybille Steinbacher in this volume.
92. Ordinance on the Employment of Jews, RGBl. 1941 I, 675.
93. On this see the corresponding chapters in this volume.
94. See here the chapters by Andreas Schulz, Ingo Loose, Sybille Steinbacher, and Wolf Gruner in this volume.
95. See the conclusion in Gruner, *Jewish Forced Labor*.
96. BArch, R 43 II/583, fol. 60. See Wolf Gruner, "Greater Germany," in *The Oxford Handbook of Holocaust Studies*, ed. Peter Hayes and John Roth (New York, 2010), 293–309.
97. On the deportations, see Alfred Gottwaldt and Diana Schulle, *Die "Judendeportationen" aus dem Deutschen Reich 1941–1945" Eine kommentierte Chronologie* (Wiesbaden, 2005).
98. Surprisingly, thus far only Hoffmann's activities in the Gau of Westphalia-South have been the subject of biographical research: Ralf Blank, "Albert Hoffmann als Reichsverteidigungskommissar im Gau Westfalen-Süd, 1943–1945: Eine biografische Skizze," in *"Bürokratien": Initiative und Effizienz*, ed. Wolf Gruner and Armin Nolzen, Beiträge zur Geschichte des Nationalsozialismus, vol. 17 (Berlin, 2001),189–210; Ralf Blank, "Albert Hoffmann: Gauleiter und Reichsverteidigungskommissar in Westfalen-Süd 1943–1945," in *Westfälische Lebensbilder* 17, ed. Friedrich Gerhard Hohmann (Münster, 2005) 255–290.
99. Law on the Confiscation of Communist Assets of 26 May 1933 and the Law on the Confiscation of Assets Hostile to the People and the State of 14 July 1933, RGBl. 1933 I, 293, 479.
100. Eleventh Ordinance on the Reich Citizen Law of 25 November 1941, RGBl. 1941 I, 722–724.

Review of the Literature and Research on the Individual Regions

Wolf Gruner and Jörg Osterloh

In the decades after the Second World War, the historiography in Germany initially developed along trajectories that were as divided as the nation itself. Efforts in the Federal Republic[1] and the GDR to grapple with the Nazi persecution of the Jews began in the 1960s, starting with the publication in the GDR of an important edition of documents on the persecution of the Jews in occupied Poland that also included the regions annexed by the Reich.[2] The period from the 1960s to the 1980s also witnessed the publication in both countries of the first isolated studies and documentations on the policies of the Nazi regime in the annexed regions—in West Germany, for example, the books by Martin Broszat and Detlef Brandes, respectively on Poland and the Protectorate of Bohemia and Moravia, which were dedicated above all to the history of the occupation.[3] Investigations that also examined anti-Jewish policy in the annexed regions first appeared in the 1980s; due, on the one hand, to a lack of academic interest and, on other hand, to the almost total inability of researchers from the West to access archives in Socialist countries, these investigations were mostly conducted by indigenous researchers.[4] This period also featured the East-German publication of the first books of the multivolume edition of documents entitled *Europa unterm Hakenkreuz*[5] (the project remained incomplete upon German reunification), which assigned a prominent role to the subject of this present anthology. But the first studies based on broad source materials that examined the annexed regions—often conducted as part of dissertations—did not appear in Germany until more than a decade later.[6] In addition, a number of anthologies more systematically examined various aspects of Nazi occupation policy in Europe.[7]

For all of the regions studied in this volume, *Die Verfolgung und Ermordung der europäischen Juden durch das nationalsozialistische Deutschland 1933–1945*—an edition of source material planned for sixteen volumes and produced through the collaboration of the German Federal Archives, the Institute of Contemporary History Munich–Berlin, and the Chair for Modern and Contemporary History at the University of Freiburg/Breisgau (Albert-Ludwigs-Universität Freiburg)—has recently made available in printed form central and exemplary documents from German and other European archives, as well as from archives in Israel and United States.[8] An anthology recently published by Christoph Buchheim and Marcel Boldorf deals with economic aspects of the persecution of the Jews, including in the regions annexed by Germany between 1938 and 1945.[9]

In the 1970s and 1980s, historical scholarship in the German Federal Republic concentrated on the establishment of Nazi rule in Germany and on accounts of the Jewish population's deportation. This applies in much the same way to historiography about the Saarland,[10] although Albert Marx submitted a well-founded overview of Jewish history in this region in the longue durée from the Ancien Régime to the Second World War as a dissertation, which admittedly did not appear in print until 1992.[11] Since the 1990s, we have been able to observe differentiation taking place here as well.[12] Nonetheless, a specific interest in the early regional deportations of 1940 still continued to dominate any research into anti-Jewish policy in the Saarland.[13]

Unique among the countries and territories annexed by Germany and dealt with in this volume, Austria figures prominently to this day in Holocaust research because of the radicalization of Jewish policy in the first weeks after the Anschluss, the impact of these developments on the Reich government's policies, and the massive involvement of Austrians in the destruction of the Jews.[14] Even so, the number of detailed studies on the Nazi persecution of the Jews in Austria itself remained limited for a long time; Austrian researchers often only mentioned this persecution in the margins of their work.[15] And this despite the fact that Herbert Rosenkranz published a rather large study in 1978 on the fate of the Austrian Jews from the perspective of the Vienna Israelite Community.[16] As of the late 1980s, historians in Austria first focused more sharply on particular aspects of anti-Jewish policy:

the plundering of assets,[17] housing policy,[18] the perpetrators,[19] and persecutions at regional levels.[20] Knowledge about persecution policies and their impact on the Jewish population improved significantly with two individual studies presented by Doron Rabinovici and Wolf Gruner in 2000.[21] The Historical Commission appointed by the Austrian Republic dealt intensively with the "Aryanization" and restitution of Jewish assets as well as with a number of persecutory institutions.[22] Most recently, works have appeared that investigate the fate of the Hungarian Jews deported to Austria.[23]

While almost every survey of the Third Reich has dealt with anti-Jewish policies in Austria, the persecution of the Jews in the annexed Czech territories—namely, the Sudetenland and the Protectorate of Bohemia and Moravia—figure neither in the early overviews by Raul Hilberg and Uwe Dietrich Adam nor in the more recent studies by Peter Longerich, Christopher Browning, and Saul Friedländer.[24] Thus the events in the Sudetenland between 1938 and 1945 were kept in the dark—in the German Federal Republic also probably in an effort to avoid damaging the self-portrayal of Sudeten-German ethnic groups.[25] Scholarship concentrated primarily on the German-Czech nationality conflicts and the historical developments leading to the Munich Agreement.[26] The first foundational studies on the Sudetenland during the Nazi period did not appear until the 1990s.[27] Czech historiography, too, only started focusing attention on the fate of the Jews in this region since this time.[28] Jörg Osterloh presented the first comprehensive and source-based study on the persecution of the Jews in the Sudetenland in 2006.[29] In September 2008, an international conference of historians in Munich summarized the state of research regarding the background, realization, and consequences of the Munich Agreement; the results appeared in print in 2013.[30]

Neither have the events in the Protectorate of Bohemia and Moravia received very much attention, even to this day—this notwithstanding Gerhard Jacoby's early publication in 1944 in the United States of one of the first studies of the occupation and persecution, expressively entitled the *Racial State*.[31] After the war, many historians admittedly dealt with the Theresienstadt (Terezín) ghetto, located in the Protectorate, but only because German Jews were deported to this site. From the German perspective, the Protectorate only seemed interesting as an example of Nazi Germanization policy or—in the GDR—of resistance against the Nazi occupation.[32] International research had been dealing with the Jewish population in Bohemia and Moravia[33] for a long time, but prior to 1990 had rarely examined Nazi occupation. With his book published in 1969 on Nazi rule in the Protectorate—still considered a key work—Detlef Brandes placed a stumbling block in the way of more intensive research into anti-Jewish policy by assuming that the Czechs had refused to issue anti-Jewish laws, and that this was why such laws were issued by the German Reich Protector of Bohemia and Moravia.[34] Only recently have studies appeared in Germany offering different assessments of both the development of anti-Jewish policy and the role of the Czech government.[35] Academic corporate histories have recently described the plunder of Jewish assets with respect to Bohemia and Moravia as well.[36] Meanwhile, in the Czechoslovakian Republic, early accounts of persecution policy came from authors—H. G. Adler, for example—who were themselves victimized by such policies.[37] Systematic research began as of the mid 1970s, due to the efforts of Miroslav Kárný.[38] Since the beginning of the 1990s, the topic—along with the hitherto predominant fate of non-Jewish Czechs and their resistance against the occupation—drew substantially more attention.[39] Unfortunately, important monographs that have since been published are often only available in Czech.[40] In contrast, Livia Rothkirchen's comprehensive account on the history of the Jews in the Protectorate, published in 2005, does not contain an analysis of anti-Jewish policies, nor does it examine the impact of such policies on the population.[41] Isabel Heinemann's pioneering study on the SS's Race and Settlement Main Office deals also with the "racial" population surveys in Bohemia and Moravia; Detlef Brandes has recently analyzed the Nazi regime's *Volkstumspolitik*—ethnic policies—in the region.[42] *Volkstumspolitik* and Jewish policy as segments of Nazi occupation policy in Bohemia and Moravia are also examined in René Küpper's biographical studies about Karl Hermann Frank, the Reich Protector's State Secretary, respectively as of 1943 the State Minister in the Protectorate, and in Robert Gerwarth's biographical study about Reinhard Heydrich, who until his death in early June 1942 managed the Reich Protector's affairs.[43] Recent research has more closely examined questions regarding national identity and cohabitation—cooperating, coexisting, and competing—of Czechs, Germans, and Jews in Bohemia and Moravia and also particularly in Prague.[44]

The literature about the Jewish population in the Memel Territory is extremely sparse, both in Germany as well as Lithuania. Historians have predominantly focused on German-Lithuanian relations prior to the annexation.[45] Due to losses during the war, the source material is also very thin. Well-founded research about Nazi rule and the persecution of the Jews has yet to appear,[46] although Ruth Leiserowitz has recently presented the first larger overview of the history of the Jews in the East Prussian–Lithuanian border region.[47]

For Poland—along with a Black Book already published by Polish government in exile in 1942—important Polish documentations appeared soon after the war; pertaining to specific aspects of occupation and Jewish policy, they also included regions such as the Warthegau.[48] In the 1960s, Martin Broszat and Czesław Madajczyk presented the first foundational analysis of the Nazi occupation.[49] While many local and regional studies were published in Poland, research in Germany on this topic—as in other European countries—only began in the mid 1990s, made possible above all by the now unhindered access to sources. Studies of anti-Jewish policies are now available for three of the five districts of the General Government.[50]

The status of research regarding the Polish regions annexed by the German Reich varies substantially. The few older accounts of the history of the Jews in Danzig and West Prussia hardly deal with the persecution,[51] while more recent studies only investigate the fate of the Jews in the Stutthof concentration camp.[52] For the part of Northern Mazovia annexed by the Reich in 1939 as the Government District of Zichenau, the standard work still today remains the study by Michał Grynberg, which advances the thesis—long established in Polish historiography—that the extermination of the Jews had already been planned when the war began.[53] The status of research for the Warthegau and East Upper Silesia is somewhat better. Götz Aly's 1995 study of the "Final Solution" already referred especially to the Warthegau.[54] In 2006, Michael Alberti published his well-founded investigation of the murder of the Jews in this region.[55] Catherine Epstein's biographical study about the region's NSDAP Gauleiter Arthur Greiser also delivered important findings regarding the policies of occupation and persecution in the Warthegau.[56] Apart from various Polish studies about the Warthegau,[57] works appearing in Germany dealt chiefly with the Litzmannstadt (Łódź) ghetto. Along with an initial investigation by Josef Wulf from the early 1960s and an exhibition catalog by the Jewish Museum in Frankfurt from 1990, today we also have the results of research by Michal Unger, Andrea Löw, and Peter Klein.[58] The Polish historian Alfred Konieczny presented multiple studies on Upper Silesia.[59] Jewish forced labor in this region was and is being investigated by a number of researchers.[60] In her dissertation published in 2000, Sybille Steinbacher ultimately examines the connections between Germanization plans and the murder of the Jews in East Upper Silesia.[61] Meanwhile, the number of studies about the

Auschwitz concentration—and extermination—camp, located in the territory, is legion.[62] A conference report published on behalf of the German Historical Institute Warsaw provides an initial overview of the annexed Polish regions, comparing the Nazi policies pursued here with those in the General Government. The persecution of the Jews, however, is just one of many aspects.[63] Researchers have continued to deal intensively with the ghettos in occupied Poland,[64] motivated in large part by the debates surrounding the Federal Republic's Ghetto Pensions Act from 2002.[65] An atlas published by Polish specialists also illustrates the migrations—resettlements, expulsions, and flights—in the annexed Polish regions from 1939 to 1945.[66] Germanization policies constitute the focal point of a new German study.[67]

In contrast, the situation with respect to research into anti-Jewish policy in the regions annexed in the West looks rather poor. Even today, a survey of the history of the Jews in Luxembourg does not exist. A Festschrift written by Grand Rabbi Charles Lehrmann on the occasion of the consecration of the new synagogue in Luxembourg appeared in 1953.[68] In the 1970s and 1980s, Paul Cerf dealt with the persecutions during the occupation period.[69] Meanwhile, in his dissertation published in 1985, Paul Dostert critically examined the occupation, Germanization policy, resistance, and collaboration, while at the same time also dealing with the persecution of the Luxembourg Jews.[70] Starting in the 1990s, interest increased both domestically and abroad.[71] The subject of Jewish persecution features in the volume devoted to Luxembourg in the East German documentation *Europa unterm Hakenkreuz*.[72] Since the end of the 1990s, smaller and larger publications have appeared in Luxembourg itself, such as exhibition catalogs[73] and studies on specific aspects, such as the "Jewish Old Age Home" in Fünfbrunnen[74] and individual Jewish communities.[75] The Commission spéciale pour l'étude des spoliations des biens juifs au Luxembourg pendant les années de guerre 1940–1945, under the direction of Paul Dostert, began its work in 2002, investigating the "Aryanizations" and expropriations in Luxembourg under the German occupation. The Commission presented its final report in 2009.[76] Only recently, a more general study on Luxembourg during the Second World War appeared, with which Hans-Erich Volkmann examines the German occupational and economic policies in detail.[77]

In Belgium the research situation is even more problematic. Whereas the history of Eupen-Malmedy and the German-speaking community in Belgium has been investigated during the last ten years, this does not apply to the persecution of the Jews.[78] The level of knowledge regarding the persecution of the Jews in Alsace-Lorraine is not much better. With the exception of individual features, the occupation period and the persecution in this region remain insufficiently explored. The standard work continues to be Lothar Kettenacker's study from 1973 on *Volkstumspolitik* in Alsace,[79] while Christopher J. Fischer has more recently conducted closer investigations into the "prehistory" of this policy between 1870 and the eve of the German occupation.[80] References to anti-Jewish policy can also be found in studies on the persecutions in France, where the expelled Alsatian Jews were treated as a category of persecuted individuals.[81]

Thus overall, apart from a few exceptions, the anti-Jewish policies during the occupation in many of the regions annexed by Germany still require major research even today. Generally speaking, since the 1990s, in the course of the old bloc system's collapse and the national redefinitions within the European framework, as well as with the differentiated focuses and internationalization of Holocaust research, a tendency has emerged both in Germany and most other countries to more openly welcome this research, even if it raises painful questions about the collaboration and cooperation of indigenous populations with the Nazi state.

Notes

The editors thank the authors for their preliminary work for the individual sections of this literature review.

1. For example, Wolfgang Scheffler, *Judenverfolgung im Dritten Reich* (Berlin, 1960). On this, see also Dieter Pohl, "Die Holocaustforschung und Goldhagens Thesen," *Vierteljahrshefte für Zeitgeschichte* 45 (1997): 1–48, here 3f.
2. Jüdisches Historisches Institut Warschau, Berlin (DDR), ed., *Faschismus—Getto—Massenmord: Dokumentation über Ausrottung und Widerstand der Juden in Polen während des Zweiten Weltkrieges* (East Berlin, 1960). See, as an overview, Joachim Käppner, *Erstarrte Geschichte: Faschismus und Holocaust im Spiegel der Geschichtswissenschaft und Geschichtspropaganda der DDR* (Hamburg, 1999).
3. Martin Broszat, *Nationalsozialistische Polenpolitik 1939–1945* (Stuttgart, 1961); Detlef Brandes, *Die Tschechen unter deutschem Protektorat*, part I: *Besatzungspolitik, Kollaboration und Widerstand im Protektorat Böhmen und Mähren bis Heydrichs Tod (1939–1942)* (Munich, 1969); part II: *Besatzungspolitik, Kollaboration und Widerstand im Protektorat Böhmen und Mähren von Heydrichs Tod bis zum Prager Aufstand (1942–1945)* (Munich, 1975).
4. On this, see the foreword by Hans Lemberg in Ralf Gebel, *"Heim ins Reich!" Konrad Henlein und der Reichsgau Sudetenland (1838–1945)* (Munich, 1999), IX.
5. See, for example, *Europa unterm Hakenkreuz: Die faschistische Okkupationspolitik in Österreich und der Tschechoslowakei (1938–1945)*, document selection and introduction by Helma Kaden, with the collaboration of Ludwig Nestler et al. (East

Berlin, 1988); *Europa unterm Hakenkreuz: Die faschistische Okkupationspolitik in Polen (1939–1945)*, document selection and introduction by Werner Röhr, with the collaboration of Elke Heckert et al. (East Berlin, 1989).

6. Thus, for example, Sybille Steinbacher, *"Musterstadt" Auschwitz: Germanisierungspolitik und Judenmord in Ostoberschlesien* (Munich, 2000); Wolf Gruner, *Zwangsarbeit und Verfolgung: Österreichische Juden im NS-Staat 1938–45* (Innsbruck, 2000); Jörg Osterloh, *Nationalsozialistische Judenverfolgung im Reichsgau Sudetenland 1938–1945* (Munich, 2006); Michael Alberti, *Die Verfolgung und Vernichtung der Juden im Reichsgau Wartheland 1939–1945* (Wiesbaden, 2006).

7. See, for example, Richard J. Overy et al., eds., *Die "Neuordnung" Europas: Die Wirtschaftspolitik in den besetzten Gebieten* (Berlin, 1997); Wolfgang Benz et al., eds., *Die Bürokratie der Okkupation: Strukturen der Herrschaft und Verwaltung im besetzten Europa* (Berlin, 1998); Johannes Houwink ten Cate and Gerhard Otto, eds., *Das organisierte Chaos: "Ämterdarwinismus" und "Gesinnungsethik": Determinanten nationalsozialistischer Besatzungsherrschaft* (Berlin, 1999); Gerhard Paul and Klaus-Michael Mallmann, eds., *Die Gestapo im Zweiten Weltkrieg: "Heimatfront" und besetztes Europa* (Darmstadt, 2000); Gregor Thum, *Traumland Osten: Deutsche Bilder vom östlichen Europa im 20. Jahrhundert* (Göttingen, 2006); Wolfgang Wippermann, *Die Deutschen und der Osten: Feindbild und Traumland* (Darmstadt, 2007).

8. Of the volumes that have appeared thus far, the ones relevant to the regions treated in this volume are: *Die Verfolgung und Ermordung der europäischen Juden durch das nationalsozialistische Deutschland 1933–1945 (VEJ)*, vol. 2: *Deutsches Reich, 1938-August 1939*, ed. Susanne Heim (Munich, 2009); *VEJ*, vol. 3: *Deutsches Reich und Protektorat September 1939—September 1941*, ed. Andrea Löw (Munich, 2012); *VEJ*, vol. 4: *Polen September 1939—Juli 1941*, ed. Klaus-Peter Friedrich (Munich, 2011); *VEJ*, vol. 5: *West- und Nordeuropa 1940—Juni 1942*, ed. Michael Mayer, Katja Happe, and Maja Peers (Munich, 2013); *VEJ*, vol. 10: *Die eingegliederten polnischen Gebiete Sommer 1941–1945*, ed. Ingo Loose (Munich, 2014). An overview of the publishing project can be found at http://www.edition-judenverfolgung.de/neu/index.php?option=com_content&view=article&id=55&Itemid=27 (accessed 12 August 2014).

9. Christoph Buchheim and Marcel Boldorf, eds., *Europäische Volkswirtschaften unter deutscher Hegemonie 1938–1945* (Munich, 2012).

10. Fritz Jacoby, *Die nationalsozialistische Herrschaftsübernahme an der Saar: Die innenpolitischen Probleme der Rückgliederung des Saargebietes bis 1935* (Saarbrücken, 1973); Editha Bucher, "Die Listen der am 22. Oktober 1940 aus der Pfalz und dem Saarland nach Gurs deportierten Juden," in *Dokumente des Gedenkens*, ed. Franz-Josef Heyen (Koblenz, 1974), 115–118; Hans-Walter Herrmann, "Das Schicksal der Juden im Saarland 1920 bis 1945," in *Die nationalsozialistische Judenverfolgung in Rheinland-Pfalz 1933 bis 1945*, Dokumentation zur Geschichte der jüdischen Bevölkerung in Rheinland-Pfalz und im Saarland von 1800 bis 1945, vol. 6 (Koblenz, 1974), 259–491; Werner Knopp, "Jüdische Bevölkerung in Bürgermeistereien des Saargebietes nach der Volkszählung vom 19. Juli 1927," in *Statistische Materialien zur Geschichte der jüdischen Bevölkerung*, Dokumentation zur Geschichte der jüdischen Bevölkerung in Rheinland-Pfalz und im Saarland von 1800 bis 1945, vol. 5 (Koblenz, 1975), 149–151; Heinrich Rudnick, "Nachforschungen über das weitere Schicksal der am 22. Oktober 1940 aus dem Saarland nach Gurs verschickten Juden und der Träger des Judensterns im Saarland," *Jahrbuch für westdeutsche Landesgeschichte* 1 (1975): 337–372.

11. Albert Marx, *Die Geschichte der Juden an der Saar: Vom Ancien Régime bis zum Zweiten Weltkrieg* (Saarbrücken, 1992).
12. Dieter Muskalla, *NS-Politik an der Saar unter Josef Bürckel: Gleichschaltung, Neuordnung, Verwaltung* (Saarbrücken, 1995). On the Jews in the Saar region's second-largest city, see Dieter Blinn, *Juden in Homburg: Geschichte einer jüdischen Lebenswelt 1330—1945* (Homburg-Saarpfalz, 1993).
13. Erhard R. Wiehn, ed., *Oktoberdeportation 1940: Die sogenannte "Abschiebung" der badischen und saarpfälzischen Juden in das französische Internierungslager Gurs und andere Vorstationen von Auschwitz* (Konstanz, 1990); Gerhard J. Teschner, *Die Deportation der badischen und saarpfälzischen Juden am 22. Oktober 1940: Vorgeschichte und Durchführung der Deportation und das weitere Schicksal der Deportierten bis zum Kriegsende im Kontext der deutschen und französischen Judenpolitik* (Frankfurt, 2002).
14. The first general accounts of the Nazi persecution of the Jews, however, did not address the radicalizing influence of the events in Austria and especially Vienna in the spring of 1938. See, for example, Gerald Reitlinger, *The Final Solution: The Attempt to Exterminate the Jews of Europe 1939–1945* (London, 1952); Raul Hilberg, *The Destruction of the European Jews* (Chicago, 1961); Uwe Dietrich Adam, *Judenpolitik im Dritten Reich* (Düsseldorf, 1972). In contrast, Austria always occupies an important place in more recent accounts, for example Peter Longerich, *Holocaust: The Nazi Persecution and Murder of the Jews* (Oxford, 2010) (German original: Munich 1998); Saul Friedländer, *Nazi Germany and the Jews*, vol. 1: *The Years of Persecution, 1933–1939* (New York, 1997), and *Nazi Germany and the Jews, 1939–1945: The Years of Extermination* (New York, 2007).
15. Emmerich Tálos et al., eds., *Die NS-Herrschaft in Österreich 1938–1945* (Vienna, 1988); Dokumentationsarchiv des österreichischen Widerstandes, ed., *"Anschluß" 1938: Eine Dokumentation* (Vienna, 1988); Dokumentationsarchiv des österreichischen Widerstands, ed., *Widerstand und Verfolgung in Oberösterreich 1934–1945: Eine Dokumentation*, vol. 2 (Vienna, 1982); Dokumentationsarchiv des österreichischen Widerstands, ed., *Widerstand und Verfolgung in Wien 1934–1945: Eine Dokumentation*, vol. 3: *1938–1945*, 2nd ed. (Vienna, 1984).
16. Herbert Rosenkranz, *Verfolgung und Selbstbehauptung: Die Juden in Österreich 1938 bis 1945* (Vienna, 1978).
17. Hans Safrian and Hans Witek, *Und keiner war dabei: Dokumente des alltäglichen Antisemitismus in Wien 1938* (Vienna, 1988).
18. Gerhard Botz, *Wohnungspolitik und Judendeportation in Wien 1938 bis 1945: Zur Funktion des Antisemitismus als Ersatz nationalsozialistischer Sozialpolitik* (Vienna and Salzburg, 1975); Herbert Exenberger et al., *Kündigungsgrund Nichtarier: Die Vertreibung jüdischer Mieter aus den Wiener Gemeindebauten in den Jahren 1938–1939* (Vienna, 1996).
19. Hans Safrian, *Eichmann's Men* (Cambridge, 2009) (German original: 1993); David Cesarani, *Eichmann: His Life and Crimes* (London, 2004).
20. For example, Friedrich Polleroß, ed., *"Die Erinnerung tut zu weh." Jüdisches Leben und Antisemitismus im Waldviertel* (Horn, 1996); Robert Streibel, *Plötzlich waren sie alle weg: Die Juden der "Gauhauptstadt Krems" und ihre Mitbürger* (Vienna, 1991); August Walzl, *Die Juden in Kärnten und das Dritte Reich* (Klagenfurt, 1987).
21. Doron Rabinovici, *Eichmann's Jews: The Jewish Administration of Holocaust Vienna, 1938–1945* (Cambridge, 2011) (German original: 2000); Wolf Gruner, *Zwangsarbeit und Verfolgung: Österreichische Juden im NS-Staat 1938–1945* (Innsbruck, 2000).

22. See, for example, Gabriele Anderl and Dirk Rupnow, *Die Zentralstelle für jüdische Auswanderung als Beraubungsinstitution* (Vienna, 2004); Shoshana Duizend-Jensen, *Jüdische Gemeinden, Vereine, Stiftungen und Fonds: "Arisierung" und Restitution* (Vienna, 2004).
23. Eleonore Lappin-Eppel, *Ungarisch-Jüdische Zwangsarbeiter und Zwangsarbeiterinnen in Österreich 1944/45- Arbeitseinsatz—Todesmärsche—Folgen* (Vienna, 2010); Walter Manoschek, ed., *Der Fall Rechnitz: Das Massaker an Juden im März 1945* (Vienna, 2009).
24. Hilberg, *The Destruction of the European Jews*; Adam, *Judenpolitik*; Longerich, *Holocaust*; Christopher Browning, *The Origins of the Final Solution: The Evolution of Nazi Jewish Policy, September 1939–March 1942* (Lincoln, NE, 2004); Friedländer, *Nazi Germany and the Jews*. See also Martin Dean et al., eds., *Robbery and Restitution: The Conflict over Jewish Property in Europe* (New York, 2007).
25. Gebel, *"Heim ins Reich!"* 5; Detlef Brandes and Václav Kural, "Der Weg in die Katastrophe: Forschungsstand und -probleme," in *Der Weg in die Katastrophe: Deutsch-tschechoslowakische Beziehungen 1938–1947*, ed. Detlef Brandes and Václav Kural (Essen, 1994), 17.
26. Johann Wolfgang Brügel, *Tschechen und Deutsche*, vol. 1: *1918–1938* (Munich, 1967), vol. 2: *1939–1946* (Munich, 1974); Rudolf Jaworski, *Vorposten oder Minderheit? Der sudetendeutsche Volkstumskampf in den Beziehungen zwischen der Weimarer Republik und der ČSR* (Stuttgart, 1977); Boris Čelovský, *Das Münchener Abkommen 1938* (Stuttgart, 1958); appearing shortly thereafter, the markedly nationalist-conservative study by Helmuth K. Rönnefarth, *Die Sudetenkrise in der internationalen Politik: Entstehung, Verlauf, Auswirkung* (Wiesbaden, 1961).
27. Volker Zimmermann, *Die Sudetendeutschen im NS-Staat: Politik und Stimmung der Bevölkerung im Reichsgau Sudetenland (1938–1945)* (Essen, 1999); Gebel, *"Heim ins Reich!"*
28. Ludomír Kocourek, "Das Schicksal der Juden im Sudetengau im Licht der erhaltenen Quellen," *Theresienstädter Studien und Dokumente* (1997): 86–104. An anthology that appeared in 2002 in the Czech Republic about "the 'people of the Sudetenland' under the swastika" also deals with the persecution of the Jews in a few scattered pages; Václav Kural et al., *"Sudety" pod Hákovým Křížem* (Ústí nad Labem, 2002), in particular 65ff., 81f. On the critique of Czech historiography, see Eva Hahn, "Verdrängung und Verharmlosung: Das Ende der jüdischen Bevölkerungsgruppe in den böhmischen Ländern nach ausgewählten tschechischen und sudetendeutschen Publikationen," in *Der Weg in die Katastrophe*, ed. Brandes and Kural, 135–150.
29. Jörg Osterloh, *Nationalsozialistische Judenverfolgung im Reichsgau Sudetenland 1938–1945* (Munich, 2006).
30. Regarding this subject, see Jörg Osterloh, "Die nationalsozialistische Politik gegen Juden und Tschechen im Sudetenland 1938–1945," in *Das Münchener Abkommen 1938 in europäischer Perspektive*, ed. Jürgen Zarusky and Martin Zückert (Munich, 2013), 291–306.
31. Gerhard Jacoby, *Racial State: The German Nationalities Policy in the Protectorate of Bohemia-Moravia* (New York, 1944).
32. See also *Europa unterm Hakenkreuz: Die faschistische Okkupationspolitik in Österreich und der Tschechoslowakei (1938–1945)*, document selection and introduction by Helma Kaden (East Berlin, 1988).
33. An overview is provided in "Bibliografie zur Geschichte der böhmischen Juden," in Rudolf M. Wlaschek, *Juden in Böhmen: Beiträge zur Geschichte des europäischen Judentums im 19. und 20. Jahrhundert*, 2nd ed. (Munich, 1997), 239–281. In the

United States, a multivolume work about the Jews in Czechoslovakia began appearing in 1968, which also included the Nazi period: Avigdor Dagan et al., eds., *The Jews of Czechoslovakia: Historical Studies and Surveys*, 3 vols. (Philadelphia, 1968, 1971, and 1984); one of the first surveys in Germany was Ferdinand Seibt, ed., *Die Juden in den böhmischen Ländern: Vorträge der Tagung des Collegium Carolinum in Bad Wiessee vom 27. bis 29. November 1981* (Munich, 1983).

34. He did so, for example, with respect to the ordinance from 21 June 1939, but without any further sources or other evidence; Brandes, *Die Tschechen unter deutschem Protektorat*, part 1, 45.

35. Wolf Gruner, "Protektorát Čechy a Morava a protižidovská politika v letech 1939–1941," in *Terezínské Studie a Dokumenty 2005* (Prague, 2005), 25–58 (German: "Das Protektorat Böhmen/Mähren und die antijüdische Politik 1939–1941: Lokale Initiativen, regionale Maßnahmen und zentrale Entscheidungen im 'Großdeutschen Reich,'" *Theresienstädter Studien und Dokumente 2005* (Prague, 2006), 27–62); see also the chapter "The Protectorate of Bohemia and Moravia," in Wolf Gruner, *Jewish Forced Labor under the Nazis: Economic Needs and Racial Aims (1938–1944)* (New York, 2006), 141–176. An effort that unfortunately remains analytically superficial and uses limited sources is Marc Oprach, *Nationalsozialistische Judenpolitik im Protektorat Böhmen und Mähren: Entscheidungsabläufe und Radikalisierung* (Hamburg, 2006).

36. See a number of the articles in Dieter Ziegler, ed., *Banken und "Arisierungen" in Mitteleuropa während des Nationalsozialismus* (Stuttgart, 2002); also Christoph Kreutzmüller and Jaroslav Kučera, "Die Commerzbank und die Vernichtung der jüdischen Gewerbetätigkeit in den böhmischen Ländern und den Niederlanden," in *Die Commerzbank und die Juden 1933–1945*, ed. Ludolf Herbst and Thomas Weihe (Munich, 2004), 173–222; Harald Wixforth, *Die Expansion der Dresdner Bank in Europa* (Munich, 2006), in collaboration with Johannes Bär et al., 306–350; Drahomír Jančík, Eduard Kubů, and Jiří Šouša, *Arisierungsgewinnler: Die Rolle der deutschen Banken bei der "Arisierung" und Konfiskation jüdischer Vermögen im Protektorat Böhmen und Mähren (1939–1945)* (Wiesbaden, 2011).

37. H. G. Adler provided the first important work on the Protectorate in 1955 with his monumental study of the "old-age ghetto" Theresienstadt: H. G. Adler, *Theresienstadt 1941–1945: Das Antlitz einer Zwangsgemeinschaft: Geschichte, Soziologie, Psychologie* (Tübingen, 1955); H. G. Adler, ed., *Die verheimlichte Wahrheit. Theresienstädter Dokumente* (Tübingen, 1958).

38. A survey of Kárnýs Œuvre is provided in "Auswahlbibliographie der Arbeiten von Miroslav Kárný 1971–2001," *Theresienstädter Studien und Dokumente* (2002): 33–44.

39. The focus on the latter topics, however, still persists uninterrupted. On the legal and political aspects of National Socialist occupation administration in the Protectorate of Bohemia and Moravia, see Pavel Maršálek, *Protektorát Čechy a Morava: Státoprávní a politické aspekty nacistického okupačního režimu v českých zemích 1939–1945* (Prague, 2002); a study of the Czech resistance and Czech collaboration is provided in Jan Boris Uhlíř, *Ve stínu říšské orlice: Protektorát Čechy a Morava, odboj a kolaborace* (Prague, 2002). On the historiography, see also Chad Bryant, *Prague in Black: Nazi Rule and Czech Nationalism* (Cambridge, 2007), 6ff.

40. Miroslav Kárný presented an initial study on the persecution and murder of the Czech Jews: Miroslav Kárný, *"Konečné řešení": Genocida českých Židů v německé protektorátní politice* (Prague, 1991); also relevant to the topic: Milena Janišová, ed., *Osud Židů v protektorátu 1939–1945* (Prague, 1991); the legal status of the Jews in the Protectorate is dealt with by Helena Petrův, *Právní postavení židů*

v *Protektorátu Čechy a Morava (1939–1941)* (Prague, 2000); sources on Reinhard Heydrich's impact on the Protectorate are provided by Miroslav Kárný and Jaroslava Milotová, eds., *Protektorátní politika Reinharda Heydricha* (Prague, 1991), published in German as Miroslav Kárný et al., ed., *Deutsche Politik im "Protektorat Böhmen und Mähren" under Reinhard Heydrich 1941–1942: Eine Dokumentation* (Berlin, 1997); see also the edition of documents compiled by Helena Krejčová et al., eds., *Židé v Protektorátu: Hlášení Židovské náboženské obce v roce 1942: Dokumenty* (Prague, 1997).

41. Livia Rothkirchen, *The Jews of Bohemia and Moravia: Facing the Holocaust* (Lincoln, NE, and Jerusalem, 2005).
42. Isabel Heinemann, *"Rasse, Siedlung, deutsches Blut": Das Rasse- und Siedlungshauptamt der SS und die rassenpolitische Neuordnung Europas* (Göttingen, 2003); Detlef Brandes, *"Umvolkung, Umsiedlung, rassische Bestandsaufnahme": NS-"Volkstumspolitik" in den böhmischen Ländern* (Munich, 2012).
43. René Küpper, *Karl Hermann Frank (1898–1946): Politische Biographie eines sudetendeutschen Nationalsozialisten* (Munich, 2010); Robert Gerwarth, *Hitler's Hangman: The Life of Heydrich* (New Haven, 2011).
44. Kateřina Čapková, *Czechs, Germans, Jews? National Identity and the Jews of Bohemia* (New York, 2012) (Czech original: 2005); Ines Koeltzsch, *Geteilte Kulturen: Eine Geschichte der tschechisch-jüdisch-deutschen Beziehungen in Prag (1918–1938)* (Munich, 2012).
45. Seppo Myllyniemi, *Die baltische Krise 1938–1941* (Stuttgart, 1979); Joachim Tauber, *Die deutsch-litauischen Beziehungen im 20. Jahrhundert* (Lüneburg, 1993); Vytautas Žalys, *Ringen um Identität: Warum Litauen zwischen 1923 und 1939 im Memelgebiet keinen Erfolg hatte* (Lüneburg, 1993); Alvydas Nikzentaitis, "Germany and the Memel Germans in the 1930s (On the Basis of Trials of Lithuanian Agents before the Volksgerichtshof, 1934–45)," *The Historical Journal* 39 (1996): 771–783; Joachim Tauber, ed., "Im Wandel der Zeiten: Die Stadt Memel im 20. Jahrhundert," special issue of *Nordost-Archiv* 10 (2001); Vytautas Vareikis, "Klaipėdos krašto praradimas: Tarp iliuzijų ir *Realpolitik*," in *Kultūros barai* 1, no. 3 (2009): 68–75.
46. Joachim Tauber, "Das Memelgebiet (1919–1945) in der deutschen und litauischen Historiographie nach 1945," *Nordost-Archiv* 10 (2001): 11–44. See, however, the chapter on the Memel Terriority in Christian Rohrer, *Nationalsozialistische Macht in Ostpreußen* (Munich, 2006), 497–532.
47. Ruth Leiserowitz, *Sabbatleuchter und Kriegerverein: Juden in der ostpreußisch-litauischen Grenzregion 1812–1942* (Osnabrück, 2010).
48. Polish Ministry of Information, *The Black Book of Poland* (New York, 1942); also, among others, Nachman Blumental, ed., *Dokumenty i Materiały*, vol. 1: *Obozy* (Lodz, 1946); Tatiana Berenstein et al., eds., *Eksterminacja Żydów na ziemiach polskich w okresie okupacji hitlerowskiej: Zbiór dokumentów* (Warsaw, 1957). On the early research in Poland, see also Pohl, "Holocaustforschung," 1f.
49. Broszat, *Nationalsozialistische Polenpolitik*; Czesław Madajczyk, *Polityka III Rzeszy w okupowanej Polsce* (Warsaw, 1970), published in German as *Die Okkupationspolitik Nazideutschlands in Polen 1939–1945* (East Berlin, 1987).
50. Dieter Pohl, *Von der "Judenpolitik" zum Judenmord: Der Distrikt Lublin des Generalgouvernements 1939–1944* (Frankfurt, 1993); idem, *Nationalsozialistische Judenverfolgung in Ostgalizien 1941–1944: Organisation und Durchführung eines staatlichen Massenverbrechens* (Munich, 1996); Thomas Sandkühler, *"Endlösung in Galizien": Der Judenmord in Ostpolen und die Rettungsinitiativen von Berthold Beitz 1941–1944* (Bonn, 1996); Bogdan Musiał, *Deutsche Zivilverwaltung und Judenverfolgung im Generalgouvernement: Eine Fallstudie zum Distrikt Lublin*

1939–1944 (Wiesbaden, 1999); Robert Seidel, *Deutsche Besatzungspolitik in Polen: Der Distrikt Radom 1939–1945* (Paderborn, 2006); Jacek Andrzej Młynarczyk, *Judenmord in Zentralpolen: Der Distrikt Radom im Generalgouvernement 1939–1945* (Darmstadt, 2007). Furthermore, Melanie Hembera is working on a dissertation project about the Krakow district at the Ruprecht Karl University of Heidelberg, with the working title "Die Shoah im Distrikt Krakau des Generalgouvernements: Eine Fallstudie am Beispiel der Stadt Tarnów."

51. Max Aschkewitz, *Zur Geschichte der Juden in Westpreußen* (Marburg an der Lahn, 1967); Grzegorz Berendt, "Die Danziger, Zoppoter und Gdinger Juden im 20. Jahrhundert: Ein historischer Vergleich," in *Zur Geschichte und Kultur der Juden in Ost- und Westpreußen*, ed. Michael Brocke et al. (Hildesheim, 2000), 187–201; Daniel Bogacz, *Fremde in einer freien Stadt: Deutsche, Polen und Juden in Danzig 1920–1939* (Bonn, 2004); Samuel Echt, *Die Geschichte der Juden in Danzig* (Leer, 1972); Sophia Kemlein, "Zur Geschichte der Juden in Westpreußen und Danzig (bis 1943)," in *Danzig—Gdańsk: Deutsch-polnische Geschichte, Politik und Literatur*, ed. Akademie für Lehrerfortbildung et al. (Dillingen, 1996), 94–109; Kozlowska, Kamila, *Die Juden in der Freien Stadt Danzig: Integrations- und Ausgrenzungsprozesse zwischen 1919 und 1933* (Munich, 2011). An exception is Ernst Sodeikat, "Die Verfolgung und der Widerstand der Juden in der Freien Stadt Danzig von 1933 bis 1945," *Bulletin des Leo Baeck Instituts* 8 (1965): 107–149.

52. Danuta Drywa, *The Extermination of Jews in Stutthof Concentration Camp 1939–1945* (Gdańsk, 2004); Aldo Coradello, *Co się działo w Stutthofie* (Warsaw, 2011).

53. The book is based on statements by Jewish survivors found in the Ringelblum archive; Michał Grynberg, *Żydzi w Rejencji Ciechanowskiej 1939–1942* (Warsaw, 1984). For more on economic and social life, see Bożena Gorzyńska-Przybyłowicz, *Życie Gospodarczo-Społeczne na ziemiach polskich włączonych do Prus Wschodnich w okresie okupacji hitlerowskiej* (Ciechanów, 1989); and on German ethnic policies, see Witold Pronobis, *Polityka narodowościowa Okupanta niemieckiego w Rejencji Ciechanowskiej 1939–1945* (diss., Uniwersytet Mikołaja Kopernika, Toruń, 1976). A recent account based on new research: Jan Grabowski, "Holocaust in Northern Mazovia (Poland) in the Light of the Archive of the Ciechanów Gestapo," *Holocaust and Genocide Studies* 18, no. 3 (2004): 460–476.

54. Götz Aly, *"Final Solution": Nazi Population Policy and the Murder of the European Jews* (London, 1999) (German original: 1995).

55. Michael Alberti, *Die Verfolgung und Vernichtung der Juden im Reichsgau Wartheland 1939–1945* (Wiesbaden, 2006).

56. Catherine A. Epstein, *Model Nazi: Arthur Greiser and the Occupation of Western Poland* (Oxford, 2010).

57. On the status of research on Poland, see ibid., 5–10.

58. Josef Wulf, *Lodz: Das letzte Ghetto auf polnischem Boden* (Bonn, 1962); Hanno Loewy and Gerhard Schoenberner, eds., *"Unser einziger Weg ist Arbeit": Das Getto in Łódź 1940–1944*, an exhibit by the Jewish Museum of Frankfurt in conjunction with Yad Vashem et al. (Vienna, 1990); Michal Unger, ed., *The Last Ghetto: Life in the Lodz Ghetto 1940–1944* (Jerusalem, 1995); Andrea Löw, *Juden im Getto Litzmannstadt: Lebensbedingungen, Selbstwahrnehmung, Verhalten* (Göttingen, 2006); Peter Klein, *Die "Gettoverwaltung Litzmannstadt" 1940–1944: Eine Dienststelle im Spannungsfeld von Kommunalbürokratie und staatlicher Verfolgungspolitik* (Hamburg, 2009).

59. See, for example, Alfred Konieczny, *Pod rządami wojennego prawa karnego Trzeciej Rzeszy: Górny Śląsk 1939–1945* (Warsaw, 1972); idem "Polenlager—obozy dla wysiedlonej ludności polskiej na Górnym Śląsku w latach 1942–1945," *Studia Śląskie: Seria nowa* 21 (1972): 155–178; on the Jewish population in Silesia in light

of the 1939 census, idem, "Ludność żydowska na Śląsku w świetle spisu z 17 maja 1939 roku," *Acta Universitatis Wratislaviensis Nr. 1207: Studia nad Faszyzmem i Zbrodniami Hitlerowskimi* 16 (1992): 185–201.

60. Alfred Konieczny, "Die Zwangsarbeit der Juden in Schlesien im Rahmen der 'Organisation Schmelt,'" in *Sozialpolitik und Judenvernichtung: Gibt es eine Ökonomie der Endlösung?*, ed. Götz Aly et al., Beiträge zur nationalsozialistischen Gesundheits- und Sozialpolitik, vol. 5 (Berlin, 1987), 91–110; Wolf Gruner, *Jewish Forced Labor under the Nazis: Economic Needs and Racial Aims (1938–1944)* (New York, 2006), 214–229; Stephan Lehnstaedt, "Coercion and Incentive: Jewish Ghetto Labor in East Upper Silesia," *Holocaust and Genocide Studies* 24 (2010): 400–430; Andrea Rudorff, "Arbeit und Vernichtung *reconsidered*: Die Lager der Organisation Schmelt für polnische Jüdinnen und Juden aus dem annektierten Teil Schlesiens," *Sozial.Geschichte Online* 7 (2012): 10–39.

61. Sybille Steinbacher, *"Musterstadt" Auschwitz: Germanisierungspolitik und Judenmord in Ostoberschlesien* (Munich, 2000).

62. Bernd C. Wagner, *IG Auschwitz: Zwangsarbeit und Vernichtung von Häftlingen des Lagers Monowitz 1941–1945* (Munich, 2000); Norbert Frei et al., eds., *Standort- und Kommandanturbefehle des Konzentrationslagers Auschwitz 1940–1945*, published on behalf of the Institut für Zeitgeschichte (Munich, 2000); Robert Jan van Pelt and Debórah Dwork, *Auschwitz: Von 1270 bis heute* (Zürich, 1998); Sybille Steinbacher, *Auschwitz: Geschichte und Nachgeschichte* (Munich, 2004).

63. Jochen Böhler and Jacek Andrzej Młynarczyk, eds., *Der Judenmord in den eingegliederten polnischen Gebieten 1939–1945* (Osnabrück, 2010). On the situation and conduct of ethnic Germans, see also Jerzy Kochanowski and Maike Sach, eds., *Die "Volksdeutschen" in Polen, Frankreich, Ungarn und der Tschechoslowakei: Mythos und Realität* (Osnabrück, 2006).

64. Among others, see recent works by Christoph Dieckmann and Babette Quinkert, eds., *Im Ghetto 1939—1945: Neue Forschungen zu Alltag und Umfeld*, Beiträge zur Geschichte des Nationalsozialismus, vol. 25 (Göttingen, 2009); Dan Michman, *The Emergence of Jewish Ghettos during the Holocaust* (Cambridge, 2011); Stephan Lehnstaedt and Jürgen Hensel, eds., *Arbeit in den nationalsozialistischen Ghettos* (Osnabrück, 2013).

65. On this, see above all Jürgen Zarusky, ed., *Ghettorenten: Entschädigungspolitik, Rechtsprechung und historische Forschung* (Munich, 2010); Stephan Lehnstaedt, *Geschichte und Gesetzesauslegung: Zu Kontinuität und Wandel des bundesdeutschen Wiedergutmachungsdiskurses am Beispiel der Ghettorenten* (Osnabrück, 2011); Kristin Platt, *Bezweifelte Erinnerung, verweigerte Glaubhaftigkeit: Überlebende des Holocaust in den Ghettorenten-Verfahren* (Munich, 2012).

66. German edition: Grzegorz Hryciuk, Małgorzata Ruchniewicz, Bożena Szaynok, and Adrzej Żbikowski, *Umsiedlungen, Vertreibungen und Fluchtbewegung 1939–1959: Atlas zur Geschichte Ostmitteleuropas* (Bonn, 2009).

67. Gerhard Wolf, *Ideologie und Herrschaftsrationalität: Nationalsozialistische Germanisierungspolitik in Polen* (Hamburg, 2012).

68. Charles Lehrmann and Graziella Lehrmann, *La Communauté juive du Luxembourg dans le passé et dans le present* (Esch-sur-Alzette, 1953). An anthology published in 2001 contains a number of articles about the Jewish communities from the Middle Ages to the postwar period: Laurent Moyse and Marc Schoentgen, *La présence juive au Luxembourg—du Moyen Âge au XXe siècle* (Luxembourg, 2001).

69. Paul Cerf, *Longtemps j'aurai mémoire: Documents et témoignages sur les Juifs du Grand-Duché de Luxembourg durant la seconde guerre mondiale* (Luxembourg, 1974); idem, *L'étoile juive au Luxembourg* (Luxembourg, 1986).

70. Paul Dostert, *Luxemburg zwischen Selbstbehauptung und nationaler Selbstaufgabe: Die deutsche Besatzungspolitik und die Volksdeutsche Bewegung 1940–1945* (Luxembourg, 1985).
71. Numerous interesting but difficult to access contributions come from genealogists and dedicated local historians, such as, for example, Arthur Muller, "Jüdische Bevölkerung in Ettelbruck," *Ettelbruck: 100 Joer Stad 1907–2007* (Ettelbruck, 2008), 267–271. Also worth mentioning is an article about the largely forgotten history of Luxembourg as a place of refuge for Jews: Serge Hoffmann, "Luxemburg—Asyl und Gastfreundschaft in einem kleinen Land," in *Solidarität und Hilfe für Juden während der NS-Zeit: Regionalstudien I: Griechenland, Luxemburg, Norwegen, Polen, Rumänien, Schweiz*, ed. Wolfgang Benz and Juliane Wetzel (Berlin, 1996), 187–204.
72. *Europa unterm Hakenkreuz: Die faschistische Okkupationspolitik in Belgien, Luxemburg und den Niederlanden (1940–1945)*, document selection and introduction by Ludwig Nestler, with the collaboration of Heidi Böhme et al. (East Berlin, 1990).
73. The Mémorial de la Déportation, which opened on 29 May 1996, has published a brochure on National Socialist Jewish policy in Luxembourg: André Hohengarten, *Die nationalsozialistische Judenpolitik in Luxemburg*, 2nd ed. (Luxembourg, 2002). Academic publications also accompanied the major exhibitions organized by the Musée d'histoire de la Ville de Luxembourg (for example, in 2002). In 2007, a highly esteemed exhibition took place in the Centre National de Littérature on the topic of Luxembourg as county of refuge. See the exhibition catalog by Germaine Goetzinger et al., *Exilland Luxemburg 1933–1947: Schreiben—Auftreten—Musizieren—Agitieren—Überleben* (Mersch, 2007).
74. Marc Schoentgen, "Das 'Jüdische Altersheim' in Fünfbrunnen," in *Terror im Westen: Nationalsozialistische Lager in den Niederlanden, Belgien und Luxemburg 1940–1945*, ed. Wolfgang Benz and Barbara Distel (Berlin, 2004), 49–71.
75. Marc Schoentgen, "Die jüdische Gemeinde in Medernach: Einwanderung, Integration und Verfolgung," in *Fanfare Miedernach 1930–2005* (Medernach, 2005), 299–366; Paul Dostert, "Les juifs vivants dans le canton d'Esch (1830–1940)," *Nos Cahiers: Lëtzebuerger Zäitschrëft fir Kultur* 27 (2006): 209–218; also Paul Cerf and Isi Finkelstein, *Les juifs d'Esch: Déi Escher Judden: chronique de la communauté juive de 1837 à 1999* (Esch-sur-Alzette, 1999). Additional works are in progress.
76. *La Spoliation des Biens Juifs au Luxembourg 1940–1945*, http://www.gouvernement.lu/salle_presse/communiques/2009/07-juillet/06-biens-juifs/rapport_final.pdf (accessed 24 August 2013).
77. Hans-Erich Volkmann, *Luxemburg im Zeichen des Hakenkreuzes: Eine politische Wirtschaftsgeschichte 1933 bis 1944*, ed. Militärgeschichtliches Forschungsamt, Potsdam, in collaboration with Centre de Documentation et de Recherche sur la Résistance (Paderborn, 2010).
78. Carlo Lejeune, *Die Säuberung*, vol. 1: *Ernüchterung, Befreiung, Ungewissheit (1920–1944)* (Büllingen, 2005), 25–59; Christoph Brüll, "Un passé mouvementé: L'histoire de la Communauté germanophone de Belgique," in *La Communauté germanophone de Belgique—Die Deutschsprachige Gemeinschaft Belgiens*, ed. Katrin Stangherlin (Brussels, 2005), 17–47; Ulrich Tiedau, "Die Rechtslage der deutschsprachigen Bevölkerung in Belgien nach dem Zweiten Weltkrieg," in *Deutschsprachige Minderheiten 1945: Ein europäischer Vergleich*, ed. Manfred Kittel et al. (Munich, 2007), 435–522, here 439–452; Peter M. Quadflieg, *"Zwangssoldaten" und "Ons Jongen": Eupen-Malmedy und Luxemburg als Rekrutierungsgebiet der deutschen Wehrmacht im Zweiten Weltkrieg* (Aachen, 2008), 20–41.
79. Lothar Kettenacker, *Nationalsozialistische Volkstumspolitik im Elsaß* (Stuttgart, 1973).

80. Christopher J. Fischer, *Alsace to the Alsatians? Visions and Divisions of Alsatian Regionalism, 1870–1939* (New York, 2010).
81. Serge Klarsfeld, *Vichy—Auschwitz: Die Zusammenarbeit der deutschen und französischen Behörden bei der "Endlösung der Judenfrage« in Frankreich* (Nördlingen, 1989); Simon Schwarzfuchs, *Aux prises avec Vichy: Histoire politique des Juifs de France 1940–1944* (Paris, 1998); Ahlrich Meyer, *Die deutsche Besatzung in Frankreich 1940–1944: Widerstandsbekämpfung und Judenverfolgung* (Darmstadt, 2000); idem, *Täter im Verhör: Die "Endlösung der Judenfrage" in Frankreich 1940–1944* (Darmstadt, 2005).

Glossary

Bezirksamt	Mid-tier administrative unit in certain German states (i.e., Bavaria) corresponding to the Kreise.
BGBl. (Austria); Bundesgesetzblatt für den Bundesstaat Österreich	Federal Law Gazette for the Federal State of Austria
CdZ; Chef der Zivilverwaltung	Head of the Civil Administration
DCVP; Deutsche Christlichsoziale Volkspartei	German Christian Social People's Party
DNVP; Deutschnationale Volkspartei	German National People's Party
DSVP; Deutsch-Saarländische Volkspartei	German-Saarland People's Party
Einsatzgruppe	Deployment groups; mobile task forces from the SiPo and SD that followed German armies to secure newly conquered territories and implement initial occupation measures (which notably in the East included mass killings).
Einsatzkommando	unit within an Einsatzgruppe
Freikorps	German volunteer militia unit
Gau, pl. Gaue	An administrative region of the NSDAP

Gauleiter, pl. Gauleiter	Party leader of a regional branch of the NSDAP, i.e. head of a Gau or Reichsgau
Gauleitung	Gau administrative office
Gendarmerie	Rural police
Gestapo; Geheime Staatspolizei	Secret State Police
HF; Heimattreue Front	Patriotic Front
Inspektion der Konzentrationslager	Concentration Camps Inspectorate
KPD; Kommunistische Partei Deutschlands	Communist Party of Germany
Kreis, pl. Kreise; Landkreis, Stadtkreis	Mid-tier administrative units within the (federal) states; Landkreise (rural districts) consist of numerous municipalities; Stadtkreise (urban districts) assume Kreis responsibilities for a single larger city
Kreisleiter	NSDAP district leader
Kriminalpolizei	Criminal police
KZ; Konzentrationslager	Concentration camp
Landesdirektor	Director of a provincial committee (Provinzialausschuss), i.e., the government of a Prussian province.
Landeshauptmann	Head of a state government in Austria
Landrat, pl. Landräte	District administrator in charge of a Kreis
Ministerialdirektor	Senior official at a high government authority at the Reich or state level
NSDAP; Nationalsozialistische Deutsche Arbeiterpartei	National Socialist German Workers' Party
Oberabschnitt	Senior district; regional districts of the SS (and the SD).

Oberführer	High-level SA and SS rank (comparatively between that of a colonel and a major general)
Obergruppenführer	Second highest general rank in the SS
Oberpräsident	Upper President (official designation of the highest administrative officials in the Prussian provinces)
Ordnungspolizei	Order police, Reich-level uniformed police organization during the Nazi period, directly subordinate to the SS-Reichsführer Himmler since 1936
Referat	Department; section
Regierungsbezirk	Government District; administrative districts in Prussia
Regierungspräsident	Government District President; president of a Prussian Regierungsbezirk
Reichsbeauftragter	Reich administrator
Reichsamtsleiter	Director of an NSDAP Reich office (a party institution at the level of the Reich, generally seated in Munich); for example, the Reichsamt für Agrarpolitik (agriculture policy)
RGBl.; Deutsches Reichsgesetzblatt	German Reich Legal Gazette
RGBl. (Austria); Reichsgesetzblatt für die im Reichsrathe vertretenen Königreiche und Länder	Reich Legal Gazette for the Kingdoms and Countries represented in the Imperial Council
Reichsführer-SS	Reich Leader of the SS; highest rank in the SS
Reichskommissar	Reich Commissioner; Commissioners granted extensive authorities by the Reich government to deal with complex administrative tasks.

Reichskommissariat	Reich Commissariat; Office of a Reichskommissar
Reichsorganisationsleiter	Reich Organizational Leader of the NSDAP
RM; Reichsmark	Currency in Germany from 1924 to 1948 and in Austria from 1938 to 1945.
Reichsstatthalter	Reich Governor; heads of the German states (excluding Prussia)
RMdI; Reichsministerium des Innern	Reich Interior Ministry
RSHA; Reichssicherheitshauptamt	Reich Security Main Office
RVJD; Reichsvertretung der Deutschen Juden / Juden in Deutschland	Reich's Deputation of the German Jew/Jews in Germany (founded in 1933, renamed in 1935); in July 1939 replaced with the Reichsvereinigung der Juden in Deutschland (Reich's Association of the Jews in Germany) (until 1943)
RWM; Reichswirtschaftsministerium	Reich Ministry of the Economy
SA; Sturmabteilung	Storm Detachment; paramilitary wing of the NSDAP
Schutzpolizei	Protection police; the state-level regular uniformed police; became part of the Order police during the Nazi period
SD; Sicherheitsdienst	Security Service; intelligence and security agency of the SS
SdP; Sudetendeutsche Partei	Sudeten German Party
SFK; Sudetendeutsches Freikorps	Sudeten German Freikorps
SiPo; Sicherheitspolizei	Security Police; i.e. Gestapo; formally merged in the RSHA in September 1939
SPD; Sozialdemokratische Partei Deutschlands	Social Democratic Party of Germany

SS Rasse- und Siedlungshauptamt	SS Race and Settlement Main Office
Standartenführer	Paramilitary rank used by various NSDAP organizations, including the SS and SA; the equivalent of full colonel
Stapo; Staatspolizei	State Police—Stapo(leit)stellen constituted the district offices of the Gestapo in various larger cities; Stapo refers to the Gestapo.
Stillhaltekommissar für Vereine, Organisationen und Verbände	Liquidation Commissar for Associations, Organizations, and Societies
Überleitungskommissar	Transition commissar
Westforschung	West Research; the term used during the Weimar and National Socialist period to refer to scholarly and popular research into eastern and north-eastern France, Switzerland, the Netherlands, Belgium, and Luxemburg, as well as the western border regions of the German Reich.
Volksgemeinschaft	People's Community; a concept central to Nazi ideology of a racially defined ethnic-national community.
Untersturmführer	SS rank, equivalent of Wehrmacht lieutenant

Contributors

Christoph Brüll received his Ph.D. in 2008 from the Friedrich-Schiller-University of Jena, Germany. He is currently a postdoctoral researcher supported by the National Fund for Scientific Research at Liège University, Belgium. His has published numerous works on the Belgo-German border region, including *Belgien im Nachkriegsdeutschland: Besatzung, Annäherung, Ausgleich 1944–1958* (2009) and, as editor, *ZOOM 1920–2010: Nachbarschaften neun Jahrzehnte nach Versailles* (2012).

Jean-Marc Dreyfus is a reader in Holocaust Studies at the University of Manchester, United Kingdom. He earned his Ph.D. at the University of Paris I–Panthéon–Sorbonne and held postdoctoral fellowships at Harvard University's Center for European Studies and the Centre Marc-Bloch in Berlin. He has written four books, including *Nazi Labor Camps in Paris: Austerlitz, Lévitan, Bassano* (2011), coauthored with Sarah Gensburger. He is one of the editors of the volumes on Western Europe for the sixteen-volume series *Die Verfolgung und Ermordung der europäischen Juden 1933–1945*, published by the German Federal Archives and the Institute für Zeitgeschichte Munich/Berlin. He is also a co-organizer of the ERC research program "Corpses of Mass Violence and Genocide."

Wolfgang Gippert received his Ph.D. from the University of Cologne, Germany, in 2004. Currently, he is a research fellow at the University of Cologne's Faculty of Human Sciences. His research and teaching focuses on historical education and gender history. His publications include the book *Kindheit und Jugend in Danzig 1920 bis 1933: Identitätsbildung im sozialistischen und im konservativen Milieu* (2005). As a coeditor he also published *Transkulturalität: Gender- und bildungshistorische Perspektiven* (2008).

Wolf Gruner holds the Shapell-Guerin Chair in Jewish Studies and is a professor of history and the founding director of the USC Shoah Foundation Center for Advanced Genocide Research at the University of Southern California, Los Angeles. He is the author of eight books on the Holocaust, including *Jewish Forced Labor under the Nazis: Economic Needs and Nazi Racial Aims* (2006), and has a new book forthcoming in Spanish on the discrimination against the indigenous people in the Republic of Bolivia from 1825 to 1890. He has held postdoctoral fellowships at Harvard, the U.S. Holocaust Memorial Museum, Yad Vashem Israel, and Women's Christian University Tokyo. He is currently working on individual Jewish defiance against Nazi persecution.

Ruth Leiserowitz has been the deputy director at the German Historical Institute in Warsaw, Poland, since 2009. She earned her Ph.D. in history at the Humboldt University of Berlin and held a postdoctoral research fellowship at the Berlin School for European Comparative History at the Free University of Berlin. Her research concentrates on nineteenth- and twentieth-century Europe, focusing on transnational and Jewish history. Her recent book *Sabbatleuchter und Kriegerverein: Juden in der ostpreußisch-litauischen Grenzregion 1812–1942* (2010) examines transnational Jewish life in a border region. She also coedited the volume *Women and Men at War: A Gender Perspective on World War II and its Aftermath in Central and Eastern Europe* (2012).

Albert Lichtblau is a professor of history at the University of Salzburg, Austria, where he is the vice-chair of the Center for Jewish Cultural History. His areas of research include contemporary history; Holocaust, genocide, and migration studies; as well as oral and audiovisual history. His current projects include a documentary history of escapees from Nazi Germany in African countries. His books include *"Arisierungen", beschlagnahmte Vermögen, Rückstellungen und Entschädigungen in Salzburg* (2004) and the recent volume coedited with Birgit Kirchmayr, *Marko M. Feingold: Wer einmal gestorben ist, dem tut nichts mehr weh; eine Überlebensgeschichte* (2012).

Ingo Loose has taught contemporary history at the Humboldt University of Berlin, Germany, for more than ten years. Since 2010 he has been a researcher for the sixteen-volume edition of Holocaust-related documents *Die Verfolgung und Ermordung der europäischen Juden 1933–1945* at the Institute für Zeitgeschichte Munich-Berlin, specializing in Polish and Yiddish sources. He is one of the authors of a forthcoming study about the Reich Economics Ministry in the Third Reich. His publications include *Kredite für NS-Verbrechen: Die deutschen Kreditinstitute in Polen und die Ausraubung der polnischen und jüdischen Bevölkerung 1939–1945* (2007). As an editor, he also published the diary *Jakub Poznański: Tagebuch aus dem Ghetto Litzmannstadt* (2011).

Jörg Osterloh is a research fellow at the Fritz Bauer Institute and teaches contemporary history at Goethe-University in Frankfurt, Germany. He received his Ph.D. at the Technical University of Dresden, Germany, in 2004. His numerous publications include a history of the prisoner-of-war camp in Zeithain, Saxony, entitled *Ein ganz normales Lager: Die Geschichte des Kriegsgefangenen-Mannschaftsstammlagers 304 (IV H) Zeithain bei Riesa/Sa. 1941–1945* (1997) and *Nationalsozialistische Judenverfolgung im Reichsgau Sudetenland 1938–1945* (2006), which examines the Nazi persecution of the Jews in the Sudeten-Area. He also coauthored the study *Flick: Der Konzern, die Familie, die Macht* (2009) about Friedrich Flick and his trust and coedited *NS-Prozesse und deutsche Öffentlichkeit: Besatzungszeit, frühe Bundesrepublik und DDR* (2011).

Marc Schoentgen is a historian, who teaches at a public secondary school in Luxembourg, and a member of the Luxembourg Auschwitz Committee. Until 2009, he served on the Commission d'études sur la spoliation des biens juifs pendant les années de guerre 1940–1945, created by the Luxembourg government to research the expropriation and restitution of Jewish assets. He has published articles about Fünfbrunnen and the Jewish Community of Medernach and coedited the books *Erlebtes-Erlittenes: Von Mönchengladbach über Luxemburg nach Theresienstadt; Tagebuch eines deutsch-jüdischen Emigranten* (2007) and *J'avais 20 ans: J'avais connu l'enfer; mémoires d'un rescapé des camps nazis* (2009).

Andreas Schulz has studied History, Polish, and Eastern and Southeast European Studies at the University of Leipzig, Germany. From mid 2006 until the beginning of 2009 he worked as an assistant faculty member at the Department of Eastern European History at the Humboldt University of Berlin and conducted research on the Gestapo and its victims in Zichenau in occupied Poland from 1939 to 1945. He subsequently left academia to work as a public administrator and currently pursues a successful career in the commercial recruitment industry. His main research interests focus on ethnic violence and collaboration in Eastern Europe during and after the Second World War.

Sybille Steinbacher is a professor of contemporary history at the University of Vienna, Austria. She was a visiting fellow at Harvard University's Center for European Studies, a senior fellow at the United States Holocaust Memorial Museum in Washington, DC, and a visiting professor at the Fritz Bauer Institute in Frankfurt, Germany. Her numerous publications include *Auschwitz: A History* (2005) and *Dachau: Die Stadt und das Konzentrationslager in der NS-Zeit; die Untersuchung einer Nachbarschaft* (1994). She also edited the volumes *Holocaust und Völkermorde: Die Reichweite des Vergleichs* (2012) and *"Volksgenossinnen": Frauen in der NS-Volksgemeinschaft* (2007).

Gerhard J. Teschner (1935–2013) initially had a career as an engineer and manager of a French mechanical engineering company, serving as an executive director of the company's German branch since 1982. He began studying art history and modern history at the University of Heidelberg in 1994, where he earned a Ph.D. in history. He published his book *Die Deportation der badischen und saarpfälzischen Juden am 22. Oktober 1940* in 2002.

Selected Bibliography

General

Aly, Götz. *"Final Solution": Nazi Population Policy and the Murder of the European Jews*. London, 1999. First published in German, 1995.
Anderl, Gabriele. "Die 'Zentralstellen für jüdische Auswanderung' in Wien, Berlin und Prag—ein Vergleich." *Tel Aviver Jahrbuch für deutsche Geschichte* 23 (1994): 276–299.
Barkow, Ben, Raphael Gross, and Michael Lenarz, eds. *Novemberpogrom 1938: Die Augenzeugenberichte der Wiener Library, London*. Frankfurt, 2008.
Benz, Wolfgang, ed. *Dimension des Völkermords: Die Zahl der jüdischen Opfer des Nationalsozialismus*. Munich, 1991.
Benz, Wolfgang et al., eds. *Die Bürokratie der Okkupation: Strukturen der Herrschaft und Verwaltung im besetzten Europa*. Berlin, 1998.
Böhler, Jochen. *Auftakt zum Vernichtungskrieg: Die Wehrmacht in Polen 1939*. Frankfurt, 2006.
Brandes, Detlef. *"Umvolkung, Umsiedlung, rassische Bestandsaufnahme": NS-"Volkstumspolitik" in den böhmischen Ländern*. Munich, 2012.
Browning, Christopher. *The Origins of the Final Solution: The Evolution of Nazi Jewish Policy, September 1939–March 1942*. Lincoln, NE, 2004.
Cesarani, David. *Eichmann: His Life and Crimes*. London, 2004.
Die Verfolgung und Ermordung der europäischen Juden durch das nationalsozialistische Deutschland 1933–1945 (VEJ). Vol. 2, *Deutsches Reich, 1938-August 1939*, ed. Susanne Heim (Munich, 2009). Vol. 3, *Deutsches Reich und Protektorat September 1939—September 1941*, ed. Andrea Löw (Munich, 2012). Vol. 4, *Polen, September 1939—Juli 1941*, ed. Klaus-Peter Friedrich (Munich, 2011). Vol. 10, *Die eingegliederten polnischen Gebiete Sommer 1941–1945*, ed. Ingo Loose (Munich, 2014).
Friedländer, Saul. *Nazi Germany and the Jews*. Vol. 1, *The Years of Persecution, 1933–1939*. New York, 1997.
———. *Nazi Germany and the Jews*. Vol. 2, *The Years of Extermination, 1939–1945*. New York, 2007.
Gerwarth, Robert. *Hitler's Hangman: The Life of Heydrich*. New Haven, 2011.

Gruner, Wolf. "Von der Kollektivausweisung zur Deportation der Juden aus Deutschland (1938–1945): Neue Perspektiven und Dokumente." In *Die Deportation der Juden aus Deutschland. Pläne, Praxis, Reaktionen 1938–1945*. Beiträge zur Geschichte des Nationalsozialismus, vol. 20, ed. Birthe Kundrus and Beate Meyer, 21–62. Göttingen, 2004.

———. *Jewish Forced Labor under the Nazis: Economic Needs and Racial Aims (1938–1944)*. New York, 2006.

Heinemann, Isabel. *"Rasse, Siedlung, deutsches Blut": Das Rasse- und Siedlungshauptamt der SS und die rassenpolitische Neuordnung Europas*. Göttingen, 2003.

Houwink ten Cate, Johannes, and Gerhard Otto, eds. *Das organisierte Chaos: "Ämterdarwinismus" und "Gesinnungsethik": Determinanten nationalsozialistischer Besatzungsherrschaft*. Berlin, 1999.

Institute of Jewish Affairs of the American Jewish Congress, World Jewish Congress. *Hitler's Ten-Year War on the Jews*. New York, 1943.

Institut Theresienstädter Initiative, ed. *Theresienstädter Gedenkbuch: Die Opfer der Judentransporte aus Deutschland nach Theresienstadt 1942–1945*. Prague, 2000.

The Jewish Black Book Committee. *The Black Book: The Nazi Crime against the Jewish People*. New York, 1946.

Jüdisches Historisches Institut Warschau, ed. *Faschismus—Getto—Massenmord: Dokumentation über Ausrottung und Widerstand der Juden in Polen während des zweiten Weltkrieges*. East Berlin, 1960.

Kaden, Helma, ed. *Europa unterm Hakenkreuz: Die faschistische Okkupationspolitik in Österreich und der Tschechoslowakei (1938–1945)*. East Berlin, 1988.

Lehnstaedt, Stephan, and Jürgen Hensel, eds. *Arbeit in den nationalsozialistischen Ghettos*. Osnabrück, 2013.

Lemkin, Raphael. *Axis Rule in Occupied Europe: Laws of Occupation, Analysis of Government, Proposals for Redress*. Clark, New Jersey, 2008. First published in 1944.

Longerich, Peter. *Holocaust: The Nazi Persecution and Murder of the Jews*. Oxford, 2010. First published in German, 1998.

Loose, Ingo. *Kredite für NS-Verbrechen: Die deutschen Kreditinstitute in Polen und die Ausraubung der polnischen und jüdischen Bevölkerung 1939–1945*. Munich, 2007.

Madajczyk, Czesław. *Die Okkupationspolitik Nazideutschlands in Polen 1939–1945*. East Berlin, 1987.

Majer, Dietmut, *"Non-Germans" under the Third Reich: The Nazi Judicial and Administrative System in Germany and Occupied Eastern Europe with Special Regard to Occupied Poland, 1939–1945* Baltimore, 2003.

Mallmann, Klaus-Michael, et al., eds. *Einsatzgruppen in Polen: Darstellung und Dokumentation*. Darmstadt, 2008.

Meinen, Insa/Ahlrich Meyer. *Verfolgt von Land zu Land: Jüdische Flüchtlinge in Westeuropa 1938–1944*. Paderborn, 2013.

Michman, Dan. *The Emergence of Jewish Ghettos during the Holocaust*. Cambridge, 2011.

Młynarczyk, Jacek Andrzej, and Bogdan Musiał, eds. *Genesis des Genozids: Polen 1939–1941*. Darmstadt, 2004.

Młynarczyk, Jacek Andrzej, and Jochen Böhler, eds. *Der Judenmord in den eingegliederten polnischen Gebieten 1939–1945*. Osnabrück, 2010.

Nestler, Ludwig, ed. *Europa unterm Hakenkreuz: Die faschistische Okkupationspolitik in Belgien, Luxembourg und den Niederlanden (1940–1945)*. Berlin, 1990.

Paul, Gerhard, and Klaus-Michael Mallmann, eds. *Die Gestapo im Zweiten Weltkrieg: "Heimatfront" und besetztes Europa*. Darmstadt, 2000.

Pohl, Dieter. "Die Reichsgaue Danzig-Westpreußen und Wartheland: Koloniale Verwaltung oder Modell für die zukünftige Gauverwaltung?" In *Die NS-Gaue: Regionale*

Mittelinstanzen im zentralistischen "Führerstaat", ed. Jürgen John et al., 395–405. Munich, 2007.
Rieß, Volker. *Die Anfänge der Vernichtung "lebensunwerten Lebens" in den Reichsgauen Danzig-Westpreußen und Wartheland 1939/40*. Frankfurt, 1995.
Ringelblum, Emanuel. *Polish-Jewish Relations during the Second World War*. Jerusalem, 1974.
Rosenkötter, Bernhard. *Treuhandpolitik: Die "Haupttreuhandstelle Ost" und der Raub polnischer Vermögen 1939–1945*. Essen, 2003.
Rossino, Alexander B. *Hitler Strikes Poland: Blitzkrieg, Ideology, and Atrocity*. Lawrence, KS, 2003.
Safrian, Hans. *Eichmann's Men*. Cambridge, 2009. First published in German, 1993.
Strippel, Andreas. *NS-Volkstumspolitik und die Neuordnung Europas: Rassenpolitische Selektion der Einwandererzentralstelle des Chefs der Sicherheitspolizei und des SD (1939–1945)*. Paderborn, 2011.
Umbreit, Hans. *Deutsche Militärverwaltungen 1938/39: Die militärische Besetzung der Tschechoslowakei und Polens*. Stuttgart, 1977.
Wolf, Gerhard. *Ideologie und Herrschaftsrationalität: Nationalsozialistische Germanisierungspolitik in Polen*. Hamburg, 2012.
Ziegler, Dieter, ed. *Banken und "Arisierungen" in Mitteleuropa während des Nationalsozialismus*. Stuttgart, 2002.

Saar Region

Blinn, Dieter. *Juden in Homburg: Geschichte einer jüdischen Lebenswelt 1330–1945*. Homburg-Saarpfalz, 1993.
Herrmann, Hans-Walter. "Beiträge zur Geschichte der saarländischen Emigration 1935–1939." *Jahrbuch für westdeutsche Landesgeschichte* 4 (1978): 357–412.
———. "Das Schicksal der Juden im Saarland 1920 bis 1945." In *Dokumentation zur Geschichte der jüdischen Bevölkerung In Rheinland-Pfalz und im Saarland von 1800 bis 1945*, vol. 6, ed. Landesarchivverwaltung Rheinland-Pfalz in conjunction with Landesarchiv Saarbrücken, 259–491. Koblenz, 1974.
———. "Die Deportation nach Gurs." In *Oktoberdeportation 1940*, ed. Erhard R. Wiehn, 493–510. Konstanz, 1990.
Jacoby, Fritz. *Die nationalsozialistische Herrschaftsübernahme an der Saar: Die innenpolitischen Probleme der Rückgliederung des Saargebietes bis 1935*. Saarbrücken, 1973.
Marx, Albert. *Die Geschichte der Juden an der Saar: Vom Ancien Régime bis zum Zweiten Weltkrieg*. Saarbrücken, 1992.
Muskalla, Dieter. *NS-Politik an der Saar unter Josef Bürckel: Gleichschaltung, Neuordnung, Verwaltung*. Saarbrücken, 1995.
Teschner, Gerhard J. *Die Deportation der badischen und saarpfälzischen Juden am 22. Oktober 1940: Vorgeschichte und Durchführung der Deportation und das weitere Schicksal der Deportierten bis zum Kriegsende im Kontext der deutschen und französischen Judenpolitik*. Frankfurt, 2002.
Wiehn, Erhard R., ed. *Oktoberdeportation 1940: Die sogenannte "Abschiebung" der badischen und saarpfälzischen Juden in das französische Internierungslager Gurs und andere Vorstationen von Auschwitz*. Konstanz, 1990.
Zenner, Maria. *Parteien und Politik im Saargebiet unter dem Völkerbundsregime 1920–1935*. Saarbrücken, 1966.

Austria

Anderl, Gabriele, and Dirk Rupnow. *Die Zentralstelle für jüdische Auswanderung als Beraubungsinstitution*. Veröffentlichungen der Österreichischen Historikerkommission: Vermögensentzug während der NS-Zeit sowie Rückstellungen und Entschädigungen seit 1945 in Österreich, vol. 20/1. Vienna, 2004.

Botz, Gerhard. *Nationalsozialismus in Wien: Machtübernahme, Herrschaftssicherung, Radikalisierung 1938/39*. Vienna, 2008.

———. *Wohnungspolitik und Judendeportation in Wien 1938 bis 1945: Zur Funktion des Antisemitismus als Ersatz nationalsozialistischer Sozialpolitik*. Vienna, 1975.

Brugger, Eveline, et al. *Geschichte der Juden in Österreich*. Supplementary volume to *Österreichische Geschichte*, ed. Herwig Wolfram. Vienna, 2006.

Duizend-Jensen, Shoshana. *Jüdische Gemeinden, Vereine, Stiftungen und Fonds: "Arisierung" und Restitution*. Veröffentlichungen der Österreichischen Historikerkommission: Vermögensentzug während der NS-Zeit sowie Rückstellungen und Entschädigungen seit 1945 in Österreich, vol. 21/2. Vienna, 2004.

Ellmauer, Daniela, et al. *"Arisierungen," beschlagnahmte Vermögen, Rückstellungen und Entschädigungen in Oberösterreich*. Veröffentlichungen der Österreichischen Historikerkommission: Vermögensentzug während der NS-Zeit sowie Rückstellungen und Entschädigungen seit 1945 in Österreich, vol. 17. Vienna, 2004.

Exenberger, Herbert, et al. *Kündigungsgrund Nichtarier: Die Vertreibung jüdischer Mieter aus den Wiener Gemeindebauten in den Jahren 1938–1939*. Vienna, 1996.

Fellner, Günter. *Antisemitismus in Salzburg 1918–1938*. Vienna, 1979.

Freund, Florian, and Hans Safrian. "Die Verfolgung der österreichischen Juden 1938–1945: Vertreibung und Deportation." In *NS-Herrschaft in Österreich: Ein Handbuch*, ed. Emmerich Tálos et al., 767–788. Vienna, 2001.

Fuchs, Gerhard. "Die Vermögensverkehrsstelle als Arisierungsbehörde jüdischer Betriebe." Ph.D. diss., University of Economics Vienna, 1989.

Gruner, Wolf. *Zwangsarbeit und Verfolgung: Österreichische Juden im NS-Staat 1938–45*. Innsbruck, 2000.

Jabloner, Clemens et al. *Schlussbericht der Historikerkommission der Republik Österreich: Vermögensentzug während der NS-Zeit sowie Rückstellungen und Entschädigungen seit 1945 in Österreich*. Vienna, 2003.

Kolonovits, Dieter et al. *Staatsbürgerschaft und Vertreibung*. Veröffentlichungen der Österreichischen Historikerkommission: Vermögensentzug während der NS-Zeit sowie Rückstellungen und Entschädigungen seit 1945 in Österreich, vol. 7. Vienna, 2004.

Lappin-Eppel, Eleonore. *Ungarisch-Jüdische Zwangsarbeiter und Zwangsarbeiterinnen in Österreich 1944/45: Arbeitseinsatz—Todesmärsche—Folgen*. Vienna, 2010.

Loewy, Hanno, and Gerhard Milchram, eds. *"Hast du meine Alpen gesehen?" Eine jüdische Beziehungsgeschichte*. Hohenems, 2009.

Maderegger, Sylvia. *Die Juden im österreichischen Ständestaat 1934–1938*. Vienna, 1973.

Mang, Thomas. *"Gestapo-Leitstelle-Wien: Mein Name ist Huber": Wer trug die lokale Verantwortung für den Mord an den Juden Wiens?* Münster, 2003.

Manoschek, Walter, ed. *Der Fall Rechnitz: Das Massaker an Juden im März 1945*. Vienna, 2009.

Moser, Jonny. *Demographie der jüdischen Bevölkerung Österreichs 1938–1945*. Vienna, 1999.

Mühl, Dieter J. "'Immer war Wahlkampf': Robert Stricker (1879–1944); Ein Beitrag zur jüdischen Politik in Österreich." *Aschkenas* 11 (2001): 121–160.

Niklas, Martin. "... *die schönste Stadt der Welt*": *Österreichische Jüdinnen und Juden in Theresienstadt*. Schriftenreihe des Dokumentationsarchivs des österreichischen Widerstandes zur Geschichte der NS-Gewaltverbrechen, vol. 7. Vienna, 2009.
Pauley, Bruce F. *From Prejudice to Persecution: A History of Austrian Anti-Semitism*. Chapel Hill, NC, 1992.
Rabinovici, Doron. *Eichmann's Jews: The Jewish Administration of Holocaust Vienna, 1938–1945*. Cambridge, 2011. First published in German, 2000.
Rosenkranz, Herbert. *Verfolgung und Selbstbehauptung: Die Juden in Österreich 1938–1945*. Vienna, 1978.
Safrian, Hans, and Hans Witek. *Und keiner war dabei: Dokumente des alltäglichen Antisemitismus in Wien 1938*. Vienna, 1988.
Schmid, Kurt, and Robert Streibel, eds. *Der Pogrom 1938: Judenverfolgung in Österreich und Deutschland*. Vienna, 1990.
Wachter, Andrea. "Antisemitismus im österreichischen Vereinswesen für Leibesübungen 1918–1938 am Beispiel der Geschichte ausgewählter Vereine." Ph.D. diss., University of Vienna, 1983.
Walzl, August. *Die Juden in Kärnten und das Dritte Reich*. Klagenfurt, 1987.
Welzig, Werner, ed. *"Anschluss"—März/April 1938 in Österreich*. Vienna, 2010.

Sudetenland

Benešová, Miroslava. "Das Konzentrationslager in Leitmeritz und seine Häftlinge." *Theresienstädter Studien und Dokumente* (1995): 217–240.
Česká křesťanská akademie and Ackermann-Gemeinde, ed. *Židé v Sudetech/Juden im Sudetenland*. Prague, 2000.
Fedorovič, Tomáš. "Die Gemeinde Schönwald und ihre unfreiwilligen Einwohner." *Theresienstädter Studien und Dokumente* (2001): 269–286.
Grossmann, Kurt R. "Refugees to and from Czechoslovakia." In *The Jews of Czechoslovakia: Historical Studies and Surveys*, vol. 2, ed. Society for the History of Czechoslovak Jews, 565–581. Philadelphia and New York, 1971.
Heumos, Peter. *Die Emigration aus der Tschechoslowakei nach Westeuropa und dem Nahen Osten 1938–1945: Politisch-soziale Struktur, Organisation und Asylbedingungen der tschechischen, jüdischen, deutschen und slowakischen Flüchtlinge während des Nationalsozialismus; Darstellung und Dokumentation*. Munich, 1989.
Iggers, Wilma A. "Die Emigration der deutschen und österreichischen Juden in die Tschechoslowakei." In *Judenemanzipation—Antisemitismus—Verfolgung in Deutschland, Österreich-Ungarn, den Böhmischen Ländern und in der Slowakei*, ed. Jörg K. Hoensch et al., 143–154. Essen, 1999.
———. "Juden zwischen Tschechen und Deutschen." *Zeitschrift für Ostforschung* 37 (1988): 428–442.
Kaiser, Vladimír. "Die jüdische Gemeinde in Aussig/Ústí nad Labem im 19. und 20. Jahrhundert." In *Židé v Sudetech/Juden im Sudetenland*, 235–254. Prague, 2000.
Kárný, Miroslav. "Der Holocaust und die Juden in Böhmen und Mähren." In *Tschechen, Deutsche und der Zweite Weltkrieg: Von der Schwere geschichtlicher Erfahrung und der Schwierigkeit ihrer Aufarbeitung*, ed. Robert Maier, 39–56. Hanover, 1997.
Kocourek, Ludomír. "Das Schicksal der Juden im Sudetengau im Licht der erhaltenen Quellen." *Theresienstädter Studien und Dokumente* (1997): 86–104.
Kryl, Miroslav, and Ludmila Chládková, eds. *Pobočky koncentračního tábora Gross-Rosen ve lnářských závodech Trutnovska za nacistické okupace*. Trutnov, 1981.

Luh, Andreas. *Der Deutsche Turnverband in der Ersten Tschechoslowakischen Republik: vom völkischen Vereinsbetrieb zur volkspolitischen Bewegung.* Munich, 1988.
Osterloh, Jörg. *Nationalsozialistische Judenverfolgung im Reichsgau Sudetenland 1938–1945.* Munich, 2006.
Šebek, Jaroslav. "Der Antisemitismus im sudetendeutschen katholischen Milieu 1918–1938." In *Židé v Sudetech / Juden im Sudetenland,* published by the Česká křesťanská akademie and the Ackermann-Gemeinde, 93–99. Prague, 2000.
Skriebeleit, Jörg. "Die Außenlager des KZ Flossenbürg in Böhmen." In *KZ-Außenlager— Geschichte und Erinnerung,* special issue, *Dachauer Hefte* 15 (1999): 196–217.
Wlaschek, Rudolf M. *Juden in Böhmen: Beiträge zur Geschichte des europäischen Judentums im 19. und 20. Jahrhundert.* 2nd ed. Munich, 1997.
Zimmermann, Volker. *Die Sudetendeutschen im NS-Staat: Politik und Stimmung im Reichsgau Sudetenland (1938–1945).* Essen, 1999.

Protectorate of Bohemia and Moravia

Adler, H. G. *Theresienstadt 1941–1945: Das Antlitz einer Zwangsgemeinschaft; Geschichte, Soziologie, Psychologie.* Tübingen, 1955.
———, ed. *Die verheimlichte Wahrheit: Theresienstädter Dokumente.* Tübingen, 1958.
Bartož, Josef. "Die Arisierung jüdischen Vermögens in Olmütz im Jahre 1939." *Theresienstädter Studien und Dokumente* (2000): 282–296.
Bodensieck, Heinrich. "Das Dritte Reich und die Lage der Juden in der Tschecho-Slowakei nach München." *Vierteljahrshefte für Zeitgeschichte* 9, no. 3 (1961): 249–261.
Bondy, Ruth. "Chronik der sich schließenden Tore: Jüdisches Nachrichtenblatt—Židovské Listy (1939–1945)." *Theresienstädter Studien und Dokumente* (2000): 86–103.
Brandes, Detlef. *Die Tschechen unter deutschem Protektorat.* Part 1, *Besatzungspolitik, Kollaboration und Widerstand im Protektorat Böhmen und Mähren bis Heydrichs Tod (1939–1942).* Munich, 1969.
Brandes, Detlef, and Václav Kural, ed. *Der Weg in die Katastrophe: Deutsch-tschechoslowakische Beziehungen 1938–1947.* Essen, 1994.
Čapková, Kateřina. *Czechs, Germans, Jews? National Identity and the Jews of Bohemia.* New York, 2012. First published in Czech 2005.
———. "Czechs, Germans, Jews—Where is the Difference? The Complexity of National Identities of Bohemian Jews, 1918–1938." *Bohemia* 46, no. 1 (2005): 7–14.
Gruner, Wolf. "Das Protektorat Böhmen und Mähren und die antijüdische Politik 1939–1941: Lokale Initiativen, regionale Maßnahmen, zentrale Entscheidungen im 'Großdeutschen Reich.'" *Theresienstädter Studien und Dokumente* (2005): 27–62.
Hájková, Alena. "Erfassung der jüdischen Bevölkerung des Protektorats." *Theresienstädter Studien und Dokumente* (1997): 50–62.
Hampel, Jens. "Das Schicksal der jüdischen Bevölkerung der Stadt Iglau 1938–1942." *Theresienstädter Studien und Dokumente* (1998): 70–99.
Heimann, Mary. *Czechoslovakia: The State That Failed.* New Haven, 2011.
Heumos, Peter. "Flüchtlingslager, Hilfsorganisationen, Juden im Niemandsland: Zur Flüchtlings- und Emigrationsproblematik in der Tschechoslowakei im Herbst 1938." *Bohemia* 25, no. 2 (1984): 243–275.
Jacoby, Gerhard. *Racial State: The German Nationalities Policy in the Protectorate of Bohemia-Moravia.* New York, 1944.
Kárný, Miroslav. "Die 'Judenfrage' in der nazistischen Okkupationspolitik." *Historica* 21 (1982): 137–192.

———. "Die Protektoratsregierung und die Verordnungen des Reichsprotektors über das jüdische Vermögen." *Judaica Bohemiae* 29 (1993): 54–66.
———. *"Konečné řešení": Genocida českých Židů v německé protektorátní politice*. Prague, 1991.
———. "Zur Statistik der jüdischen Bevölkerung im sogenannten Protektorat." *Judaica Bohemiae* 22 (1986): 9–19.
Kárný, Miroslav, et al., eds. *Deutsche Politik im "Protektorat Böhmen und Mähren" unter Reinhard Heydrich 1941–1942: Eine Dokumentation*. Berlin, 1997.
Koeltzsch, Ines. *Geteilte Kulturen: Eine Geschichte der tschechisch-jüdisch-deutschen Beziehungen in Prag (1918–1938)*. Munich, 2012.
Krejčová, Helena, et al., eds. *Židé v Protektorátu: Hlášení Židovské náboženské obce v roce 1942; Dokumenty*. Prague, 1997.
Kreutzmüller, Christoph, and Jaroslav Kučera. "Die Commerzbank und die Vernichtung der jüdischen Gewerbetätigkeit in den böhmischen Ländern und den Niederlanden." In *Die Commerzbank und die Juden 1933–1945*, ed. Ludolf Herbst and Thomas Weihe, 173–222. Munich, 2004.
Küpper, René. *Karl Hermann Frank (1898–1946): Politische Biographie eines sudetendeutschen Nationalsozialisten*. Munich, 2010.
Lexa, John G. "Anti-Jewish Laws and Regulations in the Protectorate of Bohemia and Moravia." In *The Jews of Czechoslovakia: Historical Studies and Surveys*, vol. 3, ed. Avigdor Dagan et al., 75–103. Philadelphia, 1984.
Milotová, Jaroslava. "Der Okkupationsapparat und die Vorbereitung der Transporte nach Lodz." *Theresienstädter Studien und Dokumente* (1998): 40–69.
———. "Die Zentralstelle für jüdische Auswanderung in Prag: Genesis und Tätigkeit bis zum Anfang des Jahres 1940." *Theresienstädter Studien und Dokumente* (1997): 7–30.
———. "Zur Geschichte der Verordnung Konstantin von Neuraths über das jüdische Vermögen." *Theresienstädter Studien und Dokumente* (2002): 75–115.
Osterloh, Jörg, and Harald Wixforth. "Die 'Arisierung' im Protektorat Böhmen und Mähren: Rahmenbedingungen und gesetzliche Vorgaben." In Harald Wixforth, *Die Expansion der Dresdner Bank in Europa*, in collaboration with Johannes Bär et al., 306–348. Munich, 2006.
Osud Židů v protektorátu 1939–1945. Prague, 1991.
Petrův, Helena. *Právní postavení židů v Protektorátu Čechy a Morava (1939–1941)*. Prague, 2000.
Potthast, Jan Björn. *Das jüdische Zentralmuseum der SS in Prag: Gegnerforschung und Völkermord im Nationalsozialismus*. Frankfurt, 2002.
Rothkirchen, Livia. *The Jews of Bohemia and Moravia: Facing the Holocaust*. Lincoln, NE, and Jerusalem, 2005.
———. "The Protectorate Government and the 'Jewish Question' 1939–1941." *Yad Vashem Studies* 27 (1999): 331–362.

Memel Territory

Bartusevičius, Vincas, Joachim Tauber, and Wolfram Wette, eds. *Holocaust in Litauen: Krieg, Judenmorde und Kollaboration im Jahre 1941*. Cologne, 2003.
Birger, Trudi. *Im Angesicht des Feuers: Wie ich der Hölle des Konzentrationslagers entkam*. Munich, 2002.
Ganor, Solly (Sally Genkind). *Das andere Leben: Kindheit im Holocaust*. Frankfurt, 1997.

Leiserowitz, Ruth. *Sabbatleuchter und Kriegerverein: Juden in der ostpreußisch-litauischen Grenzregion 1812–1942*. Osnabrück, 2010.
Levin, Dov. *The Litvaks: A Short History of the Jews in Lithuania*. Jerusalem, 2000.
Livio Isaak Sirovich. *Ihr Lieben, schreibt mir nicht alles: Eine jüdische Familie in Litauen 1935–1941*. Munich, 2001.
Plieg, Ernst-Albert. *Das Memelland 1920–1939: Deutsche Autonomiebestrebungen im litauischen Gesamtstaat*. Würzburg, 1962.
Tauber, Joachim. "Das Dritte Reich und Litauen 1933–1940." In *Zwischen Lübeck und Novgorod: Wirtschaft, Politik und Kultur im Ostseeraum vom frühen Mittelalter bis ins 20. Jahrhundert*, ed. Ortwin Pelc and Gertrud Pickhan, 477–499. Lüneburg, 1996.
———. *Die deutsch-litauischen Beziehungen im 20. Jahrhundert*. Lüneburg, 1993.
Žostaustaitė, Petronėlė. *Klaipėdos kraštas 1923–1939*. Vilnius, 1992.

Danzig-West Prussia

Andrzejewski, Marek. "Antyżydowski terror w Wolnym Mieście Gdańsku (1937–1939): Materiały." *Biuletyn Żydowskiego Instytutu Historycznego w Polsce* 141 (1987): 123–126.
Aschkewitz, Max. *Zur Geschichte der Juden in Westpreußen*. Marburg am Lahn, 1967.
Berendt, Grzegorz. "Die Danziger, Zoppoter und Gdinger Juden im 20. Jahrhundert: Ein historischer Vergleich." In *Zur Geschichte und Kultur der Juden in Ost- und Westpreußen*, ed. Michael Brocke et al., 187–201. Hildesheim, 2000.
Bogacz, Daniel. *Fremde in einer freien Stadt: Deutsche, Polen und Juden in Danzig 1920–1939*. Bonn, 2004.
Coradello, Aldo. *Co się działo w Stutthofie*. Warsaw, 2011.
Drywa, Danuta. *The Extermination of Jews in Stutthof Concentration Camp 1939–1945*. Gdańsk, 2004.
———. "Stutthof—Stammlager." In *Der Ort des Terrors: Geschichte der nationalsozialistischen Konzentrationslager*, vol. 6, *Natzweiler, Groß-Rosen, Stutthof*, ed. Wolfgang Benz and Barbara Distel, 477–529. Munich, 2007.
Echt, Samuel. *Die Geschichte der Juden in Danzig*. Leer, 1972.
Jezierska, Maria Elżbieta. "Straceni w obozie Stutthof." *Zeszyty Muzeum Stutthof* 7 (1987): 79–199.
Kemlein, Sophia. "Zur Geschichte der Juden in Westpreußen und Danzig (bis 1943)." In *Danzig—Gdańsk: Deutsch-polnische Geschichte, Politik und Literatur*, ed. Akademie für Lehrerfortbildung Dillingen et al., 94–109. Dillingen, 1996.
Kozlowska, Kamila. *Die Juden in der Freien Stadt Danzig: Integrations- und Ausgrenzungsprozesse zwischen 1919 und 1933*. Munich, 2011.
Lichtenstein, Erwin. *Die Juden der Freien Stadt Danzig unter der Herrschaft des Nationalsozialismus*. Tübingen, 1973.
Rojowska, Elżbieta, and Monika Tomkiewicz. *Gdynia 1939–1945 w świetle źródeł niemieckich i polskich: Aresztowania—egzekucje—wysiedlenia ludności cywilnej narodowości polskiej*. Gdynia, 2009.
Schenk, Dieter. *Danzig 1930–1945: Das Ende einer Freien Stadt*. Berlin, 2013.
Schenk, Dieter. *Hitlers Mann in Danzig: Albert Forster und die NS-Verbrechen in Danzig-Westpreußen*. Bonn, 2000.
Sodeikat, Ernst. "Die Verfolgung und der Widerstand der Juden in der Freien Stadt Danzig von 1933 bis 1945." *Bulletin des Leo Baeck Instituts* 8 (1965): 107–149.

Wartheland

Alberti, Michael. "'Exerzierplatz des Nationalsozialismus': Der Reichsgau Wartheland 1939–1941." In *Genesis des Genozids: Polen 1939–1941*, ed. Klaus-Michael Mallmann and Bogdan Musial, 111–126. Darmstadt, 2004.

———. "'Nikczemna perfidia, niska, bezmierna chciwość oraz zimne, wyrachowane okrucieństwo'—ostateczne rozwiązanie kwestii żydowskiej w Kraju Warty." In *Zagłada Żydów na polskich terenach wcielonych do Rzeszy*, ed. Aleksandry Namysło, 69–84. Warsaw, 2008.

———. *Die Verfolgung und Vernichtung der Juden im Reichsgau Wartheland 1939–1945*. Wiesbaden, 2006.

Baranowski, Julian. "Likwidacja Żydów z getta łódzkiego w obozie zagłady w Chełmnie nad Nerem." In *Ośrodek zagłady Żydów w Chełmnie nad Nerem w świetle najnowszych badań: Materiały z sesji naukowej*, 3–8. Konin, 2004.

———. *Łódzkie getto 1940–1944: Vademecum*. Łódź, 1999.

Dąbrowska, Danuta. "Zagłada skupisk żydowskich w 'Kraju Warty' w okresie okupacji hitlerowskiej." *Biuletyn Żydowskiego Instytutu Historycznego* 13–14 (1955): 122–184.

Epstein, Catherine A. *Model Nazi: Arthur Greiser and the Occupation of Western Poland*. Oxford, 2010.

Feuchert, Sascha, Erwin Leibfried, and Jörg Riecke, eds. *Die Chronik des Gettos Lodz/Litzmannstadt*. In cooperation with Julian Baranowski et al., and collaboration with Imke Janssen-Mignon et al. Göttingen, 2007.

Gerson, Daniel. "Antisemitische Erfahrungen in Lodz zwischen den beiden Weltkriegen." In *Polen, Deutsche und Juden in Lodz 1820–1939: Eine schwierige Nachbarschaft*, ed. Jürgen Hensel, 257–268. Osnabrück, 1999.

Kershaw, Ian. "Improvised Genocide? The Emergence of the 'Final Solution' in the 'Warthegau'." *Transactions of the Royal Historical Society* 6th Series, no. 2 (1992): 51–78.

Klein, Peter. *Die "Gettoverwaltung Litzmannstadt" 1940–1944: Eine Dienststelle im Spannungsfeld von Kommunalbürokratie und staatlicher Verfolgungspolitik*. Hamburg, 2009.

Krakowski, Shmuel. *Das Todeslager Chełmno/Kulmhof: Der Beginn der "Endlösung."* Jerusalem, 2007.

Loose, Ingo. "Die Berliner Juden im Getto Litzmannstadt 1941–1944." In *Berliner Juden im Getto Litzmannstadt 1941–1944: Ein Gedenkbuch*, ed. Ingo Loose, 44–63. Berlin, 2009.

———. "'Stimmungsmäßig schwierig sind die Ostgebiete überhaupt nicht': Deutsche, Polen und Juden im Kreis Kalisch (Reichsgau Wartheland) in Stimmungsberichten des SD." *Vierteljahrshefte für Zeitgeschichte* (forthcoming, 2015).

Löw, Andrea. *Juden im Getto Litzmannstadt: Lebensbedingungen, Selbstwahrnehmung, Verhalten*. Göttingen, 2006.

Melezin, Abraham. *Przyczynek do znajomości stosunków demograficznych wśród ludności żydowskiej w Łodzi, Krakowie i Lublinie podczas okupacji niemieckiej*. Łódź, 1946.

Młynarczyk, Jacek Andrzej. "Wpływ inicjatyw oddolnych Arthura Greisera i Odilona Globocnika na decyzję o wymordowaniu Żydów." In *Zagłada Żydów na polskich terenach wcielonych do Rzeszy*, 14–33. Warsaw, 2008.

Montague, Patrick. *Chelmno and the Holocaust: The History of Hitler's First Death Camp*. New York, 2012.

Rubin, Icchak (Henryk). *Żydzi w Łodzi pod niemiecką okupacją 1939–1945*. London, 1988.

Rutowska, Maria. *Wysiedlenia ludności polskiej z Kraju Warty do Generalnego Gubernatorstwa 1939–1941*. Poznań, 2003.
Trunk, Isaiah. *Łódź Ghetto: A History*. Bloomington, 2006.
Weiss, Yfaat. *Deutsche und polnische Juden vor dem Holocaust: Jüdische Identität zwischen Staatsbürgerschaft und Ethnizität 1933–1940*. Munich, 2000.
Ziółkowska, Anna. "Transporty powrotne (Rücktransporte). Eliminacja więźniów niezdolnych do pracy z obozów pracy przymusowych dla Żydów w Wielkopolsce." In *Ośrodek zagłady Żydów w Chełmnie nad Nerem w świetle najnowszych badań: Materiały z sesji naukowej*, ed. Łucja Pawlicka-Nowak, 37–43. Konin, 2004.
——— . "Żydzi poznańscy w pierwszych miesiącach okupacji hitlerowskiej." In *Poznańscy Żydzi*, ed. Jacek Wiesiołowski. 378–393. Poznań, 2006.

Zichenau

"Do dziejów ludności żydowskiej w Płocku podczas okupacji hitlerowskiej." *Biuletyn Żydowskiego Instytutu Historycznego* 52 (1964): 72–77.
Górczyńska-Przybyłowicz, Bożena. *Życie gospodarczo-społeczne na ziemiach polskich włączonych do Prus Wschodnich w okresie okupacji Hitlerowskiej*. Ciechanów, 1989.
Grabowski, Jan. "Die antijüdische Politik im Regierungsbezirk Zichenau." In *Der Judenmord in den eingegliederten polnischen Gebieten 1939–1945*, ed. Jacek Andrzej Młynarczyk and Jochen Böhler, 99–116. Osnabrück, 2010.
——— . "Holocaust in Northern Mazovia (Poland) in the Light of the Archive of the Ciechanów Gestapo." *Holocaust and Genocide Studies* 18, no. 3 (2004): 460–476.
Grynberg, Michał. *Żydzi w Rejencji Ciechanowskiej 1939–1942*. Warsaw, 1984.
Gumkowski, Janusz. "Obóz hitlerowski w Działdowie." *Biuletyn Głównej Komisji Badania Zbrodni Hitlerowskich w Polsce* 10 (1958): 57–88.
Juszkiewicz, Ryszard. *Losy Żydów mławskich w okresie II-ej wojny światowej*. Mława, 1994.
——— . "Obozy w rejencji ciechanowskie." *Notatki Płockie* 1 (1968): 32–38.
Lapierre, Nicole, ed. *Das gerettete Buch des Simcha Guterman*. 2nd ed. Hamburg, 1996.
Meindl, Ralf. *Ostpreußens Gauleiter: Erich Koch—eine politische Biographie*. Osnabrück, 2007.
Owsiewski, Miron. *Pułtuscy Żydzi Okresu Międzywojennego*. Pułtusk, 1989.
Sokolnicki, Andrzej. "Region Pułtuski w latach okupacji hitlerowskiej 1939–1945." In *Pułtusk, Studia i materiały z dziejów miasta i region*, vol. 1, 209–276. Warsaw, 1969.

East Upper Silesia

Aly, Götz, and Susanne Heim. *Architects of Annihilation: Auschwitz and the Logic of Destruction*. Princeton, 2002. First published in German, 1991.
Fulbrook, Mary. *A Small Town near Auschwitz: Ordinary Nazis and the Holocaust*. Oxford, 2012.
Gutterman, Bella. *A Narrow Bridge to Life: Jewish Forced Labor and Survival in the Gross-Rosen Camp System, 1940–1945*. New York and Oxford, 2008.
Konieczny, Alfred. "Die Zwangsarbeit der Juden in Schlesien im Rahmen der 'Organisation Schmelt'." *Beiträge zur nationalsozialistischen Gesundheits- und Sozialpolitik* 5 (1987): 91–110.

Piper, Franciszek. *Die Zahl der Opfer von Auschwitz: Aufgrund der Quellen und der Erträge der Forschung 1945 bis 1990*. Oświęcim, 1993.
Rudorff, Andrea. "Arbeit und Vernichtung *reconsidered*: Die Lager der Organisation Schmelt für polnische Jüdinnen und Juden aus dem annektierten Teil Schlesiens." *Sozial.Geschichte Online* 7 (2012): 10–39.
Steinbacher, Sybille. *"Musterstadt" Auschwitz: Germanisierungspolitik und Judenmord in Ostoberschlesien*. Munich, 2000.
Szternfinkiel, Natan Eliasz. "Zagłada Żydów sosnowieckiego getta." In *Żydzi w Zagłębie Śląskim: żyli wśród nas, mieszkali i zginęli*. Sosnowiec, 1993.
Volnerman, Chaim, et al., eds. *The Book of Oshpitsin*. Jerusalem, 1977.
Wagner, Bernd C. *IG Auschwitz: Zwangsarbeit und Vernichtung von Häftlingen des Lagers Monowitz 1941–1945*. Munich, 2000.
Weiser, Adelheid. "Der Schutz der jüdischen Rechte in Oberschlesien unter dem Mandat des Völkerbundes 1933–1945." In *Geschichte der Juden in Schlesien im 19. und 20. Jahrhundert: Dokumentation einer Tagung in Breslau*, ed. Friedrich Carl Schultze-Rhonhof, 37–53. Hanover, 1995.
———. "Juden in Oberschlesien. Ein historischer Überblick." In *Juden in Oberschlesien Teil 1: Historischer Überblick—Jüdische Gemeinden (I.)*, ed. Peter Maser and Adelheid Weiser, 13–63. Berlin, 1992.

Eupen-Malmedy

Arntz, Hans-Dieter. *Judenverfolgung und Fluchthilfe im deutsch-belgischen Grenzgebiet: Kreisgebiet Schleiden: Euskirchen—Monschau—Aachen—Eupen/Malmedy*. Euskirchen, 1990.
Brüll, Christoph, "Un passé mouvementé: L'histoire de la Communauté germanophone de Belgique." In *La Communauté germanophone de Belgique—Die Deutschsprachige Gemeinschaft Belgiens*, ed. Katrin Stangherlin, 17–47. Brussels, 2005.
Caestecker, Frank. "Onverbiddelijk, maar ook clement: Het Belgische immigratiebeleid en de Joodse Vlucht uit nazi-Duitsland, maart 1938-augustus 1939." *Bijdragen tot de Eigentijdse Geschiedenis* 13–14 (2004): 99–139.
Cremer, Freddy, and Werner Mießen. *Spuren: Materialien zur Geschichte der Deutschsprachigen Gemeinschaft Belgiens: Einführung*. Eupen, 1996.
Kartheuser, Bruno. *Die 30er Jahre in Eupen-Malmedy: Einblick in das Netzwerk der reichsdeutschen Subversion*. Neundorf, 2001.
Kirschgens, Stefan. *Wege durch das Niemandsland: Dokumentation und Analyse der Hilfe für Flüchtlinge im deutsch-belgisch-niederländischen Grenzland in den Jahren 1933 bis 1945*. Cologne, 1998.
Lejeune, Carlo. *Die Säuberung*, vol. 1, *Ernüchterung, Befreiung, Ungewissheit (1920–1944)*. Büllingen, 2005.
Meinen, Insa, and Ahlrich Meyer, "Transitland Belgien: Jüdische Flüchtlinge in Westeuropa während der Zeit der Deportationen 1942." *Theresienstädter Studien und Dokumente* (2007): 378–431.
Müller, Thomas. "Die Formierung des 'Grenzraums': Die 'Abteilung G' des Reichsinspekteurs und Landeshauptmanns Haake." In *Griff nach dem Westen: Die "Westforschung" der völkisch-nationalen Wissenschaften zum nordwesteuropäischen Raum (1919–1960)*, vol. 2, ed. Burkhard Dietz, Helmut Gabel, and Ulrich Tiedau, 763–790. Münster, 2003.

Ruland, Herbert. "Faschistische Bewegungen," in *Ostbelgien und der 10. Mai 1940: Zeitgeschichte, Verdrängung und Aktualität: Kolloquium in Büllingen am 12. Mai 1990*, ed. Volkshochschule der Ostkantone, 37–41. N.c., 1990.

———."Faschistische Bewegungen, Widerstand und Flüchtlingsschicksale in Neu-Belgien in der Zwischenkriegszeit." http://www.grenzgeschichte.eu/archiv/faschNeu-Belgien.pdf (accessed 1 October 2009).

———. "Fluchtbewegungen an der deutsch-belgischen Grenze und in Innerbelgien vor dem Hintergrund der zeitgeschichtlichen Entwicklung 1914–1945." http://www.grenzgeschichte.eu/archiv/FLUCHT1.pdf (accessed 1 October 2009).

———. "Horst Naftaniel–ein Überlebender des Konzentrationslagers Auschwitz-Monowitz," in *Zwischen Hammer und Amboß: Eupen, Malmedy, St. Vith und die "zehn Gemeinden" von 1939–1945*, ed. Herbert Ruland et al. Eupen, 1996.

———. "Spuren jüdischen Lebens in Eupen 1930–1949: Rosa Schalit-Mendelzwaig: eine gebürtige Eupenerin überlebt den Holocaust." *GrenzGeschichte DG. Rundbrief* (February 2011): 2–7. http://www.grenzgeschichte.eu/rundbriefe/Rundbrief-Nr.-11_kl.pdf (accessed 26 December 2012).

Schärer, Martin R. *Deutsche Annexionspolitik im Westen: Die Wiedereingliederung Eupen-Malmedys im Zweiten Weltkrieg*. 2nd ed. Frankfurt, 1978.

Schreiber, Marion. *Stille Rebellen: Der Überfall auf den 20. Deportationszug nach Auschwitz*. Berlin, 2000.

Van Doorslaer, Rudi, et al. *La Belgique docile: Les autorités belges et la persécution des Juifs en Belgique durant la Seconde Guerre mondiale*. Vol. 1. Brussels, 2007.

Wynants, Jacques. "Les autorités belges et la situation des Cantons de l'Est 1940–1944." *Bulletin d'information du Centre liégeois d'Histoire et d'Archéologie Militaires* 9, no. 1 (March 2004): 15–26.

Luxembourg

Artuso, Vincent. *La collaboration au Luxembourg durant la Seconde Guerre mondiale (1940–1945): Accommodation, adaptation, assimilation*. Luxembourg, 2013.

Blau, Lucien. "L'antisémitisme au Grand-Duché de Luxembourg pendant l'entre-deux-guerres." *Galerie* 10 (1992): 48–71.

Cerf, Paul. *L'étoile juive au Luxembourg*. Luxembourg, 1986.

———. *Longtemps j'aurai mémoire: Documents et témoignages sur les Juifs du Grand-Duché de Luxembourg durant la seconde guerre mondiale*. Luxembourg, 1974.

Dostert, Paul. *Luxemburg zwischen Selbstbehauptung und nationaler Selbstaufgabe: Die deutsche Besatzungspolitik und die Volksdeutsche Bewegung 1940–1945*. Luxembourg, 1985.

Goetzinger, Germaine, et al., eds. *Exilland Luxemburg 1933–1947: Schreiben—Auftreten—Musizieren—Agitieren—Überleben*. Mersch, 2007. Exhibition catalog.

Heumann, Hugo. *Erlebtes—Erlittenes: Von Mönchengladbach über Luxemburg nach Theresienstadt; Tagebuch eines deutsch-jüdischen Emigranten*, ed. Germaine Goetzinger and Marc Schoentgen. Mersch 2007.

Hoffmann, Serge. "Luxemburg—Asyl und Gastfreundschaft in einem kleinen Land." In *Solidarität und Hilfe für Juden während der NS-Zeit: Regionalstudien I: Griechenland, Luxemburg, Norwegen, Polen, Rumänien, Schweiz*, ed. Wolfgang Benz and Juliane Wetzel, 187–204. Berlin, 1996.

———. "Die Reichskristallnacht im Spiegel der Presse: Auswirkungen auf Luxembourg und dessen Nachbarregionen." *Galerie: Revue culturelle et pédagogique* 6 (1988): 379–390.

Hohengarten, André. *Die nationalsozialistische Judenpolitik in Luxemburg.* 2nd ed. Luxembourg, 2004.
Krier, Emile. "Deutsche Besatzung in Luxembourg 1940–1944." In *Die Bürokratie der Okkupation: Strukturen der Herrschaft und Verwaltung im besetzten Europa,* ed. Wolfgang Benz et al., 27–48. Berlin, 1998.
———. "Die deutsche Volkstumspolitik in Luxembourg und ihre sozialen Folgen." In *Zweiter Weltkrieg und sozialer Wandel: Achsenmächte und besetzte Länder,* ed. Wacław Długoborski, 224–241. Göttingen, 1981.
Moyse, Laurent, and Marc Schoentgen, eds. *La présence juive au Luxembourg: du Moyen Âge au XXe siècle.* Luxembourg, 2001.
Schoentgen, Marc. "Das Einsatzkommando der Sicherheitspolizei und des Sicherheitsdienstes in Luxemburg und die Judenverfolgung im Jahre 1940." In *Du Luxembourg à l'Europe: Hommages à Gilbert Trausch à l'occasion de son 80e anniversaire,* ed. Jacques P. Leider, 301–326. Luxembourg, 2011.
———. "Das 'Jüdische Altersheim' in Fünfbrunnen." In *Terror im Westen: Nationalsozialistische Lager in den Niederlanden, Belgien und Luxemburg 1940–1945,* ed. Wolfgang Benz and Barbara Distel, 49–71. Berlin, 2004.
———. "Die jüdische Gemeinde in Medernach: Einwanderung, Integration und Verfolgung." In *Fanfare Miedernach 1930–2005,* 299–366. Medernach, 2005.
———. "Luxemburger und Juden im Zweiten Weltkrieg: zwischen Solidarität und Schweigen." In *... et wor alles net esou einfach: Questions sur le Luxembourg et la Deuxième Guerre mondiale; Contributions historiques accompagnant l'exposition / Fragen an die Geschichte Luxembourgs im Zweiten Weltkrieg: ein Lesebuch zur Ausstellung,* ed. Musée d'histoire de la Ville de Luxembourg, 150–163. Luxembourg, 2002.
———. "Mouvement Antisémitique Luxembourgeois." In *Handbuch des Antisemitismus: Judenfeindschaft in Geschichte und Gegenwart,* vol. 5, *Organisationen, Institutionen, Bewegungen,* ed. Wolfgang Benz, 408–410. Munich, 2012.

Alsace-Lorraine

Arzalier, Francis. *Les perdants: La dérive fasciste des mouvements autonomistes et indépendantistes au XXe siècle.* Paris, 1990.
Boitel, Anne. *Le camp de Rivesaltes 1941–1942: Du centre d'hébergement au "Drancy de la zone livre."* Perpignan, 2000.
Caron, Vicki. *Between France and Germany: The Jews of Alsace-Lorraine, 1871–1918.* Stanford, CA, 1988.
Daltroff, Jean. *1898–1940: La synagogue consistoriale de Strasbourg.* Strasbourg, 1996.
Dreyfus, Jacky, and Daniel Fuks. *Le mémorial des Juifs du Haut-Rhin, martyrs de la Shoah.* Colmar, 2006.
Dreyfus, Jean-Marc. *Pillages sur ordonnances: Aryanisation et restitution des banques en France 1940–1953.* Paris, 2003.
Goodfellow, Samuel Huston. *Between the Swastika and the Cross of Lorraine: Fascisms in Interwar Alsace.* DeKalb, IL, 1998.
Grynberg, Anne. *Les camps de la honte: Les internés juifs des camps français 1939–1944.* Paris, 1991.
Gutman, René. *Le Memorbuch: mémorial de la déportation et de la Résistance des Juifs du Bas-Rhin.* Strasbourg, 2005.
Kettenacker, Lothar. *Nationalsozialistische Volkstumspolitik im Elsass.* Stuttgart, 1973.

Klarsfeld, Serge. *Le calendrier de la persécution des Juifs de France.* Paris, 1993.

———. *Les transferts de Juifs du camp de Rivesaltes et de la région de Montpellier vers le camp de Drancy en vue de leur déportation, 10 août 1942–6 août 1944.* Paris, 1993.

Laharie, Claude. *Le camp de Gurs: Un aspect méconnu de l'histoire du Béarn.* Pau, 1985.

Peschanski, Denis. *La France des camps: L'internement, 1938–1946.* Paris, 2002.

Samuel, Jean, and Jean-Marc Dreyfus. *Il m'appelait Pikolo: Un compagnon de Primo Levi raconte.* Paris, 2007.

Schwarzfuchs, Simon. *Le 15 juillet 1940: La dernière expulsion des Juifs d'Alsace.* Webpage of *judaïsme alsacien.* http://judaisme.sdv.fr/histoire/shh/expuls/exp1.htm (accessed 13 March 2010).

Steegmann, Robert. *Struthof: le KL-Natzweiler et ses kommandos, une nébuleuse concentrationnaire des deux côtés du Rhin 1941–1945.* Strasbourg, 2005.

Strauss, Léo. "Exil, exclusion, extermination: Les juifs alsaciens en zone sud." In "La Guerre totale, 1943," special issue, *Saisons d'Alsace* 121 (Fall 1993): 183ff.

INDEX OF PLACES

As a rule, places commonly referred to in English are indexed according to their English names; other locations are listed according to their German names during the occupation period, along with their original names in brackets.

Italicized page numbers refer to illustrations.

Aachen, 274, 275, 278, 281, 282, 357
Alsace, 7, 30, 81, 299, 305, 313n20, 316–323, 325–333, 334n18, 334n22, 335n35, 336n46, 337n70, 341–343, 345, 346, 348, 351, 355, 362, 369, 377
Alsace-Lorraine, 7, 8, *277*, 299, 315, 316–323, 321, 322, 331, 332, 337n62, 345, 363, 377
Altkirch, 326
Annaberg, 256
Ansbach, 74
Antwerp, 280
Asch (Aš), 71, 73
Auschwitz (Oświęcim), 1, 32, 241, 248, 258, 356
Auschwitz(-Birkenau), concentration and extermination camp, 1, 32, 34, 49, 57, 59, 87, 120, 151, 178, 204, 229, 230, 232, 233, 234, 252, 255, 256, 257, 259–260, 287n48, 306, 328, 330, 331, 361, 364, 365, 376
Aussig (Ústí nad Labem), 70, 74, 79, 82–86
Australia, 53

Austria/Austria-Hungary, 1–6, 8, 26, 39–67, *40*, 69, 70, 72–74, 76, 79–82, 87, 88, 94n71, 100, 102, 105, 108, 113, 116, 118, 146, 148, 152, 168, 191, 196, 252, 280, 281, 323. 340–344, 346–352, 354, 355, 357, 358, 359, 361, 363, 372, 373, 379n14

Baden, 29, 30–32, 37n104, 299, 323, 332, 323, 327, 329, 337, 346
Baden Baden, 330
Baden-Alsace (Gau), 323
Badenweiler, 318
Barr, 318
Basel, 22
Basses-Pyrénées (Département), 30
Bavaria, 14, 21, 79
Bavarian Ostmark (Gau), 81
Bełchatów, 203
Belfort, 325
Belgium, 1, 7, 8, 14, 53, 267, 268, 270, 271, 274, 276, 277, 278, 281–283, 283n1, 284n6, 288n68, 293, 294, 298, 301, 310, 311, 363, 376
Belzec (Bełżec), extermination camp, 205

Bendzin (Będzin, Bendsburg), 86, 241, 244, *246*, 249, 252, 253, 255–257, 259, 350
Benfeld, 326
Berchtesgaden, 80
Berent (Kościerzyna), 170
Bergreichenstein (Kašperské Hory), 81
Berlin, 3, 4, 6, 9, 26, 36n75, 50, 52, 56, 57, 73, 76, 79, 80, 82, 84, 85, 87, 88, 90n11, 103, 110, 113, 114, 138, 139, 146, 148, 155n68, 168, 171, 193, 203, 204, 210, 211n22, 241, 244, 249, 251, 265n59, 271, 274, 279, 281, 300, 302, 308–310, 318, 329, 344, 348, 350, 353, 354, 357, 360, 362, 372
Bessarabia, 8, 230
Beuthen (Bytom), 240
Białystok, 7, 349
Bielsk, labor camp, 230
Biesheim, 330
Bissau (Bysewo), 186
Black Forest, 318
Bohemia (Čechy), 1, 11n23, 68, 69, 71, 76, 79–81, 88, 90n14, 92n44, 99–101, 103–104, 107, 111, 115, 118, 120, 121, 340–343, 351, 355, 358, 361, 363, 373, 374
Bohemia and Moravia (Protectorate), 2, 3, 4, 6, 8, 57, *69*, 81, 86, 87, 99–135, 340, 344, 348, 355, 366n26, 371, 373, 374, 381
Bolivia, 165, 167
Bregenz, 41
Breslau, 86, 90n11, 241, 243, 247, 248, 250, 259, 260n3, 262n23, 263n41
Bromberg (Bydgoszcz), 171, 173–175, 185n77, 186n81
Brotdorf, 27, 29
Brünn (Brno), 101, 108, 111, 114, 117–119, 246
Brussels, 269, 272, 274, 280
Budweis (České Budějovice), 111
Bukovina, 254
Burgenland, 39, 40, 41, 49, 88, 206, 343
Burgundy, 322

Canada, 14, 148, 160, 165
Carinthia, 41
Carpathian Ruthenia, 100, 101, 103
Chalon-sur-Saône, 30, 327
Chile, 165

China, 53
Chorzellen (Chorzele), 237
Cologne, 19, 270, 273, 276, 281, 302
Compiègne, transit and internment camp, 32
Crottingen (Kretinga), 146
Cuba, 165
Czechoslovakia (Czechoslovak Republic/ČSR), 1, 4, 6, 8, 11n23, 68, 70–73, 78, 90n13, 92n44, 99–104, 148, 341–343, 350, 363, 374, 381n33
Czeladź, 257
Czerwinsk an der Weichsel (Czerwińsk nad Wisłą), 228–230, 233, 237n58

Dachau, concentration camp, 49, 54, 75, 87, 151
Danzig (Gdańsk), 6, 137, 157–188, *158*, 192, 249, 342, 362, 375
Danziger Werder (Żuławy Gdańskie), 177
Danzig-West Prussia (Gau), 157–188, *172*, 192, 193, 196, 207, 228, 248, 341, 342, 345, 347, 351, 352, 355, 356, 366n26
Darbėnai, 146
Debrecen, 59
Dessau, 29
Deutsch-Gabel (Jablonné v Podještědí), 96
Diedenhofen (Thionville), 330
Dijon, 37n104
Dillingen, 26, 27
Dirschau (Tczew), 170, 175
Dlaschkowitz (Dlažkovice), labor and transit camp, 85
Dobrin (Dobrzyn), 228
Dole, 326
Dombrowa (Dąbrowa Górnicza), 239, 241, 249, 252, 256, 257, 259
Drancy, collection and transit camp, 32, 280, 328, 331
Dresden, 279
Dux (Duchcov), 76

East Prussia, 11n19, 136, 143, 144, 147, 160, 221, 227, 230, 248, 349, 366n26, 375
East Upper Silesia, 1, 3, 6, 8, 55, 86, 112, 232, 239–266, *240*, 341, 345, 347, 350, 352, 353, 356, 359–361, 365, 366n26, 375
Eger (Cheb), 73, 75, *77*, 105, 106
Eifel, 273, 274, 281, 283

Eisenbach (Vyhne), 130n94
Eisenstadt, 41
Elbing (Elbląg), 160
England, 143, 145, 167
Esch/Alzette (Esch-Uelzecht), 290, 294, 302, 312n15
Espenthor (Olšová Vrata), camp, 76, 92n48
Estonia, 198, 214n61
Ettelbrück (Ettelbréck), 290, 312n15
Eupen, 267–270, *268*, 272, 274–276, 279–282
Eupen-Malmedy, 7, 267–288, 341–343, 345, 347, 376

Faulbrück (Mościsko), forced labor camp, 264n52
Flossenbürg, concentration camp, 87
Forbach, 30
France, 1, 6, 7, 8, 10n7, 14, 15, 19, 20, 21, 29, 30, 32, 33, 34, 53, 73, 102, 136, 185n76, 256, 274, 277, 293, 294, 298, 299, 301, 310, 311, 316–318, 321, 322, 325–328, 331–333, 335n38, 342, 348, 361, 363, 377
Frankfurt, 90n11, 141, 241, 317, 375
Frankfurt an der Oder, 202
Frauenkirchen, 49
Fünfbrunnen, Jewish old age home, transit camp, 306, 315n58, 376
Fürth, 162

Galicia, 43, 198, 247, 251, 290
Gdingen (Gdynia; Gotenhafen), 166, 170, 171, 187n95
General Government (for the Occupied Polish Territories), 6, 27, 60, 173–176, 179, 187n92, 193, 195–199, 201, 202, 206, 208, 227–234, 247, 249, 251, 254, 356, 359, 361, 375, 376
Geneva, 23, 164
German Bohemia, 68
German Democratic Republic (GDR), 236, 371, 373
Germany, 1–8, 11n19, 14–16, 19–21, 26, 29, 30, 32–34, 41, 42, 44–51, 53, 54, 55, 58, 60, 61, 66n94, 69–73, 77, 89n2, 91, 99, 102, 106, 108, 109, 115, 116, 118, 120, 123n6, 137–140, 143, 145, 146, 148, 156n94, 157, 160–163, 165, 167, 168, 180n14, 189–191, 198, 202, 221, 231, 241, 244, 267, 269–276, 280–283, 292, 293, 298, 299, 301, 317, 319, 320, 321, 329, 331, 332, 340, 341, 342, 349, 350, 352, 354, 356, 358, 359, 361–365, 371, 372, 374, 375, 377, 381n33
Gleiwitz (Gliwice), 240, 244
Görtzen (Żuromin), 228
Goworowo, 222
Graudenz (Grudziądz), 160, 175, 185n77
Graz, 41, 54
Great Britain, 6, 53, 73, 102
Greece, 7
Greimerath (bei Wittlich), labor camp, 302
Grenzdorf (Graniczna Wieś), 168, 176, 184n68
Grevenmacher (Gréiwemaacher), 290
Groß Kosel (Koźle), 256
Groß-Rosen, concentration camp, 87, 257
Grussenheim (Grüssa), 330
Gumbinnen, 11n19, 147, 150
Gurs, 30, 31, 32, 34, 327

Halle an der Saale, 29
Hamm in Westphalia, 93n61
Harnau (Raciąż), 228
Hastatt, 330
Haut-Rhin (Département), 318, 321, 326, 331
Heydekrug, 150, 151
Hindenburg (Zabrze), 144, 240
Hinzert, SS camp, 302
Hirsingen (Hirsingue), 326
Hohenburg (Wyszogród), 223, 228, 230, 237n58
Hohenems, 40
Hohensalza, 190, 196, 197
Holleschau (Holešov), 100
Homburg, 13, 18, 29
Hüneburg, 320
Hungary, 4, 11n14, 39, 44, 49, 53, 63n21
Hunsrück, 302

Iglau (Jihlava), 106, 111, 113
Illingen, 26, 29
Innsbruck, 41, 44, 54
Israel, 311, 372
Italy, 6, 53, 73, 156n94, 335n38
Izbica, 57, 206

Kalisch, 196, 197, 208
Karlsbad (Karlovy Vary), 70, 73, 75, 76, 79, 82, 83, 92n48, 93n61, 105
Karthaus (Kartuzy), 170
Kassel, 104
Kattowitz (Katowice), 55, 207, 239, 240, 243, 247–251, 253, 256–258, 366n26
Kaunas (Kowno), 138, 151, 155n68
Kladno, 119
Klagenfurt, 41
Koblenz, 279, 293, 304
Koblenz-Trier (Gau), 296, 305, 309
Kolmar (Colmar), 319, 321
Komotau (Chomutov), 73
Königsberg, 143, 148, 150, 221
Königsberg an der Eger (Kynšperk nad Ohří), 106
Königshütte (Chorzów), 239, 240
Konin, 197
Kraków, 192
Krenau (Chrzanów), 241
Kruszwica, 193
Kulm (Chlumec), 108
Kulmhof am Ner (Chełmno nad Nerem), extermination camp, 205, 206, 208, 210, 216n104
Kutno, 197, 198

Langfuhr (suburb of Danzig), 164, 165, 180n3
Lask (Łask), 197
Latvia, 143, 175, 198, 214n61, 230
Lauffen (Bieżuń), 228, 237n58
Le Récébédou, 31
Leitmeritz (Litoměřice), 85
Leitmeritz (Litoměřice), secondary concentration camp, 87
Lentschütz (rural district), 216n104
Leslau (Włocławek), 197
Lidice, 205
Liegnitz (Legnica), 247
Linz, 41, 52, 79, 349
Lisbon, 301
Lithuania/Lithuanian Soviet Socialist Republic, 6, 11n23, 136, 138, 140–146, 148–152, 153n12, 156n88, 156n96, 175, 228, 230, 342, 374, 375
Lodz (Łódź, Litzmannstadt), 57, 117, 175, 190, 192, 196–199, 201–206, 208, 210, 303, 314n43, 349, 350, 359, 360, 361, 375
Łomża, 222

London, 119, 206, 294
Lons-le-Saunier, 326
Lorraine, 7, 30, 81, *295*, 299, 305, 313, 316–339, 344, 345, 348, 351, 355
Löwenstadt (Brzeziny), 198, 203
Lower Austria (state), 39–41, 43, 74
Lower Bavaria-Upper Palatinate (Gau), 79
Lower Danube (Gau), 59, 94n70, 105
Lower Silesia, 86, 242, 245, 252, 256, 262n23, 263n41
Lower Styria, 345, 346
Lublin, 56, 175, 178, 246
Lublinitz (Lubliniec), 240
Ludweiler, 18
Luxembourg, 1, 7, 8, *277*, 289–315, *295*, 341–343, 345, 346, 348, 350, 352, 355, 360, 363, 366n28, 376, 385n71
Luxembourg City, 297, 301, 302, 308
Lyon, 30, 37n104

Mâcon, 30, 37n104
Majdanek, concentration and extermination camp, 178
Makow (Maków Mazowiecki), 226, 228, 232, 237n58
Malmedy, 267, 268, 270, 275, 280, 286n36
Maribor (Marburg an der Drau), 7
Marienbad (Mariánské Lázně), 76
Marienwerder (Kwidzyn), 174
Markstädt (Laskowitz), forced labor camp, 264n52
Markt Eisenstein (Železná Ruda Městys), 81
Mauthausen, concentration camp, 59
Mazovia, 6, 219, 221, 222, 229, 232, 234, 345, 375
Mechelen, 329
Medernach (Miedernach), 290, 308
Memel (Klaipėda), 7, 136–156
Memel Territory/Memelland, 3, 6, 7, 11n23, 136–156, *137*, *149*, 341–343, 350, 351, 362, 366n26, 374
Mersch (Miersch), 301
Merzig, 13, 26, 27, 29, 35n50
Metz, 316, 317, 321, 323, 331
Mielau (Mława), 223, 228, 229, 232, 237n58
Minsk, 57, 117, 361
Modlin (fortress in Pomiechowek), 229, 230, 231
Mogilno, 193

Mondorf (Munnerëf), 290
Montzen, 282
Moravia, 1–4, 6, 8, 11n23, 55, 57, 68,
    69, 71, 79, 80, 81, 86, 87, 98–135,
    340–344, 346, 348, 355, 358, 361,
    363, 366n26, 371, 373, 374
Moravian Ostrava (Mährisch-Ostrau,
    Moravská Ostrava), 101, 106, 111
Moresnet, 280, 283n1
Moscow, 255
Moselle (Département), 317, 318, 321,
    323, 328, 331
Mülhausen (Mulhouse), 37n104, 321, 325

Nachod (Náchod), 108
Nalbach, 18
Nancy, 321, 322, 331, 335n31
Nasielsk, 227
Natzweiler-Struthof, concentration camp,
    330
Netherlands, 7, 53, 81, 256, 281, 283n1,
    289, 354, 355, 391
Neufahrwasser (Nowy Port), 168, 176,
    184n68
Neuhof (Nowy Dwór), 222, 223, 228–232,
    237n58
Neunkirchen, 26
Neustadt (Nowe Miasto), 230, 232,
    237n58
Neustadt (Wejherowo), 175
Neuteich (Nowy Staw), 160, 180n6
Neutral Moresnet, 283n1
New York, 144
New Zealand, 58
Nimmersatt (Nemirsatė), 136
Nisko, 56, 246, 247, 361
Noé, 31
Nuremberg, 25, 72, 102, 237

Oberkrain, 11n22
Olmütz (Olomouc), 101, 106, 108, 109,
    111, 114
Oloron-Sainte-Marie, 31, 327
Oppeln (Opole), 70, 74, 241, 247, 250, 256
Ottweiler, 13, 27, 29

Pabianice (Pabianitz), 201, 203
Palatinate, 16, 18, 22, 27, 29, 30, 32, 33,
    323, 327, 337n56, 357
Palestine, 22, 53, 101, 146, 156n94, 160,
    165, 166, 167, 174
Pardubitz (Pardubice), 108

Paris, 4, 19, 23, 32, 321, 322
Parzymiechy, 253
Pau, 30, 31
Penza, 141
Perpignan, 31, 327
Petersdorf, 106
Piasnitz (Piaśnica), 186
Pilsen (Plzeň), 101, 115, 118
Pleß (Pszczyna), 240
Plock (Płock), 219, 224, 226, 228, 229,
    236, 237n58
Plöhnen, 230, 232, 233, 237n58
Poddębice, 216n104, 217n108
Pogegen (Pagėgiai), 145, 150, 156n91
Poland, 1–8, 20, 27, 29, 53, 56, 69, 111,
    118, 153n12, 159–161, 164, 166–170,
    172, 173, 180n14, 183n49, 183n63,
    184n74, 185n74, 185n75, 185n77,
    187n95, 189–192, 194, 195, 198, 202,
    210n8, 211n14, 214n68, 219–223,
    226, 227, 231, 233, 235n22, 239–241,
    243, 247, 250, 252, 274, 278, 301,
    302, 340, 342, 343, 349, 350, 355,
    358, 361, 363, 371, 375, 376
Polangen (Palanga), 146
Pomerania, 173, 180n8, 180n13, 184n72,
    187n96
Pomerelia, 166
Pomiechowek (Pomiechówek), 229–231
Portugal, 297, 299–301
Posen (Poznań), 190, 192, 196–198,
    200–204, 208, 249
Potulitz (Potulice), 175
Prachatitz (Prachatice), 81
Prague, 6, 7, 9, 27, 52, 55, 64, 70–73, 100–
    108, 110–121, *110*, 130n108, 242,
    246, 302, 346, 349, 350, 353–355,
    359, 360, 374
Praschnitz (Przasnysz), 221
Preußisch Stargard (Starogard Gdański),
    170
Prussia, 13, 14, 48, 180n3, 196, 275,
    283n1, 345
Przytyk, 210n5
Pułtusk (Ostenburg), 220–222
Putzig (Puck), 170

Radom, 210n5, 230
Radomsko, 198
Radzanow (Radzanów), 237
Rakonitz (Rakovnik), 119
Ramat Gan, 155n68

Ratibor (Racibórz), 240
Ravensbrück, concentration camp, 87
Rechovot, 155n65, 156n86
Regensburg, 79
Rehlingen, 26
Reichenberg (Liberec), 70, 78–80, 82, 93n61, 355
Reichenfeld (Drobin), 224, 237n58
Riga, 57, 117, 118, 133, 361
Rippin (Rypin), 228
Rivesaltes, 327
Romania, 199, 254
Russia, 140, 160, 247, 263
Rybnik, 240

Saar region/Saarland/Saar, 5, 6, 13–48, *17*, 104, 322–325, 327, 341, 342, 344, 346, 352, 357, 366n26, 372
Saarbrücken, 13, 15, 19, 22–24, 26, 27, 29, 30, 35n37, 35n50, 323
Saarlautern (Saarlouis), 13, 26, 27, 29
Saar-Palatinate (Gau), 27, 29, 31, 32, 48, 299, 327
Saarwellingen, 26, 27
Sachsenhausen, concentration camp, 274
Saint-Dié-des-Vosges (Sankt Didel), 326
Salzburg, 41, 52, 346
Saybusch, 251
Scharfenwiese (Ostrołęka), 222, 223
Schaulen (Šiauliai), 146, 155n68
Schirmeck, 326
Schirps (Sierpc/Sichelberg), 223, 224, 226–228, 230, 237n58, 359
Schleiden, 268
Schneidemühl, 74
Schönbruch, 26
Schönwald im Erzgebirge (Krásný Les), labor and transit camp, 85
Schwarzort (Juodkrantė), 114
Schwetz (Świecie), 173
Serock, 227
Shanghai, 53, 165, 167
Sieradz, 198
Silesia, 86, 100–103, 106, 113, 239–242, 244, 245, 247, 248, 251, 258, 262n23, 263n41, 366n26
Slovakia, 11n14, 100–103, 130n94, 322
Sobibór, extermination camp, 57, 204
Soldau (Działdowo), 230
Soldau (Działdowo), transit and concentration camp, 228, 231, 235n21

Sosnowitz (Sosnowiec), 86, 112, 241, 249, 250, 252–257, 259, 350
South Africa, 148
Soviet Union (USSR), 6, 7, 56, 57, 104, 115, 116, 141, 152, 198, 204, 231, 254, 258, 303, 341, 349
Spain, 234n8, 299
Spengawsken (Szpęgawsk), 186
Speyer, 14
Sporwitten (Bodzanów) 273
St. Ingbert, 13
St. Vith, 267, 268, 270, 275
St. Wendel, 26, 27
St.-Germain-en-Laye, 41
Strasbourg, 316, 317–325, *324*, 330, 339n93
Strasshof, concentration camp, 59
Striegenau (Strzegowo), 228, 229, 232, 237n58
Strzelno, 193
Stuttgart, 267, 284n2, 320
Stutthof, concentration camp, 151, 168, 170, 176–178, 184n68, 184n69, 185n79, 375
Styria, 41, 346
Sudetenland (Sudetengau/Reichsgau Sudetenland), 2, 6–8, 11n23, 68–98, *69*, 102–105, 118, 152, 196, 245, 252, 336n43, 341–344, 346–355, 357, 358, 361, 363, 366n26, 373
Suwałki (Suwalken, Sudauen), 11n19
Switzerland, 53, 328
Szeged, 59
Szolnok, 59
Szreńsk, 228, 237n58

Tarnowitz (Tarnowskie Góry), 240
Tauroggen (Tauragė), 146
Teplitz-Schönau (Teplice-Šanov), 70, 82, 85
Theresienstadt (Terezín), ghetto, 32, 49, 57, 86, 87, 89, 118–122, 178, 306, 350, 361, 373
Thoiry, 15
Thorn (Toruń), 160, 175
Thuringia, 29
Tichau (Tychy), 257
Tiegenhof (Nowy Dwór Gdański), 160, 180n6
Tilsit, 139, 147
Toul, 316

Toulouse, 31, 37n104
Trautenau (Trutnov), 86
Treblinka, extermination camp, 53, 120, 205, 232–234
Trianon, 11n14
Trier, 13, 14, 23, 297, 302, 314n43
Troppau (Opava), 79, 82, 83, 245
Tyrol, 41, 54

Übermemel, 145
Ungarisch Brod (Uherský Brod), 108
United States of America, 1, 8, 53, 148, 160, 165, 301, 372, 373
Upper Austria (state), 40, 41, 79
Upper Danube (Gau), 70, 94n70
Upper Franconia, 29
Upper Palatinate, 70, 79
Upper Silesia (Górny Śląsk), 86, 102, 173, 175, 239–244, 249–252, 361, 375

Verdun, 316
Versailles, 4, 5, 11, 13–16, 19, 20, 33, 136, 138, 139, 151, 160, 161, 167, 239, 244, 269, 278, 342, 344
Verviers, 269
Vichy, 30, 31, 327, 331
Vienna, 4, 27, 39, 41–44, 47–49, 51–59, 61, 70, 79, 90n11, 104, 106, 107, 110, 111, 114, 246, 289, 302, 346, 349–355, 359, 379n14
Volhynia, 175, 198, 199
Vorarlberg (state), 40, 41

Wallerfangen, 26

Warnsdorf (Varnsdorf), 73
Warsaw, 173, 178, 190, 191, 206, 219, 221, 229, 233, 281
Warthbrücken (Koło), 197
Warthegau (Reichsgau Wartheland), 3, 6, 8, 117, 172, 173, 175, 181n17, 189–218, 194–197, *195*, 199–202, 204–210, 211n22, 214n61, 226, 227, 248, 262n24, 303, 341, 345, 347, 350, 352, 355–361, 363, 366n26, 375
Wasselnheim (Wasselonne), 335n27
Weißenburg (Wissembourg), 330
Wesetin (Vsetín), 106
West Prussia, 6, 157, 159, 160, 170, 175, 176, 179, 184n68, 185n75, 186n87, 226, 227, 375
Wieluń, 198
Wiesbaden, 30, 327
Witkowitz (Vítkovice), 105
Würzburg, 22

Yugoslavia, 4, 7, 53

Zagórze, 257
Zakroczym, 228, 237n58
Zichenau (Ciechanów), 3, 6, 207, 219–238, *220*, *225*, 342, 343, 350, 359, 360, 366n26, 375
Zielun (Zieluń), 228, 237n58
Żnin, 193
Zoppot (Sopot), 160, 163, 165, 166, 180n6, 383
Zweibrücken, 13

Index of Names

Abetz, Otto, 321
Ackermann, Josef, 300
Adler, Viktor, 42
Alexander, Leopold, 141
Aloisi, Baron Pompeo, 20
Altschul, Moritz, 139
Alvensleben, Ludolf von, 172, 173, 179, 186n80
Andrzejewski, Marek, 167
Arlt, Fritz, 250, 251

Bachmann, Friedrich, 74, 79
Bach-Zelewski, Erich von dem, 245, 249, 258, 263n37
Baltia, Herman, 269
Bar, Jacques Israel, 281
Barroso, José M., 1
Barth, Karl, 16, 22, 27
Beneš, Edvard, 103, 105, 119
Beran, Rudolf, 103, 106, 107
Bernheim, Franz, 242
Bertsch, Walter, 117
Bethke, Hermann, 221
Betke, Willy, 148
Bettauer, Hugo, 44
Beutel, Lothar, 171
Beyer, Hans Joachim, 267
Bickler, Armand (Hermann), 319, 320, 323, 335n31, 335n38
Bilger, Joseph, 320, 321
Binder, Richard, 16, 22
Birger, Trudi, 141

Bloch, Joseph Samuel, 42
Boch, Alfred von, 14
Bock, Max, 173
Böhme, Horst, 116, 117, 127n62, 128n72, 132n152
Bormann, Martin, 262n21, 337n64
Boruchowicz, Lejzor, 223
Bourquin, Maurice, 20
Bracht, Fritz, 245, 250, 253, 257, 347
Brandt, Karl, 265n55
Brauchitsch Walther von, 80, 94n66
Braun, Max, 23
Breitscheid, Rudolf, 23
Briand, Aristide, 15
Brindlinger, Wilhelm, 147
Buhrke, Wilhelm, 275
Bürckel, Josef, viii, 16, 18, 21–26, 27, 29, 33, 48, 50–52, 56, 104, 107, 295, 299, 322, 323, 326, 327, 332, 335n35, 344, 346, 347, 353, 357, 358, 362
Burckhardt, Carl Jakob, 169, 183n53
Burgsdorff, Curt Ludwig Ehrenreich von, 127n65
Butschek, Hans, 265n59

Cahen, Marcel, 307, 311n4
Chvalkovský, František, 103
Clémenceau, George, 136
Craushaar, Harry von, 79

Dahlet, Camille, 318, 334n12
Daluege, Kurt, 119, 121

Damzog, Ernst, 222
Dannecker, Theodor, 127n64
David, Herbert, 93n57
Dollfuß, Engelbert, 45, 46
Dorer, Gottfried, 94n77
Dorgères, Roland, 321
Dreyfus (mother of Léon D.), 326
Dreyfus, Léon, 326

Eberhardt, Friedrich Georg, 168
Ehmke, Heinz, 276
Ehrlich, Jakob, 49
Ehrnrooth, Leo, 16
Eichmann, Adolf, 27, 30, 47, 48, 52, 55, 60, 61, 110, 111, 114, 117, 119, 204, 216n95, 227, 246, 300, 301, 327, 346, 352–354, 359
Eimann, Kurt, 168, 170, 175, 183n60
Eliáš, Alois, 106, 108, 116, 119
Ernst, Robert, 319, 322, 334n22

Falke (Mayor of Zichenau), 224
Falkenhausen, Alexander von, 294
Fayot, Ben, 311n5
Felina Mannheim (company), 203
Feuchtwanger, Lion, 23
Fischböck, Hans, 4
Fitzner, Otto, 250
Forst, Abraham Mendel, 225
Forster, Albert, 159, 162, 163, 169, 171, 173, 174, 176, 178, 179, 181n20, 183n54, 185n79, 186n84, 186n87, 188n107, 193
Frank, Hans, 193, 199, 202, 227, 249
Frank, Karl Hermann, 74, 78, 105, 116, 117, 121, 131n121, 132n137, 133n163, 134n173, 374
Frantz, Constantin, 319
Fremerey, Gustav, 78
Frick, Wilhelm, 22, 78–81, 121, 133n162, 286n39, 347, 350
Friedmann, Desider, 45, 46, 49
Friedmann, František, 120
Froböß, Helmut, 164, 178
Funk, Walther, 78
Futterweit, Norbert, 44

Genten, Franz, 275
Gierets, Stefan, 276, 279, 287n60
Globocnik, Odilo, 60
Goebbels, Joseph, 81 183n54

Goethe, Johann Wolfgang von, 141
Goren, Cherie (Sara Fleischmann), 141, 143
Göring, Hermann, 4, 82, 95n89, 107, 162, 196, 227, 249, 347, 350, 351, 353, 368n63
Götze, Hans-Friedemann, 168
Gotzmann (Deputy Commander of the Protection Police in the Regierungsbezirk of Zichenau), 232
Greifelt, Ulrich, 265n55
Greiser, Arthur, 162, 178, 181n17, 181n20, 192–194, 196, 199, 202, 204–207, 210, 216n99, 262n22, 347
Grohé, Josef, 273, 287n51
Grünebaum, Kurt, 317
Guterman, Simcha, 224

Hácha, Emil, 103, 105, 106, 108, 109, 116, 117
Hagen, Herbert, 127n64, 128n79
Hanke, Karl, 263n41
Harand, Irene, 46, 63
Hartmann, Fritz, 297
Heine, Heinrich, 141
Helbing, Herbert, 236n33
Henlein, Konrad, 71–73, 78–80, 82, 84, 93n60, 94n66, 102, 104, 107, 347, 358
Hennes, Fritz, 274
Hermann, Erich, 96n109
Herwanger, Karl, 276
Herzog, David, 54
Heß, Rudolf, 347
Hetzel, Paul Hermann, 74
Heydrich, Reinhard, 30, 47, 75, 85, 108, 110, 112, 116–119, 133n162, 185n77, 194, 201, 204, 222, 228, 231, 359, 366n31, 374
Hildebrandt, Richard, 172, 175, 176, 179
Hillmann, Maurice, 141, 154n34
Himmler, Heinrich, 47, 56, 63, 76, 79, 86, 112, 120, 172, 174–177, 186n79, 186n86, 186n87, 195, 198, 202, 204, 205, 213n56, 227, 243, 245, 247, 250–252, 254, 256, 257, 259, 262n23, 263n37, 264n47, 265n55, 265n60, 303, 345, 348, 361
Hindenburg, Paul von, 144
Hirsch, Emil, 281
Hirschfeld, Max, 52, 53
Hirt, August, 330

Hitler, Adolf, 3,5–7, 10, 11n17, 16, 18, 21, 39, 46–49, 55, 56, 59, 60, 72–74, 78, 80, 102, 103, 104, 107, 108, 116, 117, 119, 121, 122, 138, 141, 143, 145–147, 162, 169, 174, 175, 186n86, 189, 191, 192, 194, 195, 199, 202, 204, 226, 243, 245, 247, 261n13, 262n21, 262n23, 262n30, 269, 278, 296, 309, 313n19, 319, 320, 322, 323, 326, 330, 332, 334n22, 335n35, 340, 341, 344, 346, 348, 355, 360, 361, 363
Hoffmann, Albert, 80, 81, 94n75, 346, 355, 362, 370n98
Hohenstein, Alexander, 216n104, 217n108
Höller, Franz, 78, 93n57
Höppner, Rolf-Heinz, 204, 216n95
Höß, Rudolf, 264n54, 265n64, 266n71
Huber, Charles, 319, 335n31
Hudson, Manley O., 20, 35n44

Innitzer, Theodor, 48

Jäger, August, 196
Jagusch, Walter, 276
Jakob, Arthur, 250
Jawschitz, Feiwel, 141
Ježek, Josef, 117 132n145
Jolas, Heinrich, 16
Jost, Heinz, 79, 93n60, 221
Jung, Jakob, 16,
Jung, Rudolf, 71

K., Hubert (escape agent), 281
Kahn (business man), 23
Kahn, Mendel (merchant), 156n91
Kalfus, Josef, 358
Kaplan, Rebekka, 156n86
Karstadt, Rudolph (company), 203
Kerkhofs, Louis-Joseph, 270
Kernert (SS-Sturmbannführer, Regierungsrat), 93n61
Kerres, Josef, 286
Klapka, Otakar, 106, 116
Klauser, Klaus-Dieter, 283
Kliment, Josef, 132n145
Kluge, Günther von, 170
Klumpar, Vladislav, 125n31
Knox, Geoffrey George, 15, 16
Koch, Erich, 147, 221, 226, 227, 232, 237n62

Köllner, Fritz, 78
Konikoff, Efim, 141
Koppe, Wilhelm, 216n99
Korherr, Richard, 134n174, 256
Koßmann, Bartholomäus, 16
Kowohl (Mayor of Bendzin), 255, 265n63
Krämer, Salo, 118, 120
Kratzenberg, Damian, 294
Kraus, Erich, 120
Krebs, Hans, 79, 84
Kreißl, Anton, 78
Krejčí, Jaroslav, 106
Küchler, Georg von, 169, 170, 221
Kummer (Head of the Civil Administration with Army Group Command 5), 74

Lambert, Jacques, 14
Lammel, Richard, 93n57
Lammers, Hans Heinrich, 132n137, 262n21
Landau, Marion, 156n86
Lange, Herbert, 192, 205
Laval, Pierre, 327
Lejeune, Carlo, 283
Levy, Ludwig, 330
Ley, Robert, 251
Leyser, Ernst Ludwig, 27
Linnemann (Division Head with the Liquidation Commissar), 80
Lölgen, Jakob, 171
Löwenherz, Josef, 48, 52, 57, 131n120, 134n168
Löwinsohn, Rywa, 281
Ludwig, Siegfried, 109, 128n74
Lueger, Karl, 42
Lutze, Viktor, 276
Luxemburg, Charlotte von (Grand Duchess), 308

Mählich (Police Chief in Karlsbad), 93n61
Mann, Heinrich, 23
Marcuse, Fritz, 155n68
Masaryk, Tomáš G., 100, 102
Matuschka, Michael Graf von, 250
Mayer, Otto Eugen, 272
Medicus, Franz Albrecht, 275
Meiler, Egon, 94n77
Meinert (Commander of Protection Police in the Regierungsbezirk of Zichenau), 232

Merin, Moshe, 251, 256, 264n44
Michel, Henri, 271, 274
Moïse (Mayor of Barr), 318
Moltke-Hvitfeldt, Adam Gottlob Carl Graf, 14
Moravec, František, 116
Morize, Jean, 16
Moser, Hans, 139
Müller, Heinrich, 55
Müller, Karl, 79

Nafthal, Nathan, 141,143, 150
Neckermann, Josef (company), 203
Neuburg, Hermann, 80, 94n77, 94n78
Neumann, Ernst, 138, 144, 145, 147
Neurath, Konstantin Freiherr von, 21, 104, 108, 109, 110, 111, 116, 121, 128n79, 131n115, 353
Nölle, Wilhelm, 297
Nussbaum, Albert, 299, 301

Obama, Barack, 1
Odry, Dominique Joseph, 137
Oppenheimer, Alfred, 306, 314n51
Oppenheimer, Erich, 23

Papen, Franz von, 16, 18
Pauly, Max, 168, 176
Peirotes, Jacques, 318
Petschek (family), 70
Pfeffer-Wildenbruch, Karl von, 79
Pfitzner, Josef, 89n4, 106, 133n163, 134n173
Pfundtner, Hans, 193, 212n31
Piłsudski, Józef, 241, 243
Pirro, Jakob, 18
Pitzak, Rudolf, 13n115

R., Hedwig (escape agent), 281
Rabinowitz, Mika, 15n68
Radowitz, Otto von, 293
Rafelsberger, Walter, 50
Rasch, Otto, 104, 126n42, 230
Rath, Ernst vom, 274
Rathenau, Walther, 145
Rault, Victor, 13, 15
Rauschning, Hermann, 162, 178, 181n20
Renner, Karl, 48
Rexroth, Walther, 275, 279, 287n60, 287n61, 287n63
Richter, Wolfgang, 78, 83

Ricklin, Eugène, 318
Ringelblum, Emanuel, 191
Rohde, Herbert, 147
Rohling, August, 42
Roos, Karl, 322, 334n22
Rost, Nico, 274
Rostovsky, Leon, 139
Rothschild, Lothar, 22, 26
Rothstock, Otto, 44
Rudeitzki, Siegfried, 150
Rüdiger (Head of the Civil Administration with Army Group Command 1), 74, 79
Rumkowski, Mordechai Chaim, 203

Saal, Gabriel, 276
Saß, Theodor Freiherr von, 138
Scharitzer, Karl, 56
Scheel, Gustav Adolf, 346
Schickelé, René, 318
Schiller, Friedrich von, 141
Schmalz, Oskar, 298
Schmauser, Ernst-Heinrich, 263n37, 265n55
Schmelt, Albrecht, 86, 87, 250–253, 255–257, 259, 260, 264n54, 265n64, 266n71, 359
Schmidt, Franz, 300, 355
Schneider, Heinrich, 16, 17
Scholz, Günther, 80
Schönerer, Georg von, 71
Schönfeldt, Jost von, 79
Schönwälder, Josef, 255, 265n62
Schubert, Dietrich, 283
Schulenburg, Fritz-Dietlof Graf von der, 245, 248, 250, 254, 258, 259, 262n22, 265n60
Schuschnigg, Kurt, 46
Schwager, Karl, 52
Schwarz, Günter (company), 203
Sebekowsky, Wilhelm, 78
Segalowitz, Erna, 144
Serebrenik, Robert, 294, 300, 301, 309, 311n3, 312n16
Seulen, Felix, 276, 279, 287n60
Sever, Albert, 43
Seyß-InquarFt, Arthur, 46, 47, 168
Simon, Gustav, 293, 295–300, 302, 304, 305, 309, 310, 332
Smetona, Antanas, 149
Somerhausen, Marc, 269

Späth (Plenipotentiary for Assets Hostile to the Volk and Reich in Alsace), 328
Speer, Albert, 255
Spieser, Friedrich, 319, 320, 334n20, 334n22
Springorum, Walter, 248, 265n62
Stahlecker, Franz Walter, 27, 52, 104, 110, 126n42, 346, 353, 362
Stalin, Josef W., 151, 243
Stangl, Franz, 53
Stephens, George Washington, 15
Sternberg, Louis, 300
Stier, Rudolf, 128n74
Stosberg, Hans, 258
Stresemann, Gustav, 15
Stricker, Robert, 42, 49
Sturmann, Hilde (née Nafthal), 141
Syrový, Jan, 103

Thedieck, Franz, 272
Thorez, Maurice, 319
Toller, Ernst, 23
Tröger, Rudolf, 171
Turner, Harald, 74

Uebelhoer, Friedrich, 200, 205
Uiberreither, Sigfried, 346
Urbšys, Juozas, 146

Valsonokas, Rudolfas, 139

Vermeil, Edmond, 319
Voss, August, 282

Wagner, Josef, 244–246, 258, 259, 262n22, 262n23, 350
Wagner, Robert, 299, 322, 323, 325, 327, 328, 330, 332, 335n35, 346
Waldheim, Kurt, 60
Wanie, Paul, 96n96
Warsow, Max, 94n77
Waugh, Richard Deans, 14
Wedelstädt, Helmuth von, 221
Weill-Samuel (family), 335n27, 335n34
Weinmann (family), 70
Welsch, Heinrich, 23
Wendt (Mayor of Neuhof), 223
Werson, Joseph, 275
Wetzlar, Robert, 279
Wilson, Woodrow, 68
Wilton, Ernest C., 15
Woedtke, Alexander von, 255, 263n37, 265n61
Woyrsch, Udo von, 243, 244

Zalman, Moriz, 46
Żeligowski, Lucjan, 153n12
Zippelius, Friedrich, 79
Zoricic, Milovan, 16
Zygielbojm, Szmul, 206

War and Genocide

General Editors: Omer Bartov, Brown University
A. Dirk Moses, University of Sydney

Volume 1
The Massacre in History
Edited by Mark Levene and Penny Roberts

Volume 2
National Socialist Extermination Policies: Contemporary German Perspectives and Controversies
Edited by Ulrich Herbert

Volume 3
War of Extermination: The German Military in World War II, 1941–44
Edited by Hannes Heer and Klaus Naumann

Volume 4
In God's Name: Genocide and Religion in the Twentieth Century
Edited by Omer Bartov and Phyllis Mack

Volume 5
Hitler's War in the East, 1941–1945
Rolf-Dieter Müller and Gerd R. Ueberschär

Volume 6
Genocide and Settler Society: Frontier Violence and Stolen Indigenous Children in Australian History
Edited by A. Dirk Moses

Volume 7
Networks of Nazi Persecution: Bureaucracy, Business and the Organization of the Holocaust
Edited by Gerald D. Feldman and Wolfgang Seibel

Volume 8
Gray Zones: Ambiguity and Compromise in the Holocaust and Its Aftermath
Edited by Jonathan Petropoulos and John K. Roth

Volume 9
Robbery and Restitution: The Conflict over Jewish Property in Europe
Edited by Martin Dean, Constantin Goschler and Philipp Ther

Volume 10
Exploitation, Resettlement, Mass Murder: Political and Economic Planning for German Occupation Policy in the Soviet Union, 1940–1941
Alex J. Kay

Volume 11
Theatres of Violence: Massacre, Mass Killing and Atrocity in History
Edited by Philip G. Dwyer and Lyndall Ryan

Volume 12
Empire, Colony, Genocide: Conquest, Occupation, and Subaltern Resistance in World History
Edited by A. Dirk Moses

Volume 13
The Train Journey: Transit, Captivity, and Witnessing in the Holocaust
Simone Gigliotti

Volume 14
The "Final Solution" in Riga: Exploitation and Annihilation, 1941–1944
Andrej Angrick and Peter Klein

Volume 15
The Kings and the Pawns: Collaboration in Byelorussia during World War II
Leonid Rein

Volume 16
Reassessing the Nuremberg Military Tribunals: Transitional Justice, Trial Narratives, and Historiography
Edited by Kim C. Priemel and Alexa Stiller

Volume 17
The Nazi Genocide of the Roma: Reassessment and Commemoration
Edited by Anton Weiss-Wendt

Volume 18
Judging "Privileged" Jews: Holocaust Ethics, Representation, and the "Grey Zone"
Adam Brown

Volume 19
The Dark Side of Nation-States: Ethnic Cleansing in Modern Europe
Philipp Ther

Volume 20
The Greater German Reich and the Jews: Nazi Persecution Policies in the Annexed Territories 1935-1945
Edited by Wolf Gruner and Jörg Osterloh

Volume 21
The Spirit of the Laws: The Plunder of Wealth in the Armenian Genocide
Edited by Taner Akçam and Umit Kurt
Translated by Aram Arkun

Volume 22
Genocide on Settler Frontiers: When Hunter-Gatherers and Commercial Stock Farmers Clash
Edited by Mohamed Adhikari

Volume 23
The Making of the Greek Genocide: Contested Memories of the Ottoman Greek Catastrophe
Erik Sjöberg

Volume 24
Microhistories of the Holocaust
Edited by Claire Zalc and Tal Bruttmann

Volume 25
Daily Life in the Abyss: Genocide Diaries, 1915-1918
Vahé Tachjian

Volume 26
Let Them Not Return: Sayfo – The Genocide Against the Assyrian, Syriac, and Chaldean Christians in the Ottoman Empire
Edited by David Gaunt, Naures Atto, and Soner O. Barthoma

www.ingramcontent.com/pod-product-compliance
Lightning Source LLC
Chambersburg PA
CBHW072141100526
44589CB00015B/2025